Second Edition

MACROECONOMICS

Practice, Engage, and Assess

- **Enhanced eText**—The Pearson eText gives students access to their textbook anytime, anywhere. In addition to note-taking, highlighting, and bookmarking, the Pearson eText offers interactive and sharing features. Students actively read and learn through auto-graded practice, real-time data-graphs, figure animations, author videos, and more. Instructors can share comments or highlights, and students can add their own, for a tight community of learners in any class.

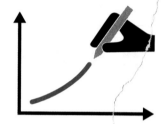

- **Practice**—Algorithmically generated homework and study plan exercises with instant feedback ensure varied and productive practice, helping students improve their understanding and prepare for quizzes and tests. Draw-graph exercises encourage students to practice the language of economics.

- **Learning Resources**—Personalized learning aids such as Help Me Solve This problem walkthroughs and Figure Animations provide on-demand help when students need it most.

- **Personalized Study Plan**—Assists students in monitoring their own progress by offering them a customized study plan based on Homework, Quiz, and Test results. Includes regenerated exercises with unlimited practice, as well as the opportunity to earn mastery points by completing quizzes on recommended learning objectives.

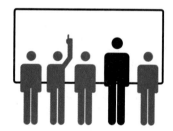

- **Dynamic Study Modules**—With a focus on key topics, these modules work by continuously assessing student performance and activity in real time and, using data and analytics, provide personalized content to reinforce concepts that target each student's particular strengths and weaknesses.

- **Digital Interactives**—Digital Interactives are engaging assessment activities that promote critical thinking and application of key economic principles. Each Digital Interactive has progressive levels where students can explore, apply, compare, and analyze economic principles. Many Digital Interactives include real time data from FRED® that displays, in graph and table form, up-to-the-minute data on key macro variables. Digital Interactives can be assigned and graded within MyEconLab, or used as a lecture tool to encourage engagement, classroom conversation, and group work.

P **Pearson**

with MyEconLab®

- **NEW: Math Review Exercises in MyEconLab**—MyEconLab now offers an array of assignable and auto-graded exercises that cover fundamental math concepts. Geared specifically toward principles and intermediate economics students, these exercises aim to increase student confidence and success in these courses. Our new Math Review is accessible from the assignment manager and contains over 150 graphing, algebra, and calculus exercises for homework, quiz, and test use.

$$P = c + dQ_S$$

- **Real-Time Data Analysis Exercises**—Using current macro data to help students understand the impact of changes in economic variables, Real-Time Data Analysis Exercises communicate directly with the Federal Reserve Bank of St. Louis's FRED® site and update as new data are available.

- **Current News Exercises**—Every week, current microeconomic and macroeconomic news articles or videos, with accompanying exercises, are posted to MyEconLab. Assignable and auto-graded, these multi-part exercises ask students to recognize and apply economic concepts to real-world events.

- **Experiments**—Flexible, easy-to-assign, auto-graded, and available in Single Player and Multiplayer versions, Experiments in MyEconLab make learning fun and engaging.

- **Reporting Dashboard**—View, analyze, and report learning outcomes clearly and easily. Available via the Gradebook and fully mobile-ready, the Reporting Dashboard presents student performance data at the class, section, and program levels in an accessible, visual manner.

- **LMS Integration**—Link from any LMS platform to access assignments, rosters, and resources, and synchronize MyLab grades with your LMS gradebook. For students, new direct, single sign-on provides access to all the personalized learning MyLab resources that make studying more efficient and effective.

- **Mobile Ready**—Students and instructors can access multimedia resources and complete assessments right at their fingertips, on any mobile device.

The Pearson Series in Economics

Abel/Bernanke/Croushore
*Macroeconomics**

Acemoglu/Laibson/List
*Economics**

Bade/Parkin
*Foundations of Economics**

Berck/Helfand
The Economics of the Environment

Bierman/Fernandez
Game Theory with Economic Applications

Blanchard
*Macroeconomics**

Boyer
Principles of Transportation Economics

Branson
Macroeconomic Theory and Policy

Bruce
Public Finance and the American Economy

Carlton/Perloff
Modern Industrial Organization

Case/Fair/Oster
*Principles of Economics**

Chapman
Environmental Economics: Theory, Application, and Policy

Daniels/VanHoose
International Monetary & Financial Economics

Downs
An Economic Theory of Democracy

Farnham
Economics for Managers

Fort
Sports Economics

Froyen
Macroeconomics

Fusfeld
The Age of the Economist

Gerber
*International Economics**

Gordon
*Macroeconomics**

Greene
Econometric Analysis

Gregory/Stuart
Russian and Soviet Economic Performance and Structure

Hartwick/Olewiler
The Economics of Natural Resource Use

Heilbroner/Milberg
The Making of the Economic Society

Heyne/Boettke/Prychitko
The Economic Way of Thinking

Hubbard/O'Brien
*Economics**

*InEcon
Money, Banking, and the Financial System**

Hubbard/O'Brien/Rafferty
*Macroeconomics**

Hughes/Cain
American Economic History

Husted/Melvin
International Economics

Jehle/Reny
Advanced Microeconomic Theory

Keat/Young/Erfle
Managerial Economics

Klein
Mathematical Methods for Economics

Krugman/Obstfeld/Melitz
*International Economics: Theory & Policy**

Laidler
The Demand for Money

Lynn
Economic Development: Theory and Practice for a Divided World

Miller
*Economics Today**

Understanding Modern Economics

Miller/Benjamin
The Economics of Macro Issues

Miller/Benjamin/North
The Economics of Public Issues

Mishkin
*The Economics of Money, Banking, and Financial Markets**

*The Economics of Money, Banking, and Financial Markets, Business School Edition**

*Macroeconomics: Policy and Practice**

Murray
Econometrics: A Modern Introduction

O'Sullivan/Sheffrin/Perez
*Economics: Principles, Applications and Tools**

Parkin
*Economics**

Perloff
*Microeconomics**

*Microeconomics: Theory and Applications with Calculus**

Perloff/Brander
*Managerial Economics and Strategy**

Pindyck/Rubinfeld
*Microeconomics**

Riddell/Shackelford/Stamos/ Schneider
Economics: A Tool for Critically Understanding Society

Roberts
The Choice: A Fable of Free Trade and Protection

Scherer
Industry Structure, Strategy, and Public Policy

Schiller
The Economics of Poverty and Discrimination

Sherman
Market Regulation

Stock/Watson
Introduction to Econometrics

Studenmund
Using Econometrics: A Practical Guide

Todaro/Smith
Economic Development

Walters/Walters/Appel/ Callahan/Centanni/Maex/ O'Neill
Econversations: Today's Students Discuss Today's Issues

Williamson
Macroeconomics

*denotes MyEconLab titles   Visit www.myeconlab.com to learn more.

iv

Second Edition

MACROECONOMICS

Daron Acemoglu
Massachusetts Institute of Technology

David Laibson
Harvard University

John A. List
University of Chicago

 Pearson

New York, NY

Vice President, Business Publishing: Donna Battista
Director of Portfolio Management: Adrienne D'Ambrosio
Senior Portfolio Manager: Christina Masturzo
Development Editor: Cydney Westmoreland
Editorial Assistant: Courtney Paganelli
Vice President, Product Marketing: Roxanne McCarley
Strategic Marketing Manager: Deborah Strickland
Product Marketer: Tricia Murphy
Senior Field Marketing Manager: Carlie Marvel
Manager of Field Marketing, Business Publishing: Adam Goldstein
Field Marketing Assistant: Kristen Compton
Product Marketing Assistant: Jessica Quazza
Vice President, Production and Digital Studio, Arts and Business: Etain O'Dea
Director of Production, Business: Jeff Holcomb
Managing Producer, Business: Alison Kalil

Content Producer: Nancy Freihofer
Operations Specialist: Carol Melville
Creative Director: Blair Brown
Manager, Learning Tools: Brian Surette
Managing Producer, Digital Studio, Arts and Business: Diane Lombardo
Digital Studio Producer: Melissa Honig
Digital Studio Producer: Alana Coles
Digital Content Team Lead: Noel Lotz
Digital Content Project Lead: Courtney Kamauf
Full-Service Project Management and Composition: Cenveo® Publisher Services
Interior Design: Cenveo® Publisher Services
Cover Design: Cenveo® Publisher Services
Printer/Binder: LSC Communications, Inc
Cover Printer: Phoenix Color/Hagerstown

Library of Congress Cataloging-in-Publication Data

Names: Acemoglu, Daron, author. | Laibson, David I., author. | List, John A.
Title: Macroeconomics / Daron Acemoglu, Massachusetts Institute of
   Technology, David Laibson, Harvard University, John A. List, University
   of Chicago.
Description: Second Edition. | New York : Pearson, [2017] | Revised
   edition of the authors' Macroeconomics, [2015] | Includes bibliographical
   references and index.
Identifiers: LCCN 2017023432 | ISBN 9780134492056 | ISBN 0134492056
Subjects: LCSH: Macroeconomics.
Classification: LCC HB172.5 .A28 2017 | DDC 339—dc23
LC record available at https://lccn.loc.gov/2017023432

2   18

ISBN 10:   0-13-449205-6
ISBN 13: 978-0-13-449205-6

Dedication

*With love for Annika, Aras, Arda, Eli,
Greta, Mason, Max, and Noah,
who inspire us every day.*

About the Authors

Daron Acemoglu is the Elizabeth and James Killian Professor of Economics in the Department of Economics at the Massachusetts Institute of Technology. He has received a B.A. in economics from the University of York, 1989; an M.Sc. in mathematical economics and econometrics from the London School of Economics, 1990; and a Ph.D. in economics from the London School of Economics in 1992.

He is an elected fellow of the National Academy of Sciences, the American Academy of Arts and Sciences, the Econometric Society, the European Economic Association, and the Society of Labor Economists. He has received numerous awards and fellowships, including the inaugural T. W. Schultz Prize from the University of Chicago in 2004, the inaugural Sherwin Rosen Award for outstanding contribution to labor economics in 2004, the Distinguished Science Award from the Turkish Sciences Association in 2006, and the John von Neumann Award, Rajk College, Budapest, in 2007.

He was also the recipient of the John Bates Clark Medal in 2005, awarded every two years to the best economist in the United States under the age of 40 by the American Economic Association, and the Erwin Plein Nemmers Prize, awarded every two years for work of lasting significance in economics. He holds honorary doctorates from the University of Utrecht and Bosporus University.

His research interests include political economy, economic development and growth, human capital theory, growth theory, innovation, search theory, network economics, and learning.

His books include *Economic Origins of Dictatorship and Democracy* (jointly with James A. Robinson), which was awarded the Woodrow Wilson and the William Riker prizes, *Introduction to Modern Economic Growth*, and *Why Nations Fail: The Origins of Power, Prosperity, and Poverty* (jointly with James A. Robinson), which has become a *New York Times* bestseller.

David Laibson is the Chair of the Harvard Economics Department and the Robert I. Goldman Professor of Economics at Harvard University. He is also a member of the National Bureau of Economic Research, where he is Research Associate in the Asset Pricing, Economic Fluctuations, and Aging Working Groups. His research focuses on the topics of behavioral economics, intertemporal choice, macroeconomics, and household finance, and he leads Harvard University's Foundations of Human Behavior Initiative. He serves on several editorial boards, as well as the Pension Research Council (Wharton), Harvard's Pension Investment Committee, and the Board of the Russell Sage Foundation. He has previously served on the boards of the Health and Retirement Study (National Institutes of Health) and the Academic Research Council of the Consumer Financial Protection Bureau. He is a recipient of a Marshall Scholarship and a Fellow of the Econometric Society and the American Academy of Arts and Sciences. He is also a recipient of the T. W. Schultz Prize from the University of Chicago and the TIAA-CREF Paul A. Samuelson Award for Outstanding Scholarly Writing on Lifelong Financial Security. Laibson holds degrees from Harvard University (A.B. in economics), the London School of Economics (M.Sc. in econometrics and mathematical economics), and the Massachusetts Institute of Technology (Ph.D. in economics). He received his Ph.D. in 1994 and has taught at Harvard since then. In recognition of his teaching excellence, he has been awarded Harvard's Phi Beta Kappa Prize and a Harvard College Professorship.

John A. List is the Kenneth C. Griffin Distinguished Service Professor in Economics at the University of Chicago, and Chairman of the Department of Economics. He received his B.S. in economics from the University of Wisconsin–Stevens Point and his Ph.D. in economics from the University of Wyoming. Before joining the University of Chicago in 2005, he was a professor at the University of Central Florida, University of Arizona, and University of Maryland. He also served in the White House on the Council of Economic Advisers from 2002–2003, and is a Research Associate at the NBER.

List was elected a Member of the American Academy of Arts and Sciences in 2011, and a Fellow of the Econometric Society in 2015. He also received the Arrow Prize for Senior Economists in 2008, the Kenneth Galbraith Award in 2010, the Yrjo Jahnsson Lecture Prize in 2012, and the Klein Lecture Prize in 2016. He received an honorary doctorate from Tilburg University in 2014 and from the University of Ottawa in 2017. In addition, List was named a Top 50 Innovator in the Non-Profit Times for 2015 and 2016 for his work on charitable giving.

His research focuses on questions in microeconomics, with a particular emphasis on using field experiments to address both positive and normative issues. For decades his field experimental research has focused on issues related to the inner workings of markets, the effects of various incentive schemes on market equilibria and allocations, and how behavioral economics can augment the standard economic model. This includes research into why inner city schools fail, why people discriminate, why people give to charity, why firms fail, why women make less money than men in labor markets, and why people generally do what they do.

His research includes over 200 peer-reviewed journal articles and several published books, including the 2013 international best-seller, *The Why Axis: Hidden Motives and the Undiscovered Economics of Everyday Life* (with Uri Gneezy).

Brief Contents

Contents

PART V   SHORT-RUN FLUCTUATIONS AND MACROECONOMIC POLICY   280

Chapter 12: Short-Run Fluctuations   280

Chapter 13: Countercyclical Macroeconomic Policy   308

PART VI   MACROECONOMIC IN A GLOBAL ECONOMY   336

Chapter 14: Macroeconomics and International Trade   336

CHAPTERS ON THE WEB

Web chapters are available on MyEconLab.

WEB Chapter 1 Financial Decision Making

WEB Chapter 2 Economics of Life, Health, and
the Environment

WEB Chapter 3 Political Economy

Preface

We love economics. We marvel at the way economic systems work. When we buy a smartphone, we think about the complex supply chain and the hundreds of thousands of people who played a role in producing an awe-inspiring piece of technology that was assembled from components manufactured around the globe.

The market's ability to do the world's work without anyone being in charge strikes us as a phenomenon no less profound than the existence of consciousness or life itself. We believe that the creation of the market system is one of the greatest achievements of humankind.

We wrote this book to highlight the simplicity of economic ideas and their extraordinary power to explain, predict, and improve what happens in the world. We want students to master the *essential* principles of economic analysis. With that goal in mind, we identify three key ideas that lie at the heart of the economic approach to understanding human behavior: optimization, equilibrium, and empiricism. These abstract words represent three ideas that are actually highly intuitive.

The breakneck speed of modern technological change has, more than ever, injected economics into the lives—and hands—of our students. The technologies that they use daily illustrate powerful economic forces in action: Uber users observe real-time congestion in the transportation market when they confront surge pricing, and Airbnb travelers explore the relationships among location, convenience, and price by comparing listings near different subway stops in the same city.

As educators, it's our job to transform economic concepts into language, visual representations, and empirical examples that our students understand. Today, markets are much more interactive than they were only a decade ago, and they exemplify that it is not just competitive markets with perfect information that are relevant to our economic lives. Our students routinely take part in auctions, purchase goods and services via organized platforms such as Uber, have to struggle with pervasive informational asymmetries as they participate in online exchanges, and have to guard themselves against a bewildering array of mistakes and traps that are inherent in these new transactions.

In this ever-changing world, students must understand not just well-known economic concepts such as opportunity cost, supply, and demand, but also modern ones such as game theory, auctions, and behavioral mistakes. It is these modern concepts, which are small parts in most Principles textbooks, that occupy center stage in ours. Today economic analysis has expanded its conceptual and empirical boundaries and, in doing so, has become even more relevant and useful.

This new world provides incredible opportunities for the teaching of economics as well, provided that we adjust our Principles canon to include modern and empirically based notions of economics. This has been our aim from day one and continues to be our goal in this second edition.

New to the Second Edition

In our new edition of *Macroeconomics*, we have completely revised the macro portion of the course, not just to bring it up to date with the firehose of current data and events, but, just as importantly, to re-evaluate and improve the pedagogy for the students.

The most important conceptual change begins in Chapter 9 (Employment and Unemployment), which then enables substantial pedagogical improvements in Chapters 12 (Short-Run Fluctuations) and 13 (Countercyclical Macroeconomic Policy). Our framework for the analysis of economic fluctuations centers on the labor market. In this framework, downward wage rigidity plays a vital role as a central mechanism preventing wages from adjusting to a negative labor demand shock and thus generating increases in unemployment during economic contractions.

In the previous edition, we went through most examples of the labor market *twice*: first with and then without downward nominal wage rigidity. We have now eliminated much of this repetition by studying both cases in Chapter 9, but then in Chapters 12 and 13 focusing the analysis on the case in which downward nominal wage rigidity is present.

To implement this strategy, we frequently deploy an empirically realistic and pedagogically effective two-part labor supply curve, which has a downward nominal wage tied to the current wage and is infinitely inelastic beyond full employment. Accordingly, the two-part labor supply curve is first horizontal (at the current nominal wage) and then vertical (at full employment). This enables us to present a much simpler unified approach that is far easier to understand and has enabled us to overwhelmingly streamline the analysis in Chapters 12 and 13. We have eliminated some of the most complex figures without loss of conceptual richness.

Our two-part labor supply curve also emphasizes why further rightward shifts of the labor demand curve in the middle of an expansion will not increase employment by very much, and instead will primarily contribute to increases in wages and prices.

The two-part labor supply curve is used consistently in Chapters 12 and 13 in our discussion of short-run fluctuations and fiscal and monetary policy designed to offset such fluctuations.

In addition, we have enriched the macro split with new features, exhibits, and sections that illustrate economic concepts with recent events of interest. These include:

- New **Choice & Consequence** that forces students to wrestle with the question of causality. We discuss a recent research paper that reports a positive correlation between expensive weddings and high rates of divorce. We ask our students to use this finding as a springboard from which to wrestle with the difference between correlation and causality, and to understand the role of omitted variables (Chapter 2).
- New **Letting the Data Speak** that tells the story of the fracking revolution and its remarkable impact on oil and gasoline prices. Supply and demand come alive when students can see how the recent rightward shift in the oil supply curve, due to the development of fracking technologies, has played a role in halving the equilibrium price of oil (Chapter 4).
- New section describing the growth of economic inequality, and emphasizing that inequality is not measured in economic aggregates, such as GDP (Chapter 5).
- New **Choice & Consequence** about the societal consequences of the expulsion of Jewish faculty from universities in Nazi Germany (Chapter 6).
- New **Letting the Data Speak** on the great productivity puzzle, discussing how we may be experiencing a slow-down of aggregate productivity despite the rapid introduction of a range of new technologies in the economy (Chapter 7).
- New **Letting the Data Speak** on democracy and growth, showing the positive impact of democratic political institutions on economic growth (Chapter 8).
- Expanded **Choice & Consequence** on Luddite resistance to new technology and what this can teach us about the disruption that new and more productive robots are bringing to the economy today (Chapter 9).
- New **Choice & Consequence** on minimum wage laws and employment (Chapter 9).
- New **Letting the Data Speak** feature on financing start-ups (Chapter 10).
- New **Choice & Consequence** on obtaining reserves outside of the federal funds market (Chapter 11).
- New **Letting the Data Speak** on the response of consumption to tax cuts (Chapter 13).
- New **Choice & Consequence** on the Trump administration's fiscal policy proposals (Chapter 13).
- New **Choice & Consequence** about the political forces that influence trade policy (Chapter 14).
- New graphical Exhibit describing the relationship between interest rates and net capital outflows, unifying material from several chapters for the analysis of open economy macroeconomics (Chapter 15).

Introductory economics classes draw students with diverse interests and future career paths: with this textbook, we show them how to apply economic thinking creatively to improve their work, their choices, and their daily lives.

One of our main objectives in writing this textbook was to show that the fundamentals of economics are not just exciting, but also alive with myriad personal applications. In the first edition, the themes of optimization, equilibrium, and empiricism were our primary tools for communicating both the surprising power and broad applicability of economics. We believe that the intervening years have confirmed these conceptual priorities; these concepts have become even more relevant for our students.

At a time when competing empirical claims abound and news sources across the political spectrum are denounced as "fake," our students need the skills to systematically question and evaluate what they read. That is why, in our Evidence-Based Economics segments, we examine both the implications *and the limitations* of academic studies. We hope that our textbook will help form a new generation of careful thinkers, smart decision-makers, engaged citizens, and even a few future economists!

Our Vision: Three Unifying Themes

The first key principle is that people try to choose the best available option: *optimization*. We don't assume that people always successfully optimize, but we do believe that people try to optimize and often do a relatively good job of it. Because most decision makers try to choose the alternative that offers the greatest net benefit, optimization is a useful tool for predicting human behavior. Optimization is also a useful prescriptive tool. By teaching people how to optimize, we improve their decisions and the quality of their lives. By the end of this course, every student should be a skilled optimizer—without using complicated mathematics, simply by using economic intuition.

The second key principle extends the first: economic systems operate in *equilibrium*, a state in which everybody is simultaneously trying to optimize. We want students to see that they're not the only ones maximizing their well-being. An economic system is in equilibrium when each person feels that he or she cannot do any better by picking another course of action. The principle of equilibrium highlights the connections among economic actors. For example, Apple stores stock millions of iPhones because millions of consumers are going to turn up to buy them. In turn, millions of consumers go to Apple stores because those stores are ready to sell those iPhones. In equilibrium, consumers and producers are simultaneously optimizing, and their behaviors are intertwined.

Our first two principles—optimization and equilibrium—are conceptual. The third is methodological: *empiricism*. Economists use *data* to test economic theories, learn about the world, and speak to policymakers. Accordingly, data play a starring role in our book, though we keep the empirical analysis extremely simple. It is this emphasis on matching theories with real data that we think most distinguishes our book from others. We show students how economists use data to answer specific questions, which makes our chapters concrete, interesting, and fun. Modern students demand the evidence behind the theory, and our book supplies it.

For example, we begin every chapter with an empirical question and then answer that question using data. One chapter begins by asking:

Why are you so much more prosperous than your great-great-grandparents were?

Later in that chapter, we demonstrate the central role played by technology in explaining U.S. economic growth and why we are much better off than our relatives a few generations ago.

In our experience, students taking their first economics class often have the impression that economics is a series of theoretical assertions with little empirical basis. By using data, we explain how economists evaluate and improve our scientific insights. Data also make concepts more memorable. Using evidence helps students build intuition, because data move the conversation from abstract principles to concrete facts. Every chapter sheds light on how economists use data to answer questions that directly interest students. Every chapter demonstrates the key role that evidence plays in advancing the science of economics.

Features

All of our features showcase intuitive empirical questions.

- In **Evidence-Based Economics (EBE)**, we show how economists use data to answer the question we pose in the opening paragraph of the chapter. The EBE uses actual data from field experiments, lab experiments, or naturally occurring data, while highlighting some of the major concepts discussed within the chapter. This tie-in with the data gives students a substantive look at economics as it plays out in the world around them.

  The questions explored aren't just dry intellectual ideas; they spring to life the minute the student sets foot outside the classroom—*Is Facebook free? Is college worth it? Are tropical and semitropical areas condemned to poverty by their geographies? What caused the recession of 2007–2009? Are companies like Nike harming workers in Vietnam?*

EVIDENCE-BASED ECONOMICS

Q: Why are you so much more prosperous than your great-great-grandparents were?

The theoretical discussion in the previous section supports the central role of technology in explaining sustained growth. We will now see that empirical evidence also bolsters the conclusion that technology plays a key role.

To evaluate the sources of U.S. economic growth, we follow the same strategy as in Chapter 6. There, we used the aggregate production function and estimates of the physical-capital stock and the efficiency units of labor across different countries to evaluate their contributions to cross-country differences in GDP (PPP-adjusted). The only major difference here is that higher-quality U.S. data enable us to conduct the analysis for real GDP per hour worked rather than real GDP per worker, thus allowing us to measure the labor input more accurately. We start the analysis in 1950.

• **Letting the Data Speak** is another feature that analyzes an economic question by using real data as the foundation of the discussion. Among the many issues we explore are such topics as life expectancy and innovation, living in an interconnected world, and why Chinese authorities historically kept the yuan undervalued (but no longer do so).

LETTING THE
DATA SPEAK

Technology and Life Expectancy

Technology has not improved our lives just by increasing real GDP per capita. It has also improved the health and longevity of billions of people around the world.

Life expectancy around the world was much lower 70 years ago than it is today.[3] In 1940, child and infant mortality rates were so high and adult diseases, such as pneumonia and tuberculosis, were so deadly (and without any cure) that life expectancy at birth in many nations stood at less than 40 years. For example, the life expectancy at birth of an average Indian was an incredibly low 30 years. In Venezuela, it was 33; in Indonesia, 34; in Brazil, 36.

In the course of the next three or four decades, this picture changed dramatically. As we saw in Chapter 6, while the gap in life expectancy between rich and poor nations still remains today, health conditions have improved significantly all over the world, particularly for poorer nations. Life expectancy at birth in India in 1999 was 60 years, almost twice as high as the country's life expectancy in the 1940s. It was also 50 percent higher than life expectancy at birth in Britain in 1820 (around 40 years), which at the time had approximately the same PPP-adjusted GDP per capita as India in 1999. How did this tremendous improvement in health conditions in poor nations take place?

The answer lies in technology and in scientific breakthroughs that took place in the United States and Western Europe throughout the twentieth century. First came a wave of global drug innovation, most importantly the development of antibiotics, which produced many products that were highly effective against major killers in developing countries. Penicillin, which provided an effective treatment for a range of bacterial infections, became widely available by the early 1950s. Also important during the same period was the development of new vaccines, including those for yellow fever and smallpox.

The second major factor was the discovery of DDT (dichloro-diphenyl-trichloroethane). Although eventually the excess use of DDT as an agricultural pesticide would turn out to be an environmental hazard, its initial use in disease control was revolutionary. DDT allowed a breakthrough in attempts to control one of the major killers of children in relatively poor parts of the world—malaria. Finally, with the establishment and help of the World Health Organization, simple but effective medical and public health practices, such as oral rehydration and boiling water to prevent cholera, spread to poorer countries.

Some economists believe that improvements in health and life expectancy directly translate into greater productivity and higher real GDP per capita.[4] The spectacular narrowing of the gap in life expectancy between rich and poor countries during the several decades following World War II does not support this view—there was no corresponding narrowing of the gaps in real GDP per capita.[5] But at some level this is secondary. Even though it is no easy fix to the problem of poverty, the agenda of continued healthcare innovations is a potent weapon in our efforts to improve the quality of life for billions of people around the world.

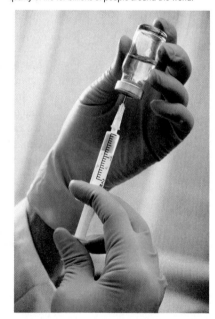

• In keeping with the optimization theme, in a feature entitled **Choice & Consequence** we ask students to make a real economic decision or evaluate the consequences of past real decisions. We then explain how an economist might analyze the same decision. Among the choices investigated are such questions and concepts as the power of exponential growth, foreign aid and corruption, and policies that address the problem of banks that are "too big to fail."

Organization

Part I Introduction to Economics lays the groundwork for understanding the economic way of thinking about the world. In **Chapter 1**, we show that the principle of *optimization* explains most of our choices. In other words, we make choices based on a consideration of benefits and costs, and to do this we need to consider trade-offs, budget constraints, and opportunity cost. We then explain that *equilibrium* is the situation in which everyone is simultaneously trying to individually optimize. In equilibrium, there isn't any perceived benefit to changing one's own behavior. We introduce the free-rider problem to show that individual optimization and social optimization do not necessarily coincide.

Because data plays such a central role in economics, we devote an entire chapter—**Chapter 2**—to economic models, the scientific method, empirical testing, and the critical distinction between correlation and causation. We show how economists use models and data to answer interesting questions about human behavior. For the students who want to brush up their graphical skills, there is an appendix on constructing and interpreting graphs, which is presented in the context of an actual experiment on incentive schemes.

Chapter 3 digs much more deeply into the concept of optimization, including an intuitive discussion of marginal analysis. We use a single running example of choosing an apartment, which confronts students with a trade-off between the cost of rent and the time spent commuting. We demonstrate two alternative approaches—optimization using total value and optimization using marginal analysis—and show why economists often use the latter technique.

Chapter 4 introduces the demand and supply framework via a running example of the market for gasoline. We show how the price of gasoline affects the decisions of buyers, like commuters, and sellers, like ExxonMobil. As we develop the model, we explore how individual buyers are added together to produce a market demand curve and how individual sellers are added together to generate a market supply curve. We then show how buyers and sellers jointly determine the equilibrium market price and the equilibrium quantity of goods transacted in a perfectly competitive market. Finally, we show how markets break down when prices aren't allowed to adjust to equate the quantity demanded and the quantity supplied.

Part II Introduction to Macroeconomics provides an introduction to the field. In **Chapter 5** we explain the basic measurement tools. Here we explore the derivation of the aggregate output of the economy, or the gross domestic product (GDP), with the production, expenditure, and income methods, explaining why all these methods are equivalent and lead to the same level of total GDP. We also consider what *isn't* measured in GDP, such as production that takes place at home for one's family. Finally, we discuss the measurement of inflation and the concept of a price index.

In *Chapter 6* we show how income (GDP) per capita can be compared across countries using two similar techniques—an exchange rate method and a purchasing power method. We explain how the aggregate production function links a country's physical capital stock, labor resources (total labor hours and human capital per worker), and technology to its GDP and thus draw the link between income per capita and a country's physical capital stock per worker, human capital, and technology. We then use these tools to investigate the roles of physical capital, human capital, and technology in accounting for the great differences in prosperity across countries.

In **Part III, Long-Run Growth and Development**, we turn to a comprehensive treatment of growth and development. In *Chapter 7*, we show that economic growth has transformed many countries over the past 200 years. For example, in the United States today, GDP per capita is about 25 times higher than it was in 1820. In this discussion, we explain the "exponential" nature of economic growth, which results from the fact that new growth builds on past growth, and implies that small differences in growth rates can translate into huge differences in income per capita over several decades. We explain how sustained economic growth relies on advances in technology and why different countries have experienced different long-run growth paths. We also emphasize that economic growth does not benefit all citizens equally. For some citizens, poverty is the unintentional by-product of technological progress. For the instructors who want a more in-depth treatment of growth and the determinants of GDP, we present a simplified version of the Solow Model in an optional appendix to the chapter.

Why do some nations not invest enough in physical and human capital, adopt the best technologies, and organize their production efficiently? Put another way, why isn't the whole world economically developed? *Chapter 8* probes this question and considers the fundamental causes of prosperity. We discuss several potential fundamental causes, in particular, geography, culture, and institutions, and argue why the oft-emphasized geographic factors do not seem to account for much of the wide cross-country gaps in economic prosperity.

In **Part IV, Equilibrium in the Macroeconomy**, we discuss three key markets that play a central role in macroeconomic analysis: the labor market, the credit market, and the market for bank reserves. *Chapter 9* begins with the labor market—labor demand and labor supply. We first describe the standard competitive equilibrium, where the wage and the quantity of labor employed are pinned down by the intersection of the labor demand and labor supply curves. We then show how downward rigid wages lead to unemployment. We use this framework to discuss the many different factors that influence unemployment, including both frictional and structural sources.

Chapter 10 extends our analysis by incorporating the credit market. We explain how the modern financial system circulates funds from savers to borrowers. We describe the different types of shocks that can destabilize a financial system. We analyze how banks and other financial intermediaries connect supply and demand in the credit market, and we use banks' balance sheets to explain the risks of taking on short-term liabilities and making long-term investments.

Chapter 11 introduces the monetary system. We begin by explaining the functions of money. The chapter then introduces the Federal Reserve Bank (the Fed) and lays out the basic plumbing of the monetary system, especially the role of supply and demand in the market for bank reserves. We explain in detail the Fed's role in controlling bank reserves and influencing interest rates, especially the interest rate on bank reserves (the federal funds rate). The chapter explains the causes of inflation and its social costs and benefits.

In **Part V, Short-Run Fluctuations and Macroeconomic Policy**, we use a modern framework to analyze and explain short-run fluctuations. Our analysis is inclusive and integrative, enabling us to combine the most relevant and useful insights from many different schools of economic thought. We believe that the labor market is the most informative lens through which first-year economics students can understand economic fluctuations. We therefore put the labor market and unemployment at the center of our analysis. In this part of the book, we also extend our discussion of the role of financial markets and financial crises. We present a balanced perspective that incorporates the diverse range of important insights that have emerged in the last century of theoretical and empirical research.

Chapter 12 lays the foundations of this approach, showing how a wide range of economic shocks cause short-run fluctuations and how these can be studied using the labor market. We trace out the impact of technological shocks, shocks to sentiments (including animal spirits), and monetary and financial shocks that work through their impact on the interest rate or by causing financial crises. In each case, we explain how multipliers amplify the impact of the initial shock. We also explain how downward wage rigidity affects the labor market responds to these shocks. We apply our labor market model to both economic contractions and expansions and look at the problems that arise when the economy grows too slowly or too quickly.

Chapter 13 discusses the wide menu of monetary and fiscal policies that are used to partially offset aggregate fluctuations. We describe the most important strategies that have recently been adopted by central banks. We then discuss the role of fiscal policy and provide an analytic toolkit that students can use to estimate the impact of countercyclical expenditures and taxation.

In **Part VI, Macroeconomics in a Global Economy**, we provide a wide-angle view of the global economy and the relationships that interconnect national economies. In *Chapter 14* we show how international trade works, using the key concepts of specialization, comparative advantage, and opportunity cost. We study the optimal allocation of tasks inside a firm and show that firms should allocate their employees to tasks—and individuals should choose their occupations—according to comparative advantage. We then broaden the picture by focusing on the optimal allocation of tasks across countries and show that here, too, the same principles apply. We analyze international flows of goods and services and the financial consequences of trade deficits. We describe the accounting identities that enable economists to measure the rich patterns of global trade. We also discuss the critical role of technology transfer.

Chapter 15 studies the determinants of exchange rates—both nominal and real—between different currencies and how they impact the macroeconomy. We describe the different types of exchange rate regimes and the operation of the foreign exchange market. Finally, we study the impact of changes in the real exchange rate on net exports and GDP.

MyEconLab®

MyEconLab's powerful assessment and tutorial system works hand-in-hand with the Second Edition of *Macroeconomics*. It includes comprehensive homework, quiz, test, interactive, engagement and tutorial options which allow students to test their knowledge and instructors to manage all of their assessment and engagement needs in one program. Students and instructors can register, create and access all of their MyLab courses at www.pearsonmylab.com.

Key Features in the MyEconLab for *Macroeconomics,* Second Edition include the following resources for instructors and students:

Personalized Learning

Not every student learns the same way or at the same rate. With the growing need for acceleration through many courses, it's more important than ever to meet students where they learn. Personalized learning in the MyEconLab gives you the flexibility to incorporate the approach that best suits your course and your students.

Interactive Graphs

The Interactive Graphs in MyEconLab enhance the student learning experience. Students can manipulate the coordinates and parameters of these graphs and watch the graphs change in real time, thereby deepening their conceptual understanding of the material.

Study Plan

The Study Plan acts as a tutor, providing personalized recommendations for each of your students based on his or her ability to master the learning objectives in your course. This allows students to focus their study time by pinpointing the precise areas they need to review, and allowing them to use customized practice and learning aids—such as videos, eText, tutorials, and more—to get them back on track. Using the report available in the gradebook, you can then tailor course lectures to prioritize the content for which students need the most support—offering you better insight into classroom and individual performance.

With comprehensive homework, quiz, test, activity, practice, and tutorial options, instructors can manage all their assessment and online activity needs in one program. MyEconLab saves time by automatically grading questions and activities and tracking results in an online gradebook.

Each chapter contains two preloaded homework exercise sets that can be used to build an individualized study plan for each student. These study plan exercises contain tutorial resources, including instant feedback, links to the appropriate chapter section in the eText, pop-up definitions from the text, and step-by-step guided solutions, where appropriate. Within its rich assignment library, instructors will find a vast array of assessments that ask the students to draw graph lines and shifts, plot equilibrium points, and highlight important graph areas, all with the benefit of instant, personalized feedback. This feedback culminates, when needed, with the correct graph output alongside the student's personal answer, creating a powerful learning moment.

After the initial setup of the MyEconLab course for Acemoglu/Laibson/List, there are two primary ways to begin using this rich online environment. The first path requires no further action by the instructor. Students, on their own, can use MyEconLab's Study Plan problems and tutorial resources to enhance their understanding of concepts. The online gradebook records each student's performance and time spent on the assessments, activities, and the study plan and generates reports by student or chapter.

Alternatively, instructors can fully customize MyEconLab to match their course exactly: reading assignments, homework assignments, video assignments, current news assignments, digital activities, experiments, quizzes, and tests. Assignable resources include:

- Preloaded exercise assignment sets for each chapter that include the student tutorial resources mentioned earlier.
- Preloaded quizzes for each chapter.
- Assignable and gradable exercises that are similar to the end-of-chapter questions and problems and numbered exactly as in the book to make assigning homework easier.
- *Real-Time Data Analysis Exercises* allow students and instructors to use the very latest data from the Federal Reserve Bank of St. Louis's FRED site. By completing the exercises, students become familiar with a key data source, learn how to locate data, and develop skills in interpreting data.
- In MyEconLab, select exhibits labeled MyEconLab Real-Time Data display updated graphs with real-time data from FRED.
- *Current News Exercises* provide a turnkey way to assign gradable news-based exercises in MyEconLab. Each week, Pearson scours the news, finds current economics articles, creates exercises around the news articles, and then automatically adds them to MyEconLab. Assigning and grading current news-based exercises that deal with the latest economics events and policy issues have never been more convenient.
- *Econ Exercise Builder* allows you to build customized exercises. Exercises include multiple-choice, graph drawing, and free-response items, many of which are generated algorithmically so that each time a student works them, a different variation is presented.
- Test Item File questions that allow you to assign quizzes or homework that will look just like your exams.

MyEconLab grades every problem type (except essays), even problems with graphs. When working homework exercises, students receive immediate feedback, with links to additional learning tools.

- *Experiments in MyEconLab* are a fun and engaging way to promote active learning and mastery of important economic concepts. Pearson's Experiments program is flexible and easy for instructors and students to use.
- Single-player experiments allow your students to play against virtual players from anywhere at any time so long as they have an Internet connection.
- Multiplayer experiments allow you to assign and manage a real-time experiment with your class.

Pre- and post-questions for each experiment are available for assignment in MyEconLab.

Dynamic Study Modules

Dynamic Study Modules help students study effectively on their own by continuously assessing their activity and performance in real time. Here's how it works: students complete a set of questions with a unique answer format that also asks them to indicate their confidence level. Questions repeat until the student can answer them all correctly and confidently. Once completed, Dynamic Study Modules explain the concept using materials from the text. These are available as graded assignments prior to class, and accessible on smartphones, tablets, and computers. NEW! Instructors can now remove questions from Dynamic Study Modules to better fit their course.

Enhanced eText

The Enhanced eText keeps students engaged in learning on their own time, while helping them achieve greater conceptual understanding of course material. The concept checks, animations, and interactive graphs bring learning to life, and allow students to apply the very concepts they are reading about. Combining resources that illuminate content with accessible self-assessment, MyEconLab with Enhanced eText provides students with a complete digital learning experience—all in one place.

And with the **Pearson eText 2.0 mobile app** students can now access the Enhanced eText and all of its functionality from their computer, tablet, or mobile phone. Because students' progress is synced across all of their devices, they can stop what they're doing on one device and pick up again later on another one—without breaking their stride.

Digital Interactives

Economic principles are not static ideas, and learning them shouldn't be a static process. Digital Interactives are dynamic and engaging assessment activities that promote critical thinking and application of key economic principles.

Each Digital Interactive has 3 to 5 progressive levels and requires approximately 20 minutes to explore, apply, compare, and analyze each topic. Many Digital Interactives include real-time data from FRED™ allowing professors and students to display, in graph and table form, up-to-the-minute data on key macro variables.

Digital Interactives can be assigned and graded within MyEconLab or used as a lecture tool to encourage engagement, classroom conversation, and group work.

Learning Catalytics

Learning Catalytics helps you generate class discussion, customize your lecture, and promote peer-to-peer learning with real-time analytics. As a student response tool, Learning Catalytics uses students' smartphones, tablets, or laptops to engage them in more interactive tasks and thinking.

- Help your students develop critical thinking skills.
- Monitor responses to find out where your students are struggling.
- Rely on real-time data to adjust your teaching strategy.
- Automatically group students for discussion, teamwork, and peer-to-peer learning.

LMS Integration

You can now link from Blackboard Learn, Brightspace by D2L, Canvas, or Moodle to Pearson MyEconLab. Access assignments, rosters, and resources, and synchronize grades with your LMS gradebook.

For students, single sign-on provides access to all the personalized learning resources that make studying more efficient and effective.

Instructor Resources

The **Instructor's Manual** for *Macroeconomics* was updated by Rashid Al-Hmoud of Texas Tech University and includes:

- A chapter-by-chapter outline of the text
- Lecture notes highlighting the big ideas and concepts from each chapter
- Teaching Tips on how to motivate the lecture
- Common Mistakes or Misunderstandings students often make and how to correct them
- Short, real-world Alternative Teaching Examples, different from those in the text

Active Learning Exercises, included online and at the end of each Instructor's Manual chapter, were updated by Rashid Al-Hmoud and include:

- 5 to 10 Active Learning Exercises per chapter that are ideal for in-class discussions and group work

The **Solutions Manual**, updated by Maggie Yellen, includes solutions to all end-of-chapter Questions and Problems in the text. It is available as downloadable Word documents and PDFs.

Three flexible **PowerPoint Presentation** packages make it easy for instructors to design presentation slides that best suit their style and needs:

- Lecture notes with some animated text figures and tables, as well as alternative examples with original static figures
- Figures from the text with step-by-step animation
- Static versions of all text figures and tables

Each presentation maps to the chapter's structure and organization and uses terminology used in the text. Rashid Al-Hmoud of Texas Tech University updated the Lecture PowerPoint presentation. Paul Graf of Indiana University, Bloomington, scripted and recorded the animations in MyEconLab.

The **Test Bank** for *Macroeconomics* was updated by Paul Holmes of Ashland University, Ross vanWassenhove of University of Houston, Alexandra Nica of University of Iowa, and Gregory Glipin of Montana State University. The Test Bank contains approximately 2,600 multiple-choice, numerical, short-answer, and essay questions. These have been edited and reviewed to ensure accuracy and clarity, and include terminology used in the book. Each question can be sorted by difficulty, book topic, concept covered, and AACSB learning standard to enhance ease of use. The Test Bank is available in Word, PDF, and TestGen formats.

TestGen is a computerized test generation program, available exclusively from Pearson, that allows instructors to easily create and administer tests on paper, electronically, or online. Instructors can select test items from the publisher-supplied test bank, which is organized by chapter and based on the associated textbook material, or create their own questions from scratch. With both quick-and-simple test creation and flexible and robust editing tools, TestGen is a complete test generator system for today's educators.

Instructor's Resource Center

Instructor resources are available online via our centralized supplements Web site, the Instructor Resource Center (**www.pearsonhighered.com/irc**). For access or more information, contact your local Pearson representative or request access online at the Instructor Resource Center.

Acknowledgments

As the three of us worked on this project, we taught each other a lot about economics, teaching, and writing. But we learned even more from the hundreds of other people who helped us along the way. For their guidance, we are thankful and deeply humbled. Their contributions turned out to be critical in ways that we never imagined when we started, and our own ideas were greatly improved by their insights and advice.

Our reviewers, focus group participants, and class testers showed us how to better formulate our ideas and helped us sharpen our writing. Through their frequently brilliant feedback, they corrected our economic misconceptions, improved our conceptual vision, and showed us how to write more clearly. Their contributions appear in almost every paragraph of this book. All of their names are listed below.

Our research assistants—Alec Brandon, Justin Holz, Josh Hurwitz, Xavier Jaravel, Angelina Liang, Daniel Norris, Yana Peysakhovich, Maggie Yellen, and Jan Zilinsky—played a critical role at every phase of the project, from analyzing data to editing prose to generating deep insights about pedagogical principles that are woven throughout the book. We learned to trust their instincts on every element of the book, and quickly realized that their contributions were indispensable to the project's success. We are especially indebted to Josh Hurwitz and Maggie Yellen, who have earned our eternal gratitude for many late work nights and for their brilliant editorial and economic insights.

We are also deeply grateful to the many inspiring economists who contributed major components of the project. Maggie Yellen contributed extensively to the updates of the end-of-chapter questions and problems, which stand out as examples of inspiring pedagogy. Rashid Al-Hmoud of Texas Tech University updated the innovative and intuitive Instructor's Manual and Active Learning Exercises. Rashid Al-Hmoud of Texas Tech University and Paul Graf of Indiana University, Bloomington, updated the outstanding PowerPoint slides and animations that illuminate and distill the key lessons of the book. Paul Holmes, Ross vanWassenhove of University of Houston, Alexandra Nica of University of Iowa, and Gregory Glipin of Montana State University updated the expansive test bank.

Most importantly, we acknowledge the myriad contributions of our editors and all of our amazing colleagues at Pearson. They have marched with us every step of the way. We wouldn't dare count the number of hours that they dedicated to this project, including evenings and weekends. Their commitment, vision, and editorial suggestions touched every sentence of this book. Most of the key decisions about the project were made with the help of our editors, and this collaborative spirit proved to be absolutely essential to our writing. Dozens of people at Pearson played key roles, but the most important contributions were made by Adrienne D'Ambrosio, Director of Portfolio Management; Christina Masturzo, Senior Portfolio Manager; Cydney Westmoreland, Development Editor; Nancy Freihofer, Content Producer; Heidi Allgair, Project Manager; Noel Lotz, Digital Content Team Lead; and Melissa Honig, Digital Studio Producer.

We are particularly grateful to Adrienne, who has been deeply committed to our project from the first day and has tirelessly worked with us on every key decision. We also wish to thank Denise Clinton, who first got us started, and Donna Battista, Vice President, Business Publishing, who championed the project along the way. All of these publishing professionals transformed us as writers, teachers, and communicators. This book is a testimony to their perseverance, their dedication, and their brilliant eye for good (and often bad!) writing. Their commitment to this project has been extraordinary and inspirational. We are profoundly grateful for their guidance and collaboration.

Finally, we wish to thank our many other support networks. Our own professors, who first inspired us as economists and showed, through their example, the power of teaching and the joy that one can take from studying economics. Our parents, who nurtured us in so many ways and gave us the initial human capital that made our entire careers possible. Our kids, who implicitly sacrificed when our long hours on this book ate into family life. And, most profoundly, we thank our partners, who have been supportive, understanding, and inspirational throughout the project.

This book is the product of many streams that have flowed together and so many people who have contributed their insights and their passion to this project. We are deeply grateful for these myriad collaborations.

Reviewers

The following reviewers, class test participants, and focus group participants provided invaluable insights.

Adel Abadeer, Calvin College

Ahmed Abou-Zaid, Eastern Illinois University

Temisan Agbeyegbe, City University of New York

Carlos Aguilar, El Paso Community College

Rashid Al-Hmoud, Texas Tech University

Frank Albritton, Seminole Community College

Sam Allgood, University of Nebraska, Lincoln

Neil Alper, Northeastern University

Farhad Ameen, Westchester Community College

Catalina Amuedo-Dorantes, San Diego State University

Lian An, University of North Florida

Samuel Andoh, Southern Connecticut State University

Brad Andrew, Juniata College

Len Anyanwu, Union County College

Robert Archibald, College of William and Mary

Ali Arshad, New Mexico Highlands University

Robert Baden, University of California, Santa Cruz

Mohsen Bahmani-Oskooee, University of Wisconsin, Milwaukee

Scott L. Baier, Clemson University

Rita Balaban, University of North Carolina

Mihajlo Balic, Harrisburg Area Community College

Sheryl Ball, Virginia Polytechnic Institute and State University

Spencer Banzhaf, Georgia State University

Jim Barbour, Elon University

Scott Barkowski, Clemson University

Hamid Bastin, Shippensburg University

Clare Battista, California State Polytechnic University, San Luis Obispo

Jodi Beggs, Northeastern University

Eric Belasco, Montana State University

Susan Bell, Seminole State University

Valerie Bencivenga, University of Texas, Austin

Pedro Bento, West Virginia University

Derek Berry, Calhoun Community College

Prasun Bhattacharjee, East Tennessee State University

Benjamin Blair, Columbus State University

Douglas Blair, Rutgers University

John Bockino, Suffolk County Community College

Andrea Borchard, Hillsborough Community College

Luca Bossi, University of Pennsylvania

Gregory Brock, Georgia Southern University

Bruce Brown, California State Polytechnic University, Pomona

David Brown, Pennsylvania State University

Jaime Brown, Pennsylvania State University

Laura Bucila, Texas Christian University

Don Bumpass, Sam Houston State University

Chris Burkart, University of West Florida

Julianna Butler, University of Delaware

Colleen Callahan, American University

Fred Campano, Fordham University

Douglas Campbell, University of Memphis

Cheryl Carleton, Villanova University

Scott Carrell, University of California, Davis

Kathleen Carroll, University of Maryland, Baltimore

Regina Cassady, Valencia College, East Campus

Shirley Cassing, University of Pittsburgh

Suparna Chakraborty, University of San Francisco

Catherine Chambers, University of Central Missouri

Chiuping Chen, American River College

Susan Christoffersen, Philadelphia University

Benjamin Andrew Chupp, Illinois State University

David L. Cleeton, Illinois State University

Cynthia Clement, University of Maryland

Marcelo Clerici-Arias, Stanford University

Bently Coffey, University of South Carolina, Columbia

Rachel Connelly, Bowdoin College

William Conner, Tidewater Community College

Kathleen Conway, Carnegie Mellon University

Patrick Conway, University of North Carolina

Jay Corrigan, Kenyon College

Antoinette Criss, University of South Florida

Sean Crockett, City University of New York

Patrick Crowley, Texas A&M University, Corpus Christi

Kelley Cullen, Eastern Washington University

Scott Cunningham, Baylor University

Muhammed Dalgin, Kutztown University

David Davenport, McLennan Community College

Stephen Davis, Southwest Minnesota State University

John W. Dawson, Appalachian State University

Pierangelo De Pace, California State University, Pomona

David Denslow, University of Florida

Arthur Diamond, University of Nebraska, Omaha

Timothy Diette, Washington and Lee University

Isaac Dilanni, University of Illinois, Urbana-Champaign

Oguzhan Dincer, Illinois State University

Ethan Doetsch, Ohio State University

Murat Doral, Kennesaw State University

Kirk Doran, University of Notre Dame

Tanya Downing, Cuesta College

Mitchell Dudley, University of Michigan, Ann Arbor

Gary Dymski, University of California, Riverside

Kevin Egan, University of Toledo

Eric Eide, Brigham Young University, Provo

Harold Elder, University of Alabama, Tuscaloosa

Michael Ellerbrock, Virginia Tech

Harry Ellis, University of North Texas

Noha Emara, Columbia University

Lucas Engelhardt, Kent State University, Stark

Erwin Erhardt, University of Cincinnati

Hadi Esfahani, University of Illinois, Urbana-Champaign

Molly Espey, Clemson University

Jose Esteban, Palomar College

Hugo Eyzaguirre, Northern Michigan University

Jamie Falcon, University of Maryland, Baltimore

Liliana Fargo, DePaul University

Leila Farivar, Ohio State University

Sasan Fayazmanesh, California State University, Fresno

Bichaka Fayissa, Middle Tennessee State University

Virginia Fierro-Renoy, Keiser University

Donna Fisher, Georgia Southern University

Paul Fisher, Henry Ford Community College

Todd Fitch, University of California, Berkeley

Mary Flannery, University of Notre Dame

Hisham Foad, San Diego State University

Mathew Forstater, University of Missouri, Kansas City

Irene Foster, George Mason University

Hamilton Fout, Kansas State University

Shelby Frost, Georgia State University

Timothy Fuerst, University of Notre Dame

Ken Gaines, East-West University

John Gallup, Portland State University

William Galose, Lamar University

Karen Gebhardt, Colorado State University

Gerbremeskel Gebremariam, Virginia Polytechnic Institute and State University

Lisa George, City University of New York

Gregory Gilpin, Montana State University

Seth Gitter, Towson University

Brian Goegan, Arizona State University, Tempe

Rajeev Goel, Illinois State University

Bill Goffe, State University of New York, Oswego

Julie Gonzalez, University of California, Santa Cruz

Paul Graf, Indiana University, Bloomington

Philip Graves, University of Colorado, Boulder

Lisa Grobar, California State University, Long Beach

Fatma Gunay Bendas, Washington and Lee University

Michael Hammock, Middle Tennessee State University

Michele Hampton, Cuyahoga Community College

Moonsu Han, North Shore Community College

F. Andrew Hanssen, Clemson University

David Harris, Benedictine College

Robert Harris, Indiana University-Purdue University Indianapolis

Julia Heath, University of Cincinnati

Jolien Helsel, Youngstown State University

Matthew Henry, Cleveland State University

Thomas Henry, Mississippi State University

David Hewitt, Whittier College

Wayne Hickenbottom, University of Texas, Austin

Jannett Highfill, Bradley University

Michael Hilmer, San Diego State University

John Hilston, Brevard College

Naphtali Hoffman, Elmira College and Binghamton University

Kim Holder, University of West Georgia

Robert Holland, Purdue University

Don Holley, Boise State University

Paul Holmes, Ashland University

James A. Hornsten, Northwestern University

Gail Hoyt, University of Kentucky

Jim Hubert, Seattle Central Community College

Scott Hunt, Columbus State Community College

Kyle Hurst, University of Colorado, Denver

Ruben Jacob-Rubio, University of Georgia

Joyce Jacobsen, Wesleyan University

Kenneth Jameson, University of Utah

Kevin Jasek-Rysdahl, California State University, Stanislaus

Andres Jauregui, Columbus State University

Brian Jenkins, University of California, Irvine

Sarah Jenyk, Youngstown State University

Robert Jerome, James Madison University

Deepak Joglekar, University of Connecticut

Paul Johnson, Columbus State University

Ted Joyce, City University of New York

David Kalist, Shippensburg University

Lilian Kamal, University of Hartford*

Leonie Karkoviata, University of Houston, Downtown

Kathy Kelly, University of Texas, Arlington

Nathan Kemper, University Arkansas

Colin Knapp, University of Florida

Yilmaz Kocer, University of Southern California

Ebenezer Kolajo, University of West Georgia

Janet Koscianski, Shippensburg University

Justin Krieg of Minneapolis Community & Technical College

Robert Krol, California State University, Northridge

Daniel Kuester, Kansas State University

Patricia Kuzyk, Washington State University

Sumner La Croix, University of Hawaii

Rose LaMont, Modesto Community College

Carsten Lange, California State University, Pomona

Vicky Langston, Columbus State University

Susan Laury, Georgia State University

Myoung Lee, University of Missouri, Columbia

Sang Lee, Southeastern Louisiana University

Phillip K. Letting, Harrisburg Area Community College

John Levendis, Loyola University

Steven Levkoff, University of California, San Diego

Dennis P. Leyden, University of North Carolina, Greensboro

Gregory Lindeblom, Brevard College

Alan Lockard, Binghamton University

Joshua Long, Ivy Technical College

Linda Loubert, Morgan State University

Heather Luea, Kansas State University

Rotua Lumbantobing, Western Connecticut State University

Rita Madarassy, Santa Clara University

James Makokha, Collin County Community College

Liam C. Malloy, University of Rhode Island

Christopher Mann, University of Nebraska, Lincoln

Paula Manns, Atlantic Cape Community College

Vlad Manole, Rutgers University

Hardik Marfatia, Northeastern Illinois University

Lawrence Martin, Michigan State University

Norman Maynard, University of Oklahoma

Katherine McClain, University of Georgia

Scott McGann, Grossmont College

Kim Marie McGoldrick, University of Richmond

Shah Mehrabi, Montgomery Community College

Aaron Meininger, University of California, Santa Cruz

Saul Mekies, Kirkwood Community College

Kimberly Mencken, Baylor University

Diego Mendez-Carbajo, Illinois Wesleyan University

Thomas Menn, United States Military Academy at West Point

Catherine Middleton, University of Tennessee, Chattanooga

Nara Mijid, Central Connecticut State University

Laurie A. Miller, University of Nebraska, Lincoln

Edward Millner, Virginia Commonwealth University

Ida Mirzaie, Ohio State University

David Mitchell, Missouri State University, Springfield

Michael Mogavero, University of Notre Dame

Robert Mohr, University of New Hampshire

Barbara Moore, University of Central Florida

Thaddeaus Mounkurai, Daytona State College

Usha Nair-Reichert, Emory University

Camille Nelson, Oregon State University

Michael Nelson, Oregon State University

John Neri, University of Maryland

Andre Neveu, James Madison University

Jinlan Ni, University of Nebraska, Omaha

Eric Nielsen, St. Louis Community College

Jaminka Ninkovic, Emory University

Chali Nondo, Albany State University

Richard P. Numrich, College of Southern Nevada

Andrew Nutting, Hamilton College

Grace O, Georgia State University

Norman Obst, Michigan State University

Scott Ogawa, Northwestern University

Lee Ohanian, University of California, Los Angeles

Paul Okello, Tarrant County College

Ifeakandu Okoye, Florida A&M University

Alan Osman, Ohio State University

Tomi Ovaska, Youngstown State University

Caroline Padgett, Francis Marion University

Zuohong Pan, Western Connecticut State University

Peter Parcells, Whitman College

Cynthia Parker, Chaffey College

Mohammed Partapurwala, Monroe Community College

Robert Pennington, University of Central Florida

David Perkis, Purdue University, West Lafayette

Colin Phillipps, Illinois State University

Kerk Phillips, Brigham Young University

Goncalo Pina, Santa Clara University

Michael Podgursky, University of Missouri

Greg Pratt, Mesa Community College

Guangjun Qu, Birmingham-Southern College

Fernando Quijano, Dickinson State University

Joseph Quinn, Boston College

Reza Ramazani, Saint Michael's College

Ranajoy Ray-Chaudhuri, Ohio State University

Mitchell Redlo, Monroe Community College

Javier Reyes, University of Arkansas

Teresa Riley, Youngstown State University

Nancy Roberts, Arizona State University

Malcolm Robinson, Thomas More College

Randall Rojas, University of California, Los Angeles

Sudipta Roy, Kankakee Community College

Jared Rubin, Chapman University

Jason C. Rudbeck, University of Georgia

Melissa Rueterbusch, Mott Community College

Mariano Runco, Auburn University at Montgomery

Nicholas G. Rupp, East Carolina University

Steven Russell, Indiana University-Purdue University-Indianapolis

Michael Ryan, Western Michigan University

Ravi Samitamana, Daytona State College

David Sanders, University of Missouri, St. Louis

Michael Sattinger, State University of New York, Albany

Anya Savikhin Samek, University of Wisconsin, Madison

Peter Schuhmann, University of North Carolina, Wilmington

Robert M. Schwab, University of Maryland

Jesse Schwartz, Kennesaw State University

James K. Self, Indiana University, Bloomington

Katie Shester, Washington and Lee University

Mark Showalter, Brigham Young University, Provo

Dorothy Siden, Salem State University

Mark V. Siegler, California State University, Sacramento

Carlos Silva, New Mexico State University

Timothy Simpson, Central New Mexico Community College

Michael Sinkey, University of West Georgia

John Z. Smith, Jr., United States Military Academy, West Point

Thomas Snyder, University of Central Arkansas

Joe Sobieralski, Southwestern Illinois College

Sara Solnick, University of Vermont

Martha Starr, American University

Rebecca Stein, University of Pennsylvania

Liliana Stern, Auburn University

Adam Stevenson, University of Michigan

Cliff Stone, Ball State University

Mark C. Strazicich, Appalachian State University

Chetan Subramanian, State University of New York, Buffalo

AJ Sumell, Youngstown State University

Charles Swanson, Temple University

Tom Sweeney, Des Moines Area Community College

James Swofford, University of South Alabama

Kevin Sylwester, Southern Illinois University

Vera Tabakova, East Carolina University

Saleh S. Tabrizy of University of Oklahoma

Emily Tang, University of California, San Diego

Mark Tendall, Stanford University

Jennifer Thacher, University of New Mexico

Charles Thomas, Clemson University

Rebecca Thornton, University of Houston

Jill Trask, Tarrant County College, Southeast

Steve Trost, Virginia Polytechnic Institute and State University

Ty Turley, Brigham Young University

Nora Underwood, University of Central Florida

Mike Urbancic, University of Oregon

Don Uy-Barreta, De Anza College

John Vahaly, University of Louisville

Ross vanWassenhove, University of Houston

Don Vandegrift, College of New Jersey

Nancy Virts, California State University, Northridge

Cheryl Wachenheim, North Dakota State College

Jeffrey Waddoups, University of Nevada, Las Vegas

Parag Waknis, University of Massachusetts, Dartmouth

Donald Wargo, Temple University

Charles Wassell, Jr., Central Washington University

Matthew Weinberg, Drexel University

Robert Whaples, Wake Forest University

Elizabeth Wheaton, Southern Methodist University

Mark Wheeler, Western Michigan University

Anne Williams, Gateway Community College

Brock Williams, Metropolitan Community College of Omaha

DeEdgra Williams, Florida A&M University

Brooks Wilson, McLennan Community College

Mark Witte, Northwestern University

Katherine Wolfe, University of Pittsburgh

William Wood, James Madison University

Jadrian Wooten, Pennsylvania State University

Steven Yamarik, California State University, Long Beach

Guy Yamashiro, California State University, Long Beach

Bill Yang, Georgia Southern University

Young-Ro Yoon, Wayne State University

Maggie Yellen

Madelyn Young, Converse College

Michael Youngblood, Rock Valley College

Jeffrey Zax, University of Colorado, Boulder

Martin Zelder, Northwestern University

Erik Zemljic, Kent State University

Kevin Zhang, Illinois State University

Macroeconomics: Flexibility Chart

Core Approach	Emphasis on Long-Run Growth	Emphasis on International
Chapter 1: The Principles and Practice of Economics	**Chapter 1:** The Principles and Practice of Economics	**Chapter 1:** The Principles and Practice of Economics
Chapter 2: Economic Methods and Economic Questions (optional)	**Chapter 2:** Economic Methods and Economic Questions (optional)	**Chapter 2:** Economic Methods and Economic Questions (optional)
Chapter 2 Appendix: Constructing and Interpreting Charts and Graphs	**Chapter 2 Appendix:** Constructing and Interpreting Charts and Graphs	**Chapter 2 Appendix:** Constructing and Interpreting Charts and Graphs
Chapter 3: Optimization: Doing the Best You Can (optional)	**Chapter 3:** Optimization: Doing the Best You Can (optional)	**Chapter 3:** Optimization: Doing the Best You Can (optional)
Chapter 4: Demand, Supply, and Equilibrium	**Chapter 4:** Demand, Supply, and Equilibrium	**Chapter 4:** Demand, Supply, and Equilibrium

Macroeconomics: Flexibility Chart

Core Approach	Emphasis on Long-Run Growth	Emphasis on International
Chapter 5: The Wealth of Nations: Defining and Measuring Macroeconomic Aggregates	**Chapter 5:** The Wealth of Nations: Defining and Measuring Macroeconomic Aggregates	**Chapter 5:** The Wealth of Nations: Defining and Measuring Macroeconomic Aggregates
Chapter 6: Aggregate Incomes	**Chapter 6:** Aggregate Incomes	**Chapter 6:** Aggregate Incomes
Chapter 7: Economic Growth	**Chapter 7:** Economic Growth	**Chapter 7:** Economic Growth
Chapter 8: Why Isn't the Whole World Developed? (optional)	**Chapter 8:** Why Isn't the Whole World Developed?	**Chapter 8:** Why Isn't the Whole World Developed? (optional)
Chapter 9: Employment and Unemployment	**Chapter 9:** Employment and Unemployment	**Chapter 9:** Employment and Unemployment
Chapter 10: Credit Markets	**Chapter 10:** Credit Markets	**Chapter 10:** Credit Markets
Chapter 11: The Monetary System	**Chapter 11:** The Monetary System	**Chapter 11:** The Monetary System
Chapter 12: Short-Run Fluctuations	**Chapter 12:** Short-Run Fluctuations	**Chapter 12:** Short-Run Fluctuations
Chapter 13: Countercyclical Macroeconomic Policy	**Chapter 13:** Countercyclical Macroeconomic Policy	**Chapter 13:** Countercyclical Macroeconomic Policy
Chapter 14: Macroeconomics and International Trade (optional)	**Chapter 14:** Macroeconomics and International Trade (optional)	**Chapter 14:** Macroeconomics and International Trade
Chapter 15: Open Economy Macroeconomics (optional)	**Chapter 15:** Open Economy Macroeconomics (optional)	**Chapter 15:** Open Economy Macroeconomics

1 The Principles and Practice of Economics

Is Facebook free?

Facebook doesn't charge you a penny, so it's tempting to say "it's free."

Here's another way to think about it: what do you give up when you use Facebook? Facebook may not take your money, but it does take your time. If you spend an hour each day on Facebook, you are giving up some alternative use of that time. You could spend that time playing soccer, watching Netflix, napping, studying, or listening to music. You could also spend it *making* money. A typical U.S. college student employed 7 hours per week earns almost $4,000 in a year—enough to pay the annual lease on a sports car. A part-time job is just one alternative way to use the time that you spend on Facebook. In your view, what is the best alternative use of *your* Facebook time? That's the economic way of thinking about the cost of Facebook.

In this chapter, we introduce you to the economic way of thinking about the world. Economists study the choices that people make, from big decisions like choosing a career to daily decisions like logging onto Facebook. To understand those choices, they often focus on the costs and benefits involved.

CHAPTER OUTLINE

1.1 The Scope of Economics

Economics involves far more than money. Economists study *all* human behavior, from a person's decision to lease a new sports car, to the speed the new driver chooses as she rounds a hairpin corner, to her decision not to wear a seat belt. These are all choices, and they are all fair game to economists. Choice—not money—is the unifying feature of all the things that economists study.

In fact, economists think of almost all human behavior as the outcome of choices. For instance, imagine that Dad tells his teenage daughter that she *must* wash the family car. The daughter has several options: she can wash it, she can negotiate for an easier chore, she can refuse to wash it and suffer the consequences, or she can move out (a drastic response, sure, but still an option). Obeying your parents is a choice, though it may not always feel like one.

> Choice—not money—is the unifying feature of all the things that economists study.

Economic Agents and Economic Resources

Saying that economics is all about choices is an easy way to remember what economics is. To give you a more precise definition, we first need to introduce two important concepts: *economic agents* and *resource allocation*.

An **economic agent** is an individual or a group that makes choices. Let's start with a few types of individual economic agents. For example, a *consumer* chooses to eat bacon cheeseburgers or tofu burgers. A *parent* chooses to enroll her children in public school or private school. A *student* chooses to attend his classes or to skip them. A *citizen* chooses whether or not to vote, and if so, which candidate to support. A *worker* chooses to do her job or pretend to work while texting. A *criminal* chooses to hotwire cars or mug little old ladies. A *business leader* chooses to open a new factory in Chile or in China. A *senator* chooses to vote for or against a bill. Of course, you are also an economic agent, because you make an enormous number of choices every day.

> An **economic agent** is an individual or a group that makes choices.

Not all economic agents, however, are individuals. An economic agent can also be a group—a government, an army, a firm, a university, a political party, a labor union, a sports team, or a street gang (Exhibit 1.1). Sometimes economists simplify their analysis by treating these groups as a single decision maker, without worrying about the details of how the different individuals in the group contributed to the decision. For example, an economist might say that Apple prices the iPhone to maximize its profits, glossing over the fact that many employees participated in the analysis—including the arguments and disagreements—that led to the choice of the price.

1.1

1.2

1.3

1.4

1.5

1.6

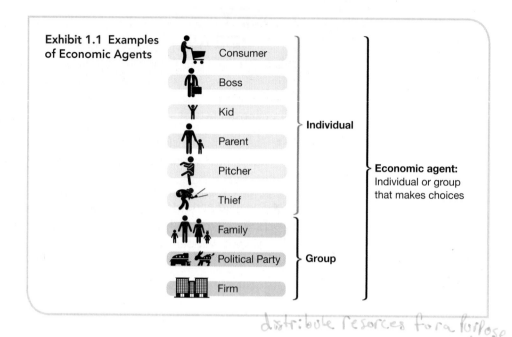

Exhibit 1.1 Examples of Economic Agents

Consumer
Boss
Kid
Parent
Pitcher
Thief
} Individual

Family
Political Party
Firm
} Group

Economic agent: Individual or group that makes choices

distribute resources for a purpose

Scarce resources are things that people want, where the quantity that people want exceeds the quantity that is available.

Scarcity is the situation of having unlimited wants in a world of limited resources.

The second important concept to understand is that economics studies the allocation of *scarce resources*. **Scarce resources** are things that people want, where the quantity that people want (if the resources were being given away for free) exceeds the quantity that is available. Gold wedding bands, Shiatsu massages, Coach handbags, California peaches, iPhones, triple-chocolate-fudge ice cream, and rooms with a view are all scarce resources. But a resource doesn't need to be luxurious to be scarce—everyday goods are also scarce, like toilet paper, subway seats, and clean drinking water. **Scarcity** exists because people have unlimited wants in a world of limited resources. The world does not have enough resources to give everyone *everything* they want (for free). Consider sports cars: if sports cars were given away at a zero price, there would not be enough of them to go around. So how does society determine who gets the limited supply of sports cars? In general, how does society allocate all of the scarce resources in the economy?

In a modern economy, consumers like you play a key role in this resource allocation process. You have 24 hours to allocate each day—this is your daily budget of time. You choose how many of those 24 hours you will allocate to Facebook. You choose how many of those 24 hours you will allocate to other activities, including school work and/or a job. If you have a job, you choose whether to spend your hard-earned wages on a sports car. These types of decisions determine how scarce resources are allocated in a modern economy: to the consumers who are able and willing to pay for them.

Economists don't want to impose our tastes for sports cars, hybrids, electric vehicles, SUVs, or public transportation on you. We are interested in teaching you how to use economic reasoning so that *you* can compare the costs and benefits of the alternative options and make the choices that are best for you.

Definition of Economics

Economics is the study of how agents choose to allocate scarce resources and how those choices affect society.

We are now ready to define economics precisely. **Economics** is the study of how agents choose to allocate scarce resources and how those choices affect society.

Our earlier examples all emphasized people's *choices,* and choices play a key role in the formal definition of economics. However, the definition of economics also adds a new element to our discussion: the effects of any individual agent's choices on society. For example, the sale of a new sports car doesn't just affect the person driving off the dealer's lot. The sale generates sales tax, which the government uses to fund projects like highways and hospitals. The purchase of the new car also generates some congestion—that's one more car in rush-hour gridlock. It's another car that might grab the last parking spot on your street. If the new owner drives recklessly, the car may generate risks to other drivers. Economists study the original choice and its multiple consequences for other people in the world.

Positive Economics and Normative Economics

We now have an idea of what economics is about: people's choices. But why study these choices? Part of the answer is that economists are just curious, but that's only a small piece of the picture. Understanding people's choices is practically useful for two key reasons. Economic analysis

1. Describes what people *actually* do (positive economics)
2. Recommends what people, including society, *ought* to do (normative economics)

The first application is descriptive, and the second is advisory.

Economics is the study of choice.

Positive economics is analysis that generates objective descriptions or predictions, which can be verified with data.

Normative economics is analysis that recommends what an individual or society ought to do.

Prescriptive economics
what is best for the
individual economic
agent.

Positive Economics Describes What People Actually Do   *Not influenced by feelings or opinions*   Descriptions of what people actually do are (objective) statements about the world—in other words, statements that can be confirmed or tested with data. For instance, it is a fact that in 2014, 50 percent of U.S. households earned less than $54,462 per year.[1] Of course, these earnings were related to the choices that those households made, including whether to work for pay, which jobs to apply for, and how many hours to work at those jobs. Describing what has happened or predicting what will happen is referred to as **positive economics** or positive economic analysis.

For instance, consider the prediction that in 2025, U.S. households will invest about half of their retirement savings in the stock market. This forecast can be compared to future data and either confirmed or disproven. Because a prediction is eventually testable—after the passage of time—it is part of positive economics.

Normative Economics Recommends What People Ought to Do   **Normative economics**, the second of the two types of economic analysis, advises individuals and society on their choices. Normative economics is about what people ought to do. *influenced by feelings or opinions*   Normative economics is almost always dependent on (subjective) judgments, which means that normative analysis depends at least in part on personal feelings, tastes, or opinions. So whose subjective judgments do we try to use? Economists believe that the people being advised should determine the preferences to be used.

For example, consider an economist who is helping a worker to decide how much risk to take in her investments. The economist might ask the worker about her own preferences regarding investment risk. Suppose the worker said that she wouldn't sleep well at night if her retirement savings were invested in the stock market, which does fall sharply from time to time. The economist would explain that eliminating risk comes at a cost—riskless investments have a lower average rate of return than investments in the stock market. Stocks have had an annual average return that is about 6 percentage points higher per year than the return on riskless investments. If the worker acknowledged this difference and still wanted the riskless investments, the economist would help the worker find such riskless investments. Here the economist plays the role of engineer, finding the investment portfolio that will deliver the level of risk that the worker wants.

And that's the key—*what the worker wants*. In the mind of most economists, it is legitimate for the worker to choose any level of risk, as long as she understands the implications of that risk for her average rate of return—less risk implies a lower average rate of return. When economic analysis is used to help *individual* economic agents choose what is in their personal best interest, this type of normative economics is referred to as *prescriptive economics*.

Sometimes the normative analysis gets more complicated, because there are many economic agents in the picture. We turn to these harder normative analyses next.

Normative Analysis and Public Policy   Normative analysis also generates advice to society in general. For example, economists are often asked to evaluate public policies, like taxes or regulations. When public policies create winners and losers, citizens tend to have opposing views about the desirability of the government program. One person's migratory bird sanctuary is another person's mosquito-infested swamp. Protecting a wetland with environmental regulations benefits bird-watchers but harms landowners who would like to develop that land.

Economic agents have divergent views on the future of this swamp. The owner of the property wants to build housing units. An environmentalist wants to preserve the wetland to protect the whooping crane, an endangered species. What should happen?

Microeconomics is the study of how individuals, households, firms, and governments make choices, and how those choices affect prices, the allocation of resources, and the well-being of other agents.

Macroeconomics is the study of the economy as a whole. Macroeconomists study economy-wide phenomena, like the growth rate of a country's total economic output, the inflation rate, or the unemployment rate.

When a government policy creates winners and losers, economists need to make some ethical judgments to conduct normative analysis. Economists must make ethical judgments when evaluating policies that make one group worse off so another group can be made better off.

Ethical judgments are usually unavoidable when economists think about government policies, because there are few policies that make everyone better off. Deciding whether the costs experienced by the losers are justified by the benefits experienced by the winners is partly an ethical judgment. Is it ethical to create environmental regulations that prevent a real estate developer from draining a swamp so he can build new homes? What if those environmental regulations protect migratory birds that other people value? Are there possible compromises—should the government, for example, try to buy the land from the real estate developer? These public policy questions—which all ask what society *should* do—are normative economic questions.

Microeconomics and Macroeconomics

There is one other distinction that you need to know to understand the scope of economics. Economics can be divided into two broad fields of study, though many economists do a bit of both.

Microeconomics is the study of how individuals, households, firms, and governments make choices, and how those choices affect prices, the allocation of resources, and the well-being of other agents. In general, microeconomists are called on when we want to understand a small piece of the overall economy, like the market for coal-fired electricity generation.

For example, some microeconomists study pollution generated by coal-fired power plants. A microeconomist might predict the level of coal-based pollution over the next decade, basing her forecast on the overall demand for electricity and likely technological developments in the energy industry—including solar- and wind-energy substitutes for coal-fired power plants. Predicting future levels of pollution from coal-fired plants is part of positive economic analysis.

Some microeconomists undertake normative analysis of coal-based pollution. For example, because global warming is largely caused by carbon emissions from coal, oil, and other fossil fuels, microeconomists design new government policies that attempt to reduce the use of these fuels. For example, a "carbon tax" targets carbon emissions. Under a carbon tax, relatively carbon-intensive energy sources—like coal-fired power plants—pay more tax per unit of energy produced than energy sources with lower carbon emissions—like wind farms. Some microeconomists have the job of designing interventions like carbon taxes and determining how such interventions will affect the energy choices of households and firms.

Macroeconomics is the study of the economy as a whole. Macroeconomists study economy-wide phenomena, like the growth rate of a country's total economic output, the percentage increase in overall prices (the inflation rate), or the fraction of the labor force that is looking for work but cannot find a job (the unemployment rate). Macroeconomists design government policies that improve overall, or "aggregate," economic performance.

For example, macroeconomists try to identify the best policies for stimulating an economy that is experiencing a sustained period of negative growth—in other words, an economy in recession. During the 2007–2009 financial crisis, when housing prices were plummeting and banks were failing, macroeconomists had their hands full. It was their job to explain why the economy was contracting and to recommend policies that would bring it back to life.

1.2 Three Principles of Economics

You now have a sense of what economics is about. But you might be wondering what distinguishes it from the other social sciences, including anthropology, history, political science, psychology, and sociology. All social sciences study human behavior, so what sets economics apart?

Optimization means picking the best feasible option, given whatever (limited) information, knowledge, experience, and training the economic agent has. Economists believe that economic agents try to optimize but sometimes make mistakes.

> People make choices that are motivated by calculations of benefits and costs.

Equilibrium is the special situation in which everyone is simultaneously optimizing, so nobody would benefit personally by changing his or her own behavior, given the choices of others.

Empiricism is analysis that uses data—evidence-based analysis. Economists use data to develop theories, to test theories, to evaluate the success of different government policies, and to determine what is causing things to happen in the world.

Economists emphasize three key concepts.

1. Optimization: We have explained economics as the study of people's choices. The study of all human choices may initially seem like an impossibly huge and diverse topic. At first glance, your decision to log on to Facebook tonight does not appear to have much in common with a corporate executive's decision to build a $500 million laptop factory in China. However, economists have identified some powerful concepts that unify the enormous range of choices that economic agents make. One such insight is that most choices are tied together by the concept of *optimization*: picking the best feasible option. Economists do *not* believe that people actually do pick the best feasible option. Rather, economists believe that people *try* to pick the best feasible option. People don't always succeed in optimizing—we are not calculating machines—but people generally try to optimize. There is a great deal of discussion among economists about how well people optimize, a discussion that we will return to in Chapter 2.

Optimization is the first principle of economics. Economists believe that people's goal of optimization—picking the best feasible option—explains most choices that people make, including minor decisions like accepting an invitation to see a movie and major decisions like deciding whom to marry. Of course, these decisions aren't made with a crystal ball. People often make mistakes, but they try to do as well as they can, given the limited information, knowledge, experience, and training that they have.

2. Equilibrium: The second principle of economics holds that economic systems tend to be in *equilibrium*, a situation in which no agent would benefit personally by changing his or her own behavior, given the choices of others. The economic system is in equilibrium when each agent cannot do any better by picking another course of action. In other words, equilibrium is a situation in which everyone is simultaneously optimizing.

3. Empiricism: The third principle of economics is an emphasis on *empiricism*—evidence-based analysis. In other words, analysis that uses data. Economists use data to develop theories, to test theories, to evaluate the success of different government policies, and to determine what is causing things to happen in the world.

1.3 The First Principle of Economics: Optimization

Let's now consider our first principle in more detail. Economics is the study of choices, and economists have a leading theory about how choices are made. Economists believe that people try to optimize, meaning that economic agents try to choose the best feasible option, given whatever (limited) information, knowledge, experience, and training the economic agents have. Feasible options are those that are available and affordable to an economic agent. If you have $10 in your wallet and no credit/debit/ATM cards, then a $5 burrito is a feasible dinner option, while a $50 lobster is not.

The concept of feasibility goes beyond the financial budget of the agent. Many different constraints can determine what is feasible. For instance, it is not feasible to work more than 24 hours in a day. It is not feasible to attend meetings (in person) in New York and Beijing at the same time.

> In the cases where agents make mistakes, normative economic analysis can help them realize their mistakes and make better choices in the future.

Any decision can depend only on the information available at the time of the choice. For example, if you choose to drive from San Diego to Los Angeles and your car is hit by a drunk driver, you are unlucky, but you haven't necessarily failed to optimize. Optimization means that you weigh the information that you have, not that you perfectly foresee the future. When someone chooses the best feasible option *given the information that is available*, economists say that the decision maker is being rational or, equivalently, that he or she is exhibiting rationality. Rational action does not require a crystal ball, just a logical appraisal of the costs, benefits, and risks that are known to the economic agent.

However, if you decide to let a friend drive you from San Diego to Los Angeles and you know that your friend has just had a few beers, this is likely a case in which you are not choosing the best feasible option. Again, evaluating the rationality of a decision means examining the quality of your initial decision, not the outcome. Even if you and your drunk driver arrive at your destination without a crash, your choice to let your friend drive is still a suboptimal choice. Fortunately, you got lucky despite making a bad decision.

We devote much of this book to the analysis of optimization. We explain how to choose the best feasible option, and we discuss some evidence that supports the theory that economic agents often do choose the best feasible option (or something close to it). We also discuss important cases where people fail to choose the best feasible option. In cases where agents make mistakes, prescriptive economic analysis can help them realize their mistakes and make better choices in the future.

Finally, it is important to note that *what* we optimize varies from person to person and group to group. Most firms try to maximize profits, but most individual people are not trying to maximize their personal income. If that were our goal, we'd all work far more than 40 hours per week and we'd keep working well past retirement age. Most households are trying to maximize their overall well-being, which involves a mix of income, leisure, health, and a host of other factors, like social networks and a sense of purpose in life. Most governments, meanwhile, are optimizing a complex mix of policy goals. For most economic agents, then, optimization is about much more than money.

Trade-offs and Budget Constraints

An economic agent faces a **trade-off** when the agent needs to give up one thing to get something else.

All optimization problems involve trade-offs. **Trade-offs** arise when some benefits must be given up in order to gain others. Think about Facebook. If you spend an hour on Facebook, then you cannot spend that hour doing other things. For example, you cannot work at most part-time jobs at the same time you are editing your Facebook profile.

A **budget constraint** shows the bundles of goods or services that a consumer can choose given her limited budget.

Economists use budget constraints to describe trade-offs. A **budget constraint** is the set of things that a person can choose to do (or buy) without breaking her budget.

Here's an illustration. To keep the analysis simple, suppose that you can do only one of two activities with your free time: surf the Web or work at a part-time job. Suppose that you have 5 free hours in a day (once we take away necessities like sleeping, eating, bathing, attending classes, doing problem sets, and studying for exams). Think of these 5 free hours as your budget of free time. Then your budget constraint would be:

$$5 \text{ hours} = \text{Hours surfing the Web} + \text{Hours working at part-time job.}$$

This budget constraint equation implies that you face a trade-off. If you spend an extra hour surfing the Web, you need to spend one less hour working at a part-time job (unless you secretly use Facebook while you are being paid for a job—in this case, keep your boss off your friend list). Likewise, if you spend an extra hour working at the part-time job, you need to spend one less hour surfing the Web. More of one activity implies less of the other. We can see this in Exhibit 1.2, where we list all the ways that you could allocate your 5 free hours.

Exhibit 1.2 Possible Allocations of 5 Free Hours (Round Numbers Only)

Each row reports a different way that a person could allocate 5 free hours, assuming that the time must be divided between surfing the Web and working at a part-time job. To keep things simple, the table only reports allocations in round numbers.

Budget	Hours Surfing the Web	Hours at Part-Time Job
5 hours	0 hours	5 hours
5 hours	1 hours	4 hours
5 hours	2 hours	3 hours
5 hours	3 hours	2 hours
5 hours	4 hours	1 hours
5 hours	5 hours	0 hours

Budget constraints are useful economic tools, because they quantify trade-offs. When economists talk about the choices that people make, the economist always takes into account the budget constraint. It's important to identify the feasible options and the trade-offs—the budget constraint gives us that information.

Opportunity Cost

We are now ready to introduce another critical tool in the optimization toolbox: opportunity cost. Our Web surfing example provides an illustration of the concept. The time that we spend on the Web is time that we could have spent in some other way. In the illustrative example just discussed, the only two alternative activities were surfing the Web and working at a part-time job. But in real life, there are an enormous number of activities that might get squeezed out when you surf the Web—for instance, playing soccer, jogging, daydreaming, sleeping, calling a friend, catching up on e-mail, texting, or working on a problem set. You implicitly sacrifice time on some alternative activities when you spend time surfing the Web.

Generate your own list of alternative activities that are squeezed out when you surf the Web. Think about the best alternative to Web surfing, and put that at the top. Pause here and write that alternative activity down. Calling a friend? Studying for an exam? Going for a jog? What is your best alternative to an hour of Web surfing?

We face trade-offs whenever we allocate our time. When we do one thing, something else gets squeezed out. Joining the fencing team might mean dropping lacrosse. During exam week, an extra hour of sleep means one less hour spent studying or decompressing with friends. You can't write a term paper and update your Facebook page at the same moment. And postponement is not an escape hatch from this economic logic. For example, even if you only postpone writing that term paper, something has got to give when the paper deadline rolls around. (Perhaps studying for your economics final?)

> **Opportunity cost** is the best alternative use of a resource.

Evaluating trade-offs can be difficult, because so many options are under consideration. Economists tend to focus on the *best* alternative activity. We refer to this best alternative activity as the **opportunity cost**. This is what an optimizer is effectively giving up when she allocates an hour of her time. Recall your own best alternative to surfing the Web. That's your opportunity cost of time online.

Here's another example to drive home the concept. Assume that your family is taking a vacation over spring break. Your choices are a Caribbean cruise, a trip to Miami, or a trip to Los Angeles. (Assume that they all have the same monetary cost and use the same amount of time.) If your first choice is the cruise and your *second* choice is Miami, then your opportunity cost of taking the cruise is the Miami trip.

The concept of opportunity cost applies to all trade-offs, not just your time budget of 24 hours each day. Suppose that a woodworker has a beautiful piece of maple that can be used to make a sculpture, a bowl, or a picture frame. (Assume that they all use the same amount of wood and take the same amount of time.) If the woodworker's first choice is the sculpture and the second choice is the bowl, then the bowl is the opportunity cost of making the sculpture.

Assigning a Monetary Value to an Opportunity Cost   Economists often try to put a monetary value on opportunity cost. One way to estimate the monetary value of an hour of your time is to analyze the consequences of taking a part-time job or working additional hours at the part-time job you already have.

The opportunity cost of an hour of your time is at least the value that you would receive from an hour of work at a job, assuming that you can find one that fits your schedule. Here's why. A part-time job is one item in the long list of alternatives to surfing the Web. If the part-time job is at the top of your list, then it's the best alternative, and the part-time job is your opportunity cost of surfing the Web. What if the part-time job is not at the top of your list, so it's not the best alternative? Then the best alternative is even better than the part-time job, so the best alternative is worth more than the part-time job. To sum up, your opportunity cost is either the value of a part-time job or a value that is even greater than that. To turn these insights into something quantitative, it helps to note that the median wage for U.S. workers between 16 and 24 years of age was $11.00 per hour in 2015—this statistic is from the U.S. Bureau of Labor Statistics. A job has many attributes other than the wage you are paid: unpleasant tasks (like being nice to obnoxious customers), on-the-job training, friendly or unfriendly coworkers, and resume building, to name just a few.

If we ignore these non-wage attributes, the value of an hour of work is just the wage (minus taxes paid). However, if the positive and negative non-wage attributes don't cancel each other, the calculation is much harder. To keep things simple, we'll focus only on the after-tax wage in the analysis that follows—about $10 per hour for young workers—but we urge you to keep in mind all of the non-wage consequences that flow from a job.

Cost-Benefit Analysis

Cost-benefit analysis is a calculation that identifies the best alternative, by summing benefits and subtracting costs, with both benefits and costs denominated in a common unit of measurement, like dollars.

Let's use opportunity cost to solve an optimization problem. Specifically, we want to compare a set of feasible alternatives and pick the best one. We call this process *cost-benefit analysis*. **Cost-benefit analysis** is a calculation that identifies the best option by summing benefits and subtracting costs, with both benefits and costs denominated in a common unit of measurement, like dollars. Cost-benefit analysis is used to identify the alternative that has the greatest **net benefit**, which is the sum of the benefits of choosing an alternative minus the sum of the costs of choosing that alternative.

Net benefit is the sum of the benefits of choosing an alternative minus the sum of the costs of choosing that alternative.

To see these ideas in action, suppose that you and a friend are going to Miami Beach from Boston for spring break. The only question is whether you should drive or fly. Your friend argues that you should drive, because splitting the cost of a rental car and gas "will only cost $200 each." He tries to seal the deal by pointing out "that's much better than a $300 plane ticket."

To analyze this problem using cost-benefit analysis, you need to list all benefits and costs of driving compared to the alternative of flying. Here we'll express these benefits and costs comparatively, which means the benefits of driving compared to flying and the costs of driving compared to flying. We'll need to translate those benefits and costs into a common unit of measurement.

From a benefit perspective, driving saves you $100—the difference between driving expenses of $200 and a plane ticket of $300. We sometimes refer to these direct costs as "out-of-pocket" costs. But out-of-pocket costs aren't the only thing to consider. Driving also costs you an extra 40 hours of time—the difference between 50 hours of round-trip driving time and about 10 hours of round-trip airport/flying time. Spending 40 extra hours traveling is a cost of driving, even if it isn't a direct out-of-pocket cost.

We're now ready to decide whether it is optimal to drive or fly to Florida. We need to express all benefits and costs in common units, which will be dollars for our example. Recall that driving will take an additional 40 hours of travel time. To complete the analysis, we must translate this time cost into dollars. To make this translation, we will use a $10 per hour opportunity cost of time. The net benefit of driving compared to flying is the *benefit* of driving minus the *cost* of driving:

$$(\$100 \text{ Reduction in out-of-pocket costs}) - (40 \text{ Hours of additional travel time}) \times (\$10/\text{hour})$$
$$= \$100 - \$400 = -\$300.$$

Hence, the net benefit of driving is overwhelmingly negative. An optimizer would choose to fly.

Your decision about travel to Miami is a simple example of cost-benefit analysis, which is a great tool for collapsing all sorts of things down to a single number: a dollar-denominated net benefit. This book will guide you in making such calculations. When you are making almost any choice, cost-benefit analysis can help.

To an economist, cost-benefit analysis and optimization are the same thing. When you pick the option with the greatest net benefits, you are optimizing. So cost-benefit analysis is useful for *normative* economic analysis. It enables an economist to determine what an individual or a society should do. Cost-benefit analysis also yields many useful positive economic insights. In many cases, cost-benefit analysis correctly predicts the choices made by actual consumers.

EVIDENCE-BASED ECONOMICS

1.1
1.2
1.3
1.4
1.5
1.6

Q: Is Facebook free?

We can now turn to the question posed at the beginning of the chapter. By now you know that Facebook has an opportunity cost—the best alternative use of your time. We now estimate this cost. To do this, we're going to need some data. Whenever you see a section in this textbook titled "Evidence-Based Economics," you'll know that we are using data to analyze an economic question.

In 2016, Web users worldwide spent over 500 million hours on Facebook each day. On a per person basis, each of the over 1.7 billion Facebook users allocated an average of 20 minutes per day to the site.[2] College students used Facebook more intensively; the average college student spends about an hour per day on Facebook.

We estimate that the time spent worldwide on Facebook has an *average* opportunity cost of $5 per hour. We generated this estimate with a back-of-the-envelope—in other words, approximate—calculation that averages together all Facebook users' opportunity costs.

Here's how we did the calculation. First, we assume that users in the developed world—which represents wealthy countries, such as France, Japan, Singapore, and the United States—have an opportunity cost of $9 per hour, which is a typical minimum wage in a developed country. For example, the minimum wages in France and the United States are $12 per hour and $7.25 per hour, respectively. Employers are legally required to pay at least the minimum wage, and most workers in developed countries get paid much more than this. Even people who choose not to work still value their time, since it can be used for lots of good things like napping, texting, dating, studying, playing Angry Birds, and watching movies. It's reasonable to guess that these nonworkers—for instance, students—will also have an opportunity cost of at least the minimum wage.

In the developing world, which represents all countries other than the developed ones, the calculations get a bit trickier. These countries have much lower minimum wages, minimum wages that aren't enforced, or no minimum wage at all. For example, the minimum wage in China varies by region and averages just under $1 per hour. For the purposes of this analysis, we assume that Facebook users in developing countries have an opportunity cost of $1 per hour, reflecting less favorable employment opportunities than those in the developed world.

About half of Facebook users live in developed countries and half live in developing countries, so, given our assumptions, the average opportunity cost is $(1/2) \times \$9 + (1/2) \times \$1 = \$5$ per hour. Accordingly, the *total* opportunity cost of time spent on Facebook is calculated by multiplying the total number of hours spent on Facebook each day by the average opportunity cost of time per hour:

$$\left(\frac{500 \text{ million hours}}{\text{day}} \right) \left(\frac{\$5}{\text{hour}} \right) = \left(\frac{\$2.5 \text{ billion}}{\text{day}} \right).$$

Multiplying this by 365 days per year yields an annualized opportunity cost of over $900 billion. This is an estimate of the cost of Facebook. As you have seen, this is only a crude approximation, since we can't directly observe the opportunity cost of each person's time.

We can also think about this calculation another way. If people had substituted their time on Facebook for work with average pay of $5 per hour, the world economy would have produced about $900 billion more of measured output in 2016. This is more than the annual economic output of Austria.

Finally, we can also estimate the opportunity cost of a typical U.S. college student who spends 1 hour per day on Facebook. Assuming that this student's opportunity cost is equal to $10 per hour, the opportunity cost is $3,650 per year.

$$(\$10/\text{hour}) \times (365 \text{ hours/year}) = \$3,650 \text{ per year.}$$

We chose $10 per hour for the opportunity cost, since the median before-tax wage of 16- to 24-year-old U.S. workers was $11 per hour in 2015, and such low-income workers don't pay much in taxes.

So far, we have gone through a purely positive economic analysis, describing the frequency of Facebook usage and the trade-offs that this usage implies. None of this analysis, however, answers the related question: Are Facebook users optimizing? We've seen that the time spent on sites like Facebook is costly, because it has valuable alternative uses (see Exhibit 1.3). But Facebook users are deriving substantial benefits that may justify this allocation of time. For example, social networking sites keep us up-to-date on the activities of our friends and family. They facilitate the formation of new friendships and new connections. And Facebook and similar sites are entertaining.

Because we cannot easily quantify these benefits, we're going to leave that analysis to you. Economists won't tell you what to do, but we will help you identify the trade-offs that you are making in your decisions. Here is how an economist would summarize the normative issues that are on the table:

Assuming a $10 per hour opportunity cost, the opportunity cost of using Facebook for an hour per day is $3,650 per year. Do you receive benefits from Facebook that exceed this opportunity cost? If the benefits that you receive are less than $3,650, you should scale down your Facebook usage.

Economists don't want to impose their tastes on other people. In the view of an economist, people who get big benefits from intensive use of Facebook should stay the course. However, we do want economic agents to recognize the implicit trade-offs that are being made. Economists are interested in helping people make the best use of scarce

	Cost per unit	Number of units	Total cost
Starbucks cappuccino	$4	52 cups	$208
iPhone	$400	1	$400
Round trip: NYC to Paris	$1,000	1	$1,000
Hotel in Paris	$250	4 nights	$1,000
Round trip: NYC to U.S. Virgin Islands	$300	1	$300
Hotel in Virgin Islands	$180	4 nights	$720
Eleven iPhone apps	$2	11	$22
Total			$3,650

Exhibit 1.3 What Could You Buy with $3,650?

Everyone would choose to spend $3,650 in their own particular way. This list illustrates one feasible basket of goods and services. Note that this list includes just the monetary costs of these items. A complete economic analysis would also include the opportunity cost of the time that you would need to consume them.

resources like budgets of money and leisure time. In many circumstances, people are already putting their resources to best use. Occasionally, however, economic reasoning can help people make better choices.

Question

Is Facebook free?

Answer

No. The opportunity cost of Facebook was over $900 billion dollars in 2016.

Data

Facebook usage statistics provided by Facebook. Minimum wage data from around the world.

Caveat

We can only crudely estimate the opportunity cost for Facebook's 1.7 billion worldwide users.

1.4 The Second Principle of Economics: Equilibrium

In most economic situations, you aren't the only one trying to optimize. Other people's behavior will influence what you decide to do. Economists think of the world as a large number of economic agents who are interacting and influencing one another's efforts at optimization. Recall that *equilibrium* is the special situation in which everyone is optimizing, so nobody would benefit personally by changing his or her own behavior.

An important clarification needs to accompany this definition. When we say that nobody would benefit personally by changing his or her own behavior, we mean that nobody *believes* he or she would benefit from such a change. In equilibrium, all economic agents are making their best feasible choices, taking into account all of the information they have, including their beliefs about the behavior of others. We could rewrite the definition by saying that in equilibrium, nobody perceives that they will benefit from changing their own behavior.

In equilibrium

Out of equilibrium

In equilibrium, everyone is simultaneously optimizing, so nobody would benefit by changing his or her own behavior.

To build intuition—which means understanding—for the concept of equilibrium, consider the length of the regular checkout lines at your local supermarket (ignore the express lines). If any line has a shorter wait than the others, optimizers will choose that line. If any line has a longer wait than the others, optimizers will avoid that line. So the short lines will attract shoppers, and the long lines will drive them away. And it's not just the length of the lines that matters. You pick your line by estimating which line will move the fastest, an estimate that incorporates everything you can see, including the number of items in each person's shopping cart. Sometimes, you might end up waiting longer because of twists you didn't anticipate: a customer who takes five minutes to find the right change, or someone with a sea of tiny items at the bottom of his cart. Still, economists say that "in equilibrium," all checkout lines will have roughly the same wait time. When the wait times are expected to be the same, no shopper has an incentive to switch lines. In other words, nobody perceives that they will benefit by changing their behavior.

Here's another example. Suppose the market price of gasoline is $2 per gallon and the gasoline market is in equilibrium. Three conditions will need to be satisfied:

1. The amount of gasoline produced by gasoline sellers—oil companies—will equal the amount of gasoline purchased by buyers.
2. Oil companies will only operate wells where they can extract oil and produce gasoline at a cost that is less than the market price of gasoline: $2 per gallon.
3. The buyers of gasoline will only use it for activities that are worth at least $2 per gallon—like driving to their best friend's wedding—and they won't use it for activities that are worth less than $2 per gallon.

In equilibrium, both the sellers and the buyers of gasoline are optimizing, given the market price of gasoline. Nobody would benefit by changing his or her own behavior.

Notice that we've started to think about what happens when many economic agents interact. This could be two chess players, thirty participants in an eBay auction, millions of investors buying and selling shares on the New York Stock Exchange, or billions of households buying gasoline to fuel their tractors, trucks, mopeds, motorcycles, and cars. In all these cases, we assume that everyone is constantly simultaneously optimizing—for instance, at every move in a chess game and during every trade on the New York Stock Exchange. Combined, these choices produce an equilibrium—and economists believe that this kind of equilibrium analysis provides a good description of what actually happens when many people interact.

The Free-Rider Problem

Let's use the concept of equilibrium to analyze an economic problem that may interest you: roommates. Assume that five roommates live in a rented house. Each roommate can spend some of his or her time contributing to the general well-being of all the roommates by throwing away empty pizza boxes and soda cans. Or each roommate can spend all his or her time on activities that only benefit him or herself—for instance, watching YouTube videos or listening to Pandora.

Imagine that one roommate hates the mess, and starts spending time cleaning up the kitchen. Although the other roommates appreciate it, they have no incentive to chip in! If he spends 30 minutes doing the dishes, all the other roommates benefit without having to lift a finger. It would be beneficial to each of the roommates if everyone chipped in and did a little cleaning. But each of the five roommates has an incentive to leave that to others. Consequently, rentals with lots of roommates are often a mess. The *equilibrium* prediction is that when people live in large rooming groups, they will have messier apartments than if the same people each had their own apartment.

Roommates who leave the cleaning to others are an example of something that economists call the *free-rider problem*. Most people want to let someone else do the dirty work. We would like to be the free riders who don't contribute but still benefit from the investments that others make.

Sometimes free riders get away with it. When there are few free riders and lots of contributors, the free riders might be overlooked. For example, a small number of people sneak onto public transportation without paying. These turnstile jumpers are so rare that they

A free rider in the New York subway system. Are you paying for him to ride the subway?

don't jeopardize the subway system. But if everyone started jumping turnstiles, the subway would soon run out of cash.

In the subway system, free riding is discouraged by security patrols. In rooming groups, free riding is discouraged by social pressure. Even with these "punishment" techniques, free riding is sometimes a problem, because it's not easy to catch the free rider in the act. It's possible to slip over a turnstile in a quiet subway station. It's easy to leave crumbs on the couch when nobody is watching.

People's private benefits are sometimes out of sync with the public interest. Jumping the subway turnstile is cheaper than paying for a subway ticket. Watching YouTube is more fun than sweeping up the remains of last night's party. Equilibrium analysis helps us predict the behavior of interacting economic agents and understand why free riding occurs. People sometimes pursue their own private interests and don't contribute voluntarily to the public interest. Unfortunately, selfless acts—like those of a war hero—are exceptional, and selfish acts are more common. When people interact, each individual might do what's best for himself or herself instead of acting in a way that optimizes the well-being of society.

Equilibrium analysis helps us design special institutions—like financial contracts—that reduce or even eliminate free riding. For example, what would happen in the rooming group if everyone agreed to pay $5 per week so the roommates could hire a cleaning service? It would be easier to enforce $5 weekly payments than to monitor compliance with the rule "clean up after yourself, even when nobody is here to watch you." Pizza crumbs don't have identity tags. So equilibrium analysis explains why individuals sometimes fail to serve the interest of society and how the incentive structure can be redesigned to fix these problems.

1.5 The Third Principle of Economics: Empiricism

Economists test their ideas with data. We refer to such evidence-based analysis as empirical analysis or *empiricism*. Economists use data to determine whether our theories about human behavior—like optimization and equilibrium—match up with actual human behavior. Of course, we want to know if our theories fail to explain what is happening in the world. In that case, we need to go back to the drawing board and come up with better theories. That is how economic science, and science in general, progresses.

Economists are also interested in understanding what is *causing* things to happen in the world. We can illustrate what causation is—and is not—via a simple example. Hot days and crowded beaches tend to occur at the same time of the year. What is the cause and what is the effect here? It is, of course, that high temperatures cause people to go swimming. It is not that swimming causes the outside air temperature to rise.

But there are some cases when cause and effect are hard to untangle. Does being relatively smart cause people to go to college, or does going to college cause people to be relatively smart? Perhaps both directions of causation apply. Or perhaps some other factor plays the causal role—for instance, a love for reading might cause people to become smarter *and* cause them to go to college.

We'll come back to the topic of empiricism in general, and causality in particular, in great detail in Chapter 2. Sometimes causes are easy to determine, but sometimes identifying cause and effect requires great ingenuity.

1.6 Is Economics Good for You?

Should you take this course? Let's think about this using cost-benefit analysis.

Let's begin by assuming that you've already chosen to go to college. So we can assume that tuition costs and room and board are *sunk costs* (they won't be affected by your decision to take economics). With those costs accounted for, are there any other costs associated with this course? The key opportunity cost of this course is another course that you won't be able to take during your time spent as a student. What other course did economics crowd out? Japanese history? Biochemistry? Russian poetry? If you are taking the two-semester version of this course, then you need to consider the two other courses that economics is crowding out.

> Learning to make good choices is the biggest benefit you'll realize from learning economics.

Now consider the benefits of an economics education. The benefits come in a few different forms, but the biggest benefit is the ability to apply economic reasoning in your daily life. Whether you are deciding where to go on vacation or how to keep an apartment with four other roommates clean, economic reasoning will improve the quality of your decisions. These benefits will continue throughout your life as you make important decisions, such as where to invest your retirement savings and how to secure the best mortgage.

Most decisions are guided by the logic of costs and benefits. Accordingly, you can use positive economic analysis to predict other people's behavior. Economics illuminates and clarifies all human behavior.

We also want you to use economic principles when you give other people advice and when you make your own choices. This is normative economics. Learning how to make good choices is the biggest benefit you'll realize from learning economics. That's why we have built our book around the concept of decision making. Looking at the world through the economic lens puts you at an enormous advantage throughout your life.

We also think that economics is a lot of fun. Understanding people's motivations is fascinating, particularly because there are many surprising insights along the way.

To realize these payoffs, you'll need to connect the ideas in this textbook to the economic activities around you. To make those connections, keep a few tips in mind:

- You can apply economic tools, such as trade-offs and cost-benefit analysis, to any economic decision, so learn to use them in your own daily decisions. This will help you master the tools and also appreciate their limitations.
- Even if you are not in the midst of making a decision, you will learn a lot of economics by keeping your eyes open when you walk through any environment in which people are using or exchanging resources. Think like an economist the next time you find yourself in a supermarket or at a used-car dealership, a soccer match, or a poker game.
- The easiest way to encounter economic ideas is to keep up with what's happening in the world. Go online and read a national newspaper like the *New York Times* or *The Wall Street Journal*. News magazines will also do the job. There's even a newsmagazine called *The Economist*, which is required reading for prime ministers and presidents. Almost every page of any magazine—including *People*, *Sports Illustrated*, and *Vogue*—describes events driven by economic factors. Identifying and understanding these forces will be a challenge. Over time, though, you'll find that it gets easy to recognize and interpret the economic story behind every headline.

Once you realize that you are constantly making economic choices, you'll understand that this course is only a first step. You'll discover the most important applications outside class and after the final exam. The tools of economics will improve your performance in all kinds of situations—making you a better businessperson, a better consumer, and a better citizen. Keep your eyes open and remember that every choice is economics in action.

Summary

- Economics is the study of how agents choose to allocate scarce resources and how those choices affect society. Economics can be divided into two kinds of analysis: positive economic analysis (what people actually do) and normative economic analysis (what people ought to do). There are two key topics in economics: microeconomics (individual decisions and individual markets) and macroeconomics (the total economy).

- Economics is based on three key principles: optimization, equilibrium, and empiricism.

- Choosing the best feasible option, given the available information, is called optimization. To optimize, an economic agent needs to consider many issues, including trade-offs, budget constraints, opportunity costs, and cost-benefit analysis.

- Equilibrium is a situation in which nobody would benefit personally by changing his or her own behavior, given the choices of others.

- Economists test their ideas with data. We call such evidence-based analysis empirical analysis or empiricism. Economists use data to determine whether our theories about human behavior—like optimization and equilibrium—match actual human behavior. Economists also use data to determine what is causing things to happen in the world.

Key Terms

economic agent *p. 3*
scarce resources *p. 4*
scarcity *p. 4*
economics *p. 4*
positive economics *p. 5*
normative economics *p. 5*

microeconomics *p. 6*
macroeconomics *p. 6*
optimization *p. 7*
equilibrium *p. 7*
empiricism *p. 7*
trade-off *p. 8*

budget constraint *p. 8*
opportunity cost *p. 9*
cost-benefit analysis *p. 10*
net benefit *p. 10*

Questions

All questions are available in MyEconLab for practice and instructor assignment.

1. Why do we have to pay a price for most of the goods we consume?

2. Many people believe that the study of economics is focused on money and financial markets. Based on your reading of the chapter, how would you define economics?

3. Examine the following statements and determine whether they are normative or positive in nature. Explain your answers.

   a. Car sales in Europe rose 9.3 percent from 2014 to 2015.

   b. The U.S. government should increase carbon taxes to reduce carbon emissions that cause global warming.

4. How does microeconomics differ from macroeconomics? Would the supply of iPhones in the United States be studied under microeconomics or macroeconomics? What about the growth rate of total economic output in the national economy?

5. What does a budget constraint represent? How do budget constraints explain the trade-offs that consumers face?

6. This chapter introduced the idea of opportunity cost.

   a. What is meant by opportunity cost?

   b. What is the opportunity cost of taking a year after graduating from high school and backpacking across Europe? Are people who do this being irrational?

7. The costs of many environmental regulations can be calculated in dollars—for instance, the cost of "scrubbers" that reduce the amount of air pollution emitted by a coal factory. The benefits of environmental regulations often are most directly expressed in terms of lives saved (reduced mortality) or decreases in the incidence of a particular disease (reduced morbidity). What does this imply about the cost-benefit analysis of environmental regulations? There is an old saying "You can't put a price on a human life." Do you agree or disagree? Explain.

8. Suppose the market price of corn is $3.50 per bushel. What are the three conditions that will need to be satisfied for the corn market to be in equilibrium at this price?

9. Economists are often concerned with the free-rider problem.

    a. What is meant by free riding? Explain with an example.

    b. Explain why dropping trash on a city street is an example of the free-rider problem.

10. Explain the concept of causation with the help of a simple real-life example.

11. Identify cause and effect in the following examples:

    a. A rise in the worldwide price of peaches and a drought in California;

    b. A surge in cocoa prices and a pest attack on the cocoa crop.

Problems

All problems are available in MyEconLab *for practice and instructor assignment.*

1. You have already purchased (non-refundable and unsellable) tickets to a concert on Friday night. A friend also invites you to her birthday party on Friday. While you like your friend, you politely decline because you really want to go to the concert.

    a. You learn that your friend is serving flank steak at her party, all-you-can eat and at no charge. Flank steak is your favorite food. Should this affect your decision to go to the concert? Explain by using the term "opportunity cost."

    b. Suppose instead that you notice that the non-refundable concert ticket (that you already purchased) cost you $10; previously you had mistakenly believed the price was $100. Should learning this information affect your decision to go to the concert?

2. You are thinking about buying a house. You find one you like that costs $200,000. You learn that your bank will give you a mortgage for $160,000 and that you will have to use all of your savings to make the down payment of $40,000. You calculate that the mortgage payments, property taxes, insurance, maintenance, and utilities would total $950 per month. Is $950 the cost of owning the house? What important factor(s) have you left out of your calculation of the cost of ownership?

3. You have 40,000 frequent flier miles. You could exchange your miles for a round-trip ticket to Bermuda over spring break. Does that mean your flight to Bermuda would be free? Explain your reasoning.

4. You have decided that you are going to consume 600 calories of beer and snacks at a party Saturday night. A beer has 150 calories and a snack has 75 calories.

    a. Create a table that shows the various combinations of beer and snacks you can consume. To keep things simple, use only round numbers (for example, you could choose 1 or 2 beers but not 1.5 beers).

    b. What is the opportunity cost of a beer?

5. Suppose you are ready to check out and see two lines: Line A has 3 people, while line B has 5 people.

    a. Assume people just chose lines at random and have not yet had a chance to switch lines. Would you consider this situation to be in equilibrium? Why or why not?

    b. Assume that all 8 shoppers are optimizing (i.e., they have had a chance to switch), and that the situation is in equilibrium. What conclusions would you draw?

    c. Of all 8 shoppers, whose behavior is the most informative?

6. Consider the following three statements:

    a. You can either stand during a college football game or you can sit. You believe that you will see the game very well if you stand and others sit but that you will not be able to see at all if you sit and others stand. You therefore decide to stand.

    b. Your friend tells you that he expects many people to stand at football games.

    c. An economist studies photos of many college football games and estimates that 75 percent of all fans stand and 25 percent sit.

Which of these statements deals with optimization, which deals with equilibrium, and which deals with empiricism? Explain.

7. In 2014, California was in its third year of a major drought. With water supplies dwindling, Governor Brown issued a plea for a voluntary 20 percent reduction in water use. This target was not reached. In early 2015 Governor Brown issued an executive order requiring local water agencies to reduce water use by 25 percent, but no enforcement mechanism was specified. No taxes or fines were in the executive order. State officials hoped that they could achieve compliance without resorting to fines.[3]

    a. From an individual homeowner's perspective, what are the costs and benefits of using water during a drought? Why do you think that the voluntary reduction order in 2014 didn't work?

b. Using concepts from this chapter, explain how you might get individual homeowners to reduce water use during a drought.

c. Eventually, many communities began levying fines on water use. However, while many middle income families dramatically cut water use, wealthy households cut back their water use relatively little.[4] How can you explain this phenomenon from an economic perspective?

8. An economist observes that many students spend $100,000 to go to college. This researcher could ask whether such spending is worth it, or she could *assume* that it is worth it. In other words, she could *assume* that students are optimizing and that the education system is in equilibrium. If we assume that students are optimizing, what can the economist conclude about the value of a college education?

9. It is the night before your economics final exam and you must decide how many hours to study. The total benefits in the following table shows how many more points you will earn because of increased knowledge. The total cost column shows how many points you will lose because of careless errors due to lack of sleep. (The "marginal" columns show the effect of each additional hour spent studying. These marginal numbers are calculated by taking the difference within a column from one row to the next row.)

Hours Spent Studying	Total Benefit	Marginal Benefit	Total Cost	Marginal Cost
0	0	–	0	–
1	10	10	0	0
2	16	6	3	3
3	20	4	8	5
4	20	0	15	7

a. If you study in an optimal way, how many points will you earn on the test?

b. Explain how you can find the optimal number of hours for which you should study by using the marginal benefits and marginal costs columns.

2 Economic Methods and Economic Questions

Is college worth it?

If you are reading this book, there is a good chance that you are either in college or thinking about taking the plunge. As you know, college is a big investment. During the 2015–2016 academic year, tuition averaged $3,435 for community colleges, $9,410 for in-state public colleges, $23,893 for out-of-state public colleges, and $32,405 for nonprofit private colleges.[1] And that's not the only cost. Your time, as we have seen, is worth $10 or more per hour—this time value adds at least $15,000 per year to the opportunity cost of a college education.

Why sit in class, then, when you could travel the world or earn money at a job? As with any other investment, you'd like to know how a college education is going to pay you back. What are the "returns to education," and how would you measure them? In this chapter, you'll see that you can answer such questions with models and data.

CHAPTER OUTLINE

2.1 The Scientific Method

In Chapter 1, we explored optimization and equilibrium, the first two principles of economics. Now, to better tie those concepts to the "real world," we turn to the third principle: empiricism.

Empiricism—using data to analyze the world—is at the heart of all scientific analysis. The **scientific method** is the name for the ongoing process that economists, other social scientists, and natural scientists use to:

> The **scientific method** is the name for the ongoing process that economists and other scientists use to (1) develop models of the world and (2) evaluate those models by testing them with data.

1. Develop models of the world
2. Evaluate those models by testing them with data

Testing models with data enables economists to separate the good models—those that make predictions that are mostly consistent with the data—from the bad models. When a model is overwhelmingly inconsistent with the data, economists try to fix the model or replace it altogether. By cycling through the two steps—developing models and then testing them—economists can move toward models that better explain the past and even partially predict the future. Given the complexity of the world, we do not expect this process to generate a perfect model—we'll never be able to precisely predict the future! However, economists do expect to identify models that are useful in understanding the world. In this section, we explain what a model is and how it can be tested with data.

Models and Data

Before the discoveries of the ancient Greek philosophers, everyone believed that the earth was flat. We now know that it is more like a beach ball than a Frisbee. Yet a flat-earth *model* is still actively used. Ask for directions from Google Maps, and you'll be using maps of a flattened planet. For driving directions, nobody keeps a globe in the glove compartment.

Flat maps and spherical globes are both models of the surface of the earth. A **model** is a simplified description of reality. Sometimes economists will refer to a model as a *theory*. These terms are usually used interchangeably.

> A **model** is a simplified description of reality. Sometimes economists will refer to a model as a *theory*. These terms are usually used interchangeably.

Because models are simplified, they are not perfect replicas of reality. Obviously, flat maps are not perfectly accurate models of the surface of the earth—they distort the curvature. If you are flying from New York to Tokyo, the curvature matters. But if you are touring around New York City, you don't need to worry about the fact that the earth is shaped like a sphere.

Scientists—and commuters—use the model that is best suited to analyzing the problem at hand. Even if a model/map is based on assumptions that are known to be false, like the flatness of the earth, the model may still help us to make good predictions and good plans for the future. It is more important for a model to be simple and useful than it is for the model to be precisely accurate.

> Scientific models are used to make predictions that can be checked with empirical evidence.

Exhibit 2.1 Flying from New York to Tokyo Requires More Than a Flat Map

This flat map is a model of part of the earth's surface. It treats the world as perfectly flat, which leads the map maker to exaggerate distances in the northern latitudes. It is useful for certain purposes—for instance, learning geography. But you wouldn't want to use it to find the best air route across the Pacific Ocean. For example, the shortest flight path from New York to Tokyo is not a straight line through San Francisco. Instead, the shortest path goes through Northern Alaska! The flat-earth model is well suited for some tasks (geography lessons) and ill-suited for others (intercontinental flight navigation).

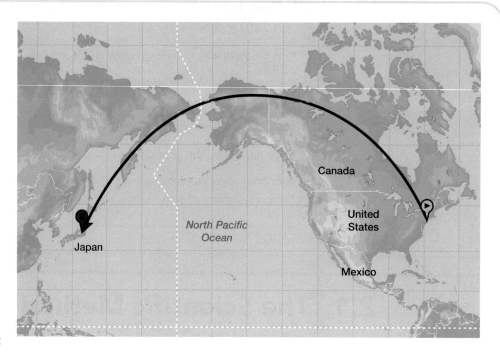

Exhibit 2.2 New York City Subway Map

This is a model of the subway system in New York City. It is highly simplified—for example, it treats New York City as a perfectly flat surface, and it also distorts the shape of the city—but it is nevertheless very useful for commuters and tourists.

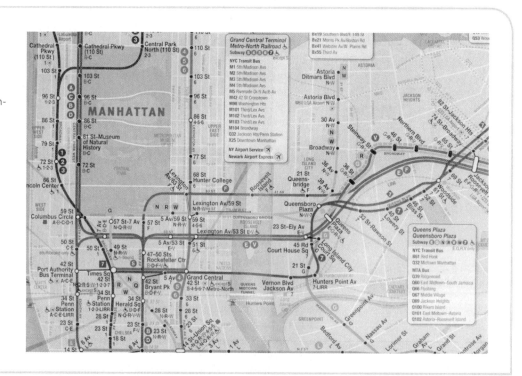

Empirical evidence consists of facts that are obtained through observation and measurement. Empirical evidence is also called **data**.

Scientific models are used to make predictions that can be checked with **empirical evidence**—in other words, facts that are obtained through observation and measurement. We also refer to empirical evidence as **data**. Recall from Chapter 1 that economists often describe themselves as empiricists, or say that we practice empiricism, because we use empirical evidence. Empiricists use data to answer questions about the world and to test models. For example, we could test the New York City subway map by actually riding the subway and checking the map's accuracy.

When conducting empirical analyses, economists refer to a model's predictions as **hypotheses**. Whenever such hypotheses are contradicted by the available data, economists return to the drawing board and try to come up with a better model that yields new hypotheses.

An Economic Model

Let's consider an example of an economic model. We're going to study an extremely simple model to get the ball rolling. But even economic models that are far more complicated than this example are also simplified descriptions of reality.

All models begin with assumptions. Consider the following assumption about the returns to education: *each additional year of education causes your future wages to rise by 10 percent.* Let's put the assumption to work to generate a model that relates a person's level of education to her wages.

Increasing a wage by 10 percent is the same as multiplying the wage by $(1 + 0.10) = 1.10$. Thus, the returns-to-education assumption implies that someone with an extra year of education earns 1.10 times as much as she would have earned without the extra year of education. For example, if someone earns $15 per hour with 13 years of education, then we predict that a 14th year of education will cause her hourly wage to rise to $1.10 \times \$15$, or $16.50.

Economists use assumptions to derive other implications. For example, the returns-to-education assumption implies that 2 additional years of education will increase earnings by 10 percent twice over—once for each extra year of education—producing a 21 percent total increase:

$$1.10 \times 1.10 = 1.21.$$

Consider another example. Four additional years of education will increase earnings by 10 percent four times over, implying a 46 percent total increase:

$$1.10 \times 1.10 \times 1.10 \times 1.10 = (1.10)^4 = 1.46.$$

This implies that going to college would increase a college graduate's income by 46 percent compared to what she would have been paid if she had ended her education after finishing high school. In other words, a prediction—or hypothesis—of the model is that college graduates will earn 46 percent more than high school graduates.

In principle, we can apply this analysis to any number of years of education. We therefore have a general model that relates people's educational attainment to their income. The model that we have derived is referred to as the returns-to-education model. It describes the economic payoff of more education—in other words, the return on your educational investment. Most economic models are much, much more complex than this. In most economic models, it takes pages of mathematical analysis to derive the implications of the assumptions. Nevertheless, this simple model is a good starting point for our discussion. It illustrates two important properties of all models.

First, economists know that *a model is only an approximation* and accordingly understand that the model is not exactly correct. Taken literally, the model implies that each person would increase their future wages by exactly 10 percent if they obtained an extra year of education, but this precise prediction is surely false. For example, the final year of college does much more to increase your wages than the second-to-last year of college because that final year earns you the official degree, which is a key line on your resume. Likewise, your college major importantly impacts how much you will earn after college. Those who major in economics, for example, tend to earn more than graduates in most other majors. Our simple model overlooks such distinctions. Just as a flat subway map is only an approximation of the features of a city, the returns-to-education model is only an approximation of the mapping from years of education to wages. The model's predicted relationship between education and wages is a simplification that overlooks lots of special considerations.

Second, *a model makes predictions that can be tested with data*—in this case, data on people's education and earnings. We are now ready to use some data to actually evaluate the predictions of the returns-to-education model.

EVIDENCE-BASED ECONOMICS

Q: How much more do workers with a college education earn?

To put the model to the test we need data, which we obtain from the 2014 Current Population Survey, a government data source. This survey collects anonymized data on earnings, education, and many other characteristics of the general population and is available to anyone who wants to use it. When data are available to the general public, they are called "public-use data."

Exhibit 2.3 summarizes the average annual earnings for our test. The returns-to-education model does not match the data perfectly. The exhibit shows that for 30-year-old U.S. workers with 12 years of education, which is equivalent to a high school diploma, average annual earnings are $32,912. For 30-year-old U.S. workers with 16 years of education, which is equivalent to graduation from a 4-year college, average annual earnings are $51,215.

If we simply divide these two average wages—college wage over high school wage—the ratio is 1.56:

$$\frac{\text{Average annual earnings of 30-year-olds with 16 years of education}}{\text{Average annual earnings of 30-year-olds with 12 years of education}} = \frac{\$51,215}{\$32,912} = 1.56.$$

Recall that the returns-to-education model says that each additional year of education raises the wage by 10 percent, so 4 extra years of education should raise the wage by a factor of $(1.10)^4 = 1.46$.

We can see that the model does not exactly match the data. Going from 12 years of education to 16 years is associated with a 56 percent increase in income. However, the model is not far off—the model predicted a 46 percent increase.

Exhibit 2.3 Average Annual Earnings of 30-Year-Old Americans by Education Level (2014 Data)

People who stop going to school after obtaining their high school diplomas have average annual earnings of $32,912, whereas those who stop going to school after obtaining a 4-year college degree earn $51,215.

Source: 2014 Current Population Survey.

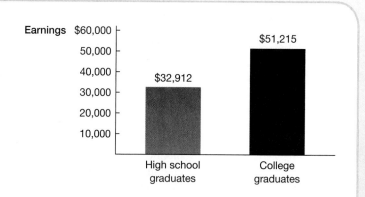

Question

How much more do workers with a 4-year college education earn compared to workers with a high school degree?

Answer

Average earnings for a college graduate are 56 percent higher than average earnings for a high school graduate.

Data

Wages from the Current Population Survey (2014). Compare average wages for 30-year-old workers with different levels of education.

Caveat

These are averages for a large population of individuals. Each individual's experience will differ.

Means and Medians

The **mean** (or **average**) is the sum of all the different values divided by the number of values.

You may wonder how the data from the Current Population Survey were used to calculate the wages reported above. We used the concept of the *mean*, or *average*. The **mean** (or **average**) is the sum of all the different values divided by the number of values and is a commonly used technique for summarizing data. Statisticians and other scientists use the terms *mean* and *average* interchangeably.

We can quickly show how the mean works in a small example. Say that there are five people: Mr. Kwon, Ms. Littleton, Mr. Locke, Ms. Reye, and Ms. Shephard, each with a different hourly wage:

$$Kwon = \$26 \text{ per hour},$$
$$Littleton = \$24 \text{ per hour},$$
$$Locke = \$8 \text{ per hour},$$
$$Reye = \$35 \text{ per hour},$$
$$Shephard = \$57 \text{ per hour}.$$

If we add the five wages together and divide by 5, we calculate a mean wage of $30 per hour:

$$\frac{\$26 + \$24 + \$8 + \$35 + \$57}{5} = \$30.$$

The **median** value is calculated by ordering the numbers from least to greatest and then finding the value half-way through the list.

In addition to calculating the mean value of a group (or "set") of numbers, scientists also frequently calculate the median value of the numbers, which is the "middle" value of the group. Specifically, the **median** value is calculated by ordering the numbers from least to greatest and then finding the value halfway through the list. For example, ordering the data that we just analyzed produces the list: $8, $24, $26, $35, $57. The middle value— the median—is $26. (When there are an even number of items in the list, the median is the midpoint between the two middle values. So the median of the numbers $8, $24, $26, and $35 is the midpoint between $24 and $26: $25.)

Summing up, the median is the value in the middle of a group of numbers, and the mean is the average value of the group of numbers. When the group of numbers has one or more extreme values, the median and the mean pull apart. For example, suppose that Shephard is extremely highly paid—she might be a corporate lawyer—with an hourly wage of $257 (instead of the original value of $57 per hour). Then the group mean rises to $70 per hour, but the median doesn't change at all: $26 per hour is still the middle wage. Hence, the mean is affected by outliers, which are extreme numbers that are dissimilar to the rest of the numbers in the list, whereas the median is not affected by outliers.

This analysis of a small sample—only five people—illustrates the concepts of means and medians, but convincing data analysis in economics relies on using a large sample. For example, a typical economic research paper uses data gathered from thousands of individuals. So a key strength of economic analysis is the amount of data used. When we showed that education raises earnings, we didn't rely on a handful of *observations*—economists call each piece of data an "observation." Instead, we used data from thousands of surveyed 30-year-olds. Using lots of observations strengthens the force of an empirical argument, because the researcher can make more precise statements.

To show you how to make convincing empirical arguments, this course uses lots of real data from large groups of people. Credible empirical arguments, based on many observations, are a key component of the scientific method.

Argument by Anecdote

Education is not destiny. There are some people with lots of education who earn very little, and there are some people with little education who earn a lot. When we wrote this book, Bill Gates, a Harvard dropout who founded Microsoft, was the richest person in the world. Mark Zuckerberg, the Facebook CEO, also dropped out of Harvard.

With these two examples in mind, it might be tempting to conclude that dropping out of college is a great path to success. However, it is a mistake to use two anecdotes, or any small sample of people, to try to judge a statistical relationship.

If you study two randomly chosen 30-year-olds, there is almost a one-third chance that the person with only a high school diploma has higher earnings than the one with a 4-year college degree. This fact highlights that there is much more than education that determines your earnings, although getting a college degree will usually help make you money.

When you look at only a small amount of data, it is easy to jump to the wrong conclusion. Keep this warning in mind the next time a newspaper columnist tries to sway you with a few anecdotes. If the columnist backs up her story with data reflecting the experiences of thousands of people, then she has done her job and may deserve to win the argument. But if she rests her case after sharing a handful of anecdotes, remain skeptical. Be doubly skeptical if you suspect that the anecdotes have been carefully selected to prove the columnist's point. Argument by anecdote should not be taken seriously.

There is one exception to this rule. Argument by example is appropriate when you are contradicting a *blanket* statement. For example, if someone asserts that every National Basketball Association (NBA) player has to be tall, just one counterexample is enough to prove this statement wrong. In this case, your proof would be Tyrone "Muggsy" Bogues, a 5-foot 3-inch (133-pound) dynamo who played point guard in the NBA for 15 seasons.

2.2 Causation and Correlation

Unfortunately, even reporting that relies on *large* data sets can be misleading. Consider our returns-to-schooling example. Using our large data set on wages and years of education, we've seen that on average, wages rise roughly 10 percent for every year of additional education. Does that mean that staying in school one more year will cause *your* future wages to rise by 10 percent? Not necessarily. Let's think about why this is not always the case with an example.

The Red Ad Blues

Imagine a department has hired you as a consultant. You have developed a hypothesis about ad campaigns: you believe that campaigns using the color red are good at catching people's attention. To test your hypothesis, you assemble empirical evidence from historical ad campaigns, including the color of the ad campaign and how revenue at the store changed during the campaign.

Your empirical research confirms your hypothesis! Sales go up 25 percent during campaigns with lots of red images and only 5 percent during campaigns with lots of blue images. You race to the chief executive officer (CEO) to report this remarkable result. You are a genius! Unfortunately, the CEO instantly fires you.

What did the CEO notice that you missed?

The red-themed campaigns were mostly concentrated during the Christmas season. The blue-themed campaigns were mostly spread out over the rest of the year. In the CEO's words,

> The red colors in our advertising don't cause an increase in our revenue. Christmas causes an increase in our revenue. Christmas also causes an increase in the use of red in our ads. If we ran blue ads in December, our holiday season revenue would still rise by about 25 percent.

Unfortunately, this is actually a true story, though we've changed the details—including the name of the firm—to protect our friends. We return, in the appendix, to a related story in which the CEO was not as sharp as the CEO in this story.

Causation versus Correlation

Causation occurs when one thing directly affects another.

As in the misguided ad analysis, people often mistake *correlation* for *causation*. **Causation** occurs when one thing directly affects another. You can think of it as the path from cause to effect: turning on the stove *causes* the water in the kettle to boil.

A **variable** is a changing factor or characteristic.

Scientists refer to a changing factor or characteristic, like the temperature of water in a tea kettle, as a **variable**. Scientists say that causation occurs when one variable (for instance, the volume of natural gas burning on a stovetop) causes another variable (the temperature of water in a tea kettle) to change.

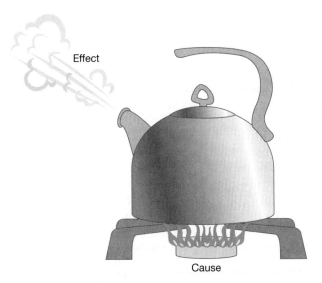

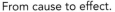
Effect

Cause

From cause to effect.

Does jogging cause people to be healthy? Does good health cause people to jog? In fact, both kinds of causation are simultaneously true.

[Think of causation as the path from cause to effect.]

Correlation means that two variables tend to change at the same time.

Correlation means that two variables tend to change at the same time—as one variable changes, the other changes as well. There is some kind of connection. It *might* be cause and effect, but correlation can also arise when causation is not present. For example, students who take music classes score better on their SATs than students who do not take music classes. Some music educators have happily jumped to the conclusion that this relationship is causal: more music causes higher SAT scores.

But don't buy a clarinet for your younger sibling just yet. There is scant evidence of a causal relationship, and there are many alternative explanations for the correlation between music lessons and high SAT scores. Maybe the students who play musical instruments have high levels of general patience, which explains why they thrive in long musical practice sessions *and* why they perform better in school (including studying for the SATs). Maybe students with high levels of general intelligence find musical instruments more appealing, and their intelligence also tends to raise their SAT scores. Maybe the students who play musical instruments tend to have wealthier parents who can pay for tutors that raise their kids' SAT scores.

When two variables are correlated, it suggests that causation may be possible and that further investigation is warranted—it's only the beginning of the story, not the end. Interestingly, when researchers have tried to document a *causal* link from music lessons to higher cognitive ability, they have almost always failed.[2] Accordingly, if a trombone player lost her trombone and dropped out of music class, this would not cause her future SAT scores to fall. Can you think of other situations in which correlation is confused with causality?

Correlations are divided into three categories: *positive correlation*, *negative correlation*, and *zero correlation*. **Positive correlation** implies that two variables tend to move in the same direction—for example, surveys reveal that people who have a relatively high income are more likely to be married than people who have a relatively low income. In this situation, we say that the variables of income and marital status are positively correlated. **Negative correlation** implies that the two variables tend to move in opposite directions—for example, people with a high level of education are less likely to be unemployed. In this situation, we say that the variables of education and unemployment are negatively

Positive correlation implies that two variables tend to move in the same direction.

Negative correlation implies that two variables tend to move in opposite directions.

When the variables have movements that are not related, we say that the variables have **zero correlation**.

correlated. When two variables are not related, we say that they have a **zero correlation**. The number of friends you have likely has no relation to whether your address is on the odd or even side of the street.

When Correlation Does Not Imply Causality   There are two main reasons we should not jump to the conclusion that a correlation between two variables implies a particular causal relationship:

1. Omitted variables
2. Reverse causality

An **omitted variable** is something that has been left out of a study that, if included, would explain why two variables that are in the study are correlated.

An **omitted variable** is something that has been left out of a study that, if included, would explain why two variables are correlated. Recall that the amount of red content in the store's ads is positively correlated with the growth rate of their sales. However, the red color does not necessarily cause the store's sales to rise. The arrival of the Christmas season causes both the store's ads to be red and month-over-month sales revenue to rise. Thus, the Christmas season is an omitted variable that explains why red ads tend to occur at around the time that sales tend to rise. (See Exhibit 2.4.)

Is there also an omitted variable that explains why education and income are positively correlated? One possible factor might be an individual's tendency to work hard. What if workaholics tend to thrive in college more than others? Perhaps pulling all-nighters to write term papers allows them to do well in their courses, encouraging them to stay in school. These same tendencies would also allow workaholics to earn more money than others—by staying late on the job, for example, or working on weekends. Does workaholism cause you to earn more and, incidentally, to graduate from college rather than drop out? Or does staying in college cause you to earn those higher wages? What is cause and what is effect?

Reverse causality occurs when we mix up the direction of cause and effect.

Reverse causality is another problem that plagues our efforts to distinguish correlation and causation. Reverse causality occurs when we mix up the direction of cause and effect. For example, consider the fact that relatively wealthy people tend to be relatively healthy, too. This has led some social scientists to conclude that greater wealth causes better health—because, for instance, wealthy people can afford better healthcare. However, this could be a case of reverse causality: better health may cause greater wealth. For example, healthy people can work harder and have fewer healthcare expenditures than less healthy people. It turns out that both causal channels seem to exist: greater wealth causes better health and better health causes greater wealth!

In our analysis of the returns to education, could it be that reverse causality is at play? That is, could higher wages at age 30 cause you to get more education at age 20? We can logically rule this out. Assuming that you don't have a time machine, it is unlikely that your wage as a 30-year-old causes you to obtain more education in your 20s. So in the returns-to-education example, reverse causality is probably not a problem. But in many other analyses—for example, the wealth-health relationship—reverse causality is a key consideration.

Exhibit 2.4 An Example of an Omitted Variable

The amount of red content in the store's ads is positively correlated with the growth of the store's revenue. In other words, when ads are red themed, the store's month-over-month sales revenue tends to grow the fastest. However, the redness does not cause the store's revenue to rise. The Christmas season causes the store's ads to be red and the Christmas season also causes the store's sales revenue to rise. The Christmas season is the omitted variable that explains the positive correlation between red ads and revenue growth.

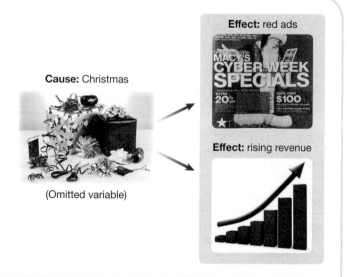

Cause: Christmas

(Omitted variable)

Effect: red ads

Effect: rising revenue

CHOICE
&CONSEQUENCE

Spend Now and Pay Later?

In a recent paper, two economists, Andrew Francis and Hugo Mialon, used U.S. survey data to calculate the empirical relationship between wedding spending and rates of divorce.[3] They found that more spending on a wedding ceremony or the engagement ring predicts a higher rate of divorce (holding other factors constant). For example, in their sample of women whose weddings cost more than $20,000, the annual likelihood of divorce is 3.5 times higher compared to women whose weddings cost between $5,000 and $10,000.

That's an entertaining piece of empirical evidence. Does this prove that the key to a long marriage is a small wedding, or better yet, an elopement? Does spending more on a wedding actually cause the couple to divorce? Or are there omitted variables at work? What omitted variables might cause people to have fancy weddings and also cause them to end up divorced? Vanity? Pride? Materialism?

Or perhaps expensive weddings create financial strains for the newlyweds, and these strains might cause divorce. So there *might* be a causal path from wedding expenses to divorce rates.

In fact, the authors of this paper aren't claiming to prove that expensive weddings cause divorce. They understand that correlation need not imply causation. With complex examples like this in mind, can we ever determine what is correlation and what is actually causation? Economists have developed a rich set of tools for identifying cause and effect. We turn to some of these tools next.

Do expensive weddings cause divorce? Or is something else going on?

Experimental Economics and Natural Experiments

An **experiment** is a controlled method of investigating causal relationships among variables.

One method of determining cause and effect is to run an **experiment**—a controlled method of investigating causal relationships among variables. Though you may not read much about economic experiments in the newspaper, headlines for experiments in the field of medicine are common. For example, the Food and Drug Administration requires pharmaceutical companies to run carefully designed experiments to provide evidence that new drugs work before they are approved for use by the general public.

To run an experiment, researchers usually create a treatment (test) group and a control group. Participants are assigned randomly to participate either as a member of the treatment group or as a member of the control group, which is not treated in a special way. **Randomization** is the assignment of subjects by chance, rather than by choice, to a treatment group or to a control group. The treatment group and the control group are treated identically, except along a single dimension that is intentionally varied across the two groups. Ultimately, the purpose of the experiment is to determine the impact of this variation.

Randomization is the assignment of subjects by chance, rather than by choice, to a treatment group or a control group.

If we want to know whether a promising new medicine helps patients with diabetes, we could take 1,000 patients with diabetes and randomly place 500 of them into a treatment group—those who receive the new medicine. The other 500 patients would be in the control group and receive the standard diabetes medication that is already widely used. Then we would follow all of the patients and monitor their health changes over the next few years. This experiment would test the causal hypothesis that the new drug is better than the old drug.

Now, consider an economics experiment. Suppose that we want to know what difference a college degree makes. We could take 1,000 high school students who cannot afford college but would like to attend college (if it were free) and randomly place 500 of them into a treatment group, where they had all their college expenses paid. The other 500 students would be placed in the control group. Then we would keep track of all of the original 1,000 students—including the 500 control-group students who weren't able to go to college because they couldn't afford it. We would use periodic surveys during their adult lives to see how the wages in the group that got a college education compare with the wages of the group that did not attend college. This experiment would test the hypothesis that a college education causes wages to rise.

One problem with experimentation is that experiments can sometimes be very costly to conduct. For instance, the college-attendance experiment that we just described would cost tens of millions of dollars, because the researchers would need to pay the college fees for 500 students. Another problem is that experiments do not provide immediate answers to some important questions. For example, learning about how one more year of education affects wages over the entire working life would take many decades. Another problem is that experiments are sometimes run poorly. For example, if medical researchers do not truly randomize the assignment of patients to medical treatments, then the experiment may not teach us anything at all. For instance, if patients who go to cutting-edge research hospitals tend to be the ones who get prescribed the newest kind of diabetes medication, then we cannot identify causation; we don't know whether it was the medication or something else at the fancy hospitals that caused those patients to get better. In a well-designed experiment, randomization alone would determine who got the new medicine and who got the old medicine.

When research is badly designed, economists tend to be very skeptical of its conclusions. We say "garbage in, garbage out" to capture the idea that bad research methods invalidate a study's conclusions.

If we don't have the budget or time to run an experiment, how else can we identify cause and effect? One approach is to study historical data that has been generated by a natural *experiment*. A **natural experiment** is an empirical study in which some process—out of the control of the experimenter—has assigned subjects to control and treatment groups in a random or nearly random way. In many situations, natural experiments are literally the only kind of experiment that we have from which to draw a conclusion. For instance, generals don't randomly choose villages on which to drop bombs—if they did, they would be court martialed. But sometimes, random factors cause some villages to be bombed and other villages to be spared. Melissa Dell, an economist, has explored such a natural experiment to determine the effect of different bombing policies during the Vietnam War. Most natural experiments are far less ethically complex. In a moment, we'll discuss a natural experiment—in this case, a change in mandatory education laws—that led some kids to get an extra year of education.

Economists have found and exploited natural experiments to answer numerous major questions. This methodology can be useful for providing a more definitive answer to our question at hand: What are you getting from your education?

A **natural experiment** is an empirical study in which some process—out of the control of the experimenter—has assigned subjects to control and treatment groups in a random or nearly random way.

EVIDENCE-BASED ECONOMICS

Q: How much do wages increase when mandatory schooling laws force people to get an extra year of schooling?

Many decades ago, compulsory schooling laws were much more permissive, allowing teenagers to drop out well before they graduated from high school. Philip Oreopoulos studied a natural experiment that was created by a change in these compulsory schooling laws.[4] Oreopoulos looked at an educational reform in the United Kingdom in 1947 that increased the minimum school leaving age from 14 to 15. As a result of this change, the fraction of children dropping out of school by age 14 fell by 50 percentage points between 1946 and 1948.

In this way, those kids reaching age 14 before 1947 are a "control group" for those reaching age 14 after 1947. Oreopoulos found that the students who turned 14 in 1948 and were therefore compelled to stay in school one extra year earned 10 percent more on average than the students who turned 14 in 1946.

Natural experiments are a useful source of data in empirical economics. In many problems, they help us separate correlation from causation. Applied to the returns to education, they suggest that the correlation between years of education and higher income is not due to some omitted variable but reflects the causal influence of education. The returns-to-education model thus obtains strong confirmation from the data. Does a 10 percent return to each additional year of education increase your appetite for more years of schooling?

Question

How much do wages increase when an individual is compelled by law to get an extra year of schooling?

Answer

On average, wages rise by 10 percent when kids are compelled to stay in school an extra year.

Data

United Kingdom General Household Survey. Compare kids in the United Kingdom who were allowed to drop out of school at age 14 with others who were compelled to stay in school an extra year due to changes in compulsory schooling laws.

Caveat

Factors other than the change in the compulsory schooling laws might explain why the kids who were compelled to stay in school eventually earned more in the workforce (this is an example of an omitted variable).

2.3 Economic Questions and Answers

Economists like to think about our research as a process in which we pose and answer questions. We've already seen a couple of these questions. For example, in the current chapter, we asked, "How much do wages increase when mandatory schooling laws force people to get an extra year of schooling?" and in Chapter 1, we asked, "What is the opportunity cost of your time?"

Good questions come in many different forms. But the most exciting economic questions share two properties.

1. *Good economic questions address topics that are important to individual economic agents and/or to our society.* Economists tend to think about economic research as something that contributes to society's welfare. We try to pursue research that has general implications for human behavior or economic performance. For example, understanding the returns to education is important, because individuals invest significant resources to obtain an education. The United States spends nearly a tenth of its economic output on education—$1.5 trillion per year. It is useful to quantify the payoffs from all this investment. If the returns to education are very high, society may want to encourage even more educational investment. If the returns to education are low, we should share this important fact with students who are deciding whether or not to stay in school. Knowing the returns to education will help individuals and governments decide how much of their scarce resources to allocate to educational investment.

2. *Good economic questions can be answered.* In some other disciplines, posing a good question is enough. For example, philosophers believe that some of the most important questions don't have answers. In contrast, economists are primarily interested in questions that can be answered with enough hard work, careful reasoning, and empirical evidence.

Here are some of the economic questions that we discuss in this book. As you look over the set, you will see that these are mostly big questions with significant implications for you and for society as a whole. The rest of this book sets out to discover answers to these questions. We believe the journey will be exhilarating. Let's get started!

Chapter	Questions
1	Is Facebook free?
2	How much more do workers with a college education earn? How much do wages increase when mandatory schooling laws force people to get an extra year of schooling?
3	How does location affect the rental cost of housing?
4	How much more gasoline would people buy if its price were lower?
5	In the United States, what is the total market value of annual economic production?
6	Why is the average American so much richer than the average Indian?
7	Why are you so much more prosperous than your great-great-grandparents were?
8	Are tropical and semitropical areas condemned to poverty by their geographies?
9	What happens to employment and unemployment if local employers go out of business?
10	How often do banks fail?
11	What caused the German hyperinflation of 1922–1923?
12	What caused the recession of 2007–2009?
13	How much does government spending stimulate GDP?
14	Are companies like Nike harming workers in Vietnam?
15	How did George Soros make $1 billion?
Web Chapter 1	Do investors chase historical returns?
Web Chapter 2	What is the value of a human life?
Web Chapter 3	Do governments and politicians follow their citizens' and constituencies' wishes?

Summary

- The scientific method is the name for the ongoing process that economists and other scientists use to (1) develop models of the world and (2) evaluate those models by testing them with data.

- Empirical evidence is facts that are obtained through observation and measurement. Empirical evidence is also called data.

- Economists try to uncover causal relationships among variables.

- One method used to determine causality is to run an experiment—a controlled method of investigating causal relationships among variables. Economists now actively pursue experiments both in the laboratory and in the field. Economists also determine causality by studying historical data that have been generated by a natural experiment.

Key Terms

scientific method *p. 21*
model *p. 21*
empirical evidence (data) *p. 22*
hypotheses *p. 23*
mean (average) *p. 25*
median *p. 25*

causation *p. 26*
variable *p. 27*
correlation *p. 27*
positive correlation *p. 27*
negative correlation *p. 27*
zero correlation *p. 28*

omitted variable *p. 28*
reverse causality *p. 28*
experiment *p. 29*
randomization *p. 29*
natural experiment *p. 30*

Questions

All questions are available in MyEconLab *for practice and instructor assignment.*

1. What does it mean to say that economists use the scientific method? How do economists distinguish between models that work and those that don't?

2. What is meant by empiricism?

3. What are two important properties of economic models? Models are often simplified descriptions of a real-world phenomenon. Does this mean that they are unrealistic?

4. Suppose 5,000 people bought scoops of ice cream on a hot summer day. If the mean number of scoops bought is 2, how many total scoops were sold that day?

5. How does the sample size affect the validity of an empirical argument? When can only one example be enough to prove your point?

6. Explain why correlation does not always imply causation. Does causation always imply *positive* correlation? Explain your answer.

7. Give an example of a pair of variables that have a positive correlation, a pair of variables that have a negative correlation, and a pair of variables that have zero correlation.

8. What is meant by randomization? How does randomization affect the results of an experiment?

9. This chapter discussed natural and randomized experiments. How does a natural experiment differ from a randomized one?

10. Suppose you had to find the effect of seat belt rules on road accident fatalities. Would you choose to run a randomized experiment, or would it make sense to use natural experiments here? Explain.

Problems

All problems are available in MyEconLab *for practice and instructor assignment.*

1. Although the mean and median are closely related, the difference between the mean and the median is sometimes of interest.

   a. Suppose country A has five families. Their incomes are $10,000, $20,000, $30,000, $40,000, and $50,000. What is the median family income in A? What is the mean income?

   b. Country B also has five families. Their incomes are $10,000, $20,000, $30,000, $40,000, and $150,000. What is the median family income in B? What is the mean income?

   c. In which country is income inequality greater, A or B?

   d. Suppose you thought income inequality in the United States had increased over time. Based on your answers to this question, would you expect the ratio of the mean income in the United States to the median income to have risen or fallen? Explain.

2. Consider the following situation: your math professor tells your class (of five students) that the mean score on the final exam is 80 but the median is 100. How is that possible? Explain.

3. Suppose you come across a study that has discovered a correlation between reading books and life expectancy: People who read more books live longer. Come up with at least one plausible way that this correlation exists even though there is no direct causal link.

4. Some studies have found that people who owned guns were more likely to be killed with a gun. Do you think this study is strong evidence in favor of stricter gun control laws? Explain.

5. As the text explains, it can sometimes be very difficult to sort out the direction of causality.

   a. Why might you think that more police officers would lead to lower crime rates? Why might you think that higher crime rates would lead to more police officers?

b. In 2012, the *New England Journal of Medicine* published research that showed a strong correlation between the consumption of chocolate in a country and the number of Nobel Prize winners in that country. Do you think countries that want to encourage their citizens to win Nobel Prizes should increase their consumption of chocolate?

c. A recent article in the *Journal of Applied Physiology* found that elderly runners had healthier muscles than a comparison group of the same age. Although the members of the comparison group were all still living independently, they had lower muscle mass and muscle strength than the athletes. The popular press framed the article as proof that exercise causes people to be healthier. Is that the only way to interpret causality in this example?

6. This chapter shows that in general, people with more education earn higher salaries. Economists have offered two explanations of this relationship. The human capital argument says that high schools and colleges teach people valuable skills, and employers are willing to pay higher salaries to attract people with those skills. The signaling argument says that college graduates earn more because a college degree is a signal to employers that a job applicant is diligent, intelligent, and perse-

vering. How might you use data on people with 2, 3, and 4 years of college education to shed light on this controversy?

7. You decide to run an experiment. You invite 50 friends to a party. You randomly select 25 friends and tell them that there will be free food; most of them show up to your party. For the other 25 friends you do not mention the free food; none of these friends show up. Based on the correlation in your data, you conclude that free food causes people to come to parties. A buddy points out "be careful, correlation does not imply causation." How should you respond?

8. Oregon expanded its Medicaid coverage in 2008. Roughly 90,000 people applied, but the state had funds to cover only an additional 30,000 people (who were randomly chosen from the total applicant pool of 90,000). How could you use the Oregon experience to estimate the impact of increased access to healthcare on health outcomes?

9. A simple economic model predicts that a fall in the price of bus tickets means that more people will take the bus. However, you observe that some people still do not take the bus even after the price of a ticket fell.

a. Is the model incorrect?

b. How would you test this model?

Appendix

Constructing and Interpreting Charts and Graphs

As you start to learn economics, it's important that you have a good grasp of how to make sense of data and how to present data clearly in visible form. Graphs are everywhere—on TV, on the Web, in newspapers and magazines, in economics textbooks. Why are graphs so popular?

A well-designed graph summarizes a large amount of information—as the saying goes, "a picture is worth a thousand words." In this book, you will find many graphs, and you will see that they provide a way to supplement the verbal description of economic concepts.

Indeed, visualization can be extremely useful at every stage of economic analysis. As you'll see throughout this book, simple charts and graphs reveal the relationships between variables in a model. Charts and graphs make complicated databases more intuitive by giving the researchers a sense of important underlying properties in the data, like time trends. To demonstrate how data visualizations enhance economic analysis, we will walk you through a recent study that one of us—John List—co-authored, presenting data visualizations along the way.

> A well-designed graph summarizes a large amount of information—as the saying goes, "a picture is worth a thousand words."

A Study about Incentives

Would you study harder for this economics class if we paid you $50 for earning an A? What if we raised the stakes to $500? Your first impulse might be to think "Well, sure...why not? That money could buy a new iPhone or maybe a ticket to a Nicki Minaj concert."

As we learned in Chapter 1, though, there are opportunity costs of studying more, such as attending fewer music concerts or spending less time at your favorite coffee house talking with friends. Such opportunity costs must be weighed against the benefits of earning an A in this course. You might conclude that because this question is hypothetical anyway, there's no need to think harder about how you would behave.

But what if the question weren't imaginary?

Over the past few years, thousands of students have actually been confronted with such a financial offer. Sally Sadoff, Steven Levitt, and John List carried out an experiment at two high schools in the suburbs of Chicago over several years in which they used incentives to change students' behavior. Such an experiment allows us to think about the relationship between two *variables*—in this case, how an increase in a financial reward affects student test scores. And it naturally leads to a discussion of cause and effect, which we have just studied in this chapter: we'll examine simple correlations between variables and identify a causal relationship. Both correlation and causation are powerful concepts in gaining an understanding of the world around us—and, as we'll see, data visualizations are crucial tools for this analysis.

Experimental Design

There are two high schools in Chicago Heights, and both have a problem with student dropout rates. It is not uncommon for more than 50 percent of incoming ninth-graders to drop out before receiving a high school diploma. These problems are not unique to Chicago Heights; many urban school districts face a similar problem.

How can economists help? Some economists have devised incentive schemes to lower the dropout rates and increase academic achievement in schools. In this instance, students were *paid* for improved academic performance.[1]

Let's first consider the experiment to lower the dropout rate. Each student was randomly placed into one of the following three groups:

Treatment Group with Student Incentives: Students would receive $50 for each month they met special academic standards (explained below) established by the experimenters.

Treatment Group with Parent Incentives: Students' *parents* would receive $50 for each month the special academic standards were met by their child.

Control Group: Neither students nor parents received financial compensation linked to academic performance.

A student was deemed to have met the monthly standards if he or she:

1. did not have a D or an F in any classes during that month,
2. had no more than one unexcused absence during that month, and
3. had no suspensions during that month.

Describing Variables

Before we discover how much money these students actually made, let's consider more carefully the variables that we might be interested in analyzing. As its name suggests, a variable is a factor that is likely to vary or change; that is, it can take different values in different situations. In this section, we show you how to use three different techniques to help graphically describe variables:

1. Pie charts
2. Bar charts
3. Time series graphs

Pie Charts

A **pie chart** is a circle split into slices of different sizes. The area of each slice represents the relative importance of non-overlapping parts that add up to the whole.

Understanding pie charts is a piece of cake. A **pie chart** is a circle split into slices of different sizes. The area of each slice represents the relative importance of non-overlapping parts that add up to the whole. Pie charts show how some economic variable can be divided into components that each represent a fraction of the total and that jointly add up to 100 percent.

For example, consider the ethnicity of the students in our experiment. In Exhibit 2A.1, we learn that 59 percent of ninth-graders in the study identify as African American. We therefore differentiate 59 percent of our pie chart with the color blue to represent the proportion of African-American participants in the study. We see that 15 percent of the students identify as non-Hispanic whites, represented by the red piece of the pie. We continue breaking down participation by ethnicity until we have filled in 100 percent of the circle. The circle then describes the ethnic composition of the participants in the study.

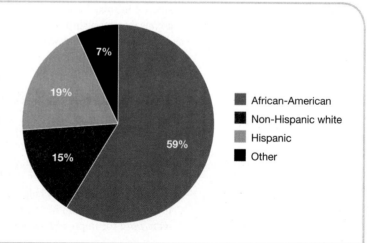

Exhibit 2A.1 Chicago Heights Study Participants by Ethnicity

The pie segments are a visual way to represent the fractions of all Chicago Heights high school students in the experiment that make up the four different ethnic categories. Just as the numbers add up to 100 percent, so do all of the segments add up to the complete "pie."

- African-American
- Non-Hispanic white
- Hispanic
- Other

7%
19%
59%
15%

Bar Charts

A **bar chart** uses bars of different heights or lengths to indicate the properties of different groups.

Another type of graph that can be used to summarize and display a variable is a bar chart. A **bar chart** uses bars (no surprise there) of different heights or lengths to indicate the properties of different groups. Bar charts make it easy to compare a single variable across many groups. To make a bar chart, simply draw rectangles side by side, making each rectangle as high (or as long, in the case of horizontal bars) as the value of the variable it is describing.

For example, Exhibit 2A.2 captures the overall success rates of students in the various experimental groups. In the exhibit we have the **independent variable**—the variable that the experimenter is choosing (the treatment group or control group in the study to which each student is randomly assigned)—on the horizontal or x-axis. On the vertical or y-axis is the **dependent variable**—the variable that is potentially affected by the experimental treatment. In the exhibit, the dependent variable is the proportion of students meeting the academic standards. Note that 100 percent is a proportion of 1, and 30 percent is a proportion of 0.30.

An **independent variable** is a variable whose value does not depend on another variable; in an experiment it is manipulated by the experimenter.

A **dependent variable** is a variable whose value depends on another variable.

We find some interesting experimental results in Exhibit 2A.2. For instance, we can see from the bar chart that 25.1 percent of students in the Control group (students who received no incentives) met the academic standards. In comparison, 32.5 percent of students in the Parent Incentive group met the standards. This is a meaningful increase in the number of students meeting the standards—evidence that incentives can work.

Time Series Graphs

A **time series graph** displays data at different points in time.

With pie charts and bar charts, we can summarize how a variable is broken up into different groups, but what if we want to understand how a variable changes over time? For instance, how did the proportion of students meeting the standards change over the school year? A **time series graph** can do the trick. A time series graph displays data at different points in time.

As an example, consider Exhibit 2A.3, which displays the proportion of students meeting the standards in each month in the Control and Parent Incentive groups. Keep in mind that although there are multiple months and groups, we are still measuring only a single variable—in this case, the proportion meeting the standard. As Exhibit 2A.3 makes clear, the number of students meeting the standard is higher in the Parent Incentive treatment group than in the Control group. But notice that the difference within the Parent Incentive and Control groups changes from month to month. Without a time series, we would not be able to appreciate these month-to-month differences and would not be able to get a sense for how the effectiveness of the incentive varies over the school year. As you read this book, keep in mind that the variables we discuss can change over time—and that time series graphs are invaluable in tracking these changes.

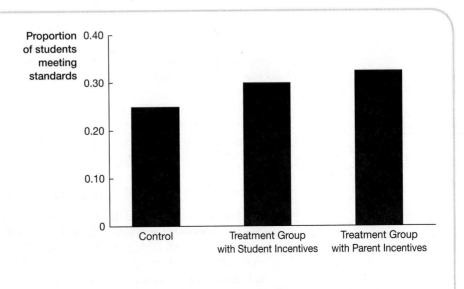

Exhibit 2A.2 Proportion of Students Meeting Academic Standards by Experimental Group

The bar chart facilitates comparing numbers across groups in the experiment. In this case, we can compare how different groups perform in terms of meeting academic standards by comparing the height of each bar. For example, the Parent Incentive group's bar is higher than the Control group's bar, meaning that a higher proportion of students in the Parent Incentives group met the standards than in the Control group.

Exhibit 2A.3 Participants Meeting All Standards by Month

The time series graph takes some of the information that was in the bar chart and shows how it changes depending on the month of the school year during which the experiment was conducted. The points are connected to more clearly illustrate the month-to-month trend. In addition, by using a different color or line pattern, we can represent two groups (Control and Parent Incentives) on the same graph, giving the opportunity to compare the two groups, just as with the bar chart in the previous exhibit.

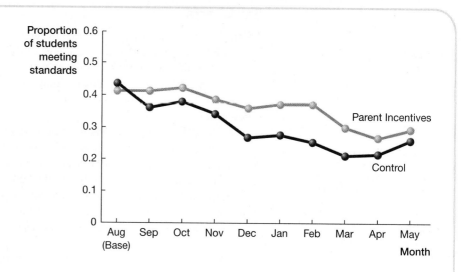

Cause and Effect

We've written about both causation and correlation in this chapter. Economists are much more interested in the former. Causation relates two variables in an active way—*a* causes *b* if, because of *a*, *b* has occurred.

For example, we can conclude in our experimental study that paying money for the students' performance *causes* them to improve their academic performance. This would not necessarily be the case if the experiment were not properly implemented—for example, if students were not randomly placed into control and treatment groups. For instance, imagine that the experimenters had placed all of the students who had achieved poorly in the past in the control group. Then the relatively poor performance of the control group might be due to the composition of students who were assigned to the control group, and not to the lack of financial incentives. Any relationship between academic achievement and payment stemming from such an experiment could be interpreted as a correlation because all other things were not equal at the start of the experiment—the control group would have a higher proportion of low achievers than the other groups.

Fortunately, the Chicago Heights experiment was implemented using the principle of randomization discussed earlier in this chapter. The experimenters split students into groups randomly, so each experimental group had an equal representation of students—that is, attributes like average student intelligence were similar across groups. Accordingly, any difference between the groups' academic performance during the experiment was due to the different experimental conditions, such as differences in financial incentives.

This means that we can claim that the cause of the difference between the performance of the Student Incentive group and that of the Control group is that students in the Student Incentive group were given an incentive of $50, whereas students in the Control group received no incentive for improvement.

Correlation Does Not Necessarily Imply Causality

Often, correlation is misinterpreted as causation. While correlation can certainly indicate potential causation—a reason to look more closely—it's only a first step. As an example, not long ago, a high-ranking marketing executive showed us Exhibit 2A.4 (the numbers are changed for confidentiality reasons). He was trying to demonstrate that his company's retail advertisements were effective in increasing sales: "It shows a clear positive relationship between ads and sales. When we placed 1,000 ads, sales were roughly $35 million. But see

Exhibit 2A.4 Advertisements and Sales

Just looking at the line chart of sales versus number of advertisements, we would be tempted to say that more ads cause more sales. However, without randomization, we risk overlooking the role of a third variable that is omitted from the chart, which increases sales and is associated with advertising. Is such an omitted variable lurking here?

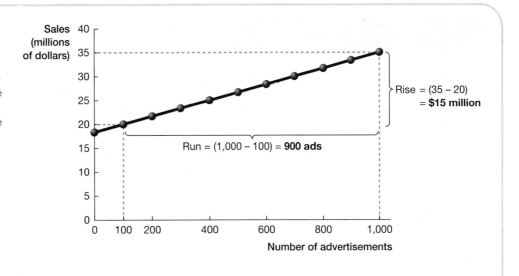

how sales dipped to roughly $20 million when we placed only 100 ads? This proves that more advertisements lead to more sales."

Before discussing whether this exhibit proves causality, let's step back and think about the basic characteristics of Exhibit 2A.4. In such an exhibit we have:

1. The *x*-variable plotted on the horizontal axis, or *x*-axis; in our figure the *x*-variable is the number of advertisements.
2. The *y*-variable plotted on the vertical axis, or *y*-axis; in our figure the *y*-variable is the sales in millions of dollars.
3. The origin, which is the point where the *x*-axis intersects the *y*-axis; both sales and the number of advertisements are equal to zero at the origin.

In the exhibit, the number of advertisements is the independent variable, and the amount of sales is the dependent variable. When the values of both variables increase together in the same direction, they have a positive relationship; when one increases and the other decreases, and they move in opposite directions, they have a negative relationship.

So in Exhibit 2A.4, we find a positive relationship between the two variables. What is the strength of that positive relationship? This is called the slope. The **slope** is the change in the value of the variable plotted on the *y*-axis divided by the change in the value of the variable plotted on the *x*-axis:

> The **slope** is the change in the value of the variable plotted on the *y*-axis divided by the change in the value of the variable plotted on the *x*-axis.

$$\text{Slope} = \frac{\text{Change in } y}{\text{Change in } x} = \frac{\text{Rise}}{\text{Run}}.$$

In this example, the increase in the number of advertisements from 100 to 1,000 was associated with an increase in sales from $20 million to $35 million. Thus, the rise, or the change in sales (*y*), is $15 million and the run, or change in *x*, is 900 ads. Because both are rising (moving in the same direction), the slope is positive:

$$\text{Slope} = \frac{\$35,000,000 - \$20,000,000}{1000 \text{ ads} - 100 \text{ ads}} = \frac{\$15,000,000}{900 \text{ ads}} = \$16,667 \text{ per ad.}$$

Thus, our exhibit implies that one more advertisement is associated with $16,667 more in sales. But, does this necessarily mean that if the retailer increases the number of advertisements by one, this will cause sales to increase by $16,667?

Unfortunately, no. While it is tempting to interpret the sales increasing with ads as a causal relationship between the two variables, we cannot be sure that this relationship is causal. In this case, the marketing executive forgot to think about *why* his company so drastically increased its advertisement volume to begin with—after all, the amount of advertising was not determined randomly in an experiment. As it turns out,

Exhibit 2A.5 Ice Cream Production and Drownings in the United States

We depict the relationship between monthly ice cream production and monthly drownings. Each of the 12 points represents a single month in 2011. Is this relationship causal or is there an omitted variable that is causing these two variables to move together? Hint: the point in the upper right corner of the exhibit is July and the point in the lower left corner of the exhibit is December!

Sources: Based on Centers for Disease Control and Prevention, and Brian W. Gould, University of Wisconsin Dairy Marketing and Risk Management Program.

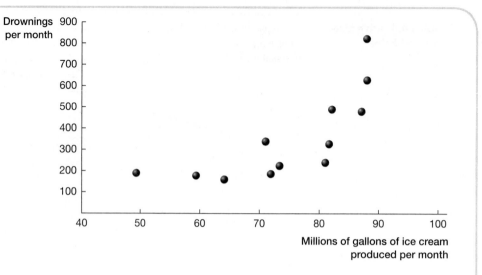

the company did so because of the holiday season, a time when sales would presumably have been high anyway.

So, after some further digging (we'll spare you the details), what the data actually say is that the retailer placed more ads during times of busy shopping (around Thanksgiving and in December), but that is exactly when sales would normally be high—because of the holiday shopping season. Similar to what happened in the department store red/blue ad example in this chapter, taking into account seasonal variation wipes out the causal relationship between ads and sales.

This example shows that you should be careful when you connect a few points in a graph. Just because two variables move together (a correlation), they are not necessarily related in a causal way. They could merely be linked by another variable that is causing them both to increase—in this case, the shopping season.

To see the general idea of what is happening more clearly, let's instead graph the quantity of ice cream produced against the number of monthly drownings in the United States. Using data across months in 2011, we constructed Exhibit 2A.5. In Exhibit 2A.5, we see that in months when ice cream production is relatively high, there are a lot of drownings. Likewise, in months when there is relatively little ice cream production, there are far fewer drownings. Does this mean that you should not swim after you eat ice cream?

Indeed, parents persuaded by such a chart might believe that it's causal, and never let their kids eat ice cream near swimming pools or lakes! But luckily for us ice cream lovers, there is an omitted variable lurking in the background. In the summertime, when it is hot, people eat more ice cream *and* swim more. More swimming leads to more drowning. Even though people eat more ice cream cones in the summer, eating ice cream doesn't *cause* people to drown.

Just as a heightened shopping season was the omitted variable in the retailer advertisement example, here the omitted variable is heat—it causes us to swim more *and* to eat more ice cream cones. While the former causes more drownings (as we would all expect), the latter has nothing to do with drowning, even though there is a positive correlation between the two, as shown in Exhibit 2A.5.

Beyond an understanding of how to construct data figures, we hope that this appendix gave you an appreciation for how to interpret visual displays of data. An important lesson is that just because two variables are correlated—and move together in a figure—does not mean that they are causally related. Causality is the gold standard in the social sciences. Without understanding the causal relationship between two variables, we cannot reliably predict how the world will change when the government intervenes to change one of the variables. Experiments help reveal causal relationships; for example, we learned from the Chicago Heights experiment that incentives can affect student performance.

Appendix Key Terms

pie chart *p. 36*
bar chart *p. 37*

independent variable *p. 37*
dependent variable *p. 37*

time series graph *p. 37*
slope *p. 39*

Appendix Problems

A1. How would you represent the following graphically?

   a. Income inequality in the United States has increased over the past 10 years.

   b. All the workers in the manufacturing sector in a particular country fit into one (and only one) of the following three categories: 31.5 percent are high school dropouts, 63.5 percent have a regular high school diploma, and the rest have a vocational training certificate.

   c. The median income of a household in Alabama was $43,464 in 2012, and the median income of a household in Connecticut was $64,247 in 2012.

A2. Consider the following data that show the quantity of coffee produced in Brazil from 2004 to 2012.

Year	Production (in tons)
2004	2,465,710
2005	2,140,169
2006	2,573,368
2007	2,249,011
2008	2,796,927
2009	2,440,056
2010	2,907,265
2011	2,700,440
2012	3,037,534

   a. Plot the data in a time series graph.

   b. What is the mean quantity of coffee that Brazil produced from 2009 to 2011?

   c. In percentage terms, how much has the 2012 crop increased over the 2009–2011 mean?

A3. Suppose the following table shows the relationship between revenue that the Girl Scouts generate and the number of cookie boxes that they sell.

Number of Cookie Boxes	Revenue
50	$200
150	$600
250	$1,000
350	$1,400
450	$1,800
550	$2,200

   a. Present the data in a scatter plot.

   b. Do the two variables have a positive relationship or do they have a negative relationship? Explain.

   c. What is the slope of the line that you get in the scatter plot? What does the slope imply about the price of a box of Girl Scout cookies?

3 Optimization: Doing the Best You Can

How does location affect the rental cost of housing?

Suppose you have just landed a job near the center of a city and you now need to decide where to live. If you live close to the city center, your round-trip commute will be 15 minutes. If you live in the distant suburbs, your round-trip commute will be 60 minutes. Where will the apartments be relatively less expensive? How will you choose where to live? How should you make the best decision given the trade-offs you face?

In this chapter, we'll dig into the concept of optimization—choosing the best feasible option. You will learn how to optimize by using cost-benefit analysis. And we will apply this knowledge to an example that we revisit throughout the chapter—choosing an apartment.

CHAPTER OUTLINE

3.1 Optimization: Choosing the Best Feasible Option

In Chapter 1, we described economics as the study of choice. Economists usually assume that people make choices by trying to select the best feasible option, given the available information. In other words, people try to optimize. Recall that optimization is the first principle of economics.

> Economists use optimization to predict most of the choices that people, households, businesses, and governments make.

Economists use optimization to predict most of the choices that people, households, businesses, and governments make. To an economist, seemingly unrelated decisions—for example, where a college student will travel on spring break, which apartment a worker will rent, or what price Apple charges for an iPhone—are all connected by the unifying principle of optimization. Whatever choices people face, economists believe that they will try to choose optimally. However, economists don't assume that people always *successfully* optimize—an issue that we will return to below.

Of course, optimization need not be easy, and optimization is often quite complex. To illustrate the complexity, consider the choice of an apartment. In large cities there are hundreds of thousands of rental apartments, each with different characteristics to consider, such as the number of bedrooms, location, views, and neighborhood amenities.

Making an optimal decision, then, involves juggling multiple trade-offs. For example, how do you compare two apartments, one of which has the benefit of lower rent and one of which has the benefit of a shorter commute? How would you determine which apartment is a better choice for you? In this chapter, we are going to see how to optimally evaluate such trade-offs. We introduce you to the most important optimization tools that economists use.

We have a lot to say about choosing a rental apartment, but remember that the choice of an apartment is just one illustration of the general concept of optimization. We can use the principal of optimization to analyze any decision that an economic agent faces, from the trivial—for instance, the choice of how many miles to jog in a workout—to the profound—how many years of education will you obtain?

Optimization can be implemented using many different techniques. In this chapter, we show you how to optimize using two different techniques, which yield *identical* answers. The first technique simply calculates the total value of each feasible option and then picks the option with the greatest total value. The second technique—*marginal analysis,* which we explain later in the chapter—focuses on differences among the feasible options and finds the best option by analyzing these differences. Because the two optimization techniques yield identical answers, you can decide to use whichever technique you find easier for each particular problem.

CHOICE —
&CONSEQUENCE

Do People Really Optimize?

With all of this talk about optimization, you might be wondering whether people actually do optimize. Do economic agents always pick the best feasible option? Of course not! So why do economists use optimization to predict their choices?

Economists believe that optimization is a useful approximation of some economic behavior, even if people don't *consistently* hit the optimization bull's-eye. Economists are interested in identifying situations in which optimization is a good approximation of behavior and those in which optimization is a bad approximation of behavior.

There is even a branch of economics that specializes in studying this question. **Behavioral economics** explains why people optimize in some situations and fail to optimize in others. Behavioral economists model this range of behavior by combining economic and psychological theories of human decision making.

Several special situations are associated with behavior that is not optimal. For example, when people have self-control problems—like procrastination, or, far worse, addiction—optimization is not a good description of behavior.

People also tend to fail as optimizers when they are new to a task. For instance, the first time individuals play poker, they tend to play poorly—they make rookie mistakes. Consequently, optimization is a better description of behavior when people have lots of experience. For example, as investors gain more years of experience, they tend to make fewer mistakes.

John Campbell, Tarun Ramadorai, and Benjamin Ranish documented this pattern of improving performance in a 2014 research paper. They obtained anonymized data that summarized the activity of 11.6 million investors in India. The researchers found that experienced investors (those with brokerage accounts that have been open a relatively long time) have annual returns that are on average 4.6 percentage points higher than those of their inexperienced peers.[1] The authors named their paper after the Beatles song "Getting Better" and began the paper with this lyric: "It is a little better all the time. (It can't get no worse.)"

Because people aren't born perfect optimizers, optimization is a useful skill to develop. Economists show people how to be better optimizers—such advice amounts to prescriptive economic analysis.

We hope that you use the concept of optimization in two ways: to describe the behavior of knowledgeable decision makers and to identify and improve suboptimal decisions—especially your own!

Behavioral economics jointly analyzes the economic and psychological factors that explain human behavior.

3.2 Optimization Application: Renting the Optimal Apartment

Let's explore the theory of optimization in more depth. To illustrate ideas, we return to our opening example, in which you are an apartment hunter.

Imagine that you have narrowed your rental choice to four possible apartments—your "short list." Exhibit 3.1 summarizes this short list, including two key pieces of information for each apartment—the monthly rent and the amount of commuting time per month. Exhibit 3.1 assumes that rent decreases the farther you are from work; as rent falls, commuting time increases, generating a trade-off. Later in this chapter, we explain why economic forces predict this inverse relationship between rent and distance from work. We'll also show you empirical evidence that confirms this prediction.

You might wonder about everything that was left out of the summary of information in Exhibit 3.1. What about other differences among these apartments, like how long it takes to walk to the neighborhood laundromat or whether there is a park nearby? We also omitted commuting costs other than time, like the direct dollar cost of public transportation or, if you drive yourself, gasoline and tolls. Shouldn't all these considerations be part of the comparison?

To keep things simple, we will omit other factors for now, even though they *are* important in practice. We omit them to keep the calculations simple and so that the basic economic concepts are easier to understand. As you'll discover in the problems at the end of

Exhibit 3.1 Apartments on Your Short List, Which Differ Only with Regard to Commuting Time and Rent and Are Otherwise Identical

Many cities have a single central business district—which is often referred to as the city center—where lots of employers are concentrated. In most cities, apartments near the city center cost more to rent than otherwise identical apartments that are far away. Why is this so?

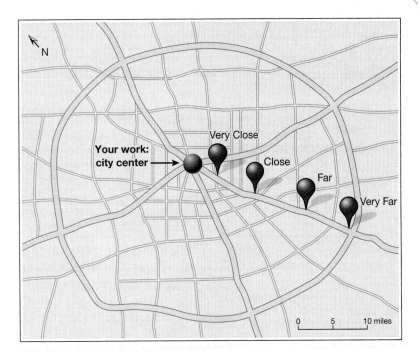

Apartment	Commuting Time (hours/month)	Rent ($/month)
Very Close	5 hours	$1,180
Close	10 hours	$1,090
Far	15 hours	$1,030
Very Far	20 hours	$1,000

The proximity of local amenities should also go into a complete optimization analysis, because these amenities change the net benefits of an apartment.

the chapter, once you understand the basic ideas, it is easy to add more details. For now, we will assume that the four apartments—Very Close, Close, Far, and Very Far—are identical except for the differences listed in Exhibit 3.1.

Note, too, that we are focusing only on costs in this example—the cost of commuting time and the cost of rent. We are assuming that the benefits of these apartments are the same—for instance, size or views. If the benefits are the same, then cost-benefit analysis becomes simpler. In normal cost-benefit analysis, the decision maker finds the alternative with the highest value of *net benefit*, which is benefit minus cost. When the benefits are the same across all the alternatives, cost-benefit analysis simplifies to finding the alternative with the lowest cost. That's what we are going to do next.

Exhibit 3.1 contains the information that we need, but, on its own, it does not enable us to choose the best apartment. First, we need to sum the cost of rent and the cost of commuting time to calculate the *total* cost of each apartment. The total cost includes the *direct* cost of rent and the *indirect* cost of commute time.

To sum these two costs, we first need to decide on a common unit of account. Let's pick dollars per month for now. Because rent is already expressed in dollars per month, half of our work has been done for us. All that remains is to translate the indirect cost—commuting time—into the same unit of measurement.

To do this, we use the concept of opportunity cost, which we introduced in Chapter 1. Let's begin by assuming that the opportunity cost of commuting time is $10/hour. This is the hourly value of the alternative activity that is crowded out when you spend more time

Exhibit 3.2 Commuting Cost and Rental Cost Expressed in Common Units, Assuming an Opportunity Cost of Time of $10/hour

To optimize, it is necessary to convert all of the costs and benefits into common units. In this example, the common unit is dollars per month. The optimum—in bold—is Far, which has the lowest total cost.

Apartment	Commuting Time (hours/month)	Commuting Cost ($/month)	Rent ($/month)	Total Cost: Rent + Commuting ($/month)
Very Close	5 hours	$50	$1,180	$1,230
Close	10 hours	$100	$1,090	$1,190
Far	**15 hours**	**$150**	**$1,030**	**$1,180**
Very Far	20 hours	$200	$1,000	$1,200

commuting. The fact that it is a dollar value doesn't imply that this time would have been spent at work if it weren't spent commuting. An extra hour of time has value to you regardless of what you might choose to do with that time, including napping, socializing, watching videos, taking longer showers, or working.

If the round-trip commute takes 20 hours/month and the opportunity cost of time is $10/hour, then the dollar cost of that commute is

$$\left(\frac{20 \text{ hours}}{\text{month}}\right)\left(\frac{\$10}{\text{hour}}\right) = \left(\frac{\$200}{\text{month}}\right).$$

The first term on the left is commute time per month, which is expressed in hours per month, just as it is in Exhibit 3.1. The term just before the equal sign is the opportunity cost of time, which is expressed as dollars per hour. The "hours" units cancel, leaving a final cost expressed as dollars per month.

Now we are ready to rewrite Exhibit 3.1. Using the calculations that we just illustrated for 20 hours of monthly commuting time, we can calculate costs for a commute of any duration. Exhibit 3.2 reports this commuting cost in dollars per month for all four apartments.

Exhibit 3.2 gives us the answer to our optimization problem. "Far" is the best apartment for a consumer with an opportunity cost of time of $10/hour. This apartment has the lowest total cost—$1,180—taking into account both direct rental costs and indirect time costs of commuting.

We also easily see this result by plotting the total costs. Exhibit 3.3 plots the total cost of each of the four apartments—and, as the dip in the curve clearly shows, Far is the best choice.

Exhibit 3.3 Total Cost Including Both Rent and Commuting Cost, Assuming an Opportunity Cost of Time of $10/hour

If the consumer chooses optimally, he or she will select Far. This apartment has the lowest total cost, which is the sum of the direct rental cost and the indirect commuting cost (see breakdown in Exhibit 3.2). The commuting cost is calculated by using the consumer's opportunity cost of time, which is $10/hour in this example.

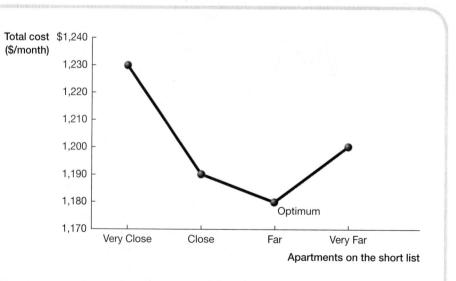

The **optimum** is the best feasible choice. In other words, the optimum is the optimal choice.

Economists call the best feasible choice the **optimum**, which you can see labeled on the total cost curve.

To sum up our discussion so far, *optimization using total value* has three steps:

1. Translate all costs and benefits into common units, like dollars per month.
2. Calculate the *total* net benefit of each alternative.
3. Pick the alternative with the highest net benefit.

Before and After Comparisons

If apartment hunters make optimal choices, then the choice of an apartment will be affected by a change in the opportunity cost of time. Until now we have assumed that the opportunity cost of time is $10/hour. Let's instead assume that the opportunity cost of time is $15/hour. Why might opportunity cost rise? For example, a freelance worker's opportunity cost of time would rise if his or her hourly wage rose.

How does this increase in the opportunity cost of time change the predicted behavior? Before we take you through it step-by-step, try to use your intuition. How would a change in the value of time affect the optimal decision of where to live? Should commuters with a higher value of time move closer to where they work or farther away?

To answer this question, we again need to translate the indirect cost—commuting time— into the same units as the direct cost of rent, which are dollars per month. Accordingly, we rewrite Exhibit 3.2, assuming instead a $15/hour opportunity cost of time. Exhibit 3.4 reports this commuting cost in dollars per month for all four apartments.

Exhibit 3.4 provides the answer to our new optimization problem. The best apartment for a consumer with an opportunity cost of time of $15/hour now shifts from Far to Close. Close has the lowest total cost—$1,240—taking into account both direct rental costs and indirect time costs of commuting.

Exhibit 3.5 plots the total cost of each of the four apartments assuming a $15/hour opportunity cost of time. Close is the best choice—the optimum.

When the opportunity cost of time increases from $10/hour to $15/hour, it becomes more valuable for the commuter to choose an apartment that reduces the amount of time spent commuting. So the optimal choice switches from a relatively inexpensive apartment with a longer commute—Far—to a relatively expensive apartment with a shorter commute—Close.

Exhibit 3.6 takes the two different cost curves from Exhibits 3.3 and 3.5 and plots them in a single figure. The purple line represents the total cost curve for the commuter with an opportunity cost of $10/hour. The orange line represents the total cost curve for the commuter with an opportunity cost of $15/hour. Two key properties are visible in Exhibit 3.6:

1. The $10/hour cost curve lies below the $15/hour cost curve. The $10/hour curve has lower commuting costs for each apartment, so the total cost, which takes into account both the direct cost of rent and the indirect cost of commuting, is lower for all apartments.

Exhibit 3.4 Commuting Cost and Rental Cost Expressed in Common Units, Assuming an Opportunity Cost of Time of $15/hour

To optimize, it is necessary to convert all costs and benefits into common units. In this example, the common unit is dollars per month. The optimum—in bold—is Close, which has the lowest total cost.

Apartment	Commuting Time (hours/month)	Commuting Cost ($/month)	Rent ($/month)	Total Cost: Rent + Commuting ($/month)
Very Close	5 hours	$75	$1,180	$1,255
Close	**10 hours**	**$150**	**$1,090**	**$1,240**
Far	15 hours	$225	$1,030	$1,255
Very Far	20 hours	$300	$1,000	$1,300

Exhibit 3.5 Total Cost Including Both Rent and Commuting Cost, Assuming an Opportunity Cost of Time of $15/hour

Given the opportunity cost of $15/hour, the optimal choice is Close. This apartment has the lowest total cost, which is the sum of the direct rental cost and the indirect commute cost.

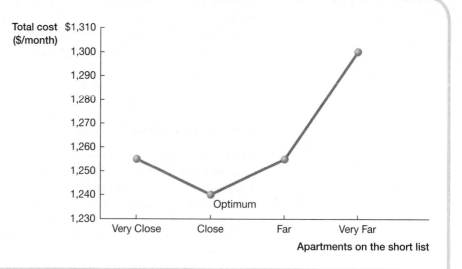

Exhibit 3.6 Total Cost Curves with the Opportunity Cost of Time Equal to $10/hour and $15/hour

As the opportunity cost of time rises from $10/hour to $15/hour, the optimal apartment shifts closer to the city center. Employees with a higher opportunity cost of time should choose the apartment with a shorter commute.

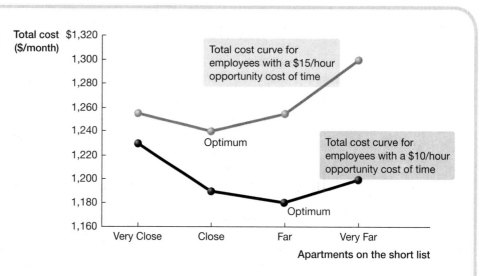

2. The $10/hour curve has a minimum value for Far, while the $15/hour curve has a minimum value for Close. In other words, the optimal apartment switches from Far to Close when the opportunity cost of time rises from $10/hour to $15/hour.

3.3 Optimization Using Marginal Analysis

Until now, we have studied the apartment-hunting problem by calculating the total value of each apartment. We are now going to discuss an alternative optimization technique: *optimization using marginal analysis*. Optimization using marginal analysis is often faster to implement than optimization using total value, because optimization using marginal analysis focuses only on the ways that alternatives differ.

Optimization using marginal analysis breaks an optimization problem down by thinking about how costs and benefits *change* as you hypothetically move from one alternative to another. For example, consider two alternative vacations at the same hotel in Miami: a 4-day trip versus a 5-day trip. Suppose that you are choosing between these two options. If you optimize using total value, you evaluate the *total* net benefit of a 4-day trip and compare it to the *total* net benefit of a 5-day trip. Alternatively, you could think only about the *differences* between the two trips. In other words, you could think only about the costs and benefits of the extra day. An optimizer will take the 5-day vacation if the benefit of vacationing for the fifth day exceeds the cost of the fifth day. In choosing between the 4- and 5-day options, the optimizer doesn't necessarily need to worry about the first 4 days, since those 4 days are shared by both the 4-day trip and the 5-day trip. The optimizer can focus on the one thing that differentiates the two vacations: the fifth day.

Economists use the word *marginal* to indicate a difference between alternatives, usually a difference that represents one "step" or "unit" more. The fifth day of vacation is the difference, or margin, between a 4-day vacation and a 5-day vacation.

Marginal analysis is a cost-benefit calculation that studies the difference between one feasible alternative and the next feasible alternative.

A cost-benefit calculation that focuses on the difference between one feasible alternative and the next feasible alternative is called **marginal analysis**. Marginal analysis compares the consequences—costs and benefits—of doing one step more of something. Thinking back to our apartment example, marginal analysis can be used to study the costs and benefits of moving one apartment farther away from the city center.

> **Marginal analysis will never change the ultimate answer to the question "what is optimal?" but it will clarify the way that you think about optimization.**

Marginal analysis will never change the ultimate answer to the question "what is optimal?" but it will help clarify the way you think about optimization. Marginal analysis forces us to focus on what is changing when we compare alternatives. Marginal analysis provides another way of finding the optimal choice. Because it gives us insight into the concept of optimization and because we can use it for optimization, marginal analysis is one of the most important concepts in economics.

Marginal Cost

Let's return to the problem of choosing the best apartment. We go back to this problem to preserve continuity with our earlier analysis; keep in mind, though, that you can use these techniques to optimize in pretty much any situation.

When we studied the problem of choosing a rental apartment, we did not use marginal analysis. Instead, we solved the problem by calculating and comparing the total cost—including direct and indirect costs—of the four apartments. We'll now solve the same apartment-selection problem using marginal analysis. The optimum won't change—we'll confirm that below—but the way that you think about the problem will.

Again consider the commuter with a $10/hour opportunity cost of time. Instead of thinking about each of the apartments in isolation, let's now think about the apartments comparatively. Specifically, let's focus on what changes as we hypothetically "move" from one apartment to the next, stepping farther away from the city center. What is the difference between each pair of apartments?

Exhibit 3.7 helps you think about these changes. The "Commuting Cost" column reports the monthly commuting cost for each apartment, assuming a $10/hour opportunity cost of

Exhibit 3.7 Cost and Marginal Cost (Assuming a $10/hour Opportunity Cost of Time)

We can break the problem down by studying the marginal costs of moving farther from the city center. At what point does it make sense to stop moving farther from the city center?

Apartment	Commuting Cost	Marginal Commuting Cost	Rental Cost	Marginal Rental Cost	Total Cost	Marginal Total Cost
Very Close	$50	—	$1,180	—	$1,230	—
Close	$100	$50	$1,090	−$90	$1,190	−$40
Far	$150	$50	$1,030	−$60	$1,180	−$10
Very Far	$200	$50	$1,000	−$30	$1,200	$20

3.3

Marginal cost is the extra cost generated by moving from one feasible alternative to the next feasible alternative.

time. The "Marginal Commuting Cost" column reports the value of the extra monthly commuting time that is generated by moving one apartment farther from the city center. For example, to move from Close to Far generates additional commuting costs of $50/month. In other words, the "Marginal Commuting Cost" column reports the difference between two commuting costs in adjacent positions on the list. In this particular example, the marginal commuting cost is always the same—the commuting cost rises by the same amount with each move farther away from the city center. This won't generally be the case, but we've set it up this way in this problem to keep things simple. In general, **marginal cost** is the extra cost generated by moving from one feasible alternative to the next feasible alternative.

Now turn to the column labeled "Rental Cost," which reports the monthly rent for each apartment. The "Marginal Rental Cost" column reports the change in the rental cost generated by moving from one apartment to the next apartment—one step farther from the city center. For example, to move from Very Close to Close would save you $90/month, so the marginal rental cost is a negative number, −$90. Likewise, if you moved from Close to Far, you would save an additional $60/month, so the marginal rental cost is −$60.

Finally, we'd like to know the marginal value of total cost. It turns out that we can calculate the marginal value of total cost in two alternative ways. First, we can add up the marginal commuting cost and the marginal rental cost to obtain the marginal total cost. For example, look at the first set of marginal cost numbers and confirm that

$$\$50 + -\$90 = -\$40.$$

In other words, a move from Very Close to Close raises commuting costs by $50 and changes rent by −$90, producing a combined change of −$40.

Alternatively, we could calculate total cost itself. This is done in the column labeled "Total Cost." For instance, for Very Close, the commuting cost is $50 and the rental cost is $1,180, so the total cost is $1,230. For Close, the commuting cost is $100 and the rental cost is $1,090, so the total cost is $1,190. Total cost *falls* by $40 when we move from Very Close, with total cost $1,230, to Close, with total cost $1,190.

Both methods confirm that the marginal total cost is −$40 when moving from Very Close to Close:

$$\text{Marginal commuting cost} + \text{Marginal rental cost} = \$50 + -\$90 = -\$40$$
$$\text{Total cost of Close} - \text{Total cost of Very Close} = \$1,190 - \$1,230 = -\$40.$$

The fact that we calculated −$40 in both cases is no accident. The match is exact, because it doesn't matter how we decompose costs to calculate marginal total cost. It doesn't matter whether we calculate marginal total cost by summing marginal costs category by category or whether we calculate marginal total cost by subtracting the *total* cost of one apartment from that of the other. Because the answer is the same, you should calculate marginal total cost whichever way is easier for you.

The last column of Exhibit 3.7—marginal total cost—contains all the information that we need to optimize. Start at the top of the column and think about how each "move" away from the city center affects the worker. The first move, from Very Close to Close, has a marginal cost of −$40/month, so it is cost cutting. That move is worth it.

The second move, from Close to Far, has a marginal cost of −$10/month. That move is also cost cutting and thus also worth taking.

The third move, from Far to Very Far, has a marginal cost of $20/month. So that move is not worth taking, because it represents an increase in costs.

To sum up, the first two moves more than paid for themselves and the final move did not. Very Far can't be an optimum, since moving from Far to Very Far made the worker worse off. Very Close can't be an optimum either, since moving from Very Close to Close made the worker better off. Finally, Close can't be an optimum, since moving from Close to Far made the worker better off.

We conclude that Far is the optimum—the best feasible choice. Moving from Close to Far made the worker better off. But moving from Far to Very Far made the worker worse off. Far is the only apartment that satisfies the following property: moving to the apartment makes the worker better off and moving away from the apartment makes the worker worse off. In other words, Far has the virtue that it is a better option than its "neighbors."

Exhibit 3.8 Total Cost of Each Apartment and the Marginal Cost of Moving Between Apartments (Assuming an Opportunity Cost of $10/hour)

The cost-minimizing choice is Far. We can see this by looking at total cost (in purple) or by looking at marginal cost (in red). Total cost is falling when marginal cost is negative. Total cost is rising when marginal cost is positive. Far is the only apartment that is better than all of its neighbors. Marginal cost is negative when moving to Far and marginal cost is positive when moving away from Far. Thus, Far is the only apartment that satisfies the Principle of Optimization at the Margin.

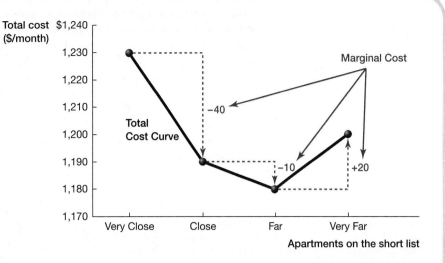

The **Principle of Optimization at the Margin** states that an optimal feasible alternative has the property that moving to it makes you better off and moving away from it makes you worse off.

The optimizer's goal is to make himself as well off as possible—at an optimum, he cannot do any better. In this example—where we are holding all else fixed—the apartment that is better than all its feasible alternatives is also the apartment that minimizes total costs. This is an example of the **Principle of Optimization at the Margin**, which states that an optimal feasible alternative has the property that moving to it makes you better off and moving away from it makes you worse off.

It helps to visualize these ideas. Exhibit 3.8 plots the total cost of each apartment and the marginal cost of moving, one apartment at a time, farther away from the center of town. For instance, moving from Very Close to Close lowers total cost by $40. The vertical portion of the dashed red line shows a change of −$40 between the total cost of Very Close and the total cost of Close.

Optimization using marginal analysis will always pick out a single optimal alternative when the total cost curve has the bowl-like shape in Exhibit 3.8. Where the *total* cost (in purple) is falling, marginal cost (in red) will be negative and marginal analysis will recommend moving farther away from the city center, thereby lowering total cost. After total cost bottoms out, marginal cost will afterward be positive, implying that the renter should move no farther out.

When the total cost curve is not bowl shaped, the calculations get more complicated, but, even in this case, marginal analysis ultimately identifies the same optimum that would emerge if we found the option with the lowest total cost.

Since marginal analysis always picks out the same optimum as minimization of total cost, you can use whichever method is easier for the particular problem that you are analyzing. However, it is important to understand why economists mostly use marginal analysis. Optimization at the margin is simple because you can ignore everything about two alternatives that are being compared except the particular attributes that are different. Marginal analysis reminds you to exclude information that is not relevant to your decision.

To sum up, marginal analysis has three steps:

1. Translate all costs and benefits into common units, like dollars per month.
2. Calculate the marginal consequences of moving between alternatives.
3. Apply the Principle of Optimization at the Margin by choosing the best alternative with the property that moving to it makes you better off and moving away from it makes you worse off.

Marginal analysis—in other words, the three steps outlined above—can be used to solve any optimization problem. Marginal analysis is most commonly used when there is a clear sequence of feasible alternatives. For example, how many hours should you sleep tonight? Six? Seven? Eight? Or Nine? More sleep makes you more rested, but sleep has an opportunity cost—some other activity must be sacrificed if you are going to get more sleep—for instance, breakfast or your 9 a.m. economics lecture. Moving from 6 to 7 to 8 to 9 hours of sleep generates a clear set of steps that can be used for marginal analysis. For example, is it a net benefit to move from 6 to 7 hours of sleep? Is it a net benefit to move from 7 to 8 hours of sleep? Is it a net benefit to move from 8 to 9 hours of sleep? At the optimum, moving up to that number of sleeping hours makes you better off and moving past that number of sleeping hours makes you worse off.

Here are a few more examples in which it is natural use marginal analysis to calculate the optimum. How many hours should you study tomorrow? How many weeks should you be employed this summer? How many miles should you jog in your next workout?

EVIDENCE-BASED ECONOMICS

Q: How does location affect the rental cost of housing?

Throughout this chapter, we've been assuming that rental prices are higher near the city center, holding the quality of the apartment fixed. You may have wondered whether we had our facts right.

People often imagine dingy apartments downtown and nice houses out in the country. However, if we want to isolate the effect of location, we need to hold apartment quality constant—for instance, apartment size—and vary *only* location.

Economists Beth Wilson and James Frew assembled a database that contains information on many apartments that were available for rent in Portland, Oregon.[2] They used statistical techniques to effectively compare apartments near the city center to similar apartments that were farther away. Such analysis reveals a strong negative relationship between distance and rent, which is plotted in Exhibit 3.9.

Exhibit 3.9 Apartment Rent in Portland, Oregon, Depends on Distance from the City Center

This plot is drawn for apartments that are identical except for their distance from the city center. The blue line is the approximate location of a ring of highways that encircles most of Portland.

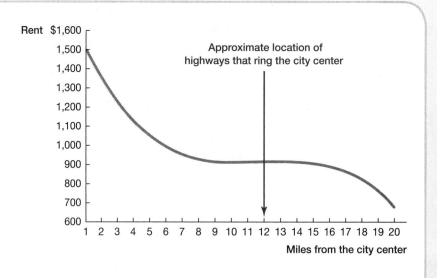

Exhibit 3.9 was calculated for apartments that all have the following features—one bedroom, one bathroom, laundry unit in the apartment, covered parking, cable, and air conditioning—and have none of the following features—a fireplace, access to an exercise room, or access to a pool. The analysis compares the rent of these apartments, holding all their features constant except for the distance to the city center.

Exhibit 3.9 confirms that proximity to the city center raises rents. The closer you get to the city, the higher the rent goes. For example, at a distance of 6 miles from the city center, the typical rent for an apartment with the specified features is nearly $1,000. For an apartment that is 1 mile from the city center, the rent for the "same" apartment is $1,500.

Exhibit 3.9 also displays a noticeable flattening around 12 miles from the city center. Can you guess why rents stop changing in this region? The answer follows from considerations about the opportunity cost of time and the structure of Portland's highway system. Like most large cities, Portland has a ring of fast highways—a "ring road"—about 12 miles from the center of the city. People who live within a few miles of the ring road have the advantage of being near a highway system that speeds up travel time. Because of the ring roads, commute times change relatively little as you go from 9 miles to 14 miles away from the city center.

Scarcity, Prices, and Incentives

We can now come full circle and return to an important question that we asked previously. Why do rental prices fall as you move farther from the city center? What does this have to do with the topic of this chapter: optimization?

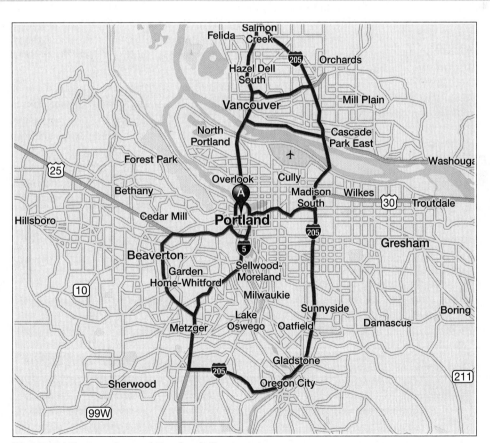

Ring Road System Around Portland, Oregon

Like most large cities, Portland has a ring of fast highways—a "ring road"—about 12 miles from the center of the city.

Mt. Hood rises to the east of Portland and presents a beautiful view to apartment dwellers lucky enough to face that way. But not everyone has such spectacular views. Some apartments are on low floors, and some apartments face the less awesome views to the west. Eastern-facing apartments on high floors rent for about 20 percent more than similar apartments that don't have the killer views. To an economist, this price differential is a good way of measuring the dollar value of a scarce resource: a room with a view.

In our analysis, we saw that optimizing commuters would love to live in the city center, but only if the rental prices are the same downtown as they are in distant neighborhoods. But not everyone can live downtown, and not everyone can have a short commute; there just aren't enough downtown apartments to go around. That is an example of economic scarcity—one of the first concepts we studied in Chapter 1.

As we'll see in Chapter 4, the market for apartments determines who gets to have the short commute. Markets allow optimizing landlords and optimizing renters to freely negotiate the rental price of apartments. In the marketplace, the rental price of apartments is determined by market forces rather than by politicians or regulators. The renters with the highest opportunity cost of time bid up the rental price of apartments with the shortest commutes.

As the price of downtown apartments rises, only workers with the highest opportunity cost of time will be willing to rent them. Most other workers will choose to move farther away and accept the consequences of a longer commute. That's a trade-off—more time commuting in exchange for a lower monthly rent.

Market prices have the effect of allocating the downtown apartments to the people who are willing to pay the most for them. This allocation mechanism implies that mostly highly paid workers—and others with a high opportunity cost of time—tend to rent the apartments with the best locations.

Some critics of markets complain that markets are unfair—why should the highest-paid workers also get the apartments with the best locations? The defenders of markets respond that people are paying for the privilege of having a good apartment—the apartments with the best locations have higher rents—and the market allocation mechanism guarantees that people who are willing to pay the most for the best apartments get them.

Understanding how the market allocation process works is the subject of Chapter 4 and many other chapters in this book. As we begin to discuss these issues, we want you to think about how society *should* determine the price of scarce resources, like downtown apartments. Should we have a system that allows landlords and renters to negotiate freely to determine rental prices for apartments? What if this produces a system in which the highest-paid workers are the only ones who can afford to live in the most convenient apartments? Is that inequitable? Can you think of a better way to allocate apartments?

Question	**Answer**	**Data**	**Caveat**
How does location affect the rental cost of housing?	In most cities, though not all, the farther you are from the city center, the more rental costs fall (holding apartment quality fixed). For example, in Portland, Oregon, rents fall by 33 percent as you move from the city center to otherwise identical apartments 6 miles out of town.	Rental prices in Portland, Oregon.	Though the analysis uses special statistical techniques to compare similar apartments located at different distances from the city center, it is possible that some important apartment characteristics were not held fixed in the comparison. This would bias the calculations.

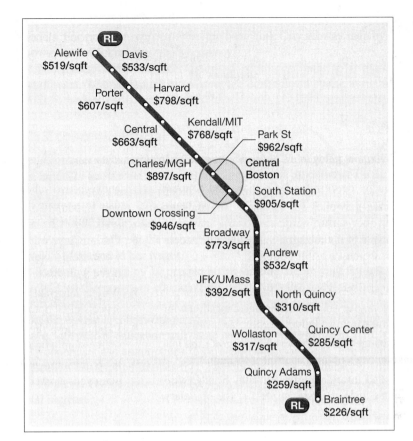

In almost all cities, rent per square foot generally falls with distance to the city center. Here we report the rent per square foot at different stops on Boston's "Red Line," part of the city's subway system. The stop with the highest rent per square foot—Park St—is in the middle of the city. Rent generally falls from there as the line passes out to the suburban subway stops of Alewife (to the north) and Braintree (to the south).

Summary

- Economists believe that optimization describes, or at least approximates, many of the choices economic agents make. However, economists don't take optimization for granted. A large body of economic research attempts to answer the questions: when do people optimize (or nearly optimize) and when do people fail to optimize? Using optimization to describe and predict behavior is an example of positive economic analysis.

- Optimization also provides an excellent toolbox for improving decision making that is not already optimal. Using optimization to improve decision making is an example of prescriptive economic analysis.

- Optimization using total value has three steps: (1) translate all costs and benefits into common units, like dollars per month; (2) calculate the *total* net benefit of each alternative; and (3) pick the alternative with the highest net benefit.

- Marginal analysis evaluates the change in net benefits when you switch from one alternative to another. Marginal analysis calculates the consequences of doing one step more of something.

- Marginal cost is the extra cost generated by moving from one alternative to the next alternative.

- Optimization using marginal analysis has three steps: (1) translate all costs and benefits into common units, like dollars per month; (2) calculate the marginal consequences of moving between alternatives; and (3) apply the Principle of Optimization at the Margin by choosing the best alternative with the property that moving to it makes you better off and moving away from it makes you worse off.

- Optimization using total value and optimization using marginal analysis yield the same answer. These techniques are two sides of the same coin.

Key Terms

behavioral economics *p. 44*
optimum *p. 47*

marginal analysis *p. 49*
marginal cost *p. 50*

Principle of Optimization at the
Margin *p. 51*

Questions

All questions are available in MyEconLab *for practice and instructor assignment.*

1. What is meant by optimization? Compare and contrast optimization using total value and optimization using marginal analysis.

2. Does the principle of optimization imply that real people always choose the best feasible option?

3. Some people choose to live close to the city center; others choose to live away from the city center and take a longer commute to work every day. Does picking a location with a longer commute imply a failure to optimize?

4. Why does a change in one's opportunity cost of time imply a change in one's optimal apartment location?

5. Suppose you had information on the sales of otherwise identical homes just east and just west of the boundary between two school districts. How could you use those data to estimate the value parents place on the quality of their children's schools?

6. There is a proverb that states, "anything worth doing is worth doing well." Do you think an economist would agree with this proverb?

7. Why is marginal analysis helpful for identifying the key aspects of an optimization problem?

8. Explain how the market for apartments allocates the scarce supply of apartments near the city center.

9. Is optimization analysis positive, normative, or both? Explain your answer.

Problems

All problems are available in MyEconLab *for practice and instructor assignment.*

1. Advances in wireless communication technology reduce the non-financial costs of long commutes: People who ride trains can get work done, and people who drive cars have more entertainment options. If this statement is true, explain the effect on the geographic area of cities. Focus on a person who must decide how close to live to the city center.

2. You are hired as a consultant for a local restaurant. It is considering whether to close at 9:00 p.m., or whether to stay open an extra hour (10:00 p.m.). Based on wages and utility bills, the added cost (the marginal cost) of staying open for each additional hour is $200.

   a. If the additional revenue (the marginal revenue) during the last hour of operation is $250, what would you recommend? By how much will profit change based on your recommendation?

   b. What if the additional revenue were only $100?

   c. What would you need to learn about marginal revenue for you to conclude that 9:00 p.m. is the ideal closing time?

3. Determine whether the following statements better describe optimization using total value or optimization using marginal analysis.

   a. John is attempting to decide on a movie (all movies have the same ticket price). He determines that the new Batman movie provides him with comparatively more of a benefit than the new Spiderman movie and that both the Batman and Spiderman movies have comparatively more of a benefit than the new Superman movie.

   b. Marcia finds that the net benefit of flying from Chicago to Honolulu on a non-stop United Airlines flight is $400, and the net benefit of the same trip flying on a one-stop American Airlines flight is $200.

   c. Nikki decided to jog 3 miles for exercise by reasoning that a 3-mile jog was better than either a 2-mile jog or a 4-mile jog.

   d. At a yard sale, Reagan calculated that she was willing to pay $200 for a queen bed that was being sold for $100 (generating net benefit of $100) and that she was willing to pay $220 for a king bed that was being sold for $300 (generating net benefit of −$80).

4. You are taking two courses this semester, biology and chemistry. You have quizzes coming up in both classes. The following table shows your grade on each quiz for different numbers of hours spent studying for each quiz. (For the purposes of this problem, assume that each hour of study time can't be subdivided.) For instance, the table implies that if you spent 1 hour on chemistry and 2 hours on biology, you would get a 77 on the chemistry quiz and a 74 on the biology quiz.

Hours of Study	Chemistry	Biology
0	70	60
1	77	68
2	82	74
3	85	78

Your goal is to maximize your average grade on the two quizzes. Use the idea of optimization using marginal analysis to decide how much time you should spend studying for each quiz if you have only 1 hour in total to prepare for the two exams (in other words, you will study 1 hour for one exam and 0 hours for the other exam). How would you allocate that single hour of study time across the two subjects? Now repeat the analysis assuming that you have 2 hours in total to prepare for the two exams. How would you allocate those 2 hours across the two subjects? Finally, repeat the analysis assuming that you have 3 hours in total to prepare for the two exams. How would you allocate those 3 hours across the two subjects?

5. Your total benefits from consuming different quantities of gas each week are shown in the following table:

Gallons/Week	Total Benefit (dollar equivalent)	Marginal Benefit
0	0	—
1	4	
2	8	
3	11	
4	14	
5	16	
6	18	
7	19	
8	19	

a. Complete the marginal benefit column starting with the step from 0 gallons/week to 1 gallon/week.

b. The price of gasoline is $2.40/gallon. Use the Principle of Optimization at the Margin to find an optimal number of gallons of gas to consume each week.

c. Some policy makers have suggested taxing gasoline to reduce global warming. (Burning fossil fuels such as gasoline releases greenhouse gases, which are a cause of global warming.) Suppose the price of gasoline, including a gasoline tax, rises to $3.60/gallon. Use the Principle of Optimization at the Margin to find an optimal number of gallons of gasoline, given this new tax-inclusive price of gasoline.

6. Scott loves to go to baseball games, especially home games of the Cincinnati Reds. All else being equal, he likes to sit close to the field. He also likes to get to the stadium early to watch batting practice. The closer he parks to the stadium, the more batting practice he is able to watch (the garages all open simultaneously). Find Scott's optimal seat location and parking garage location using the information that follows.

Seat Location	Price	Value of View
Diamond Seating	$235	$200
Club Home	$95	$130
Club Seating	$85	$125
Scout Box	$79	$120
Scout	$69	$100

Parking Location	Parking Fee (game night)	Missed Batting Practice	Benefit of Arrival Time
Westin Parking Garage	$5	60 min	$0
Fountain Square South Garage	$10	50 min	$10
West River Parking	$17	25 min	$35
East River Parking	$25	10 min	$50
Under Stadium Parking	$45	0 min	$60

7. Suppose the total benefit and total cost to society of various levels of pollution reduction are as follows:

(1) Pollution Reduction (units)	(2) Total Benefit	(3) Total Cost	(4) Total Net Benefit	(5) Marginal Benefit	(6) Marginal Cost
0	$0	$0	—	—	—
1	$20	$9			
2	$38	$20			
3	$54	$33			
4	$68	$48			
5	$80	$65			
6	$90	$84			

a. Complete column (4).

b. Use total net benefit in column (4) to show that if the U.S. Environmental Protection Agency (EPA) wants to maximize total net benefit, then it should require 3 units of pollution reduction.

c. Complete columns (5) and (6), starting with the step from 0 to 1 unit of pollution reduction.

d. Show that the Principle of Optimization at the Margin also implies that the EPA should require 3 units of pollution reduction.

8. It is possible to use equations to do marginal analysis. Suppose your firm has a marginal revenue given by $MR = 10 - Q$. This means that the seventh unit of output brings in $10 - 7 = \$3$ of additional revenue. The marginal cost for your firm is $MC = 2 + Q$. This means that the seventh unit of output increases cost by $2 + 7 = \$9$.

a. Is it a good idea to produce the seventh unit of output? Why or why not?

b. Find the Q that sets marginal cost equal to marginal revenue $(MC = MR)$. As a preview of upcoming chapters, try to explain why this value maximizes profit.

4 Demand, Supply, and Equilibrium

How much more gasoline would people buy if its price were lower?

In 2016, the retail price of a gallon of gasoline in the United States fluctuated around $2 per gallon. How much gasoline do you buy now? How much would you buy if the price were lower—say, $1 per gallon? How low would it have to go to tempt you to take lots of road trips? What if the price were $0.04 per gallon, so that gasoline was practically free? Amazingly, that's what Venezuelans paid for gas in 2013, due to an extraordinary government subsidy.

In this chapter, we study how buyers and sellers respond to the changing prices of goods and services, and we use the energy market and gasoline as our leading example. How does the price of gas affect the decisions of gas buyers, like households, and gas sellers, like ExxonMobil? How do the decisions of buyers and sellers jointly determine the price of gas when it isn't dictated by government policies?

CHAPTER **OUTLINE**

4.1	**4.2**	**EBE**	**4.3**	**4.4**	**4.5**
Markets	How Do Buyers Behave?	How much more gasoline would people buy if its price were lower?	How Do Sellers Behave?	Supply and Demand in Equilibrium	What Would Happen If the Government Tried to Dictate the Price of Gasoline?

4.1 Markets

Every year over 1 billion drivers pull into gas stations around the world. These drivers almost never find that gas stations are "sold out." Most of the time, it takes less than 10 minutes to fill the tank and pull back on the road.

The efficiency of this system is amazing. Nobody tells the companies that run the gas stations how many drivers to expect, and nobody tells the drivers where to fill their tanks. No "fill 'er up" tickets are presold by Ticketmaster or Live Nation. But somehow, there is almost always enough gas for every driver who wants to fill the tank. Drivers get the gas they are willing to pay for, and gasoline companies make enough money to pay their employees and send dividends to their shareholders.

A **market** is a group of economic agents who are trading a good or service plus the rules and arrangements for trading.

This chapter is about how the gasoline market and other markets like it work. A **market** is a group of economic agents who are trading a good or service plus the rules and arrangements for trading. Agricultural and industrial goods like wheat, soybeans, iron, and coal are all traded on markets. A market may have a specific physical location—like Holland's Aalsmeer Flower Auction—or not. For example, the market for gasoline is dispersed—located on every corner you find a gas station. Likewise, Monster.com (a Web-based job market) operates wherever there's a computer and an Internet connection. To an economist, dating sites/apps like OkCupid, Match, ChristianMingle, Tinder, Hinge, Grindr, and Coffee Meets Bagel are markets, too.

We focus the discussion on markets in which all exchanges occur voluntarily at flexible prices determined by market forces (in contrast to prices fixed by the government). This chapter explains how markets use prices to allocate goods and services. Prices act as a selection device that encourages trade between the sellers who can produce goods at low cost and the buyers who place a high value on the goods.

> Prices act as a selection device that encourages trade between the sellers who can produce goods at low cost and the buyers who place a high value on the goods.

We illustrate all of this by studying the market for gasoline, which is refined from crude oil, as well as the broader market for energy. You'll see that the price of gasoline is set in a way that implies that gas stations are ready to sell a quantity of gasoline that is equal to the quantity of gasoline that drivers want to buy.

This warehouse in Aalsmeer, Holland, covers an area larger than 100 football fields and hosts thousands of daily auctions for wholesale (bulk) flowers.

If all sellers and all buyers face the same price, it is referred to as the **market price**.

In a **perfectly competitive market**, (1) sellers all sell an identical good or service, and (2) any individual buyer or any individual seller isn't powerful enough on his or her own to affect the market price of that good or service.

A **price-taker** is a buyer or seller who accepts the market price—buyers can't bargain for a lower price, and sellers can't bargain for a higher price.

Competitive Markets

Think of a city filled with hundreds of gas stations, each of which has an independent owner. The gas station on your block would lose most of its business if the owner started charging $1 more per gallon than all the other stations. Likewise, you wouldn't be able to fill your tank if you insisted on paying $1 less per gallon than the posted price; gas station attendants usually don't cut deals. Drivers of Cadillacs and Kias pay the same price for a gallon of regular unleaded.

To prove that pleading poverty and haggling for a better gas price won't work, try bargaining for a discount the next time you need to fill your tank. Try this only if you have enough gas to reach the next station.

If all sellers and all buyers face the same price, that price is referred to as the **market price**. In a **perfectly competitive market**, (1) sellers all sell an identical good or service, and (2) any individual buyer or any individual seller isn't powerful enough on his or her own to affect the market price. This implies that buyers and sellers are all **price-takers**. In other words, they accept the market price and can't bargain for a better price.

Very few, if any, markets are perfectly competitive. But economists try to understand such markets anyway. At first this sounds kind of nutty. Why would economists study a thing that rarely exists in the world? The answer is that although few, if any, markets are perfectly competitive, many markets come close. Many gas stations do have nearby competitors—often right across the street—that prevent them from charging more than the market price. There are some gas stations that don't have such nearby competitors—think of an isolated station on a country road—but such examples are the exception. If sellers have nearly identical goods and most market participants face lots of competition, then the perfectly competitive model is a good approximation of how actual markets work.

In contrast, there are some markets in which large market participants—like Microsoft in the software market—can single-handedly control market prices; we'll come to markets like that in later chapters.

When two gas stations are located at the same intersection, their prices tend to be very close, and sometimes are exactly the same.

In this chapter, our goal is to understand the properties of markets that are perfectly competitive (identical goods and market participants who can't influence the market price on their own). Along the way, we'll ask three questions.

1. How do buyers behave?
2. How do sellers behave?
3. How does the behavior of buyers and sellers jointly determine the market price and the quantity of goods transacted?

Each of the next three sections addresses one of these fundamental questions.

4.2 How Do Buyers Behave?

We start by studying the behavior of buyers. We assume that these buyers are price-takers: they treat the market price as a take-it-or-leave-it offer and don't try to haggle to lower the price. We want to study the relationship between the price of a good and the amount of the good that buyers are willing to purchase. At a given price, the amount of the good or service that buyers are willing to purchase is called the **quantity demanded**.

To illustrate the concept of quantity demanded, think about your own buying behavior. When gas prices rise, do you tend to buy less gas? For example, if gas prices rise, a student who lives off campus might bike to school instead of driving. She might join a carpool or shift to public transportation. If gas prices rise high enough, she might sell her gas guzzler altogether.

Let's quantify these kinds of adjustments. Take Chloe, a typical consumer who responds to increases in gasoline prices by reducing her purchases of gasoline. Chloe may not be able to adjust her gasoline consumption immediately, but in the long run she will use less gas if the price of gas increases—for instance, by switching to public transportation. The relationship between Chloe's purchases of gasoline and the price of gasoline is summarized in the shaded box in the upper-right corner of Exhibit 4.1. This table reports the quantity demanded at different prices and it is called a **demand schedule**. Chloe's demand schedule for gasoline tells us how Chloe's gasoline purchases change as the price of gas changes, **holding all else equal**. The phrase "holding all else equal" implies that everything other than the price of gas is held constant or fixed, including income, rent, and highway tolls. The demand schedule reveals that Chloe increases the quantity of gasoline that she purchases as the price of gasoline falls.

Quantity demanded is the amount of a good that buyers are willing to purchase at a given price.

A **demand schedule** is a table that reports the quantity demanded at different prices, holding all else equal.

Holding all else equal implies that everything else in the economy is held constant. The Latin phrase *ceteris paribus* means "with other things the same" and is sometimes used in economic writing to mean the same thing as "holding all else equal."

Exhibit 4.1 Chloe's Demand Schedule and Demand Curve for Gasoline

The lower the price of gasoline becomes, the more gasoline Chloe chooses to buy; in other words, her quantity demanded increases as the price of gasoline decreases. Thus, demand curves are downward-sloping—a high price (on the vertical axis, or *y*-axis) is associated with a low quantity demanded (on the horizontal axis, or *x*-axis) and a low price (on the *y*-axis) is associated with a high quantity demanded (*x*-axis).

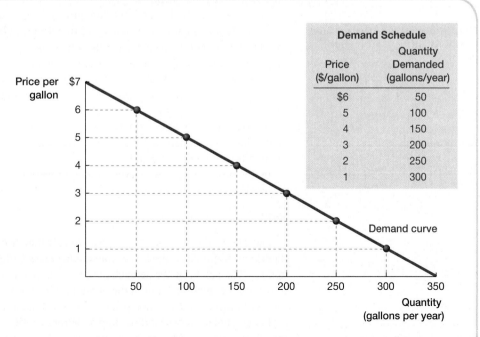

Demand Schedule	
Price ($/gallon)	Quantity Demanded (gallons/year)
$6	50
5	100
4	150
3	200
2	250
1	300

The GM Hummer (H2) weighs more than 3 tons and gets about 10 miles per gallon, among a handful of the most fuel *inefficient* personal vehicles in the world. From 2005 to 2008, gasoline prices rose by 30 percent, and Hummer sales fell by 50 percent. At that time, no other car brand experienced sales declines that were this steep. Hummer demand fell so quickly that General Motors shut down the brand in 2010. Gasoline prices plummeted in 2014 and have stayed low since then. As gasoline prices fell, demand for (second-hand) Hummers has risen![1]

Demand Curves

The demand curve plots the quantity demanded at different prices. A demand curve plots the demand schedule.

We'll often want to plot a demand schedule. That is what the demand curve does. The **demand curve** plots the relationship between prices and quantity demanded (again, holding all else equal). In Exhibit 4.1, each dot plots a single point from the demand schedule. For example, the leftmost dot represents the point at which the price is $6 per gallon and the quantity demanded is 50 gallons of gasoline per year. Similarly, the rightmost dot represents the point at which the price is $1 per gallon and the quantity demanded is 300 gallons of gasoline per year. Notice that the *x*-axis represents the quantity demanded. The *y*-axis represents the price per gallon. Economists always adopt this plotting convention—quantity demanded on the *x*-axis and price on the *y*-axis. Economists usually "connect the dots" as we have in Exhibit 4.1, which implies that prices and quantities demanded don't always have to be round numbers.

Two variables are **negatively related** if the variables move in opposite directions.

The demand curve has an important property that we will see many times. The price of gasoline and the quantity demanded are **negatively related**, which means that they move in opposite directions. In other words, when one goes up, the other goes down, and vice versa. In Chloe's case, a gas price of $6 per gallon generates a quantity demanded of 50 gallons per year, and a price of $1 per gallon generates a much greater quantity demanded of 300 gallons per year. The price of gas and the quantity demanded move in opposite directions.

Law of Demand: In almost all cases, the quantity demanded rises when the price falls (holding all else equal).

Almost all goods have demand curves that exhibit this fundamental negative relationship, which economists call the **Law of Demand**: the quantity demanded rises when the price falls (holding all else equal).

In this book all demand curves, demand schedules, and graph labels related to demand are in blue.

Willingness to Pay

Chloe's demand curve can also be used to calculate how much she is willing (and able) to pay for an additional gallon of gasoline. One extra gallon of gasoline is called a "marginal gallon." The height of her demand curve at any given quantity is the amount she is willing to pay for that marginal unit of the good. In other words, the height of her demand curve is the value in dollars that Chloe places on that last gallon of gasoline.

For example, Chloe is willing to pay $4 for her 150th gallon of gasoline. In other words, with 149 gallons already at her at her disposal in one year, Chloe's willingness to pay for

Willingness to pay is the highest price that a buyer is willing to pay for an extra unit of a good.

Diminishing marginal benefit: as you consume more of a good, your willingness to pay for an additional unit declines.

The process of adding up individual behaviors is referred to as **aggregation**.

an additional gallon of gasoline is $4. **Willingness to pay** is the highest price that a buyer is willing to pay for an extra unit of a good.

In contrast, Chloe is willing to pay only $3 for a marginal gallon of gasoline if she already has 199 gallons (for use that year). Chloe's willingness to pay for an additional gallon is negatively related to the quantity that she already has—this is the quantity on the *x*-axis in Exhibit 4.1. The more gasoline that she already has, the less she is willing to pay for an additional gallon. For most goods and services, this negative relationship applies. The more you have of something—for instance, slices of pizza—the less gain there is from acquiring another unit of the same good.

This is an example of a concept called **diminishing marginal benefit**: as you consume more of a good, your willingness to pay for an additional unit declines. An easy way to remember this concept is to think about donuts. My first donut in the morning is worth a lot to me, so I am willing to pay a lot for it. My fourth donut in the same sitting is worth much less to me, so I am willing to pay less for it. In general, the more donuts I eat, the less I am willing to pay for an extra donut.

From Individual Demand Curves to Aggregated Demand Curves

So far we've talked about a single consumer, Chloe. But we can easily extend the ideas that we have discussed to all buyers of gasoline, including consumers and firms.

Think about the worldwide market for energy. Chloe's demand curve implies that she will increase her use of gasoline when the price of gasoline goes down. Other gasoline users will also increase their consumption of gasoline as its price falls.

Though almost all individual demand curves are downward-sloping, that's about all they have in common. For example, a schoolteacher in Kenya may earn $1,000 per year. For any given price of gasoline, the schoolteacher probably won't consume nearly as much gasoline as a typical worker in the United States (who has about 50 times as much income to spend).

This leaves us with a challenge. How do we account for the gasoline demand of billions of consumers worldwide? Their individual demand curves will obey the Law of Demand, but otherwise they won't look alike. To study the behavior of the worldwide energy market, economists need to study the worldwide demand curve for gasoline, which is equivalent to the sum of all individual demand curves. Economists call this adding-up process the **aggregation** of the individual demand curves.

We begin by showing you how to add up the demand of just two individual buyers. We'll first teach you how to do it with demand schedules. Then we'll show you what that implies for plotted demand curves. Remember that these different ways of thinking about demand are equivalent. Each method reinforces the other.

Exhibit 4.2 contains two individual demand schedules and a total demand schedule. To calculate the total quantity demanded at a particular price, simply add up Sue's and Carlos's quantity demanded at that price. For example, at a price of $4 per gallon, Sue has a quantity demanded of 200 gallons per year. At that same price, Carlos has a quantity demanded of 400 gallons per year. So the aggregate level of quantity demanded at a price of $4 per gallon is 200 + 400 = 600 gallons per year.

Conceptually, aggregating quantity demanded means fixing the price and adding up the quantities that each buyer demands. It is important to remember that quantities are being added together, not prices. Here's an example to help you remember this point. Consider a bakery selling donuts at $1 each. Suppose that two hungry students walk into the bakery and each wants one donut (at the posted price). The total quantity demanded by the two students would be two donuts at a price of $1 per donut (*not* one donut at a price of $2 per donut). Remember this tale of two donuts and you'll avoid getting confused when you calculate total demand schedules.

Exhibit 4.2 also contains plotted demand curves. When a demand curve is a straight line, as in this exhibit, the relationship between price and quantity demanded is said to be linear. Economists often illustrate demand curves with straight lines, because they are easy to explain and easy to express as equations. However, real-world demand curves don't tend to be perfectly straight lines, so the linear model is mostly used as an illustrative case.

The plotted demand curves in Exhibit 4.2 can be aggregated in the same way that the demand schedules are aggregated. Again, look at the quantities demanded at a single price, say $4 per gallon. Sue's demand curve has a quantity demanded of 200 gallons per year.

Exhibit 4.2 Aggregation of Demand Schedules and Demand Curves

Demand schedules are aggregated by summing the quantity demanded at each price on the individual demand schedules. Likewise, demand curves are aggregated by summing the quantity demanded at each price on the individual demand curves.

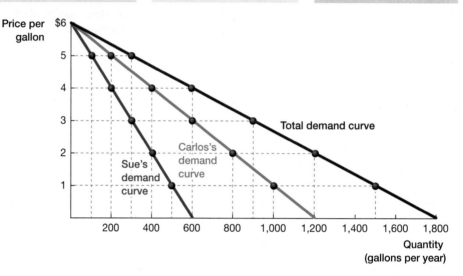

Sue's Demand Schedule	
Price ($/gallon)	Quantity Demanded (gallons/year)
$5	100
4	200
3	300
2	400
1	500

Carlos's Demand Schedule	
Price ($/gallon)	Quantity Demanded (gallons/year)
$5	200
4	400
3	600
2	800
1	1,000

Total Demand Schedule	
Price ($/gallon)	Quantity Demanded (gallons/year)
$5	300
4	600
3	900
2	1,200
1	1,500

Carlos's demand curve has a quantity demanded of 400 gallons per year. Total quantity demanded at a price of $4 per gallon is the sum of the two individual quantities demanded: 200 + 400 = 600 gallons per year.

Building the Market Demand Curve

Exhibit 4.2 shows you how to add up demand curves for just two buyers. We would like to study the demand of all buyers in a market. Economists refer to this as the **market demand curve**. It is the sum of the individual demand curves of all potential buyers. The market demand curve plots the relationship between the total quantity demanded and the market price, holding all else equal.

Billions of economic agents purchase gasoline every year. If we added up the total quantity of gasoline demanded at a particular market price, we could calculate the market demand for gasoline at that price. But economists rarely study the market demand for gasoline. Economists who study energy markets recognize that the gasoline market is very closely tied to all the other markets for products produced from crude oil. Jet fuel, diesel fuel, and automobile gasoline are all produced from oil. Accordingly, when economists study the market for gasoline, we aggregate to the total market for oil. Exhibit 4.3 reports a rough approximation of the worldwide demand curve for billions of barrels of oil (there are 42 gallons per barrel), which is the unit of measurement commonly used in this market.

Finally, note that the demand curve in Exhibit 4.3 is not a straight line, and therefore looks a bit different from the straight demand curves that you saw earlier. This serves as a reminder that the key property of a demand curve is the negative relationship between price and quantity demanded. Demand curves can exhibit this negative relationship without being straight lines.

Exhibit 4.3 also contains a horizontal dashed line that represents the market price of oil in 2016: $50 per barrel. The horizontal price line crosses the demand curve at a point labeled with a dot. At this intersection the buyers' willingness to pay (the height of the demand curve) is equal to the market price of oil. Buyers keep purchasing oil as long as their willingness to pay is greater than the price of oil. At quantities to the left of 35 billion barrels per

The **market demand curve** is the sum of the individual demand curves of all potential buyers. It plots the relationship between the total quantity demanded and the market price, holding all else equal.

Exhibit 4.3 Market Demand Curve for Oil

The price of a barrel of oil averaged about $50 per barrel in 2016. At that market price, worldwide demand for oil was around 35 billion barrels per year. This demand curve plots the relationship between the price of oil and the quantity demanded.

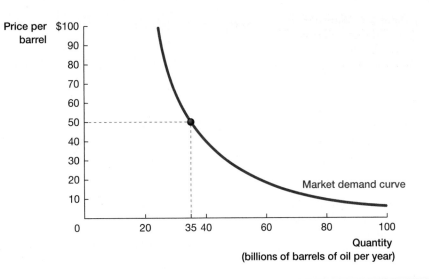

year, willingness to pay (the vertical height of the demand curve) exceeds the market price of $50 per barrel, so buyers gain by purchasing more oil. Oil purchases continue until the buyers reach a quantity demanded of 35 billion barrels per year. At that point, their willingness to pay equals the market price, and they no longer benefit by buying more oil.

Shifting the Demand Curve

When we introduced the demand curve, we explained that it describes the relationship between price and quantity demanded, holding all else equal. It's now time to more carefully consider the "all else" that is being held fixed.

The demand curve shifts when these five major factors change:

- Tastes and preferences
- Income and wealth
- Availability and prices of related goods
- Number and scale of buyers
- Buyers' beliefs about the future

Changes in Tastes and Preferences   A change in tastes or preferences is simply a change in what we personally like, enjoy, or value. For example, your demand for oil products would fall (holding price fixed) if you became convinced that global warming was a significant global problem and it was your ethical duty to use fewer fossil fuels. Because your willingness to buy oil products decreases as a result of your growing environmental worries, your demand curve shifts to the left. We refer to this as a "leftward" shift in the demand curve, because a lower quantity demanded for a given price of oil corresponds to a leftward movement on the *x*-axis. If many people have experiences like this—say the Greenland ice sheet starts to rapidly melt, convincing millions of drivers to buy hybrids—then the market demand curve will experience a shift to the left. See Exhibit 4.4 for an example of a leftward shift in a demand curve.

Naturally, a taste change could also shift a demand curve to the right, corresponding to an increase in the quantity demanded at a given market price. For example, this would happen to your individual demand curve if you started dating someone who lives a few towns away, thereby increasing your transportation needs. Exhibit 4.4 also plots a rightward shift in a demand curve.

This example illustrates two key concepts:

The **demand curve shifts** only when the quantity demanded changes at a given price.

If a good's own price changes and its demand curve hasn't shifted, the own price change produces a **movement along the demand curve**.

- The **demand curve shifts** only when the quantity demanded changes at a given price. Leftward and rightward shifts are illustrated in panel (a) of Exhibit 4.4.
- If a good's own price changes and its demand curve hasn't shifted, the own price change produces a **movement along the demand curve**. Movements along the demand curve are illustrated in panel (b) of Exhibit 4.4.

Exhibit 4.4 Shifts of the Demand Curve versus Movement along the Demand Curve

Many factors other than a good's price affect the quantity demanded. If a change in these factors reduces the quantity demanded at a given price, then the demand curve shifts left as in panel (a). If a change in these factors increases the quantity demanded at a given price, then the demand curve shifts right, which is also illustrated in panel (a). In contrast, if only the good's own price changes, then the demand curve does not shift, and we move along the demand curve, as in panel (b).

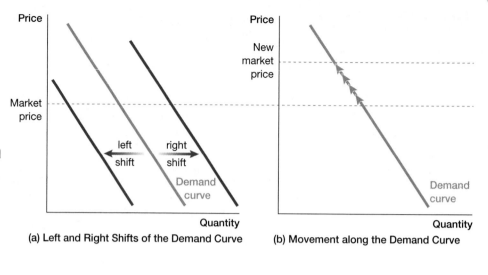

(a) Left and Right Shifts of the Demand Curve

(b) Movement along the Demand Curve

It is important to master these terms, because they will keep coming up. Use Exhibit 4.4 to confirm that you know the difference between a "shift of the demand curve" and a "movement along the demand curve." It helps to remember that if the quantity demanded changes at a given price, then the demand curve has shifted.

We now continue with a discussion of the key factors, other than tastes and preferences, that shift the demand curve.

For a **normal good**, an increase in income shifts the demand curve to the right (holding the good's price fixed), causing buyers to purchase more of the good.

Changes in Income and Wealth   A change in income or a change in wealth affects your ability to pay for goods and services. Imagine that you recently got your first full-time job and went from a student budget to a $40,000 annual salary. You might buy a car and the gas to go with it. You'd probably also start taking more exotic vacations: for instance, flying to Hawaii rather than taking the bus to visit your friends in Hackensack. Your willingness (directly and indirectly) to buy fuel will now be higher, holding the price of fuel fixed, implying that your demand curve shifts to the right. For a **normal good**, an increase in income shifts the demand curve to the right (holding the good's price fixed), causing buyers to purchase more of the good.

In contrast, consider a good like Spam, which is canned, precooked meat. In the developed world, as people's incomes rise, they are likely to consume fewer canned foods and more fresh foods. If rising income shifts the demand curve for a good to the left (holding the good's price fixed), then the good is called an **inferior good**. This seemingly insulting label is actually only a technical term that describes a relationship between increases in income and leftward shifts in the demand curve.

For an inferior good, rising income shifts the demand curve to the left. No insult intended to Spam lovers.

For an **inferior good**, an increase in income shifts the demand curve to the left (holding the good's price fixed), causing buyers to purchase less of the good.

Two goods are **substitutes** when a rise in the price of one leads to a rightward shift in the demand curve for the other.

Changes in Availability and Prices of Related Goods   Even if the price of oil hasn't changed, a change in the availability and prices of related goods will also influence demand for oil products, thereby shifting the demand curve for oil. For example, if a city raises the price of public transportation, drivers are likely to increase use of their cars. This produces a rightward shift in the demand curve for gasoline. Two goods are said to be **substitutes** when a rise in the price of one leads to a rightward shift in the demand curve for the other. Public transportation and gas are **substitutes** because a rise in the price of public transportation leads people to use public transportation less and drive their cars more, producing a rightward shift in the demand curve for gasoline.

In contrast, there are some related goods and services that play the opposite role. For example, suppose that a ski resort located 200 miles from where you live decreases its lift ticket prices. The price cut will lead some people to increase their visits to the ski resort, thereby increasing their transportation needs and shifting their demand curve for gasoline to the right. Two goods are said to be **complements** when a fall in the price of one good leads to a rightward shift in the demand curve for the other good.

Two goods are complements when a fall in the price of one leads to a rightward shift in the demand curve for the other.

Changes in Number and Scale of Buyers
When the number of buyers increases, the demand curve shifts right. When the number of buyers decreases, the demand curve shifts left. The scale of the buyers' purchasing behavior also matters. For example, if the mayor of a small town switches all of the town buses from gasoline to battery power, this will have a much smaller impact on worldwide gasoline demand than a switch by the mayor of the world's largest city, Tokyo.

Changes in Buyers' Beliefs about the Future
Changes in buyers' beliefs about the future also influence the demand curve. Suppose that some people begin losing their jobs during the first months of an economy-wide slowdown. Even if you hadn't lost your job, you might still be worried. You could lose your job at some point in the near future, and anticipating this possibility might lead you to build up a rainy-day fund right now. To do this, you might cut your spending by carpooling or eliminating weekend trips to local ski resorts. Such belt-tightening tends to reduce gas usage and shifts the demand curve for oil to the left.

Summary of Shifts in the Demand Curve and Movements along the Demand Curve

The demand curve shifts when these factors change:

1. Tastes and preferences
2. Income and wealth
3. Availability and prices of related goods
4. Number and scale of buyers
5. Buyers' beliefs about the future

The *only* reason for a movement along the demand curve:

A change in the price of the good itself

EVIDENCE-BASED ECONOMICS

Q: How much more gasoline would people buy if its price were lower?

We've explained that the quantity of gasoline demanded falls as the price rises. We're now ready to study empirical evidence that backs this up.

Brazil and Venezuela share a border, and they had similar levels of income per person in 2013. Both are also large oil producers—each produced about 3 million barrels per day in 2013. However, they had radically different energy policies. Like most countries, Brazil heavily taxed the sale of gasoline. In contrast, Venezuela aggressively subsidized the sale of gasoline. To compare their policies, we report the U.S. dollar price of gasoline in 2013, when Brazilian drivers paid $5.58 per gallon and Venezuelan drivers paid only $0.04 per gallon. The Venezuelan government provided enough of a subsidy to make gasoline practically free. The Venezuelan government is a major oil producer and supplied enough gasoline to meet consumer demand, even though the price was $0.04 per gallon.

The Law of Demand predicts that a lower price should be associated with a higher quantity demanded, all else held equal. In fact, per person gasoline consumption was almost five times higher in Venezuela than in Brazil in 2013.

EVIDENCE-BASED ECONOMICS

(continued)

Exhibit 4.5 plots the 2013 price of gasoline on the *y*-axis (including taxes and subsidies) and the 2013 quantity of gasoline demanded on the *x*-axis. As you can see, there is a negative relationship between price and quantity demanded. We've also added Mexico to this figure to give you a sense of how another Latin American country (with similar per person income at that time) compares. Mexico provided a small subsidy on gasoline and consequently fell between the other two countries. The Law of Demand predicts a negative relationship between price and quantity demanded, and the data confirm that prediction.

Venezuela's extreme gasoline subsidies were costing the Venezuelan government an enormous amount of forgone revenue (an opportunity cost): they were selling gasoline domestically at a fraction of what they could have received by exporting it. At first, the government reacted by rationing gasoline. Eventually, the authorities realized that the subsidy itself was the real problem. In 2016 the Venezuelan government announced that it would soon reduce or end the subsidy.

But that's not the end of the story. Many other oil-producing countries also aggressively subsidize domestic gasoline consumption—for example, Kuwait and Qatar. As you would expect, these countries have extremely high per capita energy use relative to other wealthy countries.[2]

Exhibit 4.5 The Quantity of Gasoline Demanded (per person) and the Price of Gasoline in Brazil, Mexico, and Venezuela (2013)

There is a negative relationship between price and quantity demanded in the gasoline market.

Source: Data from quantity demanded is from the Organisation for Economic Development and Co-ordination. After-tax, after-subsidy gasoline prices are from AIRINC.

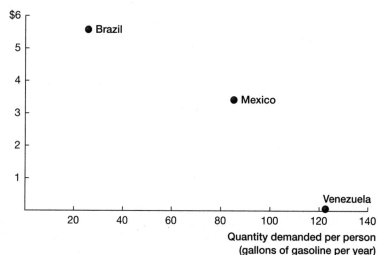

Question	Answer	Data	Caveat
How much more gasoline would people buy if its price were lower?	Venezuelans, who paid only $0.04 per gallon of gas in 2013, purchased five times as much per person as Brazilians, who paid $5.58 per gallon.	We compare the quantities of gasoline demanded in Latin American countries with similar levels of income per person and very different gas prices. The variation in gas prices was caused by differences in taxes and subsidies.	Though income levels per person are similar in these countries, the countries have other differences that are not accounted for in this analysis.

4.3   How Do Sellers Behave?

You now understand the behavior of buyers. To understand the complete picture of a market, we also need to study sellers. The interaction of buyers and sellers in a marketplace determines the market price.

Quantity supplied is the amount of a good or service that sellers are willing to sell at a given price.

We want to analyze the relationship between the price of a good and the amount of the good that sellers are willing to sell or supply. At a given price, the amount of the good or service that sellers are willing to supply is called the **quantity supplied**. Note that in this book, all supply curves, supply schedules, and graph labels relating to supply are in red.

To build intuition for the concept of quantity supplied, think about a company like ExxonMobil. As the price of oil goes up, ExxonMobil increases its willingness to supply oil that is relatively expensive for the company to discover and extract. Some oil is in deep-water locations where the ocean depth is 2 miles and the oil is another 8 miles below the seafloor. Such wells are drilled by specialized ships two football fields long, which are staffed by hundreds of workers and equipped with robotic, unmanned submarines. Because of the enormous expense, such wells are only drilled when the price of oil is over $60 per barrel.

Drilling for oil from offshore platforms above the Arctic Circle is even more costly. If a single small iceberg could sink the *Titanic*, imagine the challenge of building and protecting stationary oil rigs in areas where tens of thousands of large icebergs pass each year. Offshore oil wells within the Arctic Circle are only drilled when the price of oil is over $70 per barrel. As recently as 2014, oil prices were $100 per barrel, and many of these challenging locations were being developed. The higher the price of oil goes, the greater the number of drilling locations that will be profitable for ExxonMobil. Many observers talk about oil and warn that we are running out of it. In fact, companies like ExxonMobil are only running out of cheap oil. There is more oil under the surface of the earth than we are ever going to use. The problem is that much of that oil is very expensive to extract and deliver to the market.

Drilling from offshore platforms above the Arctic Circle is not profitable unless the price of oil exceeds $70 per barrel. At the other extreme, oil from the deserts of Saudi Arabia costs less than $15 per barrel to extract.

Supply Curves

ExxonMobil responds to increases in the price of oil by developing new oil fields in ever more challenging locations. Likewise, ExxonMobil responds to decreases in the price of oil by scaling back its exploration program and idling oil rigs. The relationship between ExxonMobil's production of oil and the price of oil is summarized in the boxed supply schedule in Exhibit 4.6. A **supply schedule** is a table that reports the quantity supplied at different prices, holding all else equal. The supply schedule shows that ExxonMobil increases the quantity of oil supplied as the price of oil increases. Exhibit 4.6 also plots ExxonMobil's **supply curve**, which plots the quantity supplied at different prices. In other words, a supply curve plots the supply schedule.

A **supply schedule** is a table that reports the quantity supplied at different prices, holding all else equal.

The **supply curve** plots the quantity supplied at different prices. A supply curve plots the supply schedule.

Two variables are **positively related** if the variables move in the same direction.

Law of Supply: In almost all cases, the quantity supplied rises when the price rises (holding all else equal).

The supply curve in Exhibit 4.6 has a key property: the price of oil and the quantity supplied are *positively related*. By **positively related** we mean that the variables move in the same direction—when one variable goes up, the other goes up, too. In the graph, we can easily identify this property, because the curve slopes upward. In almost all cases, quantity supplied and price are positively related (holding all else equal), which economists call the **Law of Supply**.

ExxonMobil starts to produce oil when the price exceeds a level of $10 per barrel. An oil price of $25 per barrel generates a quantity supplied of 0.6 billion barrels per year. A higher oil price of $50 per barrel generates a higher quantity supplied of 1.0 billion barrels per year. At $75 per barrel, the quantity supplied rises to 1.2 billion barrels per year.

Willingness to Accept

If ExxonMobil is optimizing, the firm should be willing to supply one additional barrel of oil if it is paid at least its marginal cost of production. Recall from the chapter on optimization (Chapter 3) that marginal cost is the extra cost generated by producing an additional

Exhibit 4.6 ExxonMobil's Supply Schedule for Oil and Supply Curve for Oil

As the price of oil rises (on the y-axis), the quantity of oil supplied increases (on the x-axis), so price and quantity supplied are positively related. Equivalently, we could say that the supply curve is upward-sloping. In this figure, the supply curve is curved, which reflects the fact that ExxonMobil owns only a limited amount of oil reserves and finds it more and more difficult to expand production as the quantity supplied rises.

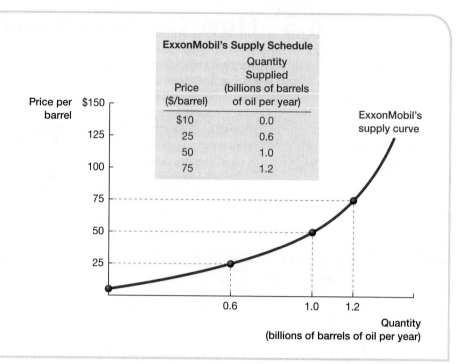

ExxonMobil's Supply Schedule	
Price ($/barrel)	Quantity Supplied (billions of barrels of oil per year)
$10	0.0
25	0.6
50	1.0
75	1.2

unit. As long as an oil producer is paid at least its marginal cost per barrel, it should be willing to supply an additional barrel of oil.

For an optimizing firm, the height of the supply curve is the firm's marginal cost. For example, ExxonMobil's supply curve implies that if the price of oil is $50, then the quantity supplied is 1.0 billion barrels per year. We can turn this around and say it another way—ExxonMobil is willing to accept $50 to produce its 1 billionth barrel of oil. That's what the supply curve tells us. Economists call this ExxonMobil's **willingness to accept**, which is the lowest price that a seller is willing to get paid to sell an extra unit of a good. For an optimizing firm, willingness to accept is the same as the marginal cost of production. ExxonMobil is willing to accept $50 for an additional barrel because $50 is ExxonMobil's marginal cost when it produces its 1 billionth barrel in a year. If ExxonMobil were to accept less than $50 for its 1 billionth barrel, it would be losing money on that unit of production.

Willingness to accept is the lowest price that a seller is willing to get paid to sell an extra unit of a good. At a particular quantity supplied, willingness to accept is the height of the supply curve. Willingness to accept is the same as the marginal cost of production.

From the Individual Supply Curve to the Market Supply Curve

When we studied buyers, we summed up their individual demand curves to obtain a market demand curve. We're now ready to do the same thing for the sellers. Adding up quantity supplied works the same way as adding up quantity demanded. We add up quantities at a particular price. We then repeat this at every possible price to plot the *market supply curve*. The **market supply curve** plots the relationship between the total quantity supplied and the market price, holding all else equal.

Let's start with an aggregation analysis that assumes there are only two oil companies, ExxonMobil and Chevron. Assume that they have the supply schedules listed in Exhibit 4.7. At a price of $50 per barrel, the quantity supplied by Chevron is 0.7 billion barrels of oil per year and the quantity supplied by ExxonMobil is 1.0 billion barrels of oil per year. So the total quantity supplied at the price of $50 per barrel is 0.7 billion + 1.0 billion = 1.7 billion barrels of oil per year. To calculate the total supply curve, we repeat this calculation for each price. The resulting total supply curve is plotted in Exhibit 4.7.

The **market supply curve** is the sum of the individual supply curves of all the potential sellers. It plots the relationship between the total quantity supplied and the market price, holding all else equal.

Of course, the market contains thousands of oil producers, not just ExxonMobil and Chevron. The market supply curve is the sum of the individual supply curves of all these thousands of potential sellers, just as the market demand curve is the sum of the individual demand curves of all the potential buyers.

Aggregating the individual supply curves of thousands of oil producers yields a market supply curve like the one plotted in Exhibit 4.8. We've included a dashed line at $50 per barrel, which is the approximate market price that prevailed in the world oil market in 2016. At this price, the total quantity supplied is 35 billion barrels of oil per year.

Exhibit 4.7 Aggregation of Supply Schedules and Supply Curves

To calculate the total quantity supplied at a particular price, add up the quantity supplied by each supplier at that price. Repeat this for each price to derive the total supply curve.

Chevron's Supply Schedule	
Price ($/barrel)	Quantity Supplied (billions of barrels of oil per year)
$10	0.0
25	0.4
50	0.7
75	0.9

ExxonMobil's Supply Schedule	
Price ($/barrel)	Quantity Supplied (billions of barrels of oil per year)
$10	0.0
25	0.6
50	1.0
75	1.2

Total Supply Schedule	
Price ($/barrel)	Quantity Supplied (billions of barrels of oil per year)
$10	0.0
25	1.0
50	1.7
75	2.1

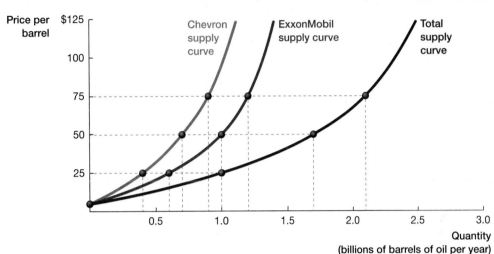

Exhibit 4.8 Market Supply Curve for Oil

The market supply curve is upward-sloping, like the supply curves of the individual sellers.

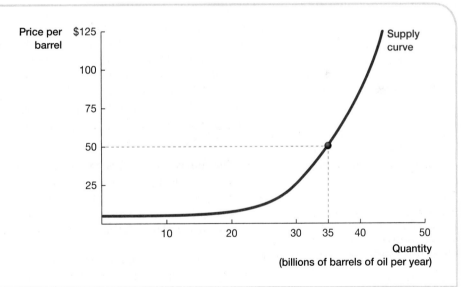

Shifting the Supply Curve

Recall that the supply curve describes the relationship between price and quantity supplied, holding all else equal. There are four major types of variables that are held fixed when a supply curve is constructed. The supply curve shifts when these variables change:

- Prices of inputs used to produce the good
- Technology used to produce the good
- Number and scale of sellers
- Sellers' beliefs about the future

Exhibit 4.9 Shifts of the Supply Curve versus Movement along the Supply Curve

Many factors other than a good's price affect the quantity supplied. If a change in these factors decreases the quantity supplied at a given price, then the supply curve shifts left, as illustrated in panel (a). If a change in these factors increases the quantity supplied at a given price, then the supply curve shifts right, which is also illustrated in panel (a). In contrast, if only the good's own price changes, then the supply curve does not shift and we move along the supply curve, which is shown in panel (b).

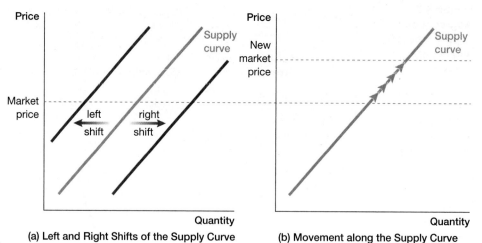

(a) Left and Right Shifts of the Supply Curve

(b) Movement along the Supply Curve

An **input** is a good or service used to produce another good or service.

Changes in Prices of Inputs Used to Produce the Good Changes in the prices of inputs shift the supply curve. An **input** is a good or service used to produce another good or service. For instance, steel is used to construct oil platforms, to create oil drilling machinery, to build pipelines, and to construct oil tankers. Hence, steel is a critical input to oil production. An increase in the price of steel implies that some opportunities to produce oil will no longer be profitable, and therefore optimizing oil producers will choose not to supply as much oil (holding the price of oil fixed). It follows that an increase in the price of steel shifts the supply curve of oil to the left. In other words, holding the price of oil fixed, the quantity of oil supplied falls. In contrast, a fall in the price of steel shifts the supply curve of oil to the right. Panel (a) of Exhibit 4.9 plots these leftward and rightward shifts in the supply curve.

This example illustrates two key concepts:

The **supply curve shifts** only when the quantity supplied changes at a given price.

If a good's own price changes and its supply curve hasn't shifted, the own price change produces a **movement along the supply curve**.

- The **supply curve shifts** only when the quantity supplied changes at a given price. Leftward and rightward shifts are illustrated in panel (a) of Exhibit 4.9.
- If a good's own price changes and its supply curve hasn't shifted, the own price change produces a **movement along the supply curve**. A movement along the supply curve is shown in panel (b) of Exhibit 4.9.

Changes in Technology Used to Produce the Good Changes in technology also shift the supply curve. In recent years, "fracking" (induced hydraulic fracturing) has revolutionized the energy industry. This technology uses pressurized fluids to create fractures in the underground rock formations that surround a drilled well. The fractures enable oil and natural gas to seep out of the rock and be drawn from the well. Fracking has caused a rightward shift in the supply curves for petroleum and natural gas.

Changes in the Number and Scale of Sellers Changes in the number of sellers also shift the supply curve. For example, in 2011 Libyan rebels overthrew Muammar Gaddafi, a dictator who had controlled the country for 42 years. Gaddafi loyalists defended his regime and the fighting dragged on for 6 months. During this period, Libya essentially stopped oil production. Before the war, Libyan wells had been producing about 550 million barrels per year. This is the scale of Libyan production. During the Libyan civil war, the worldwide supply curve shifted to the left by 550 million barrels per year.

A photograph of a Libyan oil refinery burning during the 2011 civil war that overthrew Colonel Muammar Gaddafi. During the war almost all of Libya's oil production was shut down, shifting the world oil supply curve to the left.

Changes in Sellers' Beliefs about the Future Finally, changes in sellers' beliefs about the future shift the supply curve. For example, consider the market for natural gas. Every winter, natural gas usage skyrockets for home heating. This creates a winter spike in natural gas prices. Expecting such price spikes, natural gas producers store vast quantities during the summer (when prices are low by comparison). In other words, natural gas producers use much of their summer natural gas production to build up stockpiles instead of selling all of the summer production to the public. This implies that natural gas suppliers shift the supply curve to the left in the summer. This is an optimization strategy. By pulling supply off the (low-price) summer market and increasing supply in the (high-price) winter market, natural gas suppliers obtain a higher average price. Summarizing this strategy, natural gas producers adjust their supply throughout the year in response to expectations about how the price of natural gas will move in the future.

Summary of Shifts in the Supply Curve and Movements Along the Supply Curve

The supply curve shifts when these factors change:

1. Prices of inputs used to produce the good
2. Technology used to produce the good
3. Number and scale of sellers
4. Sellers' beliefs about the future

The *only* reason for a movement along the supply curve:

A change in the price of the good itself

4.4 Supply and Demand in Equilibrium

Up to this point, we have provided tools that explain the separate behaviors of buyers and sellers. We haven't explained how to put the two sides of the market together. How do buyers and sellers interact? What determines the market price at which they trade? What determines the quantity of goods bought by buyers and sold by sellers? We will use the market demand curve and the market supply curve to answer these questions. We'll continue to study a perfectly competitive market, which we'll refer to as a "competitive market."

> Competitive markets converge to the price at which quantity supplied and quantity demanded are the same.

Competitive markets converge to the price at which quantity supplied and quantity demanded are the same. To visualize what it means to equate quantity supplied and quantity demanded, we need to plot the demand curve and supply curve on the same figure. Exhibit 4.10 does this.

In Exhibit 4.10, the demand curve (in blue) and the supply curve (in red) for the oil market cross at a price of $50 per barrel and a quantity of 35 billion barrels. Because the demand curve slopes down and the supply curve slopes up, the two curves have only one crossing point. Economists refer to this crossing point as the **competitive equilibrium**. The price at the crossing point is referred to as the **competitive equilibrium price**, which is the price at which quantity supplied and quantity demanded are the same. This is sometimes referred to as the market clearing price, because at this price there is a buyer for every unit that is supplied in the market. The quantity at the crossing point is referred to as the **competitive equilibrium quantity**. This is the quantity that corresponds to the competitive equilibrium price.

The **competitive equilibrium** is the crossing point of the supply curve and the demand curve.

The **competitive equilibrium price** equates quantity supplied and quantity demanded.

The **competitive equilibrium quantity** is the quantity that corresponds to the competitive equilibrium price.

At the competitive equilibrium price, the quantity demanded is equal to the quantity supplied. At any other price, the quantity demanded and the quantity supplied will be unequal. To see this, draw a horizontal line at any other price. Only the horizontal line at the competitive equilibrium price equates quantity demanded and quantity supplied.

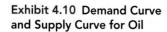

Exhibit 4.10 Demand Curve and Supply Curve for Oil

In a competitive market, the market price is the point at which the demand curve intersects the supply curve.

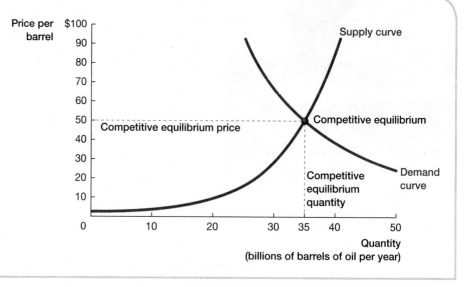

Exhibit 4.11 illustrates a case in which the market is not in competitive equilibrium, because the market price is above the competitive equilibrium price. The higher price makes selling more desirable and buying less desirable, raising the quantity supplied above its competitive equilibrium level and lowering the quantity demanded below its competitive equilibrium level. When the market price is above the competitive equilibrium price, quantity supplied exceeds quantity demanded, creating **excess supply**. For example, Exhibit 4.11 shows that at a market price of $70 per barrel for oil, the quantity supplied of 38 billion barrels of oil per year exceeds the quantity demanded of 29 billion barrels of oil per year.

When the market price is above the competitive equilibrium price, quantity supplied exceeds quantity demanded, creating **excess supply**.

If the market stayed in this situation, sellers would pump 38 billion barrels of oil per year, but buyers would purchase only 29 billion of those barrels, leaving the difference— 9 billion barrels—unsold each year. This would push down oil prices, as enormous stockpiles of oil started to build up around the world. Because existing oil storage tanks are limited in scale and expensive to build, sellers would start undercutting each other's prices to get rid of the rising inventory of unsold oil. Prices would fall. As a result, the situation in Exhibit 4.11 normally wouldn't last for long. Sellers, who are selling nearly identical

Exhibit 4.11 Excess Supply

When the market price is above the competitive equilibrium level, quantity demanded is less than quantity supplied. This is a case of excess supply. In this particular example, the excess supply is 38 − 29 = 9 billion barrels of oil per year.

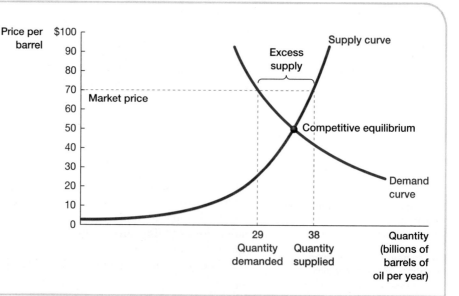

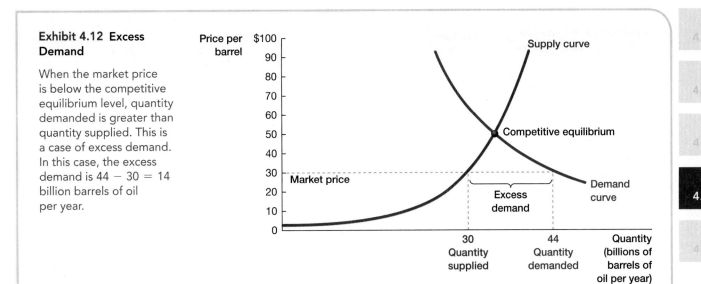

Exhibit 4.12 Excess Demand

When the market price is below the competitive equilibrium level, quantity demanded is greater than quantity supplied. This is a case of excess demand. In this case, the excess demand is 44 − 30 = 14 billion barrels of oil per year.

When the market price is below the competitive equilibrium price, quantity demanded exceeds quantity supplied, creating **excess demand**.

barrels of oil, would compete with one another for customers by cutting prices. This would continue until the market price fell back to the competitive equilibrium price. This competitive process plays an important role in pushing the market toward the aptly named competitive equilibrium.

Exhibit 4.12 illustrates the opposite case. When market price is below the competitive equilibrium price, quantity demanded exceeds quantity supplied, creating **excess demand**. In Exhibit 4.12 the quantity demanded of 44 billion barrels of oil per year exceeds the quantity supplied of 30 billion barrels of oil per year. Buyers want 44 billion barrels of oil, but there are only 30 billion barrels available on the market.

The situation in Exhibit 4.12 also normally won't last long. Buyers who aren't getting the goods they want will compete with one another by offering to pay higher prices to get the limited quantity of oil. This will continue until the market price rises to the competitive equilibrium price of $50 per barrel.

Curve Shifting in Competitive Equilibrium

We are now ready to put this framework into action. We'd like to know how a shock to the world oil market will affect the equilibrium quantity and the equilibrium price of oil.

For example, what would happen if a major oil exporter suddenly stopped production, as Libya did in 2011? This causes a leftward shift of the supply curve, as illustrated in Exhibit 4.13. Since oil has become more scarce, the price of oil needs to rise from its old level to equate quantity supplied and quantity demanded. The rise in the equilibrium oil price is associated with a movement along the demand curve (which hasn't shifted). Because the demand curve is downward-sloping, a rising price causes a reduction in the quantity demanded. In fact, the outbreak of full-scale fighting in Libya and the consequent shutdown of the Libyan oil fields did correspond with an increase in the world price of oil.

Now consider the opposite case. What would happen if a technological breakthrough shifted the supply curve to the right? This causes a rightward shift of the supply curve, as illustrated in Exhibit 4.14. Since oil has become more abundant, the price of oil needs to fall from its old level to equate quantity supplied and quantity demanded. The fall in the equilibrium oil price is associated with a movement along the demand curve (which hasn't shifted). Because the demand curve is downward-sloping, a falling price causes an increase in the quantity demanded.

We can also predict the effect of a shift in the demand curve. For example, what would happen if rising environmental concerns and new energy-saving technologies led consumers to use less oil at any given price? This change in consumer tastes and technology shifts

Exhibit 4.13 A Leftward Shift of the Supply Curve

A leftward shift of the supply curve raises the equilibrium price and lowers the equilibrium quantity. The original equilibrium is located at the grey dot. The new equilibrium is marked by the black dot, where the original demand curve and the new supply curve intersect.

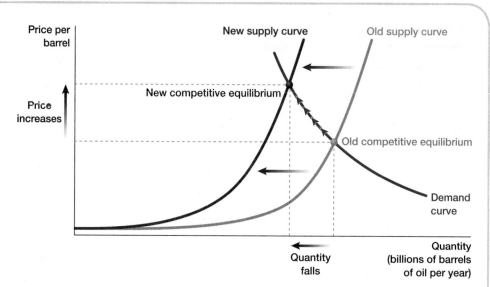

Exhibit 4.14 A Rightward Shift of the Supply Curve

A rightward shift in the supply curve lowers the equilibrium price and raises the equilibrium quantity. The original equilibrium is located at the grey dot. The new equilibrium is marked by the black dot, where the original demand curve and the new supply curve intersect.

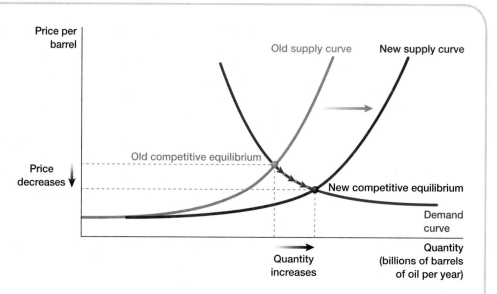

┌─ LETTING THE ─────
DATA SPEAK

Technological Breakthroughs Drive Down the Equilibrium Price of Oil

In fact, from 2011 to 2016 the supply-curve shift in Exhibit 4.14 actually occurred, due in part to a boom in fracking-based oil extraction. Recall that "fracking" uses pressurized fluids to create fractures in underground rock. To illustrate this technology, consider a single 1.5-mile-deep fracking well that BP drilled in Texas during the summer of 2016. At six different depths, BP turned the vertical drill bit 90 degrees to create three *horizontal* mile-long pipes at each depth. This system of underground hori-

zontal drilling generated over 18 miles of deep horizontal pipes, which are now being used to fracture the energy-rich rock and capture released oil and natural gas.

Fracking enabled the United States to increase oil production by 70 percent from 2011 to 2016 (from 2.1 to 3.4 billion barrels per year).[3] The fracking boom contributed to a rightward shift in the worldwide supply curve for oil. This shift played an important role in driving oil prices down from $100 per barrel in 2011 to $50 in 2016.

Exhibit 4.15 A Leftward Shift of the Demand Curve

A leftward shift in the demand curve lowers the equilibrium price and lowers the equilibrium quantity. The original equilibrium is located at the grey dot. The new equilibrium is marked by the black dot, where the original supply curve and the new demand curve intersect.

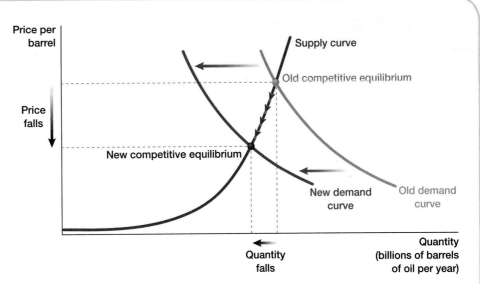

the demand curve for oil to the left, which is plotted in Exhibit 4.15. Accordingly, the price of oil needs to fall from its old level to equate quantity supplied and quantity demanded. The decrease in the equilibrium oil price is associated with a movement along the supply curve (which hasn't shifted). Because the supply curve is upward-sloping, a falling price causes a reduction in the quantity supplied.

Using demand and supply curves to study markets enables economists to resolve puzzles. For example, in Exhibit 4.14, the market price of oil drops and people buy less oil! Hearing those two facts might sound perplexing. Shouldn't a drop in the price of oil lead to an increase in oil buying? In Exhibit 4.15, you can see that the drop in the price of oil is caused by a shift of the market demand curve to the left. This leftward shift causes the price to fall and the fall in price causes the quantity supplied to fall. So the fall in price and the fall in the equilibrium quantity are both consequences of the leftward shift in the demand curve.

So far we have studied examples in which only one curve—either the demand or supply curve—shifts at a time. But life isn't always this simple. Sometimes both curves shift at the same time. For example, the fracking revolution has shifted the supply curve for oil to the right at the same time that rising environmental consciousness and energy-saving technology have shifted the demand curve for oil to the left.

We want to know what happens in such mixed cases. Exhibit 4.16 shows how simultaneous shifts in the supply and the demand curves translate into changes in the market price and the quantity of transactions. As you can imagine, there are many possible combinations of shifts. This exhibit takes you through one group of cases. The problems at the end of the chapter take you through other cases.

In all three panels of Exhibit 4.16, the demand curve shifts left and the supply curve shifts right. The three panels graph three different special cases. We represent the old demand curve in light blue (labeled D_1) and the new demand curve in dark blue (labeled D_2). Likewise, the old supply curve is light red (labeled S_1) and the new supply curve is dark red (labeled S_2). The grey dot marks the old competitive equilibrium, where the old demand curve and the old supply curve intersect. The black dot marks the new competitive equilibrium, where the new demand curve and the new supply curve intersect. The old competitive equilibrium price is P_1 and the new competitive equilibrium price is P_2. The old competitive equilibrium quantity is Q_1 and the new competitive equilibrium quantity is Q_2.

In all three panels, the equilibrium price falls: P_2 is less than P_1. However, the direction of adjustment of the equilibrium quantity depends on the relative size of the shifts in the demand and supply curves. In the panel (a), the leftward shift in demand dominates

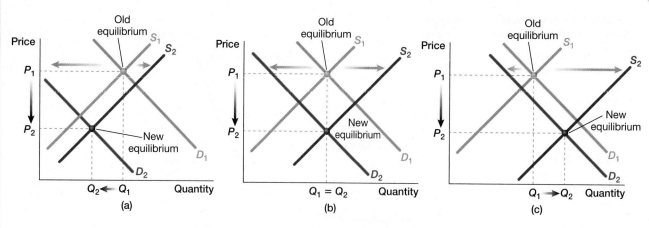

Exhibit 4.16 The Demand Curve Shifts Left and the Supply Curve Shifts Right

When the demand curve shifts left and the supply curve shifts right, the competitive equilibrium price will always decrease (P_2 is always less than P_1). However, the competitive equilibrium quantity may decrease (Q_2 less than Q_1 in panel (a)), stay the same (Q_2 equal to Q_1 in panel (b)), or increase (Q_2 greater than Q_1 in panel (c)).

and the equilibrium quantity falls from Q_1 to Q_2. In panel (b), the equilibrium quantity stays exactly the same: $Q_1 = Q_2$. In panel (c), the rightward shift in supply dominates and the equilibrium quantity rises from Q_1 to Q_2. Summing up, when the demand curve shifts left and the supply curve shifts right, the competitive equilibrium price will always decrease, but the competitive equilibrium quantity may move in either direction or stay the same.

4.5 What Would Happen If the Government Tried to Dictate the Price of Gasoline?

Our analysis has concluded that competitive markets will end up at the competitive equilibrium—the point where the supply and the demand curves cross. But this can happen only if prices are allowed to respond to market pressures.

However, some markets have prices that are set by laws, regulations, or social norms. Economists are interested in the way that all markets work, even markets that are not allowed to reach a competitive equilibrium. We illustrate these issues by considering markets without a flexible price.

Take another look at Exhibit 4.12. When the market price of gasoline is artificially held below the level of the competitive equilibrium price, the quantity of gasoline demanded exceeds the quantity supplied. Accordingly, many drivers who would like to buy gas at the market price won't be able to do so.

In a situation like this, the allocation of gasoline is determined by something other than who is willing to pay for it. During the U.S. oil crisis of 1973–1974, the U.S. government effectively capped the price of gasoline, causing quantity demanded to exceed quantity supplied. This is referred to as a price ceiling. Drivers soon realized that there was excess

At the end of 1973, the U.S. government effectively capped the price of gasoline, creating a situation of excess demand.

This photograph was taken in 1974. Why did price caps on gasoline lead to these results?

demand at the capped price, leading them to show up early to get whatever gas was available. Lines began to form earlier and earlier in the day.

A *New York Times* reporter wrote, "Everywhere lines seemed to be the order of the day. In Montclair, N.J., Mrs. Catherine Lee got up at 4:20 one morning and drove to her filling station to be first on line. She had to settle for second place—No. 1 had gotten there at 3:15. Mrs. Lee fluffed up the pillow she had brought, threw two comforters over herself, and slept for three hours until the station opened." Some drivers devised ingenious means of getting around the system. "In Bedford, Massachusetts, a businessman drove his auto into a Hertz car rental lot, ordered a car, received it complete with a full tank of gas, siphoned the gas into his own car, paid Hertz their daily rental fee—no mileage charge, of course—and drove home in his car to enjoy his full tank of gas."[4]

The lines were an optimal response by buyers who understood that there was excess demand. Because quantity demanded exceeded quantity supplied, gas stations frequently ran out of gas. During the peak of the crisis, 20 percent of stations ran out of fuel. Getting in line early—very early—was an optimal way of assuring that you'd be able to fill your own tank.

Some folks didn't like waiting in long lines, particularly when they suspected that the station was going to run out of fuel before they got their turn at the pump. "They're out of their minds, they're turning sick. They'll kill you. They're fighting amongst themselves. They'll shoot you with a gun. They're all sick." Does this sound like a scene from the latest zombie movie? It's actually a gas station attendant describing his customers during the gasoline crisis of 1973–1974. An owner of another station put it this way: "It was mayhem. They were fighting in the streets and one customer pulled a knife on another one. And that was *before* we opened."

Economic history is filled with stories of governments that try to fix the price of goods instead of letting the market generate an equilibrium price. Price controls often do not work out well and governments keep forgetting this lesson.

The following Choice & Consequence feature details one more example of a failed effort to fix a price. As you read it, ask yourself how the goods in question could have been allocated differently.

CHOICE
&CONSEQUENCE

The Unintended Consequences of Fixing Market Prices

What would happen if your town announced a first-come, first-served sale of 1,000 Apple laptops for $50 each? Would the residents form an orderly line and patiently wait their turn?

In Henrico County, Virginia, such a laptop sale was actually conducted. County residents began lining up at 1:30 A.M. on the day of the sale. When the gates opened at 7 A.M., more than 5,000 people surged into the sale site, pushing and shoving their way to get to the computers. Elderly people were trampled underneath the human tidal wave, and a baby's stroller was crushed. Eventually, about 70 police officers were called in to restore order. Seventeen people were injured and four landed up in the hospital. And after the uproar died down, more than 4,000 people were left with nothing to show for all the trouble. Of those who did manage to obtain one of the computers, many later sold them.[5]

The Henrico County computer sale resulted in a situation of excess demand. At the fixed price set by the county, $50 per laptop, the quantity demanded of 5,000 exceeded the quantity supplied of 1,000. Exhibit 4.17 illustrates the fact that there were not enough laptops to go around. The people who got laptops were not necessarily the ones who were willing to pay the most. Instead, the consumers who got the laptops were the ones who were able and willing to fight their way through the crowd. Even if we assume that the laptops were subsequently resold to other people who valued the laptops more, the stampede itself caused many injuries. A stampede is a bad way to allocate society's resources.

Economists are often asked to provide advice on how to design markets that will work well. Naturally, a flexible price would have made this market work better, and it would have raised far more revenue for Henrico County.

Alternatively, the market could have been organized as an auction with bids received by phone or e-mail. The county could have auctioned off the 1,000 laptops to the 1,000 highest local bidders.

Even a random lottery would have worked much better than the stampede. The stampede allocated the laptops to the people who were the most physically aggressive and led to numerous injuries. A random lottery would have allocated the laptops to the people who got lucky. And these lucky winners would have been free to sell their laptops to anyone who valued them more than they did.

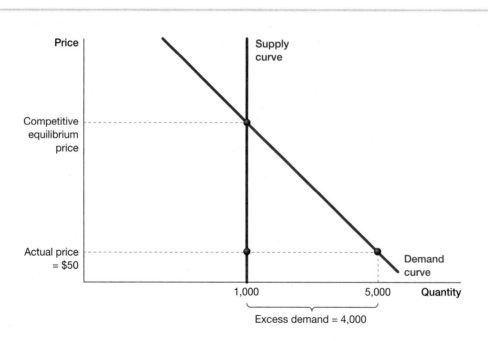

Exhibit 4.17 Excess Demand for Henrico County's Laptops

By fixing the price at $50 per laptop, Henrico County created a situation of excess demand. At this price, the quantity demanded (5,000 laptops) exceeded the quantity supplied (1,000 laptops). To equate the quantity demanded and the quantity supplied, a much higher price was needed: the competitive equilibrium price. The vertical supply curve reflects the fact that the supply of laptops at the $50 sale was fixed at 1,000 units.

Summary

- A market is a group of economic agents who are trading a good or service plus the rules and arrangements for trading. In a perfectly competitive market, (1) sellers all sell an identical good or service, and (2) individual buyers or individual sellers aren't powerful enough on their own to affect the market price of that good or service.

- Quantity demanded is the amount of a good that buyers are willing to purchase at a given price. A demand schedule is a table that reports the quantity demanded at different prices, holding all else equal. A demand curve plots the demand schedule. The Law of Demand states that in almost all cases, the quantity demanded rises when the price falls (holding all else equal).

- The market demand curve is the sum of the individual demand curves of all potential buyers: the quantity demanded is summed at each price. It plots the relationship between the total quantity demanded and the market price, holding all else equal.

- The demand curve shifts only when the quantity demanded changes at a given price. If a good's own price changes and its demand curve hasn't shifted, the own price change produces a movement along the demand curve.

- Quantity supplied is the amount of a good or service that sellers are willing to sell at a given price. A supply schedule is a table that reports the quantity supplied at different prices, holding all else equal. A supply curve plots the supply schedule. The Law of Supply states that in almost all cases, the quantity supplied rises when the price rises (holding all else equal).

- The market supply curve is the sum of the individual supply curves of all potential sellers: the quantity supplied is summed at each price. It plots the relationship between the total quantity supplied and the market price, holding all else equal.

- The supply curve shifts only when the quantity supplied changes at a given price. If a good's own price changes and its supply curve hasn't shifted, the own price change produces a movement along the supply curve.

- The competitive equilibrium is the crossing point of the supply curve and the demand curve. The competitive equilibrium price equates quantity supplied and quantity demanded. The competitive equilibrium quantity is the quantity that corresponds to the competitive equilibrium price.

- When prices are not free to fluctuate, markets fail to equate quantity demanded and quantity supplied.

Key Terms

market *p. 59*
market price *p. 60*
perfectly competitive market *p. 60*
price-taker *p. 60*
quantity demanded *p. 61*
demand schedule *p. 61*
holding all else equal *p. 61*
demand curve *p. 62*
negatively related *p. 62*
Law of Demand *p. 62*
willingness to pay *p. 63*
diminishing marginal benefit *p. 63*

aggregation *p. 63*
market demand curve *p. 64*
demand curve shifts *p. 65*
movement along the demand curve
   p. 65
normal good *p. 66*
inferior good *p. 66*
substitutes *p. 66*
complements *p. 67*
quantity supplied *p. 69*
supply schedule *p. 69*
supply curve *p. 69*

positively related *p. 69*
Law of Supply *p. 69*
willingness to accept *p. 70*
market supply curve *p. 70*
input *p. 72*
supply curve shifts *p. 72*
movement along the supply curve *p. 72*
competitive equilibrium *p. 73*
competitive equilibrium price *p. 73*
competitive equilibrium quantity *p. 73*
excess supply *p. 74*
excess demand *p. 75*

Questions

All questions are available in MyEconLab *for practice and instructor assignment.*

1. What is meant by holding all else equal? How is this concept used when discussing movements along the demand curve? How is this concept used when discussing movements along the supply curve?

2. What is meant by diminishing marginal benefits? Are you likely to experience diminishing marginal benefits for goods that you like a lot? Are there exceptions to the general rule of diminishing marginal benefits? (*Hint*: Think about batteries that you would use in a flashlight that requires two batteries.) Explain your answer.

3. How is the market demand schedule derived from individual demand schedules? How does the market demand curve differ from an individual demand curve?

4. Explain how the following factors will shift the demand curve for Gillette shaving cream.

   a. The price of a competitor's shaving cream increases.

   b. With an increase in unemployment, the average level of income in the economy falls.

   c. Shaving gels and foams, marketed as being better than shaving creams, are introduced in the market.

5. What does it mean to say that we are running out of "cheap oil"? What does this imply for the price of oil in the future?

6. What does the Law of Supply state? What is the key feature of a typical supply curve?

7. What is the difference between willingness to accept and willingness to pay? For a trade to take place, does the willingness to accept have to be lower, higher, or equal to the willingness to pay?

8. Explain how the following factors will shift the supply curve for sparkling wine.

   a. New irrigation technology increases the output of grapes in a vineyard.

   b. Following an increase in the immigration of unskilled labor, the wages of wine-grape pickers fall.

   c. The government sets a minimum wage for seasonal employment.

9. How do the following affect the equilibrium price in a market?

   a. A leftward shift in demand

   b. A rightward shift in supply

   c. A large rightward shift in demand and a small rightward shift in supply

   d. A large leftward shift in supply and a small leftward shift in demand

10. Why was a fixed price of $50 not the best way of allocating used laptops? Suggest other possible ways of distributing the laptops that would be efficient.

Problems

All problems are available in MyEconLab for practice and instructor assignment.

1. Suppose the following table shows the quantity of laundry detergent that is demanded and supplied at various prices in Country 1.

Price ($)	Quantity Demanded (million oz.)	Quantity Supplied (million oz.)
2	65	35
4	60	40
6	55	45
8	50	50
10	45	55
12	40	60
14	35	65

a. Use the data in the table to draw the demand and supply curves in the market for laundry detergent.

b. What is the equilibrium price and quantity in the market?

c. The following tables give the demand and supply schedules for two of Country 1's neighboring countries, Country 2 and Country 3. Suppose these three countries decide to form an economic union and integrate their markets. Use the data in the table to plot the market demand and supply curves in the newly formed economic union. What is the equilibrium price and quantity in the market?

Country 2

Price ($)	Quantity Demanded (million oz.)	Quantity Supplied (million oz.)
2	35	5
4	30	10
6	25	15
8	20	20
10	15	25
12	10	30
14	5	35

Country 3

Price ($)	Quantity Demanded (million oz.)	Quantity Supplied (million oz.)
2	40	10
4	35	15
6	30	20
8	25	25
10	20	30
12	15	35
14	10	40

2. Demand for books is given by the following table.

Price ($)	Quantity of Books Demanded
0	1,000
20	600
40	200
60	0

a. Plot each point on a well-labeled diagram, with quantity on the *x*-axis and price on the *y*-axis.

b. Assume that the demand curve is linear between each of the points in the demand schedule above. Using this assumption, connect the dots with straight lines. What is the quantity demanded when the price is $10?

c. Assume the Law of Demand is true. Also assume the information provided by the demand schedule is correct. However, make no other assumptions. In particular, you should no longer assume that the demand curve is linear between the points in the demand schedule. What can you say about the quantity demanded when the price is $25?

3. Explain how simultaneous shifts in demand and supply curves could explain these situations:

a. The price of insulin injection kits, used by diabetic patients, increases from $45 to $52, but the equilibrium quantity remains the same.

b. A pest attack on the tomato crop increases the cost of producing ketchup. A mild winter causes cattle herds to be unusually large, causing the price of hamburgers to fall. The equilibrium quantity of ketchup is unchanged.

4. Sketch generic supply and demand curves for the housing market and label the equilibrium price and quantity.

   a. A booming economy increases the demand for housing. Show the shift in the demand curve on your graph. What does this do to the price and quantity in the market?

   b. You and a friend both notice that more houses are built in response to this change. Your friend says, "this is a sign that the supply curve is shifting as well." You respond, "no, this is actually just a shift *along* the supply curve." To help your friend understand, demonstrate what you mean on your graph.

   c. As it turns out, there actually is a shift in the supply curve due to an unrelated breakthrough in construction that lowers the cost of building houses. In what direction does the supply curve shift? Show this on your graph.

   d. Relative to the original price and quantity, what is the overall effect of both shifts on price and quantity?

5. Brazil is the world's largest coffee producer. There was a severe drought in Brazil in 2013–2014 that damaged Brazil's coffee crop. The price of coffee beans doubled during the first 3 months of 2014.

   a. Draw and discuss a supply-and-demand diagram to explain the increase in coffee prices.

   b. Are coffee and tea substitutes or complements? Explain.

   c. What do you think the impact of this drought has been on the equilibrium price and quantity of tea? Draw a supply-and-demand diagram for the tea market to explain your answer.

6. There is a sharp freeze in Florida that damages the orange harvest and as a result, the price of oranges rises. Will the equilibrium price of orange juice rise, fall, or remain constant? Will the equilibrium quantity of orange juice rise, fall, or remain constant? Present a supply-and-demand diagram to explain your answers.

7. For each of the following situations, sketch the demand curve as accurately as possible.

   a. Appendectomy is a life-saving operation that some people need. Regardless of the price, the quantity demand is 300,000 every year.

   b. For any price above $5 absolutely nobody will buy your lemonade, but for any price below $5 you find that you are able to sell as much lemonade as you like.

   c. There is only one buyer. For any price above $100 this buyer wants nothing. For any price at or below $100 this buyer wants exactly 20 units.

8. Land in Sonoma, California, can be used either to grow grapes for pinot noir wine or to grow Gravenstein apples. The demand for pinot noir shifts sharply and permanently to the right. What will be the effect of the rightward shift in demand for pinot noir on the equilibrium price and quantity of Gravenstein apples?

9. Suppose one of your friends offered the following argument: a rightward shift in demand will cause an increase in price. The increase in price will cause a rightward shift of the supply curve, which will lead to an offsetting decrease in price. Therefore, it is impossible to tell what effect an increase in demand will have on price. Do you agree with your friend? If not, what is the flaw in your friend's reasoning?

10. New York decides to reduce the consumption of sugary soda by imposing a minimum price of $2.50 per soda. The current equilibrium price is $1.50. Sketch the supply and demand for soda and show the effect of this policy. Clearly label the excess supply in your diagram.

11. Lobsters are plentiful and easy to catch in August but scarce and difficult to catch in November. In addition, vacationers shift the demand for lobsters further to the right in August than in any other month. Compare the equilibrium price and quantity of lobsters in August to the equilibrium price and quantity of lobsters in November. Present and discuss a supply-and-demand diagram to explain your answers.

12. As part of U.S. sugar policy (in 2013), the government offered to buy raw sugar from domestic sugarcane mills at an average price of 18.75 cents per pound. This government offer was made for as much raw sugar as the sugarcane mills produced. Any raw sugar purchased by the government was not sold in the domestic market, as this might have caused raw sugar prices to fall.

a. Under this policy, what do you think the government's demand curve for sugar looks like?

b. What impact does this policy likely have on domestic sugar prices? Explain your reasoning with a supply-and-demand diagram.

13. Suppose demand in a market is described by the equation $Q_D = 6 - P$.

a. Sketch demand.

b. Write out the demand schedule for each integer price up to $6 ($0, $1, $2, . . . , $6).

c. What if another buyer shows up who is "willing to pay any amount" for one unit. If we take her word at face value, what does the new demand look like?

14. *Note: This problem requires some basic algebra.* The demand for computers is $Q_D = 15 - 2P$, where P is the price of computers. Initially, the supply of computers is $Q_S = P$.

a. Find the original equilibrium price and quantity.

b. Suppose the prices of memory chips and motherboards (two important components in computers) rise and as a consequence, the supply curve for computers becomes $Q_S = -3 + P$. Find the new equilibrium price and quantity.

5 The Wealth of Nations: Defining and Measuring Macroeconomic Aggregates

In the United States, what is the total market value of annual economic production?

Beginning with this chapter, we focus on the economy as a whole. Economists refer to the total activity in an economy as *aggregate* economic activity. *Macroeconomics* is the study of aggregate economic activity.

The field of macroeconomics has been completely transformed in the past century. Before World War I, no country even had a system for measuring aggregate economic activity. Back then, economists had to guess what was happening by looking at small pieces of the bigger picture. They studied things like the tonnage of steel that was manufactured or the volume of freight that was transported on rail lines. These indicators were used to make educated guesses about aggregate economic activity. If freight

CHAPTER **OUTLINE**

shipments were booming, it probably meant that the aggregate economy was booming too, but nobody could be certain.

Today, we no longer have to guess what is happening in the economy. Modern economies have a sophisticated system that measures the level of aggregate activity. Careful measurement has made it possible to study the aggregate economy and to design policies that improve its performance.

In this chapter, we set the stage by answering a foundational question: How does it all add up? How do we calculate the total market value of aggregate economic production?

5.1 Macroeconomic Questions

Until now we have been studying microeconomics: how individuals, households, firms, and governments make choices, and how those choices affect the prices and allocations of specific goods and services. Now it is time to turn to macroeconomics. Recall from Chapter 1 that macroeconomics is the study of economic aggregates and economy-wide phenomena, like the annual growth rate of a country's total economic output, or the annual percentage increase in the overall cost of living. Macro, which is shorthand for macroeconomics, is our new topic.

Macroeconomic analysis explains past patterns in aggregate economic activity and tries to predict future changes. For example, macroeconomists are interested in the enormous differences in income across countries and the creation of policies that would enable countries with lower income to catch up.

Income per capita—in other words, average income per person—in the United States is more than twice the level in Portugal, four times the level in China, and almost 100 times the level in Zimbabwe. The comparisons are adjusted for the cost of living in these different countries. How do we measure these cross-country differences? What causes them? How long will they persist? In Chapters 6–8 we discuss these enormous disparities across countries.

China has been catching up to the United States very quickly. China's economy has been growing four times as quickly as the U.S. economy for more than 30 years. Will

Income per capita is income per person. It is calculated by dividing a nation's aggregate income by the number of people in the country.

Zimbabwe has spectacular natural resources like Victoria Falls but has not succeeded in developing a healthy economy or a robust tourism industry. Today, most visitors to Victoria Falls stay on the Zambian side of the border, where there is a vibrant tourism industry, and never enter Zimbabwe.

A **recession** is a period (lasting at least two quarters) in which aggregate economic output falls.

A worker is officially **unemployed** if he or she does not have a job, has actively looked for work in the prior 4 weeks, and is currently available for work.

The **unemployment rate** is the fraction of the labor force that is unemployed.

China eventually match the level of U.S. income per capita? Will China surpass the United States? Or will something else happen? For example, Japan experienced a long-run slowdown in economic growth starting around 1990, when its income per capita was about to overtake that of the United States. Over two decades later, the United States is still ahead. Why does economic growth slow down as income per capita rises?

What can be done to improve living conditions in impoverished nations like Zimbabwe? Annual income per capita in Zimbabwe was $924 in 2015, barely enough for survival. Figuring out how to make low-income countries' economies grow faster is a question of enormous importance for human well-being. Malnutrition and lack of healthcare cause tens of millions of deaths annually worldwide.

To understand how to achieve long-run economic prosperity, we need to understand how different government policies augment or undermine economic growth. Corruption and confusion can lead policymakers down the wrong path. Which policies reduce long-run growth, and how can we avoid them in the future?

Macroeconomists also study the year-to-year, or "short-run," fluctuations in economic activity. Why does economic growth sometimes stall, or even temporarily turn negative? We call an economic downturn lasting at least two quarters a **recession** (a quarter is one-fourth of a year).

During recessions the *unemployment rate*, one of the most important macroeconomic variables, rises. A person is officially **unemployed** if three conditions are satisfied: he or she (1) does not have a job, (2) has actively looked for work in the prior 4 weeks, and (3) is currently available for work. Fluctuations in the **unemployment rate**—the fraction of the labor force that is unemployed—are covered in detail in Chapter 9.

To see an example of economic fluctuations, consider the U.S. recession that ran from 2007 to 2009, when the U.S. economy shrank by 4.3 percent, and the unemployment rate rose from 5 percent to 10 percent. At the same time, the world experienced a series of financial crises, including stock market crashes, collapsing housing prices, mortgage defaults, and bank failures. Why did these events occur, and what should governments have done to reduce their severity? What caused worldwide stock markets to lose over half their value in a year's time? Why did so many major banks suddenly become insolvent?

Though the recession of 2007–2009 was calamitous, it does not hold a candle to the Great Depression, which stretched from 1929 to 1939. From 1929 to 1933, production fell

During the peak of the Great Depression, 25 percent of the U.S. workforce didn't have a job. Some towns put up signs discouraging job seekers from looking for employment in the area.

by nearly 30 percent, and the unemployment rate rose from 3 percent to 25 percent of the labor force. In July 1932, the U.S. stock market reached the bottom of an 87 percent roller-coaster plunge from its peak in September 1929. Are there policies that will enable us to avoid such disasters in the future? Or are we only able to respond after the fact? Could the 2007–2009 financial crisis have turned into another Great Depression? We discuss aggregate economic fluctuations and the policies that attempt to smooth out these fluctuations in Chapters 12 and 13.

These are all important questions. To answer them, we need some special tools and new models. The first thing that we must do is measure what we are studying: a country's aggregate economy. This is a seemingly impossible task. How can we measure the total activity of millions of economic agents? A hundred years ago, nobody knew how to do this. Fortunately, economic science has progressed. Today, we have a framework called the **national income accounts**, which we use to measure the entire economy. In the United States, the formal name for this system of national accounts is the **national income and product accounts**. Once we understand how these accounts work, we will be ready to start answering the interesting and important questions posed above.

National income accounts measure the level of aggregate economic activity in a country.

The **national income and product accounts** is the system of national income accounts that is used by the U.S. government.

5.2 National Income Accounts: Production = Expenditure = Income

To measure aggregate economic activity, we will need to take both quantities and prices into account. Let's start by considering the hypothetical nation of Fordica. Fordica is a small country with only one employer, the Ford Motor Company (hereafter, "Ford"), which produces 5 million cars each year. We assume that Fordica has 200,000 citizens who are the workers in Ford's factories. We'll look at three different ways of thinking about Fordica's economy—a production approach, an expenditure approach, and an income approach.

Production

As economists, we want to measure the total market value of annual production in the nation of Fordica. To keep things simple, we assume that Ford needs only its own machines and the labor of Fordica's citizens to build cars. We won't worry right now about other inputs like steel and plastic. In fact, we'll momentarily assume that these other inputs don't exist. We'll also assume that all of Ford's plants and equipment—in other words, all its capital—are in the country of Fordica.

To determine the market value of production in Fordica, we multiply the quantity of cars produced by the market price of each car. For example, if the market price of a Ford is $30,000, then Fordica has total annual production of:

$$(5 \text{ million cars}) \times (\$30,000/\text{car}) = \$150 \text{ billion.}$$

By multiplying production quantities (during a particular year) and corresponding market prices, we have a measure that reflects the market value of the goods produced in the economy during that year. So the economy of Fordica produces goods with a market value of $150 billion per year.

Economists call this measure of aggregate economic activity **gross domestic product,** or **GDP**. We define GDP as the market value of the final goods and services produced in a country during a given period of time. GDP is always associated with a particular period of time, usually either a year or a quarter. For example, "GDP in 2018" is the market value of the final goods and services produced during the year 2018. "GDP in Q1:2018" is the market value of the final goods and services produced during the first quarter of the year 2018. When talking about aggregate economic activity, the first quarter begins in January (January–March); the second quarter begins in April (April–June); the third quarter begins in July (July–September); and the fourth quarter begins in October (October–December).

Gross domestic product (GDP) is the market value of the final goods and services produced in a country during a given period of time.

The real-life Ford Motor Company employs about 200,000 workers world-wide. It manufactures 6 million cars per year, generating annual sales of $150 billion.

The definition of GDP includes the word *final*, which signifies that we are interested in valuing the end product in a chain of production. Components that are put together to make a final product don't get counted separately, because that would imply double counting. If we are going to count the *total* value of a car, we don't need to separately count the value of the car engine. The engine is implicitly included when we value the final good, which is the complete car.

GDP is a measure of production, not a measure of sales to consumers. So something that is produced is counted in GDP even if it is not sold to a customer. For example, Ford will increase its inventory of (unsold) cars if it manufactures a car in 2018 but doesn't sell it in 2018. Production that goes into inventories counts as part of GDP.

Expenditure

There's a second way to think about the level of aggregate activity in the economy of Fordica. This second method yields exactly the same answer as the previous, production-based, method. Households and firms, some of whom reside in Fordica and some of whom reside in foreign countries, are going to buy all of the cars produced in this economy. If we add up all these car purchases, we will find that the total expenditure on Fordica's output is exactly $150 billion (again).

You might object by asking, "What if some of the goods don't get sold?" Economists reply that those unsold goods are *owned* by a firm, and those goods are therefore counted as part of the firm's inventory. In the accounting system that we are describing here, that inventory is coded as having been "purchased" by the firm. Including both households' expenditures on cars and firms' expenditures to accumulate car inventories, total expenditures again sum to $150 billion.

Income

First we focused on the market value of the goods and services that were *produced* by Ford, the sole company in the country of Fordica: $150 billion. Then we focused on the market value of the goods and services that were *purchased* from Ford: also $150 billion. Alternatively, we could have focused on what Ford's workers and Ford's owners earned—in other words, their income. Let's consider that alternative approach, which is the third way to think about the level of aggregate economic activity.

We've already calculated that Ford generates $150 billion of revenue. Assume that it pays $X to its workers, and it therefore gives the rest of its revenue ($150 billion – $X) to the people who own the company. So the income that is paid to the workers in Fordica and the income that is paid to the capital in Fordica sums up to

$$\$X + (\$150\,\text{billion} - \$X) = \$150\,\text{billion}.$$

This is the identical market value—$150 billion—that we determined the economy produced in our earlier calculations. It is also the market value of expenditures on goods and services produced in Fordica.

The fact that we keep coming up with the amount $150 billion is not a coincidence. Because of the way we've set up the system of national income accounts, every dollar of revenue must either go to a worker or an owner. So the total value of revenue must equal the total value of income received by workers and owners. This necessary equivalence is referred to as an *identity*. Two variables are related by an **identity** when the two variables are defined in a way that makes them mathematically identical. The equivalence of the value of production, the value of expenditure, and the value of income may not be apparent at first glance, but the three concepts have been defined so that they are necessarily identical.

You can now understand the following aggregate accounting identity:

$$\text{Production} = \text{Expenditure} = \text{Income}.$$

This identity is the key conceptual point of this chapter and the foundation on which most macroeconomic analysis is built. Now let's delve more deeply into the system of national income accounts.

Two variables are related by an **identity** when the two variables are defined in a way that makes them mathematically identical.

This identity [Production = Expenditure = Income] is the key conceptual point of this chapter and the foundation on which most macroeconomic analysis is built.

Circular Flows

5.1

5.2

5.3

5.4

Factors of production are the inputs to the production process.

Factors of production are the inputs to the production process. Factors of production come in two key forms: *capital* and *labor*. We'll have more to say about capital below, but for now it is helpful to simplify our analysis by thinking of capital as physical capital—for instance, land, factories, and machines.

Both physical capital and labor are "owned" by households (and some other institutions, like universities and charitable foundations, that we will lump together with "households"). Households own the physical capital in the economy, either directly or indirectly, because firms are owned by shareholders, and shareholders are households.

To understand how the three parts of the national income accounts—production, expenditure, and income—relate to one another, we need to think about the connections between households and firms. Firms, like the aircraft manufacturer Boeing, demand physical capital and labor. Firms supply goods and services, like airplanes. Households demand goods and services, like air travel. Households supply physical capital and labor.

We can explain the connections between households and firms with a circular flow diagram of the type displayed in Exhibit 5.1. This diagram highlights four kinds of economic flows that connect households and firms. It includes the three kinds of flows that we discussed in the Fordica example (Production = Expenditure = Income) and adds a fourth category, factors of production:

1. Production
2. Expenditure
3. Income
4. Factors of production

Exhibit 5.1 is admittedly a simplification of the economy, because it leaves out very important institutions like governments, markets, banks, and foreign countries. We'll have a lot to say about those critical omissions in the chapters to come. Despite these omissions, the circular flow diagram provides a useful way of understanding the basic structure of a modern economy. The circular flow diagram presents two main decision makers—firms and households—and it shows the four types of flows listed above.

Exhibit 5.1 Circular Flow Diagram

Economists have designed national income accounts that measure GDP in four equivalent ways: production, expenditure, income, and factors of production. The circular flow diagram provides a visual way of remembering the relationships among these four equivalent systems. Firms on the left produce goods and services (production), which households on the right purchase (expenditure). Firms pay households for physical capital and labor (income), which firms use as factors of production (factors). The national income accounting system is set up so that all four sets of flows are equal in market value.

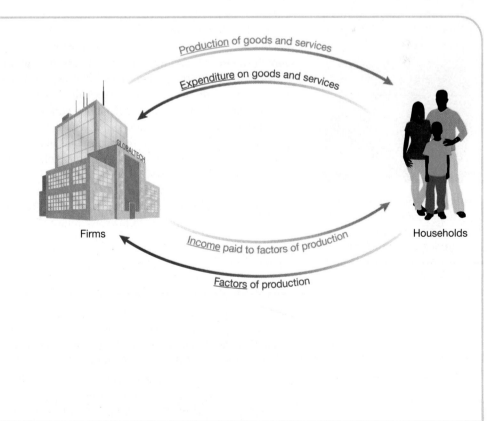

Production of goods and services

Expenditure on goods and services

Firms

Households

Income paid to factors of production

Factors of production

Production and expenditure. A Ford Mustang is produced by Ford (production), and it is purchased by Ford's customers (expenditure).

Production represents the goods and services that are produced by firms. These goods and services are ultimately sold to households. We therefore draw an arrow from the firm sector to the household sector when talking about production. For example, a Ford Mustang starts life on the factory floor and ends up in someone's garage.

Expenditure represents the payments for goods and services. These payments are made by households to firms. So we draw an arrow from the household sector to the firm sector when talking about expenditure. Continuing our earlier example, the household pays Ford $30,000 for a Mustang. Note that production and expenditure both involve goods and services, so these two flows are grouped together. They jointly represent the market for goods and services.

Income represents the payments that are made from firms to households to compensate the households for the use of their physical capital and labor (in other words, the use of the households' factors of production). These payments include things like wages, salaries, interest, and dividends. We therefore draw an arrow from the firm sector to the household sector when talking about income. For instance, the average labor compensation received by Ford's employees is about $70,000 per year.

Factors of production represent the productive resources that are owned by households and used by firms in the production process. Because factors of production—both labor and physical capital—are directly or indirectly owned by households, we draw an arrow from the household sector to the firm sector when talking about factors of production.

The remarkable thing about these four types of transactions or "flows" is that they must all be exactly the same in market value. That's where the system of national income accounts comes in. If we do the accounting correctly, the market value of expenditure must equal the market value of production. Likewise, the market value of expenditure must equal the market value of income of the households in the economy. Finally, the market value of income must equal the market value of the factors of production—labor and physical capital—that are receiving those income payments. These relationships are just mathematical consequences of the ways we define the system of national income accounts.

Although the circular flow diagram contains four sets of flows with identical market values, in the discussion that follows, we return to our earlier three-part system of national income accounts: Production = Expenditures = Income. In practice, these are the three parts of the national income accounts that government statisticians actually measure.

National Income Accounts: Production

We now revisit each of the methods for calculating national income and dig a little deeper: what happens in a world outside Fordica, where multiple firms exist? First, let's consider production-based national income accounts. Production-based accounts sum up the market value that is added by each domestic firm in the production process. More formally, production-based accounts measure each firm's **value added**, which is the firm's sales revenue minus the firm's purchases of intermediate products from other firms.

For example, consider Dell Technologies, which owns a computer company you might recognize called Dell. Three decades ago, Dell assembled almost all of its

A factor of production and a source of income. This famous image of a factory worker appeared in a poster designed to boost worker morale during World War II.

Each firm's **value added** is the firm's sales revenue minus its purchases of intermediate products from other firms.

computers at its own facilities in the United States. These days, Dell buys most of its computers from foreign manufacturers, especially in Asia. Consider Dell's value added when it sells a laptop for $1,000 directly to a U.S. consumer. In this case, Dell pays the foreign supplier $600, and Dell's value added is the difference: $400 = $1,000 − $600. This value added of $400 derives from two factors of production: Dell's domestic employees and Dell's domestic physical capital. Accordingly, the $400 is partly paid out in wages (to the employees) and partly paid out in accounting profits (to the owners of the capital).

Life gets a bit more complicated when Dell sells the same computer at the same price at a third-party retailer like Walmart, Best Buy, or Staples. In this case, Best Buy pays Dell $900 for the computer, which Dell bought from the foreign producer for $600. Now Dell's value added is $300 = $900 − $600.

Exhibit 5.2 illustrates these two transactions. Panel (a) illustrates the case of a direct sale from Dell to a consumer, generating value added of $400 for the labor and capital at Dell. Panel (b) illustrates the case of a sale from Dell to a third-party retailer (like Best Buy), generating value added of $300 for the labor and capital at Dell.

We could now ask what else gets counted as U.S. GDP in these chains of economic activity (even if it isn't counted as part of Dell's value added). The foreign factories don't count toward U.S. GDP. The production of the laptops in a foreign factory is part of a foreign country's GDP, because the factory is in that foreign country.

The production-based accounting system implies that importing some good from abroad and selling it to a U.S. consumer at the same import price doesn't add value. However,

Exhibit 5.2 Dell's Value Added

In panel (a), a U.S. consumer spends $1,000 on a Dell laptop, buying the laptop directly from Dell. Because Dell pays a foreign manufacturer $600 for the laptop, Dell's value added is $400 = $1,000 − $600. In panel (b), a U.S. consumer spends $1,000 on a Dell laptop, buying the laptop at Best Buy. Because Best Buy pays Dell $900 for the laptop and Dell pays a foreign manufacturer $600 for the laptop, Dell's value added in this case is only $300 = $900 − $600.

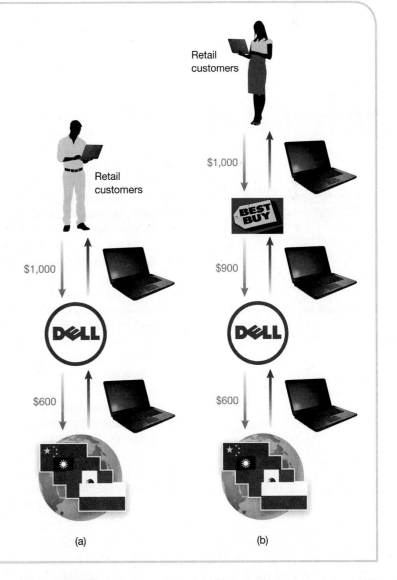

(a) (b)

importing something for $600 and reselling it for $1,000 is a source of production—$400 of value added, to be precise. Dell's ability to mark up its price relative to the import cost comes from a combination of marketing, corporate reputation, customer convenience, and bundled services like access to call centers.

Likewise, Best Buy's ability to sell Dell's computers is another source of U.S. value added. Best Buy isn't making something in a factory, but its ability to buy goods at wholesale prices and sell those goods at higher retail prices reflects its value added and consequently its contribution to GDP. Best Buy's value added is not the revenue that Best Buy receives from its customers. Best Buy's value added is the difference between the revenue that Best Buy receives when it sells Dell's computers and the amount that Best Buy pays Dell for the laptops. Accordingly, Best Buy's value added from selling a Dell laptop is $100 = $1,000 − $900. This value added is another component of U.S GDP.

Adding up the value added generated by all firms in the United States will sum to U.S. GDP.

National Income Accounts: Expenditure

Let's now turn to the second, mathematically equivalent, way of measuring GDP. Expenditure-based national income accounts measure the purchases of goods and services produced in the domestic economy. These purchases can be assigned to five categories.

(1) Consumption. This is the market value of consumption goods and consumption services that are bought by domestic households. Such consumption expenditures cover everything from Frisbees to foot massages. This category includes all consumption expenditures except expenditures that are made on residential construction (which is part of the next category). Expenditures that are made to buy a pre-existing house or apartment do not show up anywhere in the national income accounts, because such expenditures are just a transfer of an asset from one household to another and are not something that was produced in the current year or quarter.

(2) Investment. This is the market value of new physical capital that is bought by domestic households and domestic firms, including business inventories. Technically it is called *private investment*, but it is usually just referred to as investment. Such new physical capital includes residential houses, business inventories (for example, the Camaro waiting to be sold at a Chevrolet dealership, or the box of Corn Flakes waiting to be sold at Walmart), business structures (for example, office towers and factories), and business equipment (for example, computers and freight trains). When macroeconomists talk about investment, they are referring only to purchases of new physical capital and not to financial investments like purchases of stocks or bonds. This difference in usage generates confusion, because non-economists are more familiar with the everyday financial meaning of "making an investment" (for instance, buying a mutual fund or contributing money to an Individual Retirement Account), which is not what macroeconomists have in mind. In the language of macroeconomics, investment is only the purchase of new physical capital, like a new supertanker, a new factory, or a new house.

(3) Government expenditure. This is the market value of government purchases of goods and services. Tanks and bridges are two examples of government expenditure. For the purposes of the national income accounts, government expenditure excludes transfer payments (for example, Social Security payments to retirees) and also excludes interest paid on government debt. These categories are omitted because they represent payments to other agents in the economy who will use those payments to buy goods and services. To avoid double counting, these government payments to other agents are not counted as government expenditure on goods and services.

(4) Exports. This is the market value of all domestically produced goods and services that are sold to households, firms, and governments in foreign countries. We measure exports in terms of value added. If a U.S. agricultural company exports flour to Japanese supermarkets, the value of this export is the price that the U.S. company receives from the Japanese supermarket chain, not the price at which the Japanese supermarket sells the flour to Japanese households.

These first four categories are non-overlapping. In other words, they do not involve double counting. Each purchase appears in only one of the four categories above.

(5) Imports. This is the market value of all foreign-produced goods and services that are sold to domestic households, domestic firms, and the domestic government. Imports are already counted as part of consumption expenditures, investment expenditures, and government expenditures. Hence, imports overlap with the first three categories in our list. We'll explain why we need to account for this overlap in a moment. But you actually already know the answer if you remember the example of Dell selling U.S. consumers laptops manufactured in foreign factories. When calculating Dell's value added, we subtracted the payments that Dell made to the foreign manufacturers of Dell laptops. Likewise, when calculating U.S. GDP on an expenditure basis, we're going to subtract the value added of imports.

> **Imports** are the market value of all foreign-produced goods and services that are sold to domestic households, domestic firms, and the domestic government.

We are now ready to use these five categories—consumption, investment, government expenditure, exports, and imports—to calculate GDP. Let Y represent the total market value of goods and services that are produced in the domestic economy (that is, the GDP). We'll use C to represent consumption: household expenditures on consumption of goods and services, including expenditure on consumption of goods and services produced domestically and abroad. Variable I represents investment: expenditures on investment goods by private agents (excluding the government), including investment goods produced domestically and abroad. We'll let G represent government expenditure: government purchases of goods and services, including goods and services produced domestically and abroad.

If the United States were a closed economy—in other words, if the United States didn't trade with any other countries—then its GDP would simply be $Y = C + I + G$. But we do trade with other countries, so this formula isn't correct. We need to account for the fact that exports are part of U.S. GDP (but are not already contained in $C + I + G$), whereas imports are not part of U.S. GDP (but are contained in $C + I + G$). Exports are produced domestically and sold abroad, so they need to be included as another category of expenditure on U.S. production. Imports are produced abroad, so they need to be excluded from our calculation of expenditure on U.S. production. We are now ready to make these two adjustments.

> The GDP equation shows that the market value of domestic production is equal to the total expenditure of domestic economic agents ($C + I + G$), plus the expenditure of foreign agents on exports from the domestic economy (X), minus the value of domestic expenditure that was imported (M).

Let X represent exports: the value of goods and services produced in the domestic economy and purchased by economic agents in foreign countries. Let M represent imports: the value of goods and services produced in foreign countries and purchased by economic agents in the domestic economy. Finally, note that exports minus imports, or $X - M$, is the trade balance. When X is greater than M, the value of exports is greater than that of imports, so the country runs a trade surplus. When X is less than M, the value of exports is less than that of imports, so the country runs a trade deficit.

We can now calculate the total value of expenditures on goods and services produced in the domestic economy:

$$Y = C + I + G + X - M \quad \text{(national income accounting identity)}.$$

The GDP equation shows that the market value of domestic production is equal to the total expenditure of domestic economic agents $(C + I + G)$, plus the expenditure of foreign agents on exports from the domestic economy (X), minus the value of domestic expenditure that was imported (M). We subtract imports because expenditure on foreign production is already included in the terms C, I, and G. To remove this expenditure on foreign production, we subtract imports, M.

> The **national income accounting identity**, $Y = C + I + G + X - M$, decomposes GDP into consumption + investment + government expenditure + exports − imports.

This identity, which decomposes GDP into $C + I + G + X - M$, is so important that we give it a name: the **national income accounting identity**. We'll use it many times in our study of the macroeconomy.

EVIDENCE-BASED ECONOMICS

Q: In the United States, what is the total market value of annual economic production?

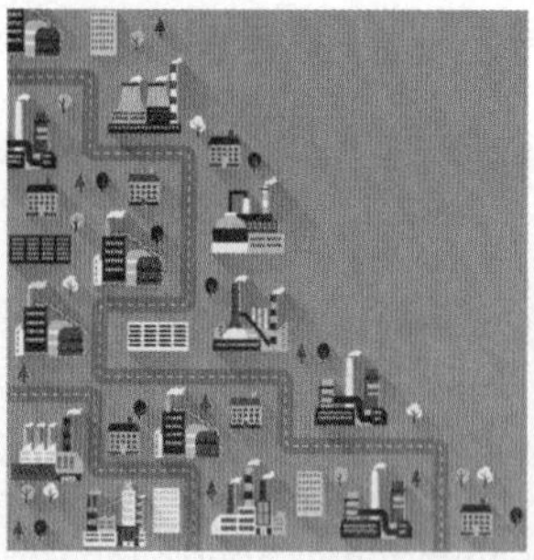

overnment statisticians carefully measure GDP, the total market value of economic output. In the United States, this work is conducted by the Bureau of Economic Analysis in the Department of Commerce. In 2015, the Bureau of Economic Analysis reported that U.S. GDP was $18.0 trillion. That year, the U.S. population was 321.8 million people. So GDP per person—in other words, GDP per capita—was about $55,620. Note that GDP per capita is equivalent to income per capita, which we introduced earlier in this chapter.

It is also valuable to study the components of GDP using the national income accounting identity that we just discussed. Exhibit 5.3 reports these data for the United States in 2015. We can observe several important properties. First, the overwhelming share of GDP is represented by household consumption. In 2015, consumption made up 69 percent of GDP. Government expenditure comes in far behind, at only 18 percent of GDP. Investment follows next with 17 percent. Exports account for 13 percent of GDP, and imports account for 16 percent of GDP. Notice that imports appear in Exhibit 5.3 with a negative sign, because when calculating GDP, imports are subtracted out after we add up all other components. You should confirm that the items in Exhibit 5.3 add up to GDP (to within the rounding error).

The fraction of GDP in each category—which is called the GDP share in that category—has been roughly constant over the past 80 years. Exhibit 5.4 reports the GDP shares from 1929 to 2015. In other words, Exhibit 5.4 reports the ratio of each expenditure category to GDP. The sum of these shares, minus the import share, must sum to one. Exhibit 5.4 shows that consumption has consistently represented about two-thirds of economic activity.

Government expenditures have consistently hovered around 20 percent of economic activity, with two exceptions. First, at the very beginning of the sample period, government expenditures accounted for only 10 percent of GDP. Large governments did not become the norm in the modern world until World War II.

Second, government expenditures temporarily absorbed a particularly large share of GDP during World War II. The high point was nearly 50 percent of GDP. It is natural that during major wars the government accounts for a much larger share of a country's economic output, because a war effort is run almost exclusively by the government. The rise in government activity during World War II is mirrored by a fall in consumption and a fall in (private) investment.

MyEconLab Real-time data

Exhibit 5.3 U.S. 2015 GDP and GDP Shares (Expenditure-Based Accounting)

U.S. gross domestic product (GDP) in 2015 was $18.0 trillion. Each component of GDP is expressed as a percentage of GDP, or a GDP "share" (component/GDP). Rounding causes the components to fail to sum to total GDP.

Source: Based on Bureau of Economic Analysis, National Income and Product Accounts.

	Value (Trillions of Dollars)	Share of GDP
Gross domestic product	18.0	100.0%
Consumption	12.3	68.3%
+ Investment	3.1	17.2%
+ Government expenditure	3.2	17.8%
+ Exports	2.3	12.8%
− Imports	−2.8	−16.0%

MyEconLab Real-time data

Exhibit 5.4 U.S. GDP Shares (1929–2015)

GDP shares have been relatively constant over time, except during World War II.

Source: Based on Bureau of Economic Analysis, National Income and Product Accounts.

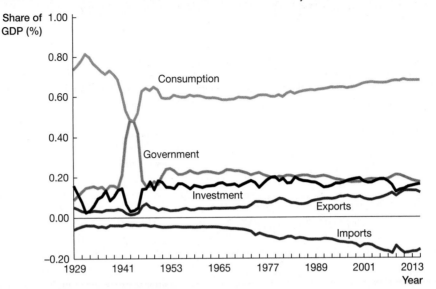

There is one final property that is important to note in Exhibit 5.4: the export and import shares have both been getting larger in absolute value over the past 80 years. Transportation technology has made it less expensive to ship goods anywhere in the world. Information technology has also made it easier for residents of one country to provide services to residents of other countries (think of call centers in India). Falling transportation and telecommunication costs have fueled an ongoing rise in trade, as optimizers look beyond their national borders to buy the goods and services that they want. Increasing exports show up as a rising share of exports. Because imports appear as a negative number in the GDP identity, rising imports show up as a movement in the import share further below zero.

Question

In the United States, what is the total market value of annual economic production?

Answer

In 2015, the Bureau of Economic Analysis reported that U.S. GDP was $18.0 trillion, or $55,620 per capita.[1]

Data

National income and product accounts compiled by the Bureau of Economic Analysis.

Caveat

National income accounts omit many types of economic production, an issue that we discuss later in this chapter.

LETTING THE
DATA SPEAK

Saving versus Investment

Economists use the national income accounting identity to study saving and investment. To derive an equation for saving, start with GDP, which is equivalent to national income, and subtract the things that households and the government consume. In other words, subtract consumption expenditures and government expenditures. We then find that

$$Saving = Y - C - G$$
$$= (C + I + G + X - M) - C - G$$
$$= I + X - M.$$

To get from the first equation to the second equation, we replaced Y with its components from the national income accounting identity: $C + I + G + X - M$. The final equation in our derivation can be written out in words:

$$Saving = Investment + Exports - Imports.$$

In most countries, exports and imports are relatively close in magnitude. In that case, exports minus imports will be close to zero, enabling us to further simplify our expression:

$$Saving = Investment.$$

This simplified expression is just an approximation, since exports and imports are never exactly the same when a country trades with other countries. However, this equation will be exactly true for a closed economy, which is an economy that does not trade with other countries. In a closed economy, exports and imports are both equal to zero.

Let's now take the last equation and divide both sides by GDP. You'll then see that the saving rate (saving divided by GDP) is equal to the investment rate (investment divided by GDP):

$$\frac{Saving}{GDP} = \frac{Investment}{GDP}.$$

Using U.S. data from 1929 to 2015, we can compare the saving rate and the investment rate year by year. Exhibit 5.5 graphs a scatter plot of these two ratios. Each point plots a single year of data: the saving rate for that year is on the x-axis, and the investment rate for that year is on the y-axis. As you can see, the saving rate and the investment rate move together very closely; the cloud of data points stays relatively close to the 45-degree line (which is plotted in red).

Exhibit 5.5 implies that saving is roughly equal to investment. We'll use this fact in Chapter 6 when we start to discuss the determinants of economic growth, including investment in physical capital.

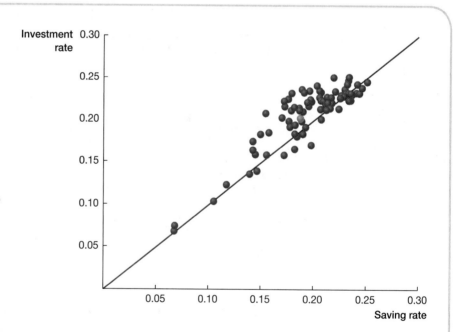

Exhibit 5.5 The Relationship Between the Saving Rate and the Investment Rate (1929–2015)

Each point plots a single year of data: the saving rate for that year is on the x-axis and the investment rate for that year is on the y-axis. The scatter plot implies that the saving rate and the investment rate tend to move together from year to year. The points stay close to the 45-degree line (which is plotted in red). The green circle represents the last year of data in the scatter plot, 2015.

Source: Based on Bureau of Economic Analysis, National Income and Product Accounts.

Home ownership is an important source of capital income. If you own your home, you don't need to pay rent (though you may need to pay interest on a mortgage). Economists consider the non-payment of rent to be a form of capital income to homeowners. The implied income from home ownership is the amount of money the owner would have needed to spend had he or she been renting the same kind of residence from a landlord.

Labor income is any form of payment that compensates people for their work.

Capital income is any form of payment that derives from owning physical or financial capital.

National Income Accounting: Income

In the previous subsections, we examined the economy by studying GDP as a production concept—the discussion of value added—and then by studying GDP as an expenditure concept—the discussion of the national income accounting identity, $Y = C + I + G + X - M$. As explained at the start of the chapter, we can also study GDP as an income concept. Recall that income-based national accounts track the income of the various agents in the economy. Recall, too, that aggregate income is identical to aggregate production and aggregate expenditure. So if aggregate expenditure was $18.0 trillion in 2015, then aggregate production and aggregate income were also each $18.0 trillion in 2015.

Income payments come in two key categories. First, there is *income paid for people's work*. We call this **labor income**. This category includes familiar items like wages, salary, workers' health insurance, and workers' pension benefits. It also includes every other way that people are directly or indirectly paid for their labor, including signing bonuses, free parking spaces at work, and the value to the CEO of being able to use the company jet on weekends.

The second category of income payments is income (or benefits) realized by the owners of physical capital (for instance, a house) or financial capital (for instance, stocks and bonds). We refer to this as **capital income**. This category includes many things: for example, dividends paid to shareholders, interest paid to lenders, earnings retained by corporations, rent payments made to landlords, and the benefits of living in your own house!

This division into labor income and capital income may encourage the misleading intuition that people who receive labor income are different from those who receive capital income. However, most people in the economy receive both. For example, a 50-year-old worker with a job, a house, and a retirement savings account will receive labor income from her job, capital income from her house (the implicit value of having a roof over her head), and capital income from her retirement savings account (dividends).

It is also important to remember that firms are owned by households. Firms can't own themselves. When a firm earns income, it is the owners of the firm who are the ultimate beneficiaries. Most large firms have shares that are traded on the stock market. In this case, the firm is owned by hundreds of millions of shareholders around the globe. The beneficiaries of capital income are these shareholders.

Finally, it is interesting to ask what fraction of income payments are labor payments and what fraction of income payments are capital payments. In the United States and other developed economies, nearly two-thirds of income payments goes to labor and one-third goes to capital.

5.3 What Isn't Measured by GDP?

Before leaving our homes in the morning, many of us go to the Web to look up the current weather conditions. Some weather Web sites report a single temperature and a simple picture.

This weather report leaves a lot of details out. Humidity, haze, wind speed, and hundreds of other factors all contribute to the actual conditions that we experience as we walk to work or sprint for the train. Nevertheless, commuters are grateful for a simple summary that tells them most of what they need to know about the local weather.

Likewise, GDP and national income accounting is a useful system for taking the temperature of the economy. It's not perfect, and it necessarily leaves out a lot of details. Nevertheless, GDP does a good job of telling us much of what we need to know about the level, fluctuations, and long-run trends in economic activity. With this tool in hand, we are ready to try to measure and predict the behavior of the entire economy.

Before we begin, though, it's important to discuss what GDP leaves out, so we know what GDP can and can't do. GDP has many quirks that limit its value as a measure of societal well-being or even of overall economic activity.

This is a simplified but useful summary of the weather. Likewise, GDP is a simplified summary of the economy.

The cruise ship *Costa Concordia* hit a reef off the Italian coast in 2012. Thirty-two people died, and the ship, which cost $600 million to build, was sold for scrap. The loss of physical capital is an example of capital depreciation. GDP does not take account of capital depreciation.

Economists are a bold breed. Measuring the production of an entire economy can't be done exactly, but we do it *anyway*. Sticking our collective heads in the sand and waiting for the perfect system of measurement to be invented is not a satisfactory alternative. We believe that it's much better to have an imperfect measure than to throw up our hands and give up.

Physical Capital Depreciation

We start by noting that GDP omits physical capital depreciation, which is the reduction of the value of physical capital due to obsolescence or wear and tear. Most productive processes cause physical capital to lose some value over time. Driving a tractor-trailer wears down the brakes and the tires. Pumping oil from the ground depletes remaining petroleum reserves.

If we want a complete picture of economic production, we might want to take into account the physical capital depreciation that accompanies production and subtract that depreciation from the value of total production.

Most governments do try to measure depreciation in their national accounts, though they do *not* subtract depreciation when calculating GDP. Depreciation analyses tend to find that depreciation is equal to about 10–20 percent of GDP. For example, the U.S. national accounts estimate that depreciation is large enough so that if it were subtracted, it would offset about 16 percent of GDP.

This sounds like a problem that has been solved, but the situation is actually more complicated. First, the depreciation estimates in the national accounts are more like sophisticated guesswork—"guesstimates"—than something that we know how to measure precisely. Second, the depreciation estimates don't even attempt to cover many hard-to-analyze categories, like depreciation of oil reserves. Third, thinking about physical capital depreciation raises many related questions. For example, changes in our health are also left out of the GDP calculations. Some productive processes make workers less healthy—for example, backbreaking work in a coal mine or exposure to toxic chemicals in a manufacturing process. If we account for physical capital depreciation, should we also try to calculate depreciation of health and *human capital* (a concept that we will return to in Chapter 6)?

In sum, trying to measure depreciation is a complicated conceptual issue, and the standard measure of GDP does not account for any type of depreciation.

Home Production

GDP also stumbles when it comes to home production, which is not included anywhere in the national income accounts. If you grow your own flowers (without buying seeds or shovels from a plant store), the bouquet you create is not measured in GDP, but if you buy domestically grown flowers from the local florist, every dollar is included in GDP. If you knit your own wool cap using wool from the sheep that you keep on your farm, nothing shows up in GDP, but if you knit a cap from the same wool and sell it to your neighbor (reporting the transaction on your taxes), every dollar counts in GDP. Sometimes the accounting rules are laughable. For example, GDP goes down if you marry your gardener.

All economists agree that excluding home production is a flaw in the GDP accounts, but we do not yet have a way to measure home production. There is no market transaction, market price, or measurable quantity that accompanies home production. What is the market value of a home-cooked meal? Families have been debating that philosophical question for a long time.

If we were talking only about a home-cooked meatloaf here and there, this omission would not be a big deal. But a large fraction of economic activity takes place in the home. Most families maintain their own homes by personally dusting, vacuuming, mopping, scrubbing, and polishing them. People often mow their own grass, rake their own leaves, and weed their own flower beds. Most families eat most of their meals at home.

Finally, there is the very important category of childcare, which is illustrated by the following example. Suppose there are two parents in different households, Avery and Micah. Suppose that they each have kids. If Avery and Micah stay home to care for their *own* kids, there is no market transaction, and the childcare is not recorded in GDP. In contrast, if Avery takes care of Micah's kids and is paid a salary of $40,000, and Micah takes care of

Should childcare be measured in GDP, even when it is not a market-based activity?

Avery's kids and receives a salary of $40,000, then annual GDP rises by the sum, $80,000. Note that the children are being cared for regardless of whether this care is measured by GDP. When each parent cares for his or her own kids, childcare is produced without a market transaction, and childcare is omitted from GDP. When each parent takes care of the *other* family's kids, childcare generates a market transaction and GDP increases by $80,000.

There are two reasons economists lose sleep worrying about all of this. First, a large fraction of the adult population does stay at home to work. We know from surveys of time use that people who are not officially employed are doing a lot more than watching reruns of *Game of Thrones*. Second, even people with formal jobs are engaged in some home production. If you hold down a day job, it is likely that you also do some cleaning, cooking, or childcare when you get home from work.

Let's quantify these effects. In the United States, where the total population was 321.8 million in 2015, approximately 150 million adults (age 16 and over) held formal jobs and another 100 million adults did not have formal jobs.[2]

Many people without formal jobs are engaged in a considerable amount of home production, including food preparation, household maintenance, and childcare. Suppose that the working-age adults without formal jobs have an average annual home production of $20,000 per person. That number averages over people with different amounts of home production. Some people who aren't in the formal labor force care for newborn triplets, and others are retirees who have lots of leisure time.

In addition, suppose that the people with formal jobs outside the home also do home production of $10,000 per year. After all, even people with formal jobs still make dinner, vacuum the rugs, and do the laundry. Indeed, many of them provide a great deal of childcare as well.

Adding up all these different sources of home production, we get annual home production in the United States of $3.5 trillion:

$$(100 \text{ million people}) \times (\$20,000/\text{person})$$
$$+ (150 \text{ million people}) \times (\$10,000/\text{person}) = \$3.5 \text{ trillion.}$$

In an economy with $18.0 trillion of market-based production, $3.5 trillion represents about 20 percent of additional economic production that has been overlooked in the GDP calculation. Many other estimates of home production are even higher.

The Underground Economy

The *underground economy*—transactions that are intentionally hidden from government statisticians—represents another hole in the GDP accounts. This includes the plumber who asks to be paid in cash and the taxicab driver who negotiates a lower rate if you would just agree to let him turn off the meter (and pay in cash). Plumbing and cab driving are perfectly legal, but some workers hide income to avoid paying taxes. In the United States, this sort of tax avoidance amounts to $500 billion per year.[3]

Earnings from legal professions may also be hidden for other reasons. For instance, if a citizen of a foreign country is working as a nanny in the United States but doesn't have a work visa, she may prefer to be paid in a way that enables her to stay off the radar screen of the U.S. government—in other words, cash only, please.

The underground economy also includes markets in illegal professions. Drug dealing and prostitution top the list (though eight states have legalized possession of small amounts of marijuana as of 2017). Illegal drug sales alone are estimated to be equal in magnitude to almost 1 percent of GDP. For the U.S. economy, that is equivalent to the value of all agricultural production.

In developed economies with excellent law enforcement systems—think of countries like Switzerland, Japan, Hong Kong, and the United States—all transactions in the underground economy add up to about 10 percent of GDP. In developing countries, the fraction of underground economic activity is generally much higher. For example, in Mexico the underground economy may be as much as half of measured GDP. In India, the underground economy is estimated to be a quarter of GDP, and India is in the midst of a campaign to push the underground economy out of the shadows. In 2016, India began a currency reform that will force people with large cash holdings (under their mattresses) to move those cash holdings into the formal banking system, where it will be measured and taxed.

Some countries (such as Ireland, Italy, and the United Kingdom) have recently started to include underground economic activity, including illicit drug purchases and prostitution, in their GDP calculations.

Negative Externalities

Negative externalities occur when an economic activity has a spillover cost that does not affect those directly engaged in the activity. Positive externalities occur when an economic activity has a spillover benefit that does not affect those directly engaged in the activity. Externalities—both negative and positive—are usually omitted from the GDP calculations. Consider a coal-powered electrical plant generating power for thousands of homes and simultaneously belching out a continuous stream of toxic airborne pollutants. GDP counts the electricity produced but fails to subtract the social cost of the pollution.

Sometimes negative externalities even get counted as *positive* contributors to economic output. For example, property crimes, like theft, lead people to purchase locks and other security devices. In some cases, property owners hire guards to safeguard their possessions. All such preventive activity counts as positive contributions to GDP.

The societal cost of pollution is not subtracted from GDP.

Gross national product (GNP) is the market value of production generated by the factors of production—both capital and labor—possessed or owned by the residents of a particular nation.

Gross Domestic Product versus Gross National Product

As we've already explained, GDP is the market value of everything produced within the borders of a country during a particular period of time. So GDP includes both the production of a country's residents and the production of visitors. For example, if a U.S. worker spends 2 months working in Singapore, her production will be counted in the GDP of Singapore and omitted from U.S. GDP. Likewise, if a Japanese auto company—like Honda—opens a plant in Alabama, the value added of this plant will be counted in U.S. GDP and not in Japanese GDP. This would be the case even if the plant were operated entirely by robots and didn't have one U.S. employee. The plant is operating within the borders of the United States, so its value added is counted in U.S. GDP.

At first glance, you might wonder whether cross-border activities amount to much. In fact, there are large amounts of such activity. For example, about 70 percent of the "Japanese" cars that are sold in the United States are now manufactured at plants in Canada, Mexico, and the United States.

With facts like this in mind, economists have constructed a measure of aggregate economic activity that includes only the output of factors of production owned by residents of a particular country: **gross national product (GNP)**. U.S. GNP includes the production of a worker who normally resides in the United States, even if the production occurred when the worker was temporarily working abroad. For example, if a U.S. professor gives a summer course at the National University of Singapore, her salary, which was paid by the National University of Singapore, would be included in U.S. GNP and excluded from Singapore's GNP.

Likewise, U.S. GNP would exclude the value added of machines owned by a Japanese car manufacturer, even if those machines operate in Alabama. In contrast, U.S. GNP would include the value added of U.S. workers who are employed in a Japanese auto plant in Alabama. U.S. GNP is carefully constructed to count only the value added of factors of production possessed or owned by U.S. residents, no matter where those factors of production operate in the world.

GNP is therefore a measure of national production, where the word *national* signifies the factors of production—like capital and labor—possessed or owned by the residents of a particular nation. To calculate GNP, begin with GDP and first add in the production of U.S.-owned factors of production that operate within the borders of foreign countries. Then subtract the production of foreign-owned factors of production that operate within the borders of the United States.

$$\text{Gross national product} = (\text{Gross domestic product})$$
$$+ (\text{Production of U.S.-owned capital and labor in foreign countries})$$
$$- (\text{Production of foreign-owned capital and labor in the United States})$$

Plugging in the actual numbers for 2015, we find that U.S. GNP ($18.2 trillion) is higher than U.S. GDP ($18.0 trillion). Specifically, the market value of production of U.S. capital and labor in foreign countries ($0.8 trillion) exceeds the market value of production of foreign capital and labor within U.S. borders ($0.6 trillion). In 2015, U.S. GNP was about 1 percent larger than U.S. GDP.[4]

For a few countries, GNP and GDP diverge much more substantially. For example, Kuwait—a wealthy oil exporter in the Persian Gulf—owns a very large portfolio of foreign assets, and residents of foreign countries own comparatively few assets inside Kuwait. The income from Kuwait's foreign assets is counted in Kuwait's GNP but excluded from Kuwait's GDP. Accordingly, Kuwait's GNP is substantially larger—generally about 10 percent larger—than its GDP. However, Kuwait's situation is uncommon. For most countries, GNP and GDP are nearly the same.

The Increase in Income Inequality

One of the biggest problems with GDP and GDP per capita is the lack of detailed information about how economic output is divided up among individual households. For example, the United States and Norway have very similar levels of per capita GDP. However, the United States has more income inequality. For instance, consider the economic fortunes of households who earn enough income to be in the top 1 percent of earners in each country. In the United States, the top 1 percent of U.S. households earn 22 percent of the nation's income, while the remaining 99 percent earn 78 percent of national income. In contrast, in Norway the top 1 percent of households earn only 7.8 percent of total Norwegian income, leaving more than 92 percent of national income to the remaining 99 percent of the population. This sharp difference in inequality implies that the vast majority of Americans are poorer than Norwegians, even though the two countries have similar levels of GDP per capita.

Inequality varies not only across countries but also over time. In most countries, income inequality has approximately followed a U-shaped pattern over the past century: falling until the 1970s and rising thereafter. For example, as we will see in greater detail in Chapter 7, in the United States, the income share of the top 1 percent of households fell from 18.0 percent of the nation's income in 1913 (when records begin) to a low of 8.3 percent in 1975 and rose back to 22.0 percent as of 2015.

The rise in inequality since the 1970s is partially reflected in the income trajectories of different educational groups. U.S. workers with only a high school degree have had flat or declining buying power of their earnings since the early 1970s. Meanwhile, the most skilled workers in the United States, especially those with a post-graduate degree, have experienced substantial gains in income.[5]

Moderate levels of inequality play a useful economic role by incentivizing people to work hard. If everyone were given (or guaranteed) exactly the same income, the incentive to work would collapse. So some reward for hard work, and the inequality that goes with it, is necessary as an incentive. Nevertheless, higher levels of inequality create economic, social, and political costs as well. Very high levels of inequality might make it impossible for all families to access high-quality education. Even more ominously, high levels of inequality might create social unrest and support for populist politicians offering unsustainable and unworkable remedies to the economic problems facing society.

Stagnating incomes, rising levels of inequality, and resentment toward economic and social "elites" may have played an important role in the recent U.S. presidential election. Voter exit polls tell the story.[6] As voters left the polls, they were asked whether their family's situation was "better today," "about the same today," or "worse today." Among those who said "better today," only 24 percent voted for candidate Donald J. Trump, now President Trump, who ran on a populist platform centered on the message "Make America Great Again." Among those voters who said that their family's situation was "about the same today," 46 percent voted for President Trump. Among those who said "worse today," 78 percent voted for President Trump.

Leisure

Leisure is another sore spot in the GDP system. The GDP accounts give an economy no credit for producing leisure. However, most people would agree that leisure is a key ingredient in human well-being. For example, in time-use surveys, people report that they are happiest when they are socializing.[7] Likewise, people report that they are the least happy when they are at work or commuting to and from work. When you think about GDP comparisons across countries, you need to remember that different countries are working at different levels of intensity. Of course, the goal in life is not to maximize your income by working every moment that you can. If that were our goal, nobody would ever retire or take a vacation. A more reasonable goal is to maximize human well-being—this is another example of optimization. GDP tells us how many material goods are being produced by an economy, but it does not tell us whether all of those material achievements are being used to optimize human happiness.

Does GDP Buy Happiness?

Despite the omission of leisure, GDP per capita is often used as a summary measure of the well-being of a society. We would like to know whether GDP per capita is actually a good predictor of human happiness. Social scientists do not have a foolproof way of measuring happiness, but we do have a crude way of gauging whether a person is satisfied with life: ask them. It's not an ideal method—for instance, people may not tell the truth: "I'm fine, how are you?"—but it's a start. When survey researchers ask about happiness in millions of interviews around the world, some remarkable patterns appear in the data.

GDP per capita turns out to be a strong predictor of life satisfaction. Exhibit 5.6 displays a positive relationship between GDP per capita and self-reports of life satisfaction in a large sample of countries. The countries with higher levels of GDP per capita report higher levels of life satisfaction. The exhibit plots GDP per capita on the *x*-axis and average life satisfaction on the *y*-axis. Life satisfaction was measured on a 10-point scale. Each circle represents a different country, and the size of the circle reflects the size of the population in that country. The large circle on the right represents the United States. The two large circles on the left are for India and China.

> GDP per capita turns out to be a strong predictor of life satisfaction.

This positive correlation between GDP and life satisfaction shows up in each country as well. In other words, when economists study household-level data on income and life satisfaction, we find that low-income households in a country report substantially lower life satisfaction than higher-income households in the same country.[8]

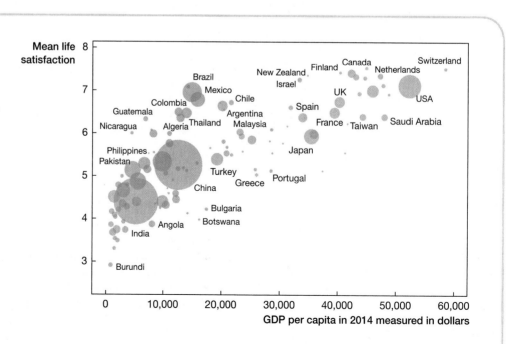

Exhibit 5.6 GDP per Capita and Life Satisfaction

A strong positive relationship is visible when we compare GDP per capita to mean life satisfaction (measured on a 10-point scale) in a large sample of countries.

Source: Data from the World Happiness Report and the Penn World Table version 9.0 (Robert C. Feenstra, Robert Inklaar, and Marcel P. Timmer, June 2016).

5.4 Real versus Nominal

GDP is particularly useful as a tool for determining how the overall economy is growing. To implement this growth analysis, we would like to separate the increase in the value of GDP that is due to overall price increases (in other words, inflation, a concept we define below) from the increase in the value of GDP that is due to increases in the quantity and quality of goods and services.

For example, suppose the country of Fordica makes ten cars in 2015 and ten identical cars in 2016. Here we make the simplifying assumption that the quality of the cars hasn't changed over time. Economists have sophisticated tools for handling improvements in quality, but we'll sidestep those issues to keep the analysis as simple as possible. Holding quality fixed, assume that the price of each car rises from $30,000 to $40,000 from 2015 to 2016. In this case, GDP in 2015 would be $(10 \text{ cars} \times \$30,000/\text{car}) = \$300,000$ and GDP in 2016 would be $(10 \text{ cars} \times \$40,000/\text{car}) = \$400,000$. At first glance, the economy has grown by 33 percent, or

$$\frac{\text{GDP in 2016} - \text{GDP in 2015}}{\text{GDP in 2015}} = \frac{\$400,000 - \$300,000}{\$300,000} = \frac{1}{3} = 0.33 = 33\%.$$

But the actual number of cars produced hasn't grown at all. It's still ten cars. If we counted the number of cars, rather than their market value, the growth rate of the economy from 2015 to 2016 would have been 0 percent. We don't want to pat ourselves on the back because prices have gone up (holding car quality fixed, as we are in this example).

Naturally, we would like to separate the growth that is due simply to price increases from the growth that is due to increases in the production of goods and services. To do this, we contrast the concepts of *nominal GDP* and *real GDP*. Nominal GDP is the standard GDP measurement that we've been discussing throughout this chapter. **Nominal GDP** is the total market value of production, using current prices to determine value per unit produced.

Real GDP is based on the same idea as nominal GDP—summing up the market value of the quantities of final goods and services—but real GDP uses prices from a base year that may be different from the year in which the quantities were produced. To illustrate this idea, let's take 2015 as the base year. In our example, the price of a Ford was $30,000 in 2015. Now let's assume that ten Fords were produced in 2015 and ten (identical) Fords were produced in 2016. To calculate real GDP, we use the 2015 prices to value the output in both 2015 and 2016. So real GDP was $300,000 in 2015 and was still $300,000 in 2016. Using the concept of real GDP, we see that there was no growth between 2015 and 2016. That makes sense—the number of cars produced did not change.

For clarity, economists use the words *nominal* or *real* in their analyses to make certain that the reader knows which of the two concepts is being discussed. However, journalists generally assume that growth of *real* GDP is the only game in town. When a headline announces, "U.S. Growth Slows to 2.2%," readers are assumed to know, without being told, that real growth is being discussed.

So far we have studied real GDP in the simple case of a one-good economy. Naturally, this concept can be applied to an economy with any number of goods and services. To get some practice using this concept, let's consider the case of an economy that manufactures two types of cars: Fords and Chevrolets. Exhibit 5.7 reports the raw data with which we will work.

Let's start by calculating nominal GDP. We simply add up the total market value of goods sold in each year, using current prices. In 2015, nominal GDP is

$$(10 \text{ Fords}) \times (\$30,000/\text{Ford}) + (5 \text{ Chevrolets}) \times (\$20,000/\text{Chevrolet}) = \$400,000.$$

In 2016, nominal GDP is

$$(10 \text{ Fords}) \times (\$40,000/\text{Ford}) + (20 \text{ Chevrolets}) \times (\$25,000/\text{Chevrolet}) = \$900,000.$$

Check these totals against the values in the column of Exhibit 5.7 labeled "Nominal GDP."

Nominal GDP is the total value of production (final goods and services), using current market prices to determine the value of each unit that is produced.

Real GDP is the total value of production (final goods and services), using market prices from a specific base year to determine the value of each unit that is produced.

Exhibit 5.7 Quantities and Prices in an Economy with Two Goods

The yellow box contains Ford's quantities and prices in years 2015 and 2016. The orange box contains Chevrolet's quantities and prices. Nominal GDP is the total value of production using prices and quantities from the same year. Real GDP in 2015 using 2015 prices is the same as nominal GDP in 2015. Real GDP in 2016 using 2015 prices is the total value of production using quantities from 2016 and prices from 2015.

Year	Ford		Chevrolet		Nominal GDP	Real GDP Using 2015 Base Prices
	Quantity Produced	Price per Car	Quantity Produced	Price per Car		
2015	10	$30,000	5	$20,000	$400,000	$400,000
2016	10	$40,000	20	$25,000	$900,000	$700,000

To calculate real GDP, we use 2015 as the base year. That means that we keep using 2015 prices in the calculation of both 2015 and 2016 real GDP. This doesn't rock the boat for 2015. Real GDP for 2015 is calculated with 2015 quantities and 2015 prices (exactly matching our calculation of nominal GDP in 2015):

$$(10\text{ Fords}) \times (\$30,000/\text{Ford}) + (5\text{ Chevrolets}) \times (\$20,000/\text{Chevrolet}) = \$400,000.$$

The boat rocking comes when we calculate real GDP in 2016, using 2015 as the base year. Now we need to use quantities from 2016 and prices from 2015. In 2016, real GDP is

$$(10\text{ Fords}) \times (\$30,000/\text{Ford}) + (20\text{ Chevrolets}) \times (\$20,000/\text{Chevrolet}) = \$700,000.$$

By holding prices constant—using prices from a single base year—we are able to make meaningful comparisons across years. Economists say that such analyses use *constant dollars*. In this case, the constant dollars are based on prices from 2015. To make the base year clear to their audience, economists say that the analysis uses "constant 2015 dollars."

Now that you understand how to calculate real GDP, we are able to talk about the growth rate of real GDP, which is usually referred to as **real GDP growth**. For example, the formula for real GDP growth in 2016 is given by

Real GDP growth is the growth rate of real GDP.

$$\text{Real GDP growth in 2016} = \frac{\text{Real GDP in 2016} - \text{Real GDP in 2015}}{\text{Real GDP in 2015}}$$

By focusing on real GDP growth—which holds prices fixed across time—we compare the total value of real output in 2015 ($400,000 in our example) and the total value of real output in 2016 ($700,000 in our example). In this example, real GDP has grown by 75 percent:

$$\frac{\$700,000 - \$400,000}{\$400,000} = \frac{3}{4} = 0.75 = 75\%.$$

The concept of real GDP growth lets us focus on the thing that we care the most about—how much the economy is producing at different points in time—without letting price movements muddy up the comparison.

Finally, don't let this teaching example mislead you. Unfortunately, actual growth rates for real GDP are much lower than they are in our illustration. Since 1929, when reliable national income accounts were first created, real GDP growth in the United States has averaged 3.2 percent per year. Even rapidly growing developing countries achieve average real GDP growth of only 5 percent to 10 percent per year. We'll analyze long-run real GDP growth in Chapter 7, and we'll study short-run fluctuations in real GDP growth in Chapter 12.

The GDP Deflator

We can also use real GDP to study the level of prices in the overall economy. Specifically, if we divide nominal GDP by real GDP in the same year and multiply the resulting ratio by 100, we end up with a measure of how much prices of goods and services produced in a country have risen since the base year. This ratio is called the **GDP deflator**:

The **GDP deflator** is 100 times the ratio of nominal GDP to real GDP in the same year. It is a measure of how prices of goods and services produced in a country have risen since the base year.

$$\text{GDP deflator} = \frac{\text{Nominal GDP}}{\text{Real GDP}} \times 100.$$

To understand why this ratio is a measure of rising prices, it helps to write out the formula. Consider again the example in Exhibit 5.7, in which we treat 2015 as the base year for calculations of real GDP. To begin, let's evaluate the GDP deflator for 2015. The expressions for nominal GDP and real GDP are written out here with the quantities shown in blue and the prices in red. Using the data in Exhibit 5.7, you can confirm the numbers used in the formula:

$$
\begin{aligned}
\text{GDP deflator}(2015) &= \frac{\text{Nominal GDP}(2015)}{\text{Real GDP}(2015)} \times 100 \\
&= \frac{\text{Cost of buying everything produced domestically in 2015 using 2015 prices}}{\text{Cost of buying everything produced domestically in 2015 using base-year prices}} \times 100 \\
&= \frac{10 \times 30{,}000 + 5 \times 20{,}000}{10 \times 30{,}000 + 5 \times 20{,}000} \times 100 \\
&= 100.
\end{aligned}
$$

This first calculation reminds us that in the base year (2015 in this example), nominal GDP matches real GDP. Consequently, in the base year, the GDP deflator is exactly equal to 100.

Now let's consider 2016, the year after the base year. Once again, you can use the data in Exhibit 5.7 to confirm the numbers in the equation:

$$
\begin{aligned}
\text{GDP deflator}(2016) &= \frac{\text{Nominal GDP}(2016)}{\text{Real GDP}(2016)} \times 100 \\
&= \frac{\text{Cost of buying everything produced domestically in 2016 using 2016 prices}}{\text{Cost of buying everything produced domestically in 2016 using base-year prices}} \times 100 \\
&= \frac{10 \times 40{,}000 + 20 \times 25{,}000}{10 \times 30{,}000 + 20 \times 20{,}000} \times 100 \\
&= \frac{900{,}000}{700{,}000} \times 100 \\
&= 128.6.
\end{aligned}
$$

In the formula for the 2016 GDP deflator, the numerator and the denominator have exactly the same quantities (in blue): 10 Fords and 20 Chevys. These are the quantities that were sold in 2016. The only numbers that change between the numerator and the denominator are the prices (in red). The numerator (top) has the 2016 prices, which are used to calculate nominal GDP in 2016. The denominator (bottom) has the 2015 prices that are used to calculate *real* GDP for 2016—recall that the 2015 prices are the base-year prices.

The numerator shows what it would cost to purchase everything that the economy produced in 2016 using 2016 prices. The denominator shows what it would cost to purchase everything that the economy produced in 2016 using 2015 prices. The GDP deflator is the ratio that reflects the rising cost of buying everything produced in 2016, holding the goods and services produced in 2016 fixed, but changing the prices from the 2016 prices (in the numerator) to the 2015 prices (in the denominator).

The 2016 GDP deflator is telling us how the 2016 prices (in red in the numerator) compare with the 2015 prices (in red in the denominator), holding the quantities fixed in the numerator and the denominator. You can think of the (blue) quantities as weights. The higher the 2016 quantity, the more weight that good or service gets in determining the overall ratio. This makes sense: goods or services with large quantities should get more weight when we form an overall measure of the price level.

Now that you understand how the GDP deflator equation works, you can see that it gives us a handy way of moving among three important variables: the GDP deflator (which is a ratio of weighted prices in a target year to weighted prices in a base year), nominal GDP (which measures the market value of output in the same target year), and real GDP (which measures the value of output in the target year using prices from the base year). If you know two of these three variables, you can easily calculate the third using the GDP deflator formula.

Economists study the percentage change in the GDP deflator from year to year. For example, the year-over-year percentage change in the GDP deflator in 2016 is given by

$$\text{Percentage change in GDP deflator in 2016}$$
$$= \frac{\text{GDP deflator in 2016} - \text{GDP deflator in 2015}}{\text{GDP deflator in 2015}}.$$

Whenever we calculate the percentage change in a variable, we divide the change in the variable by the previous level of the variable. The percentage change in the GDP deflator is a measure of the percentage change in the overall level of prices. In our illustrative example, the GDP deflator was 100 in 2015, and it was 128.6 in 2016. So an economist would conclude that prices have risen 28.6 percent:

$$\frac{128.6 - 100}{100} = \frac{28.6}{100} = 0.286 = 28.6\%.$$

Note that this overall rate of price inflation is between the rate of price inflation for Fords ($30,000 to $40,000, or a 33 percent increase) and the rate of price inflation for Chevrolets ($20,000 to $25,000, or a 25 percent increase). The relative weights of Ford and Chevy prices are determined by their quantity weights.

Exhibit 5.8 plots the value of the actual U.S. GDP deflator from 1929 to 2015, using 2009 as the base year. Because 2009 is the base year, the GDP deflator is exactly 100 in 2009. The

MyEconLab Real-time data

Exhibit 5.8 The Value of the GDP Deflator from 1929 to 2015, Using 2009 as the Base Year

Because 2009 is the base year, the GDP deflator is exactly 100 in 2009. Notice that the GDP deflator is less than 100 before 2009 and greater than 100 after 2009. The deflator is an indicator of the overall level of prices in the economy. In an economy with rising prices, the deflator rises over time. The only period of sharp declines in the GDP deflator was the period from 1929 to 1933, during the Great Depression. The series is plotted on a scale with constant proportionality, implying that changes on the y-axis of equal size represent equal proportional movements. For example, going from the level of 4 to 20 (a multiple of 5) has the same step size on the y-axis as going from the level of 20 to 100 (another multiple of 5).

Source: Based on Bureau of Economic Analysis, National Income and Product Accounts.

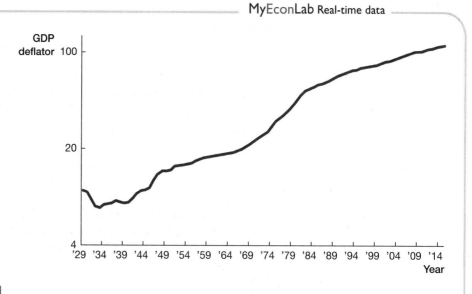

GDP deflator is less than 100 before 2009 and greater than 100 after 2009. From 1929 to 2015 the GDP deflator increased on average 2.9 percent per year, which is a measure of how quickly prices rose on average during this period.

There are many different ways to measure overall movements in prices, which causes some degree of confusion. In fact, the general public is largely unaware of the GDP deflator and its usefulness as a tool for measuring price movements. The best-known price measure is the Consumer Price Index, which we consider next.

The Consumer Price Index

As you now know, the GDP deflator is the ratio

$$\text{GDP deflator}(\text{target year}) = \frac{\text{Nominal GDP}(\text{target year})}{\text{Real GDP}(\text{target year})} \times 100$$

$$= \frac{\begin{array}{c}\text{Cost of buying everything produced domestically}\\ \text{in target year using target year prices}\end{array}}{\begin{array}{c}\text{Cost of buying everything produced domestically}\\ \text{in target year using base-year prices}\end{array}} \times 100.$$

For example, if the base year were 2009, then the prices that are used in the denominator are the prices that existed in the economy in 2009.

The Bureau of Labor Statistics calculates a related formula called the ***Consumer Price Index (CPI)***. As you can see, the CPI looks almost identical to the formula for the GDP deflator:

The **Consumer Price Index (CPI)** is 100 times the ratio of the cost of buying a basket of consumer goods using target year prices divided by the cost of buying the same basket of consumer goods using base-year prices.

$$\text{CPI}(\text{target year}) = \frac{\begin{array}{c}\text{Cost of buying a particular basket of consumer}\\ \text{goods using target year prices}\end{array}}{\begin{array}{c}\text{Cost of buying a particular basket of consumer}\\ \text{goods using base-year prices}\end{array}} \times 100.$$

As you can see, the GDP deflator and CPI formulas are nearly indistinguishable:

1. Both formulas use target year prices in the numerator and base-year prices in the denominator.
2. Both formulas contain a ratio that compares what it would cost to buy a particular set of goods in the target year (in the numerator) to what it would have cost to buy the same set of goods using base-year prices (in the denominator).
3. Both formulas have the same interpretation: a higher ratio implies a greater price increase from the base year to the target year.

The key difference between the formulas is the particular basket of goods that is being bought. The GDP deflator studies the basket of goods that is produced domestically. In other words, the GDP deflator studies the basket of goods that represents the total production of the domestic economy. We'll call this the "GDP basket."

The CPI studies a particular basket of consumer goods. This basket is constructed to reflect the types and quantities of goods that are purchased by a typical U.S. household. We'll call this the "consumer basket."

There are three key differences between the GDP basket and the consumer basket:

(1) The GDP basket includes things that households don't purchase, like coal-fired power plants, locomotives, subway stations, city buses, aircraft carriers, and nuclear submarines. Consumers use services provided by governments and firms that purchase these items, but no consumer purchases them directly, so they appear in the GDP basket (in the year they are purchased) but not in the consumer basket.

(2) The consumer basket includes things that households purchase but are not counted in GDP. For example, GDP counts only domestic production, so it does not count imports, such as the foreign value added in a laptop manufactured abroad. The Chinese value added in a laptop that is purchased by a U.S. consumer is not counted in the U.S. GDP basket but would be counted in the U.S. consumer basket.

(3) Even if a product is included in both the GDP basket and the consumer basket, it is likely to have a different weight in the two baskets. For example, housing-related expenditures are included in both baskets, but housing has a larger role in the consumer basket.

Housing—including the cost of shelter, utility bills, and household furnishings—represents more than 40 percent of the consumer basket, but these items jointly represent less than 20 percent of the GDP basket.

With all these differences, it's natural to wonder whether the GDP deflator and CPI tell very different stories about the evolution of prices in the overall economy. In fact, in practice it makes almost no difference which indicator is used, as we demonstrate next.

Inflation

The rate of increase in prices is the **inflation rate**. It is calculated as the year-over-year percentage increase in a price index.

The rate of increase in prices is the **inflation rate**. It is calculated as the year-over-year percentage increase in a price index. For example, to calculate the overall U.S. inflation rate in 2015, we use the following formula, with either the GDP deflator or the CPI as the "price index":

$$\text{Inflation rate in 2015} = \frac{\text{Price index in 2015} - \text{Price index in 2014}}{\text{Price index in 2014}}.$$

This is the same percentage change formula—the change in the variable divided by the previous level of the variable—that we used above to calculate the year-over-year percentage increase in the GDP price deflator.

It turns out that the choice of the price index doesn't have a large impact on the calculated rate of inflation. Exhibit 5.9 plots the historical rate of inflation calculated with both the GDP deflator (blue) and the CPI (dashed red line). As you can see, the two inflation series move very closely together.

This similarity may partially explain why there are relatively few news stories about the GDP deflator. The GDP deflator doesn't have much to add once we know the CPI. Moreover, CPI is released on a monthly basis, so it is more timely than the GDP deflator, which is released quarterly. Finally, CPI describes inflation that matters the most for households. In this sense, CPI has more personal relevance for the typical consumer.

Adjusting Nominal Variables

You can't make meaningful comparisons across time without adjusting nominal variables. For example, William Howard Taft was paid $75,000 per year for his service as president. He was inaugurated in 1909. In 2015, the U.S. president was paid $400,000. So who was paid more?

When we ask that question, we don't mean "Who received more dollars?" We really mean "Whose salary was worth more?" or, in the language of economics, "Who had more buying power?" There has been a lot of inflation between 1909 and 2015, so a dollar paid

MyEconLab Real-time data

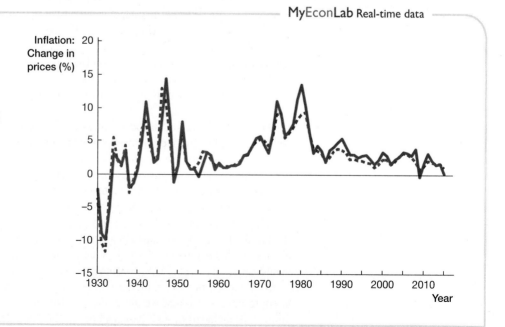

Exhibit 5.9 The Annual U.S. Inflation Rate (1930–2015)

The annual percentage change in the GDP deflator from 1930 to 2015 is plotted in blue; it is one measure of inflation. The exhibit also plots the annual percentage change in the CPI over the same period (dashed red line). This is another measure of inflation. The two measures have a very similar historical pattern.

Source: Based on Bureau of Economic Analysis, National Income and Product Accounts; and U.S. Bureau of Labor Statistics.

out in 1909 bought much more than a dollar in 2015. To compare President Taft's salary to a modern presidential salary, we need to translate President Taft's salary into current dollars.

There's a formula that enables us to do this:

$$\text{Value in 2015 dollars} = \frac{\text{Price index in 2015}}{\text{Price index in 1909}} \times \text{Value in 1909 dollars}.$$

The ratio on the right-hand side of this equation tells us how much prices have risen, enabling us to transform value expressed in 1909 dollars into value expressed in 2015 dollars. We can fill in these numbers using the 2015 CPI and a historical estimate of what the CPI was in 1909 (official government CPI calculations do not start until 1913).

$$\begin{aligned}\text{Value in 2015 dollars} &= \frac{\text{Price index in 2015}}{\text{Price index in 1909}} \times \text{Value in 1909 dollars} \\ &= \frac{237}{9} \times \$75,000 \\ &= \$1.98 \text{ million}.\end{aligned}$$

The ratio of price indices tells you that, on average, prices rose by a factor of $237/9 = 26.33$ over this time period, so having $1 in 1909 is equivalent to having $26.33 in 2015. Scaling President Taft's annual salary of $75,000 in 1909 by this ratio of price levels implies that his 1909 salary has the equivalent purchasing power of $1.98 million in 2015. President Taft's salary was worth more than 4 times Barack Obama's presidential salary in 2015. You may be curious to know whether anything has changed since then. In fact, the U.S. president's salary remains $400,000 in 2017, and the overall economy's price level continues to slowly rise (inflation is positive). Therefore, President Trump is being paid the same nominal salary as President Obama, but the march of inflation means that President Trump's presidential salary has slightly less buying power than President Obama's and far less buying power than President Taft's.

We can use the above simple formula to express any historical price (or value) in dollars for a more recent year (say, 2015). We generally have a good intuition for what 2015 dollars can buy, and we generally have a poor intuition for a dollar's buying power in 1909. Therefore, this type of transformation can come in very handy. We'll use it many times throughout this book.

Summary

- Macroeconomics is the study of economic aggregates and the economy as a whole. An aggregate is a total. Macroeconomics studies total economic activity.

- Gross domestic product (GDP) is the market value of the final goods and services produced in a country during a particular period of time (for instance, a year). GDP is defined in three equivalent ways: Production = Expenditure = Income. The circular flow diagram explains these identities and adds a fourth identical way of measuring economic activity: factors of production.

- Like a brief weather report—"92 degrees and partly cloudy"—GDP is just a summary measure of economic activity and economic well-being. GDP leaves many details out, including depreciation, home production, the underground economy, externalities, inequality, leisure, and cross-border movements of capital and labor. Nevertheless, residents of countries with relatively high levels of GDP per capita report relatively high levels of life satisfaction.

- Economists distinguish nominal values from real values. Real GDP measures the market value of economic production holding prices fixed at those of a particular base year. The GDP deflator is a measure of the overall level of prices in the economy. The Consumer Price Index (CPI) is another measure of the overall level of prices. Both the GDP deflator and the CPI can be used to measure the overall rate at which prices are rising: the inflation rate.

Key Terms

income per capita *p. 87*
recession *p. 88*
unemployed *p. 88*
unemployment rate *p. 88*
national income accounts *p. 89*
national income and product accounts *p. 89*
gross domestic product (GDP) *p. 89*
identity *p. 90*

factors of production *p. 91*
value added *p. 92*
consumption *p. 94*
investment *p. 94*
government expenditure *p. 94*
exports *p. 94*
imports *p. 95*
national income accounting identity *p. 95*

labor income *p. 99*
capital income *p. 99*
gross national product (GNP) *p. 102*
nominal GDP *p. 105*
real GDP *p. 105*
real GDP growth *p. 106*
GDP deflator *p. 107*
Consumer Price Index (CPI) *p. 109*
inflation rate *p. 110*

Questions

All questions are available in MyEconLab *for practice and instructor assignment.*

1. Find and list three recent stories in the media that would typically be studied in macroeconomics. (Cite the date and source of the stories you choose.) Discuss why they would fall within the subject matter of macroeconomics.

2. How is GDP defined?

3. What is an accounting identity? Explain the accounting identity Production = Expenditure = Income.

4. Use the circular flow diagram to show how expenditure, production, and income relate to one another.

5. How is production-based accounting used to estimate GDP? Discuss the role of value added.

6. How is GDP calculated using expenditure-based accounting?

7. Which category of expenditure accounts for the highest share of GDP in the United States?

8. How is the level of economic activity calculated using the income method?

9. If the level of aggregate expenditure was $16.8 trillion in 2013, what was the level of aggregate income? Explain your answer.

10. What is meant by capital depreciation?

11. Describe three important factors that GDP leaves out.

12. You decide to cook your own meal rather than eat in a restaurant. How will this affect GDP?

13. When would a country's GDP exceed its GNP?

14. Nobel laureate Simon Kuznets, who did significant work on national income accounts in the 1930s, said that the welfare of a nation can scarcely be inferred from a measurement of national income. Would you agree with him? Why or why not?

15. Why is it essential to differentiate between real and nominal growth rates of GDP?

16. What are the key differences between the CPI and the GDP deflator?

17. How is the CPI similar to the GDP deflator?

Problems

All problems are available in MyEconLab *for practice and instructor assignment.*

1. Which of the following would be considered a final good in the calculation of U.S. GDP? Explain your answers.

   a. Processors manufactured in California for Apple's new range of laptops (that will be sold in the United States)

   b. Foot massages at spas in California

   c. Predator drones purchased by the federal government

2. By how much would GDP change as a result of each of the following changes? Briefly explain your answers.

   a. A parent switches from buying pre-made ham-and-cheese sandwiches for a family dinner, which would have cost $20, to buying the raw ingredients, which cost only $6, and making the same ham-and-cheese sandwiches at home.

   b. On the rebound again, a famous rock star marries her butler, whom she formerly paid $50,000 a year. After they are married, her husband continues to wait on her as before, and she continues to support him as before—but as a husband rather than as an employee, that is, not with a regular salary.

   c. Tired of biking to work every day, a millennial decides to start using Uber three times a week; each one-way ride costs her $8.50.

3. To generate estimates of GDP, the Bureau of Economic Analysis must aggregate a variety of data sources, such as expenditure surveys.

   a. What measurement problems might the government face in trying to estimate GDP? Consider the three accounting methods discussed in this chapter; what kinds of information would you need for each?

   b. In its quarterly estimates, the Bureau of Economic Analysis uses both expenditures-based and income-based accounting; to differentiate between the two, it refers to the expenditures-based estimate as GDP and the income-based estimate as GDI. What would we expect the relationship between GDP and GDI to be?

c. Now go to the Bureau of Economic Analysis NIPA tables (https://www.bea.gov/iTable/index_nipa.cfm), and compare the actual estimates for GDP (table 1.1.5) and GDI (table 1.10). What are the estimates for GDP and GDI in the first quarter of 2016? What factors could explain any differences you notice?

4. Suppose there are only two small countries in the world: Ascot, with a population of 30,000 people, and Delwich, with a population of 20,000 people. Ascot's GDP is equal to $150 million, while Delwich's GDP is $250 million. Delwich's GNP has been estimated to be equal to $280 million. Use this information to calculate Ascot's GNP, the GDP per capita in Ascot, and the GNP per capita in Delwich.

5. The following table gives data for a small country, Magnolia:

Component	Expenditure (in thousands)
Social Security payments	$250
Depreciation	$ 47
Private investment	$630
Exports	$260
Imports	$300
Salaries earned by foreigners working in Magnolia	$160
Household consumption	$850
Purchases of raw materials	$270
Government purchases	$900
Capital income	$290
Salaries earned by Magnolian residents working abroad	$350

a. Use the data to calculate GDP for this economy using the expenditure method.

b. Calculate the value of Magnolia's GNP. Does Magnolia's GDP differ from its GNP? Why or why not?

6. In 2013, the value of the Consumer Price Index (CPI) in a certain country, Polonia, was 230 and median (nominal) household income was $31,200. In 1950, the CPI was 51 and median (nominal) household income was $9,500.

a. Calculate median real household income in 1950 and in 2013, using 2013 as the base year.

b. In which year was life satisfaction likely to have been higher? Explain your answer.

7. With the rise of globalization, supply chains now spread across the world. Consider the following simplified stages of production for a smartphone:

- The U.S.-based smartphone company develops the designs for the new smartphone.

- A rare minerals broker in China buys $15 billion worth of minerals from around the world, including $5 billion from U.S. mines.

- A microchip producer in Japan buys half of these minerals for $10 billion; a camera and screen producer in South Korea buys the other half for $10 billion.

- A manufacturing factory in China buys the microchip, cameras, and screens for $22 billion; it obtains the rest of the assembly materials domestically for $3 billion.

- The U.S.-based smartphone company pays the factory $28 billion for the manufactured phones. It programs and uploads the software. Any updates from previous versions of the software are available for existing phone owners as a free download.

- The company keeps $10 billion worth of smartphones in inventory, then sells the rest to U.S. retailers for $25 billion.

- The retailers sell the phones in the United States, for a total of $30 billion in revenue.

a. Calculate how much this process contributes to U.S. GDP. Explain your calculation.

b. What sources of value might not be captured in your calculation in part a.?

8. The country of Sylvania produces and consumes only three goods: Red Bull, pizza, and T-shirts. The quantity produced and price of each good in 2011 and 2012 are given in the following table:

	2011		2012	
Good	Quantity	Price	Quantity	Price
T-shirts	100	$25	110	$25
Red Bull (cans)	500	$1	500	$1.50
Pizza (slices)	1,000	$2	900	$4

a. Calculate nominal GDP for 2011 and 2012.

b. Using 2011 as the base year, calculate real GDP for 2011 and 2012.

c. Based on your answer from part (b), by what percentage did real GDP grow between 2011 and 2012?

d. Now, calculate real GDP for 2011 and 2012 using 2012 as the base year.

e. Based on your answer from part (d), by what percentage did real GDP grow between 2011 and 2012?

f. Using 2011 as the base year, what was the GDP deflator in 2011 and 2012?

g. Based on your answer from part (f), by what percentage did prices change between 2011 and 2012?

9. In addition to the national CPI discussed in this chapter, the Bureau of Labor Statistics produces several regional CPI indices. These are constructed in the same way as the national CPI, just at a smaller scale: in a given city, researchers gather prices for a bundle of goods every month and then construct an index to track price changes of that bundle within the city. The following table shows the CPI indices (base period 1982–1984 = 100) for

San Francisco–Oakland–San Jose and Los Angeles–Riverside–Orange County, from 2007 to 2014:

Year	San Francisco–Oakland–San Jose	Los Angeles–Riverside–Orange County
2007	216.048	217.338
2008	222.767	225.008
2009	224.395	223.219
2010	227.469	225.894
2011	233.390	231.928
2012	239.650	236.648
2013	245.023	239.207
2014	251.985	242.434

a. In 2014, the San Francisco–Oakland–San Jose CPI was 251.985, while the Los Angeles–Riverside–Orange County CPI was 243.434. From this information, can we assert that 2014 prices were higher in San Francisco–Oakland–San Jose than in Los Angeles–Riverside–Orange County? Explain.

b. Suppose a San Francisco resident and a Los Angeles resident each make the same nominal wage every year from 2007 to 2014: $60,000.00 a year. Using the table above, determine the percentage change in real wage in each city from 2007 to 2014 (*Hint:* Start by determining how much the $60,000 in 2007 dollars would be worth in 2014 dollars, then compare it to what was actually earned in 2014).

10. Social Security payments in the United States are currently linked to the Consumer Price Index for Urban Wage Earners and Clerical Workers (CPI-W). This means that as the CPI-W shows an increase in the price level, Social Security payments will also increase, keeping the real value of the payment constant. The following table shows the weighting given to the different components in the CPI-W consumption basket.

Item	Weight
Food and beverages	15.948
Housing	39.867
Apparel	3.623
Transportation	18.991
Medical care	5.767
Recreation	5.528
Education and communication	6.766
Other goods and services	3.510
Total	**100.000**

It has been suggested that using the CPI-W to adjust Social Security payments understates inflation for seniors. Do you agree? Why might this be the case?

11. On May 22, 2013, *Forbes* magazine reported that Bill Gates had overtaken Mexican businessman Carlos Slim as the "richest man in the world." Gates's fortune on that date was estimated at $70 billion, whereas Slim's was a mere $69.86 billion (https://www.forbes.com/sites/erincarlyle/2013/05/22/bill-gates-is-worlds-richest-bumps-slim/#314b09f1618b). But does this make Gates the richest American who ever lived?

John D. Rockefeller, the founder of Standard Oil, is usually credited with this distinction. At the time of his death in 1937, Rockefeller had an estimated net worth of $1.4 billion.

a. Go to the U.S. Bureau of Labor Statistics CPI site at http://data.bls.gov/cgi-bin/surveymost?cu. Under "Consumer Price Index—All Urban Consumers," select "US All Items, $1982 - 84 = 100$," and click the "Retrieve data" button at the bottom of the page. Adjust the years to retrieve data from 1937 through 2013. Use the data under the "Annual" column to calculate Gates's 2013 net worth measured in 1937 dollars. You should find that Gates's wealth does have more buying power than Rockefeller's wealth did.

b. Some analysts say that Rockefeller's net worth was economically equivalent to $250 billion today. However, this figure is arrived at in a particular way. First, his net worth in 1937 is calculated as a percentage of total U.S. GDP in 1937. That percentage is then multiplied by the current level of GDP to arrive at the equivalent figure in current dollars. See if you can approximate the $250 billion figure. You can find the relevant GDP figures at http://research.stlouisfed.org/fred2/data/GDPA.txt.

c. What are the pros and cons of the two different methods of adjusting Rockefeller's net worth to make it comparable to the wealth of business leaders today?

12. Recall the method of calculating real GDP detailed in the chapter. As you may already have noticed, this method has a problem: when calculating aggregate output, this method weights the output of the various goods and services by their relative prices in the base year. Say, for example, a textbook cost $100 in the base year, and a laptop cost $2,000. This means that a laptop would have 20 times the weight of a book in calculating aggregate output.

But what happens when relative prices change? As you know, the prices of most high-tech items, including laptops, have generally been decreasing over time. Suppose the price of a laptop declined from $2,000 to $1,000 in the period from the base year to the current year. Now a laptop costs only 10 times as much as a book. So, using base-year relative prices would overweight laptops when calculating real GDP in the current year.

In response to this problem, in 1996 the Bureau of Economic Analysis switched to what is called a *chain-weighted* method of calculating real GDP. Say the base year is 2008. To calculate the growth rate of real GDP between 2008 and 2009, for example, the Bureau calculates real GDP for 2008 using 2008 as the base, and then real

GDP for 2008 using 2009 as the base. Then the Bureau calculates real GDP for 2009 using 2009 as the base, and real GDP for 2009 using 2008 as the base. For each base, the growth rate is then calculated as:

$$\frac{2009\ GDP_{(2008\ Base)} - 2008\ GDP_{(2008\ Base)}}{2008\ GDP_{(2008\ Base)}},$$

$$\frac{2009\ GDP_{(2009\ Base)} - 2008\ GDP_{(2009\ Base)}}{2008\ GDP_{(2009\ Base)}}.$$

The result is two different growth rates, which are then averaged. Given this averaged growth rate, and the level of GDP in 2008 at 2008 prices, the Bureau then calculates real GDP for 2009 as 1 plus the average growth rate previously calculated, times 2008 output in 2008 dollars. The growth rate between 2009 and 2010 is then calculated similarly.

Suppose that laptops, economics textbooks, and energy drinks are the only three goods produced in the United States. The table below gives the quantity of each produced (in millions) and its price in the years from 2014 to 2016:

Year	Price of Laptops	Quantity of Laptops	Price of Textbooks	Quantity of Textbooks	Price of Energy Drinks	Quantity of Energy Drinks
2014	$1,500	7	$100	7	$2	25
2015	$1,200	9	$110	9	$4	30
2016	$1,000	9	$120	10	$4	35

a. Calculate nominal GDP and real GDP (using 2014 as the base year) for each year.

b. Calculate real GDP for 2015 and 2016 using the chain-weighted method outlined above.

6 Aggregate Incomes

Why is the average American so much richer than the average Indian?

We live in a world of great disparities. Standards of living, educational opportunities, health services, and infrastructure differ tremendously across countries. Poverty is endemic in many parts of the world, particularly in sub-Saharan Africa, South Asia, and parts of South America, while most people in the United States, Canada, Western Europe, and a few other fairly rich countries live in relative comfort, even abundance. These differences are so great that if you travel around the globe, you will be struck by the stark contrast between living conditions in some parts of the world and those back home. The realization that there are such great disparities may have been one of the factors that sparked your interest in economics in the first place. These disparities are also the reason many people from all over the world emigrate to richer countries, where standards of living are higher.

CHAPTER **OUTLINE**

KEY IDEAS

- There are very large differences across countries in GDP per capita.

- We can compare income differences across countries using GDP per capita at current exchange rates or adjusted for differences in purchasing power parity.

- The aggregate production function links a country's GDP to its capital stock, its total efficiency units of labor, and its technology.

- Cross-country differences in GDP per capita result partly from differences in physical capital per worker and the human capital of workers, but differences in technology and the efficiency of production are even more important.

Macroeconomics provides a useful conceptual framework for studying these issues and helps explain why such disparities exist. In this and the next two chapters, we study questions related to economic inequalities across countries and economic growth (sometimes called "long-run macroeconomics") before turning to the study of economic fluctuations (sometimes called "short-run macroeconomics") in the subsequent five chapters. In particular, in this chapter, we explain how to measure differences in standards of living across countries and why such disparities exist. In Chapter 7, we turn to the study of economic growth, that is, how and why an economy grows and becomes more prosperous over time. In our last chapter in this series, Chapter 8, we discuss the fundamental factors that keep poor countries poor.

6.1 Inequality Around the World

Before we can understand the variation of income across the world, we must first define our measurements. How do we quantify the differences in standards of living and economic conditions across countries? Income per capita or GDP per capita is one robust measure.

Measuring Differences in GDP per Capita

In Chapter 5, we learned how to measure aggregate income or GDP. We can do so by approaching it from the production side, from the expenditure side, or from the income side. The national income accounting identity shows that all three give exactly the same answer: gross domestic product, or GDP for short. Dividing GDP by the total population in the country gives us **GDP per capita** (per person). This quantity is also referred to as income per capita, but, to keep things simple, we use the term GDP per capita throughout.

More formally, we have:

GDP per capita is GDP divided by total population.

$$\text{GDP per capita} = \frac{\text{GDP}}{\text{Total population}}.$$

For example, the United States in 2014 had (nominal) GDP equal to about $17.35 trillion. With a total population of approximately 319 million, nominal GDP per capita was approximately $54,306.

How does this compare to the GDP per capita of other countries? Let us look to a neighboring country: Mexico. Income in Mexico is, of course, calculated in pesos instead of U.S. dollars. Thus, with a similar computation, we find GDP per capita in Mexico in the same year, 2014, to be approximately 140,101 pesos. This number is not directly comparable to the $54,306 for the United States because it is expressed in different units. Fortunately, the exchange rate allows us to convert pesos to dollars. For example, on January 1, 2014, $1 was worth 13.09 pesos, or 1 peso was worth $1/13.09 = \$0.076$. Using this ratio, we can convert the average income in Mexico into dollars as follows (where p.c. stands for "per capita"):

$$\text{Mexican GDP p.c. in \$} = \text{Mexican GDP p.c. in pesos} \times \text{\$/peso exchange rate}$$
$$= 140,101 \times 0.076$$
$$= \$10,648.$$

So the average Mexican had an income of approximately $10,648. This number is useful for thinking about how much an individual with the average Mexican income, all of which was earned in Mexico, would be able to consume in the United States.

Using this exchange-rate-based measure, we can compute GDP per capita in every country for which we have data on GDP and population. For example, in 2014, GDP per capita in Sweden was $57,440, and in Germany it was $47,407. While GDP per capita in Sweden and Germany is similar to that in the United States, large disparities emerge when we compare the United States to several other countries. For example, we have already seen that the U.S. GDP per capita is about 5 times that of Mexico. It is also 34 times greater than GDP per capita in India, 50 times greater than GDP per capita in Senegal, and approximately 94 times greater than GDP per capita in Ethiopia.

While exchange-rate-based measures allow us to compare how much money the average citizen of different countries makes, they don't tell us how much that money can buy. Put differently, they fail to account for the fact that prices vary across countries—for example, some goods, like phone calls, are cheaper in the United States than in Mexico (partly because there is a telecommunications monopoly in Mexico, keeping prices high). In contrast, other goods, like guacamole and haircuts, are cheaper in Mexico, often because labor and other inputs are cheaper. To properly take account of these price differences, we favor comparing GDP per capita across countries using *purchasing power parity*.

We saw in Chapter 5 how to adjust economic variables like GDP to correct for changes in prices over time (which led to the notion of *real GDP*). We should make a similar adjustment when comparing GDP between countries. But the exchange rate between dollars and pesos doesn't fully do this. To see why, recall that the exchange rate between the peso and the dollar was 13.09 on January 1, 2014. If instead we had used the exchange rate on January 1, 2013—12.76 pesos per dollar—the average GDP in Mexico would have been $10,980 rather than $10,648. But this fluctuation has little to do with changes in prices households face in Mexico or the United States. Rather, it is just a consequence of converting Mexican income into dollars using the current exchange rate, which (as we will see in Chapter 15) fluctuates for a variety of reasons unrelated to differences in the cost of living.

Purchasing power parity provides a better way to convert GDP in domestic currencies into common units. The idea here is very similar to the adjustment we developed for converting nominal GDP into real GDP in the previous chapter. Specifically, the **purchasing power parity (PPP)** constructs the cost of a representative basket of commodities in each country and adjusts GDP so that a dollar in each country can purchase this representative basket. The resulting measure is a country's GDP in PPP-adjusted U.S. dollars. For example, this representative basket cost $1 in the United States and 8.90 pesos in Mexico in 2014. On this basis, the PPP conversion factor between U.S. dollars and pesos is $1 for 8.90 pesos or 1 peso for

$$0.11 = 1/8.90 \text{ U.S. dollars.}$$

The **purchasing power parity (PPP)** constructs the cost of a representative basket of commodities in each country and uses these relative costs for comparing income across countries.

LETTING THE
DATA SPEAK

The Big Mac Index

In 1986, *The Economist* magazine proposed the Big Mac index as an alternative measure of exchange rates. This index would simply be the ratio of prices of a Big Mac in two countries. There were already McDonald's restaurants in many countries in 1986, so the price of a Big Mac could be computed for a large number of countries, giving an alternative measure of the exchange rate between any two of them. Though proposed tongue-in-cheek, the Big Mac index caught on and is now commonly used. In fact, there is a good reason for its popularity. The Big Mac index is a simple example of a PPP adjustment. Its shortcoming is that instead of a representative basket of diverse goods, this index compares a basket consisting of only a single good, the Big Mac, which is only a small fraction of people's consumption. Thus, this index will not reflect true cost-of-living differences across countries.

Using this procedure, GDP per capita in Mexico in PPP can be compared by multiplying GDP per capita in Mexico in pesos by the peso-dollar PPP conversion factor we just derived:

$$\text{Mexican GDP p.c. in PPP \$} = \text{Mexican GDP p.c. in pesos} \times \text{\$/peso PPP}$$
$$= 140,101 \times 0.11$$
$$= \$15,411.$$

Comparing this result for Mexico with the $10,648 obtained using the peso/dollar exchange rate, we see that there is often a significant difference between exchange-rate-based measures and PPP-based measures of GDP per capita, with the gap between the United States economy and poorer economies generally being smaller when we use PPP-based measures. This pattern reflects the lower cost of living in countries with lower GDP per capita that is, the fact that exchange-rate-based measures of GDP ignore the fact that many commodities are cheaper in poorer countries.

Inequality in GDP per capita

Very large disparities still exist across countries when we use PPP-based measures. Exhibit 6.1 shows a graph of PPP-adjusted GDP per capita across countries in 2014 (expressed in terms of 2011 constant dollars, where the notion of constant dollars was defined in Chapter 5). Note that there are five countries with less than $1,000 per capita, including Burundi, Liberia, and Niger, and another seventeen with PPP-adjusted GDP per capita of between $1,000 and $2,000, including the Democratic Republic of Congo, Ethiopia, Haiti, and Rwanda. These measures contrast sharply with those of the United States ($54,306), France ($39,374), and Germany ($47,407) in the same year.

Exhibit 6.2 complements Exhibit 6.1 by showing a map of the world with different ranges of PPP-adjusted GDP per capita shaded in different colors. Reds, oranges, and yellows correspond to lower GDP per capita and greens correspond to relatively high GDP per capita. The overall picture is similar to that shown in Exhibit 6.1, yet we can now more easily identify where the rich and the poor countries are. There are some striking patterns to the differences in incomes. For example, the African continent appears to be uniformly poorer than other continents, except for a few spots. Much of South Asia and Latin America is also quite poor. In contrast, North America and Western Europe are relatively prosperous. This map makes it clear that there are indeed major economic disparities throughout the world, and one of our purposes in this chapter is to understand the causes behind them.

GDP per Worker

We have so far talked about GDP per capita aggregate income (GDP) divided by total population. But total population includes children, the elderly, and those who are not employed, who do not take part in production (though in many less developed economies, child labor is quite common). This raises the possibility that part of the variation

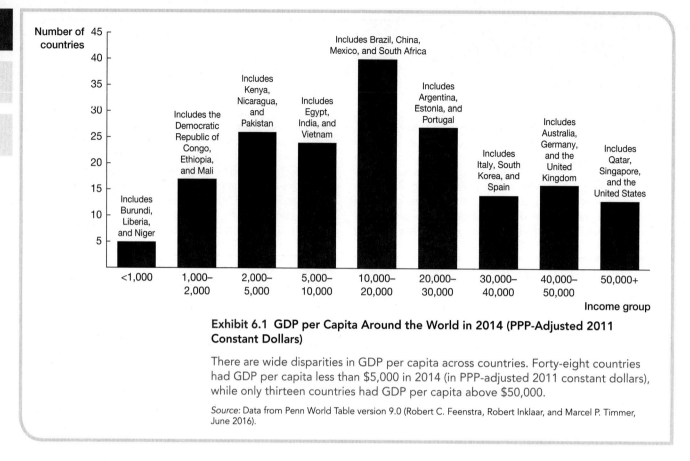

Exhibit 6.1 GDP per Capita Around the World in 2014 (PPP-Adjusted 2011 Constant Dollars)

There are wide disparities in GDP per capita across countries. Forty-eight countries had GDP per capita less than $5,000 in 2014 (in PPP-adjusted 2011 constant dollars), while only thirteen countries had GDP per capita above $50,000.

Source: Data from Penn World Table version 9.0 (Robert C. Feenstra, Robert Inklaar, and Marcel P. Timmer, June 2016).

GDP per worker is defined as GDP divided by the number of people in employment.

in GDP per capita across countries might be due to differences in what fraction of the population works. Therefore, a natural alternative that avoids this problem is to focus on **GDP per worker**, defined as GDP divided by number of "workers," meaning those in employment:

$$\text{GDP per worker} = \frac{\text{GDP}}{\text{Number of people in employment}}.$$

This measure gives us a better picture of how much each worker produces on average by excluding those who do not work.

Exhibit 6.3 is similar to Exhibit 6.1, but uses (PPP-adjusted) GDP per worker. If there were large cross-country differences in the ratio of workers to the total population, this exhibit would look very different from Exhibit 6.1. A direct comparison shows that the two exhibits are very similar, though naturally, GDP per worker is higher for every country than GDP per capita, because the denominator is always smaller for GDP per worker. For example, PPP-adjusted GDP per capita in 2014 (in 2011 constant dollars) for Mexico is $15,745 (equal to 16,725 in *current* dollars), whereas PPP-adjusted GDP per worker for Mexico in 2010 (again in 2011 constant dollars) is $38,661. For India, the two corresponding numbers are $5,224 and $13,261. As a reflection of this, the group of countries with the highest GDP per worker now corresponds to $100,000+ instead of $50,000+ as in Exhibit 6.1.

Productivity

Productivity refers to the value of goods and services that a worker generates for each hour of work.

The main reason GDP per capita or GDP per worker varies across countries is because productivity varies across countries. **Productivity** here refers to the value of goods and services that a worker generates for each hour of work. From our discussion of the national income accounting identity in Chapter 5, you will recall that the value of goods and

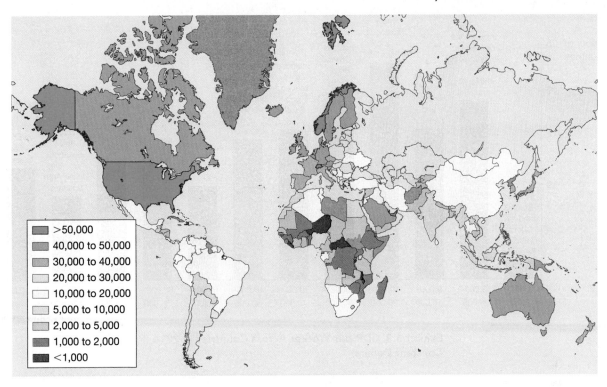

Exhibit 6.2 A Map of PPP-adjusted GDP per Capita Across the World

The large disparities in PPP-adjusted GDP per capita across countries are easily visible on this map, which also shows that the poorest countries are concentrated in Africa, parts of Asia, Central America, and the Caribbean.

Source: Data from Penn World Table version 9.0 (Robert C. Feenstra, Robert Inklaar, and Marcel P. Timmer, June 2016).

> To understand the huge differences in GDP per capita across countries, we have to look at the production side.

services produced in a country, GDP, is equal to the total income in that country. Thus productivity also measures GDP per hour of work. GDP per worker and productivity are very closely related and thus vary across countries for the same reasons. (The only reason the two concepts differ is that the total number of hours of work per worker may also vary across countries, but in practice, this variation is small.)

It is useful to focus on productivity differences across countries, because it emphasizes that to understand the huge differences in GDP per capita across countries, we have to look at the production side. In particular, we need to study the factors that make labor much more productive in some countries than in others.

Incomes and the Standard of Living

A natural question is whether GDP per capita or GDP per worker is the quantity we should focus on. The answer depends on what we are trying to measure. GDP per worker is particularly informative when we would like to understand why some economies are more productive than others, because it focuses directly on differences in GDP relative to the number of workers in employment.

Another reason we care about disparities in income across countries is that we want to measure differences in the standards of living across countries. For this purpose, GDP

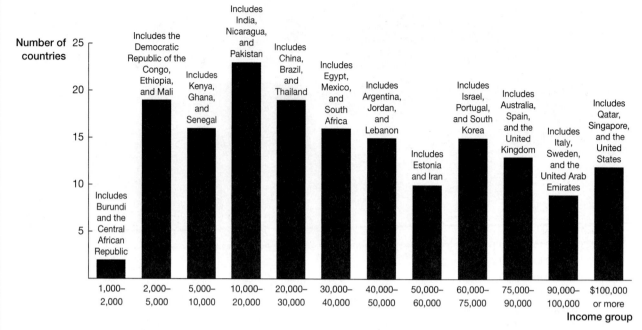

Exhibit 6.3 GDP per Worker Across Countries in 2014 (PPP-adjusted 2011 Constant Dollars)

The distribution of countries by income per worker looks similar to the distribution by GDP per capita shown in Exhibit 6.1. One visible difference is that the distribution is shifted to the right compared to Exhibit 6.1, because every country has higher GDP per worker than GDP per capita.

Source: Data from Penn World Table version 9.0 (Robert C. Feenstra, Robert Inklaar, and Marcel P. Timmer, June 2016).

per capita is a natural first step, because the conditions of the whole population, including children and the elderly, are conveyed by this measure.

People living at the poverty level.

However, there is much that is left out of GDP per capita, as you have already seen in Chapter 5. Even though, again as shown in the previous chapter, GDP per capita is a fairly good predictor of average life satisfaction in a country, we cannot capture the diverse dimensions of well-being and the standards of living of an entire population by looking at a single number. For example, income can vary widely within countries as well as across them. In the United States, the coasts are richer than the middle of the country. In Mexico, there are great differences between the north and the south. High income inequality in general prevents measures of average income (like GDP per capita) from giving a complete picture of how comfortably most people in a country actually live. Finally, as already mentioned in the previous chapter, people do not care only about income and consumption but also about factors such as pollution, the quality of healthcare, and public safety. Variations in these factors across countries are not captured by GDP per capita numbers (as you learned at the end of Chapter 5).

All of this implies that we should refrain from making sweeping generalizations about the welfare of a country's citizens solely based on its GDP per capita. Nevertheless, we can learn quite a bit from GDP per capita about the standards of living. In the previous chapter, we saw the relationship between GDP per capita and average life satisfaction. In addition, one of the things we care about when discussing a particular country is whether many people are living in extreme poverty. Researchers at the World Bank have come up with the notion of *absolute poverty*, corresponding to living on less than $1.08 per day in

Exhibit 6.4 The Relationship Between Poverty and GDP per capita in 2014 (PPP-adjusted 2011 Constant Dollars)

Absolute poverty, measured here by the fraction of the population living on less than $1.90 per day, is higher among countries with lower GDP per capita. In the exhibit, when you focus on countries with GDP per capita above $10,000, this relationship disappears, because relatively few people in these relatively prosperous countries actually live on less than $1.90 per day.

Source: Data from the World Bank DataBank and the Penn World Table version 9.0 (Robert C. Feenstra, Robert Inklaar, and Marcel P. Timmer, June 2016).

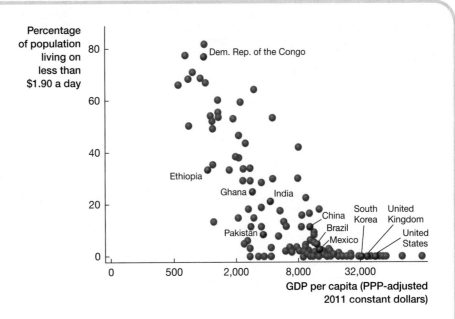

The one dollar a day per person poverty line is a measure of absolute poverty used by economists and other social scientists to compare the extent of poverty across countries.

1993—a measure commonly referred to as the **one dollar a day per person poverty line**. This measure has now been updated to $1.90 per person per day (in 2011 U.S. dollars), though it is still sometimes referred to as one dollar a day. For most of us, it is difficult to imagine how anybody could survive on such a tiny sum, but more than 899 million people in 2012 did in fact try to make do with less than $1.90 per day. Exhibit 6.4 shows a scatter plot with the fraction of a nation's population living in poverty (according to this definition) on the *y*-axis and its PPP-adjusted GDP per capita on the *x*-axis. The exhibit shows a strong association, indicating that GDP per capita gives us a fairly good idea of which countries have populations suffering from extreme poverty.

Note that in this and similar exhibits, we are using a proportional scale, which stretches the *x*-axis so that a 10 percent change in GDP per capita represents the *same* absolute distance on the horizontal scale, whether we're starting from a lower level, like $500, or a higher level, like $8,000. For example, at the point labeled $500, a 10 percent increase takes the same horizontal distance as a 10 percent increase at the point labeled $8,000. This is the same strategy we used for the vertical axis in Exhibit 5.8 in the last chapter. Our discussion

CHOICE &CONSEQUENCE

Dangers of Just Focusing on GDP per capita

A common error in comparing standards of living across countries is to focus only on GDP per capita without thinking about its composition. This error is most clearly illustrated by looking at the situation in South Africa. Until 1994, South Africa was ruled by a minority white population under a repressive system of racial segregation known as *apartheid*—a word meaning "separateness." The apartheid regime prevented blacks from participating in politics and regulated their economic activities. It also created a variety of repressive arrangements intended to keep the wages of black workers low. According to the economic historian Charles Feinstein, the result was that although the South African economy became more prosperous as a whole during much of the twentieth century, the incomes of its black citizens did not increase during this entire period[1] So if we were to look at just GDP per capita in South Africa, it would not inform us about the very low incomes and poor living conditions of most of its black citizens.

Exhibit 6.5 Relationship Between Life Expectancy at Birth and GDP per capita in 2014 (PPP-adjusted 2011 Constant Dollars)

This exhibit shows that people in countries with higher GDP per capita also have higher life expectancy at birth, meaning that on average, people in richer countries tend to live longer lives.

Source: Data from the World Bank DataBank and the Penn World Table version 9.0 (Robert C. Feenstra, Robert Inklaar, and Marcel P. Timmer, June 2016).

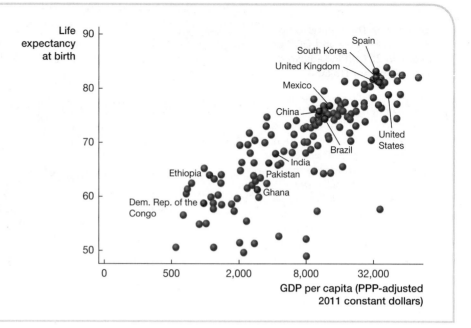

of economic growth in Chapter 6 also makes use of such proportional scales and further clarifies why using such a scale is particularly valuable in the context of economic growth.

Another reason we care about GDP per capita is that poverty often brings poor health. One way to measure the health of a nation is by looking at the average life expectancy at birth. Exhibit 6.5 shows a scatter plot with life expectancy on the *y*-axis and PPP-adjusted GDP per capita on the *x*-axis, and again there is a strong association, indicating that this non-income-based measure of the standard of living also correlates strongly with GDP per capita.

We should also take into account several other factors when measuring the standards of living across countries. One alternative measure is the United Nations' Human Development Index, which combines GDP per capita life expectancy, and measures of education to more holistically measure the standard of living. Exhibit 6.6 presents a scatter plot with the Human Development Index on the *y*-axis and PPP-adjusted GDP per capita on the *x*-axis. It shows that there is once again a strong association between GDP per capita and this measure.

Overall, the relationship between GDP per capita and several measures of the standard of living, including poverty, life expectancy, and the Human Development Index, suggests

Exhibit 6.6 Relationship Between the Human Development Index and GDP per capita in 2014 (PPP-adjusted 2011 Constant Dollars)

The Human Development Index combines information on GDP per capita life expectancy, average years of schooling for those above age 25, and the enrollment of children in school. This exhibit shows that countries with higher PPP-adjusted GDP per capita tend to have higher levels of this index.

Source: Data from the United Nations Development Programme and the Penn World Table version 9.0 (Robert C. Feenstra, Robert Inklaar, and Marcel P. Timmer, June 2016).

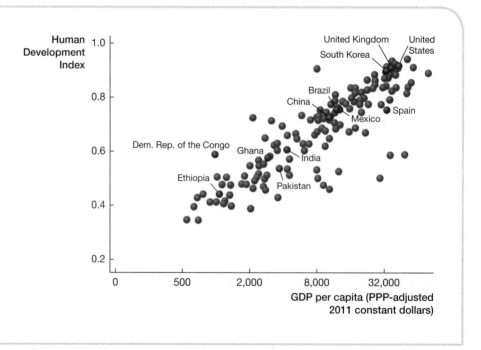

a simple strategy: first focus on GDP per capita and then look in greater detail at issues related to health, education, poverty, and inequality within and across countries. This is the strategy we adopt here.

6.2 Productivity and the Aggregate Production Function

As noted above, to understand differences in GDP per capita or GDP per worker across countries, we need to understand differences in productivity. To do so, we first outline the main sources of variation in productivity across countries. Then we turn to a more systematic analysis of these factors using the aggregate production function.

Productivity Differences

There are three main reasons productivity differs across countries, each of which we now explain in turn.

Human capital is each person's stock of skills to produce output or economic value.

1. *Human capital:* Workers differ in terms of **human capital**, which is their stock of skills to produce output or economic value. For example, a worker with a university degree in computer science will be much more productive in computer programming or Web page design than a worker with just a high school degree. Suppose, for example, that in one day, the computer scientist can do the same tasks as two workers with high school degrees. In this case, we say that she has twice the human capital as the workers with high school degrees. But this also implies that she is twice as *productive*.

Physical capital is any good, including machines and buildings, used for production.

2. *Physical capital:* **Physical capital** is any good, including machines (equipment) and buildings (structures), used for production. For example, in agriculture, aggregate production will depend on agricultural machinery, the equipment used for transporting inputs and outputs, and the buildings in which the output is stored. Though these inputs are all different, we can aggregate them into a single measure and obtain the **physical capital stock** of the economy using their dollar value. Workers will be more productive when the economy has a bigger physical capital stock, enabling each worker to work with more (or better) equipment and structures.

The **physical capital stock** of an economy is the value of equipment, structures and other non-labor inputs used in production.

Technology refers to a set of devices and practices that determine how efficiently an economy uses its labor and capital.

3. *Technology:* **Technology** refers to a set of devices and practices that determine how efficiently an economy uses its labor and capital. In particular, an economy with better technology uses its labor and capital more efficiently and thus achieves higher productivity. We will see below that an economy can have better technology either because it uses superior knowledge in production (for example, new manufacturing techniques and equipment not available to other economies) or because it organizes production more efficiently.

The Aggregate Production Function

Human capital, physical capital, and technology each play a part in determining how productive workers in an economy are. The aggregate production function is our tool for understanding how these three ingredients come together to generate GDP in an economy.

> Human capital, physical capital, and technology each play a part in determining how productive workers in an economy are.

In Chapter 5, we saw how we can aggregate tens of thousands of commodities into a single measure of GDP. For the analysis here, we can go one step further. Once we have made the simplification of aggregating everything into GDP, we can just think of GDP as if it were a single commodity. Even though this simplification ignores the *composition* of GDP, it allows us to more clearly look at what determines the *level* of GDP, which is our main purpose in this chapter.

The advantage of looking at GDP in this way is that once we start thinking of the world in terms of a single commodity, we can study the aggregate production function of the economy, which describes the relationship between GDP and its various inputs. This is similar to how we study the relationship between the output of a single firm and the inputs that it uses. For example, if we wanted to understand how much corn a farm produces, we would first specify the relationship between total corn production and its key inputs, for example, the number of workers on the farm and the equipment that the farm uses.

A key concept in our study of the aggregate production function is *factors of production*. Recall from the previous chapter that factors of production are the inputs to the production process—goods or services purchased in the market for producing other goods, in this case for producing GDP. To understand a nation's output, we will look at a production function that describes how the factors of production are combined to produce GDP. But differently from the case in which we study a single firm, our focus is not specific commodities, such as T-shirts or iPhones, but all of GDP, and we therefore refer to this function as the **aggregate production function**.

The aggregate production function is useful for understanding not only how GDP is determined but also why productivity varies across countries.

Labor

The first and most important factor of production is labor. A nation can increase output by employing more workers. For example, more workers can be deployed for tilling the soil and harvesting corn.

Remember, though, that not all workers are the same. Some will have greater human capital than others and will be able to produce more output or economic value (and this is why, as we have seen, human capital is a major determinant of productivity). Such differences in workers' human capital make looking at the total number of workers in an economy a poor indicator of how much the economy can produce. Instead, we need to know the total efficiency units of labor. **Total efficiency units of labor** is defined as the product of the total number of workers and the average human capital (efficiency) of workers. For example, suppose a computer science graduate can perform the same job as two high school graduates. Then, it would be natural to give twice the weight to her labor than to that of high school graduates. Applying the same idea more broadly, we can compute the total efficiency units of labor, denoted by H, as the product of the total number of workers in the economy, L, and the average efficiency or human capital of workers, h:

$$H = L \times h.$$

This equation implies that the total efficiency units of labor in the economy can be increased either if more workers take part in the production process (for example, because employment increases) or if each worker becomes more productive. Acquiring more skills through formal schooling is one way for a worker to increase his or her productivity.

Physical Capital and Land

The second major factor of production is physical capital, typically denoted by K (corresponding to the first letter of "Kapital," the German spelling of capital). When an economy has more physical capital, or equivalently, a greater physical capital *stock*, its workers can work with more and better equipment and structures, and thus the economy will produce more GDP.

A third factor of production is land. For example, if we think of an economy in the eighteenth century, land and other natural resources would be the key factors of production. Yet other factors of production include natural resources and the entrepreneurial talent of the economy (the skills and capabilities of its entrepreneurs and businesspeople). To simplify the discussion, we focus only on physical capital and labor (specifically, total efficiency units of labor). When we do so, the value of land and natural resources can be included in the physical capital stock (the same way that the value of buildings is). We return to the role of entrepreneurial talent in the context of our in-depth discussion of technology later in the chapter.

Technology

Another major determinant of GDP is technology, which, as you will recall, determines how efficiently the economy uses its inputs—labor, capital, and land. In the aggregate production function, technology summarizes the relationship between the factors of production and GDP.

An **aggregate production function** describes the relationship between the aggregate GDP of a nation and its factors of production.

Total efficiency units of labor is the product of the total number of workers in the economy and the average human capital of workers.

A better technology means that the economy can generate more output from the same set of inputs, and thus increases its productivity for given total efficiency units of labor and capital.

Representing the Aggregate Production Function

Let us represent the aggregate production function as

$$Y = A \times F(K, H),$$

where:

1. Y stands for GDP.
2. K is the physical capital stock of the nation.
3. H is the efficiency units of labor that the economy uses in production.
4. The function F signifies that there is a relationship between physical capital, labor, and GDP (the expression for F in the above equation is read as "F is a function of K and H"). In particular, GDP is generated through a combination of physical capital and the efficiency units of labor.
5. A is an index of technology. As A increases, the economy produces more GDP with the same level of physical capital stock and total efficiency units of labor. We discuss the role of technology in greater detail below.

As we have already emphasized, this aggregate production function is similar to the production function of an individual firm for producing a specific type of commodity. In particular:

(1) Just like the production function of a specific firm, the aggregate production function will show that GDP is increasing in both physical capital and labor—put differently, more is better. Holding labor constant, if we have a greater physical capital stock, we will be able to produce more GDP. Holding physical capital constant, if we have more labor, we will also be able to produce more GDP.

(2) The aggregate production function is also subject to the *Law of Diminishing Marginal Product* (which is related to our discussion of diminishing marginal benefit in Chapter 4). The **Law of Diminishing Marginal Product** states that the marginal contribution of a factor of production to GDP diminishes when we increase the quantity used of that factor of production (holding all other factors of production constant). We can illustrate the aggregate production function graphically by holding the total efficiency units of labor constant, as in Exhibit 6.7, or by holding the physical capital stock constant, as in Exhibit 6.8. Let's start with Exhibit 6.7.

This exhibit shows both the positive relationship between physical capital and output, and the Law of Diminishing Marginal Product. In particular, the marginal contribution of an additional unit of physical capital to output—the amount that output increases as a result of a unit increase in the physical capital stock—is decreasing with the total physical

The **Law of Diminishing Marginal Product** states that the marginal contribution of a factor of production to GDP diminishes when we increase the quantity used of that factor of production (holding all other factors constant).

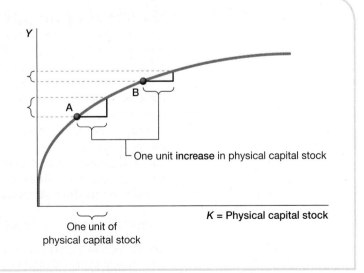

Exhibit 6.7 The Aggregate Production Function with Physical Capital Stock on the x-Axis (with the Total Efficiency Units of Labor Held Constant)

Holding the total efficiency units of labor constant, the aggregate production function shows the relationship between the physical capital stock and GDP in the economy. As the physical capital stock increases, so does GDP. But the relationship becomes less and less steep as the physical capital stock of the economy increases because of the Law of Diminishing Marginal Product. For the same one-unit increase in the physical capital stock, the increase in GDP is greater at point A (with lower physical capital stock) than at point B (with greater physical capital stock).

Exhibit 6.8 The Aggregate Production Function with the Efficiency Units of Labor on the x-Axis (with Physical Capital Stock Held Constant)

Holding the physical capital stock constant, the aggregate production function shows the relationship between the total efficiency units of labor and GDP. Once again, as the total efficiency units of labor increase, so does GDP, but consistent with the Law of Diminishing Marginal Product, the relationship becomes less and less steep as the total efficiency units of labor increase.

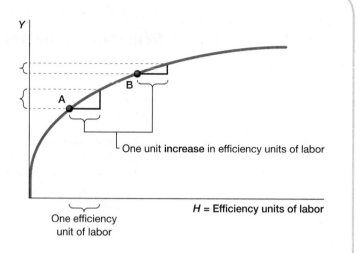

capital stock. We see this by comparing the increase in output for a unit increase in physical capital stock at two different points of the aggregate production function in Exhibit 6.7. Consider a unit increase close to the origin (point A). When there is less physical capital in the economy, the corresponding increase in output is large. When we have the same unit increase farther to the right, corresponding to more existing physical capital (point B), the resulting increase in output is smaller, as shown by the smaller vertical increase at B than at A. This visual difference captures the Law of Diminishing Marginal Product.

Exhibit 6.7 holds the efficiency units of labor, H, constant and looks at the relationship between the physical capital stock and GDP. Exhibit 6.8 does the opposite, holding the physical capital stock, K, constant and looking at the relationship between the efficiency units of labor of the economy and GDP. This relationship also satisfies the Law of Diminishing Marginal Product.

6.3 The Role and Determinants of Technology

We now discuss in more detail how technology affects the aggregate production function and the factors that influence the level of technology of an economy.

Technology

You will recall that technology determines how efficiently an economy's inputs are utilized. Exhibit 6.9 shows the implications of better technology for the aggregate production function. We once again hold the efficiency units of labor, H, constant, and plot the relationship between GDP and the physical capital stock, K. When technology improves (that is, when the economy uses better technology), the relationship between GDP and the physical capital stock shifts up. Therefore, for every level of the efficiency units of labor, a better technology implies that the economy will produce more GDP.

Our study of the aggregate production function thus clarifies why productivity depends on human capital, physical capital, and technology. Holding the total number of workers constant, greater human capital, a larger stock of physical capital, and better technology will all increase GDP. Because the total number of workers (and hours of work per worker) is constant, this also corresponds to an increase in productivity.

Dimensions of Technology

Technology, as we have defined it, is a rather broad concept, and in fact has two very distinct components. The first is *knowledge*, and the second is the *efficiency of production*.

Exhibit 6.9 The Shift in the Production Function Resulting from More Advanced Technology

As technology improves, the aggregate production function shifts upward, indicating that with the same amount of physical capital stock and total efficiency units of labor, more output can be produced. In this exhibit, the total efficiency units of labor are held constant, and for a given level of physical capital stock, the economy with more advanced technology has a higher level of GDP.

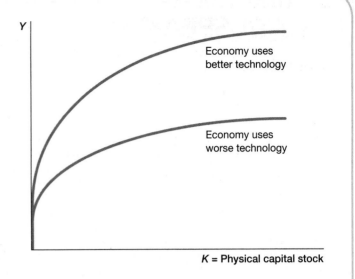

Economy uses better technology

Economy uses worse technology

K = Physical capital stock

Let us start with knowledge. Today, we know how to produce many new goods, such as smartphones and tablets, which were not available previously. In addition, this knowledge also enables us to perform certain tasks more efficiently. For example, when you use a computer for writing an essay or doing computations for a class, you are making use of the computing power, which comes from the knowledge that society has acquired and has applied to its production process. Part of this knowledge is in the human capital of the workers: workers today can perform a range of tasks more productively than their grandparents could. But an important part of this knowledge is embodied in the physical capital stock of firms: the computers that firms are using are part of the physical capital stock of the economy.

Nevertheless, there is also a sense in which technology is different from the physical capital stock of the economy. Your great-grandparents, however much they may have wished to pay for a computer, would not have been able to do so, because computers were not yet commercially sold. Your grandparents would have had to pay an enormous price for a computer with fewer capabilities than the one you are using now, and it likely would have been a giant machine rather than the small notebooks that many of you are using. Thus advances in technology—in this specific instance, in computer technology—directly increase the number of tasks we can perform and the speed at which we can accomplish them.

Research and development (R&D) refers to the activities directed at improving scientific knowledge, generating new innovations, or implementing existing knowledge in production to improve the technology of a firm or an economy.

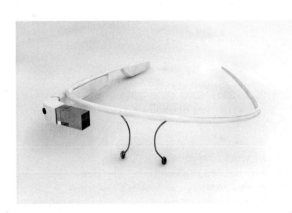

Advances in technology sometimes happen by chance, but more often, they result from the purposeful, optimizing decisions of economic agents. For example, society achieves such advances with **research and development (R&D)**, which involves a wide range of activities like research on new scientific ideas in universities and private labs, research directed at finding new ways of applying science to production on the factory floor, and development activities geared at commercializing existing knowledge and products. R&D is a major activity in the U.S. economy. Around 1.25 million people worked as researchers in 2012 (the most recent year for which this information is available), and $457 billion—2.81 percent of total GDP—was spent on research and development. Of this amount, about $278 billion was spent by businesses, while the remaining portion was spent by the U.S. government, universities, and other institutions.

Let us next turn to the second component of technology—the efficiency of production. To understand why the efficiency of production will vary and how this will resemble technological differences across countries, imagine two economies. In one, the allocation of resources is determined by the market, and in the other, resources are allocated randomly across individuals and firms. As a specific example, say that both of these economies have two types of workers, economics professors and basketball players, and two types of tasks, teaching and basketball.

> Advances in technology sometimes happen by chance, but more often, they result from the purposeful, optimizing decisions of economic agents.

LETTING THE
DATA SPEAK

Moore's Law

A long-term trend of rather remarkable regularity in the development of computer microprocessors has been observed since 1965. It's dubbed Moore's Law after Intel cofounder Gordon Moore, who predicted in that year that the number of transistors on a chip would double approximately every 2 years.[2] The number of transistors is a key determinant of how fast a computer processor is. So roughly speaking, Moore's Law implies that computer processor power should double approximately every 2 years. So far, this seems to have been borne out by developments in computer technology, as illustrated in Exhibit 6.10, which, crucially, again uses a proportional scale, so that the vertical distance between 1,000 and 10,000 is the same as that between 10 million and 100 million. The exhibit shows a striking increase in the number of transistors on a chip from about 1,000 in 1972 to over 1 billion by 2015. Several other measures of technological advances in computing have also behaved according to Moore's Law. For example, the number of pixels in digital cameras and RAM storage capacity have also doubled every 2 years or so, while power consumption of computer nodes and hard disk storage costs appear to have been halved approximately every 2 years.

Naturally, there is nothing predetermined about the relationship between time and progress in technology that would make this into an actual "law." This progress results from the investments of several companies in new computer technologies, which are in turn driven by the profitability of these investments. It also relies on government support for university and private research and on the ability of the United States and other advanced and developing nations to attract increasing numbers of young, talented students into science, engineering, and related fields. Things could change in the future, halting this rapid progress in technology. Fewer college students could choose to major in science and engineering in the future, or governments could decide to limit or even stop their support for private or university research, weakening incentives for further technological advances. Moreover, even without a major cutback in funding or a change in the profitability of research in this area, the rate of advance may slow down from its current breakneck pace. Already, the engineering community is questioning the economic and scientific feasibility of continuing to pack more transistors into chips. Nevertheless, the general relationship so far has been very accurate and, assuming it continues in the years to come, the implications for lives are enormous.

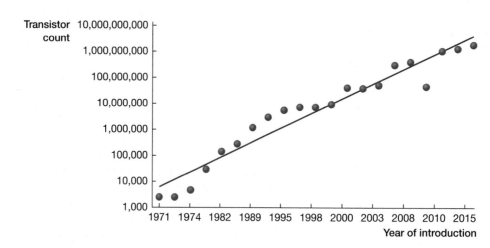

Exhibit 6.10 Moore's Law

Gordon Moore predicted in 1965 that the speed of computer processors would improve steadily. This has turned out to be a very accurate prediction, with the number of transistors packed in a computer chip doubling approximately every 2 years. This remarkable trend, which has come to be known as Moore's Law, now symbolizes the sustained technological improvements of our era.

Source: Based on Intel.

The first economy relies on the market for allocating workers to tasks. Basketball players who are better at basketball than teaching will play basketball, and economics professors will do the teaching. In the second, allocation takes place randomly. Suppose that economics professors are assigned to do the basketball playing and basketball players to do the teaching. There are no differences in the knowledge available for production between the two economies, and both have the same human capital. But the first economy will be much more successful (especially in basketball), and will produce more output (more and better basketball and perhaps even better teaching).

What is the difference between the two economies? This difference has to do with the **efficiency of production**—the ability of society to produce the maximal amount of output at a given cost or for given levels of the factors of production and knowledge. When the economy is able to increase the efficiency of production, there will be a shift in the aggregate production function similar to that shown in Exhibit 6.9. We therefore include

Efficiency of production refers to the ability of an economy to produce the maximal amount of output from a given amount of factors of production and knowledge.

CHOICE & CONSEQUENCE

Academic Misallocation in Nazi Germany

The example of economics professors assigned to playing basketball may seem droll, if not outright bizarre. But there are many instances of misallocation of resources in the real world almost as extreme—and often more consequential.

One comes from Hitler's Nazi Germany, which expelled all Jewish academics starting in 1933 from German universities and often replaced them with less-qualified ethnic Germans. In many fields, this meant a major loss of talent from German academia. For example, 18 percent of all mathematics faculty in German universities were dismissed in 1933 and 1934. The results were devastating, as many observed even at the time. When asked by the Nazi minister of education "How is mathematics in Göttingen now that it has been freed of Jewish influences?," the famous mathematician David Hilbert replied: "Mathematics in Göttingen? There is really none any more."

Fabian Waldinger studies the implications of this major dismissal of talented mathematicians on the academic performance of German universities and PhD students.[3] He measures the quality of PhD students by the probability of these students being able to publish their dissertation in an academic journal, being able to become full professors thereafter, and receiving subsequent citations to their work. Waldinger's results indicate that in universities such as Berlin, Breslau, and Göttingen, where this Nazi policy led to the expulsion of more Jewish mathematicians, there was a very significant decline in the quality of PhD students compared to universities that did not suffer such dismissals, such as Frankfurt, Hamburg, and Stuttgart. These results indicate that the consequences of sacrificing the efficiency of production are likely to be severe.

LETTING THE DATA SPEAK

Efficiency of Production and Productivity at the Company Level

Economist James Schmitz Jr. studied the experience of the iron ore industries in the United States and Canada in the face of competition from Brazilian producers.[4] His findings provide a particularly clear illustration of how changes in the organization of firms can lead to improvements in the efficiency of production—or "technology"—and thus increase productivity significantly.

Schmitz documents that productivity—for example, measured as output of iron ore per hour—was constant since at least 1970 in the Canadian and the U.S. iron ore industries when they faced little foreign competition. In the early 1980s, however, Brazilian producers entered the U.S. market and started to deliver iron ore to Chicago and other central markets. Schmitz shows that over the course of the next decade, productivity in the U.S. and Canadian iron ore industries, which had been flat for a long time, doubled. He

shows that this was not due to more intensive use of capital or materials, nor was it driven by the use of new production techniques. Rather, it resulted from a significant reorganization of production.

Iron ore production plants were heavily unionized—a fact that, according to Schmitz, prevented the plants from efficiently allocating labor across different tasks. For example, despite industry studies suggesting that there was an excess number of repair workers for a large variety of equipment, union contracts did not permit reduction in repair staff. Following the increase in competition, these work rules were changed, enabling a more productive use of labor. Schmitz provides a variety of additional evidence showing that these and other changes in work rules allowed a more flexible allocation of labor across tasks and therefore better utilization of equipment, resulting in the dramatic increase in productivity.

efficiency of production as part of our definition of technology, because it captures the differences in how much output an economy can generate with given amounts of inputs.

The importance of technology for GDP is the reason we include A and represent the aggregate production function as

$$A \times F(K, H).$$

Greater values for A correspond to better technology and increase GDP for given levels of efficiency units of labor and physical capital stock, which shifts the aggregate production function up, as shown in Exhibit 6.9. But note that A is *not* a factor of production. Although it designates the technology available to the economy, it does not correspond to an input that the producer can purchase in the marketplace.

Entrepreneurship

A particularly important reason why efficiency of production and productivity might differ across economies relates to entrepreneurship. As we discuss in greater detail in Chapter 8, various factors might influence whether individuals with a comparative advantage for entrepreneurship become entrepreneurs. When they fail to do so, the efficiency of production of an economy is lower—in the same way as the mismatch between basketball players and economics teachers, though perhaps more importantly.

LETTING THE
DATA SPEAK

Monopoly and GDP

When Mexico entered the North American Free Trade Agreement (NAFTA) with the United States in 1994, many economists predicted that Mexico's economy would grow rapidly. But in the first 15 years after signing NAFTA, Mexico's growth was much less than most analysts expected. Monopolies and barriers against the entry of new companies are just some of the reasons the country has not achieved more significant growth.

Consider the telecommunications sector in Mexico, which for a long time operated as a state monopoly. It subsequently was privatized, but turned into a private monop-oly under the ownership of Carlos Slim, who has now become one of the richest people in the world. In contrast, the telecommunications sector in the United States is very competitive, with many firms competing in both wireless and broadband. The Mexican telecommunications sector not only charges higher prices than other countries but also invests less than other comparable countries, as shown in Exhibit 6.11.

Removing monopolies and entry barriers that prevent the efficient allocation of resources is one important way of increasing GDP.

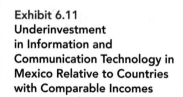

Exhibit 6.11
Underinvestment in Information and Communication Technology in Mexico Relative to Countries with Comparable Incomes

Monopolies and barriers against the entry of new companies often discourage investment and slow down technological progress. For example, Mexico, where the telecommunications sector is monopolized, invests less in information and communication technology than do other countries with similar PPP-adjusted GDP per capita.

Source: Data from World Bank DataBank.

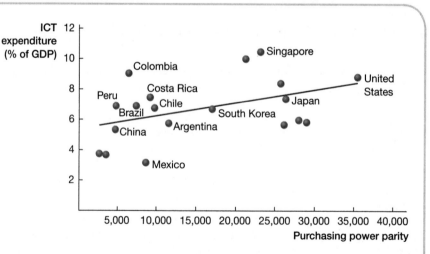

EVIDENCE-BASED ECONOMICS

Q: Why is the average American so much richer than the average Indian?

To understand the variation in productivity and PPP-adjusted GDP per worker between the United States and India (and other countries), it is useful to focus on three factors: human capital, physical capital, and technology. To see the relative importance of any one of these factors in explaining differences in PPP-adjusted GDP per worker across countries, we can compare a country's actual PPP-adjusted GDP per worker with what it *would be* if the country had access to the same human capital, physical capital stock, or technology as another country. This is exactly what we do in Exhibit 6.12, specifically, with technology.

Using data on education attainment (a key aspect of human capital) and employment, we calculate the efficiency units of labor. Column (3) records the average years of schooling per worker of each country. It shows that most countries have significantly lower levels of average schooling than the United States.

Then, using data on investment over several decades, we calculate the physical capital stock for each country. Column (4) shows the ratio of the physical capital stock per worker of each country relative to the physical capital stock per worker in the United States. Most countries have a significantly lower physical capital stock per worker than the United States (but there are also countries like Norway, not shown in the exhibit, that have higher levels than the United States).

Using estimates of the shape of the aggregate production function (we provide details of this estimation in the appendix to this chapter), we can then see how the efficiency units of labor and physical capital stock are translated into PPP-adjusted GDP per worker. Comparing these contributions of human capital and physical capital with *actual* PPP-adjusted GDP per worker (recorded in column (2) of Exhibit 6.12), we can then infer how much of a contribution technology makes to PPP-adjusted GDP per worker. Specifically, we assume that any GDP that cannot be accounted for by physical capital and labor is accounted for by technology.

Given the estimates of the aggregate production function, we can now compute what the income level of all of these countries would have been if they had had access to

Exhibit 6.12 Contribution of Human Capital, Physical Capital, and Technology to Differences in PPP-adjusted GDP per worker

Source: Data from Penn World Table (Alan Heston, Robert Summers, and Bettina Aten, Penn World Table Version 7.1).

Country (1)	PPP-adjusted GDP per worker in 2014 (2)	Average Years of Schooling (3)	Percentage of U.S. Physical Capital Stock per Worker in 2014 (4)	PPP-adjusted GDP per worker If Technology Were at U.S. Level (5)
United States	112,517.30	13.18	100.0	SAME
United Kingdom	83,611.74	12.24	86.9	102,902.90
Spain	88,944.35	10.27	81.2	91,985.66
South Korea	67,246.82	12.05	52.6	86,293.01
Mexico	38,661.51	8.79	21.0	54,766.86
Brazil	28,935.31	7.89	13.4	45,215.59
China	21,394.03	7.95	10.5	41,837.58
India	13,260.64	6.24	2.8	24,056.65
Pakistan	15,492.71	5.02	2.2	20,321.71
Ghana	7,497.48	7.00	1.7	21,407.27
Dem. Rep. of the Congo	3,757.44	3.66	1.6	16,651.50

exactly the same technology as the United States (using their actual efficiency units of labor and physical capital stock). This information is recorded in column (5) of the exhibit. The difference between actual incomes and these hypothetical numbers illustrates the contribution of technology.

The exhibit reveals some powerful facts. Consistent with the patterns we have already seen in Exhibits 6.1–6.3, PPP-adjusted GDP per worker in the United States is about 8.5 times that in India ($112,517/13,261 \approx 8.5$). We also see that Indians have average years of schooling of 6.2 compared to 13.2 in the United States, and that the physical capital stock per worker in India is about 3 percent of that of the United States.

So how much would a typical Indian worker produce with this amount of human capital and physical capital if he, hypothetically, had access to the U.S. level of technology?

Column (5) shows that the answer is $24,057. This implies that the hypothetical PPP-adjusted GDP per Indian worker if India's technology were at the U.S. level is about twice as much as its current PPP-adjusted GDP per worker. $24,057/13,261 \approx 1.8$, suggesting a sizable impact of technology differences. If, in addition, India also increased its human capital and physical capital per worker to U.S. levels, it would increase its PPP-adjusted GDP per worker to the U.S. level. (This is by construction: if India has the same level of human capital and physical capital per worker, and the same technology, as the United States, it will have the same PPP-adjusted GDP per worker as the United States.) In the Indian case, this would correspond to an increase by another 4.7 times ($112,517/24,057 \approx 4.7$).

Recall, however, that the technology differences that appear rather important (leading to a doubling of India's GDP per capita, holding its total efficiency units of labor and physical capital constant) may not just be differences in the knowledge available to the economy and to firms for production. They also reflect differences in the efficiency of production, as our example of economics professors and basketball players illustrated, and if there is any mismeasurement in factors of production, this will appear as technology differences. For example, in practice, human capital across countries differs not only because of average years of schooling but also because of major differences in the quality of schooling. If rich countries have a systematically higher quality of schooling, our methodology can lead to exaggerated technology differences.

Question	**Answer**	**Data**	**Caveat**
Why is the average American so much richer than the average Indian?	Differences in total efficiency units of labor and physical capital are important. If India had access to the same technology as the United States (including differences in the efficiency of production), its GDP per worker would be $24,057 instead of $13,261, almost twice as high. Increasing India's total efficiency units of labor and physical capital to U.S. levels would increase its PPP-adjusted GDP per worker by another 4.7 times.	Cross-country data on PPP-adjusted income per worker, schooling, and investment.	Technology differences include differences in the efficiency of production and may also reflect mismeasurement.

Summary

- GDP per capita, defined as aggregate income or gross domestic product (GDP) divided by total population, varies greatly across countries, with some nations (such as the United States and Norway) having more than 40 times the GDP per capita of other nations (such as Afghanistan, Niger, and the Democratic Republic of the Congo).

- GDP per capita across countries can be compared using exchange-rate-based measures, which rely on current exchange rates, or purchasing power parity (PPP)-based measures, which compare estimates of the cost of the representative basket of commodities in each country. The latter tend to be more reliable, as they more appropriately capture differences in relative prices across countries and are not subject to fluctuations resulting from changes in exchange rates. Though GDP per capita omits a wealth of other important information about a country (including information on health, schooling, inequality, and poverty), it provides a good summary of prosperity, and higher GDP per capita is typically correlated with higher life expectancy, better schooling, and lower poverty.

- The aggregate production function links the GDP of a nation to its total efficiency units of labor, physical capital stock, technology, and efficiency of production. Greater efficiency units of labor and physical capital, as well as better technology and efficiency of production, increase GDP.

- Though the total efficiency units of labor and physical capital stock matter a great deal for GDP, the most important determinant of cross-country differences in GDP per worker appears to be differences in technology and the efficiency of production.

Key Terms

GDP per capita *p. 117*
purchasing power parity (PPP) *p. 118*
GDP per worker *p. 120*
productivity *p. 120*
one dollar a day per person poverty line
  p. 123

human capital *p. 125*
physical capital *p. 125*
physical capital stock *p. 125*
technology *p. 125*
aggregate production function *p. 126*
total efficiency units of labor *p. 126*

Law of Diminishing Marginal Product
  p. 127
research and development (R&D)
  p. 129
efficiency of production *p. 131*

Questions

All questions are available in MyEconLab *for practice and instructor assignment.*

1. Suppose you are comparing the GDP per capita in the United States and Ghana. You first convert the values into U.S. dollars using the current exchange rate between the U.S. dollar and the Ghanaian cedi. You also convert both values to U.S. dollars using the PPP-adjusted exchange rate. Which measure is likely to give you a more accurate picture of the living standards in both countries? Explain your answer.

2. What are the disadvantages of using Big Macs to measure PPP?

3. Suppose that country A has higher GDP per capita than country B. Explain why this does not imply that most citizens of country A have higher income than most citizens of country B. Construct an example in which both countries have ten citizens to demonstrate this point.

4. Is GDP per capita more relevant to understanding differences in international living standards than GDP per worker?

5. What is the correlation between GDP per capita and welfare measures like absolute poverty and life expectancy? What does this suggest about GDP per capita as a measure of welfare?

6. What does the Human Development Index measure? What is the correlation between this index and PPP-adjusted GDP per capita in a country?

7. What is productivity? Why does it vary across countries?

8. What are the two components of technology?

9. What are factors of production? What does the aggregate production function describe?

10. What are the total efficiency units of labor? What is the relationship between this concept and human capital?

11. Use the following diagram to explain the relationship between a country's physical capital stock and GDP, holding all else constant

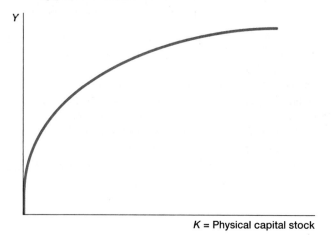

K = Physical capital stock

12. Explain the difference between the terms "physical capital" and "human capital."

13. Explain what distinguishes physical capital from natural resources.

14. How do increases in technology affect the aggregate production function?

15. What does Moore's Law state? Is Moore's Law borne out by historical data?

16. Why is the average American so much richer than the average Indian?

17. What policies can be used to raise GDP in a country?

Problems

All problems are available in MyEconLab *for practice and instructor assignment.*

1. You read a newspaper report that compares wages paid to employees at Starbucks in India and in the United Kingdom. At the time, 1 pound was equal to 87 rupees. The report says that Starbucks baristas in India are paid a mere 56 pence an hour, which is lower than the price of the cheapest coffee that Starbucks sells in the United Kingdom. A friend of yours who read the report is appalled by this information and thinks that Starbucks ought to raise its salaries substantially in India. Is your friend necessarily correct? Explain your answer.

2. The following table lists 2015 GDP per capita for four countries. The data are given in the national currencies of the countries. It also lists the price of a Big Mac burger in the local currency of each country in 2015.

Country (Local Currency)	2015 GDP per Capita	2015 Big Mac Price
Norway (krone)	600,546	46
Poland (zloty)	46,764	9.6
Turkey (Turkish lira)	29,885	10.25
United Kingdom (British pound)	28,762	2.89

Source for GDP: UNECE Statistical Database, compiled from national and international (CIS, EUROSTAT, IMF, OECD) official sources.

Source for Big Mac prices: http://www.economist.com/content/big-mac-index.

The price of a Big Mac in the United States in 2015 was $4.79. Using the Big Mac burger as a representative commodity common to the countries, calculate the PPP-adjustment factor for each country, and then the PPP level of per capita GDP in each country.

3. Let us use what we have learned in the first part of the chapter to compare living standards in the United States and a hypothetical country, Argonia, in 2008.

a. The U.S. GDP in 2008 was approximately $14 trillion, and the U.S. population was approximately 300 million. What was the per capita GDP in the United States in 2008?

b. Suppose that in the local currency, Argonian dollars, Argonia's GDP in 2008 was 1 trillion, and its population was 10 million. What was Argonia's GDP per capita in Argonian dollars? What problems do you foresee in comparing this number to the U.S. GDP per capita in U.S. dollars computed in part (a)?

c. The Argonian dollar/U.S. dollar exchange rate was equal to 6 on January 1, 2008 (meaning that 1 U.S. dollar was worth 6 Argonian dollars) and reached 9 on August 1, 2008. Compute an exchange-rate-based measure of the GDP per capita in Argonia in U.S. dollars on these two dates. Do you think the change in Argonia's exchange-rate-based measure of GDP per capita between these two dates reflects a true change in living standards?

d. McDonald's has a thriving business in Argonia and sold a Big Mac for 7 Argonian dollars in 2008, while at the same time, a Big Mac sold for $3.50 in the United States. Using this information, provide an alternative estimate of GDP per capita in Argonia. Would you trust this estimate better than the one based on exchange rates? Why or why not?

4. Suppose you are given the following information for the country Lusitania:

Characteristic	Value for Lusitania
Total population	190 million
Number employed	80 million
GDP	$2,476 billion

a. What is the GDP per capita in Lusitania?

b. What is the GDP per worker in Lusitania?

The following table gives you the same information for the country Arctica.

Characteristic	Value for Arctica
Total population	80 million
Number employed	40 million
GDP	$3,600 billion

c. What is the GDP per capita in Arctica?

d. What is the GDP per worker in Arctica?

e. Based on the given information, would Arctica be considered more productive than Lusitania? Explain your answer.

f. How would you use the information given in both these tables to compare living standards in Lusitania and Arctica?

5. Suppose that the GDP in current dollars for Polonia is higher than Ruritania's GDP. However, using PPP-adjusted dollars, Ruritania's GDP is higher than Polonia's GDP. Based on this information, what would you conclude about living standards in Polonia and Ruritania?

6. In 2011, China revised its poverty line upward to 2,300 yuan per year, or 6.3 yuan per day. At the prevailing exchange rate, this was equal to a little less than a single U.S. dollar. Some commentators felt that China's poverty line fell short of the World Bank's poverty line—which, at the time, was $1.25 per day, in 2005 PPP-adjusted U.S. dollars. Would you agree? What other information would you need to evaluate this claim?

7. In this question, use what you learned in the second part of the chapter to compare the performance of an economy in two different time periods, as a result of changes in its physical capital stock and efficiency units of labor.

a. Suppose that from period 1 to period 2, the unemployment rate in the economy increases. Everything else remains unchanged. What happens to the total efficiency units of labor? Express your results formally as an inequality, using the formula for total efficiency units of labor presented in the chapter (in particular, recall that total efficiency units of labor in two periods can be written as $H_1 = L_1 \times h_1$ and $H_2 = L_2 \times h_2$, where L is the total number of employed workers).

b. What are the consequences for GDP of this increase in unemployment? Express your results formally as an inequality, using the aggregate production function presented in the chapter.

c. What are the consequences for GDP per capita and GDP per worker?

d. Suppose that there is a technological advance from period 1 to period 2 but, at the same time, a decrease in physical capital stock. Can you say whether GDP will increase or decrease? Why or why not?

8. Assume that the country Lusitania has two industries, clothing production and computer chip production. At first, both industries have identical aggregate production functions.

The following table shows how the output of each industry is affected by a change in efficiency units of labor.

Y (in Millions of Dollars)	Stock of Physical Capital (Units)	Efficiency Units of Labor
100	15,000	16,000
150	15,000	20,000
180	15,000	24,000
200	15,000	28,000
210	15,000	32,000

a. Using the data in the table, draw a graph showing how output (on the y-axis) changes with efficiency units of labor (on the x-axis). What explains the shape of the graph? Why is it valid in this case to plot output against the efficiency units of labor and leave the stock of physical capital in the background?

b. A Lusitanian inventor has produced a new technology that doubles the output of computer chips for any combination of capital and labor. Explain, using an equation, how this invention affects the production of computer chips. Create a new table for computer chip production and compare it to the (unchanged) table for clothing production.

c. If you were a central planner, would you make any changes to the allocation of labor, holding capital fixed? If so, what factors might prevent you from implementing your policy?

9. The old Soviet Union devoted enormous resources exclusively to increasing its physical capital stock, and yet eventually the increase in the country's GDP came to an end. Based on the discussion in the chapter, explain why this was inevitable.

10. According to U.S. census projections, the percentage of U.S. citizens over the age of 65 will increase from 14.9% in 2015 to 22.1% in 2050, due, in part, to both prolonged life expectancy and declining fertility rates. How would you expect such a demographic shift to affect productivity? What about GDP per capita?

11. In the book *Dead Aid*, economist Dambisa Moyo argues that humanitarian aid—provision of food or medicine to poor families, for example—is an ineffective tool for promoting growth in the developing world. Instead, she argues in favor of foreign aid policies that encourage or subsidize foreign investment in the businesses of developing countries. Using the concepts in this chapter, evaluate her approach. Your answer should consider the short-term and long-term effects of such policies on both poverty rates and aggregate growth. If you were trying to improve macroeconomic growth and lower poverty rates in the developing world, what kind of programs would you encourage the U.S. government to fund? What trade-offs would you weigh in making your recommendation?

12. Give an algebraic and an intuitive explanation of the concept of "efficiency of production." Why is efficiency of production so important to GDP?

Appendix

The Mathematics of Aggregate Production Functions

How did we compute, in Exhibit 6.12, what the average income per worker in India would have been if India had had access to the U.S. level of technology?

We worked with the aggregate production function $Y = A \times F(K, H)$ using the following form, which is often estimated as an empirical approximation to data:

$$Y = A \times F(K, H) = A \times K^{1/3} \times H^{2/3}.$$

This form is referred to as a Cobb-Douglas function and has several attractive features. For instance, the coefficients to which K and H are raised add up to 1 $(\frac{1}{3} + \frac{2}{3} = 1)$. This ensures that the production function exhibits *constant returns to scale*: that is, increasing K and H by 1 percent would lead to a 1 percent increase in Y. Moreover, this functional form is consistent with the empirical fact that, roughly speaking, about two-thirds of national income goes to labor and one-third to physical capital.

Let us now divide both sides of the above equation by the total number of workers in the economy, L:

$$Y \times \frac{1}{L} = A \times K^{1/3} \times H^{2/3} \times \frac{1}{L}.$$

This can be rewritten as

$$y = \frac{Y}{L} = A \times K^{1/3} \times H^{2/3} \times \frac{1}{L^{1/3} \times L^{2/3}},$$

where y is income per worker, or GDP divided by the number of workers in the economy. The last term simply rewrites $1/L$ differently to derive the next equation.

Now rearranging the previous equation, we obtain

$$y = A \times \left(\frac{K}{L}\right)^{1/3} \times \left(\frac{H}{L}\right)^{2/3}.$$

Finally, recalling that $H = L \times h$, this can be rewritten as

$$y = A \times \left(\frac{K}{L}\right)^{1/3} \times h^{2/3}.$$

Stated differently:

GDP per worker
$$= \text{Technology} \times (\text{Capital per worker})^{1/3} \times (\text{Human capital per worker})^{2/3}.$$

This derivation also shows why there is a tight relationship between cross-country differences in GDP per worker and cross-country differences in productivity. For simplicity, assuming that each worker works the same number of hours in every country, the left-hand side of this equation is also GDP per hour worked and thus the productivity of a country. The equation therefore demonstrates that productivity is determined by the three ingredients we have emphasized in the text: technology, physical capital, and human capital.

We next use data on GDP per worker together with data on the physical capital stock (K), or physical capital per worker, and data on human capital per worker (h). Data on GDP are available from various sources (with original information coming from national income accounts). These sources also provide information on investment, which we can use to compute physical capital stocks. Finally, we can compute human capital differences across nations from differences in average years of schooling. In particular, we know how much more a worker with one more year of schooling earns. We can use this information to create an index, h—on the basis of differences in average years of schooling—that captures differences in human capital across nations. For example, suppose that college graduate workers will typically have 16 years of schooling and earn twice as much as workers with 6 years of schooling. Then if we set $h = 1$ for a country with 6 years of schooling on average, we would have $h = 2$ for a country with 16 years of schooling on average.

Now let us start by computing the technology for the United States, denoted by A_{US}. Using the previous equation, we arrive at:

$$A_{US} = \frac{y_{US}}{\left(\dfrac{K_{US}}{L_{US}}\right)^{1/3} \times h_{US}^{2/3}}.$$

As we have seen, the U.S. GDP per worker is given by

$$y_{US} = A_{US} \times \left(\frac{K_{US}}{L_{US}}\right)^{1/3} \times h_{US}^{2/3}.$$

The expression above is obtained simply by rearranging this equation.

In the same fashion, we can find the contribution of technology to the GDP of India, which is A_{India}:

$$A_{India} = \frac{y_{India}}{\left(\dfrac{K_{India}}{L_{India}}\right)^{1/3} \times h_{India}^{2/3}}.$$

We can then ask how the GDP of India would be different if instead of A_{India} we used A_{US} in the preceding expression. We can calculate the hypothetical GDP per worker of India in the situation in which India has the same technology term, A_{US}, as the United States:

$$y_{India \text{ with US technology}} = A_{US} \times \left(\frac{K_{India}}{L_{India}}\right)^{1/3} \times h_{India}^{2/3}.$$

Using our estimates of A_{US}, K_{India}, L_{India}, h_{India}, for example, we can compute the hypothetical GDP per worker of India, if India were able to use American technology, as $25,047. In the same way, we can plug the U.S. technology terms into the aggregate production function of any country, which enables us to do the rest of the computations in Exhibit 6.12.

7 Economic Growth

Why are you so much more prosperous than your great-great-grandparents were?

The United States was not always as prosperous as it is today. Its real GDP per capita today is about 25 times what it was in 1820. At that time, only a small fraction of the population lived in cities; most people worked in agriculture. People could not even imagine, let alone have access to, many of the goods, services, and technologies that we take for granted, including radio, television, indoor plumbing, shopping malls, cars, planes, or even trains.

The United States and several other countries have vastly increased their real GDP per capita over the past 200 years, developing new goods, services, and technologies. We call this process *economic growth*. The key questions we address in this chapter are how and why the United States and several other countries have managed to achieve such notable economic growth over the past two centuries.

CHAPTER OUTLINE

┌─ **KEY** ─────────────────────────────
│   **IDEAS**

- Economic growth measures how much real GDP per capita grows over time.

- Today's high levels of real GDP per capita in many nations are a result of rapid economic growth over the past two centuries.

- Sustained economic growth relies on technological progress.

- There are sizable differences in the historical growth rates of different economies, which are largely responsible for their differences in the levels of real GDP per capita.

- Economic growth is a powerful tool for poverty reduction.

└──

7.1 The Power of Economic Growth

We saw in Chapter 6 how aggregate incomes (GDP) are determined. We can now start using these ideas to understand why several countries, including the United States, have managed to become so much richer over the past 200 years and, in the process, we gain a new perspective on the differences across countries that we documented in the previous chapter. Throughout this chapter, we refer to *real* GDP, which uses market prices from a specific base year (in this chapter generally 2011) to express the value of production in the economy, as we discussed in Chapter 5.

A First Look at U.S. Growth

As a first step, Exhibit 7.1 depicts real GDP per capita in the United States over the past 200 years. In Chapter 6, we adjusted incomes in terms of the cost of a given basket of commodities to compare them meaningfully across countries. We saw in Chapter 5 how to make a similar adjustment for inflation to obtain real GDP, which can be meaningfully compared over time. Recall that this involves adjusting real GDP or incomes according to a base-year dollar value, which we call "constant dollars." This is what we do in this chapter also. Exhibit 7.1, for example, plots the level of real GDP per capita in the United States in 2011 constant dollars, so the income for the year 1967, for example, is expressed as what it would be equal to in year 2011 dollars.

Exhibit 7.1 clearly illustrates the *economic growth* in the U.S. economy between 1820 and 2012. **Economic growth**, or simply **growth**, refers to the increase in real GDP per capita of an economy. The exhibit shows this type of economic growth and a marked increase in real GDP per capita in the U.S. economy over the past 200 years, though the increase is not entirely steady and there are some jagged movements, corresponding to economic fluctuations. One of these stands out: the Great Depression, which started in 1929 and recorded a major contraction in U.S. real GDP per capita. Despite its importance and its impact on the lives of millions, the Great Depression was a temporary event—sustained and steady growth of real GDP per capita characterizes the U.S. economy both before and after it. In this chapter, we focus on such longer-run movements, returning to economic fluctuations like the Great Depression in subsequent chapters.

As a result of the continued economic growth depicted in Exhibit 7.1, U.S. real GDP per capita and standards of living are much higher today than they were in 1820. For example, real GDP per capita has increased from $2,806 in 1820 to $14,655 in 1950 and to $50,752 in 2014 (all numbers in 2011 constant dollars). (Notice that the *y*-axis of this exhibit has a proportional scale, similar to those we have used in several exhibits in Chapters 5 and 6; it

Economic growth, or **growth**, is the increase in GDP per capita of an economy.

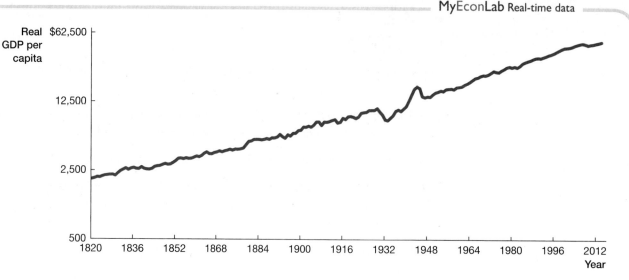

MyEconLab Real-time data

Exhibit 7.1 Real GDP per Capita in the United States (2011 Constant Dollars)

The growth of real GDP per capita in the United States has been relatively steady and sustained, except during the Great Depression and its aftermath. Note that the y-axis has a proportional scale, so that the vertical distance between 500 and 2,500 is the same as that between 2,500 and 12,500.

Source: Data from Maddison Project (1820–1959) and the Penn World Table version 9.0 (Robert C. Feenstra, Robert Inklaar, and Marcel P. Timmer, June 2016); J. Bolt and J. L. van Zanden, "The First Update of the Maddison Project; Re-Estimating Growth Before 1820," Maddison Project Working Paper 4, 2013.

ensures that the distance between $500 and $2,500 is the same as that between $2,500 and $12,500. Our discussion of exponential growth below will make it clear why this proportional scale is very convenient when studying economic growth.) Let us first specify the measurement of growth in a little more detail. A **growth rate** is defined as the change in a quantity—here, real GDP per capita—between two dates, relative to the baseline (beginning of period) quantity. Let's choose two dates (say, t and $t + 1$) and denote real GDP per capita on these two dates by y_t and y_{t+1}, respectively. Then the growth rate of real GDP per capita between these two dates is defined as

> The **growth rate** is the change in a quantity, for example, real GDP per capita, between two dates, relative to the baseline (beginning of period) quantity.

$$\text{Growth}_{t, t+1} = \frac{y_{t+1} - y_t}{y_t}.$$

Let us focus on annual differences, so that, for example, t and $t + 1$ correspond to the years 2005 and 2006, respectively. The U.S. economy had real GDP per capita of $50,512 in 2005 and $51,374 in 2006, so the growth rate between 2005 and 2006 can be computed as

$$\text{Growth}_{2005, \, 2006} = \frac{\$51,374 - \$50,512}{\$50,512} = 0.017$$

> [**Exponential growth results because new growth builds on past growth and its effects compound.**]

(or equivalently, $0.017 \times 100 = 1.7$ percent). Using this formula, we can compute growth rates of real GDP for any country.

Exhibit 7.2 depicts the annual growth rate of real GDP per capita of the U.S. economy between 1950 and 2014, which is computed using this formula. It shows that the average growth rate is positive, at approximately 2.03 percent, but economic fluctuations are also visible here, including the one starting in 2008, the Great Recession, which we discuss in greater detail in Chapter 12.

> **Exponential growth** refers to a situation in which the growth process can be described by an approximately constant growth rate of a variable such as real GDP or real GDP per capita.

Exponential Growth

Central to our discussion of economic growth is the idea of **exponential growth**, which refers to the process by which a quantity grows at an approximately constant growth rate.

Exhibit 7.2 The Annual Growth Rate of real GDP per Capita in the United States Between 1950 and 2014 (2011 Constant Dollars)

The (annual) growth rate of real GDP per capita shows the short-run fluctuations around the average growth rate.

Source: Data from the Penn World Table version 9.0 (Robert C. Feenstra, Robert Inklaar, and Marcel P. Timmer, June 2016).

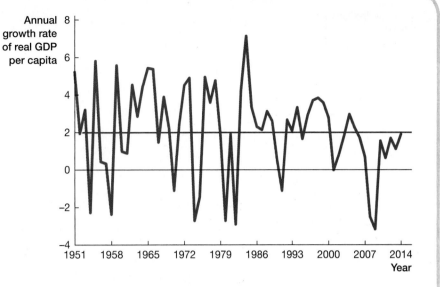

This results because the increase in the value of a variable ($y_{t+1} - y_t$ in terms of the above equation) is proportional to its current value (y_t in terms of the above equation). As we will next see, exponential growth results because new growth builds on past growth and its effects compound. This implies that relatively modest differences in growth rates translate into large differences in the level of a quantity after many years of growing.

The exponential nature of economic growth is one of the major reasons such large differences exist in real GDP per capita across countries, like the differences we saw in Chapter 6.

To understand both exponential growth and its implications, consider a simple example, where a variable Y_t starts out with the value 1 in the year 2000 and has a constant growth rate of 5 percent (0.05) in subsequent years. What will be the value of this variable in the year 2015? A first guess might be obtained by adding the increment of $1 \times 0.05 = 0.05$ to the base value 15 times (once for every year between 2000 and 2015). This would give us an increase of $15 \times 0.05 = 0.75$, thus producing the value $Y_{2015} = 1.75$.

But this is not a correct depiction of how growth takes place, because the power of compounding has to be factored in. Let's see why this is so by starting with 2001. With a growth rate of 5 percent, we will have $Y_{2001} = 1.05$. What about in 2002? The key here is that the additional 5 percent growth between 2001 and 2002 will start from 1.05—not from the initial level of 1.00. Hence, we will have $Y_{2002} = 1.05 \times 1.05 = 1.1025$. Similarly, $Y_{2003} = 1.1025 \times 1.05 = 1.1576$, and by continuing like this, we obtain $Y_{2015} = 2.0789$.

This number is greater than the naive guess of 1.75 because of compounding, the root cause of exponential growth. Exponential growth results because current growth builds on past growth. For example, to obtain Y_{2003} we started from the level at 2002, $Y_{2002} = 1.1025$, and built on it with 5 percent growth, to obtain $1.1025 \times 1.05 = 1.1576$. This implied that the increase from 2002 to 2003, $1.1576 - 1.1025 = 0.0551$, was greater than 0.05, the increase from 2000 to 2001, even though both of them corresponded to 5 percent growth. One implication of exponential growth is that to depict variables that have exponential growth (approximately constant growth rates), it is much more convenient to use an axis with a proportional scale, like the y-axis in Exhibit 7.1. This is intuitive: a 10 percent growth rate starting from a base of 1,000 will take us to 1,100, but if we had started with 100,000, it would have taken us to 110,000. The increment is very different in the two cases (100 versus 10,000), but it is the same as a *proportion* of the base value—10 percent. As a result, it is more instructive to show this change on a proportional scale where the 10 percent growth corresponds to the same distance on the y-axis regardless of whether we start from a base of 1,000 or 100,000. In contrast, Exhibit 7.3 shows how Exhibit 7.1 would look if we were to use the usual nonproportional scale. You can see that this exhibit creates a misleading impression that growth in real GDP per capita in the United States was

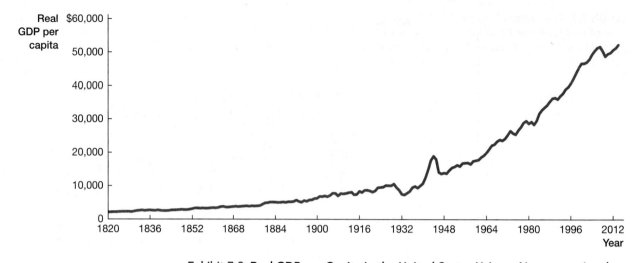

Exhibit 7.3 Real GDP per Capita in the United States Using a Nonproportional Scale (2011 Constant Dollars)

Source: Data from Maddison Project (1820–1959) and the Penn World Table version 9.0 (Robert C. Feenstra, Robert Inklaar, and Marcel P. Timmer, June 2016).

CHOICE
&CONSEQUENCE

The Power of Exponential Growth

You have two choices. You can either start a job with a salary of $1,000 per month and a 6 percent increase in your salary every month, or you can start with a salary of $2,000, but never get a raise. Which one of these two options do you prefer?

The answer might naturally vary from person to person. If you have an immediate need for money, you may be attracted by the prospect of a $2,000 paycheck. But before you rush to sign on the dotted line for the $2,000-per-month job, think of the implications of the 6 percent monthly increase. With a 6-percent-per-month increase, your monthly salary will already exceed $2,000 after only a year. After 4 years, it will be approximately $16,400 a month. So if you were thinking of staying in this job for more than a year, starting with a lower salary might be a much better idea.

The first option is attractive, at least for those of you intending to stay with it for a while, precisely because of exponential growth. The 6-percent-per-month increases in salary do not apply to the base salary (if they did, this would have increased your salary by $60 every month). Rather, they compound, meaning that each 6 percent applies to the amount that has accumulated up to that point. Thus after 1 month, your salary will be $1,060. After 2 months, it is $1,060 × 1.06 = $1,123.60. After 3 months, it is $1,123.60 × 1.06 = $1,191.02, and so on. We will next see that exponential growth plays the same role in countries' growth trajectories as in your potential income from these two hypothetical jobs.

An even more dramatic illustration of the power of exponential growth comes from the story of the invention of the game of chess in ancient India. According to legend, the inventor of the game exploited the power of exponential growth when asked for a reward for his invention by the king.[1] He proposed that the king place a single grain of wheat on the first square of the chessboard, two on the second, four on the third, and eight on the fourth. Then, continue doubling the number of grains for all sixty-four squares on the board, and he would receive the total amount of wheat on the board. The king, hearing the request, thought it trivial—but when his treasurers calculated the final tally, they returned to him in shock. The total amount, they found, was more than 18,000,000,000,000,000,000 grains of wheat—far more than they could ever produce in their entire kingdom. Indeed, today, this amount of wheat would allow you to distribute a ton of wheat to every person in the world every day for 6 months. A good story to remember both as a reminder of the power of exponential growth and as a pointer for you if you have to make choices between different options with varying growth prospects.

accelerating, whereas with a proportional scale in Exhibit 7.1, we can clearly distinguish the approximately constant rate of growth of U.S. real GDP per capita.

To see the power of exponential growth on economic growth, consider two countries with the same level of real GDP per capita in 1810, say $1,000 (in 2011 constant U.S. dollars). Furthermore, suppose that growth is exponential and, in particular, that real GDP per capita in one of these countries grows at 2 percent per year while in the other one it grows at just 1 percent. At first glance, this difference seems small. And it is true that such a difference in growth will have only small implications over 1 or 2 years.

But the implications of this difference 200 years later will be quite impressive. The country growing at 1 percent per year will achieve real GDP per capita of approximately $7,316 in 2010. In contrast, because of the exponential nature of growth, the country growing at 2 percent per year over the same period will reach a real GDP per capita of $52,485. Thus, a more than sevenfold difference results between these two countries from "just" a 1 percent difference in growth rates.

If instead of 1 percent growth per year, the second country had no growth (that is, 0 percent growth rate), then it would remain at the same level of real GDP per capita, $1,000, in 2010. The gap between the two countries, in this case, would be a truly striking fifty-two-fold! This example again illustrates the power of exponential growth—or, in this case, the lack thereof.

Patterns of Growth

Exponential growth is largely responsible for how the large differences in real GDP per capita that we observe today (and discussed in the previous chapter) emerged over time. The nations that are relatively rich today have grown steadily over the past 200 years, whereas the economies of those that are poor have failed to do so.

To see these effects of economic growth on economies in the real world, we now turn to Exhibit 7.4, which shows the patterns of growth in GDP per capita across a number of countries between 1960 and 2014 (in PPP-adjusted 2011 constant dollars, where PPP again stands for "purchasing power parity"). The third column of the exhibit summarizes growth between 1960 and 2014. Instead of showing the growth rate between these two dates using the formula we described above, this column provides the *implied* annual growth rate,

Exhibit 7.4 GDP per Capita and Growth in Selected Countries (PPP-Adjusted 2011 Constant Dollars)

GDP per capita in 2014 is determined by both GDP per capita in 1960 and the average annual growth rate of GDP per capita in between these two years. We see how Botswana is much richer than Kenya and Ghana today, even though Botswana started out poorer, because Botswana grew on average at 6.96 percent, while the average annual growth was only 0.85 percent for Kenya and 0.44 percent for Ghana. For the same reasons, today South Korea is richer than Brazil, and Singapore is richer than Spain.

Source: Data from the Penn World Table version 9.0 (Robert C. Feenstra, Robert Inklaar, and Marcel P. Timmer, June 2016).

Country	Real GDP per Capita		Implied (Average) Annual Growth
	1960	2014	
United States	$17,600.11	$52,292.28	2.04%
United Kingdom	$11,959.49	$40,241.51	2.27%
France	$10,465.52	$39,374.28	2.48%
Mexico	$5,741.75	$15,852.57	1.90%
Spain	$5,741.40	$33,864.22	3.34%
Nicaragua	$4,476.47	$4,452.81	−.01%
Ghana	$2,816.50	$3,570.19	0.44%
Singapore	$2,663.43	$72,582.99	6.31%
Brazil	$2,463.11	$14,870.58	3.39%
Democratic Republic of the Congo	$2,422.75	$1,216.95	−1.27%
Guatemala	$2,418.48	$6,850.59	1.95%
Kenya	$1,749.13	$2,768.74	0.85%
South Korea	$1,175.10	$35,103.96	6.49%
China	$1,154.19	$12,472.51	4.51%
India	$1,033.67	$5,224.02	3.05%
Rwanda	$962.58	$1,565.14	0.90%
Botswana	$427.35	$16,175.24	6.96%

which shows how much on average each country needed to grow each year to reach the 2014 level starting with the 1960 number. (Exactly how this number is computed is explained in the appendix to this chapter.)

What do these comparisons tell us? For one thing, we see that PPP-adjusted GDP per capita has increased significantly in the United States, the United Kingdom, and France; the growth rates in the last column confirm this. For example, both the United States and the United Kingdom show an average annual growth rate of about 2 percent between 1960 and 2014.

The exhibit also tells us that there has been an even greater increase in PPP-adjusted GDP per capita and correspondingly higher growth rates for Singapore, Spain, South Korea, Botswana, and China. All five of these countries were significantly poorer than the United States in 1960, but they closed some or almost all of the gap with the United States by 2014. Such success is reflected in the higher growth rates for these countries. For example, the average annual growth rates of PPP-adjusted GDP per capita in Botswana, South Korea, and Singapore during this period were above 5 percent, and China's was 4.51 percent.

The exhibit also shows other countries that have not closed the gap between themselves and richer countries, or have done so only to a limited extent. These nations include Mexico, Brazil, and India, which show similar or only slightly higher growth rates than the United States. Guatemala, Kenya, Ghana, Rwanda, and Nicaragua had even lower growth rates than the United States over this time period and thus have become relatively poorer. In fact, we see from the data in this exhibit that PPP-adjusted GDP per capita in Kenya has essentially been stagnant over this almost 50-year period, and PPP-adjusted PPP-adjusted GDP per capita in Nicaragua has declined at a rate of 0.01 percent per year, while the Democratic Republic of the Congo has seen its PPP-adjusted GDP per capita decline by 1.27 percent per year. As a result, both countries are poorer in 2014 than they were in 1960—due in part to the decades of civil war and political turmoil they have suffered.

How has PPP-adjusted GDP per capita evolved in these countries relative to the United States? Exhibit 7.5 illustrates this by taking some of the countries from Exhibit 7.4 and plotting their levels of GDP per capita divided by GDP per capita in the United States, all in PPP-adjusted 2011 constant dollars.

MyEconLab Real-time data

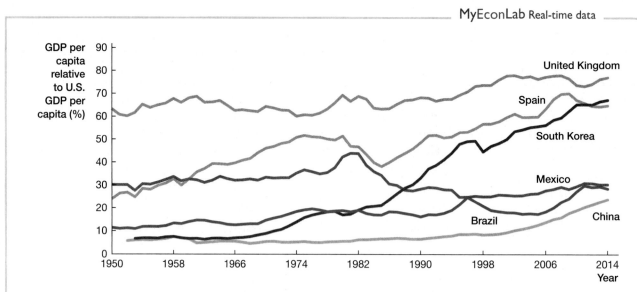

Exhibit 7.5 GDP per Capita of Selected Countries (PPP-Adjusted 2011 Constant Dollars)

Plotting the evolution of PPP-adjusted GDP per capita shows how countries such as South Korea and China have been catching up with the United States relatively steadily, while Mexico and Brazil have not.

Source: Data from the Penn World Table version 9.0 (Robert C. Feenstra, Robert Inklaar, and Marcel P. Timmer, June 2016).

The overall patterns are consistent with those shown in Exhibit 7.4, but the growth of these economies over time also reveals some interesting facts. For example, PPP-adjusted GDP per capita in the United Kingdom has remained at about 70 to 80 percent of the PPP-adjusted GDP per capita of the United States since the 1950s. Spain and South Korea showed early spurts of rapid growth, even though they started with very different income levels at the beginning of the period. By the 1980s, both countries had closed much of the gap between themselves and the United States, though they both also show periods of relative decline. Brazil also experienced relatively rapid growth in the 1950s and 1960s, closing some of the gap with the United States. But around 1980, this process went into reverse, and by 2010, PPP-adjusted GDP per capita in Brazil was about 20 percent of the GDP per capita of the United States—not much above where it started, in relative terms, in the 1950s. Finally, although there was a huge gap between the United States and China during the communist dictatorship of Mao Tse-tung (Mao Zedong), this gap started narrowing rapidly following Mao's death in 1976 and the opening of the Chinese economy in 1978.

To convey a more complete picture of growth patterns over the past 50 years, Exhibit 7.7 shows a graph of the growth rates of all countries for which we have data between 1960 and 2014. It shows that there is a wide range of growth rates. Some countries, such as Nicaragua, the Democratic Republic of the Congo, and Zimbabwe, have grown at negative rates during this period, while others, such as South Korea and Singapore, have achieved very high growth rates.

Using historical data, we can compare growth across countries even further back in time than 1960. To show these growth patterns in a simple way, Exhibit 7.8 lists levels of GDP per capita for several countries (in PPP-adjusted 2011 constant dollars) in 1820, 1870, 1920, 1970, and 2010 and their annual growth rates between 1820 and 2010 and between 1920 and 2010.

We see that income levels are not all that different across countries in 1820. For example, the United States was only about twice as rich as Mexico (U.S. PPP-adjusted GDP per capita of $1,873 versus Mexico's $863). But by 2010, there was a sizable gap between these two countries, which can be accounted for by their different growth rates. The average growth rate of the United States between 1820 and 2010 was 1.65 percent per year, while Mexico grew at an average rate of only 1.33 percent per year. The contrast between the United States and India is even starker. India started out with a little less than half of the PPP-adjusted GDP per capita of the United States in 1820. But by 2010, the gap was nearly tenfold. Once again, this is a direct consequence of the difference in the two countries' growth rates in PPP-adjusted GDP per capita.

Exhibit 7.8 also shows that in 1820, the United Kingdom was significantly richer than the United States. Yet by 2010, the United States was about 30 percent richer than the United Kingdom. This change is because of differences in growth rates: while the United States grew at 1.65 percent per year, the United Kingdom grew at only 1.29 percent per year. This relatively small difference in growth rates was sufficient for the United States to overtake the United Kingdom and become richer by 2010. We can also see from this exhibit how, by 1970, several other countries, including Spain, South Korea, and China, became poorer relative to the United States. Yet it also shows that these countries grew faster than the United States over the past 40 years, closing the gap that had opened up previously.

Part of this growth is what we call **catch-up growth**, meaning that these nations are catching up with the income and technology leader of the world, in this case the United States. Countries undergoing catch-up growth do so mostly by benefiting from available technologies but also by increasing their saving, efficiency units of labor, and efficiency of production. Catch-up growth is very important in practice, though as the examples of slow

Catch-up growth refers to a process whereby relatively poorer nations increase their incomes by taking advantage of knowledge and technologies already invented in other, more technologically advanced countries.

LETTING THE
DATA SPEAK

Levels versus Growth

Is China now poorer relative to the United States than it was in 1980? We saw in Exhibit 7.5 how Chinese PPP-adjusted GDP per capita has increased greatly over the past 30 years and closed the gap with GDP per capita in the United States. Yet now consider Exhibit 7.6, which plots PPP-adjusted GDP per capita in China and the United States since 1950. This picture creates the impression that the gap between the United States and China is opening up and that China is becoming relatively poorer. This is not the case, however. In fact, trying to decide whether China is becoming poorer or richer compared to the United States from a figure such as Exhibit 7.6 is an example of a common error: comparing *levels* of variables exhibiting exponential growth. You will have noticed that precisely to avoid this type of fallacy, in Exhibit 7.5 we used a proportional scale for the vertical axis, which provided the visual illustration of how the PPP-adjusted GDP per capita of various countries evolved relative to each other over the last 65 years.

To see the advantage of this procedure, consider two hypothetical countries. Say that the first one is twice as rich as the second and has PPP-adjusted GDP per capita of $20,000, while the second has PPP-adjusted GDP per capita of $10,000. Now suppose that they both grow by 10 percent. The first country will then have PPP-adjusted GDP per capita of $22,000 and the second one will have PPP-adjusted GDP per capita of $11,000. The ratio between the two has not changed, but the absolute gap in incomes has increased by $1,000. Thus, comparing levels of PPP-adjusted GDP is not enlightening when the growth is exponential. In the presence of exponential growth, when relative GDP remains stable, absolute gaps will increase. For this reason, looking at ratios is the right thing to do in Exhibit 7.5. It is an oft-repeated error to compare levels rather than ratios of variables exhibiting exponential growth, such as GDP or investment.

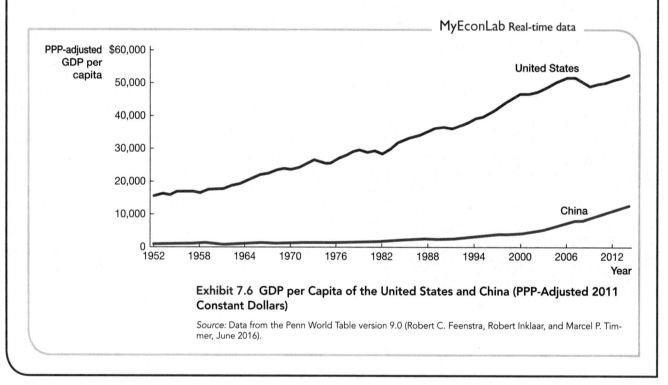

MyEconLab Real-time data

Exhibit 7.6 GDP per Capita of the United States and China (PPP-Adjusted 2011 Constant Dollars)

Source: Data from the Penn World Table version 9.0 (Robert C. Feenstra, Robert Inklaar, and Marcel P. Timmer, June 2016).

growth and stagnation in Exhibit 7.8 demonstrate, it is far from automatic. In Chapter 8, we discuss in greater detail why many countries have failed to take advantage of this type of catch-up growth.

Finally, Exhibit 7.8 drives home yet another important pattern: the approximately constant growth rates of several countries (including United States, the United Kingdom, and France) between 1820 and 2010. These countries are thus experiencing *exponential growth*. As already described, such exponential growth can have drastic implications when sustained over long periods. Given the importance of this pattern and to contrast it with *catch-up growth*, we refer to the experience of relatively steady growth over long periods of

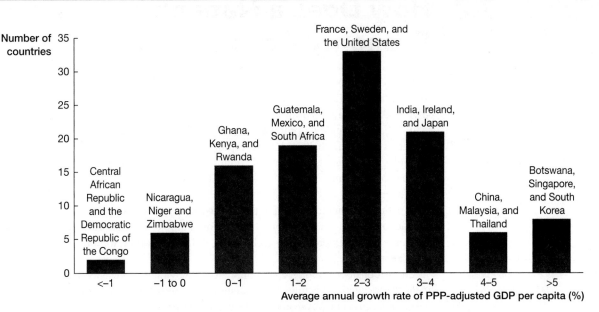

Exhibit 7.7 Average Growth Rates of GDP per Capita from 1960 to 2014 (PPP-adjusted 2011 Constant Dollars)

A few countries (in particular Botswana, Singapore, and South Korea) have grown very rapidly, with average growth rates above 5 percent, while others (such as Zimbabwe, the Democratic Republic of the Congo, and Nicaragua) have had negative growth since 1960.

Source: Data from the Penn World Table version 9.0 (Robert C. Feenstra, Robert Inklaar, and Marcel P. Timmer, June 2016).

Exhibit 7.8 GDP per Capita since 1820 in Selected Countries (PPP-Adjusted 2011 Constant Dollars)

Countries had fairly similar levels of PPP-adjusted GDP per capita in 1820. Since then, differences in PPP-adjusted GDP per capita have grown because some countries, such as the United States and the United Kingdom, have grown steadily, while others have not.

Sources: Data from Maddison Project and Bureau of Economic Analysis, National Income and Product Accounts Table 1.1.9; J. Bolt and J. L. van Zanden, "The First Update of the Maddison Project; Re-estimating Growth Before 1820," Maddison Project Working Paper 4 (2013).

Country	PPP-adjusted GDP per Capita					Average Growth	
	1820	1870	1920	1970	2010	1820–2010	1920–2010
United Kingdom	3,202	4,925	7,021	16,623	36,708	1.29%	1.85%
United States	2,101	3,775	8,571	23,204	47,074	1.59%	1.91%
France	1,752	2,896	4,982	17,615	33,157	1.56%	2.13%
Spain	1,556	1,863	3,361	9,756	25,932	1.49%	2.30%
Brazil	1,054	1,101	1,487	4,720	10,620	1.22%	2.21%
Mexico	968	1,005	2,814	6,669	11,912	1.33%	1.62%
China	926	818	852	1,201	12,400	1.37%	3.02%
India	823	823	980	1,340	5,206	0.98%	1.87%
Morocco	664	869	1,096	2,495	6,217	1.18%	1.95%
South Korea	517	520	942	3,346	33,503	2.22%	4.05%
Ghana	—	678	1,206	2,198	2,967		1.01%
Haiti	—	—	—	1,419	1,059		
Kenya	—	—	—	1,413	1,762		

Sustained growth refers to a process whereby real GDP per capita grows at a positive and relatively steady rate for long periods of time.

time as **sustained growth**. (The reason we are introducing the concept of sustained growth as well as exponential growth is that the latter term is often used to describe the idea that economic growth has an exponential, or cumulative, nature, while the former refers to the actual growth experience of several countries over the past 200 years or so.) Our next task is to understand how this type of sustained growth emerges and what factors determine the growth rate of an economy.

7.2 How Does a Nation's Economy Grow?

The aggregate production function, which we studied in Chapter 8, gives us a first answer to this question. Recall that the aggregate production function, $Y = A \times F(K, H)$, links GDP to the two factors of production: the physical capital (K) and total efficiency units of labor (H). The aggregate production function also depends on the level of technology (A), which, as we saw in the last chapter, captures the level of productivity that comes both from technological progress (for example, innovation and expansion of the knowledge available to the economy) and the efficiency of production. When A changes, the aggregate production function shifts.

A nation can increase its GDP by increasing its stock of physical capital, K; by increasing the total efficiency units of labor, H (for example, by increasing the human capital of workers); and by improving its technology, A. In this section, we look more closely at these three areas.

Let us consider the physical capital stock, K, which represents the value of all equipment (for example, machines, cars, planes, and computers) and structures (like buildings) of the economy. The physical capital stock (and therefore GDP) can be increased by investment, a process also known as *physical capital accumulation*.

You will recall from Chapter 5 that the national income accounting identity implies that $Y = C + I + G + X - M$, where C is consumption (household expenditures on consumption of goods and services), I is investment (expenditures on investment goods by private agents), G is government purchases of goods and services, X is exports, and M is imports. Recall that in a closed economy, there are no exports or imports, and if we also ignore the government (as we have done here), then we have $G = X = M = 0$. Therefore, the national income accounting identity implies

$$Y = C + I.$$

In other words, GDP is equal to the sum of aggregate consumption and investment. This equation also implies that investment comes directly from aggregate saving. This is because in our closed economy without government spending, all income will be either consumed or saved, so GDP is also equal to aggregate consumption plus aggregate saving or, in other words, $Y = C + S$. Thus

$$I = S.$$

Interpreted differently, this relationship says that all resources that households decide to save will be allocated to firms that will use them for investment (for example, by banks that will take money deposited by households and lend it to firms for investment). Consequently, a nation with a high saving rate will accumulate physical capital rapidly—that is, increase its physical capital stock rapidly—and, by the aggregate production function, increase its GDP. Thus to determine whether and how rapidly an economy will increase its physical capital stock, we need to understand the saving decisions of households, which we turn to next.

Optimization: The Choice Between Saving and Consumption

Consider the U.S. economy in 2008, when its GDP stood at $14.44 trillion. Naturally, not all of this output was consumed. Firms and the government invested some portion of it in the physical capital stock of the nation—for example, in new machines, roads, and bridges. But the resources for this investment come from the savings of households. For example, in a closed economy without the government, we have just seen that $I = S$.

Thus, to understand how the GDP of a nation is divided between consumption and investment, we need to study the preferences of consumers, who decide how much of their income will be allocated to savings. This involves studying how households trade off consumption today versus consumption tomorrow, because saving is a way of allocating some of today's resources for consumption tomorrow (or more generally, consumption in the future). This is yet another example of optimization on the part of individuals and households. Each household typically faces different priorities and needs that influence its decisions to consume its income today versus save it for tomorrow. For example, those preparing to send their children to college may save more today.

As with all optimization problems, such choices are affected by prices. In this case, the relevant price is the *interest rate*, which determines the rate of return that households expect on their savings. (How the interest rate is determined is discussed in detail in Chapter 10.) Higher interest rates typically encourage more saving. In addition, expectations of future income growth and perhaps taxes will have an impact on the saving decision. For instance, households that expect rapid income growth in the future may have less reason to save to finance future consumption (because future income growth will enable them to do this) or even to save "for a rainy day" (against potential future hardships). Conversely, if they expect high taxes in the future, households may save more in order to be able to pay these taxes without reducing future consumption.

The **saving rate** designates the fraction of income that is saved.

These trade-offs determine the **saving rate** of the economy, which corresponds to the fraction of income that is saved. (In practice, in addition to households, firms and the government also save, and we include these in the total savings of the economy.) We can compute the saving rate by dividing total savings by GDP. For example, in 2013, the level of total savings in the U.S. economy was $2.18 trillion, while GDP was $16.80 trillion (both in current dollars). Then the saving rate

$$\text{Saving rate} = \frac{\text{Total saving}}{\text{GDP}} = \frac{\$2.18 \text{ trillion}}{\$16.80 \text{ trillion}} = 0.1298, \text{ or } 12.98 \text{ percent}$$

What Brings Sustained Growth?

Can physical capital accumulation by itself generate sustained growth—where real GDP per capita grows at a positive and relatively steady rate for an extended period of time? The answer to this question is "no" for a simple reason: *the diminishing marginal product of physical capital*.

Let's look a little more closely at this reasoning. As Exhibit 6.7 from the previous chapter shows, because of the diminishing marginal product of physical capital, more and more physical capital will translate into smaller and smaller increases in real GDP. This precludes the possibility of sustained growth by just accumulating more and more physical capital.

What about steadily raising the efficiency units of labor in the economy? Can't the efficiency units of labor be raised just by increasing the number of workers in the economy? Can't we raise real GDP steadily by increasing human capital?

First consider increasing the workforce—the number of people taking part in the production process. Holding all other factors of production and technology constant, every additional worker will increase real GDP by less and less because of *diminishing marginal product of labor* (or diminishing marginal product of total efficiency units of labor). Therefore, we cannot guarantee a steady increase in real GDP per capita by just increasing the workforce either.

Note that we can also increase the efficiency units of labor for a given workforce by increasing the human capital of workers—for example, by raising their educational attainment or skill level. Although such changes will indeed increase real GDP, they will, by themselves, not achieve *sustained* growth. Because each individual has a finite life, there is a limit to how many years of schooling he or she can obtain, and, of course, more and more schooling would also imply fewer and fewer years in the workforce where an individual actively takes part in production. Thus, achieving greater and greater levels of efficiency units by continuously increasing the years of schooling of the workforce does not appear feasible.

"But hold on," you might say. "What about continuously upgrading the quality of education? Wouldn't that work toward increasing the efficiency units of labor?" Not really. Empirically, the extent to which such improvements can ensure steady growth also appears to be limited, as we will see in greater detail in the Evidence-Based Economics section of this chapter. Therefore, even though investments in education and skills do play a

CHOICE
&CONSEQUENCE

Is Increasing the Saving Rate Always a Good Idea?

Suppose that you control the saving rate in a country and your objective is to improve the standard of living of the citizens of this country in the long run. Is it always a good idea to increase the saving rate? We have seen that greater saving increases the physical capital stock of the economy and consequently raises real GDP. But this doesn't mean that increasing the saving is always good for society, even in the long run (and in the short run, a sudden increase in saving which, from the national income accounting identity, corresponds to an offsetting drop in consumption can be recessionary, as we discuss in Chapter 12). Imagine the extreme case where, as the supreme ruler of a country, you are able to encourage saving so much that every dollar earned in the country is saved. This will indeed increase real GDP. But it will not improve the standard of living of the citizens, because it will require them to consume little or nothing. In the extreme case where the saving rate reaches 100 percent, consumption drops to zero. This implies that an optimal

level of saving must exist for a society, where saving above this level would make the society worse off, because it would significantly reduce consumption.

---

major role in increasing real GDP per capita, we cannot achieve sustained growth of about 1.5–2.0 percent per year just by continuously increasing the educational achievement of the workforce.

These considerations imply that to achieve sustained growth, we need something else. And that something else is *technology*—particularly, advances in the technical knowledge used in production.

Knowledge, Technological Change, and Growth

You will recall that Moore's Law, which we first encountered in the previous chapter (Exhibit 6.10), claims that the number of transistors on memory microchips will double every 2 years, thereby increasing the computational power of computers. This trend has been true for at least the past 50 years and probably for longer. For example, around 1900, before microprocessors and other computational devices were available, it was prohibitively expensive to carry out anything but the most trivial numerical calculations. By 1950, with the technologies associated with the vacuum tube, society had access to the technology to make one computation per second at a cost of $1,000 (in today's dollars). By the 1970s, with the advent of the transistor, we could make up to 100 calculations per second for $1,000. And by the late 1990s, with the widespread use of integrated circuits, almost 10 million calculations per second could be performed for the same cost. Moore's Law is an example of *technological change*. **Technological change** is the process of new technologies and new goods and services being invented, introduced, and used in the economy, enabling the economy to achieve a higher level of real GDP for given levels of its factors of production, physical capital stock, and total efficiency units of labor.

Consider another example of technological change—the reduction in the cost of lighting over the past 200 years—as shown in Exhibit 7.9.[2] Obtaining lighting, for both firms and households, has become much cheaper over the past two centuries because of the invention of the lightbulb and ongoing improvements in the quality of lightbulbs, lighting technology, and the transmission of energy.

Technological change is the process of new technologies and new goods and services being invented, introduced, and used in the economy, enabling the economy to achieve a higher level of real GDP for given levels of physical capital stock and total efficiency units of labor.

Exhibit 7.9 The Real Price of Light over Time (in 1992 Dollars)

The source of sustained growth is technological progress, which continuously increases the amount that an economy can produce. Here we see one reflection of this technological progress, showing how improvements in lighting technology, quality of lightbulbs, and transmission of energy have reduced the cost of lighting over time.

Source: Based on William D. Nordhaus, "Do Real-Output and Real-Wage Measures Capture Reality? The History of Light Suggests Not," Cowles Foundation Discussion Paper 1078, New Haven, CT: Cowles Foundation for Research in Economics, 1994.

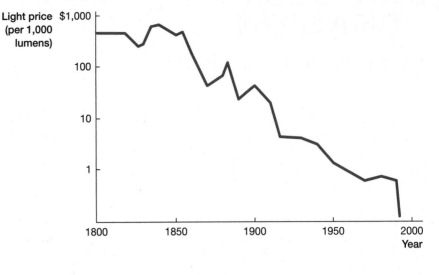

Technological change, as it turns out, is exponential. In particular, using the same definition of exponential growth from earlier in this chapter, this means that improvements in technology take place at an approximately constant rate—rather than by constant increments. There is a simple reason for this exponential nature of technological change. As we have seen, growth in real GDP per capita is exponential because growth compounds—that is, it takes place on the basis of the current level of real GDP, whose increase is already a result of past growth. A similar logic holds for technological change. Inventors of new innovations and technologies do not start from scratch in their attempts to improve the productive capacity of a firm or an economy: they build on the knowledge stock resulting from past innovations—building on the shoulders of giants, so to speak. Hence, every new innovation, instead of increasing the productive capacity of the economy by a constant amount, increases it by a constant proportional amount. For instance, when the new version of your favorite gadget (say, an iPhone or an Android device) comes to the market, it does not just add one new feature or increase the speed of just one or two items on the phone, but improves all the existing features. So the more features your previous device had and the more advanced they were, the more capacity for improvement its new version will have to build on.

This exponential nature of technological knowledge ensures that innovations improve our productive capacity in real GDP not by a constant amount but by a constant proportional amount—that is, by a constant percentage. So if we improve technology starting with a technology level that produces a real GDP per capita of $1,000, then innovations that enable us to be more productive by a certain constant percentage amount—say 10 percent—will raise real GDP per capita from $1,000 to $1,100. But if we instead start with a technology level that produces $100,000 of real GDP per capita, similar innovations bringing a 10 percent improvement will correspond to a $10,000 increase in real GDP, taking us to $110,000.

The exponential nature of technological change illustrated by these two examples is also responsible for the fact that improvements in technology need not necessarily come up against diminishing marginal product (whereas, as we have seen, increases in the use of factors of

> New innovations and technologies . . . build on the knowledge stock resulting from past innovations—building on the shoulders of giants, so to speak.

Technology and Life Expectancy

Technology has not improved our lives just by increasing real GDP per capita. It has also improved the health and longevity of billions of people around the world.

Life expectancy around the world was much lower 70 years ago than it is today.[3] In 1940, child and infant mortality rates were so high and adult diseases, such as pneumonia and tuberculosis, were so deadly (and without any cure) that life expectancy at birth in many nations stood at less than 40 years. For example, the life expectancy at birth of an average Indian was an incredibly low 30 years. In Venezuela, it was 33; in Indonesia, 34; in Brazil, 36.

In the course of the next three or four decades, this picture changed dramatically. As we saw in Chapter 6, while the gap in life expectancy between rich and poor nations still remains today, health conditions have improved significantly all over the world, particularly for poorer nations. Life expectancy at birth in India in 1999 was 60 years, almost twice as high as the country's life expectancy in the 1940s. It was also 50 percent higher than life expectancy at birth in Britain in 1820 (around 40 years), which at the time had approximately the same PPP-adjusted GDP per capita as India in 1999. How did this tremendous improvement in health conditions in poor nations take place?

The answer lies in technology and in scientific breakthroughs that took place in the United States and Western Europe throughout the twentieth century. First came a wave of global drug innovation, most importantly the development of antibiotics, which produced many products that were highly effective against major killers in developing countries. Penicillin, which provided an effective treatment for a range of bacterial infections, became widely available by the early 1950s. Also important during the same period was the development of new vaccines, including those for yellow fever and smallpox.

The second major factor was the discovery of DDT (dichloro-diphenyl-trichloroethane). Although eventually the excess use of DDT as an agricultural pesticide would turn out to be an environmental hazard, its initial use in disease control was revolutionary. DDT allowed a breakthrough in attempts to control one of the major killers of children in relatively poor parts of the world—malaria. Finally, with the establishment and help of the World Health Organization, simple but effective medical and public health practices,

such as oral rehydration and boiling water to prevent cholera, spread to poorer countries.

Some economists believe that improvements in health and life expectancy directly translate into greater productivity and higher real GDP per capita.[4] The spectacular narrowing of the gap in life expectancy between rich and poor countries during the several decades following World War II does not support this view—there was no corresponding narrowing of the gaps in real GDP per capita.[5] But at some level this is secondary. Even though it is no easy fix to the problem of poverty, the agenda of continued healthcare innovations is a potent weapon in our efforts to improve the quality of life for billions of people around the world.

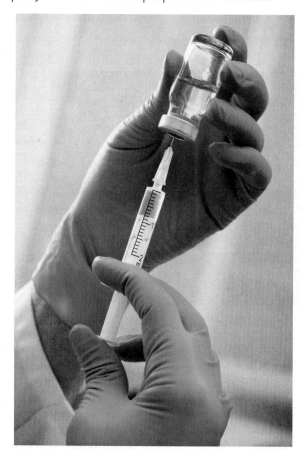

production do run into diminishing marginal product). For this reason, improvements in technology appear to be the most plausible engine of sustained growth.

By now you will have realized that there is a nice symmetry between our treatment of differences in PPP-adjusted GDP per capita across countries in the previous chapter and of differences in it over time, corresponding to growth, in this chapter. In both, the physical capital stock and efficiency units of labor play important roles, but they are insufficient to explain the major differences. Both across countries and over time, technology instead plays the central role.

LETTING THE
DATA SPEAK

The Great Productivity Puzzle

Look around your lecture halls during class, and chances are there's a phone or laptop on every desk. With the recent rise of computer and telecommunications technology, e-commerce, "big data," and more, we seem to be awash in technology. But this endless wave of new technologies has also left economists scratching their heads at another recent trend: the decline of productivity growth in advanced economies. As we learned in Chapter 6, technology should enhance a country's productivity. How can it be that, in the face of such technological wizardry around us, labor productivity has drastically slowed down? But Exhibit 7.10 shows that it has—there is a marked decline in productivity growth in Canada, France, Germany, Italy, Japan, the United Kingdom, and the United States in 2009–2014 relative to before. Some of this is due to the lingering effects of the global recession that started in 2008. But even before the onset of the global recession, we see slower productivity growth between 2001 and 2007 than in the 10 years before.

Economists have proposed several explanations for this puzzling trend. In *The Rise and Fall of American Growth*, economist Robert Gordon argues that we have reached the end of transformative new technologies: unlike the paradigm-shifting changes of the twentieth century, today's

technological development, he suggests, is more evolution than revolution. Every year brings slight improvements on, say, personal laptops, with little effect on countrywide productivity.[6] Or perhaps we simply aren't investing enough in new technologies; in the United States, for example, investment in information and communications technology as a share of real GDP declined from 4.02 percent in 2001 to 3.15 percent in 2014.[7] If we do not invest sufficiently in deploying these new technologies, they will have little impact on labor productivity even if they are potentially revolutionary. There are also other trends that could be holding labor productivity down, including a worrying decline in the rate of entry (and exit) of new firms, which are often the ones to come up with new ideas and products.[8] In the United States, for example, business start-up rates, measured as the ratio of the number of firms that have entered the market within the past two years relative to the total number of firms, have declined from 24.75 percent in 2007 to 19.58 percent in 2013.

All these causes may contribute to the slowdown—and perhaps, ultimately, it's a matter of waiting. Some economists have suggested that businesses simply haven't yet adapted their models to match technological developments.[9] In other words, maybe we need to catch up with our engineers.

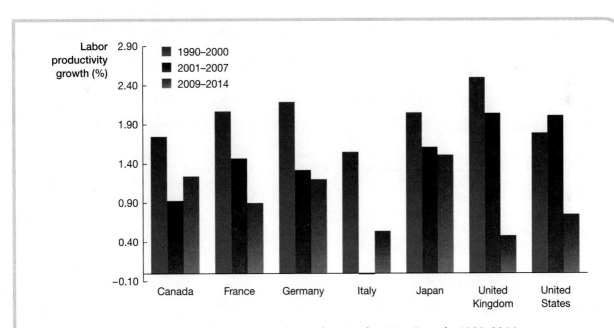

Exhibit 7.10 Trends in Labor Productivity Growth, 1990–2014

This exhibit shows the slowdown of labor productivity growth across several advanced economies. The pace of labor productivity growth is much lower in 2009–2014 than it was before. But even before the onset of the recession, productivity growth was slower in 2001–2007 than in 1990–2000.

Source: Data from Organisation for Economic Co-operation and Development, "OECD Compendium of Productivity Indicators 2016," Paris: OECD Publishing, 2006. http://dx.doi.org/10.1787/pdtvy-2016-en.

Q: Why are you so much more prosperous than your great-great-grandparents were?

The theoretical discussion in the previous section supports the central role of technology in explaining sustained growth. We will now see that empirical evidence also bolsters the conclusion that technology plays a key role.

To evaluate the sources of U.S. economic growth, we follow the same strategy as in Chapter 6. There, we used the aggregate production function and estimates of the physical capital stock and the efficiency units of labor across different countries to evaluate their contributions to cross-country differences in GDP (PPP-adjusted). The only major difference here is that higher-quality U.S. data enable us to conduct the analysis for real GDP per hour worked rather than real GDP per worker, thus allowing us to measure the labor input more accurately. We start the analysis in 1950.

Exhibit 7.11 records average real GDP per hour worked (in 2011 constant dollars), the average value of the physical capital stock per hour worked, and the most important component of the human capital of workers—the average years of schooling—for 10-year periods starting in 1950. (To remove the short-term effects of the last recession from our calculations on long-term growth, the last period is 2000–2007.) The exhibit shows the steady increase in real GDP per hour worked, physical capital stock per hour worked, and educational attainment in the United States between 1950 and 2007.

We then use a methodology similar to that used in the previous chapter to compute the contribution of physical capital, human capital (efficiency units of labor), and technology to the growth of real GDP in the United States. Once again, you should remember that, just as in Chapter 6, here "technology" captures not just the fruits of technological progress due to innovations and the deployment of better knowledge in the economy but also the level of the efficiency of production, which is affected by a range of factors. The results are recorded in columns (4), (5), and (6) of the exhibit (in percentages). Column (7) then gives the annual growth rate of real GDP per hour worked, which is the sum of the contributions of physical capital, human capital, and technology.

Period	(1) Real GDP per Hour Worked	(2) Physical Capital Stock per Hour Worked	(3) Average Years of Schooling	(4) Growth Resulting from Physical Capital (K)	(5) Growth Resulting from Human Capital (H)	(6) Growth Resulting from Technology (A)	(7) Annual Growth Rate of Real GDP per Hour Worked
1950–1959	$9.31	$115,042.24	9.38	0.89%	0.28%	2.37%	3.54%
1960–1969	$12.90	$134,163.97	10.16	0.89%	0.17%	2.20%	3.26%
1970–1979	$16.78	$144,258.27	11.15	0.88%	0.01%	1.22%	2.11%
1980–1989	$19.59	$154,406.42	12.07	0.86%	0.30%	0.45%	1.61%
1990–1999	$23.50	$161,941.80	12.77	0.84%	0.36%	0.87%	2.07%
2000–2007	$30.36	$178,097.39	13.22	0.99%	0.19%	1.29%	2.47%

Exhibit 7.11 Contributions of Factors to the Growth of real GDP per Hour Worked in the United States between 1950 and 2007 (2011 Constant Dollars)

The exhibit shows the contributions of physical capital, human capital, and technology to the growth of real GDP per hour. Column (6) is computed by subtracting columns (4) and (5) from column (7).

Sources: Data from Bureau of Labor Statistics, Bureau of Economic Analysis, and United States Census Bureau.

This exhibit highlights the central role that technology has played in U.S. growth. Let's examine the 1960s, shown in the second row. The 0.17 percent recorded as the contribution of human capital indicates that if the human capital of U.S. workers had remained constant in the 1960s, then the growth rate of real GDP per hour worked in the 1960s would have been lower by 0.17 percent (3.09 percent instead of 3.26 percent). In contrast, if technology had stayed constant, the annual growth rate of real GDP per hour worked would have been lower by 2.20 percent. The other rows of the exhibit paint a similar picture. Mirroring our findings on the role of technology in accounting for cross-country differences in the previous chapter, technology accounts for the bulk of growth in U.S. real GDP per hour worked in most periods.

Exhibit 7.12 presents the same information as the last four columns of Exhibit 7.11 in a bar chart, more clearly showing the decomposition of growth among the two factors of production and technology. It also highlights the central role of technology. The total height of each bar is the annual growth of real GDP per hour worked during the corresponding period, while the orange part of the bar shows the contribution of technology. It shows that, except between 1980 and 1989, technology was the most important contributor to U.S. growth.

The contribution of technology was somewhat lower during the 1970s and 1980s, which were decades of relatively low growth in real GDP per hour worked, while the stock of physical capital in the economy continued to increase—partly because of considerable investment in information technology capital during these decades. One reason the contribution of technology is more limited in the 1980s than in other decades is also related to this: though there was rapid investment in new equipment, especially in the area of information technology, during this decade, it plausibly took time for companies to use these new technologies to increase productivity.

An important caveat to the conclusions supported by Exhibits 7.11 and 7.12 is worth noting. As pointed out in the previous chapter and in Exhibit 7.11, the contribution of technology is obtained as the fraction of growth in real GDP not explained by physical capital and human capital. This implies that if we understate the contribution of physical

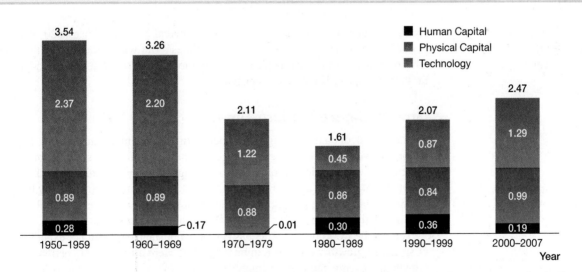

Exhibit 7.12 Shares of Factors in the Growth of Real GDP per Hour Worked in the United States Between 1950 and 2007

This exhibit shows the contribution of physical capital, human capital, and technology to growth of real GDP per hour worked in the United States. The sum of the three numbers is the growth rate in the period, indicated at the top of each bar. It is clear that technology is nearly always the single most important contributor to economic growth in the United States.

Sources: Data from Bureau of Labor Statistics, Bureau of Economic Analysis, United States Census Bureau.

capital or human capital to real GDP growth (which could happen, for example, because we do not fully take into account the improved quality of physical capital stock), then the contribution of technology may be somewhat exaggerated.

Question

Why are you so much more prosperous than your great-great-grandparents were?

Answer

It is mostly due to better technology, though greater physical capital and enhanced human capital of workers have also contributed.

Data

Estimates of real GDP per hour worked, physical capital stock per hour worked, average educational attainment, and average professional experience of the workforce in the United States between 1950 and 2007.

Caveat

If we understate the contribution of physical capital or human capital to real GDP, the contribution of technology may be somewhat exaggerated.

7.3 The History of Growth and Technology

Exhibit 7.8 depicts economic development in several countries since 1820. This 200-year period is sometimes referred to as "modern times." But what about before then? Did patterns of growth before the nineteenth century look similar to those we have documented so far in this chapter? If not, what changed?

Growth Before Modern Times

Humanity had, of course, a long history before the nineteenth century, during which several major achievements took place in science, technology, and the arts. But from an economic point of view, the period before 1800 is distinguished by one thing: a lack of sustained growth. Looking back at Exhibits 7.1 and 7.2, we see that the U.S. economy has had some downturns and one big setback during the Great Depression, but on the whole, it has experienced relatively steady economic growth in real GDP per capita.

Though the world before 1800 was certainly not stagnant, it did not experience the type of sustained growth we see in Exhibit 7.1. There were a few notable periods of economic growth and even technological improvements, some of which continued for as long as a century or even more. The periods that are best known are those in ancient Greece, ancient Rome, and Venice during the fifteenth and sixteenth centuries. During the heydays of these civilizations, standards of living improved and economic activity increased significantly. But this growth didn't last. Ancient Rome may have grown, although relatively slowly, for over 300 years, but its growth ultimately came to an end. The situation was similar in Venice.

Even though there was some economic growth during all of these eras, sustained economic growth was rare or even absent. There is a simple way to see why growth in these ancient civilizations could not have been sustained. The World Bank's definition of absolute poverty as living off the equivalent of $1.90 per day, which we discussed in the previous chapter, is not an entirely arbitrary one. An individual needs to consume a certain amount of calories in order to live, and, of course, people need shelter and clothing. Though estimates vary, it is practically impossible for a country to have real GDP per capita of much less than $500 or so per year, because this would imply that a large fraction of the population would be living on much less than $500 per person. We call this level of income per capita below which an individual cannot easily survive the **subsistence level** (even if there isn't one unique subsistence level that applies in every environment). The general idea is simple: regardless of the exact level, there exists a minimum level of income per person that is necessary for individual survival and subsistence. When income falls below this level, much of the population will starve.

Of course, no national income and product accounts were kept 10,000 years ago, 1,000 years ago, or even 200 years ago. All the same, we know that income per capita in all places in which there were human civilizations could not have been much less than $500 per capita in today's dollars. Moreover, we know from Exhibit 7.8 that at the beginning of the nineteenth century, incomes in much of the world were not much higher than $500 per capita. In the United States, for example, real GDP per capita was about $1,873, and in Western Europe, it was only a little higher. Therefore, there cannot have been much sustained growth before 1800.

Two reasons account for this lack of sustained growth before modern times. The first—the more important one—is related to the major factor that explains sustained growth: technology. Before 1800, although there were some important technological breakthroughs, the pace of technological change was much slower, almost stagnant, compared to what came thereafter. Second, whatever improvements in real GDP were realized did not typically translate into increases in real GDP per capita. This last point was the basis of the theory of Thomas Malthus, which is sometimes referred to as the "Malthusian model." We next discuss the Malthusian model and how the world broke out of it.

Malthusian Limits to Growth

Thomas Malthus had a particularly dismal view of the workings of the economy. This was partly because, writing in 1798, he had not seen a period of steady growth like the one Europe experienced in the nineteenth century.[10] Malthus thought that **fertility**—defined as the number of children per adult or per woman of childbearing age—would adjust so that income always would remain close to a subsistence level, a number like the $500 a year mentioned earlier. Malthus argued that when the standards of living rose, couples would have more children. Because he assumed that real GDP could not grow faster than population, he then concluded that increasing population would push real GDP per capita down toward—and possibly below—the subsistence level. This fall in real GDP per capita in turn would trigger famines or wars that would kill a large fraction of the population. With a given level of aggregate income, a lower population would then cause real GDP per capita to increase again. So in a pattern sometimes referred to as the **Malthusian cycle**, increased aggregate income would raise real GDP per capita above subsistence, fueling population growth, which in turn would put pressure on resources and reduce real GDP per capita back to its initial level or sometimes even below it. This pattern subsequently "corrects" the increase in population through reduced fertility and higher mortality, often due to famines.

Dismal though it may be, the Malthusian model seems to be a good representation of how the world actually was before 1800.

Around the same time or shortly thereafter, fertility declined. This process, which has both economic and social causes, is referred to as the **demographic transition**. Economists typically emphasize the importance of the transition from agriculture and rural areas to industry and cities as a major cause of the demographic transition. Urban families did not need to rely on child labor for help in the field in the same way that rural families did, and the increasing costs of rearing children, particularly when they had to stay in school longer rather than work in the fields, created incentives for smaller families.

Many historians and economists view the demographic transition as a central ingredient to modern growth, because it enabled the economies that experienced reduced fertility to break away from the Malthusian cycle. Until the demographic transition in the nineteenth century, there were recurrent Malthusian cycles. After this date, relatively sustained growth in real GDP per capita took place in many economies, particularly in the Western world.

The **subsistence level** is the minimum level of income per person that is generally necessary for the individual to obtain enough calories, shelter, and clothing to survive.

Fertility refers to the number of children per adult or per woman of childbearing age.

The **Malthusian cycle** refers to the pre-industrial pattern in which increases in aggregate income lead to an expanding population, which in turn reduces income per capita and ultimately puts downward pressure on population.

The **demographic transition** refers to the decline in fertility and number of children per family that many societies undergo as they transition from agriculture to industry.

The Industrial Revolution

But the demographic transition by itself would not have been sufficient to kick-start growth. If all that had happened was that fertility had declined and stabilized around a lower number, there would not necessarily have been any qualitative changes in the patterns of real GDP growth per capita. Instead, sustained growth was due to another major change that occurred around the same time: the *Industrial Revolution*, which opened the way for more steady and rapid technological changes that underpinned modern economic growth.

Contrary to its name, the **Industrial Revolution** was a gradual process rather than a short period of rapid disruption. It is the term coined to designate the arrival of many new machines and methods of production in Britain, starting in textile manufacturing and thereafter spreading into other sectors. The Industrial Revolution is important both as an event in itself (because it was the first time technology and scientific methods were used in production in such a coordinated manner) and also as the starting point of the wave of industrialization that spread to many other countries around the world. We have already seen that the countries that are rich today are those that have managed to achieve steady growth rates over the past 200 years. They are also the ones that have managed to benefit from the technologies brought about by the Industrial Revolution.

Although clearly new technologies and new knowledge had been created before, innovation and the application of new technologies to the production of goods and services became more systematic and pervasive during and in the aftermath of the Industrial Revolution. The available evidence thus suggests that the changes in technology that are the root cause of the sustained growth we observe today started with the Industrial Revolution at the end of the eighteenth century in Britain.

Growth and Technology Since the Industrial Revolution

Many of the technologies that we take for granted today—from railroads to automobiles and airplanes; from radio and TV to telecommunication technologies, computers, the Internet, and social networking; from electricity to almost all the technologies used on the factory floor to produce the goods we use in our everyday life; from nearly all the drugs that save hundreds of millions of lives every year around the world to basic sanitation, including indoor plumbing—have been invented and made available to us over the past 250 years. Such advances are the result of the exponential growth in our knowledge and technology since the Industrial Revolution. An important foundation of this growth has been research and development (R&D) activity, which firms, universities, and governments undertake to improve this knowledge base. The United States today spends 365 billion dollars, or 2.79 percent of its real GDP, on R&D every year. This number is even higher in some other countries—for example, 4.66 percent in Israel, 3.00 percent in Switzerland, and 3.70 percent in Sweden. To a large extent, our high standards of living today are the return on this R&D investment.

7.4 Growth, Inequality, and Poverty

The fact that an economy is growing does not necessarily imply that all citizens are benefiting equally from that growth. In fact, in recent decades, rapid growth in the U.S. economy has gone hand-in-hand with increases in inequality. There are almost always some households and individuals with significantly higher-than-average incomes and some with significantly lower-than-average incomes. In fact, economic growth is sometimes associated with increasing inequality, because only some workers and businesses benefit from the new technologies that are driving this growth.

> The fact that an economy is growing does not necessarily imply that all citizens are benefiting equally from that growth.

Growth and Inequality

There are several reasons that a society might care about inequality. Some may wish to live in a society that does not have great disparities in the living standards of its citizens. We may feel that greater inequality leads to more social polarization or even to a greater incidence of crime in society.

LETTING THE
DATA SPEAK

Income Inequality in the United States

Exhibit 7.13 shows a simple measure of inequality in the United States: the share of total U.S. income accruing to the richest 10 percent (the other 90 percent of Americans earned less than individuals in this top decile, and their aggregate earnings correspond to the remaining fraction). The data, compiled by economists Thomas Piketty and Emmanuel Saez, show that until 1940, the top 10 percent earned about 45 to 50 percent of total income.[11] This proportion then declined to about 35 percent, corresponding to a significant decline in income inequality. It then remained there until the late 1970s. Starting in the late 1970s, however, inequality started increasing, and by the end of the 1990s, the share of the top 10 percent was again up to about 50 percent. Piketty and Saez also show another interesting pattern. Before the 1970s, much of the earnings of the very rich came from capital income—that is, income from sources other than wages and salaries, like dividends, accrued wealth, income from ownership, and so on. But over the past 30 years, the contribution of wages to the income of the very rich has changed dramatically, rising to 60 percent in 2000 (though it subsequently fell to 38 percent in 2007). More and more, even the rich have to work.

So far, we have focused on real GDP per capita as the main measure of the productivity and living standards of a nation. But average income per capita of a nation at a particular point in time is not the same as the income of all individuals in that nation. As we already noted in Chapter 6, this distinction cautions us against focusing just on income per capita without taking into account the distribution of income in a given society.

While it is certainly justifiable to care about inequality in and of itself, one reason many policymakers and citizens are concerned about it is because it is associated with poverty. Poverty, particularly of the extreme sort captured by the $1.90 per day measure of the World Bank, leads to serious economic, health, and social problems. High infant mortality, child malnourishment, lack of access to education, and the inability to take part in several major economic activities are just some of the problems typically associated with extreme levels of poverty. However, it is important to distinguish between inequality and poverty, as we do in the Choice & Consequence box.

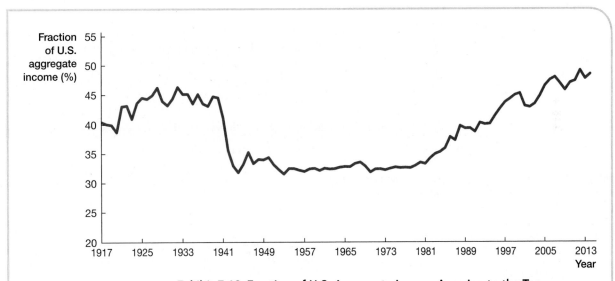

Exhibit 7.13 Fraction of U.S. Aggregate Income Accruing to the Top 10 Percent of Earners

Though growth in the United States has been relatively steady and sustained, the distribution of gains from that growth has changed considerably over time. At the beginning of the twentieth century, the richest Americans—the top 10 percent of earners—captured almost 50 percent of total income. The distribution of income became more equal in the 1940s and remained so until the mid-1970s. Inequality then started increasing again, with the share of the top 10 percent of earners in total income reaching 50 percent once again today.

Source: Data available at: http://elsa.berkeley.edu/~saez/TabFig2014prel.xls.

CHOICE & CONSEQUENCE

Inequality versus Poverty

Consider a society consisting of just two types of people: rich and poor. Suppose also that half of the population is rich and the other half is poor. Now consider two scenarios. In Scenario 1, the rich have $50,000 each, while the poor have $1,000 each. In Scenario 2, the rich have $5,000, while the poor have $500. Which society would you like to live in?

The answer to this question will naturally depend on several factors. Different people will evaluate inequality and poverty differently. Suppose first that you care only about average income and not at all about equity. Then the comparison is straightforward. You will easily compute that average income in Scenario 1 is $25,500, while it is only $2,750 in Scenario 2. The first scenario clearly dominates.

Suppose, however, that you care only about equity. One way of thinking about this is to focus just on a measure of inequality and nothing else. In that case, you will see that Scenario 1 has greater inequality, because the ratio of rich-to-poor incomes is 50. In contrast, in Scenario 2, the same ratio is only 10. So if you care only about inequality and nothing else, you may be tempted to say that Scenario 2 is preferable.

There is a fallacy here, however. Most of us care about inequality because we associate it with poverty and low living standards for part of the population. Yet Scenario 1, despite having greater inequality, also has much less poverty. In Scenario 1, the poor individuals have $1,000 each, whereas in Scenario 2, each poor individual has only $500, regardless of that economy's greater equality. Therefore, even if we strongly care about the welfare of others and the level of poverty in society, just focusing on inequality would be an error. In fact, in this case, Scenario 1 has both greater average income and lower poverty. If, instead of noticing this, we just focused on inequality, presuming that a more equal allocation would also indicate lower poverty, we would have made an error in judgment.

Growth and Poverty

What is the relationship between growth and poverty? We saw in Chapter 6 how countries with higher levels of PPP-adjusted GDP per capita have fewer people living in poverty, as measured by the $1.90 per day measure of the World Bank. Exhibit 7.14 complements this picture by showing that, on average, growth of income per capita is associated with a decline in poverty. For each country in the exhibit, the y-axis shows the percentage rise or decline in poverty between 1993 and the early 2010s (depending on data availability), while the x-axis shows the average growth between the same dates.

Exhibit 7.14
Relationship Between Growth and Change in Poverty in the Early 1990s and the Early Twenty-First Century

Economic growth tends to reduce poverty, though the relationship is noisy and less than perfect. Red dots correspond to countries identified by name.

Source: Data from Penn World Table and World Bank DataBank: World Development Indicators; Penn World Table version 9.0 (Robert C. Feenstra, Robert Inklaar, and Marcel P. Timmer, June 2016).

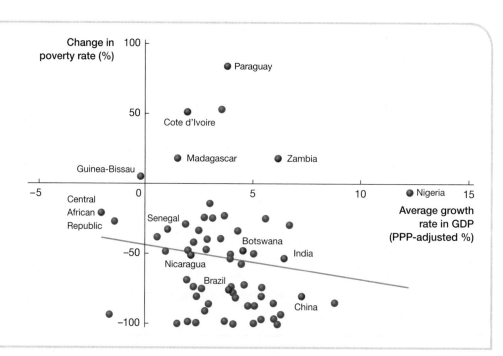

Countries in the lower right quadrant are those that have experienced positive growth and declines in poverty and include Botswana, China, India, and Brazil, among others. The exhibit also includes the line that best fits these points. Although in some countries growth and poverty have both increased significantly (such as Côte d'Ivoire and Paraguay), on the whole there is a negative association between growth over the recent decades and the fraction of the population living in poverty. Yet the exhibit also shows quite a bit of dispersion around that best-fit line, reminding us that many other factors beyond growth can influence poverty.

Even though this association does not prove that growth in income per capita is the direct cause of declining poverty, it is the type of evidence that bolsters many economists' belief that economic growth is one of the most effective ways of reducing poverty. Nevertheless, it is important to remember that economic growth does not guarantee an automatic reduction in poverty (as the cases of Côte d'Ivoire, Paraguay, Madagascar, and Zambia in the exhibit show). It will do so only if it is not associated with a significant rise in inequality.

How Can We Reduce Poverty?

Many different policies have been pursued to reduce international poverty, and, for reasons that we discuss in greater detail in Chapter 8, many have failed. Thus it is quite likely that there are no silver-bullet policies for reducing poverty around the world.

Nevertheless, economic analysis suggests several potentially useful approaches. One solution, which we explore further in Chapter 14, is international trade, which can be beneficial to all countries that take part in it. Although international trade does create losers as well as winners, the overall benefit from international trade is generally positive and significant. This is particularly so for many poor countries that have natural resources and produce agricultural goods that could be exported to the European Union or the United States but are blocked by high tariffs and prohibitive quotas. Reducing tariffs and quotas that wealthy nations impose on poor countries would be one way of creating gains in real GDP and perhaps even growth for these nations. In fact, trade might have even further benefits. If international trade also brings with it more interaction with wealthy nations, such cross-country contact might facilitate the transfer of technology.

Another important aspect of improving standards of living around the world is to continue improving the knowledge and technology available in the world economy. The United States spends a sizable fraction of its GDP on R&D, and a significant fraction of its workforce works in science and engineering. The improvements that result from these efforts in the United States and in countries such as Canada, the United Kingdom, France, and Germany improve the standards of living not only in these nations but also all around the world. For example, improvements in communications technology that originated in the United States and Western Europe now enable cell phones to be used globally, which has helped improve the lives and the business opportunities of billions of people elsewhere. Before wireless communication became available, people in many countries had to rely on wireline telephones for communication.

But the wireline telephone industry was often under state control or a private monopoly, and as a consequence, it was very expensive and not widely available. The advances in wireless technology have partly broken the hold of these monopolies on consumers and have made it possible for hundreds of millions of poor people around the world to access services they could not access before. For example, before Americans had heard of Venmo or Apple Pay, M-PESA was already transforming the lives of Kenyans. Developed in 2007 to ease microfinance repayments, M-PESA is a mobile banking application that works on the simplest of mobile phones. Even without a wifi connection or smartphone, Kenyans can pay their taxi drivers, receive government payments, or even take out a loan. By 2012, there were more mobile money accounts in Kenya than bank accounts.[12] In the meantime in South India, mobile phones have revolutionized the fish market by enabling fishermen to learn prices at various marketplaces along the coast in real time and respond to them efficiently by taking their fish to where prices are higher.[13] As the technology improves further, wireless telecommunication is expected to revolutionize healthcare in many countries. Already it is being used to help remind patients to take medications and help clinics keep track of supplies and vaccinations. Similarly, innovations in pharmaceuticals allow lives to be saved around the world, not just in the United States or Germany or France.

In this and the previous chapter, we have focused on how physical capital, human capital, and technology determine the potential for economic growth and cross-country differences in PPP-adjusted GDP per capita. We have seen how an economy—rich or poor—can grow by investing more in physical capital, upgrading the human capital of its workforce, and improving its technology and efficiency of production. The natural question, then, is why many countries in the world do not pursue such improvements but instead remain poor or submit to low growth. This is the topic of our next chapter.

Summary

- Many countries, including the United States, have experienced rapid economic growth over the past 200 years, increasing their real GDP per capita several times over. For example, current U.S. real GDP per capita is about 25 times U.S. real GDP per capita in 1820. In addition, U.S. growth has been relatively sustained, meaning that GDP per capita has grown relatively steadily, with the exception of the Great Depression and the decade following it.

- Economic growth can sometimes take place rapidly due to catch-up growth, whereby relatively poorer nations increase their real GDP per capita by taking advantage of knowledge and technologies already invented in other, more advanced countries.

- Economic growth results from an economy increasing its physical capital, raising the human capital of its workers (so that it has greater efficiency units of labor for a given workforce size), and improving its technology. Because of the diminishing marginal product of physical capital and limits to how much each worker can invest in his or her human capital before joining the workforce, sustained growth is generally impossible to achieve just by building up physical and human capital. Rather, the most plausible driver of sustained growth is technological progress. Empirical evidence also suggests that technological progress accounts for the bulk of the increase in real GDP per capita (or per hour worked) in the United States.

- Though the past 200 years have been characterized by sustained economic growth in many parts of the world, the preceding centuries did not experience steady growth. Instead, most economies during these times experienced Malthusian cycles: increases in GDP-fueled population growth, which reduced the standard of living and subsequently acted as a check on further population growth by reducing fertility and survival. The world broke out of the Malthusian cycle through the Industrial Revolution, which started a process of rapid technological progress, underpinning the sustained growth of the past two centuries.

- Economic growth has the capacity to significantly reduce poverty, provided that such growth is not associated with substantially increased inequality.

Key Terms

Questions

All questions are available in MyEconLab for practice and instructor assignment.

1. What is meant by economic growth? How has the U.S. economy grown over the past 200 years?

2. What are catch-up growth and sustained growth? Explain with examples.

3. According to the aggregate production function, how does real GDP increase?

4. The chapter emphasizes the importance of saving to economic growth.

   a. How is the saving rate in an economy defined?

   b. What factors help households decide whether to consume or save their incomes?

   c. How do household saving decisions impact investment in the economy?

5. Holding all else equal, will increasing the efficiency units of labor lead to sustained growth? Why or why not?

6. What explains economic growth in the United States over the past few decades?

7. Why was there no sustained economic growth before modern times, that is, before 1800?

8. What did Malthus predict about economic growth? Did his predictions come true? Why or why not?

9. How did the Industrial Revolution affect economic growth?

10. Does an increase in real GDP per capita of a nation imply that all its citizens have become richer? Explain.

11. Based on your understanding of the chapter, how can poverty best be reduced?

12. What factors explain the dramatic increases in life expectancy that most countries experienced in the twentieth century?

Problems

All problems are available in MyEconLab for practice and instructor assignment.

1. In the second half of the twentieth century, Japan experienced exceptional growth. According to World Bank data, in 1985, Japan's GDP was $3.67 trillion, and its annual growth rate was 6.33 percent. The GDP in this problem is in constant 2010 dollars.

   a. Assuming an exponential annual growth rate of 6.33 percent, calculate Japan's projected GDP in 2010.

   b. In fact, Japan's 2010 GDP was $5.7 trillion. What could explain any discrepancy between this number and your answer to part (a)?

2. Currently, some of the fastest-growing countries in the world remain desperately poor. For example, of the top five fastest-growing economies in 2016, three—Iraq, Burma, and Nauru—had real per capita GDPs that are 101st, 162nd, and 112th in the world, respectively. (*Source:* CIA, *The World Factbook* estimates for 2016, PPP basis.) This seems like something of a contradiction. Using the equations for growth given in the chapter, explain why a country that has a very low real per capita GDP can also have a very high growth rate.

3. The following table lists GDP per capita from 1970 to 2010 for South Korea and the United States. As you can see, both grew substantially over that 40-year period.

Year	South Korean GDP per Capita	U.S. GDP per Capita
1970	$317	$5,247
1980	$1,778	$12,598
1990	$6,642	$23,955
2000	$11,948	$36,467
2010	$22,151	$48,358

Source: Data from the World Bank, *World Development Indicators.*

   a. Plot the five data points for each country on a graph using a nonproportional scale, as in Exhibit 7.3 in the chapter. Connect the points to create a line graph.

   b. Plot the five data points for each country on a graph using a proportional scale, that is, a scale where equal distances represent equal *percentage* changes. Connect the points to create a line graph.

   c. Interpret the differences you see in the two graphs.

4. Economists Andrew McAfee and Erik Brynjolfsson have written about "The Great Decoupling"—the divergence between productivity growth and employment. Since the mid-1990s, labor productivity and real GDP have continued to increase, while employment and wages have remained

stagnant. Use the concepts from this chapter to explain how this "decoupling" might work. How could productivity and real GDP continue to increase, even with the declining employment? Why might it be the case that employment has not increased while real GDP has continued to grow? How might this dynamic influence inequality?

5. The graph below shows an index of world GDP per capita from 1000 BC to the year 2000.

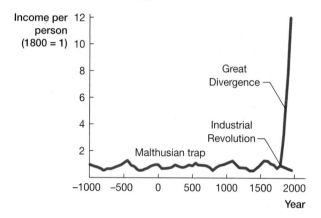

Source: Based on Jeff Speakes, *Economic History of the World,* Thousand Oaks, CA: Center for Economic Research and Forecasting, California Lutheran University, 2013.

As you can see, over most of that period, global economic growth was virtually nonexistent. While there were periods that experienced some increase in per capita income, sustained growth begins only in the mid-eighteenth century and explodes after that—by the year 2000, income per capita is 12 times what it had been 250 years before.

Explain what accounts for such a dramatic change in economic growth beginning in the 18th century.

6. Economists have long debated the causes of the slowdown in productivity (real GDP per hour worked) in the United States during the 1970s and 1980s. This slowdown can be clearly seen in Exhibits 7.10 and 7.11.

   a. Based on the data in Exhibit 7.11, is it physical capital, human capital, or technology that is most responsible for the overall decline in the annual growth rate of real GDP per hour worked in these two decades? Explain your answer with reference to the exhibit.

   b. An interesting study of the slowdown has been done by Yale economist William Nordhaus, which is summarized at http://www.nber.org/digest/jun05/w10950.html. What are the two main conclusions that Nordhaus reaches concerning the 1970s slowdown? Which industries were most affected by the slowdown, and why?

7. The concept of diminishing returns to a factor of production applies not only to physical capital but to labor as well. Use the concept of diminishing returns to labor to explain and illustrate why there was no sustained growth in living standards prior to the Industrial Revolution. Draw a graph to illustrate the relationship between population

and real GDP, where population is measured on the x-axis. Explain how your graph changes after the Industrial Revolution.

8. In 1968, Paul Ehrlich, a Stanford University professor, claimed that overpopulation would lead to famines and starvation in the 1970s and 1980s. In his book, *The Population Bomb,* he said that unless population growth was curbed, millions around the world would die. However, as we now know, this did not happen. What do you think was the flaw in Ehrlich's argument?

9. The Letting the Data Speak box "Levels versus Growth" points out how one important index of health—life expectancy—has changed in various countries over time. To see a dramatic animation of the data mentioned in the box, go to http://www.gapminder.org/videos/200-years-that-changed-the-world-bbc,/#.U8aTaJRdXTo. Hans Rosling is an expert on global health and is known for his creative presentation of statistics. Watch the brief video, and answer the following questions.

   a. What was the upper limit on life expectancy in almost all countries in 1810? Which two countries were slightly better off?

   b. Which countries failed to improve much in life expectancy and income as a result of the Industrial Revolution?

   c. As of 1948, had disparities in life expectancy and income between countries narrowed or widened? Which were some of the countries that had not made much improvement in either measure by 1948?

   d. As of 2009, what was the general situation regarding the distribution of countries in terms of health and income? What countries still lagged behind?

   e. Based on the video, how can country averages disguise the wide variation in living standards *within* a country? Give an example from the video.

10. Increasingly, independent programmers are making their code "open source." The statistical programming language "R," for example, is completely free and open; anyone can submit a new package of specialized functions. How might open source technology affect growth in developing countries? Imagine every technology company in the United States suddenly made their code open source; would this increase growth in developing countries? Explain.

11. Suppose that a 10 percent increase in the physical capital stock increases real GDP by 8 percent. Now consider an additional 8 percent increase in the physical capital stock. Will this increase real GDP by less than 8 percent, 8 percent, or more than 8 percent? Explain.

12. Challenge Problem: Refer to Exhibit 7.4. If the United States, Mexico, China, and Rwanda continue to grow at the rates given in the exhibit, how many years (starting from 2010) will it take each to catch up to the United States in terms of PPP-adjusted per capita GDP?

Appendix

The Solow Growth Model

The main tool that economists use for formally studying how GDP is determined is the *Solow model*, named after the economist Robert Solow.[14] In this appendix, we present the Solow model to show how it can be used to study the process of economic growth in greater detail. We have placed this material in the appendix rather than in the main body of the chapter because it can be skipped without interfering with the other key ideas in this chapter and elsewhere in the book. Throughout this appendix, there is no issue of prices changing, and thus changes in GDP referred to changes in real GDP.

The Three Building Blocks of the Solow Model

The Solow model consists of three building blocks. The first one is the aggregate production function, which we saw in Chapter 6. Recall that the aggregate production function, $Y = A \times F(K, H)$, links GDP to physical capital (K), total efficiency units of labor (H), and the level of technology (A). Technology includes the knowledge available to the economy and the efficiency of production; it shifts the aggregate production function.

The second building block is an equation for physical capital accumulation. Most equipment and structures making up the physical capital stock of an economy are durable. When you purchase a computer, you will be using it for several years; many household durables are typically used for much longer. Structures—buildings, roads, and bridges—last even longer. But the durability of physical capital is not infinite. Physical capital is subject to *depreciation*, meaning that any equipment or structure goes through "wear and tear" and ultimately becomes obsolete. For example, when you buy a truck and use it for a year, it will have more miles on it and its brakes may be worn out. As a result of this wear and tear, some of its value will have been lost, and you will get quite a bit less than you paid for it last year if you try to sell it. Depreciation erodes the value of physical capital, but it can be slowed or reversed by continual investment and upkeep. In the case of your truck, you could invest in it by having the brakes, oil, or tires changed. This type of investment counterbalances depreciation and increases the value of the truck.

The same is true for the physical capital stock of the economy, as captured by the following physical capital accumulation equation:

$$K_{\text{now}} = K_{\text{last year}} - K_{\text{depreciated}} + I$$

or

$$K_{\text{now}} = K_{\text{last year}} - (\text{Depreciation rate} \times K_{\text{last year}}) + I$$

or

$$K_{\text{now}} = (1 - d) \times K_{\text{last year}} + I.$$

Here, K_{now} is the physical capital stock this year. This directly depends on the physical capital stock last year, $K_{\text{last year}}$, specifically the fraction $1 - d$ of that physical capital stock that doesn't depreciate between the two dates. The remaining $d \times K_{\text{last year}}$ is the equivalent of the decline in the value of your truck. In the meantime, the firms in the economy undertake investments and purchase new machines to increase the physical capital stock of the economy, in the same way that you may have invested in new gadgets or maintenance to increase the value of your truck. In the above equations, this is represented by the investment amount I.

This equation is not only useful for the Solow growth model, but in fact is also one of the key equations that economists use to compute the actual value of physical capital stock in practice, such as in national income accounts.

Exhibit 7A.1 Aggregate Income and Aggregate Saving

The aggregate production function shows how much GDP can be produced from a given amount of physical capital stock, total efficiency units of labor, and technology. In the exhibit, this is the length of the line between the aggregate production function and the x-axis. This aggregate income is in turn divided between consumption and saving (we are ignoring government spending). Saving is also equal to investment in the aggregate.

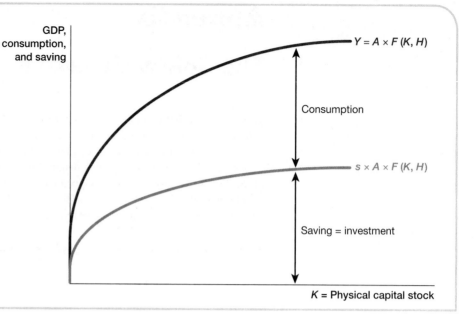

The third building block of the Solow model is saving by households. Recall from our discussion in the body of this chapter that investment is determined by household saving behavior. Then investment in the economy will be

$$I = s \times Y,$$

where, as you will recall, Y denotes GDP, s is the saving rate, and I is aggregate investment. Now, using the first building block, the aggregate production function, we can write

$$I = s \times Y = s \times A \times F(K, H).$$

This relationship is drawn in Exhibit 7A.1. The red curve represents the aggregate production function, or more specifically the relationship between GDP and the physical capital stock for given levels of efficiency units of labor and technology. This shows the same shape as Exhibit 6.7 from the previous chapter. The green curve shows the relationship between the level of investment and the physical capital stock given the saving rate of households, s. It is simply given by a downward shift of the aggregate production function—because it represents GDP times the saving rate, s. By definition, therefore, the distance between the green curve and the x-axis at a given level of physical capital stock corresponds to aggregate saving or investment, as shown in the exhibit. Because the red curve represents GDP in the economy, as shown in the exhibit, the distance between the red and green curves represents consumption (since $Y = C + I$).

Steady-State Equilibrium in the Solow Model

A natural situation for us to study is one in which the physical capital stock last year and physical capital stock now are equal:

$$K_{\text{now}} = K_{\text{last year}} = K.$$

A **steady-state equilibrium** is an economic equilibrium in which the physical capital stock remains constant over time.

We refer to such a situation as a **steady-state equilibrium**, which is similar to our usual notion of equilibrium with supply being equal to demand, but it also requires that the physical capital stock is the same between the two dates.

This equation, combined with the physical capital accumulation equation above, immediately implies that, for the physical capital stock to be unchanged between years, we need to have investment equal to a fraction d of the physical capital stock, written as follows:

$$I = d \times K.$$

(To see how to derive this equation, note that in a steady state, the physical capital accumulation equation becomes $K = (1 - d) \times K + I$, and solving this for I gives the desired equation.)

Exhibit 7A.2 Steady-State Equilibrium in the Solow Model

The steady-state equilibrium in the Solow model is given as the point of intersection of the curve denoting total saving in the economy (as a function of the physical capital stock) and the line designating the amount of investment necessary to replenish depreciated physical capital. In the exhibit, the steady-state equilibrium corresponds to the physical capital stock of K* and GDP of Y*.

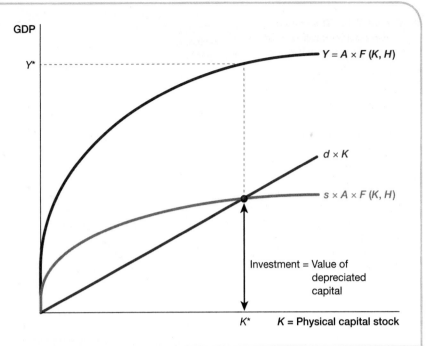

In other words, for the physical capital stock of the economy to remain constant over time, the amount of investment must equal the depreciated value of the physical capital stock, which is the depreciation rate of the economy, d, times the physical capital stock, K. Returning to our example above, the value of your truck will remain constant only if the new investment you put in is equal exactly to the depreciation—the reduction in the value of the truck due to wear and tear.

We now put the different ingredients of the Solow model together to determine the steady-state equilibrium. This can be done in Exhibit 7A.2 by also plotting the line representing the value of depreciated physical capital, $d \times K$.

The steady-state equilibrium is given by the intersection between this blue line and the green curve (which represents the investment level implied by the saving decisions of households). This follows simply because at this point of intersection, new investment, $I = s \times A \times F(K, H)$, is equal to the value of depreciated physical capital, $d \times K$.

This exhibit shows that there is a unique point where the blue straight line intersects the green curve representing investment. This intersection is the steady-state equilibrium of the Solow model. It gives the steady-state equilibrium level of physical capital stock on the x-axis, marked K*, and the steady-state equilibrium GDP level on the y-axis, Y*. The exhibit also shows the level of investment (saving) and the value of depreciated physical capital, which equal each other by definition in a steady-state equilibrium, as well as the level of consumption in this equilibrium.

Once we have the steady-state equilibrium of the Solow model, we can use it to study the determinants of GDP.

Determinants of GDP

Exhibit 7A.2 makes it clear that one of the key determinants of GDP is the saving rate, as we discussed in the text. The impact of a higher saving rate on the steady-state physical capital stock and GDP can be seen in Exhibit 7A.3, where we drop the curve for the aggregate production function, $A \times F(K, H)$, and simply show the investment level given by $I = s \times A \times F(K, H)$.

In this exhibit, we compare two economies that have access to the same aggregate production function and have the same population and same efficiency units of labor, but have different saving rates. The economy with the higher saving rate, s', is depicted by the dark green curve, while the one with the lower saving rate, s, is shown with the light green curve. (By assumption, both economies have the same rate of depreciation, so the same line

Exhibit 7A.3 The Impact of the Saving Rate on the Steady-State Equilibrium

An increase in the saving rate from s to s' rotates up the curve denoting total saving in the economy and increases the steady-state equilibrium physical capital stock and GDP level. In the exhibit, the physical capital stock increases from K^* to K^{**} and GDP from Y^* to Y^{**}. (Hence, the level of saving and investment, shown on the y-axis, increases from $s \times Y^*$ to $s' \times Y^{**}$.)

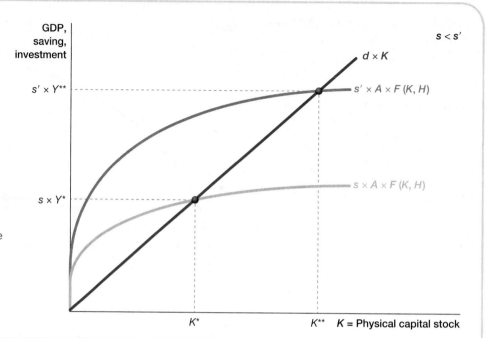

represents the value of depreciation). The exhibit shows that the economy with the higher saving rate will have a steady-state equilibrium to the right and above the original one. This corresponds to a greater physical capital stock and hence to greater GDP. Because population is kept constant in this exercise, this also translates into greater GDP per capita.

Both better technology and better human capital of workers also imply that the same amount of physical capital will translate to greater GDP. If the economy has workers with improved human capital, this will increase its efficiency units of labor, H, and given the increasing relationship between efficiency units of labor and GDP shown in Exhibit 6.8 in the previous chapter, we will have greater GDP for a given level of physical capital stock. Therefore, in terms of the relationship between GDP and the physical capital stock, greater human capital of workers implies a shift of the aggregate production function. As a result, aggregate saving shifts to the curve drawn in dark green in Exhibit 7A.4, and the

Exhibit 7A.4 Change in the Steady-State Equilibrium Resulting from an Increase in the Human Capital of Workers

When the human capital of workers increases, so does the total efficiency units of labor. This implies that the economy can produce more with the same physical capital stock and technology, so the curve for the aggregate production function shifts up. This leads to a new steady-state equilibrium with higher physical capital stock and GDP. In particular, the physical capital stock increases from K^* to K^{**} and GDP from Y^* to Y^{**}.

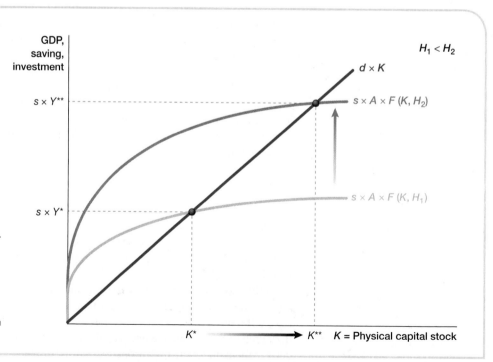

steady-state equilibrium will again be to the right and above the original one, as shown in the exhibit. This implies that higher human capital leads to both higher steady-state equilibrium physical capital stock and higher real GDP for the country. Because there has not been any change in the population (or working-age population), the higher real GDP again translates into higher real GDP per capita.

Exactly the same analysis applies to technology. Recall that better technology corresponds to higher A in terms of our aggregate production function. It can be the result of better knowledge being used in production or of greater efficiency of production. In either case, it will lead to a shift in the aggregate production function that is identical to that in Exhibit 7A.3 (except that it is now the total efficiency units of labor, not the saving rate, that is changing). Consequently, the implications are also identical. There will be a higher steady-state equilibrium level of physical capital stock and a greater steady-state equilibrium level of GDP. Because population is again constant, this will imply greater real GDP per capita.

Dynamic Equilibrium in the Solow Model

The Solow model is not only useful for understanding the determinants of steady-state equilibrium but is also the main vehicle that economists use for thinking about economic growth.

As the qualifier "steady-state" hints, we can also imagine an equilibrium that is not a steady-state equilibrium. Such an equilibrium, often referred to as a **dynamic equilibrium**, traces out the behavior of the economy over time. Therefore, a dynamic equilibrium doesn't correspond to a single point, but to a *path* (of physical capital stock and GDP levels) that will be realized over time.

A **dynamic equilibrium** traces out the behavior of the economy over time.

To understand this notion, let us look at Exhibit 7A.5, which is the same as Exhibit 7A.2 except without the curve for $A \times F(K, H)$. The steady-state equilibrium again occurs at the point where the blue straight line intersects the curve representing the investment level; thus K^* is the physical capital stock, and Y^* is GDP in this steady-state equilibrium.

Now imagine that, starting from K^*, suddenly some of the physical capital in this economy is destroyed, for example, because of war. As a result, the physical capital stock of the economy is now represented by $K_0 < K^*$. Suppose also that nothing else changes; in particular, the aggregate production function, the saving rate, the efficiency units of labor, and technology all remain the same. At this point, even though just one variable has changed, we are no longer in a steady-state equilibrium because physical capital is no longer being replenished precisely at the rate at which it is depreciating.

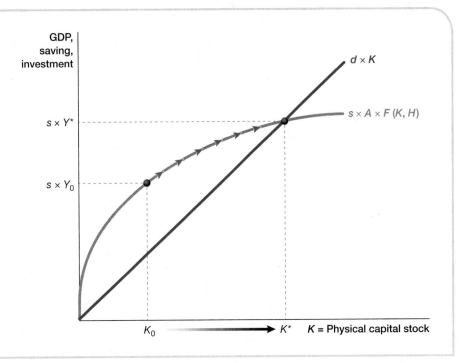

Exhibit 7A.5 Dynamic Equilibrium in the Solow Model

Suppose the economy starts with a physical capital stock of $K_0 = K^*$, that is, with a physical capital stock less than the steady-state equilibrium. What happens? The exhibit shows that at this point, saving and investment are greater than the amount of physical capital that depreciates, so the physical capital stock increases. This dynamic process takes us to the steady-state physical capital stock of K^*.

What will the level of production in the economy be now? Because the physical capital stock is now equal to K_0 but the efficiency units of labor have not changed, GDP will continue to be given by the aggregate production function at Y_0 (and corresponds to the point marked as $s \times Y_0$ on the y-axis in Exhibit 7A.5). However, this exhibit also makes it clear that at this new point (K_0, Y_0), the economy is above the straight line. Recall that, along this straight line, investment is just equal to the amount of depreciated physical capital. Above it, investment does not just make up for depreciated physical capital, but exceeds it. Recall now the physical capital accumulation equation, which tells us that $K_{\text{now}} = K_{\text{last year}} - K_{\text{depreciated}} + I$. This equation implies that, as investment exceeds depreciated physical capital (that is, $I > K_{\text{depreciated}}$), the physical capital stock will increase. Put differently, there will be a dynamic equilibrium path that takes us back toward the steady-state equilibrium at K^*. The dynamic equilibrium path is shown in Exhibit 7A.5 by the green arrows. It starts at $(K_0, s \times Y_0)$ and traces out the path of the economy toward $(K^*, s \times Y^*)$. This highlights both the fact that a dynamic equilibrium corresponds to a path showing the behavior of the economy over time and also the key result that such a dynamic equilibrium will take the economy back toward the steady-state equilibrium $(K^*, s \times Y^*)$.

Sources of Growth in the Solow Model

We can now use the Solow model to return to the discussion of sustained growth in the text. First, Exhibit 7A.6 demonstrates that increases in the saving rate and physical capital accumulation cannot be the source of sustained growth. It shows that, for given levels of total efficiency units of labor and technology, there is a maximum amount of GDP that an economy can achieve by increasing saving, since it can never go above a saving rate of 100 percent. This determines the level of GDP, Y^{MAX}, beyond which the economy cannot expand with a given aggregate production function and total efficiency units of labor.

The presence of such a maximal level of GDP, Y^{MAX}, implies that sustained growth is not possible by just increasing saving. To see this, note that if an economy grows at a constant

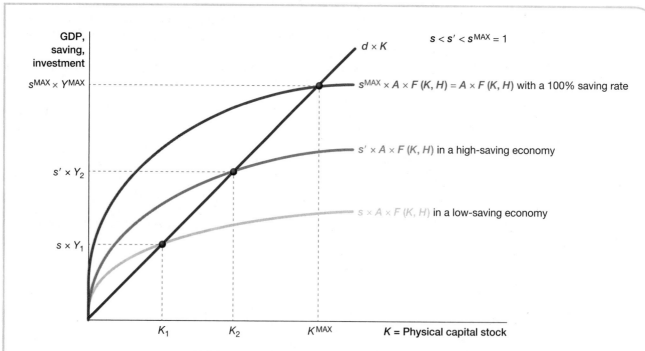

Exhibit 7A.6 Three Economies with Different Saving Rates in the Solow Model

Economies with higher saving rates have higher GDP, but increases in the saving rate cannot be the source of sustained growth. This is because there is a maximum to how much an economy can save and thus a limit to what GDP it can achieve just by saving more.

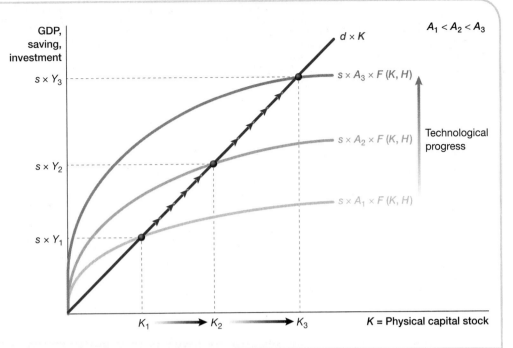

Exhibit 7A.7 Sustained Growth Driven by Technological Change

Technological progress is at the root of sustained growth in the Solow model. As technology improves, the aggregate production function shifts up, and equilibrium physical capital stock and GDP increase gradually.

rate, such as 2 percent per year, it will eventually reach and exceed any fixed level of GDP, such as Y^{MAX}. This is consistent with historical evidence. Over the past 200 years, countries have not achieved steady growth by simply increasing their saving rates. Overall, this discussion and Exhibit 7A.6 show that *increases in the saving rate can increase GDP, but they cannot generate sustained growth.*

To show how technological improvements can lead to sustained growth in the Solow model, Exhibit 7A.7 revisits our by-now-familiar figure for the determination of the steady-state equilibrium. It shows that as technology improves, the aggregate production function (and consequently the investment curve) shifts up. This raises the equilibrium levels of physical capital stock and GDP.

Notably, these improvements take place along the straight line of the steady state as shown in the exhibit. Recall that the straight line is given by the equation $d \times K$ and does not shift as a result of technological improvements.

At each point of intersection, we have $s \times Y = d \times K$. Rewriting this gives $K/Y = s/d$, which thus implies that throughout, there is a constant ratio of the physical capital stock to GDP. Therefore, the implication of the Solow model for sustained growth is that the *ratio of the physical capital stock to GDP should be constant as the economy grows.*

Exhibit 7A.8 plots the historical evolution of the value of the physical capital stock to GDP in the U.S. economy. The ratio of the physical capital stock to GDP is roughly constant over the past 50 years, with a value of about 2. This pattern is consistent with the implication of the Solow model based on sustained growth driven by technological improvements, which, as we just saw, also implies a constant ratio of physical capital stock to GDP as the economy grows.

What about catch-up growth? In contrast to sustained growth, catch-up growth can result both from the accumulation of physical capital and human capital and from technological change. The nature of catch-up growth can be illustrated by the dynamic equilibrium path of an economy starting with a level of physical capital stock such as K_0 below its steady-state equilibrium K^*, as depicted in Exhibit 7A.5. This dynamic equilibrium path represents the growth trajectory of an economy that is temporarily below its steady-state equilibrium or improves its technology and thus raises its steady-state equilibrium level of physical capital stock and GDP. This exhibit thus shows that, typically, such an economy will rapidly grow toward its steady-state equilibrium. Such rapid growth is a hallmark of the catch-up process as shown by the experiences of several countries depicted in Exhibits 7.4, 7.5, and 7.8.

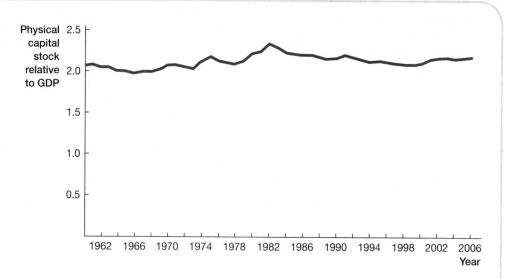

Exhibit 7A.8 The Ratio of Physical Capital Stock to GDP in the United States

Consistent with the implications of sustained growth driven by technological progress in the Solow model, the ratio of physical capital stock to real GDP in the United States has remained approximately constant over the past 50 years.

Source: Based on Bureau of Economic Analysis, National Income and Product Accounts.

Calculating Average (Compound) Growth Rates

Now let's discuss how to calculate average growth rates by returning to Exhibit 7.4. Consider the United States. Its real GDP per capita was $17,600 in 1960 and $52,292 in 2014 (in PPP-adjusted 2011 constant dollars). We can now compute the 54-year growth rate (between 1960 and 2014) as 197.11 percent, using the formula provided in the text. In particular, this number is obtained as

$$\frac{52{,}292 - 17{,}600}{17{,}600} = 1.9711,$$

corresponding to 197.11 percent growth.

One way of computing the average growth rate is to use the arithmetic average and divide this number by 54 to obtain the average annual growth rate. This would give an annual growth rate of 3.65 percent. The number in Exhibit 7.4 is different—2.0 percent. How is this number obtained, and why is it different?

The answer is related to the importance of the exponential nature of growth, which we discussed earlier in the chapter. Suppose that an economy grows at the rate of $g = 0.0365$ (that is, 3.65 percent) every year for 54 years. How much will its real GDP per capita have gone up at the end of the 54 years? To compute this, we have to note that after 1 year, its real GDP per capita will have increased by $1 + g$. From the second to the third year, it will increase by another $1 + g$, so between the first and third years, it will have gone up by $(1 + g)^2$. Continuing with this reasoning, at the end of 54 years, its real GDP per capita will have increased by $(1 + g)^{54}$. If we take $g = 0.0365$, we find that its real GDP per capita will be 6.93 times higher at the end of the 54 years, which is considerably greater than the numbers for the United States. Instead, these numbers imply that at the end of the 54 years, U.S. real GDP per capita was about 2.9711 times higher. (This number can be obtained simply as $52{,}292 / 17{,}600 = 2.9711$, that is, real GDP per capita in 2014 divided by real GDP per capita in 1960, or you can note that it is $1 + 1.9711$, where 197.11 percent was the growth rate of the U.S. economy between 1960 and 2014.)

By dividing the total growth between 1960 and 2014 by 54, we have ignored the cumulative effects of growth and overestimated the annual growth rate that would lead to the observed increase in real GDP per capita.

This discussion also indicates that a more sophisticated way of computing the average annual growth rate is by using the geometric average. In this case, we would calculate the growth rate as

$$(1 + g)^{54} = 2.9711.$$

We can then use this equation to arrive at the correct average annual growth rate, g. (More technically, we would invert this equation and compute $g = 2.9711^{1/54} - 1$.) This approximately gives the (average) annual growth rate as $g = 0.020$, as recorded in the exhibit. In most cases, using either the arithmetic or the geometric average to compute average growth rates gives similar answers, provided that we are looking at short periods. The reason the difference is sizable in this case is because we are considering a long period of time.

Appendix Key Terms

steady-state equilibrium *p. 168*

dynamic equilibrium *p. 171*

Appendix Problems

All problems are available in MyEconLab for practice and instructor assignment.
Problems marked ⊕ update with real-time data.

A1. Use a diagram to represent the Solow growth model using the aggregate production function and the relationship between the physical capital stock and aggregate saving.
   a. Which point in the figure represents the steady-state equilibrium? Why?
   b. Use the diagram to show the impact of an increase in human capital on GDP.

A2. In the 1980s, the saving rate in Japan was extremely high. Gross savings as a percentage of GDP ranged between 30 percent and 32 percent. Can such a high saving rate lead to sustained economic growth? Use the Solow model to explain your answer. (*Data source:* http://data .worldbank.org/indicator/NY.GNS.ICTR.ZS/countries/ JP?page=5&display=default.)

⊕ A3. India's GDP per capita increased from $310 in 1991 to $1,489 in 2012. (*Data source:* http://data.worldbank.org/ indicator/NY.GDP.PCAP.CD.)
   a. Calculate the arithmetic average annual rate of growth of the Indian economy during this period using the arithmetic average.
   b. Calculate the geometric average annual growth rate of India during this period. How does the number you found differ from the number given in Exhibit 7.3? Speculate on what accounts for any difference.

A4. The appendix details the important distinction between arithmetic and geometric averages when determining growth rates.
   a. Using the procedure outlined in the appendix for *geometric* average growth rates (in the section titled "Calculating Average (Compound) Growth Rates"), see if you can reproduce the "Implied (average) annual growth" figures given in the last column of Exhibit 7.4 for the following countries: France, Singapore, Botswana, India and Kenya.
   b. Using the procedure outlined in the appendix for finding *arithmetic* average growth rates, calculate the arithmetic average growth rate for the five countries. Compare these with the rates you obtained in part a. Does the arithmetic average understate or overstate the actual growth rate? Explain.

8 Why Isn't the Whole World Developed?

Are tropical and semitropical areas condemned to poverty by their geographies?

If you look back at the map of PPP-adjusted GDP per capita of the world shown in Exhibit 6.2 in Chapter 6, you will notice a striking regularity: many of the poorest nations are close to the equator in the tropical and semitropical areas of the world. Conversely, countries in the temperate areas away from the equator are much more prosperous. The Democratic Republic of the Congo, for example, is cut in the middle by the equator. In 2010, its PPP-adjusted GDP per capita was $270 (in 2011 constant dollars). Move up along the map all the way to the sixtieth parallel, and you will find Finland. In that same year, its PPP-adjusted GDP per capita was $37,008 (in 2011 constant dollars). You can do the same exercise for almost all countries around the equator. Move up the line of longitude to find the corresponding countries at the fortieth, fiftieth, or sixtieth parallels, and almost always you will see that the ones farther away from the equator are considerably richer than the ones nearest it. This pattern has led many social scientists to conjecture that there is something particularly pernicious about the economic and social conditions in the areas around the equator. Many have gone so far as to assert that tropical and semitropical geographies condemn a nation to poverty.

CHAPTER **OUTLINE**

Can this be true? Can geography determine a nation's prosperity? By the end of this chapter, we provide some answers to this intriguing question. We'll also have developed a much better understanding of why the whole world isn't developed, and why there are wide disparities in GDP per capita across countries.

8.1 Proximate Versus Fundamental Causes of Prosperity

In Chapter 6, we documented the huge differences in GDP per capita and living standards across countries. You may recall the huge gap in PPP-adjusted GDP per capita between the United States and the Democratic Republic of the Congo, Ghana, or Haiti. In that chapter, we emphasized how these gaps can be explained in terms of cross-country differences in physical capital, human capital, and technology.

Yet an explanation based on these causes alone immediately begs the question of why some countries have accumulated more physical capital, invested more in human capital, and developed and adopted better technologies than other countries. After all, if investing in physical and human capital and adopting cutting-edge technologies can lead to major improvements in GDP, wouldn't all countries in the world wish to do so? Why isn't the whole world as developed as the United States or West European nations?

These deeper questions make us realize that differences in physical capital, human capital, and technology are only *proximate causes* of economic performance. We call them **proximate causes of prosperity**, because they link high levels of prosperity to high levels of the inputs to production but without providing an explanation for why the levels of those inputs are high.

Proximate causes of prosperity are high levels of factors such as human capital, physical capital, and technology that result in a high level of real GDP per capita.

To get at the reasons some countries are either unable or unwilling to invest in different amounts of physical capital, human capital, and technology, we have to dig deeper. Causation can be complex, as we discussed in Chapter 2. We sometimes have to see what lies beneath the surface to understand the true causes of an observed phenomenon. We refer to these underlying factors as the **fundamental causes of prosperity**, which are defined as those causes that are at the root of the differences in the proximate causes of prosperity. The relationship between the fundamental and the proximate causes of prosperity is shown in Exhibit 8.1.

Fundamental causes of prosperity are factors that are at the root of the differences in the proximate causes of prosperity.

Exhibit 8.1 Fundamental and Proximate Causes of Prosperity

Societies become prosperous when they have abundant human and physical capital and use advanced technology efficiently in production. But these are proximate causes, because they are in turn shaped by other, deeper factors. Fundamental causes, such as geographic, cultural, and institutional factors, have an impact on prosperity by affecting proximate causes, such as investment in human capital, physical capital, and technology.

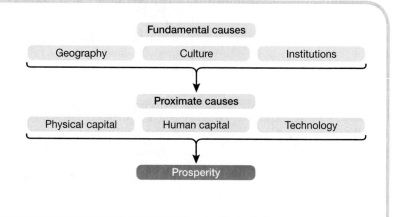

To see the distinction between proximate and fundamental causes more clearly, it is useful to consider an analogy. Say you are experiencing some symptoms of flu—sore throat, fever, and headache—that might motivate you to take drugs, such as throat decongestants or aspirin. In this example, the proximate cause of why you take these drugs is that you have a sore throat, a high fever, and a headache. But the fundamental cause—the reason you have the symptoms in the first place—is that you have the flu. The flu thus induces both the symptoms and your response of taking drugs. Similarly, if a country underinvests in human capital, physical capital, and/or technology, we should ask why. Both proximate and fundamental causes have to be considered for a complete understanding of why some nations are prosperous and others aren't.

Although there are many different theories about the fundamental causes of poverty and prosperity—theories about why poorer nations around the world have worse technologies and do not invest in physical and human capital as much as rich ones—it is useful to classify them into three categories: theories of geography, culture, and institutions. We next describe these hypotheses and then discuss whether they are consistent with empirical evidence.

Geography

The **geography hypothesis** claims that differences in geography, climate, and ecology are ultimately responsible for the major differences in prosperity observed across the world.

One approach, which we will refer to as the **geography hypothesis**, claims that differences in geography, climate, and ecology ultimately determine the large differences in prosperity across the world. According to this hypothesis, some countries have highly unfavorable geographical, climatic, or ecological circumstances that are beyond their control. Some are situated in areas where much of the soil may be inhospitable for agriculture, daytime temperatures are very high, or a lack of navigable rivers makes transport prohibitively costly. These conditions, some argue, make it impossible or unlikely for such countries to accumulate or effectively use the factors of production.

Many leading thinkers throughout the ages have advocated the geography hypothesis. One of its great proponents was the famous French philosopher Montesquieu, who argued that climate was a key determinant of work effort and thus prosperity.[1] He wrote:

> The heat of the climate can be so excessive that the body there will be absolutely without strength. So, prostration will pass even to the spirit; no curiosity, no noble enterprise, no generous sentiment; inclinations will all be passive there; laziness there will be happiness. . . . People are . . . more vigorous in cold climates. The inhabitants of warm countries are, like old men, timorous; the people in cold countries are, like young men, brave.

Another major proponent of this view was Alfred Marshall, who was the first economist to write a book (just like ours) aimed at making the principles of economics accessible to a broad population of students.[2] He stated:

> Vigor depends partly on race qualities: but these, so far as they can be explained at all, seem to be chiefly due to climate.

These views emphasizing the effect of climate on work effort and vigor are outdated (and sometimes tinged with racist overtones). But other versions of the geography hypothesis are still popular. Today, many believe that geographic characteristics determine the technology available to a society, especially in agriculture. The economist Jeffrey Sachs has been a strong proponent of this view in his academic writings.[3] Using it as the basis of his influential policy recommendations to the United Nations and the World Health Organization, Sachs, for example, argues:

> By the start of the era of modern economic growth, if not much earlier, temperate-zone technologies were more productive than tropical-zone technologies.

Jeffrey Sachs and others also argue that many parts of the world, particularly sub-Saharan Africa, are disadvantaged economically because infectious diseases, such as malaria and dengue fever, spread there more easily. When it is serious and widespread, an illness can indeed destroy a large amount of a country's human capital.

If geography is the major fundamental cause of prosperity (or its absence), then the poor nations of the world have little reason to expect much improvement in living standards.

If geography is the major fundamental cause of prosperity (or its absence), then the poor nations of the world have little reason to expect much improvement in living standards. They are permanently disadvantaged, and we should not expect them to catch up with the rest of the world and become economically developed anytime soon—or so the thinking goes. Not all variations of the geography hypothesis are equally pessimistic. In some, large-scale investments in transport technology or disease eradication may partially redress these geographic disadvantages.

Culture

The **culture hypothesis** claims that different values and cultural beliefs fundamentally cause the differences in prosperity around the world.

Another potential fundamental cause of differences in economic performance has to do with cultural differences. According to the **culture hypothesis**, different societies respond differently to incentives because of specific shared experiences, religious teachings, the strength of family ties, or unspoken social norms. Culture is viewed as a key determinant of the values, preferences, and beliefs of individuals and societies and, the argument goes, these differences play a key role in shaping economic performance. For example, some societies may have values that encourage investment, hard work, and the adoption of new technologies, while others may nurture superstition and suspicion of new technologies and discourage hard work.

The most famous link between culture and economic development was proposed by the German sociologist Max Weber, who argued that the origins of industrialization in Western Europe could be traced to Protestantism.[4] In his view, the Protestant worldview was crucial to the development of a market economy and economic growth because it encouraged hard work and saving (and thus investment).

Another common version of the culture hypothesis contrasts the Anglo-Saxon culture of the United States and the United Kingdom, which is viewed as conducive to investment and the adoption of technology, with the supposedly less dynamic and more closed-minded Iberian culture of peoples of Spanish and Portuguese origins. Many social scientists have attempted to explain the contrast between North and South America in these terms.

Almost 20 years ago, the Harvard political scientist Samuel Huntington coined the term "clash of civilizations" to capture what he thought would be the defining conflict of the twenty-first century—the conflict between the West and Islam.[5] More broadly, Huntington has supported the view that culture plays a central role in shaping prosperity. For example, his explanation for why South Korea grew rapidly in the twentieth century and Ghana did not summarizes his overall approach:[6]

> Culture had to be a large part of the explanation. South Koreans valued thrift, investment, hard work, education, organization, and discipline. Ghanaians had different values.

Of course, a society's culture is not immutable: cultures change, though they do so slowly.

Institutions

Institutions are the formal and informal rules governing the organization of a society, including its laws and regulations.

A third potential fundamental cause for the differences in prosperity involves **institutions**, the formal and informal rules governing the organization of a society, including its laws and regulations. For example, economic historian Douglass North, who was awarded the Nobel

Prize in economics largely because of his work emphasizing the importance of institutions in the historical development process, offers the following definition of institutions:[7]

> Institutions are the rules of the game in a society or, more formally, are the humanly devised constraints that shape human interaction.

This definition captures three important elements that define institutions:

1. They are determined by individuals as members of a society.
2. They place constraints on behavior.
3. They shape behavior by determining incentives.

First, institutions are humanly devised. In contrast to geography, which is largely outside of human control, and culture, which changes very slowly, institutions are determined by human-made factors. That is, institutions do not just appear out of thin air, but develop due to the choices members of a society make about how to organize their interactions.

Second, institutions place constraints on individual behavior. On the positive side, institutions constrain the ability of an individual to steal from others or to walk away from debts that he has built up. On the negative side, they might prevent people from entering into occupations or opening new businesses. Such constraints need not be absolute. Individuals around the world break laws and skirt regulations every day. For example, Apple did not own a license to sell iPads in Taiwan in 2010, so selling the device was illegal. Through online auctions, however, people were able to purchase iPad *cases*, which happened to include a "free" iPad for more than $1,000.[8]

Policies, regulations, and laws that punish or reward certain types of behavior will naturally have an effect on behavior. Though some citizens can circumvent a law that bans, for example, the adoption of certain technologies, such a law still discourages their adoption.

This observation leads us to the third important element in North's definition—institutions affect incentives. The constraints that institutions place on individuals—whether formal constraints (such as banning certain activities) or informal ones (discouraging certain types of behavior through customs and social norms)—shape human interaction and affect incentives. In some sense, institutions, much more than the other candidate fundamental causes, are about the importance of incentives.

The **institutions hypothesis** maintains that the differences in the way that humans have chosen to organize their societies—differences that shape the incentives that individuals and businesses in the society face—are at the root of the differences in their relative prosperity. For example, the economy will generate higher GDP and achieve greater prosperity when markets allocate individuals to the occupations in which their productivity is highest; when laws and regulations encourage firms to invest in physical capital and technology; and when the educational system enables and encourages people to invest in their human capital.

To sum up, the institutions hypothesis relies on the following chain of reasoning:

1. Different societies typically have different institutions.
2. These different institutions create different types of incentives.
3. The incentives help determine the degree to which societies accumulate the factors of production and adopt new technology.

The idea that the prosperity of a society depends on its institutions is not a new one. It goes back at least to Adam Smith, the father of economics, who, in *The Wealth of Nations*, emphasized the importance of markets in generating prosperity through the workings of the invisible hand and warned how constraints on markets—for example, in the form of restrictions on trade—could destroy such prosperity.[9]

The geography, culture, and institutions hypotheses are not mutually exclusive. But they are competing explanations in that if the bulk of the gaps in GDP across countries were due to geography, there would be little for culture or institutions to explain. So which one of these broad explanations accounts for most of the differences in prosperity we observe around us?

A Natural Experiment of History

The Korean peninsula is divided in two by the thirty-eighth parallel. To the south is the Republic of Korea, also known as South Korea. We saw in Chapter 7 how South Korea has

The **institutions hypothesis** claims that differences in institutions—that is, in the way societies have organized themselves and shaped the incentives of individuals and businesses—are at the root of the differences in prosperity across the world.

had one of the fastest-growing economies in the past 60 years and has by now achieved living standards comparable to those in many countries in Europe.

To the north of the thirty-eighth parallel there is another Korea: the Democratic People's Republic of Korea, or simply North Korea. Living standards in North Korea are similar to those in a sub-Saharan African country. The best estimate suggests that in 2010, real GDP per capita (in PPP-adjusted 2011 constant dollars) was $1,808 in the North, making its inhabitants worse off than the citizens of Sudan or Yemen. In contrast, in that same year real GDP per capita (in PPP-adjusted 2011 constant dollars) in the South was $29,851. What explains these large differences? Could it be geography? Culture? Highly unlikely. The North and South share the same geography, essentially the same climate, the same access to the ocean, and the same disease environments. There are also no noticeable differences between their cultures, certainly not before 1947 when the country was split into two. Korea was at that point an unusually homogeneous country, both ethnically and culturally. If we were to believe that geography or culture were important factors in determining South Korea's economic development after 1947, we would then expect a similar process of economic development in North Korea. Nothing of the sort happened.

In fact, the great disparities between the two nations did not exist before World War II, when the two parts of Korea were united. They emerged only when the two were separated and adopted very different institutions.

The separation of Korea into two halves was not something to which its citizens willingly agreed. It was an outcome of a geopolitical deal between the Soviet Union and the United States, who agreed at the end of World War II that the thirty-eighth parallel would be the dividing line for their spheres of influence in Korea and set up different governments in the North and the South.

These governments adopted very different ways of organizing their economies. In North Korea, Kim Il-Sung, a leader of anti-Japanese communist partisans during World War II, established himself as dictator. With the help of the Soviet Union, Kim Il-Sung introduced a rigid form of communism, the *Juche* system. Resources in North Korea were allocated through central planning, private property was outlawed, and markets were banned. Freedoms were curtailed not only in the marketplace but also in every sphere of North Koreans' lives—except for those who happened to be part of the very small ruling elite around Kim Il-Sung. This cronyism persisted under his son Kim Jong-Il, who ruled until his death in 2011, and continues today under Kim Il-Sung's grandson, Kim Jong-Un.

> If institutions are a major determinant of economic prosperity, then the sharply divergent institutions of the two Koreas should have led to divergent economic fortunes. And that's exactly what happened.

In the South, institutions were shaped by the Harvard- and Princeton-educated, staunchly anticommunist Syngman Rhee, with significant support from the United States. Though Rhee and his successor, General Park Chung-Hee, were autocrats, they supported a market-based economy, providing incentives to businesses for investment and industrialization and investing in the education of South Koreans. South Korea did eventually become democratic in the 1990s and further liberalized its economy.

If institutions are a major determinant of economic prosperity, then the sharply divergent institutions of the two Koreas should have led to divergent economic fortunes. And that's exactly what happened. Exhibit 8.2 shows how PPP-adjusted GDP per capita in North and South Korea has sharply diverged over the past 60 years to arrive at the great disparities that we observe today.

The Korean case depicts what we often call a natural experiment or an experiment of history. A country was split in half by a military outcome. The two newly formed, culturally identical, and geographically similar countries proceeded to develop very different institutions. While the South remained a market economy, the North adopted a very rigid form of communist rule with little room for markets, private property, or entrepreneurship. The reason this episode approximates a natural experiment is that while institutions were changing in this radical way, geography and culture remained largely unchanged. It was the changes in institutions that led to massive changes in economic prosperity, as shown in Exhibit 8.2. The Korean example thus provides strong support for the institutions hypothesis (but it does not provide direct evidence against geography and culture, because these were held fixed in this comparison).

Exhibit 8.2 GDP per Capita in North and South Korea (in PPP-adjusted 2011 Constant Dollars)

The economic fortunes of North and South Korea, starting from parity in the 1940s when they were united, have diverged sharply. South Korea, with institutions mostly based on a market economy, has reached a high level of PPP-adjusted GDP per capita. In contrast, North Korea, under a communist dictatorship, has failed to grow and has less than one-sixteenth of the level of the PPP-adjusted GDP per capita of the South.

Source: Data from Maddison Project (1820–2010); J. L. Bolt and J. L. van Zanden, "The First Update of the Maddison Project; Re-estimating Growth Before 1820," Maddison Project Working Paper 4, 2013.

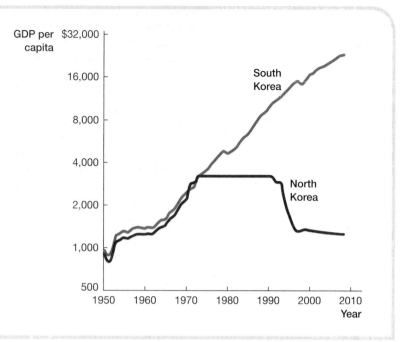

8.2 Institutions and Economic Development

Teenagers in South Korea grow up just like us. Many obtain a good education and face incentives that encourage them to exert effort and excel in their chosen vocations. South Korea is a market economy. South Korean teenagers know that, if successful, one day they can enjoy the fruits of their investments and efforts. They can buy computers, clothes, cars, houses, and healthcare. They can start businesses and bequeath their property to their offspring.

Private property rights mean that individuals can own businesses and assets and their ownership is secure.

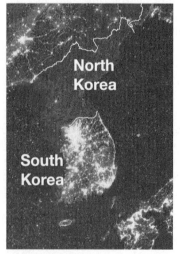

Darkness in North Korea and light in South Korea: lights at night illustrate the huge differences in prosperity between South and North Korea.

Economic institutions are those aspects of the society's rules that concern economic transactions.

This is in large part because the South has well-enforced **private property rights**, meaning that its citizens can hold property like businesses, houses, cars, and many other things without fearing that the government or anyone else will arbitrarily take it away from them. Just as in the United States, if you own a business in South Korea, you know that the income it generates is yours, other than the taxes you pay, which are often used to provide public goods and services valued by the citizens of the country. Your property is well protected because the state upholds law and order, and if you write business contracts, the courts enforce them. It is possible for entrepreneurs to borrow money from banks and financial markets, for foreign companies to enter into partnerships with South Korean firms, and for individuals to obtain mortgages to buy houses.

Teenagers in North Korea face vastly different lives from those in the South. They grow up in poverty, without high-quality education to prepare them for skilled work or entrepreneurship. Much of the education they receive at school is pure propaganda about foreign threats against North Korea and the benevolent leadership of their supreme leader and the North Korean military. But these teenagers know that they will not be able to own property, start businesses, or make much money, because there is no private property in North Korea. They also know that they will not have access to markets where they can deploy their skills or use their earnings to purchase the goods that they need and desire.

These different rules are part of the institutions under which North and South Koreans live.

Inclusive and Extractive Economic Institutions

The enforcement of private property rights, which differs so sharply between South and North Korea, is one aspect of what we refer to as *economic institutions*. **Economic institutions** are those aspects of a society's rules that concern economic transactions.

Besides the protection of property rights, economic institutions include such things as the functioning and impartiality of the judicial system, the financial arrangements that determine how individuals and businesses can borrow money, and the regulations that shape how costly it is to enter into a new line of business or a new occupation.

When a society's economic institutions provide secure property rights, set up a judicial system that enforces contracts and upholds the law, allow private parties to sign contracts for economic or financial transactions, maintain relatively open and free entry into different businesses and occupations, and enable people to acquire the education and skills to take part in such businesses and occupations, we say that they are **inclusive economic institutions**. The economic institutions in South Korea approximate these types of inclusive economic institutions. They are inclusive in the sense that they encourage the participation of the great majority of the population in economic activities in a way that best makes use of their talents and skills.

As we have seen, inclusive economic institutions do *not* describe the situation in North Korea. Economic institutions to the north of the thirty-eighth parallel fail to enforce property rights or contracts, erect prohibitive entry barriers, and all but destroy the workings of the markets. We refer to such arrangements as **extractive economic institutions**. This terminology stems from the fact that such institutions are often shaped by those who control political power to *extract resources from the rest of the society*. Extractive economic institutions are not just associated with communist North Korea. Societies ruled by monarchs, dictators, and juntas as well as several that hold elections for their parliaments and presidents have had, and still have, extractive economic institutions. In fact, most societies throughout history have had economic institutions that are closer to the extreme extractive economic institutions of North Korea than to the ideal of inclusive economic institutions we have defined here.

Examples of market economies that have extractive economic institutions include former Soviet republics (such as Azerbaijan, Turkmenistan, and Uzbekistan), Myanmar, and Pakistan in Asia; Argentina, Guatemala, and Peru in Latin America; and the Democratic Republic of the Congo, Egypt, and Kenya in Africa. Even if the specific forms of these institutions differ from the extreme form of central planning in North Korea, they share the fact that they fail to enforce property rights and instead privilege a few at the expense of the many.

Extractive economic institutions do not exist in a vacuum. It is no accident that North Korea is a repressive dictatorship. Without the political elite's tight control of the state, North Korea would not be able to maintain a system that condemns tens of millions to poverty. This meshing of political and economic power underscores the important role of **political institutions**, which determine who holds political power and what types of constraints exist on the exercise of that power. Extractive economic institutions tend to be supported by certain types of political institutions, which concentrate political power in the hands of the political elite and put little constraint on how political power can be used. Similarly, inclusive economic institutions tend to coexist with different types of political institutions that tend to distribute political power more equally in society, so that no single individual or group is able to use that political power for its own benefit at the expense of the rest of society.

How Economic Institutions Affect Economic Outcomes

The contrast between South Korea and North Korea, and between Austria and Czechoslovakia, discussed in the next Letting the Data Speak box, illustrates a general principle: *inclusive economic institutions foster economic activity, productivity growth, and economic prosperity, while extractive economic institutions generally fail to do so.*[11] Property rights are central to this principle, because only those individuals who have secure property rights will be willing to invest and increase productivity. A farmer who expects his output to be expropriated—meaning stolen, taken away, or entirely taxed away— will have little incentive to work, let alone any incentive to undertake investments and innovations. Extractive economic institutions distort incentives in exactly this fashion. Farmers, traders, businesspeople, and workers will be discouraged from investing and producing when

---

Inclusive economic institutions protect private property, uphold law and order, allow and enforce private contracts, and allow free entry into new lines of business and occupations.

Extractive economic institutions do not protect private property rights, do not uphold contracts, and interfere with the workings of markets. They also erect significant entry barriers into businesses and occupations.

Political institutions are the aspects of the society's rules that concern the allocation of political power and the constraints on the exercise of political power.

Heck. I thought you were kidding. I guess you really do want democracy.

LETTING THE — DATA SPEAK

Democracy and Growth

If political institutions shape economic institutions and economic institutions are key for economic growth, then we should expect political institutions to impact economic growth as well. As we have already noted, a key dimension of political institutions is the extent to which they distribute political power and voice broadly (and equally) in a society. Though democracies differ greatly in how (and how well) they function, they enable people to go to polling booths and elect their leaders. In this way, democracies tend to provide a more equal distribution of political power and voice than non-democratic regimes, such as monarchies (like Saudi Arabia); military regimes (like Myanmar until very recently); or dictatorships dominated by an individual, family, or narrow ethnic group (like North Korea under the Kim dynasty, Syria under the Assad family, or Iraq under Saddam Hussein until his fall). In fact, it is difficult to imagine how North Korea could have maintained its extreme extractive institutions, which we have just seen, had it been democratic and had people voted on whether to keep the Kim dynasty in power.

But hold on. Can democracy really have a positive effect on prosperity? Isn't the rapid growth of China a testament to the positive effect of non-democracies—not democracy—on economic growth? In fact, if you listen to many pundits, they will tell you how bad democracy is for economic growth.

The reality seems to be rather different, however. Recent research by Daron Acemoglu, Suresh Naidu, Pascual Restrepo, and James Robinson shows that democracy has a fairly large positive effect on GDP per capita.[10] Countries that democratize tend to grow faster in the subsequent 20 years or so and increase their GDP per capita by about 20 percent relative to those that do not democratize. Exhibit 8.3 shows where this finding comes from. It depicts the evolution of the GDP per capita of countries that democratize (switch from non-democracy to democracy) relative to those that also start out as non-democracies but remain so. Year 0 in this exhibit corresponds to the year of democratization for a country; then year −1 is the year preceding it, and year 1 is the year following it, and so on. For example, for Spain the year of democratization is 1978, following the death of its then-dictator General Franco, and thus year 1 is 1979, and so on, whereas for Brazil the year of democratization is 1985, year 1 is 1986, and so forth. The curve depicted in Exhibit 8.3

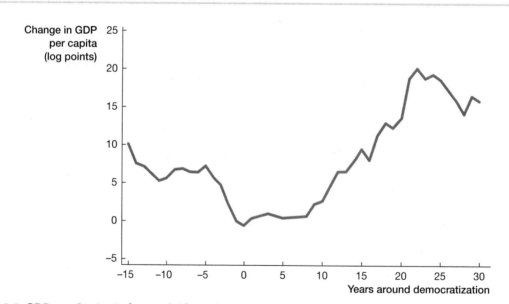

Exhibit 8.3 GDP per Capita Before and After a Democratization

When trying to identify the causal effect of democratization on GDP, we want to take into account factors other than democracy that also affect GDP. By examining a country before and after it becomes a democracy and comparing it to other non-democracies, we can isolate the role of democratization. This graph shows the results of such an analysis. The x-axis shows the number of years before/after democratization, with year 0 representing the year the country was democratized. Note that the actual historical year of "year 0" will differ across countries. The y-axis shows our variable of interest: the difference between the democratizing country's GDP and the GDP of other non-democracies.

Source: Daron Acemoglu, Suresh Naidu, Pascual Restrepo, and James Robinson, "Democracy Does Cause Economic Growth," NBER Working Paper 20004, Cambridge, MA: National Bureau of Economic Research, 2014.

is thus the difference between the GDP per capita of these countries transitioning to democracy and the GDP per capita of other non-democracies in the same year. This way of constructing the curve enables us to measure how much a country changes its GDP per capita after democratizing relative to the changes in GDP per capita of other countries remaining non-democratic in the same year. The result is fairly striking. There is a 20 percent or so increase in GDP per capita in a country switching to democracy relative to those that are not experiencing such a transition.

So why is it that many people still believe democracy to be bad for economic growth? One reason is that they sometimes simply compare non-democratic fast growers, such as China, to well-established rich democracies, like France, which are not growing as fast. Such a comparison is not particularly informative about the effect of democracy on growth, however, since there are many differences between China and France, not least their level of development (which makes it feasible for China, but impossible for France, to engage in rapid catch-up growth). For this reason, simply looking at the differences in income or economic growth between democracies and non-democracies would be focusing on correlations, not causation. Instead, Exhibit 8.3 looks at how a given country's economy is affected when it transitions from non-democracy to democracy. This exhibit also highlights another reason it has been difficult to see the positive effect of democracy: many non-democracies transition to democracy when they are having economic problems. So one fails to focus on the years following democratization but looks at a wider window that includes years before democratization, and the bad performance of non-democracies before their collapse will be confounded with the positive effects of democracy.

they have no property rights. On top of that, firms will not be able to form the trust-based relationships that are necessary to productively do business when private contracts are worth little more than the paper they are written on or when some contractual agreements are banned outright. Finally, because they erect barriers to market entry rather than create an environment that would encourage entry, extractive economic institutions tend to support inefficient firms and prevent entrepreneurs with new ideas from entering into the right lines of business and workers from working in occupations to which their skills are best suited.

Exhibit 8.5 is helpful for illustrating why extractive economic institutions discourage economic activity. There, in a hypothetical economy, we rank potential entrepreneurs in descending order according to the return they will make if they enter and start a business. The return-to-entrepreneurship curve in the exhibit (shown in blue) plots these returns. The y-axis shows the return, while the x-axis depicts the number of entrepreneurs who have at least the given rate of return (or higher).

To understand the figure, consider point A in panel (a). The y-axis shows that we are looking at a return to entrepreneurship of $75,000. The x-axis, in turn, indicates that the number of entrepreneurs with at least this return to entrepreneurship is 500. As we consider a point with a lower return to entrepreneurship, such as point B, which corresponds to a return of $25,000, naturally there will be more entrepreneurs with at least this return—in this exhibit, 900 of them. This is because, in addition to the 500 entrepreneurs with a return greater than $75,000, there are also 400 entrepreneurs with a return between $25,000 and $75,000, so the total number of entrepreneurs with a return greater than or equal to $25,000 is 900. This reasoning immediately implies that the return-to-entrepreneurship curve is downward sloping—as we consider a lower return, there will be more entrepreneurs with at least that return.

The horizontal line in red shows the opportunity cost of entrepreneurship, which is assumed to be the same for all potential entrepreneurs. This could be, for example, how much they would earn if they were to choose another occupation.

Panel (a) of Exhibit 8.5 considers the general question of entry into entrepreneurship, which is determined by whether one's returns to entrepreneurship are above or below one's opportunity cost. Consider an entrepreneur in panel (a) with a return given by point A, whom we will call Entrepreneur A. Because this point is above the horizontal line, this individual has a greater return from entrepreneurship ($75,000) than her opportunity cost, which is at $50,000 in this exhibit. Therefore, she will choose to become an entrepreneur. In contrast, an entrepreneur with a return given by point B (Entrepreneur B) will not do so because this point is below the horizontal line, and thus the return ($25,000) falls short of her opportunity cost ($50,000). This reasoning establishes that there will be entry into entrepreneurship until the point marked E_1 is reached. At this point, the return to entrepreneurship and the opportunity cost are both $50,000, so any additional entrepreneur will be indifferent between entering into or exiting entrepreneurship. Thus, point E_1 determines the equilibrium level of entrepreneurship in our economy.

LETTING THE
DATA SPEAK

Divergence and Convergence in Eastern Europe

Between 1948 and 1989, citizens of Central and Eastern European countries, just like those of North Korea, lived under a communist dictatorship. Large, state-owned enterprises were the norm in these economies. These firms did not compete in the market but instead worked toward arbitrary targets set by Communist Party officials (which they almost always failed to meet). As a consequence, shortages of food and consumer goods were common. In a market economy, companies that fail to motivate workers, produce goods of reasonable quality, or meet their production targets are ultimately driven out of the market. But state-owned enterprises under communism did not have to worry about competition or about being driven out of the market, because there was no competition, and it was the state that set prices and footed the bill if these enterprises lost money.

In 1948, Austria and Czechoslovakia, two neighbors in central Europe, each had PPP-adjusted GDP per capita of about $4,000. But in Czechoslovakia, farms were subsequently taken forcibly from their owners and collectiv-

ized, a command economy was established, and political freedoms that existed before World War II were abolished. In Austria, a market system, along with economic institutions much more inclusive than those in communist Eastern Europe, flourished. The consequences were similar to what we have seen in the case of North and South Korea. Not surprisingly, Czechoslovakia kept falling behind its neighbor, Austria, for 40 years.

The two countries, which had very similar histories, geographies, and cultures, had achieved vastly different levels of prosperity by 1989, when the communist regime finally collapsed. Those Central and Eastern European societies that had been under communist rule transitioned to democracy and a market economy, became more inclusive, and started to grow rapidly as the share of the private sector in the economy increased from 5 percent to 80 percent. Exhibit 8.4 shows the divergence between Austria and Czechoslovakia during the communist period and the convergence that started after Czechoslovakia transitioned to a market economy in the 1990s.

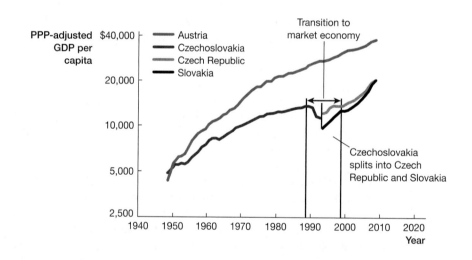

Exhibit 8.4 GDP per Capita in Austria and the Neighboring Czechoslovakia since 1948 (in PPP-Adjusted 2011 Constant Dollars)

Starting from approximately the same level of PPP-adjusted GDP per capita, the economies of Czechoslovakia and Austria diverged after 1948 while subject to different economic and political institutions. Following the collapse of communism and the subsequent transition to a market economy, first Czechoslovakia, and then the newly formed nations of Czech Republic and Slovakia after Czechoslovakia's dissolution in 1993, started growing rapidly and closing the gap with Austria.

Source: Data from Maddison Project (1820–2010); J. Bolt and J. L. van Zanden, "The First Update of the Maddison Project; Re-estimating Growth Before 1820." Maddison Project Working Paper 4, 2013.

Exhibit 8.5 How Extractive Economic Institutions Reduce the Number of Entrepreneurs

The return-to-entrepreneurship curve in panel (a) shows the number of entrepreneurs with at least the return indicated on the y-axis. It is obtained by ranking potential entrepreneurs from higher to lower return to entrepreneurship. The opportunity cost schedule indicates the value to a potential entrepreneur of her best alternate activity. The intersection of the two curves gives the equilibrium number of entrepreneurs. For example, in panel (a), all potential entrepreneurs with return greater than or equal to $50,000 choose entrepreneurship.

Extractive economic institutions shift the return-to-entrepreneurship curve to the left, as shown in panel (b). Two reasons this shift might occur are the following: first, weak property rights prevent entrepreneurs from capturing their full returns, and second, with a lack of legal backup, entrepreneurs cannot easily form reliable contracts with business partners, which can reduce profitability by making supplies more expensive and revenues more precarious.

As shown in panel (c), extractive economic institutions also shift the opportunity cost schedule upward, because they erect entry barriers that make entry into entrepreneurship more expensive. This panel shows the overall impact of extractive economic institutions on the equilibrium number of entrepreneurs resulting from a leftward shift of the return-to-entrepreneurship schedule and an upward shift of the opportunity cost schedule.

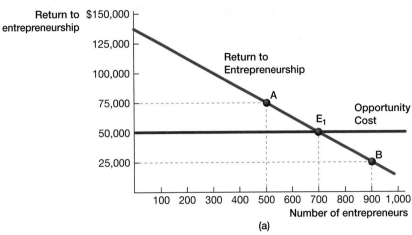

(a)

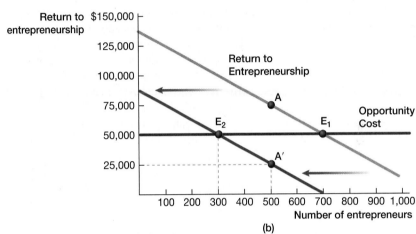

(b)

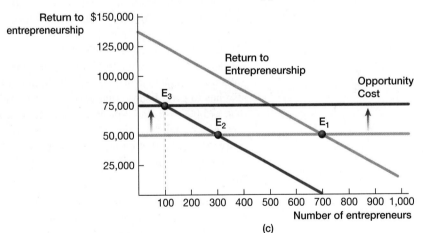

(c)

How do extractive economic institutions change this picture? First consider the implications of insecure property rights, which are investigated in panel (b). Under insecure property rights, an entrepreneur will not be able to capture all the returns that he or she creates; for example, the government or some other group may expropriate the returns of his or her enterprise. Suppose, for example, that insecure property rights imply that Entrepreneur A will be able to keep only $25,000 out of her $75,000 return, and that the remaining $50,000 will be expropriated or paid as bribes. Because all entrepreneurs similarly can keep less of what they make under insecure property rights, the return-to-entrepreneurship schedule will shift to the left.

Entrepreneur A also illustrates how extractive economic institutions affect overall entrepreneurship in the economy. This individual's return to entrepreneurship, $75,000, was initially above the opportunity cost schedule. But with insecure property rights, she can make only $25,000, which is less than her opportunity cost of $50,000, as indicated by the fact that the new point describing Entrepreneur A's situation, point A', now lies below the opportunity cost line.

We can then see that as a result of the shift, the new equilibrium will be at point E_2, which involves strictly less entrepreneurship. Less entrepreneurship implies less business creation, less technology adoption, lower returns to education and capital accumulation, and therefore a lower level of GDP. Thus one effect of extractive economic institutions, working in this instance through insecure property rights, is to reduce entrepreneurship and GDP.

Extractive economic institutions distort economic activity not only by creating insecure property rights but also by making it more costly or impossible to write contracts with suppliers, to borrow money, or to use the courts to uphold business arrangements. For example, say that an entrepreneur would make $75,000 if she could engage the right supplies for her business. But without courts to uphold her contracts, she cannot make the deals necessary for obtaining supplies, and this lack of legal backup will reduce her returns from entrepreneurship by $50,000. These effects will also shift the return-to-entrepreneurship schedule to the left, as shown in panel (b), with the same result of depressing entrepreneurship and GDP in the economy.

Finally, extractive economic institutions can create entry barriers, preventing otherwise profitable businesses from being founded, and may also encourage entrepreneurs to engage in other, nonproductive activities rather than entrepreneurship (for example, joining the underground economy). These factors thus increase the opportunity cost of entrepreneurship, as shown in panel (c) of Exhibit 8.5. Using the same numerical example as in panel (b), we can see that without entry barriers, entrepreneurs who can generate returns greater than $50,000 will open businesses (see the light red line on the graph). But if each entrepreneur also has to get a license that costs $25,000, only entrepreneurs who have returns greater than $75,000 will find it profitable to enter (see the dark red line on the graph, now shifted upward). We interpret this additional $25,000 as shifting the opportunity cost upward, because it is a cost that entrepreneurs have to pay before they enter, therefore making their second-best alternative more attractive by $25,000. Thus panel (c) simultaneously shows two possible implications of extractive economic institutions:

1. By creating insecure property rights and limiting legal backup, they make entrepreneurship less profitable and shift the return-to-entrepreneurship schedule to the left.
2. By erecting entry barriers, they make entry more costly and shift the opportunity cost schedule upward.

The resulting equilibrium, shown at E_3, now corresponds to even less entrepreneurship. As before, an economy at point E_3, with less entrepreneurship, will have lower prosperity than an economy at point E_1 because—as more potential entrepreneurs are discouraged—investment, business creation, and technological development are held back, and the economy generates a lower level of GDP.

We should also note that there are other effects of extractive institutions on entrepreneurship beyond those emphasized in Exhibit 8.5. Societies with extractive economic institutions are also unlikely to have developed the financial markets necessary to provide credit to entrepreneurs with good ideas, thus further discouraging entrepreneurship. They may also generate greater uncertainty and risk for entrepreneurs, creating yet another impediment to entrepreneurial activity.

The Logic of Extractive Economic Institutions

Exhibit 8.5 shows how extractive economic institutions tend to reduce entrepreneurship and economic activity, thus adversely affecting economic outcomes. It clarifies how there may be large differences in prosperity between two otherwise similar societies that differ in terms of their institutions—one having inclusive economic institutions similar to those in South Korea, and the other one having extractive economic institutions as in North Korea.

But why would a society adopt extractive economic institutions in the first place, particularly as these institutions seem to lead to relative poverty and a lack of economic development? It might seem obvious that everyone should have an interest in creating the type of economic institutions that will bring prosperity. Wouldn't every citizen, every politician, and even a predatory dictator want to make their countries as wealthy as they could?

Unfortunately for the citizens of many countries in the world, the answer is no. To understand why, we turn to a concept first proposed by the famous Austrian economist Joseph Schumpeter.[12] Schumpeter emphasized the notion of *creative destruction* as a central element of technological change. **Creative destruction** refers to the process by which new technologies replace old ones, new businesses replace established companies, and new skills make old ones redundant. The process of creative destruction implies that technological change, which, as we saw in Chapter 7, is the main driver of economic growth, also creates economic losers as it replaces otherwise profitable firms or technologies with new ones. Because creative destruction is an inseparable part of the process of technological change and economic growth, there will be firms and individuals that will lose as a result of this process and will be opposed to it, and this opposition to technological change can provide support for the continuation of extractive economic institutions.

Extending Schumpeter's ideas, we can also introduce the notion of **political creative destruction**, which refers to the process by which economic growth destabilizes existing regimes and reduces the political power of rulers. This might be because new technologies will also bring new actors on the scene who will make political demands, or because new economic activities may fall outside of the control of existing rulers. If the process of economic growth is also associated with political creative destruction, then we would expect that the politically powerful who fear losing their privileged positions will be opposed to this process.

In the context of North Korea, for example, the communist elites are powerful and enjoy a privileged position. The current leader, Kim Jong-Un, and his cronies could open up the economy, let markets work, allow citizens to open businesses and import technologies, and start strengthening their ties with South Korea and the West. All these initiatives would kick-start economic growth and lift millions of North Koreans out of poverty. But this process would also allow new leaders to emerge—and perhaps also discredit the old leadership that has kept the country in poverty for so long. Because Kim and his allies put their own interests ahead of those of ordinary North Koreans, they prefer to maintain the status quo rather than reform economic institutions to enhance economic growth.

In fact, fear of creative destruction and political creative destruction makes many rulers, not just communist dictators, explicitly ban the adoption of new technologies and block the process of economic development.

> **Creative destruction** refers to the process by which new technologies replace old ones, new businesses replace established companies, and new skills make old ones redundant.

> **Political creative destruction** refers to the process by which economic growth destabilizes existing regimes and reduces the political power of rulers.

> Fear of creative destruction and political creative destruction makes many rulers . . . explicitly ban the adoption of new technologies and block the process of economic development.

Inclusive Economic Institutions and the Industrial Revolution

In Chapter 7 we saw how the process of technological change gathered speed during the Industrial Revolution in Britain, which first involved a series of major innovations in textiles that then spread to other industries, resulting in the famous advances in the steam engine, which laid the foundation of modern production as well as the railroad. Economic historians have long debated why the Industrial Revolution took place in Britain rather than in France or some other European nation or in China, and why it started in the second half of the eighteenth century instead of some other time in history.

LETTING THE
DATA SPEAK

Blocking the Railways

A key technology fueling the process of economic growth during the nineteenth century was the railroad. Rapid railway construction reduced transport costs and permitted more and cheaper trade within and between countries. By 1860, Britain had laid 9,073 miles of railways, Germany 6,890 miles, and the United States 30,626 miles.

While many countries were investing rapidly in railways, two of the most powerful empires in continental Europe—Russia and Austria-Hungary—did not. Russia started doing so only after its bitter defeat in the Crimean War in 1856. Even in the early twentieth century, the number of railway journeys per inhabitant per year was 21.9 in Britain, but only 1.7 in Central and Eastern Europe.

Why did Russia and Austria-Hungary not invest in railways?

The answer is related to political creative destruction. The monarchs in both countries feared that railways and the accompanying process of industrialization would undermine their power and destabilize their regimes. For example, Francis I, who ruled Austria-Hungary in the early nineteenth century, and his right-hand man, Klemens von Metternich, were opposed to industrialization and railways. When the English philanthropist Robert Owen tried to convince the government of Austria-Hungary that some social reforms were necessary to improve the living standards of its citizens, one of Metternich's assistants, Frederick Gentz, replied:

> We do not desire at all that the great masses shall become well off and independent. . . . How could we otherwise rule over them?[13]

This attitude is likely what made Francis I and Metternich oppose railway construction—because it would make their subjects more difficult to rule.

This was also the view of Nikolai I, who ruled the Russian Empire between 1825 and 1855. He thought that the railways were the harbinger of worker unrest, industrial demands, and instability, so he opposed them. Austria-Hungary and Russia thus blocked technology adoption and economic development, because they feared the political instability that these innovations would bring.

The blocking of productive technologies is not something that just happened in the past. The Internet is one of the most important technologies of today and offers a huge amount of information to individuals and firms, as well as a platform for the expression and dissemination of ideas. But according to the organization Reporters Without Borders, Bahrain, Belarus, Cuba, Iran, Myanmar, North Korea, Saudi Arabia, Syria, Turkmenistan, and Uzbekistan seriously curtail the use of the Internet or suppress online expression. As was the case with Russia and Austria-Hungary in the nineteenth century, often these policies are aimed at curtailing political creative destruction: limiting the content that can be accessed online is a strategy to control dissent and maintain political power.

A complex social and economic process such as the Industrial Revolution seldom has a single cause. Economic historians have come up with scores of explanations for why and where it occurred. Despite this variety, though, many of these explanations either depend on Britain's relatively inclusive economic institutions or simply take them as given. This is because it would be next to impossible to imagine how the Industrial Revolution could have taken place in Britain without such inclusive economic institutions.[14] The defining characteristic of the Industrial Revolution was that new technologies were being developed and implemented by businessmen for profit. Without secure property rights, these businessmen would not have been encouraged to seek and undertake such innovations. The innovations were profitable, in turn, because Britain already had a well-developed market system, and those who could adopt new technologies to improve quality and reduce costs in textiles and other areas could reach a larger market and make sizable profits.

Britain also had a patent system that allowed the inventors of new technologies to protect their property rights not only in tangible assets but also in ideas. In fact, the protection of new ideas and innovations, just like the protection of other economic assets, was a major impetus to innovation and technological change in Britain.

Britain, in contrast to many other countries in the eighteenth century, also allowed relatively free entry into different lines of business. Although different interests tried to block entry of competitors and were sometimes successful in this endeavor (as when woolen manufacturers temporarily convinced Parliament to ban cotton imports), these entry barriers were often short lived. By international standards, Britain gradually created a much more level playing field for its potential businesspeople. These institutional features of British society were the key prerequisites for the Industrial Revolution.

Notably, British economic institutions were also supported by the appropriate political institutions. The development of these economic institutions was preceded by major political reforms, in particular the Glorious Revolution of 1688, which introduced a constitutional monarchy and considerable constraints on the political powers of the monarch. The political institutions enshrined in the Glorious Revolution and further developed in the subsequent century were the bulwarks upon which the inclusive economic institutions that underpinned the Industrial Revolution were built.

EVIDENCE-BASED ECONOMICS

Q: Are tropical and semitropical areas condemned to poverty by their geographies?

How do we determine whether tropical geographic conditions condemn a nation to poverty? We cannot do this by varying a nation's geography and seeing whether this affects its long-run economic development because, by definition, geographic conditions are largely immutable.

To gauge the importance of geographic factors in differences in prosperity and poverty, we can look at whether countries with the same geographic conditions have significantly changed their relative prosperity as their institutions have changed. We have already seen one example of the profound effect of institutions on prosperity in this chapter: North Korea and South Korea. In this section, we answer our opening question by looking at another interesting historical episode.

Europeans came to dominate much of the world starting in the late fifteenth century after they went around the southern end of Africa to reach the Indian Ocean and they discovered the New World. These events led to the process of colonization, in which European nations built new colonies around the world and came to conquer many existing empires and states. Many of the parts of the world were under Europe's command at one point or another during the 500 years between the end of the fifteenth century and the middle of the twentieth century.

Europeans set up very different institutions in various parts of the world. We in the United States live in a former European colony, and the strength of our institutions today has a lot to do with the fact that Europeans set up a very different system in North America than in other colonies. Political participation quickly became relatively broad in North America and, equally importantly, production came to be supported by fairly inclusive economic institutions. Small agricultural holders were the main producers in the early stages of the American colonies. Though many Europeans first came to North America as indentured servants who were obliged to supply their labor at a very low wage to those who paid for their passage to the new continent, most of them soon acquired economic and political rights and became citizens with relatively secure property rights.

The situation could not have been more different in other colonies. Like North America, Barbados and Jamaica were British colonies. But the British did not set up inclusive economic institutions on these islands. Rather, these colonies developed as

Are the more than 1 billion poor people in tropical and semitropical parts of the world condemned to poverty by the climate and geography of the countries they live in?

clear exemplars of extractive economic institutions: they were plantation economies, with a small minority dominating a majority brought over as slaves from Africa. Slaves had no political rights and essentially no economic rights. They were forced to work for very long hours. Their situation was so terrible that many of them died from the onerous work and the unsanitary conditions in which they were kept. These people could not effectively defend their interests because under the law of the land, the plantation owners controlled all power and all the guns.

These types of extractive economic institutions were not just confined to the Caribbean islands, where the majority of the population consisted of imported slaves. The living conditions of the native populations in areas that now correspond to Mexico, Guatemala, Peru, and Bolivia were only a little better. The descendants of the Mayas, Incas, and Aztecs were stripped of all rights (not that they had many before the Europeans arrived) and were forced to work in mines and on agricultural estates for low wages and under violent threats. These people also did not have any political representation, and their property rights were far from secure.

In sum, Europeans set up widely different economic institutions. In some places, they were inclusive; in others, highly extractive. Given this variation in institutions, we can try to evaluate whether it is the institutions that matter or whether some parts of the world are condemned to poverty by their geography. In particular, we can achieve this by examining how relative prosperity has changed after European colonization in different areas that were part of the European empire.

But there is a problem. How do we measure the GDP per capita and prosperity of places 500 years ago? Today, we can use the national income accounts, as we saw in Chapter 5. But the inhabitants of the Caribbean islands or the Aztecs and the Incas, let alone the Native Americans occupying the North American plains, did not have national income accounts. Fortunately, we can use measurements of urbanization (the fraction of the population living in urban centers with 5,000 or more inhabitants) as a fairly good proxy for measuring the prosperity of a nation. This is because only countries that can generate sufficient agricultural surplus and develop a transportation and trading network to bring this surplus to cities can support a large urban population. Much historical evidence documents a causal relationship between urbanization and prosperity. Even in the late twentieth century, when many nations around the world had long been industrialized, there was still a very strong association between GDP per capita and urbanization.

Exhibit 8.6 shows this relationship in 2014. The *y*-axis shows the GDP per capita (in PPP-adjusted 2011 constant dollars), and on the *x*-axis, we have the fraction of the population living in urban centers with 5,000 or more inhabitants. The exhibit shows that even today there is a fairly strong positive association between urbanization and PPP-adjusted GDP per capita. However, as we have emphasized several times already, correlation does not mean causation. In this exhibit, urbanization does not cause changes in PPP-adjusted GDP per capita. It is simply correlated with it, and that is why we can use it as a proxy for GDP, but we do refrain from jumping to conclusions about urbanization having a causal effect on economic growth.

Exhibit 8.7 shows the relationship between urbanization in 1500, estimated from various historical sources, and PPP-adjusted GDP per capita today. The remarkable thing that the exhibit reveals is what we call "the reversal of fortune," as shown by the best-fit line in this figure. This reversal differs from the pattern of persistent prosperity that we are generally used to seeing around the world. As we saw in Chapter 7, most of the countries that are rich today are those that were rich 50 years ago or even 100 years ago. Thus, holding all else equal, we expect to see the persistence of relative prosperity over time. We would therefore expect areas that were highly urbanized centuries ago to still be the ones that are relatively prosperous today, even if some of their advantage may have eroded.

Exhibit 8.6 Relationship Between Urbanization and GDP per Capita in 2014 (PPP-Adjusted 2011 Constant Dollars)

This exhibit shows the relationship between urbanization (as measured by the fraction of the population living in urban centers with more than 5,000 inhabitants) and GDP per capita (in PPP-adjusted 2011 constant dollars) in 2014 together with the best-fit line. It suggests that even today, urbanization is a good proxy for prosperity.

Sources: Data from Penn World Table (2014) and World Bank DataBank: World Development Indicators (2014); Penn World Table version 9.0 (Robert C. Feenstra, Robert Inklaar, and Marcel P. Timmer, June 2016).

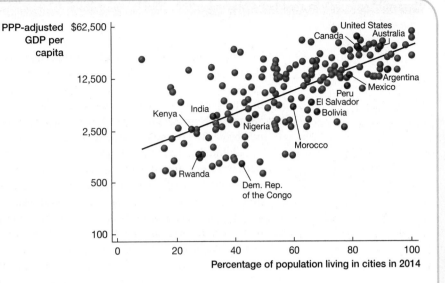

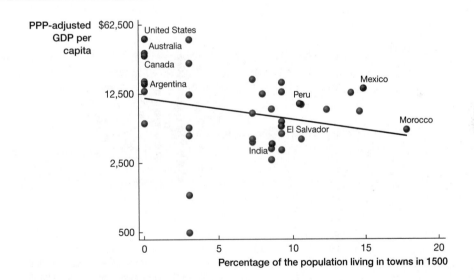

Exhibit 8.7 The Reversal of Fortune Using Urbanization (PPP-Adjusted 2011 Constant Dollars)

The former European colonies that were more prosperous in 1500, before European colonization, as proxied by their level of urbanization, are relatively less prosperous today. This can be shown by the negatively sloped best-fit line for the relationship between urbanization (percentage of the population living in towns with more than 5,000 inhabitants) in 1500 and PPP-adjusted GDP per capita in 2014. This reversal of fortune is strong evidence against the geography hypothesis, because the relative prosperity of these nations has changed greatly while potential geographic determinants of prosperity have not.

Sources: Data from Penn World Table (2014), Penn World Table version 9.0 (Robert C. Feenstra, Robert Inklaar, and Marcel P. Timmer, June 2016); and Daron Acemoglu, Simon Johnson, and James A. Robinson, "Reversal of Fortune: Geography and Institutions in the Making of the Modern World Income Distribution," *Quarterly Journal of Economics* 117(4): 2002, 1231–1294.

But Exhibit 8.7 shows something very different. The areas that were relatively more urbanized in 1500, and thus relatively more prosperous, today are generally poorer. In 1500, places like Mexico, Peru, North Africa, and India were relatively more prosperous than the parts of North America that were later to become the United States and Canada, Australia, New Zealand, and Argentina, which were sparsely populated and scarcely urbanized. Today, the picture has changed. There is a sharp reversal.

Admittedly, Exhibit 8.7 uses a limited sample that excludes countries in sub-Saharan Africa, for which we do not have urbanization data in 1500. But we can extend the sample by using another proxy. The same reasoning that led to the use of urbanization rates as a proxy for prosperity also suggests that we can use population density as a proxy. Only areas with sufficient agricultural surplus, a developed trading and transport structure, and sufficiently healthy living conditions can support a high population density. We therefore adopt this approach in Exhibit 8.8 to include data from places like sub-Saharan Africa. Even with this larger sample, the reversal of fortune persists: areas that were relatively more prosperous as measured by their population density in 1500 are today relatively less prosperous.

Understanding the Reversal of Fortune

How do we explain this reversal of fortune? One possibility could have been to appeal to geography. In fact, if we had found that such places as Mexico, India, and sub-Saharan Africa were much poorer than North America and Australia 500 years ago, it may have

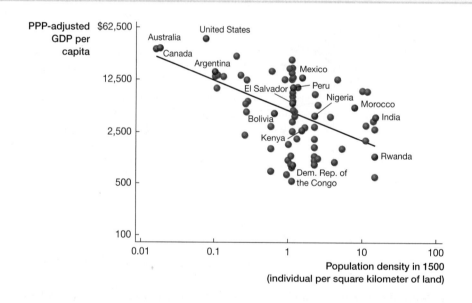

Exhibit 8.8 Reversal of Fortune Using Population Density (PPP-Adjusted 2011 Constant Dollars)

There is also a strong negative relationship between population density in 1500 (individual per square kilometer of land), another potential proxy for prosperity before European colonization, and prosperity today. Colonized areas that were capable of supporting larger populations (per acre of arable land) in 1500 are less prosperous today. This pattern is another piece of evidence against the geography hypothesis and is consistent with the role of institutions in shaping prosperity. That is, the reversal in the relative rankings of countries by prosperity since 1500 is largely a result of the fact that Europeans set up more extractive economic institutions in colonies that had higher population densities.

Sources: Data from Penn World Table (2014), Penn World Table version 9.0 (Robert C. Feenstra, Robert Inklaar, and Marcel P. Timmer, June 2016); and Daron Acemoglu, Simon Johnson, and James A. Robinson, "Reversal of Fortune: Geography and Institutions in the Making of the Modern World Income Distribution," *Quarterly Journal of Economics* 117(4): 2002, 1231–1294.

been plausible to think that these differences were due to geography. It could have been argued that agriculture was more productive in the temperate soils of North America and Australia than in the semitropical soils of Peru or India, and these differences explained why North America and Australia were richer than South America and South Asia.

But the pattern in the data shows the opposite. Five hundred years ago, many parts of South America, South Asia, North Africa, and sub-Saharan Africa were more developed than North America, Australia, and New Zealand, but today they are much poorer. Thus a geographic explanation cannot account for the patterns that we are seeing in Exhibits 8.7 and 8.8. Geographic conditions are fixed. Therefore, if the geographic conditions of Peru, India, the Caribbean, and African nations condemn them to low agricultural productivity and poverty, we should see that same poverty in 1500 as well as today. But the fact that these places were relatively more prosperous back then suggests that we must look to what actually changed between 1500 and today to understand the root of their reversal of fortune. And what changed was not these countries' geography but their institutions after European colonization.

To be fair, one could come up with more sophisticated geographical hypotheses that could account for such a reversal. For example, we could argue that geography has a time-varying effect. Perhaps the geographic characteristics that were conducive to economic growth in 1500 have become a burden.

Although this supposition is, in theory, possible, it is not plausible in practice. Today, most countries' wealth is generated by industry, trade, and services. And these are precisely the kinds of economic activities that depend less on climate and more on institutions. Diseases matter today, but we are much better at controlling them, and many semitropical areas have been able to eradicate deadly diseases, such as malaria. Thus, if anything, geographic handicaps such as poor soil quality, a worse disease environment, and more adverse transport conditions should have mattered much more 500 years ago than today. If such a sophisticated geography hypothesis were correct, today we should see these areas having a comparative advantage in industry and trade (the very opposite of what we see, where these poor nations are still largely agricultural).

These observations lead us to conclude that geographic characteristics are *not* the main reason tropical and semitropical parts of the world are today much poorer than North America and Australia.

Instead, we can view the reversal of fortune as the consequence of an institutional reversal in the sense that *Europeans established more extractive economic institutions in places that were previously more developed and set up more inclusive economic institutions in places that were previously less developed.* This pattern resulted from a simple logic. European colonialism was driven by a profit motive, and in places where Europeans encountered relatively developed civilizations, it was profitable for them to set up extractive economic institutions to funnel gold, silver, and agricultural surplus to their countries and to themselves. Most importantly, they were able to use the labor in these relatively densely populated areas to achieve their objectives, often taking over the existing institutions of the empires they dominated and setting up their own extractive economic institutions.

In contrast, in areas where they did not encounter such developed civilizations and the land was sparsely settled, such as North America, Europeans themselves went in to colonize and develop institutions under which they themselves would live. They had the incentives and the ability to structure these institutions in a more inclusive fashion. As a result, the lands of the former Aztec and Inca empires—Mexico, Peru, and their surroundings—ended up with extractive economic institutions, while Europeans who settled in the lands that were later to become the United States and Canada ended up with more inclusive economic institutions. This institutional reversal then led to the reversal of prosperity. Areas under inclusive economic institutions rapidly developed, particularly in the nineteenth century when they could readily adopt the new technologies of industry, while those under extractive economic institutions stagnated and grew much less rapidly.

We can now suggest an answer to the question posed in the title of this chapter: Why isn't the whole world developed? The answer is that inclusive economic institutions are at the root of the wealth of nations, because when market participants are not harassed by excessive regulations or paralyzed by uncertainty about the future that extractive economic institutions create, they will work, invest, innovate, and create a vibrant economy where opportunities for success feed off one another. While luck does inevitably play some role in the fate of individuals even in countries with inclusive economic institutions, an uncorrupt justice system that protects life and property and an environment where risk taking and experimentation are not frowned on are the pillars providing economic and social incentives that enrich individuals and nations.

> **Inclusive economic institutions are at the root of the wealth of nations.**

Question	**Answer**	**Data**	**Caveat**
Are tropical and semitropical areas condemned to poverty by their geographies?	No. Many of these countries were relatively more prosperous 500 years ago than countries farther from the equator that have become prosperous today. This reversal of fortune is not a reflection of changing geographic features but of different institutional structures (extractive versus inclusive) being imposed during European colonization.	Urbanization rates and data on population density in the 1500s and data on PPP-adjusted GDP per capita and urbanization rates in 2014.	The evidence presented here does not deny that geographic factors could play a role in economic development. Rather, it suggests that they are not the main cause of the poverty of tropical and semitropical areas today.

8.3 Is Foreign Aid the Solution to World Poverty?

In Chapter 7 on economic growth, we discussed certain policies that can help poor countries grow. But what about foreign aid?

Many in the Western world think that, if at all feasible, we should take steps toward improving the lives of the hundreds of millions of people who live in poverty. This conviction has led to a substantial effort over the past 60 years to provide foreign aid—in fact, "development aid"—to poor nations. Development aid, given by charitable organizations, the World Bank, and the United Nations, or sometimes by bilateral deals between countries, is meant to alleviate or even fundamentally eradicate poverty around the world.

Many in the international community—for example, high-level officials of the World Bank and the United Nations, and various journalists and commentators—have much hope pinned on development aid. But has this type of foreign aid been effective in reducing poverty around the world?

You might at first be surprised, but economists' overall verdict is that foreign aid has been on the whole ineffective in alleviating poverty. For example, over the past 50 years, hundreds of billions of dollars have been given to Africa as development aid, but as we have

A solution to world poverty? Angelina Jolie is one of many Hollywood celebrities devoting their time and money to humanitarian efforts aimed at alleviating poverty. Are these efforts likely to eradicate poverty?

seen, African nations are still much poorer than the United States or Western Europe. Why is that the case?

Though surprising at first, once we use economics to understand how foreign aid might work and recognize the difficulties faced, this conclusion turns out to be quite reasonable for three reasons. First, we know from our analysis so far that GDP per capita can be increased and economic growth can be triggered if the levels of a country's physical capital, human capital, and/or technology can be increased significantly. Although generous from the viewpoint of the donor nations, the amount of foreign aid given to even the poorest countries is not large enough to lead to a sizable increase in physical capital or to significantly increase the educational attainment of the countries' population. It also generally does not have an impact on technology or the efficiency of production. In view of this, the fact that foreign aid has not made significant progress in increasing GDP per capita among the poorest nations in the world shouldn't be too surprising.

Second, in practice, much of foreign aid does not even get invested in new technology or education. Problems related to corruption and political economy imply that money given to governments or other organizations in poor countries is often captured and distributed to corrupt officials. Studies indicate that only about 15 percent of any money given to foreign aid actually reaches its intended destination, and often it does so in a rather distorted manner.

There is also a third, and a more fundamental, reason for why foreign aid has a limited impact in alleviating poverty. If the root of poverty is the extractive economic institutions of many countries around the world, then foreign aid working within the

CHOICE &CONSEQUENCE

Foreign Aid and Corruption

In the 1990s, the government of Uganda spent a fifth of its budget on primary education. A sizable fraction of this money was provided by the international community as developmental aid.

When policymakers and academics evaluate the effectiveness of spending, they generally ask whether initial objectives were met and whether the benefits of a project exceeded its costs. But in the case of foreign and governmental aid, the money often does not even reach its intended target, precluding the chance to even try to use the money effectively. A survey by economists Ritva Reinikka and Jakob Svensson has revealed that only 13 percent of schools in Uganda actually received the grants intended for them in the period studied.[15]

The study found that a large portion of the money intended for schools was stolen by local officials. Interestingly, the schools located in the richer regions typically received more money than those schools located in the poorer areas. This disparity appears to be partly due to the fact that schools in richer areas have more resources to start with and better connections. So they may have been able to secure more of the money that was intended for them. Very few of the resources intended for students in the poorest regions actually

reached their destination. This type of corruption and siphoning off of government resources and aid money is, unfortunately, all too common and poses a formidable obstacle to the effective distribution of foreign aid in many countries. As in the Ugandan case, it may often also contribute to greater inequality of resources across regions and schools within a country.

framework of these same institutions will not fix the fundamental causes. In fact, in some instances, foreign aid funneled to dictators sitting atop of these extractive economic institutions might strengthen or enrich them, as suggested by the Choice & Consequence box.

All the evidence on the costs and limits of foreign aid does not mean that foreign aid is bad or useless. Often, foreign aid is a transfer to some of the poorest people in the world and helps alleviate their hardships, albeit temporarily, and as such serves a useful, even if limited, role. But we must also devote energy to developing policies that address the fundamental causes of prosperity—like institutions—if we wish to enduringly improve living conditions in the world's impoverished countries.

Summary

- Physical capital, human capital, and technology are proximate causes of prosperity in the sense that, though they determine whether a nation is prosperous, they are themselves determined by other, deeper factors. Put differently, if we want to understand why some nations are poor, we have to ask why they do not sufficiently invest in physical capital or human capital and why they do not adopt the best technologies and organize their production efficiently.

- The fundamental causes of prosperity include factors that potentially influence the physical and human capital investment and technology choices of nations and, via this channel, shape their prosperity.

- Three leading hypotheses about the fundamental causes of prosperity are geography, culture, and institutions. According to the geography hypothesis, geographic aspects (such as climate, topography, or disease environment) determine whether a nation can be prosperous. According to the culture hypothesis, it is the cultural values of the country's people that powerfully determine its potential for prosperity. According to the institutions hypothesis, it is the institutions (in particular, the formal and informal rules governing the organization of society and economic interactions therein) that are central to prosperity.

- Inclusive economic institutions are those that (1) provide secure property rights, (2) establish a judicial system that allows and facilitates private contracting and financial transactions, and (3) maintain relatively open and free entry into different businesses and occupations. In contrast, extractive economic institutions create insecure property rights, a partial judicial system, and entry barriers that protect the businesses and incomes of a small segment of society at the expense of the rest. According to the institutions hypothesis, inclusive economic institutions tend to generate prosperity, while extractive economic institutions do not.

- Though the inequalities in GDP per capita around the world have multiple causes, the evidence from the economic experiences of former European colonies suggests that institutional factors, and not geography, are central to explaining these disparities. In fact, the major patterns—for example, the reversal of fortune, whereby areas that were relatively prosperous became relatively less prosperous after European colonization—cannot be explained by geographic factors.

- Foreign aid can be useful to temporarily alleviate extreme poverty or manage crises but is unlikely to be a solution to poor economic development in many parts of the world. This is because aid largely fails to address the institutional roots of poverty.

Key Terms

proximate causes of prosperity *p. 177*
fundamental causes of prosperity *p. 177*
geography hypothesis *p. 178*
culture hypothesis *p. 179*
institutions *p. 179*

institutions hypothesis *p. 180*
private property rights *p. 182*
economic institutions *p. 182*
inclusive economic institutions *p. 183*
extractive economic institutions *p. 183*

political institutions *p. 183*
creative destruction *p. 189*
political creative destruction *p. 189*

Questions

All questions are available in MyEconLab *for practice and instructor assignment.*

1. How are the proximate causes of prosperity different from the fundamental causes of prosperity?

2. What does the geography hypothesis state?

3. According to the geography hypothesis, what could be done to improve incomes in poor countries?

4. What does the culture hypothesis state?

5. In the context of this chapter, what is meant by the term "institution"? What are the three important elements that define institutions?

6. How does the institutions hypothesis explain the difference in prosperity among nations?

7. What does it mean to say that private property rights are well enforced in an economy? How does enforcement of these rights foster economic development?

8. How do inclusive economic institutions differ from extractive economic institutions?

9. What does the return-to-entrepreneurship curve show? What is meant by the opportunity cost of entrepreneurship?

10. How does the existence of extractive institutions discourage entrepreneurship in an economy?

11. Suppose a country has well-enforced private property rights for entrepreneurs, but a large fraction of the population does not have access to education and thus cannot become entrepreneurs. Moreover, their productivity as workers is low. Would you say that this country has inclusive economic institutions? Is it likely to achieve a high level of economic development?

12. What is meant by political creative destruction? How would this concept explain the existence of extractive institutions?

13. Parts of the world that were relatively more prosperous 500 years ago have experienced a reversal of fortune and are relatively poorer today. What factors could explain this?

Problems

All problems are available in MyEconLab *for practice and instructor assignment.*

1. In July 2014, the founder of Facebook, Mark Zuckerberg, announced the launch of internet.org, a project aimed at spreading Internet access worldwide. Internet.org encourages mobile service providers to partner with Facebook to provide free, basic Internet services (including, of course, Facebook access) in developing countries. Over the long term, Zuckerberg hopes to deploy drones to expand access in remote areas. Discuss how this effort, if successful, might impact proximate and fundamental sources of growth—is free, ubiquitous Internet a growth panacea?

2. After World War II, Germany was divided into two parts, the German Democratic Republic (informally known as East Germany) and the Federal Republic of Germany (West Germany). East Germany was controlled by the former Soviet Union, while West Germany was controlled by the other Allied governments: the United States, the United Kingdom, and France. The war had destroyed most of Germany's economy. The Soviet Union as well as the Allied occupation forces sought to rebuild the economies of their respective parts. Before the fall of the Berlin Wall reunited East and West Germany in 1990, West Germany's economy grew at an annual average growth rate of 4.4 percent, which was about 3 times higher than East Germany's rate. Draw the parallel between the natural experiment discussed in the chapter and the case of East and West Germany. Based on the information given in the question and your own research, why do you think two otherwise similar areas had such divergent growth rates?

3. Suppose the country of Burondo is one of the poorest countries in the world. Its economy is heavily reliant on income from the export of oil. There are only two oil-extracting companies in Burondo. Both are owned by the government. A large part of the earnings from oil exports goes toward financing the president's lifestyle and entourage. Burondo has not had a single democratic election since it gained independence 50 years ago. Although Burondo is said to have abundant oil resources, only a

small proportion is extracted every year because the extraction process is so inefficient. Transporting goods in and out of the country is costly, as Burondo is surrounded by lofty mountain ranges. School enrollment in this country is very low and as a result, most of the adult population is illiterate. Life expectancy is also quite low. Agriculture is collectivized in Burondo and so food shortages are common in the country. Using the information given, distinguish between the fundamental and proximate causes of prosperity (or its absence) in Burondo.

4. Look at the following map of Nogales, a twin city that is divided by the U.S. border.

One part of Nogales lies in the United States, in Arizona, and the other part lies in Sonora, Mexico. Life in Nogales, Mexico, is very different from life in Nogales, Arizona. The average income in Nogales, Mexico, is about one-third the average income in Nogales, Arizona. Education levels, life expectancy, and health conditions are better in Nogales, Arizona, than in Nogales, Mexico. Unlike the city in Arizona, Nogales in Mexico has only recently adopted political reforms, bringing it closer to functioning as a democracy. Crime rates are also lower in Nogales, Arizona, than in Nogales, Mexico. Since both cities are located so close to each other, they share similar geographical conditions and climate. The inhabitants of both cities also share a common ancestry and enjoy the same types of food and music. Based on this information and your own research, what factors do you think can explain why Nogales, Arizona, is so much more prosperous than Nogales, Mexico?

5. Zimbabwe, formerly known as Rhodesia, was a British colony for about 90 years. It became independent in 1980. The prime minister of newly formed Zimbabwe, Robert Mugabe, implemented a forced land redistribution policy, in which commercial farms were confiscated from white farmers. Mugabe also proceeded to confiscate shares in companies owned by whites. In the following years, agricultural production in the country fell sharply. Zimbabwe, the country that used to be called the breadbasket of Africa, is now experiencing food shortages in certain parts of the country.

a. Would Zimbabwe be considered to have extractive or inclusive institutions? Explain your answer.

b. Why would a government undertake policies that would adversely affect the lives of its citizens? Explain your answer with reference to the Zimbabwean situation.

6. Since gaining independence from Malaysia in 1965, Singapore has had impressive growth performance, achieving an average annual growth rate of GDP per capita of 7.46 percent. State-owned enterprises (SOEs) have featured prominently in its burgeoning economy; even today, many of its powerful companies are partially controlled by the highly centralized government.

a. Based on what you have learned in this chapter, how would you expect the presence of SOEs to affect the returns to and opportunity cost of entrepreneurship? Use the curves developed in Exhibit 8.5 to explain.

b. Some of Singapore's SOEs have focused on developing shipping and transportation infrastructure. How might this fact change your answer to part (a)?

c. Does the example of Singapore contradict what you have learned in this chapter about institutions and growth? Explain.

7. Using a graph like that displayed in Exhibit 8.5, which shows returns to entrepreneurship and the opportunity cost of entrepreneurship, illustrate how each of the following historical events shifted one (or both) of the curves.

a. Between 1959 and 1963, the Cuban government passed a series of laws called the Agrarian Reform Laws. These laws expropriated any landholdings above a certain size and turned them over to peasants and cooperatives.

b. From independence in 1947 until the 1990s, there was in place in India what came to be known as the "Paper Raj." The term referred to a series of rules and regulations that put strict controls on business and forced business owners to navigate a bureaucratic labyrinth to start and run their companies. For example, one entrepreneur complained that simply to import a computer, he had to make fifty trips to New Delhi to get the necessary permits. Starting in the 1990s, many of these restrictions were abolished. A series of reforms made it much easier for firms to conduct business. (Based on the series *Commanding Heights*, PBS, 2002.)

c. In 2007 and 2008, the Venezuelan dictator Hugo Chavez nationalized many large firms in several key sectors of the country's economy, including telecommunications, electric utilities, steel, and banking. Subsequently, taxes on banking and other activities were also raised significantly.

8. Suppose the returns-to and cost-of entrepreneurship curves are described by the following equations (with numbers measured in the thousands):

$$R = 250,000 - 50,000 \times N,$$
$$C = 50,000 + 15,000 \times N,$$

where R = returns to entrepreneurship, C = cost of entrepreneurship, and N = number of entrepreneurs.

a. Based on the equations given, how does the cost of entrepreneurship curve differ (in overall shape) from the one displayed in Exhibit 8.5? Explain how this difference might arise.

b. Find the equilibrium number of entrepreneurs in this economy and the equilibrium returns to entrepreneurship.

c. The government enacts a license fee of $50,000 to file the paperwork necessary to start a firm. What are now the equilibrium number of entrepreneurs and the equilibrium returns to entrepreneurship?

9. Jointly published by *The Wall Street Journal* and The Heritage Foundation, "The Freedom Index" gives an annual ranking of most of the countries of the world based on their level of economic freedom. Factors considered in the rankings include the status of property rights, extent of corruption, and ease of starting and running a business. The index can be found at http://www.heritage.org/index/.

a. Go to http://www.heritage.org/index/ranking and find three countries in each of the freedom categories ("Free," "Mostly Free," and so forth). Click on the country name in the table for each country you select, and read about the rationale for its ranking. Provide a summary for the nations you selected.

b. Now go to http://www.heritage.org/index/explore?view=by-variables. Note the per capita GDP of the three countries you selected in each category, and calculate the average of the three you selected in each category. What pattern do you notice? What preliminary conclusions can you draw concerning the relationship between economic freedom and economic development? Which of the three hypotheses mentioned in the chapter do your results tend to support? Explain.

c. Sub-Saharan Africa is known to be one of the poorest regions of the world. Go to the "Interactive Freedom Heat Map" at http://www.heritage.org/index/heatmap. Into which freedom categories do the majority of the countries of the region fall? Which countries are the exceptions to the overall pattern?

10. Sometimes development aid goes toward disaster relief. For example, after the Indian Ocean tsunami of 2004, non-governmental organizations helped devastated countries to rebuild. Is this type of aid vulnerable to the criticisms explored in the chapter? Discuss.

11. Which of the three hypotheses developed in the chapter would be most likely to view foreign aid as essential for economic development? Explain.

12. In his book *The Elusive Quest for Growth*, development economist William Easterly discusses the relationship between foreign aid and investment in poor countries. He posits that to establish the effectiveness of aid in promoting investment, two tests should be passed: First, there should be a positive statistical association between aid and investment; second, aid should pass into investment 1 for 1, that is, a 1 percent (of GDP) increase in aid should result in a 1 percent (of GDP) increase in investment. Using a dataset of eighty-eight countries from 1965 to 1995, he finds that only seventeen of the eighty-eight countries pass the first test, and of them, only six pass the second. Based on the information in the chapter, and perhaps your own reading, explain why foreign aid designed to spur investment usually does not work.

9 Employment and Unemployment

What happens to employment and unemployment if local employers go out of business?

Economic shocks frequently hit local communities. A weak car market causes Ford to shutter an assembly plant. A weak regional economy causes a big-box retailer—like JCPenney, Target, or Sears—to shut one of its megastores. Falling coal prices cause a mining company to mothball an open-pit coal mine. Competition from new suppliers causes a clothing company to close a textile factory. Do the workers who lose these jobs quickly find new ones? Do the local labor markets quickly bounce back? Or do these communities experience persistent unemployment?

In this chapter, we study the determinants of employment and unemployment, and investigate how various economic shocks affect the labor market equilibrium.

CHAPTER **OUTLINE**

9.1 Measuring Employment and Unemployment

After 17 months of unsuccessful job applications, one unemployed worker wrote in a letter to the *New York Times* that "nothing stops the omnipresent feeling of loneliness, worthlessness and desperation."[1] For most people, enduring a long period of unemployment takes a terrible toll on their well-being. Long-term unemployment generates four simultaneous traumas: a loss of income, skills, social interaction, and perceived self-worth.

> Because of its enormous economic and social costs, politicians and policymakers try to limit the amount of unemployment in an economy.

Because of its enormous economic and social costs, policymakers try to limit the amount of unemployment in an economy. To do so, they must have a way of measuring and tracking unemployment over time. Unfortunately, just measuring unemployment is challenging. For example, it seems reasonable that a 30-year-old without a job who is actively looking for work should count as unemployed. But should we also count another 30-year-old who has lost a job but has decided *not* to look for work? What about full-time college students or stay-at-home parents: people who are busy and work hard but don't receive a paycheck for their labor?

Economists have agreed on a standard, though nevertheless imperfect, way of defining employment and unemployment. In the United States, this standard is set by the Bureau of Labor Statistics in the Department of Labor, which tracks the official employment statistics for the U.S. economy. We describe the Bureau of Labor Statistics definition here.

Classifying Potential Workers

The first step in measuring unemployment is to determine the population of interest. The group typically tracked for this purpose includes everyone in the general population with three exceptions: children under 16 years of age, people on active duty in the military, and people who are living in institutions where the residents have restricted mobility (for instance, facilities that provide long-term medical care or prisons). The Bureau of Labor Statistics calls the remaining population the *civilian non-institutional population 16 years old and over*. For simplicity, we refer to this as the population of **potential workers**. In January 2016, the United States had 252.4 million potential workers.

Potential workers include everyone in the general population with three exceptions: children under 16 years of age, people on active duty in the military, and people who are living in institutions where the residents have restricted personal mobility, like long-term medical care facilities or prisons.

9.1

Exhibit 9.1 The Composition of the U.S. Population of Potential Workers (January 2016)

The number of potential workers is 252.4 million people—otherwise known as the civilian non-institutional population 16 years old and older. Potential workers can be divided into three subgroups: employed workers (150.5 million), unemployed workers (7.8 million), and those not in the labor force (94.1 million). The labor force is the combination of the employed and unemployed workers (158.3 million).

Source: Based on U.S. Bureau of Labor Statistics.

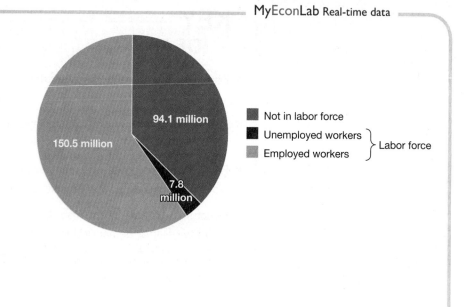

A person holding a full-time or part-time paid job is **employed**.

A worker is **unemployed** if she does not have a job, has actively looked for work in the prior four weeks, and is currently available for work.

The **labor force** is the sum of all employed and unemployed workers.

The **unemployment rate** is the percentage of the labor force that is unemployed.

The **labor force participation rate** is the percentage of potential workers who are in the labor force.

In the population of potential workers, people are classified into one of three categories: "employed," "unemployed," or "not in the labor force." Those holding full-time or part-time *paid* jobs are officially classified as **employed**. In other words, as long as a person works for pay at least part-time, she is classified as employed. Using the official definition, in January 2016, there were 150.5 million employed workers in the United States.

Potential workers are classified as **unemployed** if they do not have a paid job, have actively looked for work in the prior four weeks, and are currently available for work. This definition of unemployment makes it easy to classify the workers we had trouble considering above. Laid-off workers are only considered unemployed if they are actively looking for a new job. Similarly, students and parents who don't have a paid job are only considered unemployed if they are actively looking for a job and are currently available to work (even part time). In January 2016, there were 7.8 million unemployed workers in the United States.

The **labor force** is the sum of all employed and unemployed workers:

$$\text{Labor force} = \text{Employed} + \text{Unemployed}.$$

Finally, all potential workers who don't fit the criteria for being employed or unemployed are classified as "not in the labor force." People in this category are potential workers who don't have a paid job and aren't looking for one, such as stay-at-home parents, disabled workers, many retirees, and many students. In January 2016, 94.1 million potential workers were not in the labor force. Exhibit 9.1 breaks down the total population of potential workers into its three components: employed workers, unemployed workers, and those not in the labor force.

Calculating the Unemployment Rate

Using these classifications, economists calculate a number of statistics to describe the labor market. The **unemployment rate** is defined as the percentage of the labor force that is unemployed:

$$\begin{aligned}
\text{Unemployment rate} &= 100\% \times \frac{\text{Unemployed}}{\text{Labor force}} \\
&= 100\% \times \frac{\text{Unemployed}}{\text{Employed} + \text{Unemployed}}.
\end{aligned}$$

Similarly, the **labor force participation rate** is defined as the percentage of potential workers who are in the labor force:

$$\text{Labor force participation rate} = 100\% \times \frac{\text{Labor force}}{\text{Potential workers}}.$$

Using these equations and our numbers from before, we can calculate what the labor force, unemployment rate, and labor force participation rate were in January 2016. The components are rounded, which explains why the first sum doesn't match exactly:

$$\text{Labor force} = \text{Employed} + \text{Unemployed} = 150.5 \text{ million} + 7.8 \text{ million}$$
$$= 158.3 \text{ million}.$$

$$\text{Unemployment rate} = 100\% \times \frac{\text{Unemployed}}{\text{Labor force}} = 100\% \times \frac{7.8 \text{ million}}{158.3 \text{ million}} = 4.9\%.$$

$$\text{Labor force participation rate} = 100\% \times \frac{\text{Labor force}}{\text{Potential workers}} = 100\% \times \frac{158.3 \text{ million}}{252.4 \text{ million}}$$
$$= 62.7\%.$$

While these calculations reflect the main way that economists measure unemployment, it's important to note that they are just summaries and therefore leave out many important details. In particular, the way we officially count unemployed workers omits two important categories of workers who are frustrated by the lack of jobs: discouraged workers and underemployed workers.

Discouraged workers are potential workers who would like to have a job but have given up looking for one. Because they are not actively looking for work, these workers are not included in the unemployment rate as we defined it above. Instead, discouraged workers are counted officially as out of the labor force. There were 623,000 discouraged workers in the United States in January 2016, representing 0.4 percent of the labor force.

Similarly, we count all paid workers as employed, even if they would like to work more hours. Many workers in difficult economic circumstances would like to work more hours to support themselves and their families but don't have the option to do so. Although such workers are *underemployed*, they are not included in the official unemployment statistic. There were 6 million underemployed workers in the United States in January 2016, representing 3.8 percent of the labor force.

Trends in the Unemployment Rate

As the overall economy fluctuates, so does the unemployment rate. When the overall economy suffers a *recession*—a period in which GDP falls—the unemployment rate tends to rise. During typical U.S. recessions, the unemployment rate reaches a level between 6 percent and 9 percent. When the economy is healthy and expanding, the unemployment rate eventually reaches a level between 4 percent and 5 percent.

Severe recessions produce the largest increases in the unemployment rate. For example, in early 2007—before the start of the recession later that year—the U.S. unemployment rate hovered around 4.5 percent. The 2007–2009 recession led to a sharp rise in the unemployment rate and a peak rate of 10.0 percent in October 2009. During the Great Depression of the 1930s—the most severe contraction of the U.S. economy in the twentieth century—the unemployment rate reached 25 percent.

Exhibit 9.2 shows the evolution of the monthly unemployment rate in the U.S. economy since 1948. The unemployment rate is relatively high during and following recessions—the shaded areas on the exhibit correspond to recessions. For example, the unemployment rate was high following the oil price shocks in the mid-1970s and then again during the recession of 1981–1982. Since World War II, the peak in unemployment, 10.8 percent, occurred during the 1981–1982 recession. This peak is even higher than the 10.0 percent peak during the severe 2007–2009 recession.

> Some amount of unemployment—usually around 4 percent or 5 percent—is a necessary attribute of a well-functioning modern economy.

It is also noteworthy that the unemployment rate is never close to zero. Since 1948, the U.S. unemployment rate has gone below 3 percent during only one period in the early 1950s. Even during the economic boom in the 1990s, the unemployment rate reached a low of only around 4 percent. Later in this chapter, we explain why some amount of unemployment—usually around 4 percent or 5 percent—is a necessary attribute of a well-functioning modern economy, while an unemployment rate of 10 percent is a national crisis that policymakers aggressively try to avoid.

Exhibit 9.2 The U.S. Unemployment Rate from 1948 to 2016

The evolution of the U.S. unemployment rate is shown from January 1948 to January 2016 (monthly data). Shaded bars are recessions: periods of negative growth in the total economy. The unemployment rate increases during recessions.

Source: Based on U.S. Bureau of Labor Statistics.

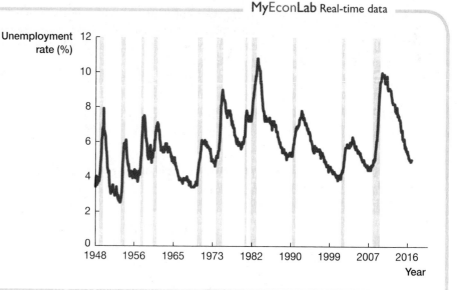

9.2 Equilibrium in the Labor Market

To study how employment and unemployment are determined, we first need to understand how the labor market works. As with any other market, we can analyze it using a model of supply and demand, which will determine the wage rate—the price of labor. We develop the demand curve for labor and the supply curve for labor separately and then put them together to describe the labor market equilibrium.

The Demand for Labor

When we first studied demand curves in Chapter 4, we discussed households demanding goods and services. Now that we are studying the *labor market*, the role of households flips. In the labor market, households *supply* labor, and firms *demand* labor. Firms are now on the demand side, because they need to hire workers for production.

Optimizing firms try to maximize profits, so they demand the quantity of labor that produces the greatest feasible *profit* (defined as revenues minus costs). How does a firm determine the profit-maximizing quantity of labor? By comparing the revenue that a worker produces with the cost of employing that worker.

The value of the marginal product of labor is the contribution of an additional worker to a firm's revenues.

To see how this works, consider a barbershop. If the barbershop has only one barber, let's assume that he'll almost always be busy cutting hair and that he'll generate revenue of $25 per hour. This $25 per hour is **the value of the marginal product of labor** of this worker, meaning his contribution to the firm's revenues. Recall that the marginal product is the amount of output that one additional worker produces, and $25 is the value of this marginal product—*value* is measured not in terms of additional haircuts, but in terms of revenue generated by these additional haircuts. For example, this barber may have a marginal product of two haircuts per hour, and, if each costs $12.50, his value of marginal product will be $25 per hour.

Let's also assume that the market wage for barbers is $15 per hour. So, by employing this first barber, the barbershop earns $10 per hour, which is the difference between the barber's value of marginal product and the barber's wage: $25 − $15 = $10 per hour. If the shop adds a second barber, the barbershop will sell more haircuts, but from time to time, there won't be enough customers to keep both barbers busy. So the addition of the second barber does not double sales at the barbershop. Suppose instead that the second barber increases sales by only $20 per hour, so that his value of marginal product is $20. Because the market wage for barbers is $15 per hour, employing the additional barber will still increase profits by $20 − $15 = $5 per hour. So an optimizing barbershop will also hire the second barber.

When this barbershop has two customers, the value of the marginal product of the third barber is zero.

Now consider what will happen if the barbershop adds a third barber. The third barber will increase sales a bit more, but will do so by even less than the addition of the second barber, because it will rarely be the case that the shop has enough customers to simultaneously keep all three barbers busy. Suppose that this third barber's value of marginal product is $10 per hour (he increases sales by only $10 per hour). Because the market wage is $15 per hour and is thus above his value of marginal product, hiring this third barber will actually *lower* the profits of the barbershop ($10 − $15 = −$5), so the shop will refrain from hiring a third barber. Summing up, the barbershop optimizes—in other words, maximizes its profits—by employing only two barbers.

The barbershop example demonstrates two important facts about labor demand. First, as we have also seen in Chapters 6 and 7, firms typically experience *diminishing marginal product* of labor. Diminishing marginal product of labor means that each additional worker creates less marginal output than the workers who were hired before. For example, additional barbers will increase the number of haircuts that the barbershop offers, but each additional barber won't be as productive as the last one, because there won't be enough customers to keep them all busy. If the barbershop faces a constant price for haircuts, the lower marginal output of additional workers also translates into diminishing value of marginal product of labor. In the barbershop, the first barber creates $25 of additional revenue (per hour), the second $20, and the third only $10. Because the value of the marginal product of each additional barber is diminishing, hiring more barbers increases the *total* revenue of the barbershop by less and less.

The second important fact illustrated by the barbershop example is that a firm hires workers until it cannot increase profits by hiring an additional worker. The firm keeps hiring as long as the revenue that an additional worker brings in for the firm—*the value of the marginal product of labor*—is at least as great as the cost of employing that worker, which is the *market wage*. To see why this is the case, consider Exhibit 9.3, which plots the value of the marginal product of labor against the number of workers employed. Because the value of the marginal product decreases as the number of workers employed increases, the curve is downward-sloping.

If the firm employs fewer workers than the optimal quantity shown in Exhibit 9.3, then it can increase profits by hiring more workers, because the revenue those workers bring in (the value of their marginal product) is greater than the cost of employing them (the market wage). Similarly, if the firm employs more workers than the optimal quantity, the firm can increase profits by laying off workers, because the revenue those workers bring in is less than the market wage, the cost of employing them.

Exhibit 9.3 The Value of the Marginal Product of Labor Is the Labor Demand Curve

Because the marginal product of labor diminishes as the quantity of labor increases, the curve that plots the value of the marginal product of labor is downward-sloping. Profit maximization implies that the firm should hire workers up to the point where the market wage is equal to the value of the marginal product of labor. The value of the marginal product of labor schedule is also the labor demand curve.

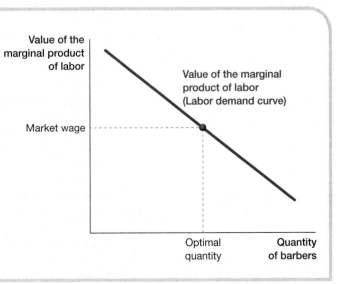

Exhibit 9.4 Downward-Sloping Labor Demand Curve

The labor demand curve, which shows the relationship between the quantity of labor demanded and the wage, is downward-sloping. The exhibit depicts left and right shifts in the labor demand curve. The labor demand curve shifts when the quantity of labor demanded changes at a given value of the wage.

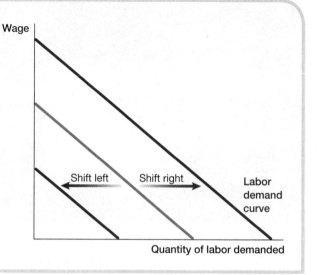

Therefore, *the profit-maximizing firm will hire the amount of labor that makes the value of the marginal product of labor equal to the market wage.* As we change the market wage, the quantity of labor demanded moves *along* the curve depicting the value of the marginal product—the firm adjusts the number of workers it employs to make the value of the marginal product equal to the wage. Thus, the downward-sloping curve in Exhibit 9.3—the value of the marginal product of labor—is also the **labor demand curve**, because it shows how the quantity of labor demanded varies with the wage.

The **labor demand curve** depicts the relationship between the quantity of labor demanded and the wage. The value of the marginal product of labor is also the labor demand curve, because they both show how the quantity of labor demanded varies with the wage.

Shifts in the Labor Demand Curve

The labor demand curve depicts the relationship between the quantity of labor demanded and the wage. A *movement along the labor demand curve* occurs when the wage changes and no other economic variables change other than the quantity of labor demanded. In contrast, many factors can change the value of marginal product of labor at each quantity of labor and thus cause the entire labor demand curve to shift to the left or right—as depicted in Exhibit 9.4.

Any change that affects the schedule relating the quantity of labor and the value of the marginal product of labor will shift the labor demand curve. We discuss four shifters in this section:

- **Changing output prices:** When the price of haircuts goes down, the value of the marginal product of barbers also declines. This implies that the firm would like to hire fewer barbers at any given wage, shifting the labor demand curve to the left.
- **Changing demand for the output good or service:** When the demand for haircuts declines, this will impact the value of the marginal product of barbers even if it does not directly change the price of haircuts. Falling demand for haircuts lowers the number of customers coming to the barbershop, leading each barber to spend more time waiting idly rather than cutting hair. Such declines in demand for output will shift the labor demand curve to the left.
- **Changing technology:** When changes in technology increase the value of the marginal product of labor, the labor demand curve shifts to the right. For example, technology that was developed in the late nineteenth century first enabled hair stylists to straighten or curl hair: "perms." The ability to offer perms increased the marginal product of hair stylists and shifted the demand curve for hair stylists to the right. Technological progress and increases in productivity typically shift the labor demand curve to the right, but in rare cases the opposite can happen. For example, machines sometimes substitute for labor and shift the labor demand curve to the left. We discuss such examples later in the chapter.
- **Changing input prices:** Businesses use labor and other factors of production, like machines and tools, to produce goods and services. When the cost of these other factors goes down, businesses purchase more of them. This usually increases the

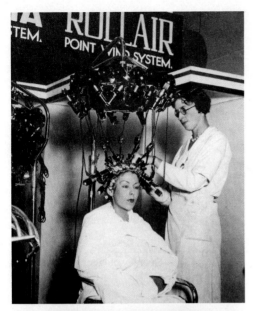

Technological innovation in the hair business. The technology for permanent waves—now called perms—was first developed in the nineteenth century and has continuously advanced since then.

marginal product of labor, shifting the labor demand curve to the right. For example, mechanical hair clippers enable barbers to cut hair more quickly. If the cost of hair clippers falls and the barbershop acquires more hair clippers, the barbers can serve more customers per hour. This will increase their value of marginal product and shift the labor demand curve to the right.

Until now, we've illustrated most ideas with the labor demand curve of a single barbershop or hair stylist. To study the level of employment and unemployment in the *total* economy, we need to analyze the labor demand curve of the entire economy. To derive this economy-wide, or "aggregate," labor demand curve, we proceed in two steps.

First, we derive the labor demand curve for each industry. For example, this is done by adding together the labor demand curves of every employer in the hair care service industry, which comprises over 100,000 businesses like barbershops and hair salons. The Bureau of Labor Statistics reports that there are about 362,000 people employed in the United States as barbers and hair stylists (Occupational and Employment Statistics, May 2015). On average these workers are paid about $14 per hour. Accordingly, the total quantity of labor demanded in the hair care industry at the wage of $14 per hour is 362,000 workers. To derive the rest of the labor demand curve for the hair care industry, we would identify the quantity of labor demanded by the businesses in this industry at every hypothetical wage.

Once we have derived the labor demand curve of each industry, we can sum these industry labor demand curves to obtain the aggregate labor demand curve. In principle, we will also need to account for spillover effects among the different industries and also between workers and firms. For example, expansion in one industry might create additional demand for the products of another industry. In addition, changing the overall level of wages and employment will affect workers' demand for the products of firms. When more workers are employed, they have more income to buy the products that other workers produce. We return to these issues in Chapter 12.

Notice that we are simplifying our model by treating the economy as if it contained a *single* aggregate labor demand curve. In practice, workers have different skills and receive different wages. Nevertheless, the simplifying assumption of a single labor market enables us to generate key insights about how the overall economy functions without having to specify how different segments of the labor market function, even if it also means that we are omitting some interesting details about the performance of these segments.

The Supply of Labor

The **labor supply curve** represents the relationship between the quantity of labor supplied and the wage.

The **labor supply curve** represents the relationship between the quantity of labor supplied and the wage. Like the labor demand curve, the labor supply curve is derived from the principles of optimization. In this case, workers optimally allocate their limited time between paid work, leisure, and other activities, which might include home production like childcare, home maintenance, cooking, or cleaning. When market wages are higher, it makes sense for workers to spend more time working outside the home. For instance, if you are paid by the hour and your employer is running overtime shifts, you can get paid 1.5 times your normal hourly wage in those special shifts. For many workers this is a tempting arrangement, leading them to work more outside the home and accordingly have less time for leisure or chores at home.

This kind of reasoning implies that as the wage increases, the quantity of labor supplied increases. Accordingly, the labor supply curve is upward-sloping, as shown in Exhibit 9.5. In this exhibit, you probably will notice that the labor supply curve changes slope as the wage increases. At a sufficiently high wage, the labor supply curve becomes (approximately) vertical. In reality, this change in slope occurs more smoothly than the kinked version you see in our figures. We use the kink to make the change in slope easier to visually recognize and analyze. The vertical portion of the labor supply curve captures the fact that it becomes much harder to further increase the quantity of labor supplied when almost all people who are interested in working have already found a full-time job.

Exhibit 9.5 Upward-Sloping Labor Supply Curve

The labor supply curve, which shows the relationship between the quantity of labor supplied and the wage, is upward-sloping. As the wage rises (holding all else equal), people's willingness to work rises. The change in slope (as the wage rises) captures the fact that it becomes much harder to keep increasing the quantity of labor supplied by further increasing the wage when almost everybody who is interested in working has already found a full-time job.

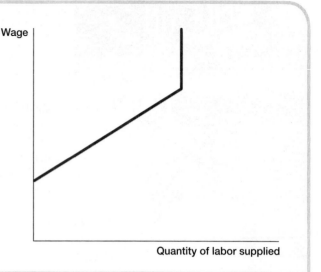

Shifts in the Labor Supply Curve

As we have noted, the labor supply curve is the relationship between the quantity of labor supplied and the wage. A *movement along the labor supply curve* occurs when the wage changes and no other economic variables change (other than the quantity of labor supplied).

In contrast, many factors can cause the entire labor supply curve to shift to the left or right, both of which are depicted in Exhibit 9.6. *Any change that affects the entire schedule relating the quantity of labor supplied and the wage will shift the labor supply curve.* We discuss three potential curve-shifting changes here:

- **Changing tastes:** Changing tastes or social norms affect people's willingness to take a paid job. For example, before World War II, working for pay outside the home was frowned on if you were a married woman. However, during World War II, most governments encouraged women to work in armaments factories as an act of patriotism. Factory work during the war was one early step in a worldwide shift toward acceptance of female labor force participation. As a result of this shift in social norms, female labor force participation in the United States rose from 25 percent in 1940 to almost 60 percent in the 1990s, corresponding to a large rightward shift in the labor supply curve. Exhibit 9.6 shows a shift of the labor supply curve to the right as a result of these changing societal norms. Note that the vertical portion of the labor supply curve also shifts to the right because of the entry of more women into the labor market.

Exhibit 9.6 Upward-Sloping Labor Supply Curve

This exhibit depicts left and right shifts in the labor supply curve. The labor supply curve shifts when the quantity of labor supplied changes at a given value of the wage.

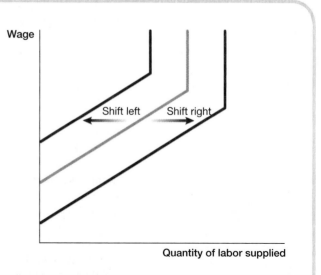

- **Changing opportunity cost of time:** Devices like vacuum cleaners, dishwashers, laundry machines, and lawnmowers lower the opportunity cost of working outside the home by freeing up time that was previously needed for home production. This sort of technology-induced change in the opportunity cost of time has been a factor contributing to the rise in female labor force participation, and it also shifts the labor supply curve to the right, as shown in Exhibit 9.6.
- **Changing population:** Increases in the size of the population, which increase the number of potential workers in the economy, also shift the labor supply curve to the right. One factor increasing population is immigration. For example, each year, the United States experiences a net immigration inflow of roughly 1 million people, implying that the population grows one-third of 1 percent per year due to immigration. This inflow shifts the domestic U.S. labor supply curve to the right.

LETTING THE
DATA SPEAK

Who Is Unemployed?

The prevalence of unemployment varies widely across different segments of the labor force. One of the most noticeable disparities is that unemployment is much higher among those with low levels of education. Exhibit 9.7 shows, for example, that the unemployment rate among those in the labor force with less than a high school diploma was 7.9 percent in 2015. For people in the labor force with a college degree, the unemployment rate was only 2.6 percent.

There are many factors that explain why more educated workers tend to have lower rates of unemployment. Their optimizing labor-supply behavior provides part of the answer. When people lose a job, they tend to spend some of their time looking for a new job and some of their time engaged in production at home. There are many "home production" activities, like cleaning out the attic or painting the house, and most of them do not require high levels of formal education. People with higher levels of education aren't necessarily more skillful in these home production activities. However, more educated workers tend to earn higher wages than less educated workers when working outside the home. This is a consequence of the fact that they have greater *human capital*, meaning that their labor is more productive, as we have seen in Chapter 6, and this translates into greater earnings for them. An unemployed cab driver might be indifferent between driving a cab and staying home for a few weeks to paint his house. An unemployed engineer might be just as good at house painting as the taxi driver, but the engineer would be much better off financially getting back to work designing robotic assembly lines, earning a relatively high income, and using some of that income to hire someone else to paint her house. Therefore, higher wages make workers with more education more eager to avoid unemployment.

Similarly, unemployment is often much lower among middle-aged workers, who tend to have more experience and skills—and therefore higher wages—than among younger workers.

MyEconLab Real-time data

Exhibit 9.7
Unemployment Rates for Different Educational Groups (2015)

Unemployment rates fall as educational attainment rises. The unemployment rates are calculated for all civilian, non-institutional U.S. adults aged 25 and over. The unemployment rates in this exhibit are for 2015.

Source: Based on U.S. Bureau of Labor Statistics and the Federal Reserve Economic Data (FRED) database.

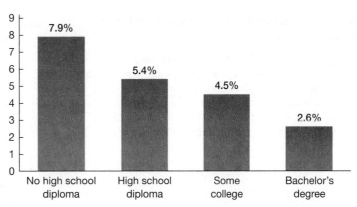

As with the labor demand curve, the labor supply curve of the entire economy (the aggregate labor supply curve) can be derived by summing over the labor supply of each potential worker in the economy.

Equilibrium in a Competitive Labor Market

Recall from Chapter 1 that we define an *equilibrium* as a situation in which nobody would benefit by changing his or her own behavior. Moreover, recall from Chapter 4 that a *competitive equilibrium* is given by the intersection of the supply and demand curves. Equilibrium in a competitive labor market works the same way: it is the point of intersection between the labor supply and labor demand curves, as shown in Exhibit 9.8. At the competitive equilibrium wage w^*, the quantity of labor supplied is equal to the quantity of labor demanded—all workers are able to work as many hours as they wish at this wage, and all firms are able to hire as many hours of labor as they find profitable. In contrast, at a wage above w^*, the quantity of labor supplied would exceed the quantity of labor demanded and push the wage down. At a wage below w^*, the quantity of labor demanded would exceed the quantity of labor supplied and push the wage up. Thus w^* is the unique wage that equates the quantity of labor supplied and the quantity of labor demanded. This *labor market equilibrium*, shown by L^* in Exhibit 9.8, is also referred to as *equilibrium employment*.

We also refer to the competitive equilibrium wage as the **market-clearing wage**. The label "market-clearing" should remind you that every worker who wants a job can (eventually) find one: the wage has adjusted so that the quantity of labor demanded matches the quantity of labor supplied. This distinguishes the market-clearing wage from the wage that results from wage rigidities, which prevent the wage from adjusting to equate the quantity of labor demanded and the quantity of labor supplied. As we'll see later in this chapter, such rigidities will generate unemployment.

We will use the labor market equilibrium depicted in Exhibit 9.8 to model the overall level of employment in an economy. As mentioned above, we are simplifying our analysis by focusing on a single type of labor. But the labor market equilibrium shown in Exhibit 9.8 can be readily applied to study equilibrium in a specific segment of the market or in a local labor market as well. For example, we could consider the supply of and demand for workers with computer programming skills and derive the equilibrium wage and employment level in that specific labor market.

It is useful to note that the labor market depicted in Exhibit 9.8 is what is sometimes referred to as a *frictionless* labor market. In a frictionless market, firms can instantly hire and fire workers, both workers and firms have complete information about each other, and the wage adjusts instantly to clear the market (setting the quantity of labor supplied equal to the quantity of labor demanded). We will see next why departures from this frictionless labor market are often useful for understanding real-world labor markets and unemployment.

> The competitive equilibrium wage is the **market-clearing wage**. At this wage, every worker who wants a job can find one: the quantity of labor demanded matches the quantity of labor supplied.

Exhibit 9.8 Competitive Equilibrium in the Labor Market

The intersection of the upward-sloping labor supply curve and the downward-sloping labor demand curve determines the market-clearing wage w^* and the equilibrium quantity of labor, or for short, equilibrium employment, L^*. At the market-clearing wage, the quantity of labor supplied is equal to the quantity of labor demanded.

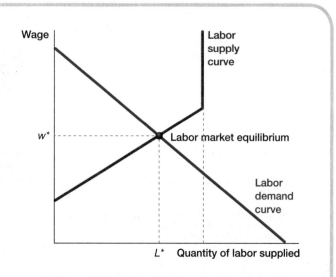

9.3 Why Is There Unemployment?

At the market-clearing wage w^* in Exhibit 9.8, the labor supply and labor demand curves intersect. Accordingly, the quantity of labor demanded equals the quantity of labor supplied—every worker who wants to work at wage w^* has a job. There are people who are not working—represented by the segment of the labor supply curve that lies above the market-clearing wage. The people on this part of the labor supply curve are only willing to work for wages above the market-clearing wage w^*.

Voluntary Unemployment

In the economy depicted in Exhibit 9.8, there are employed workers and workers who are not employed because they are unwilling to work at the market-clearing wage w^*. In a competitive equilibrium, there should be no workers looking for work (they are either employed or unwilling to work at the market-clearing wage). So in a competitive equilibrium, there shouldn't be people who are not employed and are looking for work. But then, how would we explain the fact that there were 7.8 million *officially* unemployed Americans in January 2016 who are thus counted as not employed and looking for work?

A first possibility is that the official unemployment statistics are probably counting some workers who are *voluntarily unemployed*. They are willing to work, but only for a wage above the market-clearing wage w^*. Therefore, at the equilibrium wage they are happy to remain unemployed. Because unemployment survey questions do not specify that the workers should be looking for work at the *current prevailing market wage*, some people might be counted as unemployed even though they are looking only for jobs that pay more than the current prevailing market wage.

However, the available evidence suggests that most unemployed workers are not voluntarily unemployed. Rather, most unemployed workers would be willing to work at the prevailing market wage but are unable to find employers that are willing to hire them at this wage.[2] Thus, we must find another way to explain why 7.8 million Americans couldn't find a job in January 2016.

When economic models do not predict what we observe in the world, we must ask ourselves whether the assumptions made in our model are correct. In our model of the labor market, we made an assumption that might not actually hold.

We assumed that workers and firms have full information about the job market. For instance, we assumed that they know what the equilibrium wage is, what qualifications employers are looking for, and where the jobs are. This means that workers can instantly find the right job for themselves whenever it is available and no open job will be left unfilled. However, when firms and workers lack important information about the labor market, workers cannot always be matched to open jobs, and this mismatch will cause unemployment.

We next discuss this type of unemployment, which we call *frictional unemployment*. We then turn to two other economic factors that explain why unemployment exists and also why it varies over time.

Job Search and Frictional Unemployment

In the economy described by Exhibit 9.8, any worker who wants a job at the market-clearing wage w^* can find one. Up until this point, our analysis of the labor market has assumed that the labor market is frictionless, which implies that the worker can instantly find an employer that is willing to hire her. Yet if you've ever looked for a job, you've probably discovered that finding the right job is not simple and might take a lot of legwork. It might be simple to find a summer job at McDonald's, but it's hard to land a job that is a good fit for your particular skills and capabilities.

> Because each person has specific capabilities, experience, and job preferences, finding the right match between an unemployed person and a firm usually takes time.

To find the right job, you need to determine which firms are hiring and try to learn how pay, benefits, and other job characteristics vary among them. You have to line up references and send out resumes. It also helps to network with family and friends to find some acquaintance of an acquaintance who happens to work where you are applying. You need to set up interviews and survive them. Finally, you wait for the people who conduct those interviews to finish interviewing the other leading candidates. In most cases, someone else gets chosen, and then you start all over again.

Job search refers to the activities that workers undertake to find appropriate jobs.

Economists refer to job-hunting activities as **job search**. Because each person has specific capabilities, experience, and job preferences, finding the right match between an unemployed person and a firm usually takes time.

Search frictions arise both because of the time-consuming logistics of finding, applying for, and interviewing for jobs and because firms and workers have imperfect information about each other and the state of the economy. Imagine a Detroit autoworker who loses his $40 per hour job during the 2007–2009 recession. Shortly afterward, he hears about job offers in the service sector for $20 per hour. Instead of pursuing those jobs, he keeps looking for higher-paying jobs in the auto industry. Only after months of unsuccessful searching in the auto sector does he have enough information to conclude that his best options are the $20 per hour jobs in the service sector. Examples like this illustrate that gathering information and searching for the right job take time.

Frictional unemployment refers to unemployment that arises because workers have imperfect information about available jobs and need to engage in a time-consuming process of job search.

Unemployment resulting from imperfect information about available jobs and from the time-consuming process of job search is **frictional unemployment**.

Though it might at first seem strange, you can think about the dating market in the same way that you think about the job market. It takes a long time to find a person who is a good match as a romantic partner. In this sense, people who are not in a relationship, but looking for one, are romantically unemployed. We don't expect single people to find a new romantic partner overnight, and we shouldn't expect unemployed workers to instantly find a job either.

9.4 Wage Rigidity and Structural Unemployment

Frictional unemployment resulting from job-search activities is a normal feature of every labor market. However, unemployment also arises because wages are sometimes above the market-clearing level w^*, meaning that the quantity of labor supplied is greater than the quantity of labor demanded. When wages are held fixed above the competitive equilibrium level that clears the labor market, this is referred to as **wage rigidity**. **Structural unemployment** arises when the quantity of labor supplied persistently exceeds the quantity of labor demanded. Wage rigidity is a key factor in creating such a persistent gap. Wage rigidity can occur for many reasons, which we discuss next, but the economic consequences are similar, regardless of the source of the wage rigidity: holding the market wage above the market-clearing wage causes some workers who would like to work at the market wage to be unemployed. To illustrate how wage rigidity impacts the labor market, we start with minimum wage laws, because it is easy to understand their effect using the supply and demand framework. However, other causes of wage rigidity are much more important in the U.S. labor market, and we study those in turn.

Wage rigidity refers to the condition in which the market wage is held above the competitive equilibrium level that would clear the labor market.

Structural unemployment arises when the quantity of labor supplied persistently exceeds the quantity of labor demanded.

> Holding the market wage above the market-clearing wage causes some workers who would like to work at the market wage to be unemployed.

Minimum Wage Laws

In most countries, legislation specifies a minimum level for the hourly wage. Such legislated wage floors, often called *minimum wage laws*, can prevent the market wage from falling to the market-clearing wage that equates the quantity of labor supplied with the quantity of labor demanded.

In the United States, the federal government chooses a national minimum wage and state legislatures can choose higher minimum wages for in-state jobs. In January 2016, for example, the federal minimum wage was $7.25, while the highest state minimum wage was $10.00, which applied in California and Massachusetts. Many U.S. cities and states are phasing in higher minimum wages.

Minimum wages might prevent the quantity of labor supplied from equaling the quantity of labor demanded, as depicted in Exhibit 9.9. In this exhibit, the minimum wage is labeled

CHOICE
&CONSEQUENCE

Luddites and Robots

Does technology cause unemployment? In a Phillips electronics factory in China, hundreds of employees work on an assembly line that manufactures electric shavers. Meanwhile, in the Netherlands, the same shavers are assembled by an army of 128 robotic arms. With video cameras for eyes and computer-calibrated hydraulics, these robots tirelessly go about their work. Robot-filled factories raise the possibility that technology can reduce a firm's demand for labor. Throughout history, workers have complained about technological innovation that reduces employment.

The most famous episode began in 1811, when gangs of British textile workers started burning down factories and smashing newly invented mechanized looms. The rioters also targeted inventors and mill owners, burning down their homes and in one instance conducting an assassination. These so-called Luddites—named after the worker Ned Ludd, who was reputed to have smashed textile machines several decades earlier—opposed the mechanization of production (and, for that reason, the term "Luddite" has come to refer to those opposing new technology). The riots became so frequent and so destructive that the British army was called in to restore order. Dozens of rioters were hanged, and the movement faded in 1813. Ultimately, the Luddites could not stop the mechanization of textile manufacturing.

Were new machines really destroying the livelihoods of the textile workers in 1811? The likely answer is yes. The new machines enabled workers to complete tasks in minutes that had previously taken hours. Consequently, the mills needed to employ fewer workers. Many skilled artisans lost their jobs, and their families suffered. So the Luddites were not mistaken in believing that the machines were putting some of them out of work.

Technological progress *can* destroy jobs in a single industry, such as textiles. Many famous economists, including John Maynard Keynes, worried that new machines would take jobs away from workers, creating widespread joblessness. Keynes, for example, stated in 1930: "We are being afflicted with a new disease of which some readers may not have heard the name, but of which they will hear a great deal in the years to come— namely, technological unemployment. This means unemployment due to our discovery of means of economising the use of labour outrunning the pace at which we can find new uses for labour."[3] Keynes went on to speculate that in 100 years, people would end up working only a few hours per day, even as

Workers smashing a mechanized loom in Britain during the period of the Luddite riots (1811–1813).

their quality of life continued to rise because of the great abundance provided by the new technologies.

It's still too early to judge Keynes's accuracy, as he was forecasting events in the year 2030 and beyond. Nevertheless, in some ways, Keynes may have gotten things wrong. As Keynes predicted, technological progress has increased productivity and incomes in the overall economy; however, higher incomes have not drastically reduced the number of hours worked. Instead, higher incomes have led to higher demand for goods and, consequently, higher demand for labor. As a result, workers who have lost jobs in one industry have typically found jobs in others, although for many of them this took time and some of them, like the Luddites, have ended up with lower wages in their new jobs. In developed economies like the United States, employees now work about 20 percent fewer hours per day than they did when Keynes wrote his essay in 1930, a smaller decline than Keynes predicted.[4]

However, many recent technological developments have rekindled the debate surrounding Keynes' forecasts. A new wave of digital technologies, robots, and advances in artificial intelligence is threatening millions of jobs. Consider driverless taxis and trucks, which are already in the late stages of development and are now in a testing phase. Many commentators fear that such new technologies will create technological unemployment. Should we dismiss these fears as the newest embodiment of the Luddites' spirit? Can we be certain that, just like in the past, new jobs will be created to replace those that have been automated and taken over by machines? Only time will tell, and, though history is a useful guide, there is no guarantee that the future will mirror the past.

Recent research by one of us (Daron Acemoglu) and Pascual Restrepo shows that the introduction of industrial robots *has* had a significant impact on employment.[5] Their estimates suggest that every new industrial robot reduces total employment by about five workers. Though that number sounds large, so far the effect of robots on the U.S. labor market has not been sizable, because there are still relatively few industrial robots deployed in firms. For example, according to their estimates, U.S. employment declined by only 0.5 percent between 1990 and 2007 because of robots. As employers increase the number of robots on the factory floor (and in the service sector), the impact on employment may amplify, but, as has been our experience over the past two centuries, new types of jobs might be created, providing new opportunities for those who are dislocated by technological unemployment.

Exhibit 9.9 Labor Supply and Labor Demand in a Market with a Minimum Wage

When the minimum wage (w) is above the market-clearing wage (w*), the quantity of labor supplied, Q_S, exceeds the quantity of labor demanded, Q_D, creating unemployment (quantity of labor supplied minus quantity of labor demanded). The quantity of labor demanded, Q_D, which is also the quantity of labor employed, is given by the point on the labor demand curve that intersects with the horizontal minimum wage line.

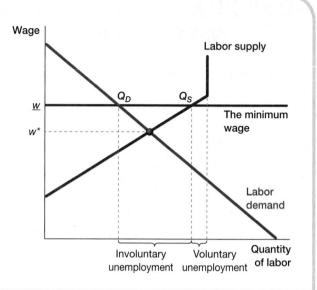

with a line beneath it to signify that the minimum wage is a wage floor: w. The point where the horizontal minimum wage line intersects with the labor demand curve determines the quantity of labor demanded, Q_D, which, in this situation, is also the quantity of labor employed. Because the minimum wage w is above the market-clearing wage w*, the quantity of labor demanded by employers is less than the quantity of labor supplied by workers, Q_S. Consequently, in this minimum-wage equilibrium, some workers—represented by the gap between the quantity supplied and the quantity demanded at w—aren't able to find jobs. These unemployed workers are willing to work at the going wage w and would even be willing to work at wages lower than w. The minimum wage legislation prevents employers from hiring these unemployed workers at wages that would equalize the quantity of labor supplied and the quantity of labor demanded. Economists sometimes refer to these workers as *involuntarily unemployed,* to contrast them with those who are *voluntarily unemployed.* In Exhibit 9.9, we can see both involuntary and voluntary unemployment: those whose opportunity cost of labor is below w, and who would thus be happy to work at this prevailing wage, are involuntarily unemployed; those who would have been happy to work only at a wage above w and who are therefore choosing not to work at the prevailing wage are voluntarily unemployed.

Finally, we want to emphasize that we are referring to the intersection of the labor demand curve with the binding minimum wage as the "equilibrium," since this is the point that informs us about both the prevailing wage (which is the minimum wage, w, in this example) and the quantity of labor transacted in the market. This equilibrium should be distinguished from the competitive labor market equilibrium, which arises when the market wage is allowed to be the wage at which the labor supply curve and the labor demand curve intersect.

Minimum wage laws are an example of a policy that creates winners and losers. The winners are the workers who get jobs at wages above the wage that equates the quantity of labor supplied and the quantity of labor demanded. The losers are the firms that have to pay the higher wage and the unemployed who would like to work but can't find a job at the prevailing wage w. The costs and benefits of the minimum wage are actively debated, with economists divided on the question of whether the United States should raise its minimum wage.

The minimum wage produces structural, involuntary unemployment, but it cannot be the only cause of unemployment. For example, in January 2016, there were 1.3 million college graduates who were unemployed. The median hourly wage for a college graduate was $28.24 per hour in 2015, four times the level of the minimum wage. Because almost all college graduates are paid far more than the minimum wage, it is not the minimum wage that prevents the labor market for college graduates from clearing.

In the overall workforce, including all education levels, only 1 percent of workers are paid the minimum wage. Accordingly, the impact of the minimum wage on the labor market is modest. The minimum wage does prevent the market for some types of low-skilled workers from clearing but has little impact on the general labor market.

Labor Unions and Collective Bargaining

Another source of wage rigidity is **collective bargaining**, which refers to the contract negotiations that take place between firms and labor unions. A labor union is an organization of workers that advocates for better working conditions, pay, and benefits for its members. Unions use the threat of going on strike—a mass work stoppage—as a bargaining chip in these negotiations. Collective bargaining often leads to equilibrium wages and benefits that are greater than what workers would have received under the market-clearing wage. Collective bargaining has the same effect on unemployment as the minimum wage laws that we analyzed in Exhibit 9.9. If they can keep the equilibrium wage above the market-clearing wage, unions can cause the quantity of labor supplied to be greater than the quantity of labor demanded, thus creating structural unemployment. Through such collective bargaining, unions benefit their members but make it difficult for non-members to find work.

However, just like the minimum wage, collective bargaining is unlikely to be the most important factor causing wage rigidity in the U.S. labor market because union membership is relatively low in the United States. For example, in 2013, 10.8 percent of employed workers in the United States were members of labor unions. Unions play a more important role in most other countries. For example, in Italy, in 2013, 37.3 percent of employed workers were members of labor unions.

Efficiency Wages

In 1914, Henry Ford, founder of the Ford Motor Company, seemed to go bonkers. Out of the blue, Ford increased the daily wage of most of his employees from $2.34 to $5.00. Why would a profit-maximizing employer double his employees' pay without any external pressure to do so?

Ford explained the wage of $5 per day as an act of self-interest. There was "no charity in any way involved," he said. "We wanted to pay these wages so that the business would be on a lasting foundation. We were building for the future."

In a frictionless, competitive labor market, paying an above-market wage (or above the wage that workers would accept) would not be optimal for a firm—in other words, it would not maximize the firm's profits. In such a "perfect" market, the firm knows everything about its workers and observes everything that they do at work. In this idealized environment, there is no need to pay workers more than the market wage to obtain their labor. But in actual markets, where workers can shirk (slack off) on the job, paying *more* than the going wage can have benefits for the firm. Ford's wage premium is an example of what economists call **efficiency wages**. By paying wages above the wage that workers were willing to accept (and in fact above the market wage), Ford was able to increase the productivity and profitability of his company.

Efficiency wages increase productivity and firm profitability for a number of reasons. First, efficiency wages reduce worker turnover. Working on an assembly line is monotonous, causing a relatively high level of turnover. Recruiting and training new workers is costly to the company. If workers are paid more than the prevailing market wage by their employer, they are more motivated to keep their job, because they would face lower wages if they tried to find a job elsewhere. Second, the fear of losing a high-paying job motivates employees to work harder than they otherwise would, increasing their hourly output. Third, some employees are grateful for an above-market wage, leading them to reciprocate this apparent generosity by working harder—another boost to their hourly output. Finally, efficiency wages also improve the quality of the pool of workers who apply for a job in the first place.

If efficiency wages increase productivity, employers like Henry Ford might find it profitable to pay a higher wage than the market-clearing wage. Like minimum wage laws and collective bargaining, this results in a form of wage rigidity. As before, this will cause the quantity of labor supplied to be greater than the quantity of labor demanded, leading to structural unemployment, just as we saw in Exhibit 9.9. One difference is worth noting, however. The minimum wage and collective bargaining force employers to pay a wage above the

In October 2010, striking teachers, postal workers, and transport workers protested the French government's proposal to raise the retirement age from 60 to 62.

Collective bargaining refers to contract negotiations between firms and labor unions.

Efficiency wages are wages above the lowest pay that workers would accept; employers use them to increase motivation and productivity.

CHOICE & CONSEQUENCE

Minimum Wage Laws and Employment

In April 2016, New York State's governor signed legislation that will slowly phase in a $15 minimum wage—more than twice as high as the federal minimum at the time. The state of California and the city of Seattle have adopted similar legislation. Some politicians, notably the 2016 Democratic primary candidate Senator Bernie Sanders, want more: a *national* (or "federal") minimum wage of $15. Over time, the federal minimum wage has increased to account for inflation and improvements in standards of living: since the Fair Labor Standards Act established a minimum wage of $0.25 in 1938, Congress has raised the amount 22 times, to $7.25 in 2009.

In the early 2010s, congressional attempts to raise the federal minimum to $10.10 failed. The main objection was the negative effects of higher minimum wages on employment, consistent with the analysis in Exhibit 9.9.

The data, however, tell a more nuanced story. The evidence collected by economists David Card and Alan Krueger indicate a very small, perhaps even a negligible, impact of the minimum wage increases of the 1980s and early 1990s on employment.[6] Most famously, they took advantage of a New Jersey minimum wage increase in 1992 from $4.25 per hour to $5.05 per hour to examine how fast food restaurants in the state responded, compared to comparable restaurants in bordering Pennsylvania (which did not have any change in its minimum wage).[7]

A $15.00 minimum wage, however, is unprecedented, and basic economic reasoning suggests caution when increasing the minimum wage to such levels—even Alan Krueger echoed this point in an editorial in the *New York Times*.[8] The minimum wage levels studied by Card and Krueger were relatively low. For example, in 1992, when New Jersey increased its minimum wage to $5.05 per hour, the average wage in the U.S. economy was $9.79, and only 7 percent of workers in New Jersey had hourly wages below $5.05 per hour and thus were directly affected by the minimum wage increase. To understand how such a low minimum wage affects employment, in Exhibit 9.10 we distinguish between the labor market for two types of workers,

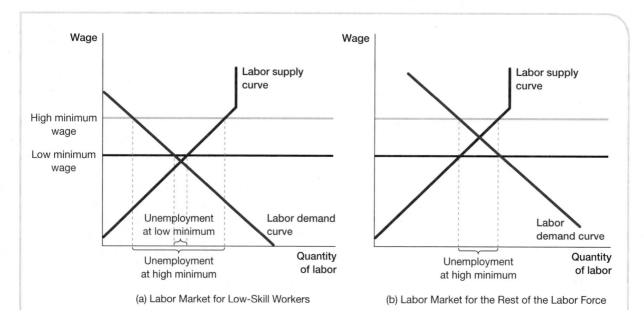

(a) Labor Market for Low-Skill Workers

(b) Labor Market for the Rest of the Labor Force

Exhibit 9.10 Effects of a Minimum Wage on the Labor Market for Workers

Panel (a) depicts the labor market for low-skill workers, while panel (b) shows the labor market for the rest of the labor force. Note that the labor demand curve is shifted to the right in panel (b). A low minimum wage (the horizontal black line) causes involuntary unemployment among low-skill workers in panel (a), but a low minimum wage is *below* the market clearing wage in panel (b) and thus does not cause any unemployment in panel (b). A high minimum wage (the horizontal green line) is above the market clearing wage in both panels and causes involuntary unemployment among both low-skill workers (panel a) and the rest of the labor force (panel b).

those with the lower earning potential ("low-skilled workers" depicted in panel (a)) and the rest of workers in the economy (panel (b)). The exhibit shows that a low minimum wage has a small effect on low-skilled workers (panel (a)) and no effect on the rest of the labor force (panel (b)).

The impact of a $15 minimum wage, however, might be very different from what occurred with the introduction of a $5.05 minimum wage in 1992. A $15 minimum wage would affect 38 percent of U.S. workers today. In terms of Exhibit 9.10, we see that a high minimum wage (the horizontal green line) impacts both the low-skilled workers (panel (a)) and the rest of the workforce (panel (b)) and thus would cause more negative consequences for employment than a low minimum wage.

market-clearing wage level, whereas with efficiency wages, the equilibrium wage is above the market-clearing level because profit-maximizing firms prefer to pay such wages.

Downward Wage Rigidity

Downward wage rigidity arises when workers resist a cut in their wage.

Another type of wage rigidity results from the fact that workers are highly averse to reductions in their wage, resulting in what economists call **downward wage rigidity**. Cuts in the wage hurt worker morale and lower productivity. As a result, many firms would rather fire workers than cut their wages. Typically, only firms on the brink of bankruptcy attempt to talk their workers into accepting wage reductions.

Downward wage rigidity, like the other forms of wage rigidity we have studied so far, causes wages to remain above the market-clearing level, leading to structural unemployment. To see this, consider the following scenario, depicted in panel (a) of Exhibit 9.11. Assume that the labor market begins in a competitive equilibrium with no unemployment (at the point labeled E_1). Next, imagine that the labor demand curve shifts to the left, for example, because there are new robots replacing workers at lower

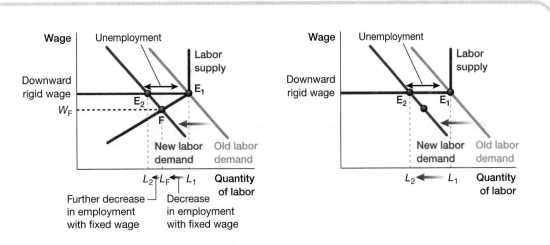

Exhibit 9.11 Shifts in Labor Demand Affect Equilibrium in the Labor Market

With flexible wages, a shift to the left in the labor demand curve reduces the equilibrium wage and employment (the economy moves from point E_1 to point F in panel a). With a downward rigid wage, the same leftward shift has a larger impact on employment (the economy moves from point E_1 to point E_2). Employment now falls all the way to L_2 instead of L_F, because none of the impact of the leftward shift in the labor demand curve is absorbed by the wage, which remains at its original (rigid) level. Moreover, downward wage rigidity causes unemployment: because the wage does not change, the quantity of labor supplied remains the same, but the quantity of labor demanded falls to L_2. The gap between the quantity of labor supplied and the quantity of labor demanded (at the rigid wage) corresponds to unemployment. Panel (b) depicts the same consequences of a downward rigid wage. However, in panel (b) we draw the labor supply curve so it is equal to the downward rigid wage until the original labor supply curve rises above the downward rigid wage. We draw the labor supply curve with this horizontal segment to simplify analysis when there is a downward rigid wage.

Exhibit 9.12 The Distribution of Wage Increases at One Large Firm in 2008

The vertical height of each bar represents the fraction of all workers with a particular pay increase. The pay increase can be read off the horizontal axis. At this firm, only forty-six workers out of about 15,000 experienced a pay cut in 2008. These forty-six workers are plotted in the exhibit, but the bars to the left of zero are too small to be seen. Over 50 percent of the workers experienced a pay freeze (corresponding to the bar at 0 percent).

Source: Nathan Hipsman, "Downward Nominal Wage Rigidity: A Double-Density Model," Harvard University Working Paper, Cambridge, MA, 2012.

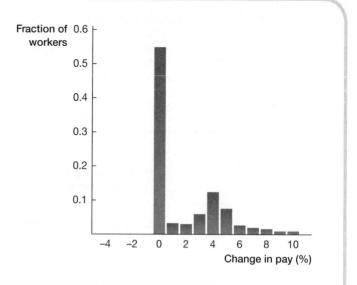

cost or because there are inexpensive imports from another country (like imports from China, which we'll discuss below).

When the wage is flexible, the leftward shift in labor demand moves the market to a new equilibrium (point F) in which the equilibrium wage is w_F, as shown in Exhibit 9.11, and the quantity of labor demanded falls to L_F. The exhibit also shows that at this new equilibrium, the quantity of labor supplied is equal to the quantity of labor demanded and so unemployment is still equal to zero.

However, when the wage is rigid, it won't fall to its market-clearing level and will instead stay at its initial level, which is labeled with a horizontal line in panel (a) of Exhibit 9.11: the "downward rigid wage." This downward wage rigidity causes the quantity of labor supplied, which is still at L_1, to be greater than the quantity of labor demanded, which has now fallen to L_2, thus leading to structural unemployment, as shown in the exhibit.

Panel (b) in Exhibit 9.11 provides a simplified version of panel (a). The labor market functions as if the labor supply curve were equal to the downward rigid wage until the point where the original labor supply curve rises above the downward rigid wage. Because a downward rigid wage has the effect of preventing the nominal wage from falling, we have redrawn the labor supply curve in panel (b) so it begins as a horizontal line at the downward rigid wage. We use this effective labor supply curve to simplify analysis of the labor market equilibrium.

The effect of downward wage rigidity can be seen in Exhibit 9.12, which shows the wage growth of workers in a large company for 2008, right in the middle of the 2007–2009 recession.[9] Each bar shows the fraction of workers whose wage grew by the percentage depicted on the horizontal axis. We see a large bulge in the distribution at zero, meaning that wages were frozen instead of being cut. Wage cuts were so infrequent (only 46 out of 15,000 employees) that they are not even visible on the graph. Although the extent of downward wage rigidity does vary from company to company and industry to industry, this type of rigidity is quite pervasive throughout labor markets and can have a significant effect on unemployment, especially during recessions, as we will see in greater detail in Chapter 12.

9.5 Cyclical Unemployment and the Natural Rate of Unemployment

As Exhibit 9.2 documents, unemployment is highly cyclical, increasing during recessions and declining during economic expansions. The labor market diagram helps us analyze this cyclical behavior. As noted earlier, the U.S. economy always has some

Exhibit 9.13 Cyclical Variation in the Rate of Unemployment

This exhibit demonstrates how expansions and downturns affect unemployment when there is a downward rigid wage. When the economy is at the natural rate of unemployment, the labor demand curve is represented by the light blue line and the level of unemployment is $L_{FE} - L_0$. FE stands for Full Employment. During a recession, the labor demand curve shifts to the left, decreasing employment and increasing unemployment to $L_{FE} - L_R$; during an economic boom, the labor demand curve shifts to the right, increasing employment and decreasing unemployment to $L_{FE} - L_B$.

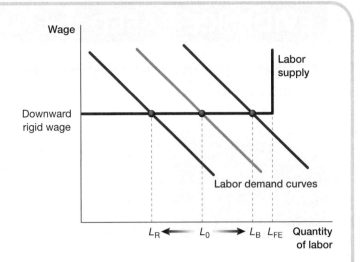

The natural rate of unemployment is the rate around which the actual rate of unemployment fluctuates.

Cyclical unemployment is the deviation of the actual unemployment rate from the natural rate of unemployment.

unemployment. In addition, the unemployment rate fluctuates considerably, as shown in Exhibit 9.2. To distinguish the "normal" rate of unemployment from fluctuations around that normal rate, economists use the concept of the *natural rate of unemployment*. The **natural rate of unemployment** is the rate around which the actual rate of unemployment fluctuates.

Exhibit 9.13 illustrates how employment fluctuations happen in an economy with downward wage rigidity. In this analysis we assume that the economy starts with the middle labor demand curve. We have drawn this exhibit to reflect pre-existing (structural) unemployment at this middle/starting labor demand curve. The initial level of unemployment is $L_{FE} - L_0$.

During a recession (cyclical downturn), the labor demand curve will shift to the left, and unemployment will increase to $L_{FE} - L_R$. (We will have much more to say on how labor demand changes cyclically in Chapter 12.) Conversely, during an economic boom (cyclical expansion), the labor demand curve will shift to the right, and unemployment will decrease to $L_{FE} - L_B$. Assume that the "average" unemployment rate coincides with the unemployment rate at the start, when the labor demand curve was in its middle position. We can think of this as the natural rate of unemployment, around which the actual unemployment rate fluctuates as labor demand shifts left and right during the economic cycle.

Cyclical unemployment is defined as the deviation of the unemployment rate from its natural rate. Cyclical unemployment rises in recessions and falls in economic booms.

The natural rate of unemployment includes frictional unemployment, which is a necessary part of any well-functioning labor market. But the natural rate of unemployment also includes *long-term* structural unemployment, which is generally considered to be economically inefficient. Accordingly, the natural rate of unemployment should not be confused with the rate of unemployment that is socially optimal or desirable—so some might say there is nothing "natural" about it. To see this, consider an economy that is subject to a significant level of downward wage rigidity. As Exhibit 9.11 shows, this economy will have a relatively high level of structural unemployment, and this will increase the long-term average rate of unemployment. This is not a desirable state of affairs, because many potential workers who could have been gainfully employed are out of work and are unable to use their labor productively. This example illustrates that the natural rate of unemployment includes some inefficient sources of unemployment.

EVIDENCE-BASED ECONOMICS

Q: What happens to employment and unemployment if local employers go out of business?

From 1990 to 2007, the unemployment rate in Pittsburgh fell by 1.8 percentage points. Pittsburgh had both good and bad economic news during this period, but one particularly lucky factor was that economic activity in Pittsburgh was concentrated in industries that were not highly exposed to Chinese imports. Pittsburgh specialized in industries such as paper, print, and metal products that had "low exposure" to competition from Chinese imports, meaning that the sectors experienced relatively slow growth of Chinese imports in the entire United States.

The experience of the Raleigh-Durham area in North Carolina, shown in a map together with Pittsburgh (Exhibit 9.14), was very different between 1990 and 2007. In the Raleigh-Durham area, unemployment *increased* by 1.9 percentage points. In addition, many workers in this area are now out of the labor force, because they have stopped looking for jobs entirely. One factor contributing to Raleigh-Durham's weakening labor market was its specialization in industries that have "high exposure" to competition from Chinese imports, such as textiles and apparel, electrical products, and computers.

By comparing *hundreds* of regions with different levels of exposure to Chinese imports (of which Pittsburgh and Raleigh-Durham are just two examples), economists David Autor, David Dorn, and Gordon Hanson were able to identify leftward shifts in labor demand caused by high exposure to Chinese imports, similar to the shift depicted in Exhibit 9.11.[10] Their analysis shows that high-exposure communities experienced sharper declines in manufacturing employment than low-exposure communities. The rate of unemployment also rose more in the areas with high exposure than in those with low exposure.

The study confirms the model of labor market analysis depicted in Exhibit 9.11, in which a leftward shift in the labor demand curve, combined with downward wage

Exhibit 9.14 A Tale of Two Cities

Pittsburgh and Raleigh-Durham have had very different changes in their local unemployment rate between 1990 and 2007. Pittsburgh saw its unemployment rate decline from 7.3 percent to 5.5 percent, while Raleigh-Durham experienced an increase in its unemployment rate from 4.0 percent to 5.9 percent. This difference arose at least partially because Raleigh-Durham has had high exposure to Chinese imports, meaning that it specialized in manufacturing industries that experienced relatively rapid growth in competition from Chinese imports. In contrast, Pittsburgh has had relatively low exposure to Chinese imports.

rigidity, reduces the number of jobs and increases the rate of unemployment. Consistent with the model's predictions about wage rigidity, the authors found no decline in manufacturing wages despite the leftward shifts in labor demand. It is therefore likely that some of the higher unemployment in high-exposure areas was due to wage rigidity, as reflected in Exhibit 9.11. However, the authors also find a significant decline in non-manufacturing wages in high-exposure areas, implying that wage rigidity only applies to a worker's existing job and does not carry over to the new jobs that unemployed workers find. Laid-off manufacturing workers are offered lower wages when they search for new jobs, and they are willing to accept those lower wages to find work.

This analysis might lead you to conclude that the United States should ban Chinese imports to increase U.S. employment, but doing so would generate far more problems than it would solve. Chinese imports are beneficial to most U.S. households, which enjoy the lower prices of the imported goods. Nevertheless, it is true that some domestic workers lose their jobs because of international trade, and much of the debate about trade revolves around the personal and economic dislocation caused by these job losses and the policies that can be used to mitigate these costs. We return to these important issues in Chapters 14 and 15, where we discuss fully the effects of international trade.

Question	Answer	Data	Caveat
What happens to employment and unemployment if local employers go out of business?	Communities with a high level of exposure to competition from Chinese imports between 1990 and 2007 experienced an increase in the local rate of unemployment relative to communities with a low level of exposure to competition from Chinese imports.	Community-level data on employment, unemployment, and industry composition. National U.S. data on industry-by-industry growth in Chinese imports. The study covers the period from 1990 to 2007.	Many factors other than competition from Chinese firms contribute to movements in unemployment rates.

Summary

- Potential workers are defined as the civilian non-institutional population aged 16 and older. Those holding a paid full-time or part-time job are classified as employed, while those without a paid job who have actively looked for work in the prior 4 weeks and are currently available for work are unemployed. Potential workers who are employed and unemployed make up the labor force, while the rest of the potential workers are classified as out of the labor force. The unemployment rate is the percentage of the labor force that is unemployed.

- The unemployment rate fluctuates significantly over time. It is higher during and in the immediate aftermath of recessions.

- Employment is determined by labor demand and labor supply. The labor demand curve is downward-sloping because of the diminishing marginal product of labor and profit maximization by firms. In contrast, the labor supply curve tends to be upward-sloping, because higher wages generally encourage workers to supply more hours to the labor market.

- The competitive labor market equilibrium is given by the intersection of the labor demand and labor supply curves. The competitive equilibrium wage is also called the market-clearing wage.

- In a competitive labor market equilibrium in which all workers know the market-clearing wage, there will be very little unemployment because every worker willing to work at the market-clearing wage can find a job. Workers who are not willing to work at the market-clearing wage will stop searching and will therefore not be counted as unemployed.

- Frictional unemployment exists because workers need time to learn about the condition of the labor market and search for a job that suits them. Even in a healthy labor market, there will always be some unemployed workers in the process of changing jobs, or finding a new job after losing their previous one, or finding their first job after entry into the labor market.

- Structural unemployment results when the market wage is above the market-clearing level, causing the quantity of labor supplied to be greater than the quantity of labor demanded. This is often referred to as wage rigidity. It can result from institutional features of the labor market like minimum wage legislation or collective bargaining. More importantly, it can result from efficiency wages or from downward wage rigidity. Efficiency wages arise when employers pay wages higher than the market-clearing wage to increase worker productivity. Downward wage rigidity arises because of the unwillingness of workers to accept wage cuts, which prevents wages from immediately falling in response to a leftward shift of the labor demand curve.

- The most important cause of unemployment fluctuations is a shifting labor demand curve. When wages are flexible, a shift to the left of the labor demand curve reduces both employment and wages but does not increase unemployment because the labor market clears. When wages are rigid, the same leftward shift creates a larger decline in employment because the wage does not decline and, as a result, unemployment increases.

- The natural rate of unemployment is the long-term average rate of unemployment. Cyclical unemployment is the difference between the current rate of unemployment and the natural rate of unemployment. Cyclical unemployment is positive in recessions and negative in economic booms.

Key Terms

Potential workers *p. 203*
Employed *p. 204*
Unemployed *p. 204*
Labor force *p. 204*
Unemployment rate *p. 204*
Labor force participation rate
  p. 204

Value of the marginal product of labor
  p. 206
Labor demand curve *p. 208*
Labor supply curve *p. 209*
Market-clearing wage *p. 212*
Job search *p. 214*
Frictional unemployment *p. 214*

Wage rigidity *p. 214*
Structural unemployment *p. 214*
Collective bargaining *p. 217*
Efficiency wages *p. 217*
Downward wage rigidity *p. 219*
Natural rate of unemployment *p. 221*
Cyclical unemployment *p. 221*

Questions

All questions are available in MyEconLab *for practice and instructor assignment.*

1. Unemployment statistics are measured and released by the Bureau of Labor Statistics, a division of the U.S. Department of Labor.

   a. When does the Bureau of Labor Statistics officially classify a person as being employed? When are potential workers classified as being unemployed?

   b. What do the following terms mean and how are they calculated?

      i. The unemployment rate

      ii. The labor force participation rate

2. Explain whether each of these individuals will be counted as a part of the labor force.

   a. Jane is working full-time toward a Ph.D. in philosophy but volunteers at nursing homes during her spare weekends.

   b. Kristen left her full-time job as a journalist to spend more time with her kids and now makes some income working part-time for a children's magazine.

   c. In the past four weeks, Harry did not respond to a call from a firm seeking to interview him for a job opening. But he recently applied for another job that he feels will better suit his qualifications.

3. Consider Exhibit 9.2. What were the two highest rates of unemployment since 1948? When did they occur?

4. What could explain why unemployment is lower among workers with a relatively higher level of education?

5. What is the value of the marginal product of labor? Explain how it is computed with an example.

6. List two factors that can cause a shift in the labor demand curve. Explain why a change in each factor can lead to a shift of the curve.

7. Why does the labor supply curve slope upward, and what can cause the labor supply curve to shift?

8. Would a country with a healthy economy have a zero unemployment rate?

9. What is meant by job search? How does it lead to frictional unemployment?

10. What is the difference between frictional and structural unemployment?

11. Sometimes new technology in production reduces the time that a worker takes to complete a task. Technological innovations can also completely replace a factory worker. Does this mean that technological progress will lead to large-scale unemployment? Explain your answer.

12. What is wage rigidity? List and explain two factors that can increase wage rigidity in the labor market.

Problems

All problems are available in MyEconLab *for practice and instructor assignment.*

1. The following table shows the annual averages of the employment level, unemployment level, and the labor force participation rate in the United States in the years from 2001 to 2011. Use the given data to complete the table and answer the following questions. (*Note*: Adult population refers to individuals 16 years and over, not in the military, and not institutionalized. All rates are in percent.)

Year	Number Unemployed (in thousands)	Number Employed (in thousands)	Labor Force Participation Rate	Employment Rate	Unemployment Rate	Labor Force	Adult Population
2001	6,830,000	136,939,000	66.8%				
2002	8,375,000	136,481,000	66.6%				
2003	8,770,000	137,729,000	66.2%				
2004	8,140,000	139,240,000	66.0%				
2005	7,579,000	141,710,000	66.0%				
2006	6,991,000	144,418,000	66.2%				
2007	7,073,000	146,050,000	66.0%				
2008	8,951,000	145,370,000	66.0%				
2009	14,301,000	139,888,000	65.4%				
2010	14,815,000	139,070,000	64.7%				
2011	13,743,000	139,873,000	64.1%				

Source: Annual averages based on data from the Bureau of Labor Statistics (Series: LNS12000000, LNS11300000, LNS13000000).

a. In which year did the economy witness the sharpest change in the unemployment rate? What could possibly explain this?

b. Use the data on the size of the labor force and potential workers to compute the percentage of adults out of the labor force for the year 2002. Verify that your calculation is equal to one minus the labor force participation rate.

c. What general trends do you observe in the data?

2. In April 2012, The *Bazanian Daily*, a leading newspaper in the country of Bazania, carried a report titled "20,000 Jobs Added in the Last Quarter; Unemployment Rate Shoots up from 5 Percent to 6.7 Percent." How could the unemployment rate in Bazania increase even when new jobs were created?

3. A new study suggests that technology might provide improved leisure options, like video games, to potential workers, and that young men with low levels of education are increasingly staying home and playing video games instead of working.[11] There has also been a concurrent decline in the labor force participation of young men with low levels of education.

a. Could the rapid rise in video game playing be a cause of the decreased labor force participation of low-education young men? What other factors might explain these two simultaneous trends? In your response, you should use the labor market equilibrium figure (e.g., Exhibit 9.8) and also utilize the concepts of voluntary and involuntary unemployment.

b. The authors of this new study also find that these young men, as a group, have experienced an increase in self-reported happiness through the 2000s (according to the General Social Survey). How does this factor into your explanations in part a?

4. Suppose Die Cast Aluminum Co. is a subcontractor for the auto industry and makes specialized auto parts. There is a bracket it manufactures that it sells for $1.50. The following table shows the number of brackets that can be produced from a given number of labor hours. Assume that the company cannot hire labor for a fraction of an hour.

Hours of Labor	Number of Brackets Manufactured
0	0
1	50
2	90
3	120
4	140
5	150
6	155
7	157

a. Find the marginal product (in brackets), and the value of the marginal product (in dollars), of each hour of labor.

b. If the wage paid to workers in Die Cast's plant is $25 per hour, how many hours of labor should the firm employ? How many hours will be employed if the wage increases to $35 per hour? Explain.

c. How many hours will be employed if the wage is $35 per hour, but the price of a bracket declines to $1?

5. In a recent study for the National Bureau of Economic Research, four researchers looked at the effect of generous unemployment benefits on the local unemployment rate. They compared the unemployment situation in adjoining counties, which happened to lie in two different states with different laws regarding the amount and duration of unemployment benefits. The authors of the study found that the unemployment rate "rises dramatically in the border counties belonging to the states that expanded unemployment benefit duration" during the Great Recession. Why might this be so?[12]

6. Every month, statistics on employment and unemployment are compiled by the Bureau of Labor Statistics.

a. The unemployed worker whose frustration was discussed at the beginning of Section 9.1 had been unemployed for 17 months. Go to www.bls.gov and consult Table A-12. Find the average (mean) duration of unemployment (seasonally adjusted) in the most recent month. Based on what you find, is 17 months higher or lower than average?

b. List some possible reasons for the quoted worker's unemployment that would make her joblessness qualify as frictional unemployment. List reasons that would fall in the category of structural unemployment.

7. In recent years, countries around the world have faced a youth unemployment crisis. According to a report by the International Labour Organization, the global youth unemployment rate in 2016 was 2.9 times higher than the global adult rate.[13]

a. In Exhibit 9.5, we compared the curves for two *types* of labor, low-skill and high-skill. Suppose that the curves show the labor market for workers over the age of 22, with a minimum wage of $10. Use new charts to demonstrate two ways in which the youth labor market might feature greater structural unemployment at the same minimum wage.

b. How would you distinguish between the two different explanations you proposed in part a: what kind of data would you need to test these different explanations?

c. Some countries, like the UK, have attempted to reduce youth unemployment by implementing a lower minimum wage for workers under the age of 20. Discuss how this might influence youth unemployment, linking your answer to the two explanations discussed in parts a and b as well as to the different types of unemployment discussed in this chapter. Do you think efforts to reduce youth unemployment by setting lower minimum wages for young workers is likely to be effective?

8. The following graph shows the demand for and supply of labor in a market with a minimum wage set at $8 per hour. Use the graph to answer the following questions.

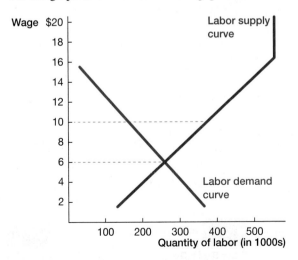

a. How many workers will be unemployed due to the minimum wage? What kind of unemployment is this?

b. What would happen to the quantity of labor demanded and supplied if the minimum wage were less than $6?

c. Who are the winners and the losers when the minimum wage is $10?

d. In the United States, does minimum wage legislation have a significant impact on unemployment in the overall labor force? Why or why not?

9. The Earned Income Tax Credit (EITC) provides low-income workers with a refundable tax credit (reducing the tax obligations of the worker). The recipient must have a job, and the amount of the credit depends on marital status, income, and number of children. How might an expansion of this policy compare to an increase in the minimum wage in terms of the impact on labor markets? What might be potential downsides of the EITC?

10. According to salary.com, the average salary for a software engineer level III (a higher-level position in software design and implementation) in the Silicon Valley area of California is $120,086. However, Google pays its level III software engineers an average salary of $132,869. Explain why Google would pay a salary higher than the equilibrium salary for equivalent positions in the same area.

11. The following figure shows the demand and supply curves in the market for workers (called "baristas") in Starbucks coffee shops. The hourly wage in this market has been fixed at $7.25 and cannot be changed.

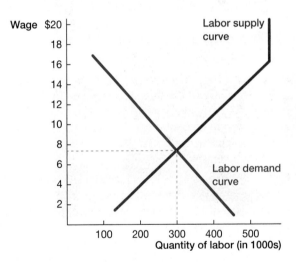

a. Suppose that, due to concerns about the high number of calories in many Starbucks drinks, the demand for Starbucks products declines. Use a graph to explain what will happen to employment in the market for baristas.

b. Now suppose the wage is flexible. How would your answer to part (a) change?

12. The period from 2007 to 2009 was a time of economic contraction that some have called the "Great Recession." During periods of recession, most firms experience a decline in demand for their product. All other things being equal, macroeconomic theory predicts that the wage of most workers should decline in recessionary periods. However, this was not the case in the 2007–2009 recession, or during many other economic downturns throughout recent history. Based on the discussion in the chapter, explain why this might be so, and what the implications are for unemployment.

10 Credit Markets

How often do banks fail?

Financial service companies, such as banks, insurance companies, and investment companies, want you to believe that they are rock-solid. They try to convey that message with stone pillars and marble lobbies. Sometimes they choose names that imply indestructibility, like Northern Rock, Blackrock, and Blackstone. Prudential, a leading insurance company, nicknamed itself "The Rock" and adopted the Rock of Gibraltar, a mountain fortress, as its corporate symbol. Those are encouraging words, but are financial institutions really impregnable?

CHAPTER **OUTLINE**

10.1 What Is the Credit Market?

You've got your first business idea, and you can't think about much else. You are going to be the founder and CEO (chief executive officer) of your own company! OK. Catch your breath. And get down to work. Most new businesses fail within 5 years, and you are going to do everything that you can to avoid becoming one of those casualties.

You want to create a taxi and limo company that uses only vehicles that are 100 percent battery powered, just the sort of thing you reckon would appeal to your fellow New Yorkers. You call your new firm BatteryPark. Everyone you know loves the idea and promises to use your start-up if you manage to get it off the ground. You've even been able to convince numerous local companies to sign up for your service for their employees and clients.

Now you need to raise money to buy or rent the necessary equipment and buildings: licenses, electric vehicles, battery-charging systems, a reservation office with computers, and a few garages spread around the city so that your taxis can easily get a fresh battery when they run out of juice. You also need to hire staff, train them, and advertise. You figure you need about $500,000 to start your business and quickly reach an efficient scale of operation. That's not a trivial amount by any stretch of the imagination, but you think it's worth taking the risk, considering what you expect to make from your new business.

But how will you raise $500,000? You certainly don't have it in your checking account, and neither do any of your friends. You think of asking your parents and grandparents, but then you imagine how you would feel if your business went bust and a family member lost his or her life savings. So what's the solution?

Borrowers and the Demand for Loans

The good news is that you are not alone in your quest for funds. Every year, hundreds of thousands of entrepreneurs in the United States and millions around the world borrow money to start new businesses. Many, many more businesses that are already in operation also borrow funds to expand their existing operations or simply to pay their bills.

Consumers, too, borrow to purchase big-ticket items like automobiles and houses. Some households borrow to pay their expenses during a temporary period of unemployment. Many people borrow to put themselves or their children through college. Almost everyone who pursues graduate studies in business, law, or medicine borrows to pay some of their bills. We refer to economic agents who borrow funds—including entrepreneurs, home buyers, and medical students—as **debtors**. And the funds that they borrow are referred to as **credit**.

Most businesses and individuals obtain credit from banks, but the credit market is much broader than banks. It includes several non-bank institutions, as well as the market for commercial debt, where well-established, large businesses obtain large loans.

Debtors, or borrowers, are economic agents who borrow funds.

Credit refers to the loans that the debtor receives.

The **interest rate** (also referred to as the **nominal interest rate**), i, is the annual cost of a $1 loan, so $i \times L$ is the annual cost of an $L loan.

Of course, borrowed money is not lent for free. You need to pay *interest*. The original amount of borrowed money is referred to as principal. The **interest rate** is the additional payment—above and beyond the repayment of principal—that a borrower needs to make on a $1 loan (at the end of 1 year). We can also say that the interest rate is the annual cost of a $1 loan.

Let's now scale up that $1 loan into an $L loan. The total interest payment a borrower needs to make for an $L loan is the loan amount multiplied by the interest rate. Put differently, if you borrow $L with a 1-year loan at an annual interest rate of i, at the end of 1 year you pay back the L dollars of principal *plus* $i \times L$ dollars in interest. To distinguish it from the real interest rate, which we define next, we'll also refer to the interest rate, i, as **the nominal interest rate**.

Let's now return to your blockbuster business idea. You have enough confidence in your plans that you would be willing to pay a 10 percent interest rate to get your loan. That means you would be willing to make an annual interest payment of $50,000 to get a $500,000 loan ($0.10 \times \$500,000 = \$50,000$). In fact, you are so confident that you would take the loan even if you had to pay 20 percent interest.

But what if the interest rate were 50 percent? An interest payment of $250,000 per year on a $500,000 loan is quite extreme. At that interest rate, there probably wouldn't be any profit left for you. Perhaps you should scale back your plans and take a smaller loan. Instead of hiring a team of twenty employees, you might want to start with just a handful of coworkers.

And what if the interest rate were 100 percent? Principal plus interest one year later would then be $500,000 + \$500,000 = \$1,000,000$ on a $500,000 loan. That is, you would need to pay back twice as much as you borrowed. If so, it might make sense for you to forget about this new idea altogether. It's hard to imagine that any business could make money if it had to finance itself this way.

In reality, most businesses do not need to pay 50 percent or 100 percent interest rates on loans. We present such cases to explain why a rise in the interest rate causes a fall in the quantity of credit demanded. As the interest rate goes up, fewer firms and individuals are willing to pay the high price to acquire credit.

Real and Nominal Interest Rates

So far, we've neglected to mention the inflation rate—the rate at which prices are increasing in the overall economy. It turns out that the inflation rate has a key role to play in influencing households' and firms' willingness to borrow money. To illustrate why the inflation rate is so important, suppose you borrowed $500,000 at a 10 percent nominal interest rate to finance your battery-powered-limo company. The 10 percent nominal interest rate implies that in 1 year's time you will have to pay back $50,000 on top of the original $500,000, or $550,000 in total. Let's assume that each limo ride generates $50 in net revenue to your firm and the inflation rate is 0 percent per year. Then you will have to book 11,000 limo rides over the next year just to earn enough revenue to pay back your loan and the interest you owe:

$$(\$50 \text{ per ride}) \times (11{,}000 \text{ rides}) = \$550{,}000.$$

Suppose instead that all prices double and your net revenue also doubles from $50 to $100 per ride. Now, you will only need to book 5,500 limo rides to pay back your creditor:

$$(\$100 \text{ per ride}) \times (5{,}500 \text{ rides}) = \$550{,}000.$$

In this example, a doubling of prices made it much easier to pay back what you owe. This example illustrates a general point: the higher the inflation rate is (holding all else equal), the higher the prices will be of the goods and services that firms sell, and the easier it will be to pay back loans at a given nominal rate of interest.

We have seen an example that illustrates why it is important to consider inflation when you think about your ability to repay a loan. In fact, there is a formula that adjusts the nominal interest rate to take account of the effects of inflation. To derive this formula, note that the *nominal interest rate* is the annual growth rate of what you owe on a loan—principal plus interest—in *nominal dollars*. For example, if the nominal interest rate is 10 percent, you owe 10 percent more in nominal dollars at the end of the year than the amount you borrowed at the beginning of the year. The inflation rate is the annual growth rate of the overall price level. To calculate the growth rate of what you owe in *real dollars*—in other words, in inflation-adjusted dollars—you need to subtract the inflation rate from the growth rate of what you owe in nominal dollars. Accordingly, the growth rate of what you owe in real dollars is

$$\text{Nominal interest rate} - \text{Inflation rate} = i - \pi.$$

In this equation, π is the inflation rate. We use the symbol r to represent this inflation-adjusted interest rate:

$$r = i - \pi = \text{Real interest rate}.$$

The real interest rate is the nominal interest rate minus the inflation rate.

Here $r = i - \pi$ is the **real interest rate**, because it adjusts for the effects of inflation. This formula is called the Fisher equation, honoring Irving Fisher (1867–1947), whose research emphasized the distinction between the nominal and real interest rates.[1]

Here is an example of the Fisher equation in action. If the nominal interest rate is 5 percent and the inflation rate is 2 percent, then the *real* interest rate is

$$3\% = 5\% - 2\%.$$

Optimizing economic agents will use the *real* interest rate, r, when thinking about the economic cost of a loan because they want to know how borrowing will generate *real* growth in what they owe. In Chapter 11 we will return to this equation and discuss the role of inflationary expectations in thinking about the real interest rate.

The relationship between the nominal and real interest rates is very similar to the relationship between nominal and real GDP growth, which we discussed in Chapter 5. To turn the nominal GDP growth rate into the real GDP growth rate, we take the nominal GDP growth rate and subtract the inflation rate. Likewise, to convert the nominal interest rate into the real interest rate, we take the nominal interest rate and subtract the inflation rate. Both adjustments are driven by the same economic logic of focusing on the growth of real buying power instead of the growth of nominal dollars. They both take a nominal growth rate—either the growth rate of nominal GDP or the growth rate of what is nominally owed on a loan—and adjust it by subtracting the growth rate of overall prices.

The Credit Demand Curve

The credit demand curve is the schedule that reports the relationship between the quantity of credit demanded and the real interest rate.

Because it is the real interest rate, r, that matters for business and individual decisions, the demand for credit will also be a function of this real interest rate. The **credit demand curve** is the schedule that reports the relationship between the quantity of credit demanded and the real interest rate.

Exhibit 10.1 plots the credit demand curve, with the quantity of credit demanded on the *x*-axis and the real interest rate on the *y*-axis. The credit demand curve slopes downward because the higher the real interest rate is, the lower the quantity of credit demanded will

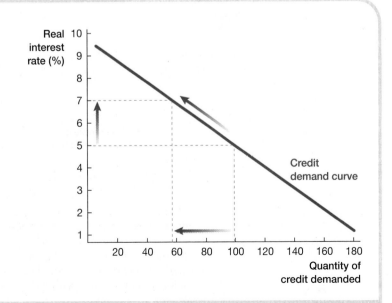

Exhibit 10.1 The Credit Demand Curve

The quantity of credit demanded is plotted on the *x*-axis and the real interest rate is plotted on the *y*-axis. As the real interest rate rises, the quantity of credit demanded falls. This is a movement along the credit demand curve.

be. As BatteryPark's demand for credit illustrates, the higher the interest rate a firm pays to borrow money is, the lower the borrower's profit will be. So, fewer borrowers will be willing to obtain a loan at a higher interest rate. This is conceptually the same as other demand curves: when the price of any good—like carrots or caviar—goes up, consumers tend to buy less of it. Credit works the same way, where the real "price" of credit is the real interest rate. The steepness of the credit demand curve tells us about the sensitivity of the relationship between the real interest rate and the quantity of credit demanded:

1. When the credit demand curve is relatively steep, the quantity of credit demanded doesn't change that much in response to variation in the real interest rate.
2. When the credit demand curve is relatively flat, the quantity of credit demanded is relatively sensitive to variation in the real interest rate.

Having emphasized that the *real* interest rate is the price that appears on the *y*-axis of Exhibit 10.1—you can think of it as the price of borrowing money—it is important to remember that almost all loans are made at a *nominal* interest rate. For example, when you apply for a loan for your limo company or for a mortgage to buy a new house, your bank will quote a nominal interest rate. The same is true for almost all businesses. However, as we have seen, what is relevant for the decisions of an optimizer is the implied real interest rate (which adjusts for the inflation rate). The real interest rate will play a central role in macroeconomic analysis in the next several chapters, especially the real interest rate for long-term borrowing (like 30-year mortgages or 10-year corporate loans). For now, we focus on the relationship between the real interest rate and the demand for credit. We return to the nominal interest rate and its relationship to the real interest rate in Chapter 11.

When using the credit demand curve, it is important to draw a very careful distinction between *movements along* the credit demand curve, as in Exhibit 10.1, and *shifts* of the credit demand curve. You have already encountered this distinction when we first introduced it in Chapter 4, and it still applies here. Exhibit 10.2 illustrates shifting demand curves. Many factors cause the demand curve to shift:

- **Changes in perceived business opportunities for firms.** Businesses borrow to fund their expansions. For example, if an airline like United Airlines notices that more and more travelers are trying to buy plane tickets, then United's demand for airplanes

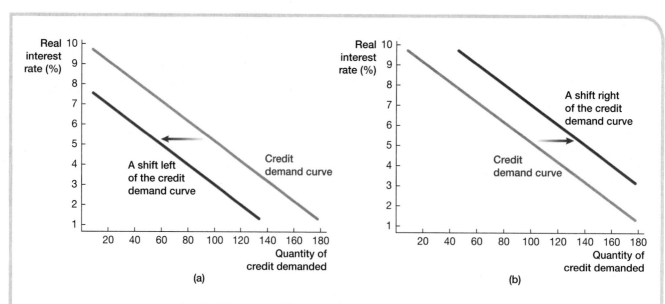

(a)

(b)

Exhibit 10.2 Shifts in the Credit Demand Curve

Changes in perceived business opportunities for firms, changes in household preferences or expectations, and changes in government policy may decrease the quantity of credit demanded for a fixed level of the real interest rate, shifting the credit demand curve to the left (panel (a)). When such changes increase the quantity of credit demanded for a fixed level of the real interest rate, the credit demand curve shifts to the right (panel (b)).

will increase. United will then have to borrow money to buy or lease more planes, so its credit demand curve will shift to the right. If other businesses are experiencing similar trends and increasing their demand for credit at a given real interest rate, then the market (or aggregate) credit demand curve will shift to the right.

- **Changes in household preferences or expectations.** Households borrow for many reasons: buying a home, a car, that gargantuan flat-screen TV, or paying college tuition bills. If household preferences change so that they would like to consume more of these goods and services, they will tend to borrow more. Likewise, they'll be more willing to borrow when they grow more optimistic about the future, for example, because they expect that they'll be in a good position to pay back those loans later. Such changes in household preferences or expectations shift the market credit demand curve to the right. Likewise, if households become more pessimistic about the future, then they will cut their desired borrowing at each interest rate, shifting the market credit demand curve to the left.

- **Changes in government policy.** Government borrowing in the credit market can swing wildly from year to year. For example, in 2007 the U.S. government ran a deficit of $0.4 trillion, which implies that it borrowed $0.4 trillion on the credit market. As the 2007–2009 recession deepened, household and business income fell; this situation in turn reduced tax revenues collected by the government. At the same time, government spending rose both to help out struggling families and to stimulate the contracting economy. By 2009, the government deficit was $1.5 trillion. Holding all else equal, an increase in government borrowing shifts the market credit demand curve to the right. (By 2015, the federal government deficit had shrunk to $0.6 trillion, representing a substantial reversal from 2009.) Finally, the government's tax policies can also shift the credit demand curve. Sometimes the government stimulates investment in physical capital by lowering taxes on profits or explicitly introducing subsidies for physical capital investment. Such tax cuts or subsidies also shift the market credit demand curve to the right.

Saving Decisions

Banks provide credit to businesses and households that wish to borrow. But where do banks obtain the money that they lend out?

> Banks play the role of middlemen, matching savers and borrowers.

Economic agents with excess cash have deposited their money in the bank. Banks use that cash to fund lending. In this sense, banks play the role of middlemen, matching savers and borrowers. Banks aren't the only middlemen in the market for credit. Many different kinds of institutions—we provide a partial list later in this chapter—play the critical role of linking people with savings to people or firms who want to use those savings.

Let's momentarily ignore the institutions that serve as the middlemen and focus on the depositors—in other words, the savers—who are the initial source of the funds that borrowers will ultimately receive. Savers have money that they are willing to lend out, because they prefer to spend it in the future rather than today. Of course, they could keep their money under a mattress or bury it under a palm tree on a deserted island. But buried treasure doesn't pay interest.

The Credit Supply Curve

People and firms with saved money obtain interest by lending the money to a bank or some other financial institution. In some cases, this "lending" takes the form of depositing the money at the bank in return for interest on a savings account. How much money are the savers willing to lend in this way? To answer this question, we need to understand the optimizing behavior of savers.

Saving results from a natural trade-off: people can spend their income on consumption today or can save it for consumption in the future. Because saving requires giving something up—current consumption—people will only save if they get something worthwhile in return. The real interest rate is the compensation that people receive for saving their money, because a dollar saved today has $1 + r$ dollars of purchasing power in a year, where r is

Buried treasure earns no interest. Savings accounts do.

The **credit supply curve** is the schedule that reports the relationship between the quantity of credit supplied and the real interest rate.

the real interest rate. Put differently, the real interest rate is the opportunity cost of current consumption—what you are giving up in terms of future purchasing power. Consequently, a higher real interest rate increases the opportunity cost of current consumption and encourages a higher level of saving.

However, a higher real interest rate might actually *lower* the saving rate. For example, if the real interest rate is relatively high, savings put aside when a person is young will grow relatively quickly, enabling a young worker to save *less* while still achieving a long-run goal of accumulating a retirement nest egg of a certain targeted size. Note, though, that in most situations this negative effect on saving is thought to be weaker than the (positive) opportunity cost effect discussed above. In other words, for most people, a higher real interest rate induces a higher saving rate.

This leads us to conclude that the **credit supply curve**, which is the schedule that reports the relationship between the quantity of credit supplied and the real interest rate, is upward-sloping. Specifically, a higher real interest rate encourages more saving, increasing the amount of funds that banks can lend and thereby increasing the quantity of credit supplied. Exhibit 10.3 plots the credit supply curve.

As before, it's important to carefully distinguish between movements along the credit supply curve, as in Exhibit 10.3, and shifts of the credit supply curve, as in Exhibit 10.4. Movements along the supply curve correspond to savers' response to changes *only* in the real interest rate. Shifts in the credit supply curve are driven by changes in the saving motives of optimizing economic agents, holding fixed the real interest rate.

- **Changes in the saving motives of households.** As discussed above, households save for many reasons—like retirement—but these motives change over time, shifting the credit supply curve. For example, if households start to predict economic hard times ahead, they will save more, because they want to build up a store of wealth to be better prepared. This shifts the credit supply curve to the right. Likewise, demographic trends can change the saving behavior of households. For example, as households approach the age of retirement, their saving rate tends to rise.

CHOICE & CONSEQUENCE

Why Do People Save?

There are five key reasons that people save for the future.

1. First and foremost, people save for retirement. When you retire, you'll only receive a fraction of the income that you received during your working life. For example, the Social Security program pays the typical U.S. household a bit less than half of the household's preretirement income. If you don't want your consumption to fall sharply when you retire, you'll need to save some of your preretirement income. Most advisers recommend that working households in the United States contribute 10 percent to 20 percent of their income to a retirement savings account—for instance, a 401(k) account or an IRA (Individual Retirement Account).

2. People save "for their kids," for example, for their weddings or their future educational investments, like college and postgraduate school. A small fraction of parents also leave significant amounts of money to their kids in their wills. (Such gifts are called *bequests*.)

3. People save to pay for predictable large expenses, like a home purchase, *durable goods* (for instance, a washing machine or a car), and vacations.

4. People save so they can invest in a personal business. Small businesses sometimes can't obtain loans from banks or other funding sources. The bank's loan officer might not believe in your latest, greatest business idea. (If you were a bank's loan officer, would you give a loan to a recent college graduate with a plan to open a new taxi and limo service like BatteryPark?) In cases where outside funding can't be obtained, small business owners must use their own savings to fund their breakthrough ideas.

5. People save for a "rainy day." Your roof might spring a leak and require an expensive repair. You might lose your job. You might have a large medical expense that is not covered by insurance. In situations like these, you'll need a fund that you can lean on to get through hard times.

Exhibit 10.3 The Credit Supply Curve

The quantity of credit supplied is plotted on the x-axis and the real interest rate is plotted on the y-axis. As the real interest rate rises, the quantity of credit supplied increases. This is a movement along the credit supply curve.

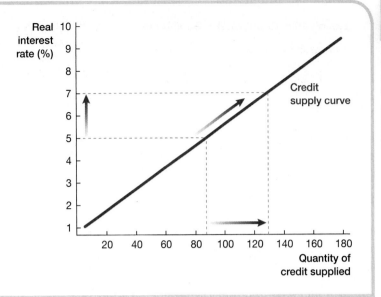

Exhibit 10.4 Shifts in the Credit Supply Curve

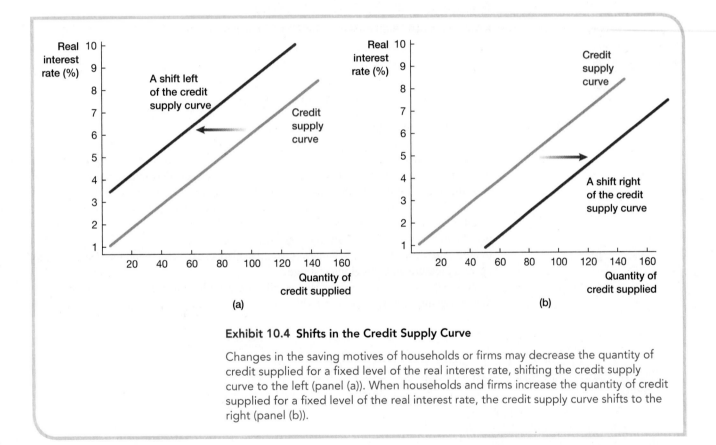

Changes in the saving motives of households or firms may decrease the quantity of credit supplied for a fixed level of the real interest rate, shifting the credit supply curve to the left (panel (a)). When households and firms increase the quantity of credit supplied for a fixed level of the real interest rate, the credit supply curve shifts to the right (panel (b)).

- **Changes in the saving motives of firms.** A firm has positive earnings if its expenses—including the cost of paying employees—are less than the firm's revenue. Some firms pass such earnings back to their stockholders—for example, by paying shareholder dividends. But some firms retain these earnings, depositing them in the firm's bank account and saving them for future investment. The magnitude of such *retained earnings* shifts over time. When firms are nervous about their ability to fund their business activities in the future, they tend to hold on to more retained earnings instead of paying them out as dividends. This shifts the credit supply curve to the right, another form of saving for a rainy day.

Exhibit 10.5 Credit Market Equilibrium

The credit market equilibrium is the real interest rate and quantity of credit at which the credit supply curve and the credit demand curve intersect.

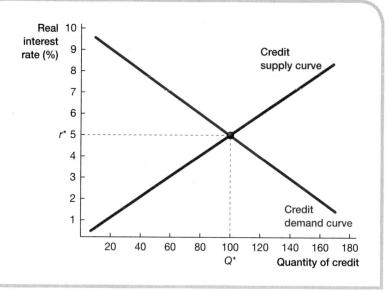

Equilibrium in the Credit Market

The **credit market** is where borrowers obtain funds from savers.

Exhibit 10.5 plots both the credit supply curve and the credit demand curve. This completes our picture of the **credit market**, where borrowers obtain funds from savers. It is sometimes referred to as the *loanable funds market*.

We've simplified the credit market by assuming that different borrowers all have identical risks of defaulting on their loans. In other words, all borrowers have the same risk of not repaying their loans. This simplification implies that there will be a single equilibrium real interest rate in the credit market. (In actual markets, borrowers with different risks of defaulting face different real interest rates to compensate lenders for these differential default risks.)

Like other markets represented by a supply curve and a demand curve, the equilibrium in the credit market is the point at which the curves intersect. This intersection determines both the total quantity of credit in the market (Q^*) and the equilibrium real interest rate (r^*). At the equilibrium real interest rate, the quantity of credit demanded is equal to the quantity of credit supplied. A real interest rate above this level would lead to an excess supply of credit, which would typically put downward pressure on the real interest rate. A real interest rate below the equilibrium level would lead to an excess demand for credit, creating upward pressure on the real interest rate.

To see this in action, consider how a shift in the credit demand curve affects the credit market equilibrium, as shown in Exhibit 10.6. For example, assume that the government

Exhibit 10.6 Effect of a Shift in the Credit Demand Curve on the Real Interest Rate and Credit

A rightward shift in the credit demand curve raises the equilibrium real interest rate and the equilibrium quantity of credit.

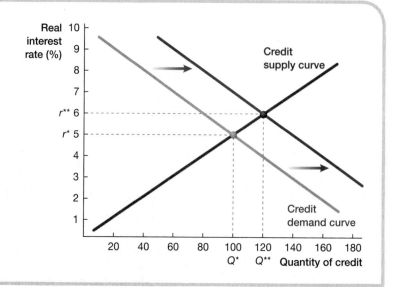

introduces a tax credit for business investment expenditures so that every dollar a firm invests by building plants or purchasing equipment reduces the taxes that it owes by 30 cents. Such a tax credit reduces the cost of investment to firms and thus raises the net benefit—benefits minus costs—of investment. As a consequence, an optimizing firm's willingness to borrow in the credit market (to fund investment in plants and equipment) will increase. Consequently, the credit demand curve shifts to the right. The new equilibrium point has a higher real interest rate (r^{**}) and a greater quantity of credit supplied and demanded (Q^{**}).

Credit Markets and the Efficient Allocation of Resources

Credit markets play an extremely valuable social role. By enabling savers to lend their excess money to borrowers, the credit market improves the allocation of resources in the economy.

There is a simple way of seeing this. Suppose there were no credit market and you had $1,000 you wanted to save for next year. What could you do with it? You could put it in a safe box in your house—"putting the money under your mattress"—in which case you would have just $1,000 next year. With no inflation, you will have received a real interest rate of zero. If there is inflation, say 5 percent, then the real interest rate you will have received is much worse, −5 percent, because inflation eroded 5 percent of the purchasing power of your money.

> By enabling savers to lend their excess money to borrowers, the credit market improves the allocation of resources in the economy.

We can also work through these examples by using the Fisher equation, which gives the formula for the real interest rate: $r = i - \pi$. If you receive no nominal interest (so $i = 0$), then the real interest rate is $r = 0 - \pi$. When the inflation rate is zero (so $\pi = 0$ percent), the real interest rate is $r = 0 - 0 = 0$ percent. When the inflation rate is 5 percent (so $\pi = 5$ percent), then the real interest rate is $r = 0 - 5 = -5$ percent.

You might do better than a 0 percent nominal interest rate by lending your money to your uncle who has some business venture in mind. But unless your uncle happens to be a good businessman, this choice might be worse than the mattress option.

Unknown to you, there could be several borrowers (possibly more reliable than your uncle!) who need that $1,000 for their investments. Without credit markets, they would also suffer, because many of them would not be able to raise the necessary funds.

The valuable social role of credit markets is to match savers like you with borrowers. When credit markets work, you will get a reasonable return on your $1,000 saving (typically an average real return of 1 percent to 5 percent, depending on how much risk you take), and worthy potential borrowers will be able to raise the funds they need.

10.2 Banks and Financial Intermediation: Putting Supply and Demand Together

Banks and other financial institutions are the economic agents connecting supply and demand in the credit market. Think of it this way: when you deposit your money in a bank account, you do not know who will ultimately use it. The bank pools all its deposits and uses this pool of money to make many different kinds of loans: credit card loans to households; mortgages to home buyers; small loans to entrepreneurs; and large loans to established companies like General Electric, Nike, and Ford. Banks even make loans to other banks that need cash.

Running a bank is a complicated operation, and, so far, we've taken it all for granted. When we discussed the market for credit in the last section, we assumed that the lenders and borrowers could easily find each other. But in real life, matching lenders and borrowers is complex. Banks are the organizations that provide the bridge from lenders to borrowers, and because of this role, they are called *financial intermediaries*. Broadly speaking,

financial intermediaries channel funds from suppliers of financial capital, like savers, to users of financial capital, like borrowers.

Financial capital comes in many different forms, including credit (which is also referred to as debt) and equity. When a saver turns her savings into *credit*, she loans her savings to another party in exchange for the promise of repayment of her loan with interest. When a saver turns her savings into *equity*, she uses her savings to become a shareholder in a company, which means that she has obtained an ownership share and a claim on the future profits of the company. These profits are paid out as dividends to the company's shareholders.

Securities are financial contracts. For example, securities may allocate ownership rights of a company (stocks), or promise payments to lenders (bonds).

Banks Are Only One of Many Types of Financial Intermediaries

Many different types of financial institutions act as financial intermediaries, channeling funds from suppliers of financial capital—in other words, savers—to users of financial capital. In addition to banks, financial intermediaries include, but are not limited to, asset management companies, hedge funds, private equity funds, venture capital funds, bank-like businesses that make up the "shadow banking system," and even pawnshops and shops that give payday loans.

Asset management companies, like Blackrock, Fidelity, and Vanguard, enable investors to use their savings to buy financial **securities** like *stocks* and *bonds*. When you buy a company's stock, you are buying a share of ownership in that company. When you buy a bond, you are effectively lending money to the company that issued the bond. Most investors, rather than picking individual stocks and bonds, make such investments through mutual funds, which in turn invest in a diversified pool of securities (mixtures of stocks in a stock mutual fund; mixtures of bonds in a bond mutual fund; and mixtures of both stocks and bonds in a fully diversified mutual fund). The value of all mutual funds in the United States in 2015 was approximately $15.9 trillion.[2]

Hedge funds are investment pools gathered from a small number of very wealthy individuals or institutions, like pension funds or university endowments. Hedge funds tend to follow risky, non-traditional investment strategies, like buying large tracts of land that can be used to grow timber, or buying stock in companies that are in financial trouble and have recently experienced large drops in their stock value. Hedge funds charge fees that are much higher than those of mutual funds. The value of all hedge funds in the United States in 2015 was approximately $2 trillion.

Private equity funds are investment pools that also typically gather funds from a small number of wealthy institutions. Private equity funds mostly hold securities that are not publicly traded—in other words, you can't buy those securities on a stock exchange. For instance, private equity funds might buy a company that is privately owned, like a family business. Alternatively, they might take a publicly traded company private by buying all of the shares in the company. The value of all private equity funds in the United States in 2015 was approximately $3 trillion.

Venture capital funds are a particular kind of private equity fund. They invest in new companies that are usually just starting up and therefore have no track record. For instance, in 1999, two venture capital funds—Kleiner-Perkins and Sequoia Capital—invested $25 million to acquire 20 percent of a start-up company with a funny name—Google—founded the previous year. Twenty percent of Google is now worth $100 billion, implying a 4,000-to-1 return on every dollar invested. However, venture capital is a highly risky type of financial intermediation, and the overwhelming majority of venture capital investments have lost money. But one big payoff can compensate for hundreds of failures.

The *shadow banking system* comprises thousands of institutions that are not officially banks, because they don't take deposits, but that nevertheless act like banks in the sense that they raise money and then make loans with those funds. Lehman Brothers, whose bankruptcy fueled the 2008 financial crisis, was one example of a shadow bank. Instead of taking common deposits, Lehman would take loans from large investors like insurance companies and use them to trade stocks and bonds, to make loans to businesses, and to create new financial products that they could sell to other institutions and wealthy investors.

LETTING THE —
DATA SPEAK

Financing Start-ups

Thanks to venture capital, many unproven but promising start-ups can get financing—without explaining their ideas to unreceptive loan officers at a bank. For example, Facebook, now worth $350 billion, owes its start, in part, to venture capital. Peter Thiel, a venture capitalist and co-founder of PayPal and Palantir, recognized Facebook's value early on. In 2004, Thiel invested in the fledgling company. In 2012, Thiel cashed out his shares, making $2,000 for every dollar that he originally invested. Not a bad rate of return!

A rapidly growing list of tech start-up companies have reached market valuations in excess of $1 billion. Companies that exceed this valuation threshold before they issue shares to the general public are referred to as *unicorns*. In 2016, unicorns included the ride-sharing company Uber, the vacation rental company Airbnb, and the social media company Snapchat. In an effort to find the next generation of unicorns, venture capital firms are placing big bets. In 2015, venture capitalists invested $74.2 billion in North American companies alone.

If you are thinking of your own start-up, perhaps your very own unicorn, you don't even have to plead with venture capitalists to obtain funding. You can now use "crowdfunding" through websites such as Kickstarter to pitch your idea to your customer base or to anybody with a bit of money to invest. For instance, the smartwatch company Pebble, unable to attract sufficient funding from venture capitalists, turned to Kickstarter in 2012, with an initial goal of raising $100,000. By the end of the campaign, it had raised over $10 *million* from an enthusiastic public. In 2015, Pebble went back to Kickstarter and raised an additional $20 million from over 75,000 individual investors.

Before you throw your hat in the ring, however, you should note that most start-ups, even those receiving substantial financing from venture capitalists and crowdfunding, are unsuccessful. The most famous recent trainwreck is Theranos, a blood-testing company that was funded by venture capital and valued at $9 billion in 2014. By the summer of 2016, Theranos was under multiple criminal investigations, and its 32-year-old founder and CEO was struggling to stave off the collapse of her company. Almost all of the company's value was wiped out when it was revealed that Theranos had misled investors and government regulators about the capabilities of its blood-testing technology. Survival isn't easy for start-ups, even for unicorns.

Assets and Liabilities on the Balance Sheet of a Bank

To understand what banks do, it helps to first look at a bank's balance sheet, which summarizes both its *assets* and its *liabilities*. Assets include the investments the bank has made; government securities the bank holds; and the money the bank is owed by borrowers, including households and firms that have taken loans from the bank. The bank's liabilities include claims that depositors and other lenders have against the bank. For example, when a household deposits $10,000 at a bank, that deposit is a liability for the bank—money that the bank owes to the depositor.

Accountants call this statement of assets and liabilities a *balance sheet* because it is set up so that the assets and liabilities are balanced one for one. Think of the words *own* and *owe* to clarify the balance sheet—the balance sheet states what the bank owns (assets) and what it owes (liabilities).

Exhibit 10.7 summarizes some key features of the balance sheet of Citibank at the end of the first quarter of 2016, following the convention of listing assets in the left-hand column and liabilities in the right-hand column. The right-hand column also lists stockholders' equity, which is defined as total assets minus total liabilities and represents the value of the owners' (stockholders') stake in the company. Let's look in a bit more detail at the key categories that make up the assets and liabilities of the balance sheet.

Assets Citibank's assets are divided into three categories: reserves, cash and cash equivalents, and long-term investments.

Bank reserves consist of vault cash and reserves held at the Federal Reserve Bank.

1. **Bank reserves** include vault cash—paper money and coins held by Citibank in its own vaults—and Citibank's holdings of reserves at the Federal Reserve Bank. Note that the Federal Reserve Bank is a *government-operated* bank that regular banks use to make transfers within the U.S. financial system. For now, you can think of Citibank's reserves at the Federal Reserve Bank as "deposits" that Citibank has

Exhibit 10.7 Citibank's Balance Sheet, March 2016 (billions of dollars)

Citibank's balance sheet from March 2016 summarizes the assets that the bank owns, as well as the claims that depositors and other financial intermediaries have against the bank—the bank's liabilities. Stockholders' equity is defined as the difference between total assets and total liabilities, so liabilities plus stockholders' equity is exactly equal to the value of total assets.

Assets		Liabilities and stockholders' equity	
Reserves	$74	Demand deposits	$935
Cash equivalents	$274	Short-term borrowing	$429
Long-term investments	$1,453	Long-term debt	$208
		Total liabilities	**$1,572**
		Stockholders' equity	$229
Total assets	**$1,801**	**Total liabilities + Stockholders' equity**	**$1,801**

Source: Data from Citigroup Inc., 2016 first quarter form 10-Q.

made at the Federal Reserve Bank. These "deposits" are owned by Citibank and are available at a moment's notice for any payments that Citibank needs to make to other banks. In Chapter 11 we will have much more to say about the Federal Reserve Bank, often called the Fed, and about bank reserves, and we will see why banks hold their money on deposit at the Fed. In Exhibit 10.7, Citibank's reserves—both vault cash and reserves at the Federal Reserve Bank—account for 74 billion of Citibank's total assets.

2. *Cash equivalents* are riskless, liquid assets that Citibank can immediately access, like deposits with other private banks. An asset is riskless if its value doesn't change from day to day. An asset is liquid if it can quickly and easily be converted into cash, with little or no loss in value. In Exhibit 10.7, cash equivalents account for $274 billion of Citibank's total assets.

3. *Long-term investments* mostly comprise loans to households and firms but also include things like the value of the real estate that the bank uses for its operations, such as its bank branches and corporate headquarters. Long-term investments account for $1,453 billion of Citibank's total assets.

Liabilities and Stockholders' Equity In Exhibit 10.7, Citibank's liabilities and stockholders' equity are divided into four categories: demand deposits, short-term borrowing, long-term debt, and stockholders' equity.

1. **Demand deposits** are funds "loaned" to the bank by depositors. Most depositors don't think of this as a loan to a bank, but rather as a deposit to a checking account. These deposits are referred to as *demand deposits* because the depositor can access the funds on demand—meaning, at any time—by withdrawing the money from an ATM or bank teller, writing a check, or using a debit card to make a store purchase. Even though demand deposits are "cash in the bank," so to speak, they are liabilities from the perspective of Citibank, because it owes this money to its depositors. Citibank owes depositors $935 billion in demand deposits. We look at these more closely in the next section.

2. *Short-term borrowing* comprises short-term loans that Citibank has obtained from other financial institutions. All these loans are part of Citibank's liabilities and need to be repaid in the next year. Some of them are overnight loans that Citibank needs to repay the next day! Usually, such overnight loans are rolled over from one day to the next, meaning that Citibank repays its overnight loans and then instantly arranges new overnight loans with the same lenders. Unfortunately, heavy reliance on short-term debt generates some fragility in the banking system. If lenders suddenly start to worry that Citibank will have difficulty paying back short-term debt, Citibank might have trouble borrowing new funds and would therefore lack the funds it needs to conduct its day-to-day operations. Despite these risks, Citibank funds its operations by borrowing $429 billion of such short-term debt.

Demand deposits are funds that depositors can access on demand by withdrawing money from the bank, writing checks, or using their debit cards.

3. *Long-term debt* is defined as debt that is due to be repaid by Citibank in a year or more to an institution that loaned the money to Citibank (Citibank's creditor). Citibank has $208 billion in long-term debt, representing 13 percent of its liabilities. This proportion contrasts sharply with the asset side of the balance sheet, where nearly 75 percent of the assets are long-term. The difference between long-term debt and long-term assets introduces a source of risk for the bank—a topic that we explore later in this chapter.
4. **Stockholders' equity** is defined as the difference between the bank's total assets and its total liabilities.

Stockholders' equity is the difference between a bank's total assets and its total liabilities.

$$\text{Total assets} - \text{Total liabilities} = \text{Stockholders' equity.}$$

This difference is equal to the estimated value of the company, or what the total value of Citibank's shares should be worth if the accountants got everything right.

We can rearrange the identity for stockholders' equity to find that

$$\text{Total assets} = \text{Total liabilities} + \text{Stockholders' equity.}$$

Looking at this equation, you can see that the two sides (left and right) of the balance sheet match up. Given the way in which accountants define stockholders' equity, the liability side of the balance sheet and the asset side of the balance sheet are always perfectly balanced.

10.3 What Banks Do

We can use the bank's balance sheet to identify three interrelated functions that banks perform as financial intermediaries:

1. Banks identify profitable lending opportunities.
2. Banks transform short-term liabilities, like deposits, into long-term investments in a process called *maturity transformation*.
3. Banks manage risk by using diversification strategies and also by transferring risk from depositors to the bank's stockholders and, in some cases, to the U.S. government.

We discuss each of these three functions in turn.

Identifying Profitable Lending Opportunities

One of the main roles of banks is to find creditworthy borrowers and channel savings of depositors to them. Thus, banks bring together the two sides of the credit market. Banks are in a good position to do this because, given their willingness to lend, they attract a large number of would-be borrowers and choose the more creditworthy among them. Banks employ armies of investment specialists and loan officers trained in identifying the best loan applications.

Maturity Transformation

Recall from Exhibit 10.7 that 87 percent of Citibank's liabilities, which are shown on the right-hand side of its balance sheet, are short-term (made up of demand deposits and short-term borrowing), while nearly 75 percent of its assets, shown on the left-hand side, are long-term investments. Citibank has transformed its short-term liabilities into long-term assets.

Maturity is the time until debt must be repaid.

Maturity is the time until debt must be repaid. Demand deposits have a 0-year maturity, because the depositor can take back her money at any time. In contrast, when banks lend to borrowers, such loans usually have a maturity ranging from several years up to 30 years. The transfer of short-term liabilities like demand deposits into long-term investments is called **maturity transformation**.

Maturity transformation is the process by which banks take short-maturity liabilities and invest in long-maturity assets (long-term investments).

Maturity transformation is what enables society to undertake significant long-term investments. But it also implies that banks wind up with a mismatch between the short-term maturities of their deposits and the long-term maturities of their loans. This maturity mismatch could get them into trouble if lots of depositors were to simultaneously ask to make withdrawals. Banks can't simply recall their long-term loans if their short-term depositors want their money back. To ensure that they can fulfill demands for withdrawals, banks do not lend out all of their deposits. They hold back some fraction of the deposit pool as *reserves* or some other form of cash-like security.

Banks have a large number of depositors, and typically only a tiny fraction of depositors demand their funds on any given day. Banks are also able to exploit the fact that withdrawals of existing deposits and inflows of new deposits are roughly offsetting on most days. Banks therefore usually need only a small pool of reserves to meet the net withdrawals of deposits. This enables them to commit most of their demand deposits to long-term investments.

Management of Risk

A bank promises that depositors will never lose a penny. This is a striking promise, since the bank makes risky loans with the depositors' savings. For example, banks often invest in *mortgages*—loans to households to purchase houses—which are risky. About 12 percent of the mortgages held by banks at the beginning of the 2007–2009 financial crisis ended up late on payments or in default.

Banks manage risk in two ways. First, they hold a *diversified* portfolio: a typical bank invests not only in mortgages but also in a diverse set of assets, including business loans, loans to other financial institutions, and government debt. A diversified portfolio is useful, because all the diverse assets of the bank are unlikely to underperform at the same time.

But diversification by itself isn't sufficient to manage risks, because sometimes a large fraction of even a diverse set of assets may underperform. Most types of assets lost value during the 2007–2009 financial crisis. But even in such extreme situations, depositors remain safe because of banks' second strategy of risk management: shifting risk to stockholders, and ultimately, during severe financial crises, to the U.S. government.

To understand how risk is transferred, consider what happens to a simplified bank balance sheet after its long-term investments lose about 10 percent of their value. To keep things simple, we analyze a bank with exactly $11 billion in assets, which is allocated to $1 billion in reserves and cash equivalents and $10 billion in long-term investments.

Panel (a) of Exhibit 10.8 reports an original balance sheet, while panel (b) of Exhibit 10.8 reports a new balance sheet with two changes. First, the value of long-term assets has decreased by 10 percent, or $1 billion. Second, the value of stockholders' equity has been reduced by $1 billion. Recall that stockholders' equity is defined as the difference between

Exhibit 10.8 Illustrative Balance Sheet (billions of dollars)

In panel (a), the bank has $11 billion in assets and stockholders' equity of $2 billion. In panel (b), a $1 billion reduction in the value of the bank's assets reduces stockholders' equity to $1 billion, as stockholders' equity is defined as total assets minus total liabilities.

(a) Before Investment Loss			
Assets		**Liabilities and stockholders' equity**	
Reserves and cash equivalents	$1	Demand deposits	$9
Long-term investments	$10		
		Total liabilities	**$9**
		Stockholders' equity	$2
Total assets	**$11**	**Total liabilities + Stockholders' equity**	**$11**

(b) After $1 Billion Investment Loss			
Assets		**Liabilities and stockholders' equity**	
Reserves and cash equivalents	$1	Demand deposits	$9
Long-term investments	$10 − $1 = $9		
		Total liabilities	**$9**
		Stockholders' equity	$2 − $1 = $1
Total assets	**$11 − $1 = $10**	**Total liabilities + Stockholders' equity**	**$11 − $1 = $10**

Seal of the U.S. Federal Deposit Insurance Corporation. The FDIC was founded in 1933. Today, it insures deposits at over 7,000 banks in the United States.

A bank becomes **insolvent** when the value of the bank's assets is less than the value of its liabilities.

A bank is **solvent** when the value of the bank's assets is greater than the value of its liabilities.

the value of assets and that of liabilities. Since the value of the demand deposits has not changed—these are contractual promises from the bank to its depositors—but the value of the assets has declined by $1 billion, the value of stockholders' equity must also fall by $1 billion.

This example illustrates that stockholders bear all the risk that the bank faces, *as long as stockholders' equity is greater than zero*. In other words, as long as the bank's assets exceed its liabilities, every change in the value of the assets is absorbed one-for-one by stockholders.

When the value of the bank's assets falls below the value of its liabilities, stockholders' equity goes to zero. Now the bank owes more than it owns. At about that moment, the government shuts down the bank. The government bank regulator—the Federal Deposit Insurance Corporation (FDIC)—steps in and takes control of the bank. The FDIC will either (1) shut down the bank's operations and make payouts to depositors or (2) transfer the bank to new ownership.

In the payout scenario, the FDIC takes over the assets of the bank and makes full payouts to all individuals with deposits at that bank up to a cap of $250,000; deposits up to $250,000 are "FDIC-insured." The FDIC may also make payouts for deposits in excess of $250,000 if sufficient funds are available. However, most other creditors and all stockholders of the bank will be wiped out, meaning that they will receive nothing.

More often, however, the FDIC does not pay out to depositors, but instead arranges for a speedy takeover by a healthy bank. Bank takeovers usually protect *all* deposits—even those greater than $250,000—but in most cases, the stockholders are still wiped out. The next business day the bank opens for business as usual, though it might have a different name on the front door. If the failed bank's depositors aren't paying attention, they may miss the fact that anything has happened at all.

These maneuvers don't always come cheap. In most cases, the failed bank has liabilities, principally demand deposits, that exceed the value of its assets. In technical terms, the failed bank is **insolvent**, meaning that the value of its assets is less than the value of its liabilities. In contrast, the healthy bank that is taking over the failed bank is **solvent**, meaning that the value of its assets is greater than the value of its liabilities. The healthy bank needs some financial inducement to take over the operations of the failed bank. The FDIC has to provide this sweetener.

Bank failures during the financial crisis of 2007–2009 cost the FDIC over $100 billion. And the buck doesn't stop there. Depositors at *all* U.S. banks implicitly pay for these bank failures, because the FDIC raises the funds that it needs by charging all banks deposit insurance premiums. These insurance premiums are a cost of doing business—in other words, a cost of taking deposits—which lowers the interest rates that banks pay their depositors.

Bank Runs

Though socially useful, the maturity and risk transformation roles played by banks also create some risks. Most importantly, maturity transformation causes many of the bank's assets to become *illiquid*—that is, by turning short-term liabilities into long-term, illiquid assets, the bank effectively locks up money that it might need to give back to depositors or other creditors on short notice.

A banking panic can be self-fulfilling—it feeds on itself.

During a banking panic, a substantial fraction of depositors may try to withdraw their deposits at the same time. If the bank has mostly long-term, illiquid assets, the bank may have a hard time coming up with the cash that it will need to pay out those withdrawals. As word gets out that the bank's cash is running low, more depositors will try to make withdrawals in the hope that they can get what little cash remains.

A **bank run** occurs when a bank experiences an extraordinarily large volume of withdrawals driven by a concern that the bank will run out of liquid assets with which to pay withdrawals.

In this way a banking panic can be self-fulfilling—it feeds on itself. An unusually large amount of withdrawals reduces the bank's cash, and this cash shortage begets even *more* withdrawals as depositors race to withdraw their deposits before the bank runs out of cash altogether. Even if a bank was healthy before the panic, it might no longer be healthy after losing many of its depositors and being forced to sell its illiquid assets in "fire sales," where the bank doesn't get a good price for the assets, because it doesn't have enough time to find the buyers who are willing to pay the highest price. The expanding panic and rising flood of withdrawals is called a **bank run**.

Northern Rock, a U.K. bank that specialized in mortgage lending, found it increasingly difficult to raise funds in late 2007. This triggered the first U.K. bank run in 150 years. A few months later, Northern Rock failed and was taken over by the U.K. government.

Bank runs have various economic costs. Most importantly, a run forces a bank to liquidate its long-term, illiquid assets prematurely. This sometimes involves abandonment or inefficient liquidation of long-term investments in physical capital, such as construction projects. In addition, since banks are key participants in the credit market, bank runs also disrupt the smooth working of the credit market.

Bank runs occurred in different forms during the 2007–2009 financial crisis, although some of the bank runs were hard for the public to see. The most visible bank run occurred in 2007 at Northern Rock, a U.K. bank that specialized in mortgage lending. Northern Rock's depositors were worried that the bank was insolvent, so they started to withdraw their deposits from the bank. These withdrawals snowballed into the first U.K. bank run in 150 years. Northern Rock desperately tried to find a stronger bank that would buy it out and instill confidence in its depositors. No such sale could be arranged, and Northern Rock was subsequently taken over by the U.K. government.

Bank Regulation and Bank Solvency

If bank runs were a frequent occurrence, the banking system would be quite unstable. Fortunately, bank runs like the one on Northern Rock—with tens of thousands of jittery depositors rushing to withdraw their money—have been relatively rare since the 1930s because of deposit insurance. If a bank fails for any reason, depositors' balances are protected up to some cap. All deposits at or below the cap are paid out in full by the relevant (government) insurance agency (the FDIC in the United States).

Deposit insurance didn't stop the bank run at Northern Rock, since the caps were relatively low in 2007 in the U.K. and many depositors had balances above the cap. Even depositors with fully insured accounts also withdrew their money, as they were afraid that the failure of Northern Rock would temporarily prevent them from accessing their money.

But households aren't the only economic agents depositing money at banks. Firms like Nike and Microsoft also hold bank accounts. Moreover, as we have seen, banks borrow money from one another. When large firms and the general banking community lose confidence in a weak bank, an institutional bank run may ensue, in which firms and banks withdraw their deposits and their short-term loans from the weak bank. FDIC insurance won't prevent institutional bank runs, because institutions make deposits and short-term loans that vastly exceed the FDIC's insurance cap of $250,000 per account. Institutional bank runs occurred frequently during the 2007–2009 financial crisis. However, because it is impossible to take a photograph of an institutional bank run, it is hard to know exactly when one of them is occurring.

We do know that the collapse of the investment bank Lehman Brothers in 2008 was preceded by an institutional bank run. Investment banks specialize in helping firms and governments make large financial transactions, especially for clients that need to raise financial capital to make investments. Investment banks are not FDIC-insured and do not take any deposits the way your neighborhood bank does. Instead, *all* liabilities on an investment bank's balance sheet are loans from other institutions, including other banks.

Many of the largest institutions that lent money to Lehman Brothers decided to stop making such short-term loans in the 2 weeks before Lehman went bankrupt. In other words, Lehman experienced an institutional bank run just before it failed. We now know that Lehman was insolvent at this time—its liabilities exceeded its assets. No wonder smart banks were unwilling to extend new loans to Lehman in the weeks before Lehman's bankruptcy.

Naturally, banks are very eager to avoid such financial meltdowns. They have many strategies at their disposal, though some of these strategies work better than others. As always, prevention is the ideal cure. The ultimate source of strength is to have lots of stockholders' equity, implying that a bank has assets that far exceed the value of its liabilities. When a bank owns far more than it owes, it is said to be well capitalized. In this case, the public should have no doubt about a bank's solvency, which reduces the likelihood of a bank run.

If a bank is running short of reserves, it can stop making new loans and it can sell its long-term investments. However, these efforts can backfire, because they may actually reveal that a bank is in trouble and can intensify the panic that may already have begun. In addition, if a bank stops lending, it reduces its ability to act as a financial intermediary and reduces its earnings at exactly the time when it needs those earnings the most.

EVIDENCE-BASED ECONOMICS

Q: How often do banks fail?

B anks work very hard to create the impression that they are bedrock institutions. But they haven't proved to be as solid as advertised. In the United States alone, nearly 20,000 banks have failed since 1900. However, most of those failures occurred before the establishment of the FDIC in 1933, which created deposit insurance and also enforced strict nationwide bank regulations. Nevertheless, even after the FDIC was established, more than 3,000 banks failed.

Bank failures appear to be a regular feature of modern market economies. The U.S. economy has observed four major waves of bank failures since the beginning of the twentieth century. The first wave of these bank failures occurred from 1919 to 1928—the decade before the Great Depression—when almost 6,000 banks failed, or 20 percent of all banks in the United States. These failures were concentrated among rural banks that issued mortgages to farms with land values that subsequently fell.

The second wave hit during the Great Depression (1929–1939), when more than 9,000 banks failed. This wave of bank failures was far more severe than the failures of the 1920s. For example, in 1933 alone, more than 25 percent of all U.S. banks failed. All told, nearly 50 percent of all U.S. banks failed during the Great Depression.

The third wave occurred during the savings and loan crisis in the 1980s and early 1990s. Savings and loan associations are one type of regional bank. During the savings and loan crisis, nearly 3,000 banks failed, comprising about 15 percent of all U.S. banks. The crisis was caused by a boom-to-bust cycle of rising and then falling agricultural and oil prices. During the period of rising prices, the banks made risky investments in local farms and businesses. When agricultural and oil prices fell unexpectedly, those investments were decimated.

The fourth wave of failures resulted from the 2007–2009 financial crisis. By year-end 2012, there were over 460 bank failures, representing less than 5 percent of all U.S. banks. At first glance, this may seem to be relatively small when compared with the earlier waves. But the 2007–2009 wave included the failure of Washington Mutual in 2008, with more than $300 billion in assets. The largest previous bank failure was Continental Illinois, which collapsed in 1984 with $40 billion in assets, which is equal to $90 billion in 2008 dollars.

Even more importantly, the 2007–2009 financial crisis coincided with the collapse of several (nonbank) financial institutions, like Lehman Brothers. As described earlier, investment banks like Lehman are not regular banks, since they don't take deposits and their lenders are not insured by the FDIC. Lehman had $600 billion of loans from other financial institutions, so its balance sheet was nearly twice as large as that of Washington Mutual.

Exhibit 10.9 plots the annual number of bank failures in the United States divided by the total number of banks in operation during that year. Although this measure is not perfect—recall that Washington Mutual counts the same as any other bank, large or small—the data do provide some useful guidance about the pattern of historical bank failures.

Two key facts jump out. First, the Great Depression remains the most severe financial crisis in U.S. history (see the huge peak for 1933 in Exhibit 10.9). Second, after the FDIC regulatory and insurance system was created in 1933, the rate of bank failures plummeted. Note that the FDIC not only insures deposits but also acts as a stringent regulator. Deposit insurance reduces the likelihood of bank runs. Regulation reduces the likelihood that banks will take irresponsible risks with their depositors' money. At least so far, the FDIC era has been relatively placid in comparison to the financial mayhem that preceded it.

MyEconLab Real-time data

Exhibit 10.9 Annual Rate of Bank Failures in the United States (1892–2015)

The graph plots the number of annual bank failures in the United States divided by the number of banks in operation.

Sources: Based on Federal Reserve Bank of St. Louis, Federal Reserve System, Federal Reserve Board of Governors, and Federal Deposit Insurance Corporation.

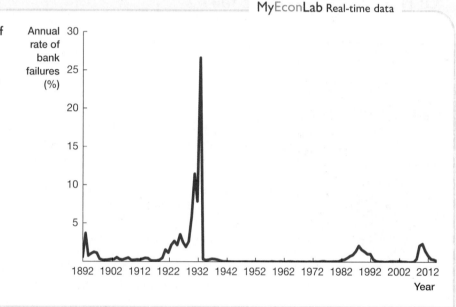

| | Question | Answer | Data | Caveat |

Question	**Answer**	**Data**	**Caveat**
How often do banks fail?	Although there have been long periods of calm, four waves of bank failures have occurred in the United States since 1900, generating around 20,000 total failures.	Historical banking data from the Federal Reserve and the FDIC.	In some ways, counting bank failures can be misleading, because the failure of one large national bank can be more destructive than the failure of hundreds of small regional banks.

CHOICE & CONSEQUENCE

Too Big to Fail

Many economists worry that extremely big banks have become too powerful. If a bank is big enough, the government will think twice before letting the bank fail, as this failure will reverberate throughout the economy. Big banks naturally have many more liabilities (and more assets) than smaller banks have. This means they owe more money to other banks, and, if they fail, all these other banks to which they owe money will also suffer losses. And the dominoes might keep falling, as one bank after another fails and the ripples of financial losses keep spreading through other banks. In theory, the failure of one megabank could bring down the whole financial system.

Systemic risk refers to the system-wide risks created by the failure of one or several financial institutions, and regulators refer to a financial institution that is large enough to pose a threat to the entire financial system as a *systemically important financial institution* (SIFI). Because of these systemic risks, regulators pay special attention to and stringently regulate SIFIs. The government faces a devilish problem with respect to its relationship to SIFIs: if a SIFI is in trouble, even if this is due to the SIFI's own irresponsible past decisions, how could a responsible government *not* bail the SIFI out? For instance, the government could lend the bank some funds (at a low interest rate), thereby enabling the bank to keep operating and avoiding the cataclysmic economy-wide consequences of the bank's failure.

Because a SIFI is "too big to fail"—meaning that the government is afraid of the consequences of its failure and will rescue the mega-bank if it gets into trouble—the SIFI might knowingly choose to take irresponsible risks. If things *do* go badly, the bank will still be OK, since the government will be forced to offer a bailout. It's the

"heads I win, tails you lose" situation, with the winner being the bank's shareholders and the loser being taxpayers, who indirectly bear the losses when the government sends in the financial cavalry to save the day.

To avoid problems like this, bank regulators have adopted three strategies. First, they require SIFIs to explain how they could be wound down in an orderly way if they were to become insolvent. These procedures are referred to as "living wills," and they spell out how the bank would sell its assets and pay off its creditors in the event that it needed to end its business operations. Such living wills are designed to make it more credible and easier for a government to shut down a failing bank.

Second, SIFIs must show that they would survive plausible *potential* economic shocks, like a deep recession or a sharp fall in housing prices. These evaluations—which are referred to as *stress tests*—have the effect of encouraging banks to hold relatively more stockholder equity and to reduce the riskiness of the assets on their balance sheet.

Third, regulators also directly require SIFIs to hold more stockholders' equity, reducing the likelihood that a large bank will become insolvent (and helping banks pass their stress tests). We return to these issues in Chapter 11.

We should also add that systemic risk is not only brought about by large banks like SIFIs. Sometimes many small banks fail at the same time and create systemic problems for the entire financial system. The spike of bank failures during the Great Depression shown in Exhibit 10.9, which brought the entire economy to a standstill, was due to the failure of many small banks, not the collapse of a handful of big banks.

CHOICE & CONSEQUENCE

Asset Price Fluctuations and Bank Failures

After hearing about the waves of failures that sometimes engulf the banking industry, you might be wondering how these waves originate. Why do so many banks go belly up at the same time?

Banks fail when they invest in long-term assets that subsequently fall in price. Since different banks tend to invest in the same types of long-term assets, banks' fortunes often rise and fall together. Even a small percentage decline in the value of a bank's long-term assets can wipe out all of a bank's stockholders' equity, causing the bank to become insolvent.

Large changes in asset values are common in economic history. For example, in the late 1920s, stock prices and land prices skyrocketed, only to plummet subsequently during the Great Depression. Likewise, the savings and loan crisis of the late 1980s was caused by a fall in asset values. One of the contributing factors was a roller-coaster ride in the prices of natural resources, particularly oil. From 1972 to 1980, the price of crude oil rose from about $20 per barrel to $100 per barrel (in 2010 constant dollars) and then fell back, ending up in 1986 where it started in 1972 (using constant dollars). When oil prices peaked in 1980, most forecasters predicted steep ongoing increases in oil prices. Consequently, the subsequent fall in oil prices was unanticipated, devastating the oil-producing regions in the United States, particularly towns in Texas, Louisiana, and Oklahoma. Local businesses lost value, and more than 10,000 of them went bankrupt. In turn, the slowdown in regional economies decimated housing prices.

The 2007–2009 financial crisis was also associated with falling asset prices. The real value of U.S. stocks halved and the real value of residential real estate fell by over a third.

Why do asset prices fluctuate so much? The most established theory of stock prices links them to *fundamentals*—rational forecasts of the future earnings prospects of companies and the future value of interest rates. This theory, often referred to as *the theory of efficient markets* and associated with Nobel Prize-winning economist Eugene Fama, asserts that stock market prices are based exclusively on fundamentals and are entirely rationally determined.[3] It implies that all movements in stock prices reflect rational appraisals of new information, not a tendency for investors to let their emotions get in the way. In the efficient markets' view, large fluctuations in asset prices are episodes in which important new information becomes available to investors, who then use this information to rationally update their beliefs about the future profitability of firms traded on the stock exchange.

An alternative view, gaining more traction over the past three decades and developed by another Nobel Prize-winning economist, Robert Shiller, links asset price fluctuations to *asset bubbles*.[4] Bubbles occur when asset prices depart from fundamentals. Some economists believe that substantial asset price bubbles arise on occasion, partly driven by psychological factors and biases, particularly during specific episodes such as extended economic and stock market booms. If bubbles can be identified while they are occurring, then subsequent market crashes will be partially predictable.

Whatever the source of crashes in asset prices, most economists agree that banking regulation plays a useful role in helping the banking sector survive these episodes. In response to the 2007–2009 financial crisis, regulators around the world drafted new rules that have improved banks' ability to withstand severe economic shocks. The chapters that follow contain extensive discussions about macroeconomic fluctuations—like recessions—and the many different policies that governments use to reduce the severity of these events.

Summary

- Credit is essential for the efficient allocation of resources in the economy; for example, credit allows firms to borrow for investment or households to borrow to purchase a house.

- The relevant price in the credit market is the real interest rate rather than the nominal interest rate. The real interest rate adjusts the price of borrowing or lending for the effects of inflation, thus reflecting the economic trade-off between the present and the future that borrowers and savers face.

- Firms, households, and governments use the credit market for borrowing. The credit demand curve summarizes the relationship between the quantity of credit demanded by borrowers and the real interest rate. The credit demand curve results from the optimizing behavior of these borrowers.

- The credit supply curve summarizes the relationship between the quantity of credit supplied and the real interest rate and also results from optimizing behavior, this time of savers. Savers trade off consumption today for consumption in the future, taking into account the reward for delaying consumption—the real interest rate.

- The intersection of the credit demand curve and the credit supply curve is the credit market equilibrium. At the equilibrium real interest rate, the quantity of credit demanded is equal to the quantity of credit supplied.

- Saving and borrowing in the credit market are intermediated by banks and other financial intermediaries. Banks play three key roles in the economy. First, they find creditworthy borrowers and channel savings of depositors to them. Second, they transform the maturity structure in the economy by collecting money from savers in the form of short-term demand deposits and investing that money in long-term projects. Third, they manage risk by holding a diversified portfolio and by transferring risk from depositors to stockholders and, in economic crises, to the government.

- Governments provide deposit insurance that reduces the likelihood of bank runs, and governments intervene to save failing banks in order to avert widespread crises. The U.S. economy has experienced four major waves of bank failures since 1900.

Key Terms

debtors *p. 229*
credit *p. 229*
interest rate or nominal interest rate *p. 230*
real interest rate *p. 231*
credit demand curve *p. 231*

credit supply curve *p. 234*
credit market *p. 236*
financial intermediaries *p. 238*
securities *p. 238*
bank reserves *p. 239*
demand deposits *p. 240*

stockholders' equity *p. 241*
maturity *p. 241*
maturity transformation *p. 241*
insolvent *p. 243*
solvent *p. 243*
bank run *p. 243*

Questions

All questions are available in MyEconLab for practice and instructor assignment.

1. What is the difference between nominal and real interest rates?

2. Firms, households, and governments use the credit market for borrowing. The credit demand curve shows the relationship between the quantity of credit demanded and the real interest rate.

   a. Why does the credit demand curve slope downward?

   b. What can cause a shift in the credit demand curve?

3. What factors explain why people save for the future?

4. Households and firms with savings lend money to banks and other financial institutions. The credit supply curve shows the relationship between the quantity of credit supplied and the real interest rate.

   a. Why does the credit supply curve slope upward?

   b. What can cause a shift in the credit supply curve?

5. What are the key categories on a bank's balance sheet? Illustrate using a table.

6. What is the shadow banking system?

7. What functions do banks perform as financial intermediaries in the economy?

8. What is maturity transformation?

9. What is stockholders' equity? Who bears the risk that a bank faces when stockholders' equity is greater than zero?

10. What is a bank run?

11. What is deposit insurance? Is deposit insurance successful in preventing bank runs?

12. As the Choice & Consequence box on "Too Big to Fail" notes, bank regulators worry about the prospect of the failure of large financial institutions, dubbed "systemically important financial institutions" (SIFIs).

a. How would the failure of a SIFI affect the economy?

b. What steps do bank regulators take to prevent SIFIs from failing or to minimize the effect of such failures?

13. Banks fail when they invest in long-term assets that subsequently fall in price. What are the two views on why asset prices fluctuate so much that they lead to financial crises and bank failures?

Problems

All problems are available in MyEconLab *for practice and instructor assignment.*

1. Optimizing economic agents use the real interest rate when thinking about the economic costs and returns of a loan.

a. Recently, the average rate paid by banks on savings accounts was 0.45 percent. However, at the same time, inflation was around 1.5 percent. What was the average saver's real rate of interest on his or her savings?

b. Banks expect that the inflation rate in the coming year will be 3 percent. They want a real return of 5 percent. What nominal rate should they charge borrowers? Explain using the Fisher equation.

2. The 1970s was a period of high inflation in many industrialized countries, including the United States.

a. Due to the increase in the inflation rate, lenders, including credit card companies, revised their nominal interest rates upward. How is the inflation rate related to the nominal interest rate that credit card companies charge? Why would lenders need to increase the nominal interest rate when the inflation rate increases?

b. Usury laws place an upper limit on the nominal rate of interest that lenders can charge on their loans. In the 1970s, in order to avoid usury laws, some credit card companies moved to states where there were no ceilings on interest rates. Why would credit card companies move to states without usury laws during a period of high inflation like the 1970s?

3. In August 1979, the annual inflation rate in the U.S. was nearly 12 percent, and the U.S. short-term nominal interest rate was nearly 10 percent. Over the next 35 years, both the inflation rate and short-term nominal interest rate tended to fall. By August 2014, the inflation rate was about 2 percent and the short-term nominal interest rate was close to 0 percent. How has the *real* short-term interest rate changed from 1979 to 2014? Why do the inflation rate and the nominal interest rate tend to move together over the long run?

4. Many kinds of loans, like student loans and mortgages, can be taken out at either a fixed or variable rate. A fixed rate loan allows the borrower to pay the same nominal interest rate for the entire lifetime of the loan, while a variable rate loan may experience changes in in the nominal interest rate as the rate that banks charge each other for overnight loans changes. For this problem, assume that this variable nominal interest rate adjusts such that the associated real interest rate remains constant over time.

a. In the first year, inflation is 2.75 percent and the nominal interest rate for both the fixed and variable rate loans is 5 percent. What is the real interest rate for the fixed rate loan? What about for the variable rate loan?

b. In the second year, inflation rises to 3 percent. Calculate the nominal and real interest rates for the fixed rate and the variable rate loans described in part a.

c. What happens if the inflation rate falls? Could a borrower end up facing a much higher real interest rate with a variable rate loan? With a fixed rate loan?

d. Suppose you are deciding between a fixed rate and a variable rate loan and that you dislike risk (variability) in the real interest rate you pay. Should you opt for a fixed rate or a variable rate loan? Are there any reasons for a borrower to dislike variability in the nominal interest rate rather than the real interest rate she faces?

5. Explain how the equilibrium real interest rate and the equilibrium quantity of credit would change in each of the following scenarios, and illustrate your answer with a well-labeled graph of the credit market.

a. As the real estate market recovers from the 2007–2009 financial crisis, households begin to buy more houses and condominiums, and they apply for more mortgages to enable those purchases.

b. Congress agrees to a reduction in the federal deficit, which results in a significant decrease in the amount of government borrowing.

c. Households begin to fear that the recovery from the 2007–2009 recession will not last, and become more pessimistic about the economy.

d. Businesses become more optimistic about the future of the economy, and decide to distribute more of their earnings as dividends to their shareholders.

6. Households, like banks, maintain balance sheets. Although these assets and liabilities may not be written down in a neat table, they still influence household decision making.

a. We saw in this chapter that for banks, assets are equal to liabilities. Do you expect the same to be true for a household? Explain.

b. What kinds of assets might the average household have? Of these, which do you think are the most liquid?

c. How would a one-time loan made to a relative affect a household's annual balance sheet? What about purchasing a car with cash?

d. During the financial crisis of 2007–2008, the federal government decided to bail out the big banks, but not any of the households that had lost money because of their investments or house purchases. What kinds of justifications might there be for this type of federal government policy?

7. Banks that practice *narrow banking* match the maturity of their investments with the term of the deposits that they collect from the public. In other words, narrow banks take short-maturity deposits and invest in assets that carry a low level of risk and are also of short-term maturity, like short-term government debt.

   a. Suppose that all FDIC-insured banks decide to adopt narrow banking. How would narrow banking reduce the level of risk in the banking system?

   b. If narrow banking reduces systemic risk, why do banks still practice maturity transformation?

8. If you have studied microeconomics, you may recall a concept called "moral hazard." Moral hazard occurs when an economic agent is incentivized to take risks because some (or all) of the losses that might result will be borne by other economic agents. Discuss how federal deposit insurance, administered by the FDIC as described in this chapter, might lead to moral hazard.

9. Recall from the chapter that banks in the United States hold a fraction of their checking deposits as reserves, either as vault cash or as deposits with the Federal Reserve (where they earn very little interest). Regulations require them to hold a certain percentage (currently 10 percent) of their checking deposits as reserves. However, banks are free to hold additional reserves if they choose. The latter are called *excess reserves*. Ordinarily, banks have held very few excess reserves. However, starting in the financial crisis of 2007–2009, the amount of excess reserves held by banks went from virtually zero to over $1.8 trillion.

   a. Explain why banks would be expected to try to minimize the amount of excess reserves that they hold.

   b. Based on what you have learned about banking in this chapter, explain why you think that the crisis prompted banks to dramatically expand the amount of excess reserves they held.

10. In this problem, consider a simple mutual fund. Households and businesses invest in the fund by buying shares; the fund uses this money, in turn, to invest in a range of assets, including equities and bonds. If an investor wishes to divest from the fund, she can "redeem" her shares. Redeeming involves selling the shares back to the mutual fund for a price called the "net asset value" (NAV). The NAV is equal to the difference between assets and liabilities, divided by the total number of investors in the fund (similar to the shareholders' equity discussed in this chapter). The NAV is updated at the end of each day. Thus every investor who redeems on a given day will get the same price.

   a. What does this fund's balance sheet look like?

   b. Suppose several large investors in the mutual fund start getting nervous about market conditions and decide to redeem, all on the same day. How will these redemptions affect the fund's balance sheet?

c. Suppose now that investors anticipate that other (large) investors will redeem. How will this affect their incentives to redeem? Link your answers to the notion of bank runs discussed in this chapter.

d. Assume that the economy has 15 other, identical mutual funds. As the fund in part b begins selling assets to pay back investors, the market price of those assets drops. How would this price drop affect the balance sheets of the other mutual funds that invest in those assets? Does this also relate to bank runs? Clarify the differences between your answers to this part and part c.

11. The Choice & Consequence box on "Asset Price Fluctuations and Bank Failures" discusses the relationship between the prices of things like oil and real estate, and the solvency of lending institutions like banks. Consider the following two scenarios. Supply the missing entries, and answer the questions that follow. Assume that Securitas Bank is a large bank in the country of Hyponatremia. The bank's *only* assets and liabilities at the beginning of the year are given in the following balance sheet:

Securitas Bank Balance Sheet (billions of dollars)			
Assets		**Liabilities**	
Reserves and cash equivalents	$20	Demand deposits	$200
Long-term investments	$330	Borrowing from other banks	$50
Total assets	?	**Stockholders' equity**	?

Philopericulum Bank is another large bank whose only assets and liabilities are summarized in its balance sheet:

Philopericulum Bank Balance Sheet (billions of dollars)			
Assets		**Liabilities**	
Reserves and cash equivalents	$10	Demand deposits	$450
Long-term investments	$650	Borrowing from other banks	$200
Total assets	?	**Stockholders' equity**	?

Assume now that due to an economic downturn, the value of each bank's long-term investments declines by 10 percent. Show the resulting situation on each bank's balance sheet. How would you describe the resulting situation for each bank? Relate your answer to the discussion in the chapter of the concept of "too big to fail."

12. The sharpest one-day percentage decline in the Dow Jones Industrial Average (DJIA) took place on October 19, 1987. The DJIA fell 23 percent on this one day. Foreign exchange markets and other asset markets also exhibit large fluctuations on a daily basis. Based on the information given in this chapter, discuss some factors that could explain why asset prices fluctuate.

11 The Monetary System

What caused the German hyperinflation of 1922–1923?

Hyperinflation occurs when a country's price level doubles within 3 years. In 1923, the inflation rate in Germany blew past this threshold. At one point, prices were doubling *every 3 to 4 days*. At that pace, prices doubled about 8 times in 1 month. For example, a single egg cost about 1 million German marks on October 1, 1923, and it cost about 256 million marks 30 days later:

8 doublings: 2, 4, 8, 16, 32, 64, 128, 256.

During the entire period of German hyperinflation, prices rose by a factor of roughly 500 billion. German currency lost so much value that a briefcase or, in some cases, a wheelbarrow was needed to carry enough paper currency to buy a day's worth of groceries. Paper currency with low denominations had so little value that it was used to make toys, such as the kite shown to the left.

You might guess that there is something unique about Germany that caused this mass hysteria. But hyperinflations have occurred in many countries over the past century, including Argentina, Austria, Brazil, Chile, China, Greece, Hungary, Poland, and Zimbabwe, to name a few. In this chapter, we examine why hyperinflations occur and explain how they can be avoided. Using these insights, most countries have avoided hyperinflations since the end of World War II. Nevertheless, not all policymakers have learned these lessons. For example, since 2011, Belarus, Iran, and Venezuela have suffered from debilitating hyperinflations. To pick one example, at the end of 2016, the International Monetary Fund predicted that Venezuelan inflation for 2017 would be 1,660 percent.

CHAPTER OUTLINE

11.1 Money

The world economy is a phenomenally complex social system. Every year, global GDP totals over $80 trillion of goods and services. **Money** is the asset that people use to conduct these transactions. We can't understand how the world economy works without first understanding how money lubricates the system.

To introduce the role of money, consider a student majoring in English who works part-time in a bookstore; he exchanges his labor for money. Assume he uses his bookstore wages to buy something he wants, say, an iPhone. In this example, money greases the wheels of the exchange: he will give up 25 hours of time in the bookstore to *eventually* obtain an iPhone. Without money, the English major would have a hard time directly trading his labor for an iPhone. It is far more efficient for Apple to take his money in exchange for an iPhone than for Apple to hire him directly and pay him with an iPhone.

Money is the asset that people use to make and receive payments when buying and selling goods and services.

The Functions of Money

Money simultaneously serves three functions in a modern economy:

1. It is a *medium of exchange*.
2. It is a *store of value*.
3. It is a measure of relative value, or a *unit of account*.

A **medium of exchange** is something that can be exchanged in return for goods and services, thereby facilitating trade. For example, when you hand the cashier $10 for a pepperoni pizza, you are using money—in this case currency—as a medium of exchange. The use of money allows for a convenient, universally acceptable way of buying and selling goods and services.

Money serves as a better medium of exchange when it is also a **store of value**—it enables people to transfer purchasing power into the future. We expect that the $10 bill we receive on Tuesday will be accepted as a form of payment on Wednesday, or even a decade from now. If pizzeria owners didn't trust that the $10 bill would be accepted in the future, they would not accept the $10 bill today.

Money simultaneously serves three functions in a modern economy. It is a *medium of exchange*. It is a *store of value*. It is a measure of relative value, or a *unit of account*.

A **medium of exchange** is an asset that can be traded for goods and services.

A **store of value** is an asset that enables people to transfer purchasing power into the future.

Money also provides the yardstick for describing prices. What does it cost to buy a pair of jeans? In principle, Levi's could report the price of stonewashed jeans in units of bananas: one pair of stonewashed jeans might be worth 112 bananas. Of course, shopping would be difficult if every store used its own yardstick for reporting prices. Bananas at Levi's. Mandarin oranges at Gap. Cucumbers at Guess. Life would be easier with a single yardstick for measuring value—a single unit of account. Modern economies use money as the **unit of account**—a universal yardstick that expresses the price of different goods and services. We measure the cost of a good by the number of dollars it takes to buy that good, not by the equivalent value in bananas.

A **unit of account** is a universal yardstick that is used for expressing the worth (price) of different goods and services.

Economic transactions are much easier to conduct when there is a medium of exchange, a store of value, and a universal unit of account. Money performs all three critical tasks simultaneously.

One Benjamin (Franklin)

Fiat money refers to something that is used as legal tender by government decree and is not backed by a physical commodity, like gold or silver.

Types of Money

Paper money was invented around 1000 AD in China, but other forms of money have existed throughout human history. Before the adoption of paper money, people used money that was valuable in and of itself. The most well-known examples are silver and gold, though goats, chickens, and horses were also used from time to time.

Modern societies have switched to using **fiat money**—something that is used as legal tender by government decree and is not backed by a physical commodity, like gold or silver. For example, paper money is valuable only because other people will accept it as money. We don't accumulate Benjamins because we like the fine portrait of Benjamin Franklin on the $100 bill. Rather, $100 bills are useful for exchange, for storing value, and for keeping accounts because we *trust that paper currency will be used for these purposes in the future*. In this sense, money is a remarkable social invention—it works because we have developed enough trust to believe that it will keep working.

In theory, any object in limited supply could play the role of fiat money, like used ticket stubs from major league baseball games or cobblestones taken from St. Peter's Square in the Vatican. But if we used things like ticket stubs or cobblestones for money, there would be a far greater risk of somebody counterfeiting them. This problem is partially resolved by having the government create fiat money that is difficult and illegal to counterfeit.

The Money Supply

How much money do you have available to purchase goods and services today? For many people, the answer would be much more than the amount of cash they have in their pocket. Suppose you have $10 of currency in your wallet and a $1,000 balance in your checking account. The minute you pull out your checkbook, the money available to you for purchases jumps from $10 to $1,010. And why stop there? You could increase the balance in your checking account by electronically transferring funds from your savings account.

Money

Hundreds of years ago

Today

CHOICE
&CONSEQUENCE

Non-Convertible Currencies in U.S. History

In 1861, at the beginning of the Civil War, the U.S. government paid its soldiers with paper currency that was convertible into gold. However, in 1862 the government ran short of gold and switched to fiat currency, which is not convertible.

You can see the difference in the following pair of images. The top image is paper currency issued in 1861, which is convertible into gold. It was called a Demand Note, because the note could be exchanged for gold "ON DEMAND"—look for those words written in an arc in the center of the note, just below the words "FIVE DOLLARS." The lower image is currency issued in 1862, which could not be exchanged into gold and omits the phrase "ON DEMAND."

When the introduction of fiat money was debated in 1862, the idea was highly controversial. Many politicians believed that money would work only if it were backed by gold or silver. However, once it was issued, the 1862 fiat money quickly gained acceptance and did not generate hyperinflation. Convertibility wasn't reintroduced until 1879.

The Civil War is just one of many periods in which fiat money has been used in the United States. The American colonies temporarily used fiat money during the Revolutionary War. The United States temporarily adopted fiat money during the War of 1812. Following each of these episodes, convertibility was eventually reinstated.

Convertibility was gradually eliminated in the twentieth century, and the last vestiges of convertibility were

A small number of firms now accept payments in bitcoin.

dropped in 1971. Since then, the system of fiat currency has performed well: the buying power of paper currency has been far less volatile than the buying power of gold. Almost no economist believes that the United States should return to a "gold standard"—a system in which paper currency is convertible into gold.

In fact, new *non-convertible* electronic currencies are now being introduced by private organizations. Because these new currencies are not endorsed by the government, they are not fiat currencies, and their future success is anyone's guess. These electronic *cryptocurrencies* are protected by computer codes (cryptography) that make theft of the currency difficult, though not impossible. The use of computer codes also hides the identities of the agents who use the currencies. The most famous—and the first—cryptocurrency is bitcoin, which is accepted by more than 100,000 businesses.[1]

Cryptocurrencies have had a controversial start. The electronic exchanges on which cryptocurrencies are traded have frequently been used for illegal transactions, such as the sale of cocaine. Moreover, several exchanges have been hacked by rogue computer programmers, resulting in electronic thefts. For example, the bitcoin exchange Mt. Gox declared bankruptcy after $477 million was stolen. The cryptocurrencies have also had volatile valuations, because the public's demand for these new currencies waxes and wanes. For example, during 2013 the value of a bitcoin rose from $13 per bitcoin at the start of the year to a peak of $1,163 in November! After that, the cryptocurrency kept trending lower, until it bottomed out at $177 in January 2015. Then, 2016 was a huge bull market for bitcoin. By January 4, 2017, bitcoin traded at $1,130. But one week later bitcoin had fallen back to $776, a decline of over 30 percent. Bitcoin has been a financial roller coaster.

Despite its price appreciation in 2016, bitcoin is still a tiny player in the overall economy. The total value of bitcoin currency is only $16 billion, which is less than 1/1,000 the value of total U.S. GDP.[2]

Examples of a demand note (top figure), which was convertible into gold, and fiat currency (bottom figure), which was not.

Some societies used large stone discs as money. This type of money is referred to as rai stones. This photo of five rai stones was taken on the island of Yap (now part of the Federated States of Micronesia) around 1900. A wooden pole—which was carried by many people—was used to transport each stone. The heaviest rai stones weigh more than 8,000 pounds.

Source: W. H. Furness, "The Stone Money of Yap, Western Caroline Islands," *Transactions of the Department of Archaeology, University of Pennsylvania* 1(1): 1904, 51.

The **money supply** adds together currency in circulation, checking accounts, savings accounts, travelers' checks, and money market accounts. It is sometimes referred to as M2.

When economists talk about money, we include most forms of assets that can be immediately drawn on to purchase goods and services. With this concept in mind, we define the **money supply** as currency in circulation, checking accounts, savings accounts, and most other types of bank accounts. You'll often hear this definition of money supply referred to as M2. Using this definition, the money supply is overwhelmingly composed of different types of bank accounts. There are several different definitions of money supply, which go by the related names M1, M2, and M3. To avoid unnecessarily complicating our discussion, we focus on M2.

At year-end 2016 in the United States, M2 was $13.2 trillion, which is almost nine times more than the amount of currency in circulation: $1.5 trillion.[3] This is not surprising once we remember how little cash we carry around compared with the balances in our bank accounts. Moreover, very few of our important financial transactions are conducted with currency. In developed countries, only drug dealers buy a house or a car with a suitcase full of cash. Indeed, even smaller transactions, like paying the rent each month, are rarely conducted with currency.

11.2 Money, Prices, and GDP

We are now ready to study the relationships among money supply, prices, and nominal GDP.

Nominal GDP, Real GDP, and Inflation

Let's start by reviewing a few definitions first introduced in Chapter 5. Nominal GDP is the total value of production (final goods and services), using prices from the year in which the output was produced. Real GDP is the total value of production (final goods and services), using fixed prices taken from a particular base year, which may or may not be the year in which the output was produced. Finally, the inflation rate is the growth rate of the overall price level in the economy.

To review these concepts, consider an illustrative economy that produces only soccer balls. Assume that in 2016, this economy produced 10 soccer balls at a market price of

$50 per ball, for total sales of $500. In 2017, total sales rise to $550. Therefore, nominal GDP has risen by $50 = $550 − $500. What has caused the $50 increase? Here are two possible scenarios:

1. The price of soccer balls is still $50 per ball, and the number of soccer balls produced has risen to 11 balls.
2. The price of soccer balls has risen to $55 per ball, and the number of soccer balls produced has stayed fixed at 10.

Under either Scenario 1 or 2, nominal GDP in 2017 is $550, 10 percent more than it was the year before.

In Scenario 1 the price hasn't changed, but the number of soccer balls produced has risen from 10 to 11 balls. In this case, we say that inflation is zero and real GDP has grown by 10 percent. In other words, using 2016 as the base year for prices, we can see that real GDP rose from 10 × $50 = $500 to 11 × $50 = $550, which is a 10 percent increase.

In Scenario 2 the price has risen from $50 to $55 per ball, but the number of soccer balls produced has stayed fixed at 10 balls in each year. In this case, we say that inflation is 10 percent and real GDP is flat. Using 2016 as the base year for prices, we can see that real GDP held steady at 10 × $50 = $500. In both years, the number of balls produced was 10.

This example illustrates a basic property of nominal GDP. Increases in nominal GDP can arise because of an increase in the price level, an increase in the level of real GDP, or a combination of the two. In fact, we can express the growth rate of nominal GDP as the sum of the growth rate in prices (the inflation rate) and the growth rate in real GDP:

$$\text{Growth rate of nominal GDP} = \text{Growth rate of prices} + \text{Growth rate of real GDP}$$
$$= \text{Inflation rate} + \text{Growth rate of real GDP}.$$

We refer to this equation as the *nominal GDP growth equation.*

We will now use this basic relationship to derive a theory that describes the connections among the growth rate of the money supply, the inflation rate, and the growth rate of real GDP.

The Quantity Theory of Money

We begin by discussing the relationship between the money supply (M2) and nominal GDP. In the historical data, these two economic variables tend to grow at the same rate. For example, consider the United States, for which high-quality money supply data go back to 1959. From 1959 to the present, money supply (M2) and nominal GDP have both grown at an average rate of approximately 7 percent per year. This common growth rate arises because nominal GDP represents the total volume of transactions (in a year) and the money supply is the medium of exchange that is used to conduct those transactions. However, note that money supply need not equal nominal GDP, because money can be used more than once in a single year. It is only the growth rate of money supply and the growth rate of nominal GDP that tend to be tied together over the long run.

The **quantity theory of money** assumes that money supply and nominal GDP grow at the same rate. Year by year this is not always the case. Accordingly, the quantity theory of money is just an approximation of how the economy behaves in the *long run* (meaning over a few decades). The available empirical evidence supports this long-run approximation:

$$\text{Growth rate of money supply} = \text{Growth rate of nominal GDP}.$$

We refer to this equation as the *quantity theory of money equation.*

We are now ready to use our first equation—the nominal GDP growth equation—which breaks down the growth rate of nominal GDP into (1) the inflation rate and (2) the growth rate of real GDP. The nominal GDP growth equation implies that we can replace the growth rate of nominal GDP on the right-hand side of the quantity theory of money equation with the inflation rate plus the growth rate of real GDP, implying that

$$\text{Growth rate of money supply} = \text{Inflation rate} + \text{Growth rate of real GDP}.$$

The **quantity theory of money** assumes that the growth rate of the money supply and the growth rate of nominal GDP are the same over the long run.

> The quantity theory of money . . . [implies] that inflation is equal to the gap between the growth rate of the money supply and the growth rate of real GDP.

Rearranging this equation to put inflation on the left-hand side by itself, we find that

$$\text{Inflation rate} = \text{Growth rate of money supply} - \text{Growth rate of real GDP}.$$

We call this the *inflation equation*.

The inflation equation is an implication of the quantity theory of money. It states that inflation is equal to the gap between the growth rate of the money supply and the growth rate of real GDP. When this gap widens, the inflation rate increases. Intuitively, this equation says that if the growth rate of money exceeds the growth rate of real output, you'll have excess money in the economy, which will drive prices up and create inflation. The inflation equation makes clear predictions that we can test.

11.3 Inflation

Recall from Chapter 5 that the inflation rate refers to the rate of increase of a price index. Of course, price movements need not always be positive. If a price level decreases, we call the rate by which it decreases **deflation**. For example, if the inflation rate is negative 1 percent, we say that the deflation rate is 1 percent. Rising price indexes have been much more common than falling prices almost everywhere in the world since World War II, though Japan has experienced 10 years of deflation interspersed over the period from 1995 to 2012.

The **deflation** rate is the rate of decrease of a price index.

What Causes Inflation?

As we have just seen, the quantity theory of money implies that inflation occurs when the growth rate of money supply exceeds the growth rate in real GDP. This is the implication of the last equation that we derived: the inflation equation.

Exhibit 11.1 tests the inflation equation with data from 110 countries during 1960–1990. As you can see, the inflation rate (plotted on the *y*-axis) is closely related to the growth rate of money supply minus the growth rate of real GDP (this difference is plotted on the *x*-axis). All these variables are annualized, which means that they are expressed as a rate of increase per year. The quantity theory of money predicts that the inflation rate should rise one-for-one with the growth rate of money supply minus the growth rate of real GDP (so if either the growth rate of money supply increases by 1 percent *or* the growth rate of real GDP decreases by 1 percent, the inflation rate should increase by 1 percent). That is what you see in Exhibit 11.1; most of the data lie close to the 45-degree line, which has a slope of 1. This empirically confirms the inflation equation, which is a key long-run prediction generated by the quantity theory of money.

You might have noticed that some of the countries plotted in Exhibit 11.1 had very high average inflation rates from 1960 to 1990. In the case of Argentina, the most extreme point in Exhibit 11.1, inflation averaged 80 percent per year from 1960 to 1990. Argentina experienced this high average inflation rate during this 30-year period because prices rose extraordinarily quickly in the 1980s, pulling up the three-decade average.

Recall from the chapter opener that during hyperinflation, a country's price level doubles within 3 years. Hyperinflationary episodes are always related to extremely rapid growth of the money supply. In almost all cases, such extreme monetary growth is brought about by (misguided) government policy responses to large government budget deficits. If a government's tax revenues fall short of its expenditures, then it meets its obligations by borrowing from the public and/or printing currency to buy goods and services. When a government prints currency and uses it to make purchases, this increases currency in circulation and thereby increases the money supply. This is how German policymakers generated the great German hyperinflation of 1922–1923.

The Consequences of Inflation

It is possible that inflation increases all prices by the same percentage. For example, increasing all prices of the goods and services that a consumer buys by 5 percent and

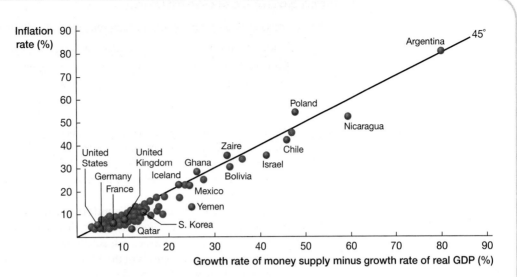

Exhibit 11.1 Testing the Long-Run Prediction of the Quantity Theory of Money

This figure empirically evaluates the long-run predictions of the quantity theory of money—the inflation equation—using data from 1960 to 1990 for 110 countries. The y-axis plots the annualized inflation rate for each country. The x-axis plots the difference on the right-hand side of the inflation equation: the annualized growth rate of money supply minus the annualized growth rate of real GDP. Each country is represented by a single point in the figure. We have also plotted the 45-degree line, which starts at the origin and has a slope of 1, and represents the relationship predicted by the inflation equation.

Source: Data from International Monetary Fund.

simultaneously increasing that worker's nominal wage by 5 percent does not change any of the relative prices or the worker's buying power. If inflation raised all prices, including all nominal wages, by the same percentage, then inflation would not matter.

However, all prices and all wages do not always move in sync, at least not in the short run. An increase in the inflation rate generates windfall losses for some and windfall gains for others. Imagine that you have negotiated a fixed 3-year nominal wage contract with your employer. If the inflation rate unexpectedly rises during this 3-year contract, you will be harmed by the unexpected inflation. In this example, though you and the other employees of the firm lose out, the shareholders of the firm benefit from the unexpected inflation, because the extra inflation lowers the real (inflation-adjusted) value of the wages that the firm pays its workers.

Next consider a retiree receiving a fixed pension that is not indexed to inflation. In other words, the pension payments do not automatically rise with the overall level of prices. A rise in inflation makes the retiree worse off, because the buying power of the pension declines. Here, too, there is a winner on the other side of the relationship: the shareholders of the firm that is paying the pension. The real (inflation-adjusted) costs of the pension payments have gone down.

As yet another example, imagine that you have a mortgage at a fixed rate of interest. In other words, you borrowed money from a bank to buy your home and you are repaying that loan back at a fixed (predetermined) interest rate. If the inflation rate rises, your *real* interest rate falls, lowering the real cost of your mortgage. In this case, the consumer is the winner and the bank's shareholders are the losers.

When contracts for wages, pensions, or mortgage payments are not indexed to inflation, an increase in inflation hurts some economic agents and helps others.

In these three examples, inflation generates specific winners and losers but no clear overall impact on society. However, some consequences of inflation are more generally harmful—almost everyone is a loser. We now turn to those cases. We then discuss some cases where inflation is generally helpful.

The Social Costs of Inflation

We first discuss two of the most important reasons that inflation is socially costly.

1. **A high inflation rate creates logistical costs.** In an environment of high inflation, firms need to frequently change their prices. Recall that during the worst months of the German 1923 hyperinflation, prices were doubling every 3 to 4 days, which means they were increasing about 1 percent per hour. Imagine trying to run a business in which you needed to post new prices for everything in your store several times a day! That's an extreme example, but even much lower rates of inflation—for instance, 20 percent per year—necessitate multiple changes to prices over the course of the year. Economists refer to a business's cost of changing its prices as "menu costs," using as a metaphor the new menus that restaurants print when prices change.

2. **Inflation sometimes leads to counterproductive policies like price controls.** Inflation generates voter anger, and politicians sometimes respond by adopting economically destructive schemes, especially price controls. In most of these cases—like the gasoline price controls of the 1970s, which were discussed in Chapter 4—the policy cure is worse than the disease. Price controls cause numerous problems, including supply disruptions. For example, in Venezuela, strictly enforced price controls have made it impossible for many firms to do business. These firms cannot profitably sell goods and services at the prices set by the government. This devastated the Venezuelan economy and has led to widespread unemployment and malnutrition. Shuttered businesses and empty store shelves are literally starving millions of Venezuelan families. Even when goods are available, price caps cause the quantity demanded to exceed the quantity supplied. The consumers who are lucky enough to obtain a good at the official capped price sometimes resell it at a higher price in the underground economy. Hence, price controls create an inefficient incentive for consumers who don't want to consume a good to wait in long lines to buy it anyway, just so they can resell it to someone else at a profit. In Venezuela, one such professional shopper/reseller described her life this way: "Every day, I have to get up at 2 in the morning and call my friends to find out where things are for sale or what is for sale." The lines start forming so long before dawn that some regional governments have tried to ban standing in line at night.[4]

Price controls in Venezuela have caused shortages of many goods.

Source: http://www.dailymail.co.uk/news/article-2912175/Empty-shelves-Venezuela-tumbling-oil-prices-create-new-industry-People-queuing-goods-probably-run-earn-professors.html.

The Social Benefits of Inflation

However, inflation does generate some social benefits. We mention two here.

1. **Government revenue is generated when the government prints currency.** While printing and spending an enormous amount of new currency leads to hyperinflation, printing/spending a modest amount of new currency can be a socially beneficial source of revenue for a government. However, this additional government revenue is a double-edged sword. The citizens gain, because their government has more money to spend; but they also lose, because the resulting inflation reduces the real value of the currency that they already hold. However, if the amount of money creation is low enough, the net social benefit is positive.

Government revenue obtained from printing currency is called **seigniorage**.

The government revenue obtained from printing currency is called **seigniorage**. This is not a major source of revenue for most governments, though it is relatively important in the United States, because there are many people around the globe—especially traders in the underground economy—who hold vast quantities of U.S. currency. Demand for U.S. currency also derives from entirely legal sources, like people in other countries with an unstable local currency who want a stable store of value. Seigniorage generates roughly $30 billion of implicit revenue for the U.S. government each year.

The fact that a government can raise revenue by printing currency makes seigniorage a candidate for abuse, and this is the reason, as we noted above, some governments running large budget deficits often rapidly expand the money supply and cause inflation—as Zimbabwe and Venezuela have done recently. Printing a lot of currency has short-term appeal for a government, but in the long run the strategy of printing currency to pay a government's bills often gets out of hand and leads to devastating episodes of hyperinflation.

2. **Sometimes inflation can stimulate economic activity.** Assume that a worker's nominal wage is above the competitive equilibrium level, and assume that the nominal wage is downwardly rigid (a case we highlighted in the labor supply and labor demand framework discussed in Chapter 9). The **real wage** is the nominal wage divided by an overall price index, like the consumer price index (CPI). A rise in the overall price index causes a fall in the real wage when the nominal wage is fixed. A fall in the real wage implies that labor has become less expensive to firms relative to the price of the firms' outputs, which rise with inflation. A fall in the real wage therefore induces firms to hire more workers.

The **real wage** is the nominal wage divided by a price index, like the consumer price index (CPI).

We can use the labor supply and labor demand to understand the aggregate implications of a rise in overall prices with a fixed nominal wage. The rise in prices shifts the labor demand curve to the right, because firms can now sell their output at a higher price. Because nominal wages remain fixed, this rightward shift in the labor demand curve increases employment and GDP.

Inflation also lowers the real interest rate. Recall from Chapter 10 that the real interest rate is the nominal interest rate minus the inflation rate. If the inflation rate rises and nominal interest rates don't respond one-for-one, then the real interest rate falls. Since the real interest rate is the inflation-adjusted cost of borrowing, a fall in the real interest rate stimulates borrowing that funds consumption and investment. An increase in consumption and investment (holding all else equal) increases GDP.

Modest inflation therefore stimulates the economy in the short run by cutting real wages (stimulating employment) and cutting real interest rates (stimulating consumption and investment).

In 2010, Zimbabwe experienced hyperinflation. That year it cost 100 billion (Zimbabwe) dollars to buy lunch.

Q: What caused the German hyperinflation of 1922–1923?

At the end of World War I, the Allies imposed heavy financial penalties on the defeated Central Powers, particularly Germany. German reparation payments were specified in the Treaty of Versailles, which was signed in 1919. Postwar Germany, which is called the Weimar Republic, did not make the required payments, and France retaliated in January 1923 by occupying the Ruhr, a German industrial region. To protest the French occupation, German workers in the Ruhr went on strike. This crippled the German economy along with the finances of the German government. As the economic situation deteriorated, the German government was able to meet only 8 percent of its financing needs with tax collection. The rest was paid by borrowing from the public and printing paper money.

Exhibit 11.2 plots the explosive growth of German currency in circulation during this episode. As implied by the quantity theory of money, the rapid increase in the German money supply (without a simultaneous increase in real GDP) prompted a surge in inflation. Economists believe that the German hyperinflation would not have occurred if the government had avoided printing so much currency, which it could have achieved by either reducing its expenditures, raising funds by borrowing more from the public, or reducing its need for funding by defaulting on its debt.

The collapse of the German economy partially set the stage for the ascent of the Nazi party. On November 8, 1923, coinciding with the height of the hyperinflation, 3,000 members of the Nazi party attempted to conduct a regional coup in Munich. This coup attempt, which came to be known as the Beer Hall Putsch, ended with Adolf Hitler's arrest and 8-month imprisonment. While in jail, Hitler wrote his autobiography, *Mein Kampf* (or *My Struggle*), which became a rallying point for the Nazi party.

A plaque commemorating the 1922–1923 German hyperinflation. The inscription reports the price, in German marks, of three basic goods on November 1, 1923: "1 pound of bread, 3 billion; 1 pound of meat, 36 billion; 1 glass of beer, 4 billion." On November, 15, 1923, a new currency, the Rentenmark, replaced the old mark at an exchange rate of 1 new mark for 1 trillion old marks.

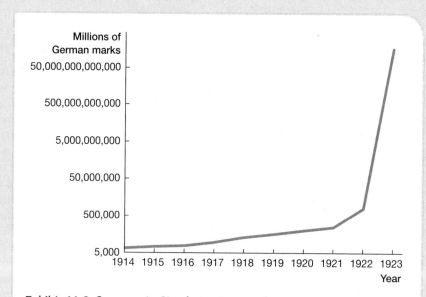

Exhibit 11.2 Currency in Circulation During the Weimar Republic

German currency in circulation exploded during the early 1920s. The *y*-axis scale is proportional, so that each upward tick represents an increase by a factor of 100.

Source: Carl-Ludwig Holtfrerich, The German Inflation 1914–1923: Causes and Effects in International Perspective, Berlin and New York: Walter de Gruyter, 1986.

Tragically, Germany's economic nightmare continued 6 years after the 1922–1923 hyperinflation ended. In 1929, the Great Depression devastated the economy, bringing a deep deflation and sky-high unemployment. Germany had now experienced three economic catastrophes in little more than a decade: the loss of World War I in 1918 (along with subsequent reparations), hyperinflation in 1922–1923, and depression/deflation in 1929. The Great Depression completed the process of economic impoverishment, catapulting the previously unpopular Nazis to power. By 1933, Hitler was chancellor of Germany.

Question	Answer	Data	Caveat
What caused the German hyperinflation of 1922–1923?	The German government could not make reparation payments to the Allies after World War I. As the German economy struggled, the government started to print more and more currency to pay its bills.	Historical money supply data, specifically, currency in circulation.	Though the German money supply and the German price level rose together in 1922 and 1923, correlation does not always imply causation. Nevertheless, in this case a large body of other supportive evidence implies that the relationship is likely to be causal.

11.4 The Federal Reserve

In each country, the monetary system is run by a central bank. We now introduce the basic operations of the central bank. We will continue this discussion in Chapter 13, when we describe how central banks counteract recessions and other economic fluctuations. In the current chapter, we introduce the most important tools at the disposal of central banks and describe the "plumbing" of the monetary system.

The Central Bank and the Objectives of Monetary Policy

The **central bank** is the government institution that monitors financial institutions, controls certain key interest rates, and indirectly controls the money supply. These activities are jointly described as **monetary policy**, and central banks are occasionally referred to as the *monetary authority*.

In the United States, the central bank is called the **Federal Reserve Bank**, or simply the **Fed**. Note that the Fed is *not* the federal government, but rather an independent regulatory agency/bank that operates almost completely autonomously from the rest of the federal government. Exhibit 11.3 shows the locations of the twelve regional Federal Reserve Banks and the Federal Reserve's Board of Governors, which is located in Washington, D.C. The Fed's most important policy decisions are made by the Federal Open Market Committee, comprising the presidents of the twelve regional Federal Reserve Banks (five of whom vote on a rotating basis) and the seven members of the Board of Governors.

Monetary policy is multifaceted, both in terms of its goals and its policy tools. At the broadest level, the Fed uses monetary policy to pursue two key goals or objectives: (1) low

The **central bank** is the government institution that monitors financial institutions, controls certain key interest rates, and indirectly controls the money supply. These activities constitute **monetary policy**.

The **Federal Reserve Bank**, or the **Fed**, is the name of the central bank in the United States.

Exhibit 11.3 Geographic Boundaries of the Federal Reserve Districts

The Federal Reserve System was founded in 1913. To avoid political concentration of the central bank's power, the Fed was divided into twelve regional Federal Reserve Banks (distinguished by color in the map) and the Board of Governors in Washington, D.C. (Alaska and Hawaii are served by the San Francisco district. Puerto Rico is served by the New York district.)

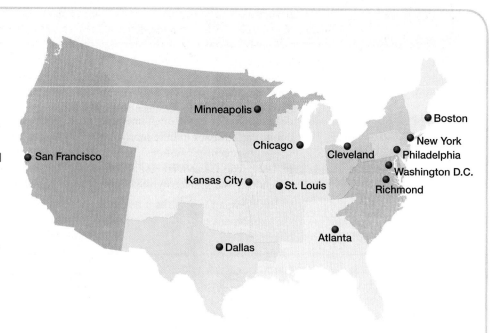

The Fed uses monetary policy to pursue two key goals or objectives: (1) low and predictable levels of inflation and (2) maximum (sustainable) levels of employment. These two goals are referred to as the Fed's *dual mandate*.

The Board of Governors of the Federal Reserve System is nominated by the president and confirmed by the Senate. President Obama nominated Janet Yellen to serve as Chair of the Board of Governors, and the Senate confirmed her nomination in February 2014. Her term as chair will end in February 2018. Most analysts expect that President Trump will not nominate her for another term as chair.

and predictable levels of inflation and (2) maximum (sustainable) levels of employment. These two goals are referred to as the Fed's *dual mandate*.

The goal of low and predictable inflation is sometimes described as "price stability," but this phrase is slightly confusing, since the Fed and almost all other central banks interpret "price stability" to mean around 2 percent annual inflation. The term *inflation targeting* refers to the policy of attempting to obtain a specific low level of inflation over the long run. Most central banks have adopted some form of official or unofficial inflation targeting.

For the European countries that use the euro—the euro-area countries—the European Central Bank (ECB) plays the role of the Fed. But the ECB places slightly greater emphasis on the goal of low and predictable inflation and slightly less emphasis on the goal of maximum employment, partly because of Germany's terrible experience with hyperinflation in the 1920s coupled with Germany's strong influence on decision making at the ECB.

What Does the Central Bank Do?

To achieve its dual mandate—low and predictable levels of inflation and maximum sustainable levels of employment—the Fed engages in three types of activities: regulation, management of interbank transfers, and management of macroeconomic fluctuations by manipulating the quantity of bank reserves. We'll begin by summarizing these three activities and then take a deeper dive into the financial plumbing that makes everything work: bank reserves held at the central bank.

Regulation   The central bank is a key regulator of private banks, particularly the largest private banks. The central bank audits the financial statements, or "books," of large private banks, requiring each bank to accurately report the value of assets and liabilities on its balance sheet.

The central bank will object if it notices that a private bank is holding a portfolio of assets that is too risky. The central bank monitors the amount of shareholders' equity in private banks, trying to ensure that shareholders' equity is adequate to safely absorb future losses in the value of the private bank's assets, even during extremely adverse economic events, like a deep recession. Such "stress tests" started in 2011 as a reaction to the 2007–2009 financial crisis. The central bank takes these stress tests seriously. For example, in

2016, two of the thirty-three banks that received a stress test flunked: the U.S. subsidiaries of Deutsche Bank and Santander were told to strengthen their balance sheets.

Such stress tests are important, because they force vulnerable banks to raise more capital during good times, so the banks are less likely to become insolvent during the next economic downturn. Bank insolvencies intensify economic crises. Rigorously implemented stress tests—with meaningful penalties for failure—incentivize banks to reduce risk and thereby reduce the likelihood of insolvencies.

Interbank Transfers   The central bank oversees the interbank payment systems. When one bank transfers money to another—for example, when a depositor writes a check and the recipient of that check deposits the proceeds at a different bank—the central bank processes this transaction using bank reserves.

Recall from Chapter 10 that bank reserves are the deposits that a private bank makes at the central bank plus cash that the private bank holds in its vault—referred to as vault cash. Note that bank reserves are not part of M2, which is the money supply that households and (non-bank) firms can use to buy goods and services. However, as we will see below, bank reserves can influence the money supply. The quantity of bank reserves plays the key role in interbank payments. Suppose a customer at JPMorgan Chase (hereafter "Chase") writes a $100 million check to a customer at Citibank. Then the Fed will clear this check by transferring $100 million from Chase to Citibank. In this way, the Fed acts as a bank for banks.

To implement these interbank transfers, the Fed uses bank reserves held on deposit at the Fed. In our illustrative example, the Fed would transfer $100 million from Chase's reserves (on deposit at the Fed) to Citibank's reserves (on deposit at the Fed). Naturally, this is only possible if Chase holds at least $100 million as reserves with the Fed in the first place. Accordingly, the Fed requires that banks keep a substantial amount of reserves on deposit so that there are always enough reserves to support the ebb and flow of interbank transactions. This system of bank reserves and the interbank payments that build on it are the monetary lifeblood of an economy.

Management of Macroeconomic Fluctuations by Manipulating the Quantity of Bank Reserves   The central bank manipulates the total quantity of bank reserves. This policy tool affects interest rates, inflation, and unemployment. As we explain in greater detail below, increasing the total quantity of bank reserves lowers interest rates, raises inflation, and lowers unemployment. Likewise, decreasing the quantity of bank reserves has the opposite effects: raising interest rates, lowering inflation, and raising unemployment. Accordingly, by manipulating the quantity of bank reserves, the Fed influences aggregate economic activity. When central banks engage in this type of macroeconomic management, it is referred to as monetary policy. The rest of this chapter explains the system of bank reserves, which serves as the key policy lever of monetary policy.

11.5   Bank Reserves and the Plumbing of the Monetary System

The management of bank reserves is one of the most important and complex roles that the Fed plays. The Fed's control of bank reserves enables it to manage the macroeconomy by influencing interest rates, the inflation rate, and the unemployment rate.

To understand how the Fed does this, we'll proceed as follows.

- We explain why private banks need to have bank reserves, revisiting some of the issues introduced in Chapter 10.
- We explain that bank reserves are traded in a market: in aggregate, private banks demand bank reserves and the central bank supplies bank reserves. We discuss the demand curve for bank reserves.
- We then discuss the supply curve for bank reserves. Having explained the demand and supply curves, we put them together to generate equilibrium in the market for bank reserves. This equilibrium pins down a key short-term interest rate, the *federal*

funds rate. At this equilibrium interest rate, the quantity of bank reserves demanded equals the quantity of bank reserves supplied.

- We then explain that an increase in the quantity of bank reserves supplied by the Fed will usually increase the money supply and inflation.
- Finally, we discuss how the short-term interest rate influences long-term interest rates that are directly relevant for households' and firms' investment decisions and the overall level of employment.

If you get lost at any point while reading the rest of the material in this chapter, reread these five bullet points to remind yourself of the big picture. Alternatively, look at Exhibit 11.11 near the end of this chapter, which summarizes the key role that bank reserves play in influencing interest rates, money supply, inflation, and employment.

Bank Reserves and Liquidity

We now study how private banks choose the quantity of reserves to hold and how they obtain extra reserves when necessary. To conduct transactions, private banks need a source of funds. Bank reserves serve this purpose.

On any given day, a private bank may have more account holders making withdrawals than new deposits coming in. For example, a large corporate account holder at a private bank might pay its employees at the end of the month by withdrawing funds from its corporate bank account. Or a large corporate depositor might withdraw $1 billion of funds from the private bank so that the corporate depositor can use those funds for an acquisition of another company.

The private bank may also need funds to make new loans, such as issuing mortgages to thousands of home buyers or making a large commercial loan to a firm building a new plant. Finally, the private bank may need funds to repay other banks from which it has borrowed money in the past.

All these scenarios imply that the private bank will need **liquidity**, meaning that it will need funds that can be used immediately to conduct transactions. We say that a private bank has enough liquidity if it has sufficient funds to conduct its day-to-day business and to meet its regulatory *reserve requirements*. Reserve requirements are set by the central bank. In the United States today, the reserve requirement is 10 percent of a private bank's demand deposits, such as checking accounts and other accounts that can be withdrawn by depositors with no notice ("on demand"). Summing up, the private bank must hold reserves (as vault cash or on deposit at the Fed) that equal at least 10 percent of the private bank's demand deposits. Reserves in excess of this regulatory minimum are referred to as *excess reserves*.

When a private bank needs funds—liquidity—to conduct transactions, its first line of defense is the reserves that it holds as vault cash or as deposits at the central bank. If the bank has ample reserves, it will use some of these to meet its daily funding needs. However, in some cases, the bank won't have enough reserves to conduct its business. If a bank cannot find a way to raise additional funds on very short notice, it may not be able to make new loans or, in a dire case, it may not be able to pay depositors who wish to withdraw their funds.

Fortunately, banks have a way of obtaining additional liquidity. They can borrow funds from other banks. If some banks face large net withdrawals, then other banks are probably experiencing large net deposits. It is possible that all banks suddenly face large net withdrawals, but most of the time the need for liquidity is not an aggregate phenomenon but specific to a limited set of banks.

To illustrate this point, think about the case of a large employer, like General Electric (GE), on payroll day. GE has 300,000 employees, earning an average salary of about $7,000 per month. To keep things simple, let's assume that GE keeps all its cash at one bank, pays its employees once per month, and makes all these employee payments electronically. On payroll day, GE's bank account shrinks by 300,000 × 7,000 = $2.1 billion, and the bank accounts of GE's employees swell by $2.1 billion. If GE and its employees all have their accounts at the same bank, this single bank will experience no net withdrawals. Withdrawals and deposits will be offsetting.

But if the accounts are at different banks, which is a more realistic scenario, then GE's bank will have a net withdrawal of $2.1 billion, and the employees' banks will receive net deposits of $2.1 billion. At this moment, GE's bank may be short of reserves, and the

The **federal funds market** refers to the market where banks obtain overnight loans of reserves from one another.

The **federal funds rate** is the interest rate that banks charge each other for overnight loans in the federal funds market. The funds being lent are reserves at the Federal Reserve Bank.

employees' banks will be swimming in excess reserves. GE's bank would like to borrow some reserves to address the shortage, and the employees' banks would like to lend out their excess reserves.

Enter the **federal funds market**. This is where banks borrow and lend reserves to one another. In this market banks typically make one-day (24-hour) loans, so the federal funds market is referred to as an *overnight market*. The loan is typically made in the morning and is repaid the next morning. The term *federal funds* refers to the fact that these are loans of bank reserves held at the Federal Reserve Bank. The interest rate in this market is referred to as the **federal funds rate**.

An overnight loan might sound strange, but large banks are so efficient at making interbank loans that they are happy to make these loans for 24 hours (or less!). You wouldn't want a 24-hour mortgage, because it would kill you to re-sign all that paperwork *every* morning for 30 years. However, large banks make billions of dollars of loans to one another each morning in the blink of an eye. Every morning, the banks assess their liquidity needs for the coming business day and borrow or lend accordingly. The following morning, the cycle repeats itself.

The Demand Side of the Federal Funds Market

Exhibit 11.4 graphs the demand curve for reserves. To be precise, these are reserves held on deposit by private banks at the Federal Reserve Bank (so we are not including vault cash held in private banks). The federal funds rate is plotted on the *y*-axis, and the quantity of reserves is plotted on the *x*-axis. It is important to emphasize that the demand curve for reserves plots the *total* quantity of reserves held by private banks (not just the borrowed reserves). So if one bank has $10 billion in reserves and loans $1 billion of reserves to another bank, the net quantity of reserves demanded is

To avoid double-counting, the $1 billion of loaned reserves is only counted as reserves for the borrowing bank. In this example, the total quantity of reserves held by private banks is $10 billion.

The demand curve relates the total quantity of reserves demanded by private banks for each level of the federal funds rate. The demand curve slopes down because optimizing banks choose to hold more reserves as the cost of holding those reserves—the interest rate that they pay to borrow reserves—falls. Reserves are a safety net for the banks, and they prefer to have a bigger safety net if the cost of that safety net falls.

Exhibit 11.4 The Demand Curve in the Federal Funds Market

The (net) demand curve for reserves is downward-sloping: a higher federal funds rate increases the cost of holding reserves and reduces the quantity of reserves demanded by optimizing banks. Conversely, a lower federal funds rate increases the quantity of reserves demanded by banks. Movements in the federal funds rate, holding all else equal, correspond to movements along the demand curve. Shifts of the entire demand curve arise because of economic expansion or contraction, a changing deposit base, or changing liquidity needs.

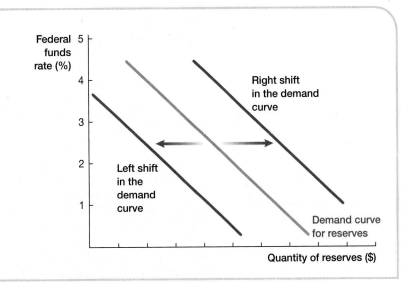

Hence, a lower interest rate increases the quantity of reserves demanded. Changes in the federal funds rate (holding all else equal) generate movements along the demand curve for reserves.

In contrast, if some factor other than the federal funds rate changes, the entire demand curve shifts. A shift in the demand curve for reserves corresponds to a change in the quantity of reserves demanded at a given federal funds rate. There are five key reasons for such shifts in the demand curve for reserves, and the last two of these reasons are under the direct control of the Fed:

- **Economic expansion or contraction.** In a booming economy, private banks need to obtain liquidity so they can make new loans to their customers—for instance, a manufacturing firm that wishes to expand production by borrowing the funds to build a new factory. Reserves provide liquidity that can be used to fund these loans. Therefore, an expansion in private banks' loan originations produces a shift to the right in the demand curve for reserves. Likewise, a contraction in private banks' loan originations produces a shift to the left in the demand curve for reserves.

- **Changing liquidity needs.** If banks expect a flood of withdrawals—for instance, a bank run—this also increases the demand for reserves. Paying out depositors requires liquidity, which is exactly what reserves provide. Hence, an anticipated flood of withdrawals shifts the demand curve for reserves to the right.

- **Changing deposit base.** The demand for reserves is proportional to the total value of bank account balances. Recall that the reserve requirement compels each bank in the United States to hold at least 10 percent of its customers' bank accounts in either vault cash or in reserves held on deposit at the Fed. So an expansion in the quantity of bank account balances produces a shift to the right in the demand curve for reserves. Conversely, the demand curve for reserves shifts to the left as a consequence of a contraction in bank account balances.

- **Changing reserve requirement.** The Fed has the authority to change the 10 percent reserve requirement. Though it rarely uses this authority, the Fed could raise the reserve requirement, thereby shifting the demand curve for reserves to the right. Likewise, the Fed could lower the reserve requirement, thereby shifting the demand curve for reserves to the left.

- **Changing interest rate paid by the Fed for having reserves on deposit at the Fed.** The Fed pays a modest interest rate when private banks deposit money at the Fed—in other words, when private banks hold reserves at the Fed. As of January 2017, the interest rate paid by the Fed to private banks with reserves on deposit at the Fed was 3/4 of 1 percent. When the Fed raises this interest rate, reserves become more beneficial to private banks, shifting the demand curve for reserves to the right. When the Fed lowers this interest rate, reserves become less valuable, shifting the demand curve for reserves to the left.

Exhibit 11.4 plots right and left shifts of the demand curve.

The Supply Side of the Federal Funds Market and Equilibrium in the Federal Funds Market

We're now ready to talk about the supply side of the federal funds market. To understand the day-to-day operations of the Fed, it is useful to model the supply curve of reserves as a vertical line that is set every morning by the Fed. However, from day to day, the Fed may move this vertical supply curve to the right or to the left—as we will see below. Exhibit 11.5 starts with the simple case in which the vertical supply curve does not respond to right or left shifts in the demand curve.

The point where the supply and demand curves cross in the federal funds market is the **federal funds market equilibrium**. Here, the equilibrium quantity of reserves demanded is equal to the equilibrium quantity of reserves supplied by the Fed. The equilibrium federal funds rate is the point at which the demand curve of private banks crosses the vertical supply curve of reserves set by the Fed.

In practice, each dollar of reserves (held at the Fed) is an electronic IOU issued by the Fed to a private bank. Private banks sell the Fed assets in exchange for these reserves. In most cases, the assets that the Fed buys are government bonds, principally bonds issued

The point where the supply and demand curves cross in the federal funds market is the **federal funds market equilibrium**.

Exhibit 11.5 Equilibrium in the Federal Funds Market

Because the Fed fixes the supply of reserves each day, we represent the supply curve of reserves as a vertical line. The intersection of the downward-sloping demand curve and the supply curve gives the equilibrium in the federal funds market. Assuming that the Fed does not shift the supply curve in response to movements in the demand curve, a shift to the left in the demand curve lowers the federal funds rate, and a shift to the right in the demand curve raises the federal funds rate.

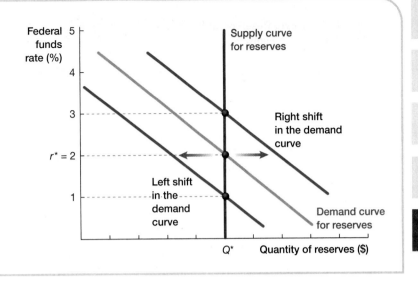

If the Fed wishes to increase the level of reserves that private banks hold, it offers to buy government bonds from the private banks, and in return it gives the private banks more electronic reserves. If the Fed wishes to decrease the level of reserves, it offers to sell government bonds to the private banks and in return the private banks give back some of their reserves. By buying or selling government bonds, the Fed shifts the vertical supply curve in the federal funds market and thereby controls the level of reserves. These transactions are referred to as **open market operations**.

directly by the federal government or entities sponsored by the federal government, like the Federal National Mortgage Association (informally called "Fannie Mae"), which provides funding to the mortgage market.

If the Fed wishes to increase the level of reserves that private banks hold, it buys government bonds from the private banks, and in return it gives the private banks more electronic reserves. If the Fed wishes to decrease the level of reserves, it sells government bonds to the private banks, and in return the private banks give back some of their reserves. By buying or selling government bonds, the Fed shifts the vertical supply curve in the federal funds market and thereby controls the level of reserves (at the Fed) held by private banks. These transactions are referred to as **open market operations**, and they are the Fed's most important monetary policy tool. The transactions associated with open market operations are illustrated in Exhibit 11.6.

The Fed chooses between two alternative strategies when it implements monetary policy. First, consider again the case in Exhibit 11.5. In this case, the Fed holds reserves fixed, even when the demand curve shifts. When this strategy is adopted, shifts in the demand curve translate into changes in the federal funds rate.

The Federal Reserve's second strategy is to find the level of reserves that achieves a particular level of the federal funds rate. Exhibit 11.7 shows how to find the level of reserves that generates a particular federal funds rate (2 percent in the exhibit). In this case, the Fed first chooses the federal funds rate and then finds that point on the demand curve that corresponds to that federal funds rate. The Fed makes available the exact level of reserves

Exhibit 11.6 Open Market Operation That Lowers the Federal Funds Rate

An open market operation is an exchange between the central bank and private banks. In the example depicted here, the Fed gives a private bank (Bank of America in this case) $1 billion in IOUs, which take the form of reserves held on deposit at the Fed. In exchange, the Fed receives $1 billion in bonds from Bank of America.

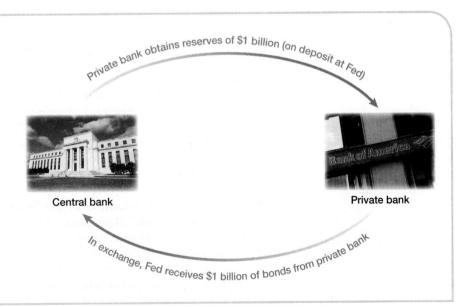

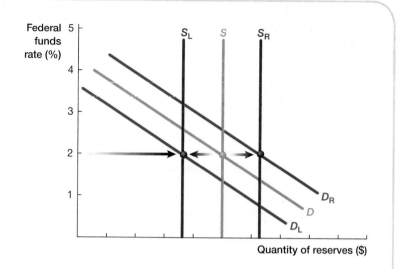

Exhibit 11.7 Picking Reserves to Keep the Federal Funds Rate Fixed

In response to shifts in the demand curve for reserves, the Fed can adjust the level of reserves to hold the federal funds rate constant. If the blue demand curve for reserves shifts to the right (from D to D_R), the Fed will need to shift the supply curve of reserves to the right by exactly the amount that will make the intersection between the new supply curve and the new demand curve remain at the same federal funds rate (S shifts to S_R). If the demand curve for reserves shifts to the left (from D to D_L), the Fed will need to shift the supply curve of reserves to the left (from S to S_L).

associated with that point on the demand curve. Using a strategy like this, the Fed can hold the federal funds rate at a particular fixed value, even as the demand curve shifts from day to day. When the demand curve shifts to the right, the Fed increases the supply of reserves to keep the federal funds rate from rising. When the demand curve shifts to the left, the Fed reduces the supply of reserves to keep the federal funds rate from falling.

Over the past 30 years, the Fed has gradually shifted toward this second strategy rather than the first strategy depicted in Exhibit 11.5. In particular, starting in 1995, the Federal Open Market Committee began making regular statements about the level (or range) of the federal funds rate that it was targeting.

Exhibit 11.7 shows how the Fed can maintain a constant federal funds rate even when the demand curve for reserves shifts. On almost all days since the late 1980s, that is exactly what the Fed has done. But from time to time, the Fed decides to change the federal funds rate in an effort to nudge the economy. As we explain in Chapter 13, raising interest rates will cause economic growth to slow down, whereas lowering interest rates will cause economic growth to speed up. We have a lot to say later in the book about why the Fed raises and lowers interest rates, but for now let's discuss how the Fed makes this happen.

Panel (a) in Exhibit 11.8 illustrates how the Fed can raise the federal funds rate by shifting the supply curve for reserves to the left. As we have seen, the Fed can shift the supply curve to the left by selling government bonds to private banks, allowing the private banks to pay for these bonds with their reserves, and thereby lowering the quantity of reserves that private banks hold at the Fed. The shift in the supply curve leads to a new equilibrium with a higher "price" for reserves—a higher equilibrium federal funds rate.

Likewise, panel (c) in Exhibit 11.8 illustrates how the Fed can lower the federal funds rate by shifting the supply curve for reserves to the right. The Fed can shift the supply curve to the right by buying government bonds from private banks and giving the private banks additional reserves in return for these bonds. The shift in the supply curve leads to a new equilibrium with a lower price for reserves—a lower equilibrium federal funds rate.

Exhibit 11.9 provides historical perspective on the behavior of the federal funds rate. It depicts fluctuations in that rate between July 1954 and January 2017. The exhibit shows that the federal funds rate can increase sharply. This volatility arises both from shifts in the supply curve of reserves (as shown in Exhibit 11.8) and from shifts in the demand curve for reserves (as shown in Exhibit 11.5).

Summary of the Fed's Control of the Federal Funds Rate   Drawing together what we've discussed so far, the Fed can influence the federal funds rate either by shifting the quantity of reserves supplied (with open market operations) or by shifting the demand curve for reserves. Recall that the Fed can shift the demand curve for reserves to the right by raising the reserve requirement (which was 10 percent of demand deposits as of January 2017) or by increasing the interest rate paid on reserves (which was 3/4 of 1 percent as of January 2017). Both of these demand-shifting policies would have the effect of increasing the equilibrium federal funds rate.

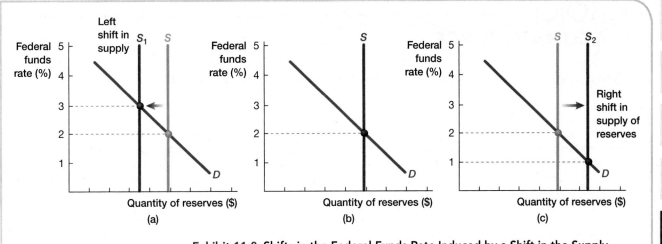

Exhibit 11.8 **Shifts in the Federal Funds Rate Induced by a Shift in the Supply of Reserves**

The Fed can raise the federal funds rate by shifting the supply curve for reserves to the left. This shift leads to a new equilibrium with a higher equilibrium federal funds rate. Likewise, the Fed can lower the federal funds rate by shifting the supply curve for reserves to the right. This shift leads to a new equilibrium with a lower equilibrium federal funds rate.

> The Fed has three basic policy levers for influencing the federal funds rate: changing the quantity of reserves supplied, changing the reserve requirement, and changing the interest rate paid on reserves.

In contrast, the Fed can shift the demand curve for reserves to the left by lowering the reserve requirement or by lowering the interest rate paid on reserves. Both of these demand-shifting policies would have the effect of lowering the equilibrium federal funds rate.

Summing up, the Fed has three basic policy levers for influencing the federal funds rate: changing the quantity of reserves supplied, changing the reserve requirement, and changing the interest rate paid on reserves. The Fed has always shifted the quantity of reserves (open market operations) to influence interest rates. In contrast, changes in reserve requirements have been phased out. The last U.S. change in the reserve requirement occurred in 1992. Paying interest on reserves was approved by Congress only in 2008, but this policy has quickly become part of the Fed's standard policy toolbox. For example, in December 2016 the Fed raised the interest rate on reserves from 1/2 of 1 percent to 3/4 of 1 percent. Many more such increases are anticipated to occur in 2017–2019.

MyEconLab Real-time data

Exhibit 11.9 The Federal Funds Rate Between July 1954 and January 2017

The federal funds rate has varied a great deal during the postwar period. During recessions—indicated by the shaded areas in the exhibit—the federal funds rate tends to fall. When the economy is weak, the Fed stimulates the economy by lowering the federal funds rate.

Source: Based on Board of Governors of the Federal Reserve System.

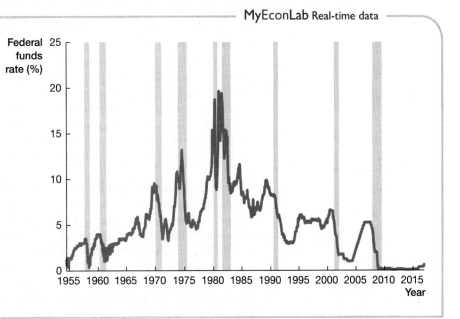

Obtaining Reserves Outside the Federal Funds Market

During normal times, the federal funds market operates without a hitch. Banks that need extra reserves borrow them, and banks that have excess reserves lend them out. But during extraordinary times, such as during a financial panic, the federal funds market can break down, because banks with excess reserves don't know whom they can trust. They don't know which banks are solvent—those that are able to pay back their lenders—and which banks are not. Accordingly, the banks with excess reserves may be unwilling to lend these reserves out.

In such a crisis, the banks that need reserves may not be able to obtain them. Fortunately, the Fed can step in and provide reserves through another channel. The Fed does this by allowing banks to borrow reserves from the Fed's "discount window." Because loans from the discount window have a higher interest rate than loans obtained on the federal funds market, the discount window is usually a private bank's *last resort* for borrowing reserves. Sometimes the Fed is referred to as the "lender of last resort." When all else fails, a bank can go directly to the Fed for a loan of reserves.

The Fed's Influence on the Money Supply and the Inflation Rate

We've now completed our discussion of the determination of the federal funds rate—a key short-term interest rate. Let us turn now to a second important channel: the Fed's influence on the money supply and on the inflation rate.

In fact, the Fed cannot directly control either the money supply or the inflation rate. Some people mistakenly think that the Fed controls the money supply because the Fed controls the quantity of bank reserves. But bank reserves are actually not part of the money supply. Instead, the money supply includes deposits by households and firms at private banks and currency in circulation.

Though the Fed doesn't directly control the money supply or inflation, the Fed does try to influence these important macroeconomic variables. Since inflation is part of the Fed's dual mandate and the money supply is not, the Fed cares a great deal about inflation and only indirectly cares about the money supply. Accordingly, if the annual inflation rate is close to the Fed's target of 2 percent, the Fed won't worry about short-run variation in the growth rate of the money supply.

In the long run, the inflation rate is approximately equal to the growth rate of the money supply minus the growth rate of real GDP, as we saw in our empirical analysis of the quantity theory of money earlier in the chapter. Because of this relationship, the Fed will try to slow down the rate of money supply growth if the inflation rate starts to rise above the Fed's inflation target.

Note that the money supply increases when banks make new loans. Consider a home buyer who takes out a $200,000 mortgage from Citibank. The person who is selling the home receives these funds from the buyer and deposits them at her bank, which may or may not be Citibank. This deposit increases the money supply by $200,000. Hence, the origination of this new mortgage increases the money supply by $200,000. Accordingly, the origination of many new loans causes the money supply to grow rapidly. When the Fed attempts to slow down the growth of the money supply, it does this by slowing down the growth of loans from private banks to households and firms.

As we explain in the next subsection, the federal funds rate influences the long-term interest rates that affect the quantity of new loans demanded by households and firms. By raising the federal funds rate, the Fed raises the interest rate that households and firms face, thereby lowering the quantity of loans demanded and lowering the growth rate of the money supply.

Summary of the Fed's Influence on the Money Supply and the Inflation Rate

The Fed raises the federal funds rate with three tools. First, the Fed can reduce the quantity of bank reserves by using open market operations. Second, the Fed can increase the reserve requirement. Third, the Fed can increase the interest rate that it pays on reserves. All these policies will increase the federal funds rate and the interest rates that households and firms face for borrowing. Consequently, a higher federal funds rate reduces the rate of loan growth to households and firms, reducing the rate at which the money supply grows and reducing the rate of inflation. Likewise, a lower federal funds rate increases the rate of loan growth to households and firms, increasing the rate at which the money supply grows and increasing the rate of inflation.

The Relationship Between the Federal Funds Rate and the Long-Term Real Interest Rate

We've now completed our discussion of the first two consequences of the Fed's management of bank reserves. We're ready to turn to a third, and final, category. By intervening in the market for bank reserves, the Fed influences both the federal funds rate and the *long-term real interest rate*. Recall that the real interest rate is defined as the real price of a loan, or, in other words, the price of a loan adjusted for inflation. It is defined as

$$\text{Real interest rate} = \text{Nominal interest rate} - \text{Inflation rate}.$$

The long-term real interest rate is the long-term nominal interest rate minus the long-term inflation rate.

Consider a firm that borrows $100 for a year at a nominal interest rate of 5 percent in an economy with a 2 percent inflation rate. One year later, the firm pays back $100 × (1 + 0.05) = $105 dollars, but inflation has chipped away at the buying power of this money. If the inflation rate is 2 percent, $105 in the payback year has buying power of only $105/(1 + 0.02), or about $103 in the year the loan was issued. This is just $3 more than the original loan amount. So the *real* cost to the borrower is only $3 of buying power, which is 3 percent of the original $100 loan. In general, the real cost of a loan is the nominal interest rate minus the inflation rate. In the current example, the real interest rate can be calculated as 5% − 2% = 3%.

Investment depends on the **long-term real interest rate**, which is the long-term nominal interest rate minus the long-term inflation rate. When we talk about the long term, we are referring to horizons that are 10 years away (or more). The long-term real interest rate is relevant for the economy, because many investments require funding for at least a decade. A home loan lasts 30 years. A major corporate research and development project—like the development of the double-decker, "superjumbo" Airbus A380—can take 20 years between the initial conceptualization and the rollout of the finished product.

Development of the A380 was started in 1988. The first aircraft was sold in 2008. Twenty-year research and development projects are **not** funded by 365 × 20 = 7,300 overnight loans. Corporations fund projects like this by issuing long-term bonds.

In contrast, the federal funds rate is a short-term nominal interest rate. So there is a mismatch between the short-term interest rate that the Fed essentially controls and the long-term real interest rates that matter for most investment decisions. To understand the potential impact of the federal funds rate on the long-term real interest rate, it is also useful to think about the real interest rate that is anticipated when the loan is made. This is potentially different from the real interest rate that is *realized* over the life of the loan. It is therefore useful to distinguish between a *realized real interest rate* and an *expected real interest rate*.

The realized real interest rate is the nominal interest rate minus the realized rate of inflation.

The **realized real interest rate** is defined as:

$$\text{Realized real interest rate} = \text{Nominal interest rate} - \text{Realized inflation rate}.$$

For example, if a borrower takes out a loan on December 31, 2010, and repays the loan on December 31, 2020, the realized real interest rate would be the nominal interest rate that the borrower agreed to on December 31, 2010, minus the actual realized inflation rate between December 31, 2010 and December 31, 2020. Note that realized inflation is the inflation that actually occurred over a particular period of time.

When the loan is first issued, the borrower doesn't yet know what the realized inflation rate will be. So the borrower won't be able to calculate the realized real interest rate until the loan ends on December 31, 2020.

But we do have beliefs, or expectations, about the inflation rate between now and then. We can use those expectations to motivate a closely related concept called the **expected real interest rate**:

The expected real interest rate is the nominal interest rate minus the expected rate of inflation.

$$\text{Expected real interest rate} = \text{Nominal interest rate} - \text{Expected inflation rate}.$$

When making loans, optimizing borrowers and lenders consider the expected real interest rate; they do not yet know what the realized inflation rate will be. The expected real interest rate

Two Models of Inflation Expectations

How do people actually form inflation expectations? Some economists believe that people's inflation expectations are determined by the level of inflation in the recent past. For example, "my forecast of the inflation rate next year is the inflation rate that was realized last year." Such *adaptive expectations* are a backward-looking form of inflation expectations. Backward-looking inflation expectations are plausible, because it is natural to believe that the future will mirror your recent past experiences.

But believing that what will happen in the future is the same as what happened in the recent past is not maximally rational. Many economists believe that people are more sophisticated than the adaptive expectations theory assumes. These critics of the adaptive expectations

model typically endorse the model of *rational expectations*, which assumes that people have inflation expectations that incorporate all the information that is available when the inflation expectations are being formed and use that information in the most sophisticated way possible. If agents have rational expectations, they are masterful forecasters who make the best possible forecast using a sophisticated understanding of the workings of the economy.

Critics of the rational expectations model complain that it overestimates the degree of human rationality. For decades, economists have debated which of these models best describes the actual inflation expectations of consumers and workers. The jury is still out.

Economic agents' **inflation expectations** are their beliefs about future inflation rates.

depends on economic agents' **inflation expectations**, which are their beliefs about future inflation rates.

We are now ready to ask how a change in the federal funds rate affects the long-term expected real interest rate. Although there is no universally accepted answer, most economists agree that changing the federal funds rate also tends to change—in the same direction—the long-term expected real interest rate.

A fall in the federal funds rate implies that private banks are able to borrow reserves in the federal funds market at a lower interest rate. Because the private banks' own borrowing costs are falling, they start to offer loans at lower interest rates too. This implies that the supply of credit from private banks shifts to the right.

> Although there is no universally accepted answer, most economists agree that changing the federal funds rate also tends to change—in the same direction—the long-term expected real interest rate.

Moreover, the long-term nominal interest rate falls, because a long-term loan is effectively made up of many short-term loans. You can think of a 10-year loan as ten 1-year loans lined up one after the other—like a freight train made up of box cars that are linked together. When the federal funds rate goes down, the first 1-year loan becomes less expensive for the private bank to make. In addition, a change in the federal funds rate is usually not reversed for at least several years, so several of the 1-year loans that are linked together in the first few years of the 10-year loan package are affected. Think of the nominal interest rate for the long-term loan as the average of these ten 1-year loans. If several of the 1-year loans decline because of a change in the federal funds rate, the long-term nominal rate will also fall.

Ten-year loan

To make this concrete, suppose that the Federal Reserve lowers the federal funds rate from 4 percent to 3 percent, and that this decrease is going to last for 2 years, at which point the federal funds rate will revert to its old level. Then the 10-year nominal interest rate, which can be thought of as the average of ten 1-year loans, will fall from 4 percent to 3.8 percent. To see why, let's take the average of ten 1-year loans, where the first two loans are made at 3 percent and the last eight loans are made at 4 percent:

$$\frac{3\% + 3\% + 4\% + 4\% + 4\% + 4\% + 4\% + 4\% + 4\% + 4\%}{10} = 3.8\%.$$

Exhibit 11.10 Effect of Open Market Operation on the Long-Term Expected Real Interest Rate

An increase in bank reserves at the Fed lowers the federal funds rate, which in turn lowers the long-term nominal interest rate. With constant inflation expectations, the long-term expected real interest rate falls by as much as the long-term nominal interest rate.

Starting point
Federal funds rate: 4%
Long-term nominal interest rate: 4%
Long-term inflation expectations: 2%
Long-term expected real interest rate: 4% − 2% = 2%

Open market operation increases bank reserves
CAUSES
Federal funds rate to fall from 4% to 3%
CAUSES
Long-term nominal interest rate to fall from 4% to 3.8%
(Assume that inflation expectations don't change)

Ending point
Federal funds rate: 3%
Long-term nominal interest rate: 3.8%
Long-term inflation expectations: 2%
Long-term expected real interest rate: 3.8% − 2% = 1.8%

To complete our analysis, we now need to determine how changes in the long-term nominal interest rate—which we just analyzed—affect the long-term expected real interest rate. This requires that we study the effect of monetary policy on both the long-term nominal interest rate and the long-term expected inflation rate.

First, imagine what would happen if inflation expectations don't change in response to a fall in the federal funds rate. If inflation expectations don't change, and nominal interest rates fall, then the expected real interest rate falls. Hence, a fall in the federal funds rate lowers the long-term nominal interest rate and lowers the expected long-term real interest rate.

Exhibit 11.10 summarizes these linkages and provides a numerical example. The exhibit begins with an increase in the reserves held at the central bank. This change results from open market operations conducted by the Fed. Specifically, the Fed buys bonds from banks and gives the banks reserves in exchange for the bonds. The rightward shift in the supply of reserves lowers the federal funds rate—in this example, from 4 percent to 3 percent. This in turn lowers the long-term nominal interest rate from 4 percent to 3.8 percent. If the long-term expected inflation rate remains at 2 percent, then the long-term expected real interest rate falls from 4 − 2 = 2 percent (before the open market operation) to 3.8 − 2 = 1.8 percent (after the open market operation).

If inflation expectations do change, the analysis gets more complicated, but even in this case, the long-term expected real interest rate often falls in response to a reduction in the federal funds rate.

Finally, we can turn to the effects on consumption, investment, and unemployment. We'll have much more to say about these effects in Chapter 13, but for now we'll whet your appetite by noting that changes in long-term real interest rates influence household and firm investment decisions. For example, a fall in the mortgage rate will increase demand for home buying and home building, stimulating employment and output in the construction industry. Likewise, a fall in corporate borrowing rates will stimulate corporate investment, increasing employment and output once again. Channels like these give the Fed a policy tool with which it can influence overall economic activity, especially in industries that are sensitive to long-run interest rates.

Summary of the Fed's Influence on Long-Term Expected Real Interest Rates The long-term real interest rate is the long-term nominal interest rate minus the long-term expected inflation rate. When the Fed influences short-term interest rates, such as the federal funds rate, this affects the long-term nominal interest rate. A long-term loan is like a combination of short-term loans. You can think of a 10-year loan as ten 1-year loans lined up one after the other. When the federal funds rate goes down, the interest rate for the first 1-year loan goes down. In addition, a change in the federal funds rate is usually not reversed for several years, so several of the 1-year loans in the 10-year loan package are affected. In most cases, when the Fed lowers the federal funds rate, this action has little impact on long-term inflationary expectations. In short, the long-term real interest rate tends to fall when the federal funds rate falls, because the long-term nominal interest rate falls and inflation expectations tend to stay roughly the same.

This completes our overview of the Fed's activities. We've discussed the Fed's core activities, but some important details have been left out. We'll fill in the rest of the picture in the next two chapters. The current chapter introduced the concept of money and the fundamental "plumbing" of the Fed's operations, especially the Fed's influence over the federal funds market. In the next two chapters, you'll see how the Fed trades off competing policy goals and how the Fed actually conducted policy during and after the financial crisis and recession of 2007–2009.

We conclude with a schematic diagram—Exhibit 11.11—that illustrates how the Fed influences macroeconomic activity by manipulating the federal funds rate. This exhibit summarizes the channels that we discussed in our analysis of the role of reserves.

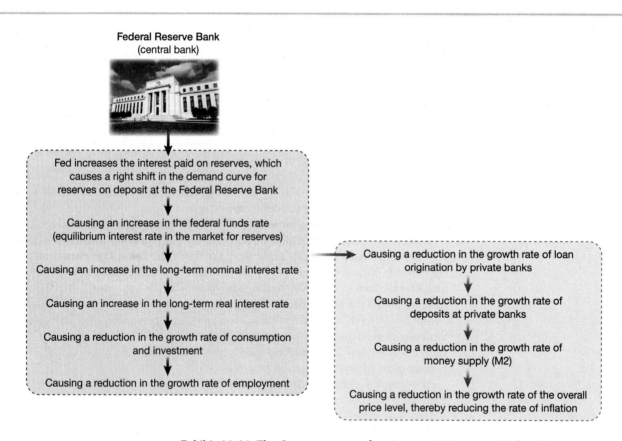

Exhibit 11.11 The Consequences of an Increase in Interest Paid on Reserves on Deposit at the Federal Reserve Bank

An increase in interest paid on reserves on deposit at the Federal Reserve Bank causes the demand curve for reserves to shift to the right. This causes the equilibrium interest rate in the federal funds market to rise: in other words, the federal funds rate rises. Following the black arrows, this leads to a rise in long-run interest rates; a rise in long-run real interest rates; and a fall in the growth rates of consumption, investment, and employment. Turning to the blue arrows, this increase also decreases the growth rate of loan originations, which in turn decreases the growth rates of deposits, the money supply, and the price level (due to the quantity theory of money). Accordingly, the rate of inflation declines.

Summary

- Money plays a vital role in our lives. It makes a range of economic transactions possible, simultaneously serving as (1) a medium of exchange that can be traded for goods and services, (2) a store of value that enables us to save and transfer purchasing power into the future, and (3) a common unit of account that expresses the price of different goods and services.

- The money supply is the quantity of money that individuals can immediately use in transactions. The money supply is defined as the sum of currency in circulation (which excludes currency in bank vaults) and the balances of most bank accounts at private banks. This measure of the money supply is referred to as M2. This measure excludes all forms of bank reserves.

- The quantity theory of money links the money supply to nominal GDP, which is the value of total output in the economy measured at current prices. The quantity theory of money implies that the long-term inflation rate equals the long-run growth rate of the money supply minus the long-run growth rate of real GDP.

- At a fixed growth rate of real GDP, faster growth of the money supply leads to inflation and, in extreme cases, to hyperinflation. Inflationary growth in the money supply generates social costs, which include "menu costs" that firms incur as they make frequent price changes and price controls that create supply disruptions, shortages, and inefficient queuing. Moderate growth in the money supply, which produces moderate inflation, generates certain benefits for society, including seigniorage and temporarily lower real wages and real interest rates, which stimulate growth of real GDP.

- Central banks, such as the Federal Reserve Bank (the Fed) in the United States, attempt to keep inflation at a low and stable level and also try to maximize the sustainable level of employment.

- The Fed regulates banks, implements interbank payments, and attempts to influence macroeconomic fluctuations.

- The Fed holds the reserves of private banks (with the exception of vault cash). The management of these private bank reserves is one of the most important roles that the Fed plays. The Fed's management of private bank reserves enables it to influence interest rates, the inflation rate, and the level of employment.

- The Fed has many policy levers that enable it to influence the market for bank reserves and, by implication, the federal funds rate, including shifting the quantity of reserves supplied (which is referred to as open market operations), changing the reserve requirement, and changing the interest rate paid on reserves.

Key Terms

money *p. 253*
medium of exchange *p. 253*
store of value *p. 253*
unit of account *p. 254*
fiat money *p. 254*
money supply *p. 256*
quantity theory of money *p. 257*
deflation *p. 258*

seigniorage *p. 261*
real wage *p. 261*
central bank *p. 263*
monetary policy *p. 263*
Federal Reserve Bank, or the Fed *p. 263*
liquidity *p. 266*
federal funds market *p. 267*
federal funds rate *p. 267*

federal funds market equilibrium *p. 268*
open market operations *p. 269*
long-term real interest rate *p. 273*
realized real interest rate *p. 273*
expected real interest rate *p. 273*
inflation expectations *p. 274*

Questions

All questions are available in MyEconLab for practice and instructor assignment.

1. List and explain the three functions of money in a modern economy

2. How does fiat money differ from commodities like gold and silver that have been used as money?

3. How is the M2 money supply defined?

4. Recall the discussion in the chapter about the quantity theory of money.

   a. Explain the quantity theory of money.

   b. Explain how predictions of the quantity theory of money are borne out by historical data.

5. What are the differences among inflation, deflation, and hyperinflation?

6. What is the most common cause of hyperinflation?

7. What are the costs associated with inflation?

8. Does inflation have any benefits? Explain.

9. What is the federal funds rate? What are the factors that would shift the demand curve for reserves?

10. What is an open market operation? Why does the Federal Reserve conduct open market operations?

11. Why is the Federal Reserve referred to as the "lender of last resort"?

12. How does the Federal Reserve influence the long-term real interest rate?

13. What are the two models that are used to describe inflationary expectations?

Problems

All problems are available in MyEconLab for practice and instructor assignment.

1. Barter is a method of exchange whereby goods or services are traded directly for other goods or services without the use of money or any other medium of exchange.

   a. Suppose you need to get your house painted. You register with a barter Web site and want to offer your car cleaning services to someone who will paint your house in return. What are the problems you are likely to encounter?

   b. Some barter Web sites allow the use of "barter dollars." The registration fee that you pay to a barter Web site gets converted into barter dollars that can be exchanged with other users to buy goods and services. Would the use of barter dollars resolve the problems you listed in part (a)? Explain.

2. Money makes a variety of economic transactions possible. In the following three situations, determine whether money is involved in the transaction.

   a. In prison camps during World War II, and in some prisons today, cigarettes circulate among prisoners. For example, a cell phone might cost 600 cigarettes, whereas a magazine might cost only two cigarettes. Discuss whether cigarettes are fulfilling all three functions of money in this case.

   b. Over the past 50 years, credit cards have become an increasingly popular way for people to purchase goods and services. Are credit cards money? Explain your reasoning.

   c. Many people have retirement savings accounts, in which they hold stocks and bonds. Do these balances constitute money? Why or why not?

3. In some parts of the world, salt—the stuff sitting on your kitchen table—was once used as currency. In ancient Ethiopia, for example, blocks of salt were used to purchase goods and pay salaries. The value of the salt block was based on weight, and it was physically transferred as part of the transaction. In part, salt was valuable because of its scarcity and its usefulness: before the introduction of refrigeration, many civilizations used salt to preserve food.

   a. Discuss how salt did or did not fulfill the three purposes of currency.

   b. Suppose several new salt mines opened in ancient Ethiopia. How would you expect the rapid infusion of currency into society to affect the economy? Explain.

4. Bitcoins are defined as a "peer-to-peer decentralized digital currency." The supply of bitcoins is not controlled by the government or any other central agency. The value of each bitcoin is determined on the basis of supply and demand and is defined in terms of dollars. New bitcoins can be generated through a process called "mining." However, new bitcoins will not be created once there are a total of 21 million bitcoins in existence. Some commentators feel that bitcoins can eventually replace most of the major currencies in the world. Would you agree? Explain your answer.

5. Imagine that the chair of the Federal Reserve announced that, as of the following day, all currency in circulation in the United States would be worth 10 times its face denomination. For example, a $10 bill would be worth $100; a $100 bill would be worth $1,000; and so forth. Furthermore, the balances in all checking and savings accounts would

be multiplied by 10. So, for example, if you had $500 in your checking account, as of the following day your balance would be $5,000. Would you actually be 10 times better off on the day the announcement took effect? Why or why not?

6. According to the BBC, inflation in the country of Zimbabwe reached an annualized rate of 231,000,000 percent in October 2008. Prices got so high that in January 2009, the country's central bank—the Reserve Bank of Zimbabwe—introduced a $100 trillion bill. (*Sources*: http://news.bbc.co.uk/2/hi/africa/7660569.stm; http://news.bbc.co.uk/2/hi/africa/7832601.stm.)

   Read the summary of Zimbabwe's experience with hyperinflation in Wikipedia (http://en.wikipedia.org/wiki/Hyperinflation_in_Zimbabwe). How does the history of hyperinflation in the country illustrate the points made in the chapter regarding the root causes, costs, and benefits of inflation? What were some of the adaptations that citizens of the country used to cope with the situation?

7. The following table shows the cost of producing dollar notes of various denominations. As you can see in the table, it costs only 15.5 cents to produce a $100 bill. Suppose the government decides that it will print new notes to fund its fiscal deficit as well as all its ongoing expenditures. What would be the effects of such a policy?

Note Denomination	Cost of Production
$1 and $2	5.4 cents per note
$5	11.5 cents per note
$10	10.9 cents per note
$20	12.2 cents per note
$50	19.4 cents per note
$100	15.5 cents per note

8. After every meeting, the Federal Open Market Committee releases a statement that summarizes their policy decisions. For this problem, we'll use the statement from December 16, 2015, which announced the beginning of "normalization." Carefully read through the statement here: https://www.federalreserve.gov/newsevents/pressreleases/monetary20151216a.htm

   a. According to the statement, what factors did the committee consider in making their decision? Explain how these factors relate to the Federal Reserve's mandate.

   b. What decision did the committee reach in this meeting?

   c. The committee used open market operations to reach its new goal. What kind of open market operations would move the federal funds rate in the desired direction? Using a chart, show the resulting change in the market for bank reserves.

   d. Ultimately, how would you expect this policy change to affect the long-term real interest rate, employment, and the money supply? Walk through the steps, as in Exhibit 11.11.

9. From 2001 to 2006, Japan's central bank, the Bank of Japan (BOJ), engaged in a monetary policy program called quantitative easing. The BOJ increased the quantity of the excess reserves that commercial banks held with the central bank by buying assets from these commercial banks. Use a graph to show how this policy is likely to have affected the "overnight call rate." The overnight call rate in Japan is similar to the federal funds rate in the United States.

10. During the financial crisis of 2007–2008, many central banks, including the Federal Reserve and the Bank of Japan, lowered their federal funds rate (or the non-U.S. equivalent) to around zero. The Bank of Japan took an additional, unusual measure: it introduced a *negative* short-term interest rate on excess reserves. Faced with a negative interest rate, banks must *pay* to lend their excess reserves to other banks. How would this policy change the incentives of banks? Based on what you learned in this chapter, why might a central bank choose to lower interest rates on reserves below zero?

11. As the U.S. economy continues to recover from the effects of the recession of 2007–2009, it is widely anticipated that the Fed will keep raising the federal funds rate. Suppose the current federal funds rate is 1.5 percent, and that this rate is expected to prevail for 1 more year. Then, the expectation is that the Fed will raise the federal funds rate by 0.5 percentage points each year for 4 years, reaching 3.5 percent in year five and then maintaining the federal funds rate at that level for another 5 years. What will be the 10-year nominal interest rate as a result of these expectations? Explain and show your work.

12. The chapter discusses different models of how people form their expectations regarding inflation. Consider the following two investors, who are trying to forecast what inflation will be for next year. Sean reasons as follows: "Inflation was 2.5 percent last year. Therefore, I think it is likely to be 2.5 percent this year." In contrast, Carlos thinks this way: "The economy has recovered from recession sufficiently that inflationary pressures are likely to build. Likewise, a weaker dollar means that imports are going to be more expensive. I don't think the Fed will risk slowing the recovery and raising unemployment by raising interest rates to fight inflation. So, in light of all these factors, I expect inflation to increase to 3 percent this year." Using the terminology mentioned in the chapter, explain how you would best describe how each investor is forming his expectations of inflation. Which description better fits your own forecasts of inflation?

12 Short-Run Fluctuations

What caused the recession of 2007–2009?

The U.S. economy, like any other, experiences economic fluctuations—in other words, the growth rate fluctuates from year to year. From 1983 to 2007, the U.S. economy tended to grow quickly and experienced only two mild recessions, achieving average growth in real gross domestic product (GDP) of 3.4 percent per year. But near the end of 2007, the economy began a deep contraction. The fall in economic activity caused significant hardship for hundreds of millions of households worldwide. In the United States alone, the number of unemployed workers rose by 7.4 million. Many families also lost a large chunk of their life savings; U.S. housing prices fell by a third, and stock prices halved. The recession that started in December 2007 lasted until June 2009, when the economy started growing again.

What caused the recession of 2007–2009? In this chapter, we examine the various factors that contributed to this economic and financial free fall. But first we explore the characteristics of economic fluctuations in general and possible causes for them. In the process, we will develop a model that can help us better understand the short-run causes and consequences of fluctuations in economic activity.

CHAPTER OUTLINE

12.1 Economic Fluctuations and Business Cycles

Modern market economies have demonstrated a remarkable ability to generate long-run growth. As we saw in Chapter 7, the U.S. economy has grown substantially over the past 100 years. But growth, even for the most developed economies, is never completely steady. Instead, there are periods of good times and bad, of ups and downs. These fluctuations tend to be hard to predict. We refer to short-run changes in the growth rate of real GDP as **economic fluctuations** or **business cycles**.

Short-run changes in the growth of GDP are referred to as **economic fluctuations** or **business cycles**.

Exhibit 12.1 plots the level of real GDP (in blue) in the United States from 1929 to 2016, using 2009 as the base year for prices. Recall that real dollars hold the overall price level fixed, implying that the effects of inflation are removed from plots of *real* variables. The plot of real GDP starts in 1929 because that is when high-quality data were first available.

Growth, even for the most developed economies, is never completely steady.

The exhibit also plots a trend line (in red), which represents the level of real GDP that the economy would attain if we could wave a wand and magically maintain a steady rate of growth, thereby avoiding fluctuations. The trend line in Exhibit 12.1 is derived by drawing a path that grows smoothly over time. Such a fluctuation-free economy is not actually feasible—economic fluctuations are a fact of life. Government policies can only reduce the severity—not the very existence—of fluctuations.

In Exhibit 12.1, two major deviations from trend are apparent: the Great Depression (lasting throughout the 1930s) and the period of U.S. participation in World War II (1941–1945). During the Great Depression, the U.S. economy fell far below trend GDP. Conversely, during World War II, the U.S. economy surged ahead of trend GDP.

Exhibit 12.2 provides an alternative way of looking at the same data by plotting the percentage deviation—that is, the difference between the blue and the red lines as a percentage of the level of the red line—between real GDP and its trend. When the difference is positive, real GDP is above its trend line. When it is negative, real GDP is below its trend line. Looking at Exhibit 12.2, we can again easily see two big events standing apart from the rest: the Great Depression and World War II. The most recent recession (2007–2009) is also visible near the right end of the plot, where the difference between real GDP and

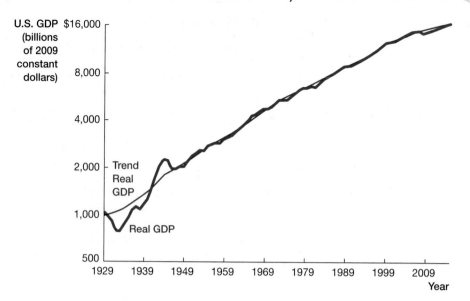

Exhibit 12.1 Real U.S. GDP and a Trend Line (1929–2016; billions of 2009 constant dollars)

Real GDP is plotted in blue. The red trend line represents the level of real GDP that the economy would attain if we could smooth out the year-to-year fluctuations. The trend line is derived by drawing a path that grows smoothly over time. The figure uses a proportional scale for the *y*-axis, so that each number on that axis represents a further doubling of real GDP. Recall from Chapter 7 that with a proportional scale, a straight line represents a constant rate of annual growth. The slowly declining slope of the trend line in this exhibit implies that the trend rate of growth for real GDP is also slowly declining over the seven decades following World War II.

Source: Based on Bureau of Economic Analysis, National Income and Product Accounts (GDP). The trend line is calculated by the authors.

Exhibit 12.2 Percentage Deviation Between U.S. Real GDP and Its Trend Line (1929–2016)

This plot shows the percentage deviation between U.S. real GDP and a trend line for U.S. real GDP (the trend line is plotted in Exhibit 12.1). The percentage deviation is calculated as $100 \times$ (Real GDP − Trend)/Trend.

Source: Based on Bureau of Economic Analysis, National Income and Product Accounts (real GDP). The trend line is calculated by the authors.

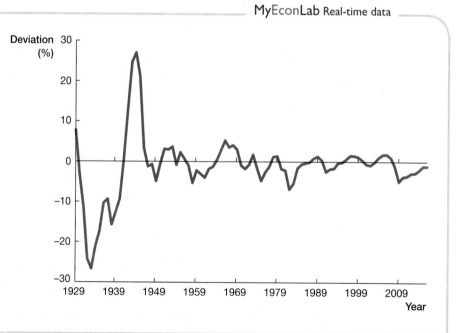

Exhibit 12.3 U.S. Recessions (1929–2016)

Since 1929, a recession has occurred about once every 6 years, and each recession has on average lasted about 1 year. The recession trough is the low point for real GDP during a recession, corresponding to the end of the recession. In most recessions, the decline in real GDP from peak to trough is less than 3 percent, though in the Great Depression of 1929–1933, the U.S. economy experienced a 26.3 percent drop in real GDP from peak to trough.

Sources: Based on National Bureau of Economic Research (recession dating) and Bureau of Economic Analysis, National Income and Product Accounts (real GDP).

Starting Month	Ending Month	Duration (months)	Decline in Real GDP from Peak to Trough
August 1929	March 1933	43	26.3%
May 1937	June 1938	13	3.3%
February 1945	October 1945	8	12.7%[1]
November 1948	October 1949	11	1.5%
July 1953	May 1954	10	1.9%
August 1957	April 1958	8	3.0%
April 1960	February 1961	10	0.3%
December 1969	November 1970	11	0.2%
November 1973	March 1975	16	3.1%
January 1980	July 1980	6	2.2%
July 1981	November 1982	16	2.5%
July 1990	March 1991	8	1.3%
March 2001	November 2001	8	0.3%
December 2007	June 2009	18	4.3%

the trend line is negative. The recovery from this recession has been slow, so real GDP is still slightly below its trend line as of year-end 2016, 7 years after the end of the recession.

In addition to comparing economic activity to its trend (as done in Exhibit 12.1), economists focus on fluctuations in the annual growth rate of GDP. We refer to periods of positive growth in GDP as *expansions* or *booms* and to episodes of negative GDP growth as *downturns*, *contractions*, or *recessions*.

As discussed in Chapter 5, recessions are periods (lasting at least two quarters) in which real GDP falls. Of course, we also care about periods of economic growth. **Economic expansions** are the periods between recessions. Accordingly, an economic expansion begins at the end of one recession and continues until the start of the next recession. During the past century, the average economic expansion has been about 4 times as long as the average recession.

Exhibit 12.3 reports the dates of the fourteen U.S. recessions that have occurred since 1929 and the decline in real GDP from peak to trough in each recession. The peak is the high point of real GDP, just before a recession begins. The trough is the low point of real GDP during the recession, which corresponds to the end of the recession. Since 1929, a recession has occurred about once every 6 years, and the average recession length has been about 1 year.

Economic expansions are the periods between recessions. Accordingly, an economic expansion begins at the end of one recession and continues until the start of the next recession.

Patterns of Economic Fluctuations

Economic fluctuations have three key properties:

1. Co-movement of many aggregate macroeconomic variables
2. Limited predictability of turning points
3. Persistence in the rate of economic growth

We now look at each of these properties in turn.

Co-Movement Many aggregate macroeconomic variables grow or contract together during economic booms and recessions. Economists refer to this pattern as *co-movement*. Exhibit 12.4 illustrates co-movement, focusing on two key variables: consumption and investment, both adjusted for inflation, which are referred to as real consumption and real investment, respectively. The *x*-axis plots the growth rate of real consumption in a

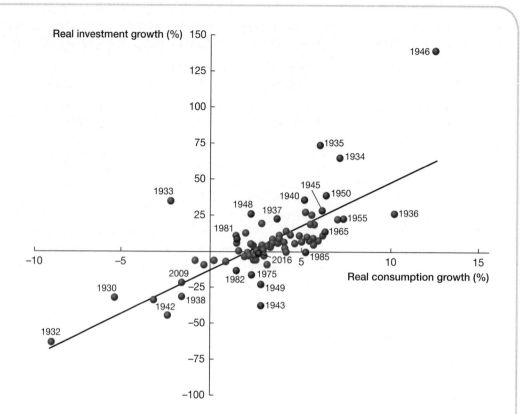

Exhibit 12.4 Real Consumption Growth Versus Real Investment Growth (1929–2016)

The x-axis plots the growth rate of real consumption in a single year, and the y-axis plots the growth rate of real investment in the same year. Each plotted point corresponds to a single year of historical data, so you can read the growth rates for real consumption and real investment by tracing a point to both x- (real consumption) and y- (real investment) axes. For example, the right-hand side of the exhibit shows a point marked "1950." That year, real consumption grew by about 6 percent (read this off the x-axis), and real investment grew by about 39 percent (read this off the y-axis). When consumption growth is relatively high, investment growth also tends to be relatively high. On the left-hand side of the exhibit is a point marked "2009." That year, real consumption grew by about –2 percent (x-axis), and real investment grew by about –22 percent (y-axis). When consumption growth is relatively low, investment growth also tends to be relatively low. Economists say that consumption and investment tend to move together—they exhibit co-movement.

Source: Based on Bureau of Economic Analysis, National Income and Product Accounts.

single year, and the *y*-axis plots the growth rate of real investment in the same year. Each plotted point is a single year of historical data, so you can read the growth rates for real consumption and real investment by tracing a point to both *x*- (real consumption) and *y*- (real investment) axes.

The exhibit shows that points tend to cluster around an upward-sloping line. This means that consumption and investment co-move. When consumption growth is high, investment growth tends to be high as well. When consumption growth is low (or negative), investment growth tends to be low (or negative). In other words, consumption and investment tend to either grow together or shrink together.

Note also that investment is more volatile than consumption. The *y*-axis ranges from −100 percent to +150 percent, while the *x*-axis ranges only from −10 percent to +15 percent. The substantial variation in investment growth occurs because firms often drastically cut investment in response to a weakening economy and then raise it rapidly when the economy is booming. However, it is optimal for households to try to *smooth* consumption over time. For example, unless you actually run out of money, you wouldn't want to postpone replacing your smashed smartphone until the economy recovers from a recession.

Employment and GDP also move together with consumption and investment, and unemployment moves negatively with GDP. For example, this implies that during contractions, real consumption, real investment, employment, and real GDP all fall, while unemployment rises.

Limited Predictability of Turning Points   The second important feature of economic fluctuations is that of *limited predictability of turning points*. A turning point is either the end of a recession (also referred to as a trough in economic output) or the beginning of a recession (also referred to as a peak in economic output). If you look back at Exhibit 12.3, showing the duration of recessions in the U.S. economy since 1929, you can see that recessions have been as short as 6 months and as long as 43 months. The 2007–2009 recession was 18 months long. Economic expansions also have highly variable lengths. Since 1929, the shortest expansion was 1 year, and the longest was 10 years.

Because recessions and expansions have such variable lengths, it is clear that they do not follow a repetitive, easily predictable cycle. In fact, even with the tools of modern economics, it is impossible to predict far in advance when a recession or an expansion will end. We call this property "limited predictability" rather than "no predictability," because by using sophisticated statistical techniques we can achieve a small degree of predictive power. Given the current state of economic science, we are usually able to accurately predict the end of a recession a month or two before its actual end. But it is practically impossible to forecast the end of a recession at the time the recession begins. What we do know is that the likelihood of experiencing a turning point ending the recession in the next month increases slightly as a recession reaches and then passes its first anniversary. Forecasters use this fact to help them predict the likely longevity of recessions. But this small degree of predictability doesn't change the fact that troughs are very difficult to foresee (no matter the age of the recession).

It is even harder to forecast when an expansion will end. Economic expansions are *not* like batteries that predictably run out of juice. The likelihood of experiencing an expansion-ending peak in the next month does not change even as the expansion gets longer.

Limited predictability is important to acknowledge, because many early theories of business cycles assumed that economic fluctuations had a pendulum-like structure with systematic swings in economic growth. Such strong predictability is a far cry from the truth.

Persistence in the Rate of Economic Growth   The third noteworthy regularity of economic fluctuations is that of *persistence*. Even though recessions begin and end at somewhat unpredictable times, economic growth is not random. When the economy is growing, it will probably keep growing the following quarter. Likewise, when the economy is contracting—in other words, when growth is negative—the economy will probably keep contracting the following quarter. So if the economy is in a recession this quarter, our best bet is that it will still be in a recession the next quarter as well. Thus there is a large amount of persistence in the rate of economic growth.

The Great Depression

One event stands out like no other in the past century of economic fluctuations. This is the **Great Depression**, which is far and away the most severe U.S. economic contraction since modern methods for measuring GDP were developed about 100 years ago. Although there is no consensus on the definition, the term **depression** is typically used to describe a prolonged recession with an unemployment rate of 20 percent or more. Although the U.S. economy has experienced dozens of recessions, only the 1929 contraction qualifies as a depression. For example, unemployment during the 2007–2009 recession peaked at 10.0 percent, less than half the level of peak unemployment during the Great Depression.

The Great Depression started in 1929, coinciding with a crash in the U.S. stock market. From 1929 to 1933, the crisis deepened as stock markets around the world continued to fall. At its bottom in 1933, the U.S. stock market was about 80 percent below its peak 4 years earlier. Millions of U.S. farmers and homeowners went bankrupt. Real GDP fell 26.3 percent below its 1929 level, and unemployment eventually rose from 3 percent in 1929 to 25 percent in 1933. From 1929 to 1933, the number of banks in the United States fell from 23,679 to 14,207. This decline was driven by failing banks that either went out of business altogether or were acquired by stronger competitors. Similar events occurred in almost all developed countries around the world, though the U.S. contraction was among the most severe.

An impoverished farm worker and three of her children, photographed in California during the Great Depression.

The **Great Depression** refers to the severe contraction that started in 1929, reaching a low point for real GDP in 1933. The period of below-trend real GDP did not end until the buildup to World War II in the late 1930s.

Although there is no consensus on the definition, the term **depression** is typically used to describe a prolonged recession with an unemployment rate of 20 percent or more.

Exhibit 12.5 The Great Depression and Its Effects on GDP, Unemployment, and the Stock Market

(a) The Great Depression started in 1929 and real GDP bottomed out in 1933—the trough. During the contraction and the long recovery, real GDP, real consumption, and real investment moved together.

Source: Based on Bureau of Economic Analysis, National Income and Product Accounts.

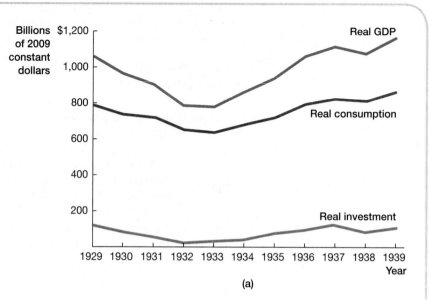

(a)

(b) The unemployment rate tracks fluctuations in GDP but moves in the opposite direction. Unemployment tends to rise when GDP falls. During the Great Depression, unemployment rose from 3 percent in 1929 to a peak of 25 percent in 1933.

Source: Based on U.S. Census Bureau, Historical Statistics of the United States, Colonial Times to 1970, U.S. Department of Commerce, no. 93 (1975).

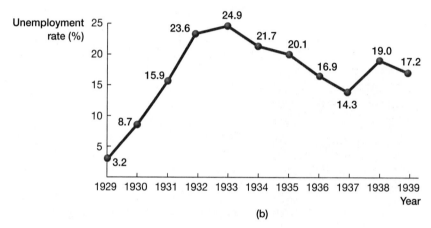

(b)

(c) Stock prices also tend to move with other measures of economic activity. The Dow Jones Industrial Average is an index that averages together the stock prices of thirty of the most important companies based in the United States.

Source: Global financial data. Dow Jones, Down Jones.655.

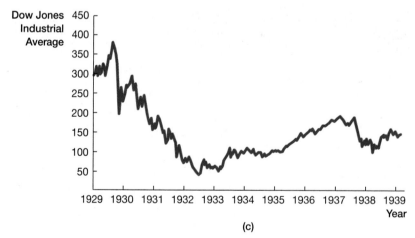

(c)

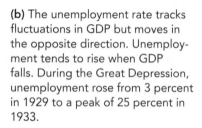

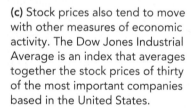

The Great Depression . . . came as a complete surprise to most economists, policymakers, and business leaders.

The Great Depression illustrates the three key properties of economic fluctuations that we just discussed. First, it featured strong co-movement in economic aggregates. Panel (a) of Exhibit 12.5 illustrates this co-movement by plotting real GDP, real consumption, and real investment from 1929 to 1939. The three series started to fall in 1929 and bottomed out in 1932 and 1933. Unemployment moved in lockstep in the opposite direction: starting at 3 percent in 1929 and peaking at 25 percent in 1933. The unemployment rate is plotted in panel (b) of Exhibit 12.5. Finally, the financial markets reflected these economic forces. Corporate accounting profits took an enormous hit during the Great Depression. The Dow Jones Industrial Average, an important stock index, mirrored the level of overall economic activity—see panel (c) of Exhibit 12.5.

The Great Depression also featured limited predictability—or in this case, *no* predictability. In fact, it came as a complete surprise to most economists, policymakers, and business leaders.[2] The preeminent economic forecaster of the late 1920s was Irving Fisher, a Yale professor and newspaper columnist, who repeatedly wrote about the strength of the economy and the low likelihood of adverse economic events. Indeed, one week before the stock market's Great Crash of October 24, 1929, Fisher stated that "stock prices have reached what looks like a permanently high plateau." Even after the initial October stock market crash, and after the broader economy had started to contract, Fisher maintained his optimism. On May 19, 1930, Fisher wrote, "It seems manifest that thus far the difference between the present comparatively mild business recession and the severe depression of 1920–1921 is like that between a thunder-shower and a tornado." Unfortunately, unfolding events would soon prove him completely wrong. The contraction of 1920–1921 turned out to be minor compared to the much deeper contraction that started in 1929.

Fisher's misplaced optimism was common. No leading economic or business forecaster foresaw the Great Depression. Consider this: on January 18, 1930, a group of eminent forecasters at Harvard wrote, "There are indications that the severest phase of the recession is over."[3] In truth, the Great Depression had barely begun.

Finally, the Great Depression featured the third property of economic fluctuations—a great deal of persistence. Indeed, the Great Depression lasted even longer than a typical recession. The period of negative growth in real GDP lasted for 4 years, starting in 1929 and ending in 1933.

12.2 Macroeconomic Equilibrium and Economic Fluctuations

Why are there economic fluctuations? Given the importance of economic fluctuations and the voluminous amount of research on the topic, you might think that we would have a convincing answer—one on which we could all agree. Alas, that is not the case. In fact, there probably isn't another topic that incites as much passionate disagreement among economists. Although this disagreement—often aired in newspaper editorials and blogs—is real, it masks the fact that economists have built up a significant body of shared knowledge about the nature of economic fluctuations. This knowledge forms the basis of the model of economic fluctuations that we now describe.

Labor Demand and Fluctuations

We begin our analysis by returning to a discussion of the labor market. Recall from Chapter 9 that the intersection of the labor demand and labor supply curves determines the labor-market equilibrium. We use the labor-market model to study fluctuations in the aggregate economy. The labor market is a particularly useful vehicle for us because we can analyze the effects of a variety of forces impacting the economy by tracing how they shift labor demand.

Exhibit 12.6 graphs the labor demand curve and the labor supply curve and their intersection. We focus on a labor market with downward wage rigidity—originally introduced in Chapter 9—which highlights the implications of shifts of labor demand for unemployment. Recall from the discussion in Chapter 9 that with downward wage rigidity, firms are unable or unwilling to cut nominal wages because of contractual restrictions or because they are concerned that wage cuts would reduce worker morale and adversely affect productivity. In Exhibit 12.6, the downward rigid wage is high enough to produce a two-part labor supply curve that is first flat (due to a downward rigid wage) and then vertical (due to a limited supply of potential workers). The two-part labor supply curve has a right angle where the flat portion intersects the vertical portion.

The labor-market equilibrium, which corresponds to the wage and employment levels given by the intersection of the labor supply and labor demand curves, is the key building block we will use to construct a model of economic fluctuations. Employment fluctuations

Exhibit 12.6 Recession Dynamics of Labor Demand and Employment

A shift to the left of the labor demand curve leads to a fall in equilibrium employment and a rise in the number of unemployed workers (the point labeled "Recession"). The flat portion of this two-part labor supply curve reflects wages that are downwardly rigid.

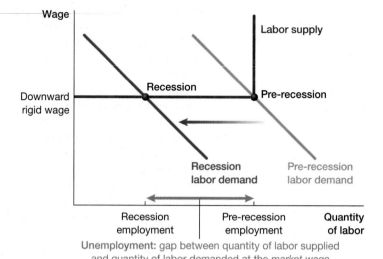

Summary of Shifts in the Labor Demand Curve

In Chapter 9, we discussed the most important sources of shifts in the labor demand curve:

1. **Changing output prices.** When the price of the output good goes down, the value of the marginal product of labor also declines. This implies that the firm would like to hire fewer workers at any given wage, shifting the labor demand curve to the left. (When the price of the product the firm produces rises, the value of the marginal product of labor goes up, shifting the labor demand curve to the right.)

2. **Changing output demand.** When demand for the product the firm produces shifts to the left, its price and thus the value of the marginal product of labor goes down, also shifting the labor demand curve to the left. (When the demand for the product the firm produces shifts to the right, the value of the marginal product of labor goes up, also shifting the labor demand curve to the right.) In addition to the factors emphasized in Chapter 9, an expansion in credit (and a decline in the interest rate) can also lead to a right shift in demand for the output good, as demonstrated in Chapter 10.

3. **Changing technology and productivity.** When the marginal product of labor falls, the labor demand curve shifts to the left. (When the marginal product of labor rises, the labor demand curve shifts to the right.)

4. **Changing input prices.** Businesses use labor and other factors of production, like physical capital and energy, to produce goods and services. When the cost of these other factors goes up, firms purchase less of them. This usually decreases the marginal product of labor, shifting the labor demand curve to the left. (When the cost of these other factors goes down, firms purchase more of them, shifting the labor demand curve to the right.) A change in the credit market equilibrium can also influence labor demand by affecting the firm's cost of financing the acquisition of physical capital.

correspond to changes in this labor-market equilibrium. Exhibit 12.6 illustrates the implications of a leftward (adverse) shift in the labor demand curve, which reduces the equilibrium quantity of labor employed. Before a recession begins, the original equilibrium is given by the point labeled "Pre-recession." After an economic shock has shifted the labor demand curve to the left, the new equilibrium, which features a lower quantity of labor demanded, is at the point labeled "Recession." Firms typically achieve the reduction in employment by cutting back new hiring and allowing the number of employees to shrink through attrition, but when this type of adjustment is not sufficient to get them quickly to their desired level of employment, as shown by the point "Recession" in the exhibit, they may also engage in mass layoffs or even shut down some of their plants.

Because firms aren't hiring, unemployed workers are unable to find jobs. Accordingly, downward rigid wages produce unemployment. At the market wage, which in this example is also the downward rigid wage, the number of workers who are willing to work exceeds the number of jobs that firms are willing to fill. The number of unemployed workers—in other words, workers who would like to work at the market wage but can't find a job—is represented by the green bar near the x-axis in Exhibit 12.6.

Fluctuations in real GDP are linked to these employment fluctuations through the aggregate production function (discussed in Chapter 6). As employment declines (due to the leftward shift in the labor demand curve), so does real GDP; there is less labor producing goods and services. Accordingly, employment and real GDP fall together. This provides another illustration of co-movement among economic aggregates.

When firms shed their workers, utilization of physical capital also falls.

In practice, falling employment is only one adjustment that occurs during an economic contraction. Laying off a worker also makes the physical capital that the worker was previously using—plant and equipment—less productive, leading firms to shutter plants and mothball equipment. The rate of utilization of physical capital is called *capacity utilization*, and recessions are usually accompanied by a reduction in capacity utilization. For example, during the depths of the 2007–2009 recession, capacity utilization in the United States fell to 67 percent from a normal rate of 80 percent, further depressing real GDP.

Although shifts in the supply of labor can also cause fluctuations in employment and unemployment, the most important source of fluctuations are shifts in the demand for labor. To understand the nature of short-run macroeconomic equilibrium, we need to know why the demand for labor fluctuates. We now turn to three theories that each explain some of the reasons for fluctuations in the labor market.

Sources of Fluctuations

Shifts in the labor demand curve are at the root of economic fluctuations. But what shifts labor demand?

Chapter 9 lists the factors shifting labor demand: (1) changes in the output price for a firm's products, (2) changes in the demand for a firm's products, (3) changes in productivity or technology, or (4) changes in the costs of a firm's inputs.

We now offer a different breakdown by discussing three schools of thought in the economics profession, each emphasizing different drivers as the key sources of aggregate economic fluctuations. What unifies these theories is that each approach describes mechanisms that ultimately affect the labor demand curve. Moreover, even though these schools of thought are sometimes presented as competing explanations of economic fluctuations, they are also complementary. In many business cycles, the mechanisms emphasized by all three are relevant, even if at times one or another might be more dominant.

These three schools of thought are:

1. *Real business cycle theory* (emphasizes changing productivity and technology)
2. *Keynesian theory* (emphasizes changing expectations about the future)
3. *Financial and monetary theories* (emphasize changes in prices and interest rates)

Each of these three schools of thought draws on one or more of the four categories of shifts in the labor demand curve discussed in Chapter 9. Most economists studying business cycles believe each school of thought has generated many key insights, and economists don't believe that any one school has all the answers.

1. Technology Shocks: Explanations from Real Business Cycle Theory Chapters 6 and 7 showed that technology differences across firms and workers in different countries help explain differences in cross-country income and growth. Accordingly, one might look for technological reasons to explain economic fluctuations within a given country. For example,

DATA SPEAK

Unemployment and the Growth Rate of Real GDP: Okun's Law

As Exhibit 12.3 shows, real GDP and unemployment often move together (and in opposite directions). The linkage between these two variables is related to an equation called **Okun's Law**, which is named after economist Arthur Okun, who first noticed in the early 1960s that there is a close connection between falling unemployment and the growth rate of real GDP.[4] Employment tends to increase and the unemployment rate tends to decline when the growth rate of real GDP is high.

In particular, let g represent the annual growth rate of real GDP in percentage points. Then the current version of Okun's Law states that:

Year-to-year change in the rate of unemployment

$$= -\frac{1}{2} \times (g - 2\%).$$

This equation implies that the unemployment rate holds steady when the growth rate of real GDP is 2 percent. The equation also implies that the unemployment rate falls when g is above 2 percent, and the unemployment rate rises when g is below 2 percent. In other words, the unemployment rate falls when real economic growth is relatively high, and the

unemployment rate rises when real economic growth is relatively low. Okun's Law is plotted as a black line in Exhibit 12.7. Although the data don't line up perfectly with the equation, Okun's Law is roughly consistent with the data.

Though the overall relationship between changes in the rate of unemployment and the growth rate of real GDP is clear in the data, these two variables do not *always* move together. Sometimes, a fall in the unemployment rate is delayed by a year or more after the growth rate of real GDP picks up at the end of a recession. This delay occurs for several reasons, but the most important one is *labor hoarding*. Labor hoarding means that because recruiting workers and training them is costly, firms may not want to lay off qualified workers during a temporary slowdown and thus keep them on the firms' payrolls even though the firms could have produced their desired level of output without these workers. Labor hoarding keeps the level of unemployment during the recession lower than it would have been otherwise. However, when the economic recovery comes and these firms increase production, they will not initially need to hire new workers, because they can start to ramp up production by fully utilizing the workers they had hoarded during the contraction.

Okun's Law states that the year-to-year change in the rate of unemployment is equal to $-\frac{1}{2} \times (g - 2\%)$, where g represents the annual growth rate of real GDP in percentage points.

Exhibit 12.7 Relationship Between the Change in the Rate of Unemployment and the Growth Rate of Real GDP (2000–2016)

This exhibit depicts Okun's Law (black line), which shows the relationship between the change in the rate of unemployment and the growth rate of real GDP (g). Also shown are annual data from 2000 to 2016.

Sources: Based on Bureau of Labor Statistics (unemployment rate) and Bureau of Economic Analysis, National Income and Product Accounts (real GDP).

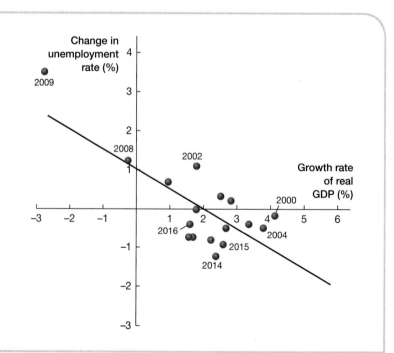

imagine that research and development (R&D) leads firms to invent more valuable products (such as smartphones replacing traditional cellular phones). This will increase the value of the marginal product of the labor that designs, manufactures, assembles, transports, and markets these valuable products, inducing firms to expand their operations and most likely leading them to increase their demand for labor. Firms will also likely seek to increase their productive capacity, raising the level of investment in the economy. These changes will lead to higher household income for three reasons: (1) employment increases, (2) wages rise, and (3) rising corporate earnings make the corporations' stockholders wealthier. For all these reasons, households will raise their consumption. Thus certain types of technological improvements can lead to increases in labor demand and increases in aggregate economic activity, including investment and consumption.

A version of this view appears in the work of classical economists, most notably, that of Arthur Cecil Pigou.[5] This idea was revived and extended in the 1980s in what came to be known as **real business cycle theory**—a school of thought that emphasizes the role of technology in causing economic fluctuations.[6]

Real business cycle theory is the school of thought that emphasizes the role of changes in technology in causing economic fluctuations.

We know from Chapters 6 and 7 that the rate of technological progress is at the root of long-run variation in economic growth. For example, a technological breakthrough can cause a rapid *increase* in a particular industry's output. However, purely technological changes have difficulty explaining situations in which real GDP falls, like a recession. "Technological regress," in which the technological capabilities of an economy deteriorate, seems an unlikely explanation for recessions. It is unlikely, for example, that negative technology shocks caused the Great Depression.

Nevertheless, the rate of technological progress is believed to play a key role in *long-term* variation in economic growth. As discussed in Chapter 7, countries that consistently develop new technologies (or import cutting-edge technologies from other countries) will attain high rates of growth. So technological progress is a very important determinant of long-term fluctuations in growth—for instance, over several decades—even though it is not the main force driving recessions.

Proponents of real business cycle theory tend to also emphasize the importance of changing input prices—especially the price of oil. We can think of an increase in the price of oil as a decrease in the productivity of firms that use oil. Because almost all firms use oil in one form or another—oil products are a key source of energy—changes in the price of oil function like technology changes. As oil price changes can be abrupt, including large increases in the price of oil, this factor does help to explain recessions. A substantial increase in the price of oil may make firms less profitable, shifting the labor demand curve to the left.

2. Sentiments and Multipliers: Explanations from John Maynard Keynes

Many modern analyses of economic fluctuations build on the insights of the British economist John Maynard Keynes (1883–1946), who was an academic, a stock market trader, and a frequent advisor to the British government. (In case you want to talk about him over dinner in your dining hall, Keynes is pronounced "cains.")

Keynes was 46 years old at the start of the Great Depression. As the Depression took hold, Keynes began to develop new theories that attempted to explain its causes. This work culminated in his groundbreaking book *The General Theory of Employment, Interest and Money*.[7] His ideas also had novel implications for government policy. Keynes was highly controversial during his time and remains so today, though few would deny his enormous influence on modern macroeconomics.

Animal spirits are psychological factors that lead to changes in the mood of consumers or businesses, thereby affecting consumption, investment, and GDP.

Keynes believed in a phenomenon that he dubbed **animal spirits**, which represents psychological factors that lead to changes in the mood of consumers and businesses, thereby affecting consumption, investment, and GDP. In Keynes's view, the animal spirits in an economy could fluctuate sharply even as the underlying fundamental features of the economy changed relatively little. For example, a period of heightened optimism could give way to a period of deep pessimism, even though the economic fundamentals—technology, physical capital, and human capital—hadn't changed much at all.

Sentiments include changes in expectations about future economic activity, changes in uncertainty facing firms and households, and fluctuations in animal spirits. Changes in sentiments lead to changes in household consumption and firm investment.

Animal spirits are in fact one example of a broader phenomenon: changing **sentiments**, which include changes in expectations and changes in the (actual or perceived) uncertainty facing firms and households. Changes in sentiments lead to changes in household consumption and firm investment.

For example, consider what happens when firms expect future demand for their products to be low. Such pessimism will have a direct effect on labor demand. When United

Airlines becomes pessimistic about future demand for air travel, it cuts back its hiring of flight attendants and pilots. It also cuts back its orders for new planes. This reduces demand for planes at manufacturers like Boeing. Consequently, labor demand at both United Airlines and Boeing shifts to the left.

Consider the effects of this pessimism on GDP. Let's begin by analyzing the fall in investment that occurs when United Airlines cuts back its orders for new planes. Recall the national income accounting identity from Chapter 5:

$$Y = C + I + G + X - M.$$

The change in the behavior of United Airlines causes a decline in investment in the economy (I) and thus also in GDP (Y). But this decline could be at least partially offset by an increase in consumption (C), government expenditure (G), or the difference between exports and imports ($X - M$). With completely *offsetting* movements in C, G, or $X - M$, it is possible for Y to remain unchanged despite a sharp decline in investment. For example, if I falls by \$5 billion, C could rise by \$5 billion, offsetting the reduction in I.

When firms are turning pessimistic and cutting back employment and investment, however, households are unlikely to increase their consumption. In fact, households face a heightened risk of losing their jobs because of the fall in investment. Accordingly, in most instances, consumption moves in the same direction as investment (consistent with the discussion of co-movement above).

The implications for employment were displayed in Exhibit 12.6. A left shift in the labor demand curve will reduce employment and raise unemployment. Summing up, an increase in negative sentiment leads to a fall in investment, triggering a leftward shift in firms' labor demand curves and reducing employment and GDP.

The implications of households becoming more pessimistic are similar: households will cut their current spending to build up their "rainy-day" savings and thereby prepare for economic problems ahead. This translates into a decline in the current demand for the products of many firms, shifting the labor demand curve of those firms to the left.

This discussion hints at another major element of Keynes's theory: the possibility that a modest shock could hit the economy and generate a cascade of follow-on effects that ultimately cause a much larger contraction. For example, an increase in pessimism among airline executives will have a series of immediate effects—for instance, reduced hiring at United Airlines—that might cascade into a series of follow-on effects—reduced hiring at aircraft manufacturers, like Boeing. The cascade keeps building as the ripples spread to more and more interconnected firms, which each start to cut back hiring and shift their own labor demand curves to the left. The pessimism might also spread to households, which, sensing fewer opportunities in the labor market, start to reduce their demand for goods and services. The economic mechanisms that cause an initial shock to be amplified by follow-on effects are called **multipliers**, or self-reinforcing feedback.

Multipliers are economic mechanisms that amplify the initial impact of a shock.

To illustrate the potential power of multipliers, imagine that a stock market decline causes a drop in consumer confidence and reduces households' willingness to spend. Such an event will cause many other dominos to fall. Firms will cut back production and lay off employees. Those newly unemployed workers will be unable to buy goods and services, leading firms that previously sold goods to these consumers to scale back production even more. According to Keynes, such a cycle could have calamitous effects as each round of layoffs further damages the economy, setting off another wave of layoffs. Such cascades of effects will amplify—or multiply—the impact of the initial shock whether the initial shock is negative or positive news. Hence a bit of good economic news can also produce a cascade of positive effects as consumers increase their demand for goods and services and firms respond by shifting the labor demand curve to the right, all of which multiplies the impact of the initial news. Keynes's theory of multipliers plays an important role in many modern economic models.

A **self-fulfilling prophecy** is a situation in which the expectations of an event (such as a left shift in labor demand in the future) induce actions that lead to that event.

It is also useful to note that the workings of multipliers involve an element of a **self-fulfilling prophecy**, since the expectation of an event (such as a leftward shift in labor demand in the future) induces actions that lead to the realization of that event (that is, firms cutting their employment now). This is because sentiments can be powerful catalysts of economic change. For example, when a large number of economic actors become pessimistic about the future state of the economy, their resulting actions can indeed reduce the level of future economic activity, partially or even fully justifying their pessimistic beliefs. Consumers might stop buying goods and services. Firms might stop investing in plants and equipment. Labor demand will then shift to the left, reducing employment and raising unemployment. This notion of a self-fulfilling prophecy also highlights that a change in expectations driven by animal spirits might turn out to be "rational"; when households and firms become pessimistic about the economy, the economy will contract as a result of people's pessimistic behavior. So the pessimism ends up justifying itself!

Finally, Keynes emphasized the idea that an economy might remain in a state of extended recession, or even depression, because of a lack of **aggregate demand**, which is the economy's overall demand for the goods and services that firms produce. Aggregate demand drives the hiring decisions of firms and consequently determines the labor demand curve. For example, falling levels of aggregate demand cause a leftward shift in the labor demand curve. Moreover, Keynes argued that such a leftward shift in labor demand could generate a long and deep economic contraction, like the Great Depression, that might not be self-correcting. Such a long contraction might be reinforced by multipliers and self-fulfilling prophecies that would leave households and firms despondent about the future. Consumers might not spend, for fear that they will run out of savings, and firms might not hire, for fear that consumers won't spend. All these contractionary forces would reinforce one another, leaving the economy permanently on its knees.

With scenarios like this in mind, Keynes believed that government had an important role to play in stimulating aggregate demand. In our modeling framework, this corresponds to a government policy that shifts the labor demand curve to the right. We will have more to say about such government policies later in this chapter and especially in the next chapter (Chapter 13).

Aggregate demand is the economy's overall demand for the goods and services that firms produce. Aggregate demand drives the hiring decisions of firms and consequently determines the labor demand curve.

3. Monetary and Financial Factors: Explanations from Milton Friedman

Monetary factors are yet another force that drives business cycles. As we saw in Chapter 11, money supply affects nominal GDP. Typically, a fall in nominal GDP, driven by a sharp decline in the money supply, will not only affect the aggregate price level but also real GDP. In this case, changes in the money supply will also drive business cycles. The major proponent of this view has been one of the few macroeconomists to rival Keynes in terms of genius and influence—Milton Friedman.[8]

To understand how monetary factors drive fluctuations in real GDP, consider a scenario in which contractionary monetary policy causes the money supply (M2) to fall sharply.

The fall in the money supply will cause the price level to fall, as predicted by the quantity theory of money (Chapter 11). A fall in the price level reduces employment because of downward wage rigidity. To understand why, note that a drop in the aggregate price level implies that firms have cut their output prices, reducing their nominal value of marginal product of labor. Consequently, each firm demands a lower quantity of labor at a given nominal wage. In other words, a fall in output prices shifts the labor demand curve to the left. Without the downward rigid (nominal) wage, firms would cut nominal wages in line with the fall in output prices, and this would enable them to maintain their level of employment they before the decrease in the money supply. However, as we have seen in Chapter 9, the downward rigid wage implies that firms cannot or will not reduce wages and will instead cut back the number of workers employed.

In addition, as shown in Chapter 11, contractionary monetary policy causes the real interest rate to rise. Recall from Chapter 10 that the real interest rate is the price that a firm pays for another one of its inputs—physical capital. A rise in the real interest rate will therefore make production more costly. Because physical capital is needed by labor, the rising cost of physical capital leads firms to hire less labor, implying a leftward shift in the demand for labor.

Disruptions in the operation of the credit market also cause economic fluctuations. In Chapter 10 we saw how the supply and demand for credit determine the equilibrium interest rate and the amount of credit in the economy. Disruptions in the credit market—for instance, bank failures or other types of financial crises—will reduce the amount of investment and consumption, thereby lowering real GDP and employment. Hence, a leftward shift in the supply of credit will shift firms' labor demand curves to the left.

Exhibit 12.8 Multipliers in a Contracting Economy

Start the feedback loop at any point on the circle. For example, a shock to consumption (at the 10 o'clock position on the feedback loop) causes the firms that produce consumption goods to reduce labor demand, shifting the labor demand curve to the left (2 o'clock on the feedback loop). The leftward shift in labor demand leads to layoffs, which in turn reduces household income (6 o'clock) and further reduces household consumption (back at 10 o'clock). The cycle continues in the same way, increasing the depth of the economic contraction with each loop around the circle. In this way, the impact of an initial shock is multiplied.

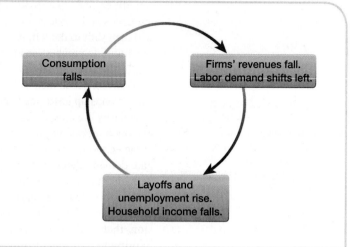

Multipliers and Economic Fluctuations

Multipliers, which we discussed in the context of changes in sentiment, can amplify the effects of any economic shock, regardless of whether the shock arises from changes in technology, sentiment, or financial markets. Exhibit 12.8 illustrates a simple self-reinforcing feedback loop that arises in a contracting economy with multipliers. A shock to consumption causes firms to reduce labor demand, shifting the labor demand curve to the left. The leftward shift in labor demand leads to layoffs, reducing household income and further reducing household consumption. The cycle continues in this way, increasing the depth of the economic contraction with each loop around the circle.

> **Multipliers . . . can amplify the effects of any economic shock, regardless of whether the shock arises from changes in technology, sentiment, or financial markets.**

The effects of multipliers on wages and employment are graphed in Exhibit 12.9 for the case of downward rigid wages. Labor supply is plotted as a two-part curve (with a right angle joining the horizontal and vertical parts) and labor demand is plotted in blue. The economy begins at the equilibrium labeled "1: Pre-recession." A shock causes the labor demand curve to shift to the left. The economy is now at a new temporary equilibrium, at the point labeled "2." We refer to this point as a temporary equilibrium, because it does not factor in multiplier effects. In particular, the first wave of layoffs leads unemployed workers to cut back their demand for goods and services, leading the businesses that provide those

Exhibit 12.9 Multipliers in an Economy with Downward Rigid Wages

The economy begins at the equilibrium labeled "1: Pre-recession." A shock causes labor demand to shift to the left. The economy is now at a new temporary equilibrium, "2," which does not include multiplier effects. Because we are assuming that the wage is downwardly rigid, only employment falls while the market wage remains fixed at this downward rigid level. The layoffs lead to additional reductions in labor demand—more leftward shifts of the labor demand curve—moving the economy to the full-blown recession equilibrium, "3: Trough." A trough is the low point of GDP in a recession.

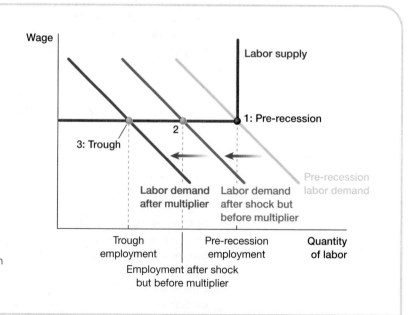

Exhibit 12.10 Additional Multipliers

Start the multiplier loop at any point on the circle. For example, a shock that lowers consumption (at the 10 o'clock position) causes the firms that manufacture consumption goods to reduce labor demand, shifting the labor demand curve to the left (2 o'clock). The weak economy leads to layoffs, declining asset prices, mortgage defaults, household bankruptcies, firm bankruptcies, and declining financial intermediation as banks struggle to survive and some banks fail (6 o'clock). All of this in turn reduces consumption and investment (bringing us back to 10 o'clock). Thus the cycle continues, increasing the depth of the economic contraction with each loop around the circle.

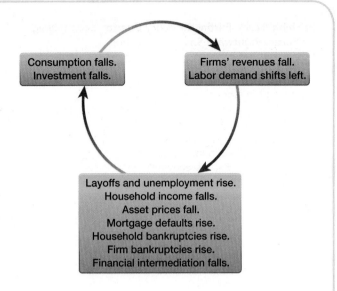

Consumption falls.
Investment falls.

Firms' revenues fall.
Labor demand shifts left.

Layoffs and unemployment rise.
Household income falls.
Asset prices fall.
Mortgage defaults rise.
Household bankruptcies rise.
Firm bankruptcies rise.
Financial intermediation falls.

goods and services to further reduce their labor demand—another leftward shift in the labor demand curve. This moves the economy to the full-blown recession equilibrium labeled "3: Trough." A trough is the low point of real GDP in a recession. This exhibit plots two shifts in the labor demand curve:

1. The initial shock to labor demand (the first shift to the left)
2. A second leftward shift of labor demand due to the layoffs resulting from the initial shock

This second shift to the left takes into account multiplier effects.

The multiplier loop depicted in Exhibit 12.8 leaves out many mechanisms that are important in a modern economy. Exhibit 12.10 adds some of these mechanisms, providing a more complete picture of the factors that multiply the impact of an initial negative shock. These mechanisms include declines in asset prices, such as the value of stocks, bonds, and housing; rising rates of mortgage defaults, which weaken banks' balance sheets; rising rates of household bankruptcies, generating defaults on numerous types of consumer credit (including credit card loans); rising rates of firm bankruptcies, causing their lenders to absorb large losses; and falling levels of financial intermediation as banks become unwilling or unable to extend new loans, even to their existing customers. All these mechanisms create additional multiplier effects and drive down the level of consumption and investment, further depressing labor demand. Falling labor demand leads to additional declines in employment and GDP, further weakening the economy and generating additional rounds of multiplier effects.

Equilibrium in the Medium Run: Partial Recovery and Full Recovery

There are many forces—some market driven and some policy driven—that tend to reverse the effects of a recession in the course of a few years. We refer to this 2- to 3-year time horizon as the *medium run* to distinguish it from the short run (which corresponds to a few quarters) and the long run (which corresponds to periods of a decade or more). In our discussion, we divide the recovery mechanisms into two categories.

i. The labor demand curve shifts back to the right due to market forces.
ii. The labor demand curve shifts back to the right due to expansionary government policies.

Let's now explore each of these in more detail.

Exhibit 12.11 Partial Recovery Due to a Partial Rightward Shift in the Labor Demand Curve

With downward rigid wages, a leftward shift in labor demand to "Labor demand at trough" takes the economy from "1: Pre-recession" to "2: Trough." A partial recovery in the labor demand curve takes the economy from "2: Trough" to "3: Partial recovery."

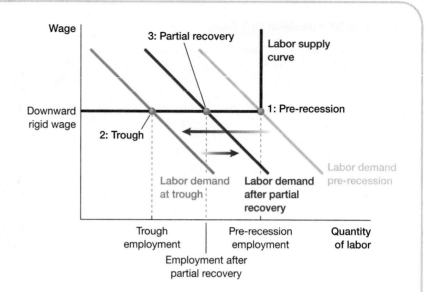

i. *The labor demand curve shifts back to the right due to market forces.* This rebound occurs for many reasons. Here are the most important ones:

- Labor demand partially recovers (shifts to the right) when excess inventory has been sold off. For example, after an excessive economic boom in housing construction, there will be little need for the construction of more new homes, causing the labor demand curve for construction workers to shift to the left. However, the inventory of unsold homes will eventually be sold off, and at that point construction of new homes will start up again, shifting the labor demand curve back to the right. This effect applies to any business that holds an inventory of unsold goods, like car or computer manufacturers. Inventories won't last forever. When they run out, the firm usually increases production. A rightward shift in the labor demand curve is plotted in Exhibit 12.11.

- Labor demand partially recovers when households that have postponed expenditures—like replacing an aging car—eventually grow frustrated with the inconvenience of the delayed purchase and come back into the market. Refrigerators, washing machines, cell phones, and furnaces eventually need to be replaced and the longer households postpone the inevitable, the more pent-up demand builds eventually reinvigorating production. Vacations can be postponed, but eventually the pressure to visit Grandma wins the day and families hit the road again, spending money on gasoline, restaurants, hotels, and airfare.

- Labor demand partially recovers when physical and human capital shift from firms that went bankrupt during the downturn to healthier firms. These newly employed factors of production generate income that supports expenditures. For instance, an unemployed worker is likely to spend much less than an employed worker. As workers transition out of unemployment into new jobs, their incomes rise and they start to buy more goods and services, shifting the overall labor demand curve to the right.

- Labor demand partially recovers when technological advances encourage firms to expand their activities. For example, after the 2007–2009 recession, new drilling technologies enabled energy companies to profitably extract natural gas and oil from oil-shale geological deposits. This led to a rapid expansion in the U.S. energy industry, including drilling activity, pipeline construction, and the growth of industries that have a comparative advantage in regions with ample energy resources.

- Labor demand partially recovers as the banking system—and the rest of the system of financial intermediation—recuperates and businesses are again able to use credit to finance their activities. During the 2007–2009 financial crisis, many small firms had a hard time obtaining loans from their banks. When the banks that survived the crisis returned to health, they became more willing to lend to businesses,

Exhibit 12.12 The Effect of Inflation on the Labor-Market Equilibrium

The downward rigid wage (represented by the horizontal line) prevents the labor market from clearing. Inflation shifts the labor demand curve to the right (firms can sell their output goods at higher prices). The post-inflation labor-market equilibrium is point *B*, where the downward rigid wage intersects the new labor demand curve.

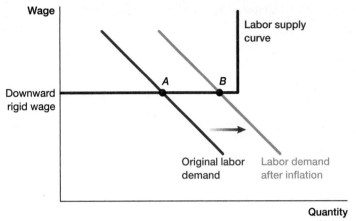

enabling those businesses to expand their operations and hire more workers. The availability of credit shifted the borrowers' labor demand curve to the right.

ii. *The labor demand curve shifts back to the right due to expansionary government policies.* The next chapter focuses exclusively on these issues. For now, we summarize the key policy levers.

- The central bank can use *monetary policy* to shift labor demand to the right. Lowering interest rates stimulates both firm investment and household consumption.

- Labor demand also shifts to the right as overall *inflation* raises firms' output prices. A rise in output price makes production, and thus increasing employment, more profitable at a given wage. This shifts the labor demand curve to the right. Exhibit 12.12 shows the implications of this inflation-driven rightward shift of the labor demand curve. With wages pinned down by the downward wage rigidity, the rightward shift of the labor demand curve causes a movement from point *A* to point *B*, which corresponds to a partial recovery in employment.

- The government also uses *fiscal policy* (government spending and taxes) to shift the labor demand curve to the right. Increasing government spending increases the demand for the products that firms produce, shifting the labor demand curve to the right. Decreasing taxes gives firms and consumers more after-tax income, thereby increasing their purchasing power and increasing demand for the products that firms produce, shifting the labor demand curve to the right.

Exhibit 12.13 puts all these market-based and policy-driven effects together to illustrate a complete cycle of contraction and recovery. Initially, the economy is at point 1. The combination of downward rigid wages and multipliers creates a rapid contraction in labor demand, which moves the economy to point 2. This is the trough of employment. The labor demand curve then starts to shift back toward its pre-recession level due to both market mechanisms and government intervention. Inflation shifts the labor demand curve to the right. At the beginning of the recovery, the equilibrium remains at the rigid wage and the economy shifts from point 2 to point 3.

Eventually, the rightward shifts in labor demand lead the economy to point 4. At this point, downward wage rigidity is no longer a constraint, because the market-clearing wage is above the downward rigid wage. The post-recession wage is above the pre-recession wage, and the economy is at full employment. At this point, the equilibrium wage has risen above the downward rigid wage. Once such a point has been reached, further rightward shifts in labor demand will increase wages but leave employment unchanged.

Exhibit 12.13 Full Recovery

The labor demand curve begins at "Labor demand pre-recession" and then shifts to the left (to "Labor demand at trough"). Because the wage is downward rigid, it does not fall and the economy transitions from point 1 to point 2. As the labor demand curve shifts back to the right ("Labor demand after partial recovery"), the level of employment partially rebounds to point 3. At this point, the downward rigid wage is still preventing the labor market from clearing. Eventually, the combination of rightward shifts in labor demand lead the economy to point 4. At this point, downward wage rigidity is no longer a constraint, because the market-clearing wage is above the downward rigid wage. Now the economy is once again at full employment.

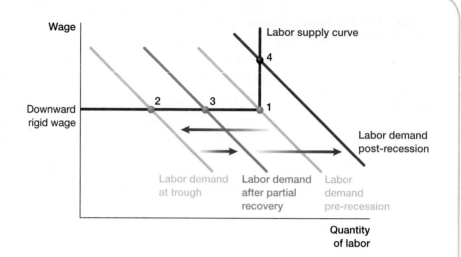

Actual wages are also called **nominal wages**, which distinguishes them from wages adjusted for inflation, or **real wages**. To calculate real wages, economists divide nominal wages by a measure of overall prices, for example the Consumer Price Index (CPI).

Nominal Wages Versus Real Wages

In this chapter (as in Chapter 9), we've conducted the analysis using the actual wages that workers are paid. Actual wages are also called **nominal wages**, which distinguishes them from wages adjusted for inflation, or **real wages**. The distinction between nominal and real wages is similar to the distinction between nominal and real GDP. To calculate real wages, we divide nominal wages by a measure of overall prices. Real wages can be interpreted as the (price-level-adjusted) buying power of nominal wages.

The entire analysis of labor demand and labor supply can be equivalently carried out using real wages. The change in variables wouldn't change the conclusions, but it would highlight different elements of the story. If we focus on real wages, we emphasize that firms base their hiring decisions on the ratio of how much they pay their workers (nominal wages) and how much they charge their customers (their output prices).

Downward rigidity in nominal wages, one of the factors that amplifies negative macroeconomic shocks, plays a similar role when we look at the labor market through the lens of real wages. In particular, downward nominal wage rigidity implies that, because nominal wages cannot fall, real wages do not immediately adjust either. As a result, the labor market does not reach the market-clearing real wage.

But in the presence of inflation, real wages can fall even if nominal wages don't. Because real wages are the ratio of nominal wages to a price index, and because inflation raises the price index, real wages will fall when (1) the price index rises and (2) nominal wages are fixed. This is exactly the scenario highlighted in Exhibit 12.12. Therefore, the analysis of real wages provides another way of explaining how modest inflation might help an economy with downward rigid nominal wages recover from a recession.

12.3 Modeling Expansions

We have so far focused on recessions. The framework we presented can also be used for studying economic booms. Returning to the same example we used earlier, suppose that now United Airlines becomes optimistic about the demand for its products. This will shift its labor demand curve to the right. When many firms become optimistic about their future demand, the aggregate labor demand curve will shift to the right, as shown in Exhibit 12.14.

One important difference from our analysis of leftward shifts is that there is no issue of rigid wages in this case because, as emphasized in Chapter 9, workers are often unwilling to accept cuts in their wages, but this has no equivalent for increases in their wages. This implies that there is downward, but not upward, wage rigidity. For this reason, in Exhibit 12.14, following the rightward shift in the labor demand curve, employment changes along a labor supply curve (and not along a horizontal line as in, for example, Exhibit 12.9).

Though the impact of the rightward shift in the labor demand curve is not exacerbated by wage rigidities, multiplier effects will continue to be present, amplifying the initial shift. For example, as United increases its purchases of airplanes and other inputs, this will cause the firms that supply United to shift their labor demand curves to the right. Increases in labor demand will tend to raise household income, causing households to start consuming more, triggering another round of multiplier effects. As a result of these multiplier effects, there is a further shift in the labor demand curve, as shown in Exhibit 12.14.

Economic expansions also have a dark side. If the labor demand curve shifts to the right when the labor market is already close to full employment (meaning that the unemployment rate is low and the economy is close to the vertical portion of the labor supply curve), there will be relatively little room for the economy to grow. If so, the boom is likely to generate a great deal of wage inflation and very little employment and output growth. This raises a trade-off that is sometimes referred to as the **Phillips curve**, which is a positive relationship between employment growth and inflation. The Phillips curve trade-off is especially unfavorable when an economy is approaching full employment.

Economic booms can lead to another problem. The optimism or other factors that originally triggered the boom may get reversed at some point. But such a reversal involves precisely the sort of leftward shift in labor demand we have analyzed in this chapter. These leftward shifts tend to create negative multiplier effects and might take the economy into a recession rather than gently back to its pre-boom level.

The **Phillips curve** describes the empirical relationship between employment growth and inflation, showing that employment growth tends to produce more inflation, especially when an economy is near full employment.

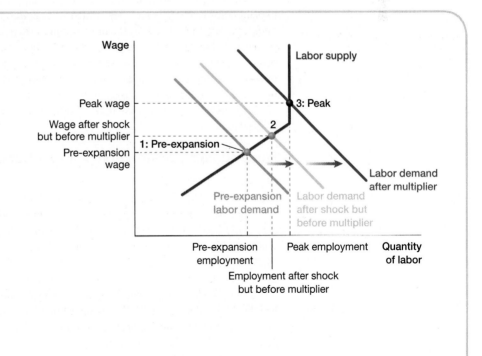

Exhibit 12.14 Rightward Shift in the Labor Demand Curve

Starting from an economy below full employment, a positive economic shock will lead to an increase in employment and an economic expansion. First, the direct impact of the positive economic shock shifts the labor demand curve to the right. This impact is amplified by multipliers. Because wages are flexible upward, all the adjustment to the shifts in the labor demand curve takes place along an upward-sloping labor supply curve. In this example, the boom is strong enough to generate full employment (which corresponds to the vertical portion of the labor supply curve).

The dark side of economic booms raises some of the most difficult challenges for policymakers. Prudent policymaking would involve attempting to control the economic booms in order to limit the potential negative effects. However, the increase in employment and the fall in unemployment accompanying economic booms increase the popularity of policymakers, encouraging them to let economic booms continue or even to fan the flames (especially during election years).

EVIDENCE-BASED ECONOMICS

What caused the recession of 2007–2009?

The causes of the recession of 2007–2009 can be likened to chains of dominos, with one negative shock setting off another in a sequence of events that cascaded throughout the American and global economies. Three key factors appear to have played the central roles in the crisis: (1) a fall in housing prices, which caused a collapse in construction of new homes; (2) a sharp drop in household consumption; and (3) spiraling mortgage defaults that caused many bank failures, leading the entire financial system to freeze up.

Let's first zoom out to take an aerial snapshot:

1. During the pre-recession years of 2000–2006, a run-up in housing prices caused a boom in housing construction, which produced a large stock of newly constructed homes. When housing prices fell sharply from 2006 to 2009, homebuilders rapidly reduced their rate of new construction, because they already held a large inventory of new homes and the falling prices made new construction unprofitable. Consequently, their labor demand curves shifted sharply to the left.

2. The decline in housing prices in turn reduced the wealth of many consumers and curtailed their ability to borrow more against their homes—a scenario that in turn sharply reduced consumption. The firms that produce the goods and services that consumers buy were suddenly faced with a substantial drop in demand for their products. Accordingly, they cut back production and their labor demand curves shifted to the left.

3. The decline in housing values led to millions of mortgage defaults (for reasons we explain below). These mortgages, which were held on the balance sheets of many large banks, pushed those banks to the brink—and in some cases over the brink—of solvency. As banks failed (or cut their lending activity to increase their reserves and strengthen their balance sheets), credit to the private sector fell, causing borrowing firms to cut their production and shifting their labor demand curves to the left. The decline in credit to households reduced their consumption and triggered another round of adverse demand shifts.

This was the big picture. We now zoom in on each of these economic events and look at the data.

Housing and Construction: A Burst Bubble

Many economists characterize the rapid rise of housing prices between the late 1990s and 2006 as a *bubble*, meaning that the significant increase in asset prices (in this case housing assets) did not reflect the true long-run value of the asset. Exhibit 12.15 plots a monthly index of housing prices adjusted for inflation in ten major U.S. cities from 1987 to 2013. Notice that the index rose sharply from 100 in January 2000 to 190 in May 2006. Then everything fell apart—the index collapsed to a value of 120 by April 2009 and continued falling a bit more after that. The bubble in housing prices had burst.

Falling housing prices had a devastating effect on the home construction industry. Exhibit 12.16 plots the real value of investments in residential real estate. Note how real investment in new home construction started falling after peaking in the third quarter of 2005. The exhibit shows that when the dust had settled in 2009, the rate of home construction had fallen by nearly 60 percent.

Exhibit 12.15 Index of Real Home Prices in Ten Major U.S. Cities (January 1987–March 2016)

Real U.S. home prices started rising precipitously in the late 1990s, with real prices more than doubling in a single decade: 1996 to 2006. Prices then fell sharply from 2006 to 2009.

Source: S&P/Case-Shiller home price index and Bureau of Labor Statistics (Consumer Price Index).

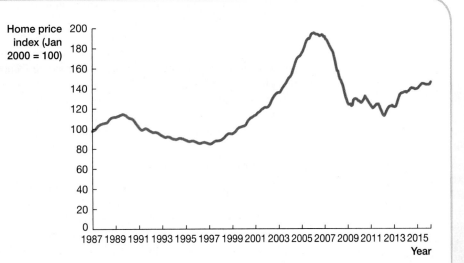

Exhibit 12.16 Real Investment in Residential Construction (1995:Q1–2016:Q1; normalized to 100 in 2009)

The flow of real investment in residential construction nearly doubled from 1995 to 2005, peaking just before housing prices peaked. Residential construction then fell sharply, falling well below its level from 1995. As the excess inventory of newly built homes was sold off, home building slowly picked up again after 2011.

Source: Based on Bureau of Economic Analysis, National Income and Product Accounts.

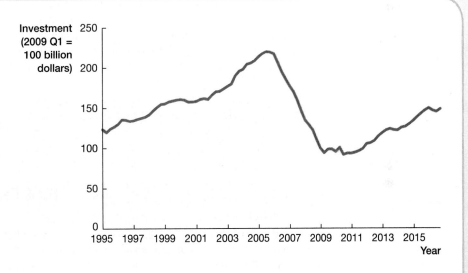

Then the other shoe dropped. As the home construction industry shrank, employment in the industry also plummeted. At its peak in April 2006, there were 3.5 million jobs in the residential construction industry. By 2010, the number of jobs had fallen to 2 million, a 43 percent decline. Related industries also got hit as all real estate prices fell, including commercial real estate (like office buildings and malls). For example, the non-residential construction industry fell from employment of 4.4 million in early 2008—at the start of the recession—to 3.4 million in 2010.

Putting all the pieces together, the sharp drop in real estate prices caused a large leftward shift in the labor demand curve for construction jobs, which then led to a sharp drop in employment in the construction industry. The key step—a leftward shift in the labor demand curve—was plotted in Exhibit 12.6.

The decline in economic activity in the construction industry also led to multiplier effects. Many construction workers lost their incomes, and many businesses that served those workers—home supply stores like Home Depot—saw demand for their products plummet. Falling home construction and home sales also lowered demand for home appliances—like washing machines and refrigerators. These multiplier effects magnified the effects of the fall in home prices, shifting the aggregate labor demand curve further leftward and deepening the fall in aggregate employment.

Cuts in Consumption

Housing price declines were also associated with large reductions in overall household consumption—the second key factor in the 2007–2009 recession.

During the early 2000s, many households had increased their consumption by using funds that they had borrowed from banks. In most cases, this borrowing took the form of mortgages—for instance, taking out a second mortgage in addition to a first mortgage. "Cash-out" refinancings were also popular—when interest rates fell, homeowners with an existing mortgage would lower their interest rate and increase the size of their mortgage, taking the difference as a cash payout. At the peak of the housing bubble, consumers used second mortgages and "cash-out" refinancing to extract $400 billion of wealth per year from their homes. Even consumers who did not take out more mortgage debt tended to increase their real consumption during the run-up in housing prices from 2000 to 2006, because home price rises increase wealth and consumers' perceptions of what they can afford to consume.

That wealthy feeling started to vanish in 2007. By March 2009, U.S. households had lost about $15 trillion in net worth—both the housing market and the stock market had crashed. Most households cut back their consumption, causing aggregate real consumption to decline by 2.7 percent from the start of the recession in the fourth quarter of 2007 to the end of the recession in the second quarter of 2009. This decline translated into a significantly lower demand for the products of firms, creating another multiplier effect that shifted the labor demand curve further to the left.

Spiraling Mortgage Defaults and Bank Failures

Falling house prices also led mortgage delinquencies to skyrocket: many borrowers stopped making their required mortgage payments. For example, suppose that a family had bought a $300,000 home with almost no down payment in 2006. If we assume that the home's value followed the ten-city index, this home would have fallen to a value of $200,000 by 2009. However, the mortgage debt would not have been affected by the fall in the home value, leaving the borrower owing nearly $300,000 (very little of the initial mortgage would have been paid off in the first 3 years of home ownership). Consequently, the family would find itself with a debt of almost $300,000 on a house worth only $200,000. Owing more on your home than it is worth is referred to as being "upside down" or "under water." If a household with an underwater mortgage sells its home, it doesn't receive enough money to repay the mortgage. In many U.S. states, households in this situation have a strong incentive to default on their mortgages—that is, stop making their mortgage payments and walk away. This incentive is further strengthened when households face economic hardship (for example, because of unemployment or other negative labor income shocks).

And walk away is exactly what millions of households did, either because they didn't have a job and couldn't afford to pay their mortgage, or because they recognized that it wasn't optimal to keep paying interest on a mortgage that vastly exceeded the value of the home. Previously, when home prices were rising, foreclosure rates stayed around 1.7 percent per year. In other words, 1.7 percent of U.S. homes with a mortgage entered foreclosure each year. Exhibit 12.17 shows that the foreclosure rate rose to 5.4 percent

Exhibit 12.17 Percentage of U.S. Home Mortgages That Began Foreclosure Proceedings (2000–2013)

This exhibit plots the annual rate of foreclosure filings in the United States. A 2 percent rate of foreclosure filing implies that 2 percent of the homes with a mortgage started foreclosure proceedings in that year.

Source: Mortgage Bankers' Association National Delinquency Survey.

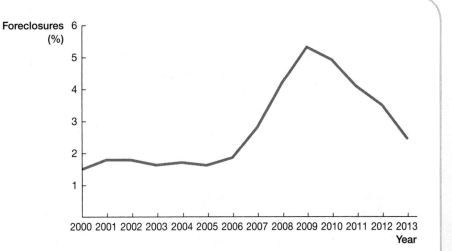

during the financial crisis. To appreciate the significance of that foreclosure rate, consider that there are approximately 75 million owner-occupied homes in the United States and about two-thirds, or 50 million, have a mortgage. So a foreclosure rate of 5.4 percent translates into almost 3 million foreclosed homes per year at the peak of the crisis. In total, about 10 million foreclosures took place from 2007 to 2012.

Home foreclosures were terrible news not only for homeowners but also for banks. When a bank seizes a home that is worth $200,000, on which the outstanding mortgage is $300,000, the bank has no way of recouping its money. At best, it can sell the house for $200,000, realizing a $100,000 loss on its $300,000 loan. In practice, the foreclosure sale yields a price significantly below $200,000. With so many homes being sold simultaneously, and with no homeowner to put flowers in window pots, mow lawns, or keep vandals from trashing the empty house or ripping out copper pipes, it's easy to sell the house for far less than $200,000.

Consequently, banks suffered enormous losses on their portfolios of mortgages. In 2005, during the run-up in home prices, banks recorded losses in their real estate portfolios equal to only 0.2 percent of the value of their real estate loans. In 2009, banks booked real estate losses that were 40 times greater—8 percent of the total value of their real estate loans.

Many banks could not withstand the extent of the hit they took on their mortgage holdings. Among the 5,000 banks regulated by the FDIC, about 400 failed from 2007 to 2011.

But the biggest story of the 2007–2009 recession was the failure of Lehman Brothers, a bank that was *not* regulated by the FDIC. Lehman did not originate home mortgages of its own, but it did originate commercial mortgages (for businesses) and it did buy mortgages of all types that other banks had issued. As those mortgages lost value in 2008, Lehman Brothers lost huge sums and, perhaps more importantly, also lost the confidence of its business partners.

Within a 2-week period in September 2008, many of Lehman's biggest institutional trading partners and lenders stopped doing business with the bank. Each new defection bred more uncertainty and a widening loss of confidence in Lehman's future. Lehman experienced an institutional bank run, a special kind of bank run that we discussed in Chapter 10. The bank customers running for the exits were large financial institutions like other large banks and hedge funds. Soon, no institutions would lend money to Lehman, and at that point Lehman was both illiquid and insolvent.

The failure of Lehman Brothers initiated a financial panic that suddenly threatened the prosperity of the world economy. Other major bank crises followed in Iceland, the United Kingdom, Greece, Ireland, Portugal, Switzerland, France, Germany, the Netherlands, Spain, Italy, and Cyprus. Suddenly, many countries teetered on the precipice of another depression.

As financial markets fell, the banking sector cut back on loans to businesses because failed banks obviously couldn't make loans. Even the surviving banks were hesitant to make loans, afraid that these new loans—to households and businesses—would soon end up in default. The retrenchment of the financial sector created yet another multiplier effect, which reduced consumption and investment and shifted the labor demand curve further to the left.

Question

What caused the recession of 2007–2009?

Answer

Real housing prices rose 90 percent from 2000 to 2006 and then quickly fell back to their 2000 level. Falling house prices led to a collapse in the home building industry, to a sharp decline in real consumption, and to a jump in mortgage defaults. Approximately 10 million U.S. home foreclosures occurred from 2007 through 2012. The defaulting mortgages caused 400 bank failures, including the spectacular failure of the investment bank Lehman Brothers.

Data

Historical data on housing prices (Case/Shiller housing price index), residential investment (National Income and Product Accounts), foreclosure rates (Mortgage Bankers Association), and bank balance sheets (FDIC and Lehman Brothers).

Caveat

Many other factors also contributed to the financial crisis.

Summary

■ All economies experience economic fluctuations—in other words, the growth rate fluctuates from year to year. During recessions, real GDP contracts and unemployment increases. On rare occasions a recession turns into a depression, like the Great Depression, which started in 1929. From 1929 to 1933, real GDP declined by 26 percent, and the rate of unemployment rose from 3 percent to 25 percent.

■ Economic fluctuations display three key properties:

1. Co-movement: Consumption, investment, GDP, and employment generally fall and rise together. Unemployment moves in the opposite direction.
2. Limited predictability of turning points: Economic fluctuations are not pendulum-like with regular up and down cycles. It is difficult to predict in advance when an economy will enter a recession (a peak) and when a recession will end (a trough).
3. Persistence: When the economy is growing, it will probably keep growing the following quarter. Likewise, when the economy is contracting—when growth is negative—the economy will probably keep contracting the following quarter.

- Many factors explain fluctuations in economic activity, most notably:

  1. Technology shocks (the theory of real business cycles): Changes in firms' productivity translate into shifts in the demand curve for labor, causing fluctuations in employment and real GDP. When the labor demand curve shifts to the left, employment and real GDP fall. When the labor demand curve shifts to the right, employment and real GDP rise.

  2. Keynesian factors:
     - Changes in sentiments, including changes in expectations, uncertainty, and animal spirits, influence firm and household behavior. If a firm becomes pessimistic, its demand curve for labor shifts to the left. If a firm's customers become pessimistic, they reduce their purchases, decreasing demand for the firm's products and shifting the firm's labor demand curve to the left.
     - An initial shift in the labor demand curve creates a cascading chain of events, multiplying or amplifying the impact of the initial shock. For example, when firms lay off workers in response to a shock, the laid-off workers cut their own consumption, reducing the demand for the products of *other* firms and leading to shifts in the labor demand curves of these firms. Financial factors create additional multiplier effects. Defaults, bankruptcies, and declines in asset prices lead banks to scale back their lending to firms and households, generating another round of adverse shifts in the labor demand curve.

  3. Monetary and financial factors: A fall in the price level is contractionary, because firms face downward wage rigidities—that is, they are either unable or unwilling to cut wages. Employment declines by more than it would have with flexible wages. In addition, monetary contractions cause the real interest rate to rise, reducing investment. Finally, financial crises reduce the credit available to firms and households. All these channels will shift the labor demand curve to the left, reducing employment and real GDP.

- Multiplier effects help us understand the sharp recession of 2007–2009. Between the late 1990s and 2006, the U.S. housing market experienced a bubble. This bubble burst in 2006, and real housing prices fell by approximately 40 percent. The construction industry, which had been booming until then, began a sharp contraction. Falling housing prices—and by implication falling wealth—led households to cut their consumption. Firms, seeing the demand for their products decline, reduced their labor demand, starting a spiral of layoffs and further reductions in household consumption. The collapse in housing prices also led to mortgage defaults and foreclosures. The defaults and foreclosures generated huge losses for many banks, which either failed or sharply cut lending, further worsening the recession.

- Economic booms tend to increase employment and reduce unemployment as the labor demand curve of the economy shifts to the right and the multiplier effects increase employment further. Economic expansions may also generate inflation, especially if the economy is already near the level of full employment. Economic booms also have a dark side, because when they reverse, the economy can overshoot and sink into a recession. For this reason, some policymakers try to control and dampen economic booms, though other factors might push policymakers and politicians to fan the flames of economic booms rather than follow a prudent course of action.

Key Terms

economic fluctuations or business cycles *p. 281*
economic expansions *p. 283*
Great Depression *p. 285*
depression *p. 285*

Okun's Law *p. 290*
real business cycle theory *p. 291*
animal spirits *p. 291*
sentiments *p. 291*
multipliers *p. 292*

self-fulfilling prophecy *p. 292*
aggregate demand *p. 293*
nominal wages *p. 298*
real wages *p. 298*
Phillips curve *p. 299*

Questions

All questions are available in MyEconLab for practice and instructor assignment.

1. What are economic fluctuations? What is the difference between an economic expansion and a recession?

2. What does it mean to say that an economic fluctuation involves the co-movement of many aggregate macroeconomic variables? Name four variables that exhibit co-movement during an economic expansion.

3. The duration of an economic fluctuation is completely unpredictable. why this statement is only partially true.

4. Does the Great Depression illustrate the three characteristics of economic fluctuations? Explain your answer.

5. How do wage flexibility and downward wage rigidity affect the extent of unemployment in the economy when the demand for labor shifts to the left?

6. How does real business cycle theory explain economic fluctuations?

7. How did John Maynard Keynes use the concepts of animal spirits and sentiments to explain economic fluctuations?

8. The concept of multipliers was one of the key elements of John Maynard Keynes's theory of fluctuations. What is a multiplier? Explain with an example.

9. How can contractionary monetary policy lead to an economy-wide recession?

10. What are two important mechanisms that reverse the effects of a recession in a modern economy?

11. How can the 2007–2009 recession be explained?

12. Between 2000 and 2006, housing prices in the United States increased by about 90 percent. As detailed in the chapter, this increase abruptly reversed.

   a. Why is the rise in housing prices between the late 1990s and 2006 characterized as a bubble by some economists?

   b. How did the fall in housing prices cause the financial system in the United States to freeze up?

Problems

All problems are available in MyEconLab for practice and instructor assignment.

1. Consider the data in Exhibit 12.3.

   a. List the recessions since 1929 by duration, with the longest recession first and the shortest last.

   b. List the recessions since 1929 according to decline in real GDP from peak to trough, with the greatest decline first and the smallest decline last. Note which recessions are first and second on your list from part (a) and first and third on your list from part (b). Can you think of a reason why the fall in real GDP at the end of World War II (1945; second recession on your list from part (b)) was so deep even though that recession was very short?

2. The University of Michigan runs monthly surveys of households around the United States. Some of the questions gauge consumer optimism by asking how households feel about their own financial situation, as well as the economy more broadly. These responses are used to generate a monthly measure of Consumer Sentiment. Look at a chart of this measure over time here: https://fred.stlouisfed.org/series/UMCSENT/. Note that the shaded areas represent recessions.

   a. How does the consumer sentiment measure behave during recessions? Explain what you see in the chart using Keynes's animal spirits view of economic fluctuations.

   b. Does this chart prove that Keynes's theory is correct? Explain. Why is it hard to determine the direction of causality? Do recessions cause drops in consumer sentiment, or do drops in consumer sentiment cause recessions?

3. The Conference Board publishes data on Business Cycle Indicators (BCI). The Composite Index of Leading Economic Indicators is one of the three components of the BCI. Changes in leading economic indicators usually precede changes in GDP. Some of the variables tracked by the index are listed below.

   i. The average weekly hours worked by manufacturing workers

   ii. The average number of initial applications for unemployment insurance

   iii. The amount of new orders for capital goods unrelated to defense

iv. The number of new building permits for residential buildings

v. The S&P 500 stock index

vi. Consumer sentiment

Consider each variable and explain whether it is likely to be positively or negatively correlated with real GDP.

4. Suppose that the mythical country Moricana has a downward rigid wage. Moricana is in a recession; capacity utilization in the economy is at an all-time low, and surveys show that firms do not expect economic conditions to improve in the coming year.

   a. Firms in the country are cutting back on capital spending and investment. Use a graph to show how this would affect the labor demand curve (ignore the effects of multipliers).

   b. Is unemployment in Moricana likely to be classified as voluntary or involuntary? Explain your answer.

5. Imagine a new technology emerged, allowing for increased productivity and driving U.S. real GDP growth from 2.5% one year to 3% in the next year.

   a. How will this change in the growth rate of GDP affect unemployment? Use Okun's Law to generate a numerical estimate.

   b. Use the real business cycle approach to explain how the new technology could affect both unemployment and GDP. Why might this new technology lead to higher unemployment than we estimated using Okun's Law?

6. Assume that labor supply and labor demand are described by the following equations:

   $$\text{Labor supply:} \quad L^S = 5 \times w$$
   $$\text{Labor demand:} \quad L^D = 110 - 0.5 \times w$$

   where w = wage is expressed in dollars per hour, and L^S and L^D are expressed in millions of workers.

   a. Find the equilibrium wage and the equilibrium level of employment.

   b. Assume that there is a shock to the economy, such that the labor demand curve is now described by the equation

   $$L^D = 55 - 0.5 \times w.$$

   If wages are flexible, what will be the new equilibrium wage and level of employment? Show your work.

   c. Now assume that wages are rigid at the level you found in part (a). What will employment be at this wage? How many workers will be unemployed?

7. In 1973, the major oil-producing nations of the world declared an oil embargo. The price of oil, a key source of energy, increased. In many countries, this led to a fall in real GDP and employment. Which of the three business cycle theories explained in the chapter—real business cycle theory, Keynesian theory, and monetary theory—would best fit this explanation of the 1973 recession?

8. An old saying goes: "Nothing succeeds like success." Explain how this could relate to Keynes's animal spirits view of economic fluctuations.

9. Use a detailed graph to show the effect of a negative shock on the labor demand curve in an economy. Assume that wages in the economy are rigid and cannot fall in the short run. Compare the point of trough employment on the graph with the point of trough employment if wages were flexible.

10. Republicans and Democrats fiercely debate the economic legacy of President Obama's presidency: Republicans point to low GDP growth during his presidency, while Democrats laud improvements in labor markets since the great recession. Recall that President Obama took office in January 2009, a few months after the collapse of Lehman Brothers in September 2008. Does it make sense to attribute the deepening of the recession—or, ultimately, its end—entirely to the actions of the president? Explain, for example, how the recession might have been alleviated in the absence of any governmental action at all.

11. In the early 1980s, the unemployment rate in the United States rose above 10 percent. The United States was in a severe recession. Both fiscal and monetary policies were used to stimulate the economy. Government spending increased by 18.9 percent, while the Federal Reserve cut interest rates by nearly 11 percentage points. How would these policies affect the labor demand curve and the overall labor market? Assuming wages are rigid, use a graph to explain your answer. Be sure to show the pre-recession equilibrium, the situation at the trough of the recession, and the effect of the government policies.

12. The Evidence-Based Economics feature in the chapter identifies three key factors that caused the recession of 2007–2009.

   a. How would Keynes's concept of animal spirits explain the creation of a housing bubble?

   b. Explain how the 2007–2009 recession affected the consumption and investment components of the national income identity.

13. Some economists stress the role of monetary policy in the period leading up to the 2007–2009 recession. Between 2001 and 2003, the Federal Reserve lowered the target federal funds rate from 6.5 percent to 1 percent and kept it there through much of 2004. This resulted in a substantial decline in real interest rates throughout the economy, including mortgage rates. Based on the chapter's discussion of monetary and financial factors, explain how the Federal Reserve's policies could have contributed to the economic "bubble" of the pre-recession years of 2000–2006.

13 Countercyclical Macroeconomic Policy

How much does government expenditure stimulate GDP?

You are a presidential adviser on economic policy: the chairperson of the Council of Economic Advisers (CEA). The CEA consists of three economists who advise the president and help formulate the administration's economic policy. These experts prepare the annual *Economic Report of the President*.

Unfortunately, you happen to be in office during an economic downturn. The president asks you, "What would happen if the government increased spending?" How would more government expenditure—for instance, repairing highways, hiring teachers, or building schools—support an economic recovery?

This chapter studies the many ways that policymakers try to smooth out fluctuations in GDP, stimulating the economy during contractions and stepping on the brakes during periods of excessively rapid economic expansion.

CHAPTER OUTLINE

13.1 The Role of Countercyclical Policies in Economic Fluctuations

Countercyclical policies attempt to reduce the intensity of economic fluctuations and smooth the growth rates of employment, GDP, and prices.

In Chapter 12, we discussed the reasons economic growth fluctuates. In this chapter, we focus on the government and the Fed's efforts to reduce those fluctuations by using what are called *countercyclical policies*. **Countercyclical policies** attempt to reduce the intensity of economic fluctuations and smooth the growth rates of employment, GDP, and prices. (In this chapter, whenever we discuss GDP, we are referring to *real* GDP.)

During a recession, *expansionary policy* aims to reduce the severity of the downturn by shifting labor demand to the right and "expanding" economic activity (GDP). Similarly, *contractionary policy* is sometimes used to slow down the economy when it grows too fast or "overheats."

Countercyclical policies come in two main categories:

Countercyclical monetary policy, which is conducted by the central bank (in the United States, the Fed), attempts to reduce economic fluctuations by manipulating bank reserves and interest rates.

1. **Countercyclical monetary policy**, which is conducted by the central bank (in the United States, the Fed), attempts to reduce economic fluctuations by manipulating bank reserves and interest rates.

Countercyclical fiscal policy, which is passed by the legislative branch and signed into law by the executive branch, aims to reduce economic fluctuations by manipulating government expenditures and taxes.

2. **Countercyclical fiscal policy**, which is passed by the legislative branch and signed into law by the executive branch, aims to reduce economic fluctuations by manipulating government expenditures and taxes.

Though countercyclical monetary and fiscal policies work in different ways and are effective in different circumstances, they also share some common features. Countercyclical monetary and fiscal policies both work by shifting the labor demand curve. During a recession, monetary and fiscal policies are used to stimulate the economy by shifting the labor demand curve to the right. During a runaway boom, monetary and fiscal policies are used to slow the economy by shifting the labor demand curve to the left.

> Countercyclical monetary and fiscal policies both work by shifting the labor demand curve.

We plot the case of a recession in Exhibit 13.1. At point 1 (pre-recession), the economy starts at full employment. Then a negative shock shifts the labor demand curve to the left. In this exhibit, we assume, as we did in the previous chapter, that there is downward wage rigidity, so the

Exhibit 13.1 The Effect of Countercyclical Policy on the Labor Market

During a recession, the labor demand curve has shifted to the left and the equilibrium is at point 2 (trough). Countercyclical policy can partially reverse this situation by shifting the labor demand curve back to the right. The equilibrium transitions from point 2 to point 3 (partial recovery). The rightward shift in the labor demand curve translates into an increase in employment.

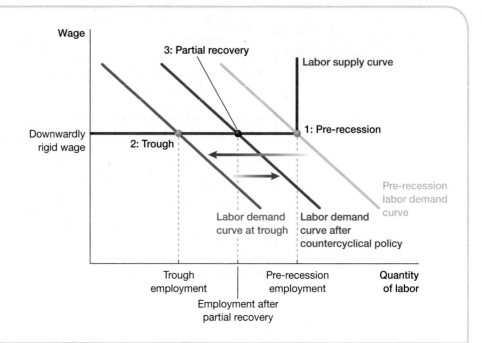

negative labor demand shock takes us along the flat portion of the labor supply curve to point 2 (trough). At this point, the level of employment is lower. Successful expansionary policy can shield the economy from the full impact of the recession by shifting the labor demand curve back to the right, taking the economy to point 3 (partial recovery).

Just as expansionary policy reduces the severity of a recession, policymakers sometimes use contractionary policy that reduces economic growth during a boom. Why would policymakers intentionally adopt a policy that has the effect of reducing GDP growth and reducing the level of employment? In some situations, the negative effects on GDP and employment are a by-product of another policy goal. For example, when inflation is consistently above the Fed's target, the Fed will raise interest rates to suppress borrowing, thereby slowing growth of the money supply and reducing the rate of inflation. The rise in interest rates will shift the labor demand curve to the left, causing employment to fall as a by-product of the Fed's efforts to reduce inflation.

In other cases, countercyclical policy may be directly targeting economic expansion. Recall from Chapter 12 that such factors as excessively optimistic sentiments about the economy can result in an unsustainable economic expansion. Left alone, such expansions may lead to a severe downturn, because optimistic sentiments can implode suddenly and severely (due to multiplier effects). In some cases, contractionary policy attempts to reduce the risks of an extreme contraction by trying to cool off the economy before it overheats. Such cooling off is achieved by putting gradual leftward pressure on the labor demand curve. Contractionary policy is sometimes referred to as "leaning against the wind."

13.2 Countercyclical Monetary Policy

We now discuss countercyclical policies in detail. Let us first focus on countercyclical monetary policy, which, as explained in Chapter 11, is conducted by the Fed.

The Fed responds to economic contractions by adopting **expansionary monetary policy**, which increases the quantity of bank reserves and lowers interest rates. Let's begin by getting a big-picture view of the impact of such policies.

The Fed influences short-term interest rates, especially the *federal funds rate*. Recall that the federal funds rate is the interest rate that banks use to make loans to one another, using reserves on deposit at the Federal Reserve Bank.

Expansionary monetary policy increases the quantity of bank reserves and lowers interest rates.

Exhibit 13.2 Expansionary Monetary Policy

These are the core ingredients of expansionary monetary policy. The first half of this chapter explores the various ways in which the Fed implements the top (red) box in this exhibit.

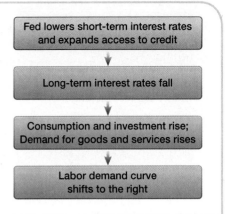

When the Fed wants to stimulate the economy, it lowers short-term interest rates. This, in turn, usually causes long-term interest rates to fall. Recall from Chapter 11 that the long-term interest rate is related to the long-term average of short-term interest rates.

A fall in long-term interest rates encourages households to buy more durable goods, like cars, because a lower interest rate implies a lower cost of a car loan. To satisfy an increase in household demand for durable goods, firms try to hire more workers, shifting the labor demand curve to the right. Likewise, a fall in long-term interest rates causes firms to engage in more investment in plants and equipment, like building a new factory, because a lower interest rate implies a lower cost of a commercial loan that will fund the construction project. Firms need workers to build and eventually operate these new factories, shifting the labor demand curve to the right. In many different ways, expansionary monetary policy shifts firms' labor demand curve to the right and increases the level of employment, as shown in Exhibit 13.1. Exhibit 13.2 provides a bird's-eye view of this process.

To better understand monetary policy, we need to discuss how the Fed lowers short-term interest rates and expands access to credit. We need to fill in the details of the red box in Exhibit 13.2. The Fed's most powerful tool in this process is its control of bank reserves and the federal funds rate, which we review next.

Controlling the Federal Funds Rate

The primary tool of monetary policy is the Fed's control of the federal funds rate. By changing the supply of bank reserves available to private banks, which is called open market operations, the Fed influences the federal funds rate. As explained in Chapter 11, in an open market operation, the Fed transacts with private banks to increase or reduce bank reserves held at the Fed. These transactions influence the federal funds rate.

For instance, by increasing the supply of bank reserves available to private banks, the Fed decreases the federal funds rate. This mechanism is shown in Exhibit 13.3. You can see in this exhibit that a shift to the right of the supply of reserves held at the Fed drives down the federal funds rate (which is the price that a bank pays to borrow another dollar of reserves).

> The primary tool of monetary policy is the Fed's control of the federal funds rate.

The following example illustrates the steps involved in an open market operation. Suppose that the Fed wants to raise bank reserves held on deposit at the Fed by $1 billion. To bring this about, the Fed finds a bank—let's say Citibank—that is willing to sell the Fed $1 billion worth of bonds in exchange for $1 billion in bank reserves that Citibank will have on deposit at the Fed. The Fed doesn't use paper currency in this transaction. Instead, the Fed creates the $1 billion in bank reserves with the stroke of a computer key. Poof! The Fed has issued an IOU to the private bank. The IOU takes the form of $1 billion of reserves that the private bank holds on deposit at the Fed.

Following these open market operations, Citibank now has $1 billion *more* in bank reserves on deposit at the Fed and owns $1 billion *less* in bonds: those are the bonds that Citibank sold to the Fed. On the assets side of its balance sheet, Citibank has an extra

Exhibit 13.3 The Federal Funds Market

A rightward shift in the reserves supply curve reduces the federal funds rate.

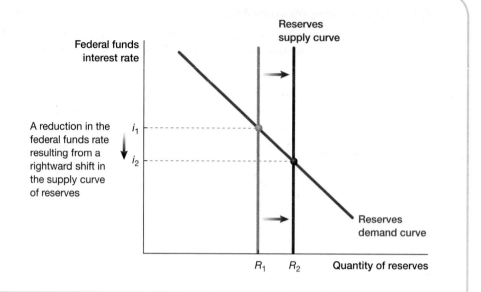

A reduction in the federal funds rate resulting from a rightward shift in the supply curve of reserves

$1 billion in bank reserves that it received in exchange for the $1 billion in bonds that are now owned by the Fed and now appear on the Fed's balance sheet. Total assets at Citibank are unchanged, though the composition of those assets has tilted away from bonds and toward bank reserves. Exhibit 13.4 illustrates this change on Citibank's balance sheet, showing how reserves on the assets side of its balance sheet increase from $100 billion to $101 billion.

The Fed's balance sheet has also changed. The Fed's assets now include $1 billion more in bonds—this amount represents the bonds that the Fed bought from Citibank. The Fed's liabilities also show a corresponding increase. In particular, the Fed's liabilities now include $1 billion more in the form of reserves—these are the reserves that the Fed electronically created and then exchanged with Citibank. Exhibit 13.5 illustrates this change on the Fed's balance sheet. Note that reserves held at the Fed are an asset to Citibank—which can draw on the reserves—and a liability to the Fed—which is on the hook to pay out the reserves if asked to do so.

Exhibit 13.4 Balance Sheet of Citibank Before and After a $1 Billion Bond Sale to the Fed

The Fed engages in an open market operation with Citibank. The Fed buys $1 billion in bonds in exchange for $1 billion in reserves that are credited to Citibank. This changes nothing on the liabilities and shareholders' equity side of Citibank's balance sheet. On the assets side, total assets don't change, but the composition of assets does (changes on the assets side are shown in blue). After the trade, Citibank has another $1 billion in reserves on deposit at the Fed and $1 billion less in bonds.

Before:	Assets		Liabilities and Shareholders' Equity	
	Reserves:	$100 billion	Deposits and other liabilities:	$800 billion
	Bonds and other investments:	$900 billion	Shareholders' equity:	$200 billion
	Total assets:	$1,000 billion	Liabilities + shareholders' equity:	$1,000 billion

After:	Assets		Liabilities and Shareholders' Equity	
	Reserves:	$101 billion	Deposits and other liabilities:	$800 billion
	Bonds and other investments:	$899 billion	Shareholders' equity:	$200 billion
	Total assets:	$1,000 billion	Liabilities + shareholders' equity:	$1,000 billion

Exhibit 13.5 Balance Sheet of the Fed Before and After $1 Billion Bond Purchase from Citibank

The Fed's balance sheet changes following its open market operation with Citibank. In return for $1 billion in bonds from Citibank, the Fed gives Citibank $1 billion in reserves on deposit at the Fed. On the liabilities and shareholders' equity side of the Fed's balance sheet, the Fed now has another $1 billion of IOUs in the form of reserves held by Citibank (changes on the liabilities side are shown in red). On the assets side, the Fed has another $1 billion in bonds received from Citibank (changes on the assets side are shown in blue).

Before:	Assets		Liabilities and Shareholders' Equity	
	Treasury bonds:	$1,000 billion	Reserves:	$1,000 billion
	Other bonds:	$1,000 billion	Currency:	$1,000 billion
	Total assets:	$2,000 billion	Total liabilities:	$2,000 billion
After:	Assets		Liabilities and Shareholders' Equity	
	Treasury bonds:	$1,001 billion	Reserves:	$1,001 billion
	Other bonds:	$1,000 billion	Currency:	$1,000 billion
	Total assets:	$2,001 billion	Total liabilities:	$2,001 billion

Historically, the stock of reserves—including both banks' vault cash and the reserves that banks hold at the Fed—fluctuated between $40 billion and $80 billion. During and after the 2007–2009 recession, however, the Fed drastically expanded the quantity of reserves banks held on deposit at the Fed.

Exhibit 13.6 plots this expansion. In August 2008, reserves totaled about $40 billion. You have to squint to see them, because they are hovering close to the x-axis. This quantity of reserves was enough to cover banks' reserve requirements, with little left to spare. In other words, the quantity of reserves was roughly equal to the amount of reserves that banks were required to hold—for large banks, 10 percent of the demand deposits of their customers.

MyEconLab Real-time data

Exhibit 13.6 Total Reserves on Deposit at the Federal Reserve Bank (Monthly Data from January 1959 through June 2016)

Shown are total reserves of private banks held on deposit at the Fed. Before 2008, reserves fluctuated between $40 billion and $80 billion, which was roughly the minimum amount of reserves that were required to be held—10 percent of demand deposits at large banks. In 2008, in response to the financial crisis, the Fed drastically increased the amount of reserves held at the Fed, causing total reserves to rise to $2.5 trillion by December 2013. This expansion was designed to drive down interest rates, thereby stimulating GDP. (Shaded areas denote recessions.)

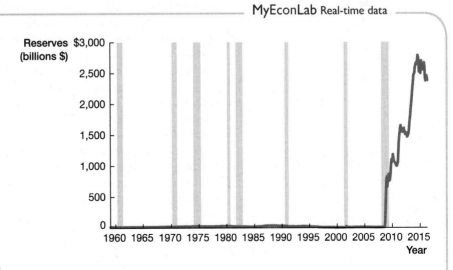

Source: Data from Board of Governors of the Federal Reserve System.

Over the next 5 years, the quantity of reserves exploded, exceeding $2.5 trillion. This vast expansion in reserves did not reflect an increase in required reserves, but rather an expansion of reserves far, far above the quantity that was required to be held. Reserves above and beyond the regulatory minimum are referred to as *excess reserves*. The Fed expanded reserves to lower the federal funds rate and so also lower long-term real interest rates. (Recall that Exhibit 13.3 shows that a rightward shift in the supply of reserves drives down the federal funds rate.) And this reduction in interest rates is exactly what this policy achieved. In early 2007, before the 2007–2009 recession, the federal funds rate was 5.25 percent. By early 2009, it was only 0.1 percent. The federal funds rate remained near 0 from 2009 up to December 2015.

Other Tools of the Fed

The Fed uses many tools to manipulate interest rates and affect the demand for goods, services, and labor. Like traditional open market operations, which we just discussed, most of these additional tools also work through the Fed's supply of bank reserves. We list these other tools here, many of which will be familiar from Chapter 11.

1. **Changing the reserve requirement.** For large private banks, the current level of required reserves is 10 percent of their customers' demand deposits. The Fed can decrease the quantity of required reserves, which shifts private banks' demand curve for reserves to the left, decreasing the federal funds rate and the long-term interest rate. (Likewise, the Fed can increase the quantity of required reserves, which shifts the demand curve for reserves to the right, increasing the federal funds rate and the long-term interest rate.)

2. **Changing the interest rate paid on reserves deposited at the Fed.** The Fed currently pays an interest rate of 0.25 percent on reserves deposited at the Fed. The Fed can change this interest rate. A decrease in the interest rate paid on reserves shifts the demand curve for reserves to the left, once again decreasing the federal funds rate and the long-term interest rate. (An increase in the interest rate paid on reserves would again have the opposite effect, increasing the federal funds rate and the long-term interest rate.)

3. **Lending from the discount window.** The Fed can lend bank reserves through its "discount window." For private banks, the discount window is an alternative to the federal funds market as a source of reserves. Lending from the discount window occurs most frequently during financial crises, when private banks are afraid to lend to one another in the federal funds market because they can't be sure that they will be paid back.

4. **Quantitative easing.** The Fed can also change the way that it conducts open market operations. Rather than buying short-term Treasury bonds, which is the usual way that the Fed increases bank reserves in an open market operation, the Fed can buy *long-term* bonds instead. Purchasing long-term bonds in an open market operation pushes up the price on the long-term bonds and thereby drives down long-term interest rates. The interest rate is the (fixed) coupon that the bond pays divided by the price of the bond, so a higher bond price implies a lower interest rate. Quantitative easing occurs when the central bank creates a large quantity of bank reserves to buy long-term bonds, simultaneously increasing the quantity of bank reserves and pushing down the interest rate on long-term bonds. Quantitative easing played a key role in the huge run-up in bank reserves that occurred from 2008 to 2014.

Central banks occasionally invent even more ways of increasing the supply of credit during financial crises by creating specialized lending channels that increase lending in the credit market and thus indirectly stimulate the demand for goods, services, and labor.

For example, immediately after the investment bank Lehman Brothers went bankrupt in September 2008, an even larger financial firm—the American International Group (AIG)—also suffered a cataclysmic liquidity crisis. AIG desperately needed cash because it had to make billions of dollars of immediate payments to hundreds of other financial firms, including many of the largest banks in the United States, Europe, and Asia. AIG was having trouble raising funds because investors feared that AIG was about to declare bankruptcy. The failure of AIG would have triggered a domino effect that could have crippled the global financial system. If AIG declared bankruptcy, any institutions that were owed money by AIG would not immediately receive the funds they were counting on, and some of these firms would be unable to meet their own financial commitments, creating ripples that might cause hundreds of interconnected financial institutions to fail.

The Fed joined forces with the U.S. Treasury Department to prop up AIG by extending AIG loans, credit lines, and other guarantees for a total of nearly $200 billion. AIG eventually recovered, and the Fed and Treasury got back their money. AIG's original shareholders were almost completely wiped out, but AIG was able to pay off its debts to other financial institutions, averting an even worse global financial meltdown.

We've now discussed the key tools that the Fed uses in its conduct of countercyclical monetary policy. However, we haven't completed the picture yet. There are several important factors that influence the way the Fed uses these tools. We turn to these issues in the next three subsections.

Expectations, Inflation, and Monetary Policy

The effectiveness of monetary policy depends on expectations about interest rates and inflation. Recall that the federal funds rate, which the Fed directly controls, is the annualized interest rate on overnight loans between banks. In contrast, the interest rate that is relevant for consumers' and firms' investment decisions—for instance, the real mortgage interest rate—is the long-term expected real interest rate:

$$\text{Long-term expected real interest rate} = \text{Long-term nominal interest rate} - \text{Long-term expected inflation rate.}$$

For the Fed to lower the long-term real interest rate, it has to either lower the long-term nominal interest rate or raise long-term expectations of the inflation rate (or both). To do this, the Fed can publicly announce that it will maintain an expansionary monetary policy in the future, by continuing to hold down the federal funds rate and continuing to prop up the inflation rate. In general, the Fed's effort to influence today's expectations about future monetary policy is referred to as *forward guidance.*

> The effectiveness of monetary policy depends on expectations about interest rates and inflation.

For example, if households and firms believe that the federal funds rate will remain low for several years, then the long-term nominal interest rate will also be low. To see why, think of the 10-year nominal interest rate as being tied to the market's expectations of the average interest rate for overnight loans over the next 10 years. If the Fed announces forward guidance that it will continue to keep the federal funds rate low for an extended period of time, then the market will believe that the interest rate for overnight loans will also tend to be low over the next 10 years, and as a consequence, today's long-term nominal interest rate will be low as well.

A similar analysis applies to long-term expectations of inflation. To many people, inflation is a four-letter word. But as already mentioned in Chapter 11, the impact of inflationary expectations on the long-term expected real interest rate implies that the Fed might wish to create expectations of inflation—if it can. In particular, the Fed might announce forward guidance that it will continue to conduct an expansionary monetary policy for an extended period of time. If the market believes this announcement, then inflationary expectations will rise. Provided that the nominal interest rate doesn't rise one-for-one with inflation, the long-term expected real interest rate will decline.

Contractionary Monetary Policy: Control of Inflation

Recall from Chapter 11 that stabilizing inflation is one of the Fed's two mandates. The Fed would like the inflation rate to hover around 2 percent per year, neither deviating far above nor far below this target.

Expansionary monetary policy can put this inflation target at risk. In normal circumstances, increasing the quantity of bank reserves enables banks to make more loans. Those loans circulate through the economy and return to the banking system as deposits. Rising bank deposits increase the amount of money in the economy, since the stock of money includes customers' bank deposits. The quantity theory of money, which we studied in Chapter 11, implies that over the long run, the inflation rate will equal the growth rate of M2 minus the growth rate of real GDP. Excessively rapid growth in M2 therefore creates a risk of high levels of inflation.

DATA SPEAK

Managing Expectations

The Fed's desire to influence long-term expectations is apparent in its monthly policy statements. In the fall of 2010, the economy was slowly recovering from the 2007–2009 recession, and consequently the Fed wanted to maintain a low long-term expected real interest rate. In its September 2010 policy announcement, the Federal Open Market Committee (FOMC)—the committee that conducts the Fed's open market operations—wrote that the federal funds rate would be held between 0 and 0.25 percent for "an extended period."

In its December 2012 announcement, the Fed announced an even clearer policy rule, by linking changes in the federal funds rate to future changes in the unemployment rate and the inflation rate:[1]

> "The committee decided to keep the target range for the federal funds rate at 0 to 1/4 percent and currently anticipates that this exceptionally low range for the federal funds rate will be appropriate at least as long as
> - the unemployment rate remains above 6.5 percent,
> - inflation between one and two years ahead is projected to be no more than a half percentage point above the Committee's 2 percent longer-run goal,
> - and longer-term inflation expectations continue to be well anchored."

In this statement, the Fed announced a specific policy rule, which increased the public's ability to forecast future interest rates. In essence, the Fed announced that it planned to keep the federal funds rate close to 0 percent as long as the unemployment rate remained above 6.5 percent and inflation remained close to the Fed's 2 percent target. At the time this announcement was made, the unemployment rate was 7.7 percent, and forecasters anticipated that it would take years for the unemployment rate to fall to the

6.5 percent threshold that the Fed set for itself. In reality, it took less than 2 years—unemployment fell below the threshold in early 2014. Still, the Fed remained steadfast, deferring any rate increases until the economy improved further.

In December 2015, with unemployment at 5 percent, the Fed finally raised the federal funds rate above zero, beginning the long process of normalization of the federal funds rate. The change was modest—the new target range for the federal funds rate was 0.25–0.5 percent—but significant, as this was the first rate increase in more than 11 years. In December 2016 and again in March 2017, the Fed raised the target range two more times—first to the range of 0.5–0.75 percent and then to the range of 0.75–1.0 percent. More increases are anticipated later in 2017 and in the years to come.

Today, the Fed continues to influence expectations of participants in the credit markets. Market participants can monitor the policy recommendations of individual members of the FOMC, which are summarized in the Fed's "dot plot" (Exhibit 13.7). In this exhibit (shown with forecasts made in December 2016), each dot represents the future federal funds rate recommended by one member of the FOMC. Each dot is plotted at the midpoint of the member's recommended target range for the future federal funds rate. However, this chart is not a fixed plan—it can (and does) change with changing economic conditions.

The chart reveals a wide variety of recommendations among the members of the FOMC. For example, the midpoints of the appropriate target ranges reported by FOMC members for 2019 vary from just less than 1 percent to just less than 4 percent. Even these experts don't agree. Nevertheless, the dot plot reduces public misunderstandings about the thinking of policymakers and thereby reduces the likelihood of policy surprises that might rattle the credit markets.

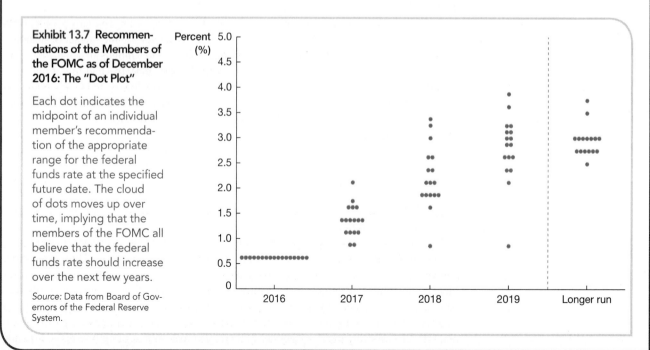

Exhibit 13.7 Recommendations of the Members of the FOMC as of December 2016: The "Dot Plot"

Each dot indicates the midpoint of an individual member's recommendation of the appropriate range for the federal funds rate at the specified future date. The cloud of dots moves up over time, implying that the members of the FOMC all believe that the federal funds rate should increase over the next few years.

Source: Data from Board of Governors of the Federal Reserve System.

Exhibit 13.8 The Path from Reserves to Inflation

Increasing the quantity of bank reserves deposited at the Fed usually leads banks to make more loans. Those loans circulate through the economy and return to the banking system as deposits. Rising bank deposits enable banks to make even more loans. The resulting total increase in deposits generates an increase in the stock of money (for instance, M2). If the stock of money grows faster than real GDP, the aggregate price level will likely rise, generating inflation. This poses a problem only when inflation persistently stays above the Fed's 2 percent target.

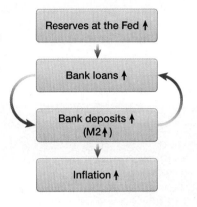

Contractionary monetary policy
slows down growth in bank reserves, raises interest rates, reduces borrowing, slows down growth in the money supply, and reduces the rate of inflation.

William McChesney Martin, Jr., was the chair of the Fed from 1951 to 1970. A teetotaler in his personal life, he described the Fed's role this way: "I'm the fellow who takes away the punch bowl just when the party is getting good."

> The Fed [plays] a countercyclical role, leaning against the prevailing economic winds.

We summarize these linkages in Exhibit 13.8. Countercyclical policy is useful for controlling current and future inflation. In particular, when inflation threatens to rise persistently above the Fed's target of 2 percent, the Fed uses **contractionary monetary policy**, which slows down growth in bank reserves, raises interest rates, reduces borrowing, slows down growth in the money supply, and prevents inflation from rising. If inflation has already risen above 2 percent, then contractionary monetary policy might be used to reduce the rate of inflation.

Contractionary monetary policy is like expansionary monetary policy, but now the Fed runs everything in reverse. The Fed will *shrink* bank reserves—or slow their growth—to *raise* the federal funds rate. It might also use forward guidance to change expectations about future monetary policy in a contractionary direction.

The Fed is currently engaged in a program of gradual interest rate increases. This episode started in December 2015, when the Fed moved from a target range of 0–0.25 percent for the federal funds rate to a new target range of 0.25–0.50 percent. A second increase occurred in December 2016, and a third increase took place in March 2017. As this textbook goes to press in the spring of 2017, more increases in the federal funds rate are anticipated. Forward guidance is being used by the Fed (see Exhibit 13.7) to communicate a longer-run aspiration to slowly increase the federal funds rate to approximately 3 percent.

In terms of our model, the Fed is hoping to avoid the situation plotted in Exhibit 12.14 (from the previous chapter), where we show how an excessive rightward shift in the labor demand curve produces a high rate of inflation. By slowly raising the federal funds rate to approximately 3 percent, the Fed hopes to prevent the labor demand curve from shifting too far to the right.

In essence, the Fed can run the engine of monetary policy either forward or backward. During a recession, the Fed employs expansionary monetary policies to partially offset the economic contraction. During a boom, particularly one that is inflationary, the Fed employs contractionary monetary policy to reduce a rising rate of inflation. In both cases, the Fed is playing a countercyclical role, leaning against the prevailing economic winds.

Though it might sound straightforward to run the engine of monetary policy backward, controlling inflation is not always easy. Once prices begin rising quickly—for instance, an inflation rate of 5 percent or more—the public starts to expect a high inflation rate in the future and the central bank has a hard time regaining its reputation as an inflation fighter. Such a loss in reputation occurred during the 1970s—a decade of high and rising U.S. inflation caused in part by expansionary monetary policy. By the end of the 1970s, the Fed's reputation as a careful steward of the monetary system was shattered. In 1979, the U.S. public expected that inflation would remain at a high level for the foreseeable future. This is when a new Fed chair, Paul Volcker, stepped in with a sharply contractionary monetary policy. To cut inflation, he drastically slowed the growth rate of the stock of money, which raised the federal funds rate to 20 percent. This started the 1981 recession, which turned out to be one of the most severe U.S. recessions since World War II. Volcker's recession generated a peak unemployment rate of 10.8 percent, even greater than the 10 percent peak during the 2007–2009 recession. Volcker believed that the benefits of lowering the rate of inflation offset the costs of this deep recession.

Volcker managed to reclaim the Fed's credibility for fighting inflation, and ever since, the Fed has retained its reputation for being serious about controlling the level of inflation.

With historical episodes like this in mind, central banks work hard to protect their reputation for keeping inflation at a low level—around 2 percent per year. Even the slightest hint that inflation is getting out of control might lead a central bank to end a policy of monetary expansion.

Paul Volcker sharply reduced the growth rate of the money stock in the early 1980s to reclaim the Fed's reputation as an inflation fighter. His actions raised interest rates and started a major recession. Despite national protests against his policies, he stayed the course, and he is now viewed as one of the greatest chairs of the Fed. This is one central banker you shouldn't mess with. (He also had the odd quirk of testifying before the Senate while puffing on cigars.[2])

Zero Lower Bound

Japan has experienced four recessions and a very low level of overall growth in real GDP since the early 1990s. Many observers refer to the 1990s and 2000s as "lost decades" for the Japanese economy. In response to these economic conditions, Japan's central bank has responded by increasing the supply of bank reserves, thereby lowering Japan's version of the federal funds rate—the interest rate for interbank loans—approximately to zero. Exhibit 13.9 plots this interbank interest rate.

When an interest rate is zero, economists say that it is at the "zero lower bound." This language implies that zero is a barrier—or a boundary line—that nominal interest rates can't cross.

To understand the zero lower bound, it is helpful to explain how bizarre a negative nominal interest rate actually is. A negative interest rate implies that a borrower eventually repays *less* money than she borrowed. For example, suppose that you go to the bank to borrow $100 million for 1 year at a negative interest rate of –1 percent. Assuming that you can store this money—for example, under a very big mattress—then borrowing at a –1 percent interest rate would present a great profit opportunity for you. You borrow $100 million. You store it for a year and then repay your loan by giving the bank $99 million back and pocketing the remaining $1 million!

Of course, lending money at a negative interest rate is a bad deal for banks; they would rather keep the money in their own vaults than lend it to you. At least then they would have $100 million at the end of the year rather than just the $99 million they would get from you.

This example ignores the fact that storing money isn't actually costless. If a bank leaves $100 million in its vault, someone might steal it. We've all seen movies with a bank heist featuring a motley crew of criminal geniuses. Accordingly, sometimes a bank or another

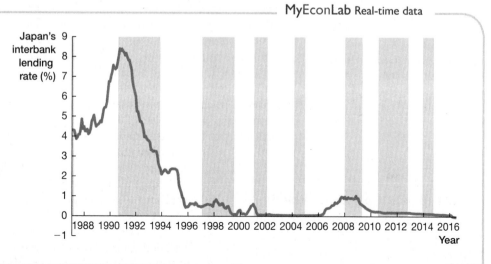

Exhibit 13.9 Japan's Interbank Lending Rate (1987–2016)

The Japanese central bank has kept the interest rate on interbank loans near zero since 1995. The rate dipped slightly below zero in 2016. The interbank lending rate is analogous to the federal funds rate in the United States. (Shaded areas correspond to Japanese recessions.)

Source: Data from Board of Governors of the Federal Reserve System.

type of investor would rather buy a government bond with a slightly negative interest rate—for instance, –0.2 percent—then leave $100 million in cash in a vault. This small negative interest rate is the price of security. Even if a government bond were stolen, the thief couldn't cash it in, and the legitimate owner would retain legal ownership and the right to collect the money from the government. Because of these considerations, some governments have managed to sell bonds with interest rates that are slightly negative. But interest rates can't get too negative, because then it would be profitable to build a bigger vault, fill it with cash, and pay a small army to guard it.

These arguments explain why banks generally won't lend money at an interest rate that is much below zero. Banks will hold onto their money rather than make loans at negative interest rates. It therefore follows that central banks can't push nominal interest rates far below zero. And that is the zero lower bound.

The zero lower bound is a problem for monetary policy when the rate of inflation is low or negative, which has also been the case in Japan since the early 1990s. Remember that households and firms make investment decisions based on the expected real interest rate. When the nominal interest rate is stuck at or just above 0 and the inflation rate is negative (also called *deflation*), the real interest rate will be positive. For example, a nominal interest rate of 0 and an expected inflation rate of –1 percent jointly imply an expected real interest rate of

$$\text{Nominal interest rate} - \text{Expected inflation rate} = 0\% - (-1\%) = 1\%.$$

If the inflation rate keeps falling (further below zero), the real interest rate will rise, squelching investment and shifting the labor demand curve to the left.

When the economy is in recession or growing only slowly, the central bank usually wants to lower the real interest rate to stimulate economic growth. But what does it do

CHOICE & CONSEQUENCE

Policy Mistakes

On occasion, policymakers fail to recognize what is happening in the economy. Sometimes they mistakenly adopt policies that increase the magnitude of economic fluctuations instead of policies that smooth things out.

Some economists believe that the severity of the 2007–2009 financial crisis and recession was in part caused by unduly expansionary monetary policy from 2002 to 2005. During this period, the Fed, under chair Alan Greenspan, lowered the federal funds rate to 1 percent, even though the economy was growing and the housing market was gripped by what we now realize was an unsustainable speculative bubble. Alan Greenspan's unwillingness to increase the federal funds rate was in part caused by his belief at the time that unsustainable speculative bubbles are extremely rare. After the collapse in housing prices, Greenspan publicly revised his views on the frequency of asset bubbles.

Asset bubbles—like the home price bubble that peaked in 2006—do occur from time to time and are often followed by recessions. In other words, asset bubbles increase, or amplify, economic fluctuations. The Fed's expansionary policies of 2002–2005 greased the wheels of the housing bubble and therefore played a partial role in causing the recession that followed. Sometimes central banks administer the wrong monetary medicine.

Central banks have studied this policy failure and many are now attempting to identify asset bubbles as they are forming. Some central banks, including the Bank of England, are also implementing policies that are designed to suppress asset price bubbles before they grow destructively large.[3]

when nominal interest rates can't be lowered much further because they are already at the zero lower bound? As discussed earlier, the central bank tries to influence expectations of future nominal interest rates and future inflation. By promising to keep nominal interest rates low for many years and promising to keep inflation at 2 percent in the long run, the central bank attempts to influence the long-term expected real rate of interest, even if the current federal funds rate is at zero and can't be lowered much further.

Policy Trade-offs

We hope you have concluded that the job of a central banker is not easy. Monetary policymakers face many conflicting considerations. For example, the Fed would like to stimulate the economy during a recession, but it does not want to risk runaway inflation. How should the Fed make this trade-off?

Many central banks set the federal funds rate in a way that is approximately described by the following formula:

$$\text{Federal funds rate} = \text{Long-run federal funds rate target} + 1.5 \times (\text{Inflation rate} - \text{Inflation rate target}) + 0.5 \times (\text{Output gap in percentage points})$$

(called the *Taylor rule* after economist John Taylor, who first suggested it).[4] This equation relates the federal funds rate to its long-run target (about 3 percent), the inflation rate, the inflation rate target (2 percent), and the output gap in percentage points. The *output gap*, which was first discussed in Chapter 12, is the difference between GDP and trend GDP divided by trend GDP:

$$\text{Output gap} = \frac{\text{GDP} - \text{Trend GDP}}{\text{Trend GDP}}.$$

An output gap of –0.05 is expressed in percentage points as –5 percent—in other words, the economy is 5 percent below trend. Recall from Chapter 12 that trend GDP is a smoothed version of actual GDP. You sometimes will see the output gap expressed with trend GDP replaced by *potential GDP*, which represents the level of GDP that would be attained if the labor force and the capital stock were fully employed in production.

It is useful to spell out the two parts of the Taylor rule:

1. The rule states that the Fed raises the federal funds rate as the inflation rate rises. A higher inflation rate causes the Fed to raise the federal funds rate, thereby reducing the degree of stimulus. Specifically, the formula indicates that every percentage point increase in the inflation rate (for a given inflation target) will translate into a 1.5 percentage point increase in the federal funds rate.
2. The rule also states that the Fed raises the federal funds rate as the output gap increases. A larger output gap—in other words, a stronger economy—leads the Fed to raise the federal funds rate, thereby reducing the degree of stimulus. The formula indicates that every percentage point increase in the output gap will translate into a half percentage point increase in the federal funds rate.

To see the Taylor rule in action, consider the state of affairs in 2016. Inflation was running at about 1 percent, and the economy was about 1 percent below its trend GDP level. Plugging these numbers into the Taylor rule (and assuming a 3 percent long-run federal funds rate target and 2 percent inflation rate target), the recommended level of the federal funds rate was:

$$\text{Federal funds rate} = 3\% + 1.5\% \times (1\% - 2\%) + 0.5 \times (-1\%) = 1\%.$$

Hence, the Taylor rule predicted a federal funds rate of 1 percent, far below its long-run target of 3 percent. In fact, the actual federal funds rate in late 2016 was within the range of 0.50–0.75 percent, only slightly below the level predicted by the Taylor rule.

The Taylor "rule" is really just a rule of thumb. Monetary policy is as much an art as a science—policymakers need to use their intuition and wisdom, not just a simple formula. However, the Taylor rule is a good starting point for their deliberations and a rough-and-ready summary of the trade-offs that central banks have made in the past.

13.3 Countercyclical Fiscal Policy

Countercyclical monetary policy, which is conducted by the central bank and aims to reduce economic fluctuations by manipulating interest rates, has been our focus so far. Countercyclical fiscal policy is the other major category of countercyclical policy. Countercyclical fiscal policy, which is passed by the legislative branch and signed into law by the executive branch, reduces economic fluctuations by manipulating government expenditures and taxes.

Expansionary fiscal policy uses higher government expenditure and lower taxes to increase the growth rate of real GDP. Like expansionary monetary policy, expansionary fiscal policy shifts the labor demand curve to the right, as Exhibit 13.1 showed. **Contractionary fiscal policy** uses lower government expenditure and higher taxes to reduce the growth rate of real GDP. Just like contractionary monetary policy, contractionary fiscal policy shifts the labor demand curve to the left.

We now discuss the reasons that macroeconomists view fiscal policy as a useful tool for offsetting macroeconomic fluctuations. We'll also explain some of its limitations.

Fiscal Policy Over the Business Cycle: Automatic and Discretionary Components

Fiscal policy can be divided into automatic and discretionary components.

1. *Automatic countercyclical components* are aspects of fiscal policy that automatically partially offset economic fluctuations. These automatic countercyclical components do not require deliberate action on the part of the government. For example, tax collection falls automatically during a recession because unemployed workers don't owe income tax. Moreover, during a recession, government expenditure automatically increases, because government transfer payments rise, including unemployment insurance and food stamps (otherwise known as the Supplemental Nutrition Assistance Program or SNAP). The less households earn, the more government transfers they receive.

   These automatic countercyclical fiscal mechanisms are often referred to as **automatic stabilizers** because they stimulate the economy during economic contractions. Such transfers help households cope with economic hardship and are widely believed to stimulate GDP by enabling millions of households to spend more during recessions.

2. *Discretionary countercyclical components* are those aspects of the government's fiscal policy that policymakers deliberately enact in response to economic fluctuations. In most cases, these new policies introduce a package of specific expenditure increases or temporary tax cuts to reduce economic hardship and stimulate GDP. For example, during the recession of 2007–2009, the U.S. Congress passed the Economic Stimulus Act of 2008—signed by President George W. Bush in February 2008—and the American Recovery and Reinvestment Act of 2009—signed by President Barack Obama in February 2009. The first package contained $152 billion in tax cuts, which were received by households in the spring of 2008. The second package cost $787 billion, with a third of the funding supporting new tax cuts and two-thirds of the funding supporting new government expenditure. The new spending was spread out over several years.

Exhibit 13.10 illustrates the behavior of fiscal policy (combining both the automatic and discretionary components) during the 2007–2009 recession. The rising budget deficit—government revenue minus government expenditure—provides a summary measure of fiscal policy, because the deficit reflects rising expenditures and falling tax collection. In the fourth quarter of 2007, which was the start of the recession, the budget deficit was $416 billion (all numbers are in constant 2009 dollars). By the end of the recession in the second quarter of 2009, the budget deficit had risen to $1,603 billion. Persistent weakness in the labor market coupled with lags in spending from the 2009 American Recovery and Reinvestment Act caused the deficit to remain high following the end of the recession.

Expansionary fiscal policy uses higher government expenditure and lower taxes to increase the growth rate of real GDP.

Contractionary fiscal policy uses lower government expenditure and higher taxes to reduce the growth rate of real GDP.

Automatic stabilizers are components of the government budget that automatically adjust to smooth out economic fluctuations.

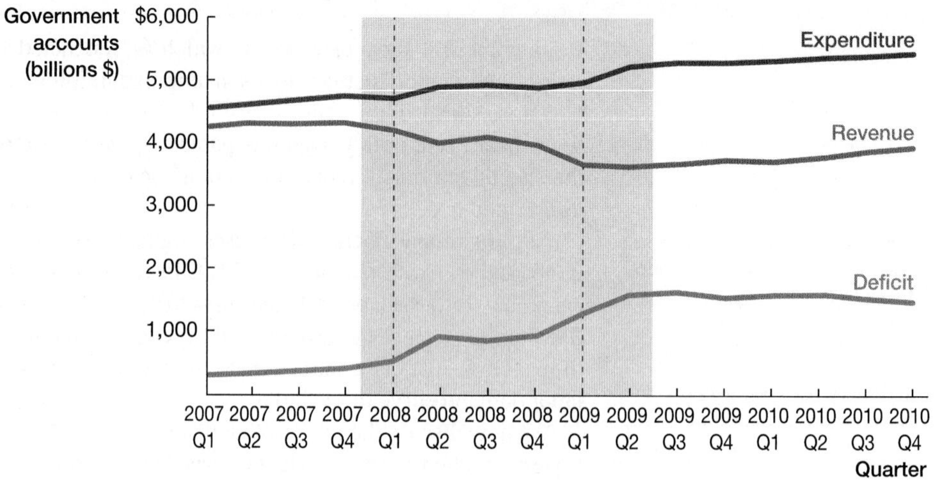

Exhibit 13.10 U.S. Government Accounts, Combining Federal, State, and Local Governments, 2007–2010 (Constant 2009 Dollars)

During the 2007–2009 recession (December 2007–June 2009, which corresponds to the shaded area), fiscal policy was implemented in two major pieces of legislation. The first act was passed in February 2008 and was principally focused on tax cuts that were paid out in the spring of 2008 (the second quarter of 2008). The second act was passed in February 2009 and included both tax cuts and spending increases. Vertical lines identify the quarter in which each piece of legislation was passed.

Source: Based on Bureau of Economic Analysis, National Income and Product Accounts; and National Bureau of Economic Research.

Such deficits have consequences. When the government borrows money to pay its bills, future taxpayers are implicitly responsible for paying back the government's debts. Ultimately, the government will have to pay what it owes. Roughly speaking, the 2007–2009 recession generated $2 trillion of automatic fiscal adjustments and $1 trillion of discretionary fiscal adjustments, implying that taxpayers are now on the hook for approximately $3 trillion of new government debt. But all of this debt was accumulated for a reason— to conduct countercyclical fiscal policy. The basic idea behind fiscal policy is that higher government expenditure and lower taxation play a useful role in recessions by increasing spending by households, firms, and governments. This increased spending translates into demand for firms' products, which in turn increases demand for labor, shifting labor demand to the right. To the extent that some of this money goes to state and local governments, it enables them to avoid laying off state and local employees.

> The basic idea behind fiscal policy is that higher government expenditure and lower taxation play a useful role in recessions by increasing spending by households, firms, and governments.

The remainder of the chapter explains why more government expenditure and lower taxation increase GDP. We first look at expenditure-based fiscal policy and then at taxation-based fiscal policy.

Analysis of Expenditure-Based Fiscal Policy

Let's begin with the national income accounting identity.

$$Y = C + I + G + X - M.$$

Here, Y is GDP, C is consumption, I is investment, G is government expenditure, X is exports, M is imports, and thus $X - M$ is net exports. To start the analysis of fiscal policy, assume (for the moment) that changing government expenditure does not change any of the other terms on the right-hand side of the equation. Then a $1 increase in government expenditure would cause a $1 increase in GDP, Y:

$$(Y + 1) = C + I + (G + 1) + X - M.$$

If a $1 change in government expenditure causes an $m change in GDP, then the **government expenditure multiplier** is m.

If we take the change in GDP (Y) and divide it by the change in government expenditure (G), we have what is known as the **government expenditure multiplier**. If government expenditure rises by $1 and causes GDP to rise by m, then the government expenditure multiplier is $m/$1 = m. For example, if $m = 1$, then a $1 increase in government expenditure generates a $1 increase in GDP (which is the case in the previous equation). In terms of our analysis of Exhibit 13.1, if $m = 1$, then increased government expenditure of $1 raises the demand for firms' goods and services and shifts the labor demand curve to the right, increasing GDP by $1.

Let's now revisit the assumption that nothing else on the right-hand side of the equation changes. Additional government expenditure might lead to higher levels of household consumption. For example, the government's extra expenditure might encourage additional business activity, which would raise employment and take-home pay and thereby increase household consumption. In this scenario, increased government expenditure levels are creating a multiplier effect of the sort discussed in Chapter 12. The multiplier effect shifts firms' labor demand curves further to the right and translates into a larger impact of government expenditure on employment and GDP.

We can illustrate this multiplier effect with the national income accounting identity. Assume that the multiplier effect raises household consumption by $1 (in addition to the original $1 increase in government expenditure). In particular:

$$(Y + 2) = (C + 1) + I + (G + 1) + X - M.$$

In this scenario, Y rises by $2—remember that the left- and right-hand sides of this equation must be equal. In this case, the government expenditure multiplier would be $2/$1 = 2. This means that GDP rises by $2 for every $1 increase in government expenditure.

Advocates of expenditure-based fiscal policy tend to believe that the government expenditure multiplier lies between 1 and 2.

Crowding Out In addition to its useful role of combating recessions as part of countercyclical fiscal policy, there is also a negative side to government expenditure. Rising government expenditures lead to more government borrowing, and such borrowing can soak up resources that would otherwise have been used by households and firms. Some economists believe that rising government expenditure "crowds out" private economic activity like consumption and investment. **Crowding out** occurs when rising government expenditure partially or even fully displaces expenditures by households and firms. In Exhibit 13.1, crowding out results in a smaller effect of countercyclical policy—in other words, crowding out implies that the labor demand curve shifts to the right less than it otherwise would.

Crowding out occurs when rising government expenditure partially or even fully displaces expenditures by households and firms.

For example, suppose that an extra $1 of government expenditure forces the government to borrow an extra $1 to pay its bills, leading $1 of private savings to switch from funding private investment to purchasing government debt. The switch occurs because the government is willing to pay whatever interest rate it takes to borrow funds, whereas private businesses tend to be more responsive to interest rate changes. As the government borrows to pay its bills, the interest rate in the credit market rises, causing a reallocation of savings from private borrowers—like households and firms—to the government. If private investment becomes too expensive for consumers and firms, it might fall by $1 when the government increases its spending by $1. In effect, the private investment is "crowded out" by government borrowing. In this scenario, countercyclical government expenditure will not shift the firms' labor demand curve to the right, because the expansionary effect of the additional government expenditure is offset by the contractionary effect of the fall in private investment. Consequently, GDP does not increase, because the $1 increase in government expenditure crowds out $1 of private investment:

$$Y = C + (I - 1) + (G + 1) + X - M.$$

In this case, the government expenditure multiplier is $(-$1 + $1)/$1 = 0$. Critics of fiscal policy emphasize the importance of crowding out and believe that the government expenditure multiplier is well below 1 and might even be close to 0 (which is the case in this illustrative example).

At this point you are probably wondering which scenario is "right." Unfortunately, we are not completely sure. Economists hold a wide range of positions on this question, and everyone in this debate has some data that partially support his or her position. Taking into account both multipliers and crowding out, the government expenditure multiplier probably lies between 0 and 1.5, depending on the state of the economy. If the economy is already running at full steam, it is likely that additional government expenditure will substantially crowd out other kinds of economic activity. For example, if all factories are already operating at full capacity, there may be little the government can do in the short run to increase GDP. Consequently, many economists believe that the government expenditure multiplier is close to zero when the economy is already booming. But that's not particularly relevant to the fiscal policy debate, because economists don't recommend expansionary fiscal policy when the economy is already growing rapidly.

The interesting question is what we should expect the government expenditure multiplier to be when the economy is contracting. For example, envision an economy suffering from an extreme contraction, and further assume that monetary policy has been rendered less effective because interest rates have already been lowered to zero and can't be lowered any further—the scenario in which monetary policy has reached the region of the zero lower bound.

This was the situation of the U.S. economy in the aftermath of the 2007–2009 recession. In such situations there will be substantial slack in productive resources, like factories running below capacity and significant numbers of unemployed workers. Accordingly, additional government expenditure might only weakly crowd out private consumption and investment. Additional government expenditures can then encourage the utilization of some of the idle capacity and unemployed workers. For instance, President Barack Obama's administration assumed a government-expenditure multiplier of 1.57 when developing the American Recovery and Reinvestment Act of 2009.[5] This number was close to, though slightly above, the estimates of other forecasters at that time.

Most economists endorse some additional government expenditures during a deep recession, but there is substantial debate on this issue. Critics of expansionary government expenditure believe that crowding out is strong even during recessions. Accordingly, the appropriate scale of countercyclical government expenditure remains an open policy question.

We'll now show you how to use the government expenditure multiplier to predict the impact of expenditure-based countercyclical policy. Let's assume that the economy is in a deep recession and that the multiplier is 1.5, approximately the top of its range. The American Recovery and Reinvestment Act of 2009 contained about $500 billion of new spending, but this new spending was spread out over many years. Only $120 billion occurred in 2009, implying an impact of

$$1.5 \times \$120 \text{ billion} = \$180 \text{ billion.}$$

Since GDP was approximately $14 trillion in 2009, a $180 billion increase in GDP amounted to an increase of about

$$\frac{\$180 \text{ billion}}{\$14 \text{ trillion}} = 1.3\%.$$

That might not seem like much, but 1.3 percentage points of extra growth do make a difference when talking about the growth rate of the entire U.S. economy. For example, in 2009 real GDP fell by 2.8 percent. A multiplier of 1.5 implies that the economy would have fallen by 4.1 percent without the impact of the new government expenditures in the American Recovery and Reinvestment Act of 2009.

Analysis of Taxation-Based Fiscal Policy

So far, we've been discussing the use of government expenditure to partially offset an economic contraction. Expansionary fiscal policy can also be implemented by cutting taxes. Let's therefore switch gears and assume that the government gives households a $1 tax cut. To illustrate this scenario let's start with the extreme assumption that consumers spend every penny of the tax cut, raising consumption (C) by $1, but nothing else changes on the

If a $1 reduction in taxation causes an m increase in GDP, then the **government taxation multiplier** is m.

right-hand side of the national income accounting identity. Then GDP would rise by $1 and the **government taxation multiplier** would be $1/$1 = 1$:

$$(Y + 1) = (C + 1) + I + G + X - M.$$

But a $1 tax cut need not increase GDP by $1. If it increases it by m, the government taxation multiplier would be $m/$1 = m$.

For instance, a $1 tax cut might have an impact that is even greater than $1 for many reasons. The rise in consumption might have multiplier effects, causing a domino effect of rising consumption, rising firm revenues, rising firm hiring, rising household income, and yet more consumption. In addition, a cut in income tax might lead workers to supply more labor, because their *after-tax* wages will have risen (though this effect is estimated to be small in magnitude). With these kinds of mechanisms in mind, suppose that a $1 decrease in taxation leads to a $2 increase in households' incomes and a $2 increase in consumption. Suppose that nothing else changes on the right-hand side of the accounting identity. In this case, GDP (Y) would rise by $2, so the government taxation multiplier would be $2/$1 = 2$.

$$(Y + 2) = (C + 2) + I + G + X - M.$$

In contrast, tax cuts might generate crowding out of the sort that we described before. As consumers try to spend more, resources that would have previously gone to investment might now be redirected to consumption. For instance, a car company might shift from manufacturing rental cars (an investment for Hertz and Avis) toward manufacturing cars that households buy:

$$(Y + 1) = (C + 2) + (I - 1) + G + X - M.$$

Likewise, as consumers try to spend more, the extra goods might be provided by an increase in imports, lowering net exports. If imports rise by $1, then net exports will fall by $1, so the national income accounting identity becomes:

$$(Y + 1) = (C + 2) + I + G + X - (M + 1).$$

If crowding-out effects are large, the government taxation multiplier will be significantly reduced. In the last two examples discussed, the government taxation multiplier would be $($2 - $1)/$1 = 1$.

Critics of using tax policy to manage short-run economic contractions point out that optimizing consumers might not actually spend much of their tax cut right away. In other words, critics worry that consumption might not rise very much as a result of a tax cut. Why might households hold back on spending their tax cuts? There are at least two reasons.

1. If consumption offers diminishing returns—a fifth slice of pizza might not taste as good as the fourth slice—consumers might try to smooth their consumption by spreading the "extra" spending over the long term rather than consuming the proceeds of a tax cut all at once.

2. Consumers might recognize that the government will have to raise taxes in the future to pay for the current tax cut. Because of this anticipated future tax hike, they may decide that a current tax cut should be saved so that they will be in a position to pay these higher taxes in the future.

The tendency to save the tax cut will be particularly pronounced among wealthy consumers who don't have an urgent reason to consume the tax cut right away. In summary, if some consumers save some or even all of a tax cut, cutting taxes will have only a small effect on consumption, and the government taxation multiplier will be small.

Economists believe that the government taxation multiplier is between 0 and 2. The administration of President Barack Obama assumed a government-taxation multiplier of 0.99 when developing the American Recovery and Reinvestment Act of 2009.[6] The act created total tax cuts of about $300 billion, but only $65 billion of those cuts took effect in 2009. Assuming a government-taxation multiplier of 1, these tax cuts raised 2009 GDP by about $65 billion, representing about 0.5 percent of GDP in 2009.

LETTING THE
DATA SPEAK

The Response of Consumption to Tax Cuts

We've discussed competing theories about the impact of tax cuts: perhaps tax cuts boost consumption, or perhaps people instead decide to save the money, leading to little macroeconomic impact. What do we find in practice? In general, it is extremely difficult to empirically isolate the effect of tax cuts on consumption. A tax cut might be introduced in response to other economic shocks that could also affect consumption, or a tax cut might be included in a complex package of other economic policies. In either case, it's hard to prove that a change in consumption was caused solely by a tax cut.

In 2001, however, the Economic Growth and Tax Relief Reconciliation Act included tax rebates that were mailed to American families at random times over a 10-week period (because it was logistically impossible to mail them all out at once). Recall from Chapter 2 that this type of randomness can be used as a "natural experiment" to help identify causation; indeed, economists David Johnson, Jonathan Parker, and Nicholas Souleles took advantage of the law to test the effect of the tax rebate on consumption.[7]

Their results indicate that households do indeed spend considerably more after receiving a rebate, particularly in the first few months after the check arrives. In particular, they found that households spend about 20–40 percent of the rebate in the first 3 months. Given the total rebate amount of $38 billion, they estimated that the rebates raised aggregate consumption by 0.8 percent in the third quarter of 2001 (when the rebates were mailed). In the next 3 months, the effects were lower but still significant according to their estimates—raising consumption by 0.6 percent in the fourth quarter of 2001. Thus, it seems that this tax policy did raise short-run consumption. A similar study of tax rebates in the 2007–2009 recession yielded even larger estimates of the effect of tax rebates on consumption.[8]

We can therefore calculate the total impact of the American Recovery and Reinvestment Act of 2009, assuming that the government's estimates of multipliers are correct. Expenditures raised GDP by 1.3 percent (see calculations on page 324) and tax cuts raised GDP by 0.5 percent. Hence, the act raised 2009 GDP by

$$1.3\% \, + \, 0.5\% \, = \, 1.8\%.$$

Actual growth in real GDP was –2.8 percent from 2008 to 2009. If the act raised GDP by 1.8 percent, then *without* the act, growth in real GDP would have been

$$-2.8\% \, - \, 1.8\% \, = \, -4.6\%.$$

So, on the basis of the government's own estimates of the multipliers, the act had a considerable impact on GDP.

Fiscal Policies That Directly Target the Labor Market

A few specific fiscal policies directly target the labor market. For example, in the midst of recessions, when many workers have lost their jobs and are unemployed, governments enact policies to lessen the terrible personal toll of joblessness. In the United States, the government extends eligibility for unemployment insurance from 26 to 52 weeks and, in some severe downturns, even to 99 weeks.

More generous eligibility rules have complex effects on the labor market. Lengthening eligibility reduces the hardships that unemployed workers suffer and gives them more time to find a job that is a good fit for their skills, but lengthened eligibility also partially reduces the incentive for unemployed workers to find new jobs. This shifts the labor supply curve to the left, which, holding all else equal, reduces employment.

However, by increasing the incomes of unemployed workers, lengthened eligibility supports household spending and thus limits the negative multiplier effects that result from falling employment. Hence, lengthened eligibility increases household consumption, and this effect shifts the labor demand curve to the right.

Adding up the different considerations, the extension of unemployment benefits probably is good policy, but this is due to the suffering that it alleviates and not its effect on GDP. Because of the multiple effects with opposing implications for employment, lengthening eligibility is likely to have only a limited effect on total employment or GDP.

During recessions, another type of fiscal policy reduces unemployment by subsidizing wages and thereby encouraging job creation. Such subsidies might be justified when unemployment remains high for a long period of time—for instance, during the Great Depression. Wage subsidies might also be justified when traditional monetary and fiscal policy have only limited success in combating unemployment. The last three U.S. recessions have been followed by "jobless recoveries," meaning that the rate of employment growth after these three recessions, although positive, has been lower than after earlier recessions.

We show the effect of a subsidy on labor demand and job creation in Exhibit 13.11. With a $1 subsidy received by employers, a wage of $10 per hour would cost employers only $9 per hour. So the subsidy shifts the labor demand curve to the right by just enough to create a $1 vertical gap between the old and new labor demand curves (drop a vertical line from one curve to the other to see the $1 gap). An employer who is willing to pay $9 for a worker without the subsidy is willing to pay $10 for that worker once the $1 government subsidy is in effect. Wage subsidies have been used commonly by European governments since the 1990s, when their economies were also beset by jobless recoveries.

LETTING THE
DATA SPEAK

A Different Type of Fiscal Policy

Not all expansionary fiscal policies look like tax cuts and increases in government spending. At the peak of the 2007–2009 financial crisis, the U.S. Congress passed emergency legislation authorizing the Treasury Department to spend $700 billion to stabilize the financial system. The Treasury Department is a government agency that resides in the executive branch and therefore is not part of the Fed. Nevertheless, the Troubled Asset Relief Program (TARP), as this program came to be known, was developed jointly by Fed and Treasury officials, and the legislation required that the Fed chair be consulted during TARP's implementation.

Of the $700 billion in TARP funds, $115 billion was used to increase the capital of the eight largest U.S. banks, which were all forced to participate. In essence, the banks were required to issue new shares that the government bought. Some of the banks didn't like this plan, since the government became a partial owner. In addition, all eight banks were obligated to limit the compensation of their senior executives. An additional $135 billion was used to increase the capital of smaller banks that applied for TARP support.

These bank capital infusions—totaling $250 billion—gave the participating banks breathing room, and the financial system as a whole stabilized. The financial system came back from the brink of a devastating financial contagion in which banks would have fallen like dominos, each failure instigating other failures as banks couldn't repay their debts to one another. TARP funding is now viewed as a successful policy, though there remain questions about whether it played a causal role in rescuing the economy or simply appeared to be successful because of coincidental timing.

The bank capital infusions ended up costing the government little, since the government was repaid with interest after the crisis had passed. In fact, the government made a small profit from its TARP investments in the banks. However, many government programs other than TARP benefited banks, so banks were net recipients of government support.

You might be wondering about the $450 billion of TARP funding that was not used to buy bank shares. Dozens of other programs were funded by TARP, including investments in the bankrupt car companies General Motors and Chrysler and the nearly bankrupt insurance company AIG. When the dust settled, the government was able to recoup most of its investment, and the government's support prevented these important companies from shutting down their operations at the peak of the crisis. Such shutdowns would have aggravated the crisis, leading to an even deeper recession.

We do not know what would have happened without TARP and the other countercyclical fiscal and monetary policies that were adopted during the financial crisis. It would be convenient if we could set up numerous identical economies to study macroeconomic policy interventions, just like a laboratory scientist would do. In one economy, we would include TARP. In another otherwise identical economy, we would not. We could then see which economy performed better. Because economists can't run experiments like that, we are stuck with making judgments based on less than perfect data and models of economic behavior. Though most economists think that TARP was a success, it is impossible to be sure.

Exhibit 13.11 The Impact of a $1 Wage Subsidy

If the government introduces a $1 per hour wage subsidy that is paid to firms, the labor demand curve shifts rightward by enough so that the new labor demand curve and the original labor demand curve are separated by a vertical distance of exactly $1. If a firm was willing to hire a worker at a wage of $w per hour without the subsidy, the firm is willing to hire the worker at a wage of $(w + 1) per hour with the subsidy. At the new equilibrium, the rightward shift of labor demand increases employment.

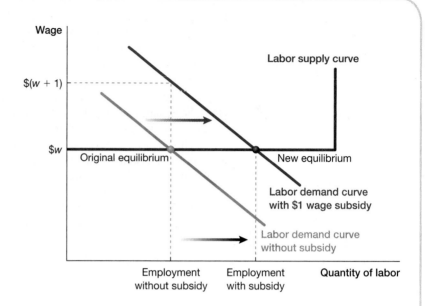

Policy Waste and Policy Lags

Though the government typically funds socially valuable projects as part of countercyclical fiscal policy, government waste is often a problem. The government frequently funds *pork barrel spending*, which is the (derogatory) name given to inefficient public spending that some politicians value, because it increases their popularity with their constituents. For example, a senator has an incentive to obtain federal funding for an infrastructure project in his or her home state, even if the project is expensive and unnecessary, such as a bridge to nowhere. Since the home state residents only pay approximately 1/50 of the cost of the project (through their federal taxes) but get most of the benefits, including local construction jobs, they are happy to see the bridge built, and the project improves the senator's in-state popularity. In this sense, the senator is personally optimizing when obtaining federal funding for almost any in-state project, even those with total social costs that exceed their total social benefits.

> Though the government typically funds socially valuable projects as part of countercyclical fiscal policy, government waste is often a problem.

The efficiency of public expenditures further deteriorates when hundreds of billions of dollars of new government expenditures need to be spent quickly. The urgency makes it harder to identify and efficiently implement the projects that are socially beneficial. In addition, many of the projects with the highest social return have been funded already, raising the chance that a new project won't be socially desirable. Finally, politics and special interests sometimes get in the way, increasing the chances that wasteful projects with negative social value get funded.

Another important determinant of the effectiveness of expenditure-based policies is the lag in implementation. Most spending projects are slow out of the starting gate. It takes a long time to build a bridge, a highway, or a school. Plans have to be drawn up. The local community has to be consulted. The relevant zoning boards need to mull over the proposals, request changes, and then evaluate the amended plans. Environmental impact studies have to be conducted. Contractors have to be hired. And only then does construction begin.

For example, when the most recent recession officially ended in June 2009, practically none of the $230 billion in infrastructure spending legislated in the American Recovery and Reinvestment Act of (February) 2009 had been spent. In June 2010—almost a full year after the recession was over—only a *quarter* of the infrastructure budget had been spent. Many of the largest infrastructure projects hadn't spent a penny one full year after the end of the recession. Lags like these raise the concern that by the time many of the projects are implemented, the economy might already be past the point where these projects would have been most useful.

The "Bridge to Nowhere" was a $398 million project to build a road to Gravina Island, Alaska, which has fifty residents and is served by a ferry. When the plan generated a national protest over pork barrel spending, the bridge project was cancelled.

In contrast, taxation-based fiscal policy can sometimes advance more quickly, for example because it doesn't take the Treasury Department long to mail every household a check. Taxation-based policies also have the advantage that the additional spending is done by households themselves, so that the money is spent on goods and services that they value. (Government expenditure also ultimately puts money in households' pockets, but in the process, it may lead to the implementation of projects of negative social value.)

Despite these concerns, expenditure-based policies are still a very useful part of countercyclical strategies. Several expenditure-based policies are not plagued by waste and lags. For example, most economists endorse federal transfers that enable state and local governments to reduce layoffs of teachers, firefighters, and police during recessions. Such countercyclical transfers from the federal government to the states are particularly useful because many states have balanced-budget rules that prevent them from borrowing during a recession. Without federal transfers, states would be forced to lay off many public employees, reducing public services and deepening the recession.

Likewise, most economists endorse infrastructure projects—like repairs to bridges and highways—that have already passed rigorous cost-benefit analysis. Such projects are said to be "shovel ready."

EVIDENCE-BASED ECONOMICS

Q: How much does government expenditure stimulate GDP?

On December 7, 1941, bombers from six Japanese aircraft carriers attacked the U.S. Pacific fleet. The bombers destroyed or damaged eight battleships, numerous other ships, and 188 aircraft. The attack on Pearl Harbor catapulted the United States into World War II.

The attack also initiated an enormous increase in war-related spending, including the rebuilding and expansion of the Pacific fleet. A few months before the attack, when the United States was not yet a combatant, analysts forecast that preparations for a possible war would cost the United States about $100 billion (1941 dollars). Immediately after the attack, estimates for war-related spending rose to $200 billion. The economic magnitude of these numbers is revealed by comparing this war spending to 1941 GDP, which was $129.4 billion.

Though terrible, wars and the expenditures they trigger can be used to identify the economic effects of government expenditure, as economist Valerie Ramey has shown.[9] She studied 63 years of news articles to identify foreign events that caused a change in U.S. government expenditure. Ramey's data include many war-related events—like the attack on Pearl Harbor—as well as other events, like the surprise launch in 1957 of the Soviet satellite *Sputnik*, the first Earth-orbiting satellite, that sparked the space race between the United States and the Soviet Union. Ramey estimated that the launch of *Sputnik* led to an expansion of $10.3 billion (1957 dollars) in the U.S. government's space program.

On December 7, 1941, Japanese bombers attacked Pearl Harbor, catapulting the United States into World War II and drastically raising the expected level of future government expenditure.

The 1957 launch of *Sputnik,* the first Earth-orbiting satellite, kicked off a space race between the United States and the Soviet Union.

Surprising foreign events that change government expenditure present us with a natural experiment—once again, recall the discussion of natural experiments in Chapter 2. In Ramey's study, a foreign shock caused the government to spend more for reasons unrelated to the state of the economy. She then compared the growth of GDP after these large random spending shocks to the growth of GDP in periods that did not experience such shocks.

Using such comparisons, Ramey estimated a government expenditure multiplier between 0.6 and 1.2. In other words, when the government raises expenditure by $1 (because of an unforeseen foreign event), GDP increases by an amount between $0.60 and $1.20. The range of possible values is large because we don't have enough historical data to pin down a more precise answer.

Question	**Answer**	**Data**	**Caveat**
How much does government expenditure stimulate GDP?	In the study by Ramey, the government expenditure multiplier is estimated to lie between 0.6 and 1.2.	National income and product account data from the United States (1939–2008) and historical news coverage in *Business Week,* the *New York Times,* and the *Washington Post.*	Ramey's analysis measures the government expenditure multiplier that arises from expenditures that are mostly war-related. The analysis might underestimate the government expenditure multiplier during periods of economic slack, like recessions.

The New Administration's Fiscal Policies

President Trump took office planning to spend $100 billion per year on infrastructure, a proposal which has so far engendered more bipartisan approval than any other major policy of his administration (we write this only a month after he took office). With the unemployment rate below 5 percent, infrastructure investment is probably not useful for short-term countercyclical purposes (to understand this, go back to Exhibit 13.1, and suppose that point 3 is very close to point 1; then any fiscal policy-induced shift in the labor demand curve will have a small impact on employment). Put differently, the government expenditure multiplier is likely to be far below its peak level. Infrastructure spending (for example, repairing ailing and overburdened bridges, roads, and public transportation systems) could also be justified because better infrastructure could improve the economy's long-run efficiency, if the right projects are targeted. However, so far the president has not provided enough details on his spending plans to know whether they will be directed to the right projects.

President Trump has also endorsed a system of permanent tax cuts, which is estimated to cost between $300 and $900 billion per year. For the same reason that fiscal policy is likely to have a small impact at a time of relatively low unemployment, these tax cuts are also likely to generate a small multiplier. Though proponents of the tax cuts argue that they will improve economic efficiency and increase the rate of long-run growth, their immediate impact will be to balloon the budget deficit, which currently stands at $559 billion per year.[10] These tax cuts will also reduce the progressivity of the tax system, further increasing economic inequality in the United States.

Summary

- Countercyclical policies attempt to reduce the intensity of economic fluctuations and smooth the growth rates of employment, GDP, and prices.

- Countercyclical monetary policy, which is conducted by the central bank (in the United States, the Fed), attempts to reduce economic fluctuations by manipulating bank reserves and interest rates.

- Open market operations refer to the Fed's transactions with private banks to increase or reduce bank reserves held on deposit at the Fed. Open market operations influence the federal funds rate—an increase in the supply of bank reserves lowers the federal funds rate, holding all else equal.

- Expansionary monetary policy increases the quantity of bank reserves and lowers interest rates, shifting the labor demand curve to the right and increasing the growth rate of GDP.

- Contractionary monetary policy slows down the growth in bank reserves and increases interest rates, shifting the labor demand curve to the left and reducing the growth rate of GDP. Contractionary monetary policy is used when inflation is rising above the Fed's long-run target of 2 percent or when the economy is growing excessively quickly.

- Countercyclical fiscal policy, which is passed by the legislative branch and signed into law by the executive branch, reduces economic fluctuations by manipulating government expenditures and taxes.

Summary (*continued*)

- Countercyclical fiscal policies might be automatic or discretionary. Automatic stabilizers are components of the government budget, like taxes owed, that automatically adjust to smooth out economic fluctuations.

- Expansionary fiscal policy uses higher government expenditure and lower taxes to increase GDP, shifting the labor demand curve to the right. Crowding out occurs when rising government expenditure partially (or even fully) displaces expenditures by households and firms.

- Contractionary fiscal policy uses lower government expenditure and higher taxes to reduce GDP, shifting the labor demand curve to the left.

Key Terms

countercyclical policies *p. 309*
countercyclical monetary policy *p. 309*
countercyclical fiscal policy *p. 309*
expansionary monetary policy *p. 310*

contractionary monetary policy *p. 317*
expansionary fiscal policy *p. 321*
contractionary fiscal policy *p. 321*
automatic stabilizers *p. 321*

government expenditure multiplier *p. 323*
crowding out *p. 323*
government taxation multiplier *p. 325*

Questions

All questions are available in MyEconLab *for practice and instructor assignment.*

1. What are the similarities and the differences between monetary and fiscal policies?

2. How do expansionary policies differ from contractionary policies?

3. Briefly explain how expansionary monetary policy shifts the labor demand curve to the right.

4. What is quantitative easing? Why do central banks undertake quantitative easing programs?

5. Other than open market operations and quantitative easing, what tools does the Federal Reserve use to manipulate interest rates in the economy?

6. Does the effectiveness of monetary policy depend on inflation expectations? Explain.

7. Briefly explain how an increase in the quantity of reserves that commercial banks hold at the Federal Reserve could lead to inflation.

8. How does the zero lower bound on interest rates affect the working of monetary policy?

9. When nominal interest rates have hit the zero lower bound, can central banks use interest rates to stimulate the economy? Explain.

10. What does the Taylor rule state?

11. According to the Taylor rule, when should the Federal Reserve lower or raise the federal funds rate?

12. What are the automatic and discretionary components of fiscal policy?

13. How can expansionary expenditure-based fiscal policy lead to crowding out in the economy?

14. What could explain why a decrease in taxes could lead to a less-than-proportionate increase in output?

15. Why is the Troubled Asset Relief Program (TARP) considered an example of a countercyclical policy that represents a mix of fiscal and monetary effects?

Problems

All problems are available in MyEconLab for practice and instructor assignment.

1. The former chairman of the Federal Reserve, Alan Greenspan, used the term "irrational exuberance" in 1996 to describe the high levels of optimism among stock market investors at the time. Stock market indexes, such as the S&P Composite Price Index, were at an all-time high. Some commentators believed that the Fed should intervene to slow the expansion of the economy. Why would central banks want to clamp down when the economy is growing? What policies could the government and the central bank use to slow down an economic expansion?

2. The following figures show the Federal Reserve's balance sheet as well as the balance sheet of a commercial bank, BHZ Bank. Suppose the Federal Reserve wants to lower bank reserves by $1 billion. Assuming that BHZ Bank is willing to transact with the Federal Reserve, show how the Fed's as well as BHZ's balance sheet will change.

The Federal Reserve

Assets		Liabilities and Shareholders' Equity	
Treasury bonds	$1,500 billion	Reserves	$1,500 billion
Other bonds	$500 billion	Currency	$500 billion
Total assets	**$2,000 billion**	**Total liabilities**	**$2,000 billion**

BHZ Bank

Assets		Liabilities and Shareholders' Equity	
Reserves	$200 billion	Deposits and other liabilities	$700 billion
Bonds and other investments	$800 billion	Shareholders' equity	$300 billion
Total assets	**$1,000 billion**	**Liabilities + shareholders' equity**	**$1,000 billion**

3. Suppose that, in the United States, the inflation rate is at 3.2 percent. Rapidly rising prices and low interest rates have spurred businesses to hire more workers and invest in new facilities.

   a. Why might the Federal Reserve be worried about these developments?

   b. Given the circumstances, what would countercyclical monetary policy seek to accomplish? Explain the different mechanisms that the Fed can use to implement this policy.

   c. Based on your answers to parts (a) and (b), explain why having an independent central bank might be useful. Do you think this countercyclical policy would still be enacted if central bankers were appointed by popular vote? What would happen if they were political appointees that could be hired and fired by the president? Explain.

4. You and a friend are debating the merits of using monetary policy during a severe recession. Your friend says that the central bank needs to lower interest rates all the way down to zero. According to him, zero nominal interest rates will boost lending and investment; consumers and firms will surely borrow and spend when interest rates are zero. Would you agree with his reasoning? How does the level of inflation affect your answer? Explain your conclusions.

5. Some pundits have advocated for a "rules-based" monetary policy. This problem considers one extreme possibility: a world in which the Federal Open Market Committee (FOMC) decides on a new federal funds rate simply by applying the Taylor rule, which we discussed at the end of Section 13.2.

   a. How will market participants form their expectations in such an environment? Suppose that the next FOMC meeting is coming up in a few days, and the official inflation and output gap numbers have just been released. The current federal funds rate is 1.25 percent, the long term fed funds rate target is 3 percent, and the inflation rate target is 2 percent. According to the release, inflation is currently at 1.25 percent and the output gap is $-.5$ percentage points. How will expectations of future inflation change based on this information? Explain.

   b. Why might the Federal Reserve not want to set their policy by mechanically applying the Taylor rule? Discuss some of the benefits and drawbacks of this approach.

6. The following graph shows trend GDP and GDP. The graph was created in 2013, so the data after 2013 is projected. The white vertical bars represent recessions. When is the output gap, defined as the percentage difference between GDP and trend GDP, negative? According to the Taylor rule, how should a negative output gap affect the federal funds interest rate?

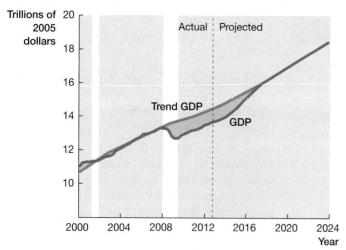

Trillions of 2005 dollars

Actual | Projected

Trend GDP

GDP

2000 2004 2008 2012 2016 2020 2024
Year

Sources: Based on Congressional Budget Office; Department of Commerce, Bureau of Economic Analysis.

7. Two economists estimate the government expenditure multiplier and come up with different results. One estimates the multiplier at 0.75, while the other comes up with an estimate of 1.25.

a. What do these different estimates imply about the consequences of government expenditure?

b. If the current value of GDP is $13.28 trillion and the government is planning to increase spending by $800 billion, what is the percentage increase in GDP for each of the two estimates for the multiplier? Assume the entire increase in spending occurs in 1 year.

8. In 2005, $320 million of the federal government's budget was allocated toward building a "Bridge to Nowhere" in Alaska that connected two small towns. In 2006, $500,000 was allocated toward a teapot museum in North Carolina, and $4.5 million toward a museum and park at an abandoned mine in Maine. These projects were requested by specific legislators in order to boost their popularity in their constituencies.

a. What is this type of expenditure called?

b. Since government spending increases employment by shifting the labor demand curve to the right, is it always a good idea for the government to increase expenditure? Explain your answer.

9. Milton Friedman, the renowned monetary economist, gave the following analogy about the Fed.

"Imagine your house is being heated by a heater. The heater is controlled by a thermostat. The way it's set up, when the house gets a little too warm, the thermostat turns off the heater; if it gets too cold, the thermostat turns the heater back on. If everything works as planned, the room temperature in the house should roughly be the targeted temperature all the time.

Now suppose the thermostat is not in the same room as the heater. In fact, it's in the last room that is affected by the heater. Say, the attic. And the radiators through which the heater works are really old, and it takes them

at least twenty minutes to react. Then, instead of making the temperature more stable, the thermostat would make the temperature swing wildly. For example, if the house is cold, then the thermostat will turn the heater on. But it will turn the heater off only when the attic is warm. By then, the entire house will be scorching hot. When it turns the heater off, it will not turn it back on until the attic is cooler. By then, the house will be freezing."

(In this analogy, the thermostat is the Fed; the house is the entire economy.)

a. What do you think Milton Friedman was trying to say about monetary policy? (*Hint*: You do not need to draw any graphs for this question.)

b. As in the thermostat analogy, what might be some possible unintended consequences of monetary policy? Might there be a similar effect for fiscal policy? If yes, how does the effect differ from that of monetary policy?

10. The European Central Bank (ECB) manages monetary policy for the eurozone. Following the financial crisis of 2007–2008, the ECB, like the Fed, lowered interest rates to around zero.

a. Using the concept of the zero lower bound, explain how low interest rates could constrain countercyclical monetary policy.

b. Though fiscal policies are controlled by individual governments in the eurozone, the European Union's Stability and Growth Pact places strict limits on country-level deficit spending. Explain how the confluence of the zero lower bound and restrictions on the fiscal deficit might be problematic for countercyclical macroeconomic policy.

11. *Challenge Problem.* The chapter mentions that an open market operation by the Fed can increase or decrease the quantity of deposits in banks and therefore the money supply. (See, for example, Exhibit 13.8.)

The expansion in the money supply from a Fed open market operation is given by the following equation (under the simplifying assumption that households don't hold cash, so the money supply is equal to demand deposits):

$$\text{Change in money supply} = (\text{Change in reserves}) \times \frac{1}{RR + ER}$$

where RR = the percentage of deposits that banks are required to keep as reserves (expressed as a decimal), and ER = the percentage of deposits that banks voluntarily hold as excess reserves (expressed as a decimal). The quantity $1/(RR + ER)$ is called the "money multiplier."

Suppose the Fed decides to sell $14 billion in Treasury bonds. Assume that the reserve requirement is 8 percent and banks hold 4 percent in excess reserves, so $RR = 0.08$ and $ER = 0.04$.

What is the total increase or decrease in the money supply that would result from the Fed's action? Explain your answer and show your calculations. Verify that the quantity of new deposits (which is the change in the money supply in this example) is backed up by an adequate quantity of new reserves:

$$(RR + ER) \times (\text{Change in deposits}) = \text{Change in reserves}.$$

12. *Challenge Problem.* Assume that the public in the small country of Sylvania does not hold any cash. Commercial banks, however, hold 5 percent of the public's checking deposits as excess reserves, regardless of the interest rate. In the questions that follow, use the "money multiplier" equation from Problem 11.

   a. Consider the balance sheet of one of several identical banks:

Assets		Liabilities and Shareholders' Equity	
Reserves	$400	Checking deposits	$2,000
Loans	$1,600	Shareholders' Equity	$0

   What is the required reserve ratio in the country of Sylvania?

   b. If the total money stock (supply) is $100,000, find the total amount of reserves held in the banking system. Show your work.

   c. The Sylvania Central Bank decides that it wants to cut the money stock in half. It is considering an open market operation. How many dollars' worth of bonds should the Central Bank buy or sell? Assume that excess reserves are 5 percent and the required reserve ratio is what you found in part (a). Show your work.

14 Macroeconomics and International Trade

Are companies like Nike harming workers in Vietnam?

Consumers love sneakers—and Nike alone sells approximately $15 billion of them each year. Nike conducts much of its production in places like Vietnam, using subcontractors who rely on low-wage workers with little education. In the 1990s, a leaked audit revealed grueling, hazardous working conditions at one such factory: for $10 per week, employees at that location worked 65 hours in a factory filled with airborne carcinogens.[1] Critical news accounts included accusations of illegal child labor. Finally, under intense public pressure, Nike's then-CEO, Philip Knight, admitted in 1998 that "the name of Nike has become synonymous with slave wages, forced overtime, and arbitrary abuse."[2] Following that speech Nike launched a highly publicized effort to clean up its act (or at least its reputation). Nevertheless, Vietnamese workers are still paid very low wages, as low as $2 per day. This situation is just the tip of the iceberg of low wages and poor working conditions throughout parts of the interconnected global economy. U.S. consumers clearly benefit from this trade as they get access to low-cost products. Are they to blame for buying sneakers manufactured in sweatshops?

CHAPTER OUTLINE

- International trade enables countries to focus on activities in which they have a comparative advantage.

- The current account includes international flows from exports, imports, factor payments, and transfers.

- If a country runs a current account deficit, it pays for this by giving its trading partners financial IOUs. If a country runs a current account surplus, it receives financial IOUs from its trading partners.

- The world has become more globalized over the past several decades.

14.1   Why and How We Trade

Trade, both within and between countries, enhances our quality of life by increasing the efficiency of production. In modern economies, goods and services are produced by individuals who specialize in their production. For example, your professor spent years mastering economics. Similarly, the engineers who work for Apple have extensive training in their particular line of work.

An Apple engineer can't produce insightful economics research or teach an economics course. Likewise, an economics professor can't design a miniaturized circuit board and a high throughput factory to manufacture it. In a market system, people try to choose an occupation that suits their talents and interests. In many cases, they develop specialized skills in their chosen industry and trade with others. Trade exploits **gains from specialization**, which are the economic gains that society obtains by having some workers specialize in specific productive activities.

Specialization won't work without trade. Economics professors can't eat economic ideas or live in them. Economists teach, then get paid with money, and then use the money to buy food and shelter. Apple engineers love the iPhone, but they can't sleep on it or drive it to work. Engineers get paid so they can buy what they want.

Without opportunities for trade, life is bleak. If your economics professor were stranded on an island, he or she would have no students to teach and no policymakers to advise. The professor would have little or no way to put economic knowledge to use. Despite all that knowledge, day-to-day life would resemble that of a Stone Age hunter-gatherer.

Gains from specialization are the economic gains that society can obtain by having some individuals, regions, or countries specialize in the production of certain goods and services.

> Without opportunities for trade, life is bleak.

Absolute Advantage and Comparative Advantage

To gain a deeper understanding of how trade works, consider the late Steve Jobs, the visionary chief executive officer (CEO) of Apple. Jobs was famous for being a great marketer and a brilliant designer.

Because of his knowledge of and love for Apple products, Jobs was a much better salesperson than most of Apple's employees. To illustrate this point, let's assume that Jobs could sell twice as many computers (per time period) compared to the typical Apple salesclerk. In this sense, Jobs had an *absolute advantage* at selling computers. A producer has an **absolute advantage** in producing a good or service if the producer can produce more units per hour than other producers can.

An economy without trade wasn't great for this castaway.

Exhibit 14.1 Productivity in Sales and Design

	Steve Jobs	Chuck Chores
Sales	2,000 sales/year	1,000 sales/year
Design	1,000 design ideas/year	1 design idea/year

A producer has an **absolute advantage** in producing a good or service if the producer can produce more units per hour than other producers can.

Of course, selling computers isn't the only skill that Jobs had. As CEO, he *designed* revolutionary new products. Relative to a typical salesclerk, Jobs was a superstar designer. Let's assume that if Jobs allocated his time to design, he would generate 1,000 design ideas per year. If a typical salesclerk worked on design, he would generate only one design idea per year.

Let's give the typical Apple salesclerk a name: Chuck Chores. Exhibit 14.1 reports the estimated productivity of Jobs in the first column of data and the estimated productivity of Chores in the final column.

By looking across the rows of Exhibit 14.1, we see that Jobs has an absolute advantage in both tasks: Jobs was capable of producing twice as many sales per year (relative to Chores) and Jobs was capable of producing 1,000 times as many useful design ideas per year (relative to Chores). Which task should Apple have asked him to do?

To answer this question, let's calculate the opportunity cost *per unit of production* or, more precisely, the opportunity cost of a design idea in terms of forgone sales. This calculation will answer the following question: how many sales are given up to produce a design idea? A worker has a *comparative advantage* in design when the opportunity cost of the worker's design idea is lower than the opportunity cost of other workers' design ideas. More generally, a worker has a **comparative advantage** in producing a good (or service) when she has a lower opportunity cost per unit produced compared to other producers.

A producer has a **comparative advantage** in producing a good (or service) when the producer has a lower opportunity cost per unit produced compared to other producers.

Exhibit 14.1 implies that Steve Jobs forgoes 2,000 sales for every 1,000 design ideas that he generates, or $2,000/1,000 = 2$ forgone sales per design idea. In contrast, Chuck Chores forgoes 1,000 sales for every design idea that he generates.

With that calculation in mind, we can determine how production should be optimally organized. Apple can produce design ideas by allocating Jobs to design, with an opportunity cost of two forgone sales per design idea. Or Apple can produce design ideas from Chores with an opportunity cost of 1,000 forgone sales per design idea. Since Jobs has a lower opportunity cost for *each* design idea (two forgone sales for Jobs versus 1,000 forgone sales for Chores), Jobs has a *comparative advantage in design ideas*. Hence, Apple should allocate Jobs to work on design and Chores to work on sales (as long as it needs both types of activities).

You can verify that the same conclusion would have been reached if we had calculated the opportunity cost of a sale in terms of forgone design ideas. Using Exhibit 14.1, we find that Jobs forgoes 1,000 design ideas for every 2,000 sales. Because $1,000/2,000 = ½$, Jobs has an opportunity cost of ½ forgone design idea per sale. Chores forgoes 1 design idea for every 1,000 sales, so Chores has an opportunity cost of 1/1,000 forgone design idea per sale. Because Chores has the lower opportunity cost per sale, he should be the one doing sales and Jobs should work on design.

Comparative advantage is the idea that *opportunity cost, not absolute advantage, should be used to determine which producer is assigned to which task.* Just relying on absolute advantage would not have been sufficient for Apple to determine whether Jobs should work in design or in sales: Jobs has an absolute advantage in working as a salesclerk *and* he has an absolute advantage in working as a designer.

Until now, we have assumed that the work allocation decision is being made by Apple. Although such decisions are sometimes made by corporations, in practice they are often the result of choices that individuals make for themselves. Jobs himself decided to found Apple and work as a designer, while many individuals such as Chores choose to become salesclerks, not designers. Why is this?

The career choices that individuals make are a consequence of comparative advantage, but, in this case, the key economic signals are market prices. In fact, one of the powerful implications of comparative advantage is that market prices will often induce individuals to choose occupations and activities that line up with their comparative advantages.

Exhibit 14.2 Wages in Sales and Design

(a) With Value Added of $50 from Sales and $50 from Design

	Steve Jobs	Chuck Chores
Sales	$100,000/year	$50,000/year
Design	$50,000/year	$50/year

(b) With Value Added of $50 from Sales and $100,000 from Design

	Steve Jobs	Chuck Chores
Sales	$100,000/year	$50,000/year
Design	$100,000,000/year	$100,000/year

(c) With Value Added of $50 from Sales and $5,000 from Design

	Steve Jobs	Chuck Chores
Sales	$100,000/year	$50,000/year
Design	$5,000,000/year	$5,000/year

To see this, suppose that Jobs and Chores sell their skills in a competitive labor market in which their wages are equal to their (personal) contribution to value added (recall from Chapter 5 that value added is defined as a firm's sales revenue minus the firm's purchases of intermediate products from other firms). To simplify the analysis, suppose that the economy consists only of workers like Jobs and Chores and that the economy needs both design and sales functions to be performed. We will now see that equilibrium prices must be such that workers with productivity similar to Jobs will choose to work in design and those with productivity similar to Chores will choose to work in sales.

Let's start by assuming that the prices in this economy are such that the value added from each computer sale is $50 and the value added from each design idea is also $50. If you multiply output in Exhibit 14.1 by value added per task, you'll generate the results in panel (a) of Exhibit 14.2. These numbers imply that both Jobs and Chores will maximize their own wages if they work in sales: $100,000 for Jobs in sales versus $50,000 for Jobs in design; $50,000 for Chores in sales versus $50 for Chores in design. Hence, workers like Jobs and workers like Chores will both work in sales. But this cannot be a market equilibrium, because the economy needs both functions—design and sales—to be performed. If everyone is working in sales, then no design ideas will be created in this economy, pushing the value added from design much higher than $50 (there would be a shortage of design, raising the relative wages of designers).

What happens if market prices for design become much higher, so that value added from each design idea now shoots up to $100,000 (holding fixed value added from sales at $50)? The resulting wages are shown in panel (b) of Exhibit 14.2. Now we have a situation in which both Jobs and Chores have higher wages in design, thus all workers in this economy will now choose design careers. But this also cannot be a market equilibrium. Now there will be no sales in the economy and a lot of design ideas. Yet again the economy needs both functions to be performed, and this will push the relative wages of salespeople higher.

You have probably already guessed that equilibrium prices will need to settle somewhere between these two extremes. Equilibrium prices should induce some people to do design and others to do sales. Take another combination of values: $50 of value added per sale and $5,000 of value added per design idea. The resulting wages are shown in panel (c) of Exhibit 14.2. At these wages, it is clear that Chores will choose to work in sales while Jobs focuses on design. Indeed, at these wages, Jobs would be greatly misallocating his time if he worked as a salesclerk.

The key insight is that market prices will adjust so that individuals choose occupations consistent with their comparative advantages. This is the sense in which trade in the market supports and reinforces comparative advantage. In fact, without such trade, we could not realize the gains from comparative advantage. For example, it is trade that allowed Steve

Steve Jobs, Apple's most productive salesclerk.

Jobs to hire other people to work as salesclerks in Apple stores, enabling him to focus on his comparative advantage: designing the next beautiful gizmo that everyone wants to have.

At this point, you might be curious about whether one could have picked a value added for each sale and a value added for each design that would make Jobs choose sales while Chores would prefer to do design. Comparative advantage implies that the answer is no. If their different opportunity costs lead Jobs and Chores to choose different tasks, comparative advantage always implies it will be Jobs who earns more in design than in sales, and Chores who earns more in sales than in design.

Comparative Advantage and International Trade

To illustrate how *international* trade exploits comparative advantage—much like the division of labor between Steve Jobs and Chuck Chores—consider a particular Apple product, the iPod. In some sense, the iPod is a U.S. product—designed by engineers in the United States by a company headquartered in the United States. However, it is not actually manufactured in the United States. Each iPod is composed of hundreds of parts, most of which are manufactured and assembled outside the United States.

Let's consider some of the key components. The iPod has a hard drive where the songs, videos, and photos are stored. This is produced in Japan. It also has a memory card, which is produced in Korea. The central processing unit, in contrast, is produced in the United States. Specialization explains this proliferation of locations. For example, the Japanese company Toshiba specializes in hard drive manufacturing and has become a world leader in the production of tiny hard drives with very low failure rates. Gains from specialization are realized by delegating production of two of these three key parts to manufacturers outside the United States. Finally, the components are combined into the final product on a Chinese assembly line.[3]

Comparative advantage in international trade explains why Chinese workers assemble iPods, even though U.S. workers have an absolute advantage in assembly. Let's begin by considering the hourly productivity of U.S. and Chinese workers in different tasks. For the moment, we'll assume that in terms of their productivity, the U.S. workers are all identical to one another and the Chinese workers are also all identical to one another—a simplifying assumption that we'll revisit later in the chapter.

The first row of Exhibit 14.3 shows that a U.S. worker would assemble 20,000 iPods per year, which is 15,000 more than a Chinese worker would assemble. The differences between U.S. and Chinese labor productivity arise for a variety of reasons. Workers in the United States currently have relatively more education and thus greater *human capital* (recall from Chapter 6 that human capital is each person's stock of ability to produce output or economic value). This greater human capital makes U.S. workers more productive in a range of tasks. In addition, U.S. workers currently have access to more physical capital per worker and better technology—for instance, robotic assembly lines—than their Chinese counterparts.

Consider another task, which we refer to as research and development (R&D). We assume that U.S. workers generate ten R&D innovations per year. We assume that Chinese workers, who currently don't have as much education as U.S. workers, would be much less effective at this, and we assume that their productivity in R&D is one innovation per year.

Exhibit 14.3 Productivity in Assembly and R&D

	U.S. Worker	Chinese Worker
Assembly	20,000 iPods/year	5,000 iPods/year
R&D	10 innovations/year	1 innovation/year

Exhibit 14.4 Wages in Assembly and R&D

	U.S. Worker	Chinese Worker
Assembly	$30,000/year	$7,500/year
R&D	$50,000/year	$5,000/year

Looking across the rows in Exhibit 14.3, we see that U.S. workers have an absolute advantage in both assembly and R&D. Considering only absolute advantage, it's tempting to guess that both assembly and R&D should be performed in the United States. But this is the wrong conclusion for the same reason that Steve Jobs shouldn't have been working as a salesclerk.

To determine the optimal allocation across industries, we again need to use the concepts of opportunity cost and comparative advantage. We can verify that U.S. workers have a comparative advantage in R&D. Their productivity in assembly relative to R&D is $20,000/10 = 2,000/1$. In other words, U.S. workers forgo the assembly of 2,000 iPods for every R&D innovation they generate. Chinese workers' productivity in assembly relative to R&D is $5,000/1$. Chinese workers forgo the assembly of 5,000 iPods for every R&D innovation they generate. The U.S. workers thus have a lower opportunity cost per R&D innovation (2,000 forgone iPods assembled) compared to Chinese workers (5,000 forgone iPods assembled). This implies that U.S. workers have a comparative advantage in R&D and should focus on R&D, while Chinese workers should (currently) specialize in assembly.

To further illustrate the allocation of tasks between U.S. and Chinese workers, suppose that workers in both economies are paid the value added they generate and that the value added from each iPod assembly is $1.50 and the value added from each R&D innovation is $5,000. Multiplying output in Exhibit 14.3 by value added per task generates the results in Exhibit 14.4, which describes annual wages of U.S. and Chinese workers in assembly and R&D.

Looking at Exhibit 14.4, you can see that the U.S. worker will choose to specialize in R&D and the Chinese worker will specialize in assembly. In fact, for the same reasons highlighted in our discussion of the allocation problem of Steve Jobs and Chuck Chores, value added and market prices cannot be such that both U.S. and Chinese workers all have greater value added in assembly or that they all have greater value added in R&D, because otherwise the world economy would not generate *both* iPod assemblies and R&D ideas. Given the current pattern of comparative advantage (in R&D for U.S. workers and in iPod assembly for Chinese workers), if these workers are choosing different tasks, then it must be the case that it is the U.S. workers who are specializing in R&D and the Chinese workers who are working in assembly.

As in our earlier example, trade is essential to achieve an efficient allocation of resources. If there were no international trade, then U.S. workers would end up spending less time on R&D and more time on assembly, lowering the value of their total output.

iPod assembly line in China.

Efficiency and Winners and Losers from Trade

By exploiting comparative advantage, international trade increases overall economic efficiency. For example, if Apple could not assemble iPods in foreign countries, it would have to do so in the United States, and the cost of making iPods would rise. As a result, iPods would likely cost 10 or 20 percent more than they do now. Consumers benefit from international trade and the resulting international division of labor.

At this point you might wonder whether foreign iPod production prevents the United States from benefiting from its own innovation. How much of the value added from iPod manufacturing goes to foreign producers and not to the iPod's U.S. inventors? Of course, even if all value added went to foreign workers, U.S. consumers would still benefit from the low cost of an iPod. But is a low retail price the only benefit that U.S. residents receive?

A study by economists Greg Linden, Kenneth Kraemer, and Jason Dedrick shows that a large part of the retail price of an iPod is ultimately received by U.S. residents.[4] For iPods sold in the United States through a retailer other than Apple, 41 percent of the value added is generated by U.S. firms other than Apple, including distributors, retailers, and component manufacturers with domestic production facilities. Another 45 percent of the value added goes to Apple, the company that designed the iPod and owns the intellectual property rights. These are not just corporate earnings, since Apple has a large team of in-house engineers, designers, and executives whose salaries are paid with Apple's revenues. The example of the iPod illustrates that international trade contributes to value added in the United States as well as to low prices for U.S. consumers.

> Though international trade achieves a more efficient allocation of resources ... in any given instance, trade will produce some winners and some losers.

The iPod story is not unusual. Other products confirm the same pattern of widely shared benefits from trade. For example, Hewlett-Packard's laptop computers are assembled in low-wage countries like China and Brazil. Nevertheless, over half of the value added from the production of these laptops accrues to residents of the United States.

This doesn't mean that everybody gains from trade. Though international trade achieves a more efficient allocation of resources and creates potential gains for society as a whole, in any given instance, trade will produce some winners and some losers. We can see this by going back to the issue of U.S.-China trade. When we discussed the gains from exploiting comparative advantage, we talked of the typical U.S. worker. In practice, of course, the United States isn't inhabited by "typical" U.S. workers, but by some U.S. workers with high levels of skill, and others with low levels of skill and a comparative advantage in assembly. International trade causes routine assembly jobs to move to developing countries like China, and, as a result, there are significantly fewer assembly jobs performed in the United States today than three decades ago. If they can no longer find assembly jobs, those U.S. workers with a comparative advantage in assembly are made worse off by the outsourcing of assembly jobs to countries like China. This is illustrated by our Evidence-Based Economics feature in Chapter 9, which showed how workers in areas specializing in products that compete with Chinese imports have experienced employment losses.

When considering the consequences of opening a country to free international trade, it is important to recognize that within that country, there will be winners and losers from increased international trade. Economists typically favor free international trade, because the efficiencies achieved by exploiting comparative advantage and specialization are large enough to outweigh the costs borne by the losers. This means, in particular, that by means of a system of government taxes and transfers, the winning households could compensate the losing households, so that everyone would be better off as a result of free trade.

In practice, however, such compensation rarely takes place. This is sometimes because politicians may not be interested in engaging in complicated tax-transfer schemes that benefit the losing households. And even if the political will to carry out such redistribution were there, it would be hard for the government to identify how much each person has gained or lost as a consequence of international trade. With no compensating redistribution by the government (or with limited compensation or imperfect targeting), some households would end up on the losing side of the economic ledger.

Since the losers are rarely compensated, it is important to recognize that, while international trade creates large gains for society, there will be those who suffer true hardship as a result of the process of globalization.

The politics of globalization is in fact even more complicated. The losing households are sometimes visible and outspoken. For example, in February 2016, a manager at the Carrier Corporation told an assembly of workers that the company was relocating an air conditioner production facility from the United States to Mexico. A video of the announcement, which featured the frustrated reactions of soon-to-be-unemployed workers, went viral, and has now been watched more than 4 million times.[5] The planned relocation of this plant became a major talking point in the 2016 U.S. presidential election, stoking anti-trade sentiment across all political parties in the United States.

In contrast, the benefits of international trade are less tangible. It's easy to overlook the fact that the goods and services that we buy would cost much more if they all needed to be produced domestically. It's also hard to find viral videos or nightly news stories about the jobs that international trade creates. Job losses are far more politically salient than job gains.

The Carrier episode is just one example of a rising voter backlash against globalization. Later in this chapter we describe the consequences of this political opposition to globalization.

How We Trade

To realize the gains from comparative advantage and specialization, the United States and China need to trade goods and services. This takes the form of *imports* and *exports*. Recall from Chapter 5 that imports refer to the goods and services that are produced abroad and sold domestically, and exports are the goods and services that are produced domestically and sold abroad. Thus exports from the United States to China are China's imports from the United States.

In theory it is possible for a country not to have any exports or imports. Such a country that doesn't trade—that is, does not have any imports or exports—is said to be a **closed economy**. Today, not a single country has an entirely closed economy, but North Korea, a totalitarian dictatorship with mostly closed borders, comes the closest.

An **open economy** allows international trade, and in most countries such trade amounts to a significant share of GDP. For example, in 2015, the United Kingdom's imports equaled 29 percent of GDP, double the import share in the United States. But neither country could compete with Hong Kong and Singapore, which had 2015 imports equaling about 150 and 200 percent of GDP, respectively. Hong Kong and Singapore have such large import shares because many of their imports are later re-exported with only modest value added domestically. For example, if a country imports $200 of electronic parts and assembles them into a $250 smart phone, then the value added is just $50. In this illustrative example, imports are four times the level of GDP (recall that only value added is counted in GDP). If the assembled phone is later exported, then exports ($250) are five times the level of value added.

Exhibit 14.5 depicts the evolution of U.S. imports and exports as a share of GDP since 1929. In 1950, imports amounted to 4 percent of GDP. In 2016, the import share was 15 percent. Economically speaking, the United States is now more closely linked to the rest of the world than at any other period in U.S. history.

A closed economy does not trade with the rest of the world.

An open economy trades freely with the rest of the world.

MyEconLab Real-time data

Exhibit 14.5 U.S. Imports and Exports as a Share of GDP (1929–2016)

The U.S. economy has become more open over the past century, with its share of imports to GDP rising from around 5 percent (in 1929) to around 15 percent (in 2016).

Source: Based on Bureau of Economic Analysis, National Income and Product Accounts (Table 1.1.5).

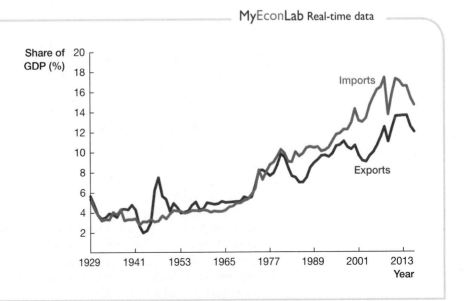

LETTING THE
DATA SPEAK

Living in an Interconnected World

Given the importance of specialization and comparative advantage, the world is highly interconnected through imports and exports. The first and most obvious facet of this interconnection is the array of goods and services we consume. Look at the shelves of your local Walmart and you will find an enormous number of items made in China, Mexico, and Brazil. Two-thirds of the goods sold in Walmart are imported. For example, Walmart annually imports over $30 billion worth of goods from China.

Check out the geography of trade whenever you go shopping. You'll be amazed at the range of countries that manufacture the goods you buy. You may think of Pakistan only as a hotbed of political and religious unrest on the border of Afghanistan. Pakistan also happens to manufacture *half* of the world's hand-stitched soccer balls. Pakistan is also an important exporter of textiles and clothing. Look at the latest fashions on display at Banana Republic or Old Navy, and you will see that much of this clothing is produced in India, Indonesia, Turkey, and Vietnam.

Many people mistakenly believe that international trade can only flow in goods. Services, however, are also getting into the act. In 2015, the United States imported $502 billion in services and exported $749 billion in services. The next time you call a computer company for advice about removing a virus or upgrading software, ask the technician where he or she is located. There's a good chance you are speaking to someone in India, where service representatives carefully hone American accents and adopt American names during working hours. Carol Miller might be Bhumika Chaturvedi.

Many of the services that now flow across international boundaries are very sophisticated. The United States exports entertainment services (such as music and movies) and financial services (for example, financial advice given by a New York investment bank to an oil exploration company in Brazil).

Even medical services can be traded internationally. An Indian radiologist—a physician specializing in reading X-rays—earns one-eighth of a U.S. radiologist's income. So an Indian radiologist has a lower opportunity cost of time than a U.S. radiologist does. There is a small group of Indian teleradiologists who read X-rays for hospitals in the United States, United Kingdom, and Singapore. Here's how it works. A patient who is a resident of the United Kingdom has an X-ray taken at a UK hospital. The images are uploaded to a teleradiologist in Bangalore, India. The teleradiologist examines the X-ray for abnormalities, like tumors, writes a report, and then sends it back to the patient's UK physician.

The increase in imports and exports as shares of GDP is not confined to the United States. Most major economies in the world have been trading more over the past 50 years. Exhibit 14.6 plots the evolution of imports as a share of GDP for Germany, China, India, and the world average, as well as for the United States.

Trade Barriers: Tariffs

Because international trade creates winners and losers, there are some opponents to trade. As a result, most countries, including the United States, impose a host of *trade barriers* that reduce their imports. The most common restrictions are tariffs, which are special taxes levied only on imports.

The average U.S. tariff on all imported products was 2.7 percent in 2014, down from over 5 percent in 1990. As we discuss in the Choice & Consequence box, this downward trend might be reversed during the administration of U.S. President Donald J. Trump, who has promised to renegotiate many trade treaties and has threatened to impose new tariffs on the imports of countries, such as Mexico and China, that export to the United States much more than they import from it.

Exhibit 14.6 The Ratio of Imports to GDP in Four Large Economies and in the Total World Economy (1960–2015)

Most major economies, including the United States, have been trading more over the past 55 years. This is a reflection of the process of globalization, which has generated a steady increase in the value of international trade flows relative to GDP.

Source: Based on Bureau of Economic Analysis, National Income and Product Accounts; and World Bank DataBank: World Development Indicators.

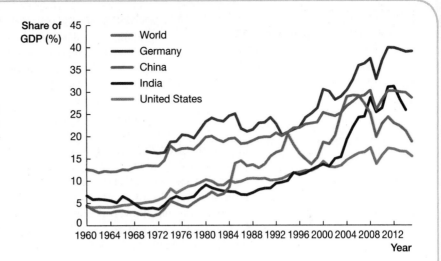

CHOICE
&CONSEQUENCE

Trade Policy and Politics

In March 2002, President George W. Bush imposed tariffs of 8 to 30 percent on steel imports. The move was widely viewed as a political decision to shore up support among industrial states that might switch party allegiance in the November midterm election. If you ran for office, would you do the same thing, even if you believed in the benefits of trade?

The U.S. trade representative, Robert B. Zoellick, admitted during a speech in Brazil that political calculations had motivated the new tariffs: "We are committed to moving forward with free trade, but, like Brazil, we have to manage political support for free trade at home. We have to create coalitions." The administration maintained the tariffs in the run-up to the election despite a flood of worldwide criticism and threats from many countries to erect punitive tariffs in response. One month after the U.S. election, the administration reversed itself and removed the tariffs.[7]

The current U.S. President, Donald J. Trump, made trade a centerpiece of his 2016 campaign. For example, candidate Trump said he would punish firms that moved production facilities from the United States to other countries. He also promised to withdraw from the Trans-Pacific Partnership (TPP, a free trade agreement for Pacific basin countries) and renegotiate the North American Free Trade Agreement (NAFTA, a free trade agreement among Canada, Mexico, and the United States). Finally, he vowed to raise tariffs on goods imported from two of the three most important U.S. trading partners, China and Mexico.[8]

Unlike President Bush, who reduced tariffs after he won the 2002 election, President Trump has followed through on his anti-globalization policy positions. His message was clear in his inauguration speech: "We will follow two simple rules: buy American, and hire American."

During his first week in office he did withdraw from the TPP and confirmed that he would renegotiate NAFTA. These measures, and the potential tariffs on Mexico and China, are expected to reduce U.S. trade. Though these policies will benefit some Americans, the policies will probably have a net negative effect on the U.S. economy. It is also possible that these aggressive policies could trigger a highly destabilizing trade war if other countries retaliate with their own tariffs against imports from the United States.

The United States isn't the only country where discontent about globalization has reached a boiling point. Anti-trade and anti-immigration policies have become increasingly popular in Europe. An unanticipated example occurred in June 2016, when the United Kingdom held a referendum on whether to exit the European Union (a union of European countries that share common economic regulations and allow free trade and open immigration among member countries). A *British exit* from the European Union—widely referred to as "Brexit"—passed with a 52 percent majority. Now the United Kingdom, led by Prime Minister Theresa May, is in the process of working out the details of this major economic separation from the rest of Europe. The economic consensus is that the United Kingdom will ultimately suffer economically as it forgoes some of the benefits of free trade with its European neighbors.

Looking around the globe, the forecast for globalization has suddenly become very cloudy.

14.1

14.2

14.3

The average 2014 tariff of 2.7 percent masked an enormous amount of variation across industries. In recent years, the average U.S. tariff on agricultural products has been 62 percent. Tariffs on tobacco have run to approximately 90 percent, while tariffs on sugar have been even higher, sometimes exceeding 100 percent. Such tariffs naturally discourage international trade. Due to tariffs and trade barriers, U.S. sugar imports have fallen 80 percent over the last 30 years.

Some *developing* countries use tariffs to raise revenue, because they don't have well-functioning tax systems and can more easily tax imports that flow through a few urban ports than they can tax domestic economic activity that is widely geographically dispersed. In contrast, *developed* countries overwhelmingly use tariffs to protect domestic producers. In fact, some tariffs are set at such a high level that they block imports completely and therefore raise no revenue, since there are no imports to tax. Powerful domestic producers lobby governments to impose tariffs that will drive out foreign competition and increase the domestic industry's profits. Of course, this benefit to the domestic industry is a cost to domestic consumers, because they end up paying higher prices.

In some cases, trade wars create comical inefficiencies. In the 1960s, Germany and France restricted imports of U.S. chickens. The U.S. retaliated with a punitive tariff on imports of European light trucks. Today, Mercedes-Benz assembles light trucks at a factory in Dusseldorf, Germany, and tests the trucks to verify that they drive properly. Then Mercedes-Benz partially disassembles the trucks by removing the engines, bumpers, driveshafts, fuel tanks, and exhaust systems. The trucks are exported to the United States, where Mercedes-Benz doesn't need to pay the U.S. tariff because the trucks aren't fully assembled. At a warehouse in South Carolina, the disassembled parts are bolted on again.[6]

14.2 The Current Account and the Financial Account

In 2015, U.S. imports of goods and services amounted to $2,761.5 billion. Of this amount, $497.8 billion was imported from China. In recent years, approximately one-seventh of U.S. imports have come from China.

In 2015, the United States exported goods and services worth $2,261.2 billion. That year, U.S. exports to China were $161.6 billion. Approximately one-twentieth of U.S. exports go to China.

To some politicians, the fact that the United States imports more from China than it exports to China is a sign of a serious problem. However, there is no reason to expect that U.S. exports to China should equal U.S. imports from China, in the same way that there is no reason to expect your own purchases from the grocery store to equal the grocery store owner's purchases from you. If you own a Ford dealership and the grocery store owner loves Cadillacs, then you'll never get a dollar of her business. But that's OK as long as there are other people who are interested in buying your Fords.

That's generally the way that markets and exchanges work. There is no need to sell our goods and services to the same people from whom we buy goods and services. Now apply that idea to a national economy. There is nothing necessarily wrong with the fact that the United States as a whole sells relatively little to China and still buys a lot from China. There are other countries, like Brazil, to which the United States sells lots of stuff and from which the United States buys relatively little. These facts lead us to the observation that trade between two specific countries—also referred to as "bilateral trade"—will rarely be balanced. This does not imply that the United States–China trade relationship is optimal, but it does suggest that a bilateral trade imbalance is neither unusual nor necessarily a bad thing.

Trade Surpluses and Trade Deficits

Trade can be unbalanced in another important sense. Sometimes a country imports more or less than it exports to the world as a whole. We'll see that even this imbalance can also be socially desirable, though it depends on the reasons for the trade imbalance.

When a country as a whole imports more from abroad than it exports abroad, the country runs a *trade deficit*. This is a case of spending on imports more than the country earns from exports. Exports minus imports is defined as **net exports** or the **trade balance**. When the trade balance is positive, it is referred to as a **trade surplus**. When the trade balance is negative, it is called a **trade deficit**. In 2016, U.S. net exports were negative, so the United States ran a trade deficit:

$$\text{Net exports} = \text{Exports} - \text{Imports}$$
$$= \$2,128 \text{ billion} - \$2,690 \text{ billion} = -\$562 \text{ billion}.$$

Net exports are the value of a country's exports minus the value of its imports. Net exports are also known as the **trade balance**.

A **trade surplus** is an excess of exports over imports and is thus the name given to the trade balance when it is positive.

A **trade deficit** is an excess of imports over exports and is thus the name given to the trade balance when it is negative.

International Financial Flows

It might appear that knowing the value of the trade balance is sufficient for understanding how payments flow from one country to another. However, a complete understanding of international financial flows requires more details. We need to study all sources of payments from foreign residents to domestic residents, and all sources of payments from domestic residents to foreign residents. Trade flows represent only one source of these financial payments.

The international accounting system is built on the concept of residency, not the concept of citizenship. In this accounting system, domestic *residents* are people who reside in the United States, whether or not they are U.S. citizens. So a Japanese citizen living in the United States is defined as a domestic resident of the United States in the official international trade accounts. Residents of foreign countries—we'll call them "foreigners"—are people who reside outside the United States (some of whom are U.S. citizens living abroad).

Income-Based Payments from Foreigners   Let's start with income-based payments from foreigners. There are three ways that domestic residents receive income-based payments from foreigners:

1. Receiving payments from the sale of goods and services to foreigners—*exports*
2. Receiving income from assets that the domestic resident owns in foreign countries— *factor payments from foreigners*
3. Receiving transfers (remittances) from individuals who reside abroad or from foreign governments—*transfers from foreigners*

Recall that *exports* are the goods and services that domestic residents produce and then sell in foreign countries. When a foreign resident receives these goods and services, he directly or indirectly makes a payment to the domestic resident who produced them.

Factor payments from foreigners represent the payments that domestic residents receive from assets owned in foreign countries. For example, if a U.S. resident owns stock in Tata Steel, one of the largest companies in India, and Tata Steel pays a dividend, that dividend payment would count as a factor payment from abroad. Likewise, if a U.S. company owns a plant in China and that plant generates earnings, those earnings would count as a factor payment from abroad. Or, if a U.S. engineer who resides in the United States spends a day working in Turin, Italy, where she consults for Fiat, the payment that she receives from Fiat would count as a factor payment from abroad. In this consulting example, the relevant factor of production is human capital.

Transfers from foreigners are "gifts" from foreign residents or foreign governments. For example, following Hurricane Katrina in 2005, China sent 104 tons of emergency supplies to New Orleans, including tents and generators, valued at $5 million. All told, foreign governments and citizens of foreign countries sent hundreds of millions of dollars of aid to support the victims of Hurricane Katrina; contributions like these are transfers from abroad.

Income-Based Payments to Foreigners Similar types of financial flows move in the opposite direction. We now list all of the sources of income-based payments *to* foreigners:

1. Making payments to foreigners in return for their goods and services—*imports*
2. Paying income on assets that foreign residents own in the domestic economy—*factor payments to foreigners*
3. Making transfers to individuals who reside abroad or to foreign governments—*transfers to foreigners*

Imports are the goods and services that foreigners produce and then sell to domestic residents. *Factor payments to foreigners* represent the payments made to foreigners who own assets in the domestic economy. *Transfers to foreigners* are "gifts," which include foreign aid from the U.S. government, donations from U.S. citizens to foreign charitable organizations, and remittances from legal and illegal residents of the United States. For example, a Mexican citizen who permanently resides in the United States and periodically transfers money back to family members in Mexico is making a transfer to foreigners. In this case, the transfer is just the money that is sent to family members in Mexico, and not the total earnings that the Mexican citizen receives for work that she does in the United States.

The Workings of the Current Account and the Financial Account

> The **current account** is the sum of net exports, net factor payments from abroad, and net transfers from abroad.

The **current account** adds together these different sources of payments into and out of a country. We start with the definitions of net exports, net factor payments from abroad, and net transfers from abroad:

$$\text{Net exports} = \text{Payments from abroad for exports} - \text{Payments to foreigners for imports,}$$

$$\text{Net factor payments from abroad} = \text{Factor payments from abroad} - \text{Factor payments to foreigners,}$$

$$\text{Net transfers from abroad} = \text{Transfers from abroad} - \text{Transfers to foreigners.}$$

With these concepts, we can now define the current account, which is the net flow of payments made to domestic residents from foreign residents. Put differently, the current account is given by the sum of net exports, net factor payments from abroad, and net transfers from abroad:

$$\text{Current account} = (\text{Net exports}) + (\text{Net factor payments from abroad}) + (\text{Net transfers from abroad}).$$

It is important to bear in mind that any of these net flows could be negative, which would correspond to a net flow of payments *to* foreign residents. In fact, in 2015, the United States did run a current account deficit of $477 billion. In other words, U.S. residents paid foreigners $477 billion more than foreigners paid U.S. residents.

Exhibit 14.7 breaks down the current account deficit for the United States in 2015 into its three components. Trade in goods and services led to net payments of $501 billion to foreigners. Factor payments led to net payments of $168 billion from foreigners to U.S. residents. Finally, net transfer payments led to net payments to foreigners of $145 billion. Adding these up, and remembering to use a negative sign when net payments are made to foreigners, we come up with a total current account *deficit* of $477 billion.

Exhibit 14.7 The Current Account of the United States in 2015 (Billions of 2015 dollars)

The current account is the sum of net exports, net factor payments from abroad, and net transfers from abroad. (The U.S. government does not break down transfer payments into gross flows, so only the net flow is reported starting with the transfer payments row.)

Source: Based on Bureau of Economic Analysis, National Income and Product Accounts.

Note: NA, Not applicable.

	Payments from Foreigners	Payments to Foreigners	Net Payments
Trade in goods and services	2,261	2,762	−501
Factor payments	769	601	+168
Transfer payments	NA	NA	−145
Current account	NA	NA	−477

What are the consequences of running a current account deficit? When U.S. residents make $477 billion of net payments to foreigners, the payments are made in U.S. dollars. These dollars enable the foreign residents to buy U.S. assets, which can be exchanged for U.S. goods and services at some point in the future.

To understand what this means in practice, consider the simple current account transaction illustrated in Exhibit 14.8. Suppose a U.S. consumer decides to buy a Chinese laptop that costs $1,000. In effect, the U.S. consumer gives the Chinese laptop manufacturer $1,000. In the U.S. current account, this amount would show up as a $1,000 payment to foreigners. Exhibit 14.8 illustrates this current account transaction by showing the purchase of the $1,000 laptop.

Now suppose that there is no offsetting transaction in which China buys goods and services from the United States, so the $1,000 payment can be thought of as a current account deficit. Instead of importing $1,000 of goods and services from the United States, China saves the $1,000, thereby preserving that purchasing power for future purchases of goods and services. For example, the Chinese company could use the $1,000 to buy a specific U.S. asset from U.S. residents—for instance, a U.S. Treasury bond. This is the case depicted in the circular flow of Exhibit 14.8.

Exhibit 14.8 Circular Flows in the U.S. International Transactions Accounts

A U.S. consumer buys a $1,000 laptop from a Chinese manufacturer. Then the Chinese manufacturer uses the $1,000 to buy a U.S. Treasury bond. At the end of the transactions, the U.S. consumer has a new laptop computer, and China has an additional U.S. Treasury bond.

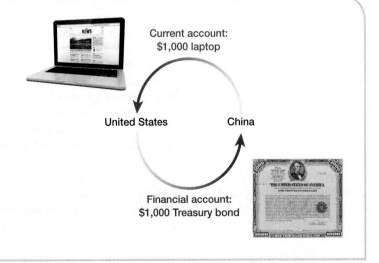

Current account: $1,000 laptop

United States   China

Financial account: $1,000 Treasury bond

The **financial account** is the increase in domestic assets held by foreigners minus the increase in foreign assets held domestically.

Let's summarize the flows in Exhibit 14.8. At the end of the international transactions depicted there, the United States has one new laptop and owns one less Treasury bond. In the current account, the U.S. has imported goods worth $1,000. In the *financial account,* the U.S. has transferred to China a Treasury bond worth $1,000. The **financial account** is defined as the increase in domestic assets held by foreigners minus the increase in foreign assets held domestically. (Note that the financial account only registers transactions that change an asset's ownership and does not measure changes in asset prices.)

The financial account is just the accounting system that records the asset purchases that domestic residents and foreigners make. The financial account is defined so that *the net flows in the financial account offset the net flows in the current account.* (To keep the analysis simple, we have omitted a few other details in the accounting rules.)

The following two equations give the definition of the financial account and describe its relationship to the current account:

$$\text{Financial account} = \text{Increase in domestic assets held by foreigners}$$
$$- \text{Increase in foreign assets held domestically,}$$

$$\text{Current account} + \text{Financial account} = 0.$$

The preceding equation has an important implication: a change in the current account balance will be matched by a change in the opposite direction in the financial account. This is intuitive. For example, when foreigners receive net payments in the current account, they can buy any type of U.S. asset in the financial account. In the example just discussed, they bought U.S. Treasury bonds. But they could also just hold the payment in dollars (in a bank account) as a claim against the United States. In either case, the current account deficit is exactly offset by a financial account surplus.

We can now talk about the specific numbers for the United States in 2015. Exhibit 14.7 shows that foreigners received $477 billion in net payments in the U.S. current account, which is called a current account deficit for the United States. To pay for this current account deficit, U.S. residents must have made net transfers of $477 billion in assets to foreigners (including dollar-denominated deposits). As required by the accounting identities, the financial account exactly offsets the current account, dollar-for-dollar.

This isn't necessarily bad news for U.S. residents. It was a trade. Residents of the United States got Sony TV sets, Louis Vuitton handbags, BMWs, and hundreds of thousands of other imported goods and services. Foreigners obtained bank deposits and other assets worth $477 billion from residents of the United States.

When a country runs a current account deficit, it is analogous to what takes place when a single household spends more than it earns. To fund this extra spending, the household either borrows or spends down assets that had previously been accumulated. For example, suppose you spend $1,000 more than you earn from all sources, including labor income, asset income, and transfers. If you already have some assets in the bank (say, $3,000 in your checking account), you could finance the extra $1,000 of consumption by running down those assets so that at the end of the year you would have only $2,000 left in your checking account. Or if you do not have such assets to spend down, you could borrow. If you start without any assets and without any debt, you would borrow $1,000, so your net asset position would become $-1,000$. Notice that regardless of what your asset position was at the beginning, you are financing your $1,000 shortfall by reducing your asset position by $1,000—either from $3,000 to $2,000 or from zero to $-1,000$.

The situation is identical for a country, which must also finance its net exports by selling some of its assets or borrowing. This fact highlights a central concept in international accounting: just like an individual household, an entire country can only spend more than it earns if it finds a way to fund the extra spending. The country must either sell assets to foreigners or borrow from foreigners. Hence, current account deficits must match financial account flows. In other words, when a country makes net purchases of goods and services from foreigners, the country must make net asset sales to foreigners to pay the bill.

Just like an individual household, an entire country can only spend more than it earns if it finds a way to fund the extra spending.

We can also conduct the analysis by focusing only on net exports (the trade component of the current account, leaving out net factor payments from abroad and net transfers from abroad) and the net capital outflows associated with net exports. In particular, from the national income accounting identity in Chapter 5, we have that

$$Y = C + I + G + NX,$$

where Y represents gross domestic product (GDP), C represents consumption of domestic residents, I represents investment of domestic residents and firms, G represents government expenditure, and NX represents exports minus imports, which we refer to as net exports. We can rearrange this identity so that

$$Y - C - G - I = NX.$$

Note also that savings (S) is income minus both consumption and government expenditure: $S = Y - C - G$. Substituting this savings equation into the last expression, we find that

$$S - I = NX.$$

At first glance, this implication of the national income accounting identity may seem strange. However, the reasoning here is conceptually the same as the logic linking the financial account to the current account. To build your intuition, suppose that Boeing manufactures and exports an additional 787 Dreamliner to All Nippon Airways (of Japan). Suppose also that U.S. imports from the rest of the world and U.S. consumption, government expenditure, and investment all remain the same. What must adjust in the national accounts? The production of the plane implies that GDP rose by the value of the plane. What else changes? The simplest scenario to consider is the one where All Nippon Airways writes an IOU to Boeing, effectively implying that Boeing is owed money by the Japanese company, which counts as Boeing *saving* the proceeds of this sale. The extra U.S. savings takes the form of an IOU from All Nippon Airways. This also counts as a capital "outflow" from the United States to Japan. A capital outflow occurs when a country (the United States, in this example) makes an investment in a foreign country (Japan, in this example).

Putting these insights together, we see that the national accounting identities imply that

$$S - I = NX = \text{Net capital outflows,}$$

Net capital outflows are the difference between investment by the home country in foreign countries and foreign investment in the home country.

where **net capital outflows** are defined as the difference between U.S. investment in foreign countries and foreign investment in the United States. Because net capital outflows are tied to net exports (NX), when U.S. firms export more, net capital outflows will increase, and when U.S. firms and consumers import more, net capital outflows will decline.

The relationship between net capital outflows and net exports has an important consequence, linking net exports to the real interest rate. This is depicted in Exhibit 14.9, which shows the relationship between net capital outflows and the real interest rate in the home country—in this case, the United States. When the real interest rate rises, the U.S. becomes

Exhibit 14.9 Relationship Between Net Capital Outflows and the Real Interest Rate

As the real interest rate increases, the home country becomes more attractive to investors, decreasing net capital outflows and thus net exports. Conversely, a decrease in the real interest rate increases net capital outflows and net exports.

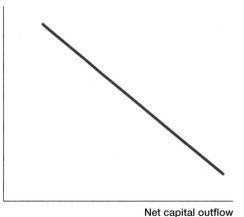

more attractive to global investors; as capital pours in, net capital outflows decrease and net exports therefore decrease. The opposite happens when the real interest rate decreases. Since net capital outflows are equal to net exports, Exhibit 14.9 shows a negative relationship between net exports and the real interest rate. In a nutshell, a rising real interest rate discourages net capital outflows and reduces net exports, while a falling real interest rate encourages net capital outflows and increases net exports.

14.3 International Trade, Technology Transfer, and Economic Growth

International trade benefits countries not just through specialization and comparative advantage. It is also a conduit for the transfer of technology from more advanced to less advanced economies, thus contributing to an increase in the recipient's productive capacity (recall the discussion in Chapter 6 on the importance of technology for productivity and living standards).

The interplay between international trade and technology transfer is illustrated by China's economic development. When the founding father of Communist China, Mao Zedong, died in 1976, Chinese PPP-adjusted GDP per capita was $882 in 2005 dollars. Under Mao, China was organized as a planned economy, so state officials decided how to allocate almost all economic resources. Free markets were banned, international travel was forbidden, international trade was very low compared to most other countries, and citizens could not own land or businesses. The Chinese state owned all important types of physical capital. From an economic perspective, human capital was also controlled by the Chinese government, because people could not choose where to work and did not receive wages that were commensurate with their value added. The economic consequences of these policies were disastrous, leading to mass starvation under Mao's leadership. Approximately 30 million people died from malnutrition during the Great Famine of 1958–1961.

In 1978, two years after Mao's death, Deng Xiaoping became the next powerful leader of China. Under Deng, China began to liberalize its economy, including opening the country to international trade. Exhibit 14.10 plots Chinese imports and exports as shares of GDP since 1970. Under Mao's leadership in the early 1970s, exports represented less than 5 percent of GDP. Over the past 10 years, the export share of the Chinese economy has averaged more than 30 percent. Chinese growth over the past 20 years has often been described as "export-led growth."

MyEconLab Real-time data

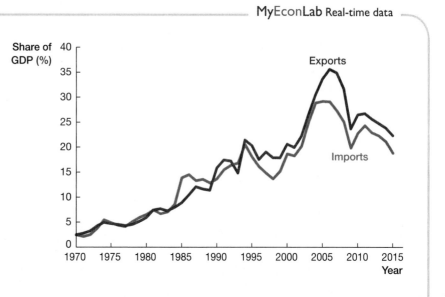

Exhibit 14.10 Chinese Imports and Exports as Shares of Chinese GDP (1970–2015)

China has transitioned from a largely closed economy in the 1970s to an open economy today.

Source: Based on World Bank DataBank: World Development Indicators.

China achieved an average annual growth rate of real GDP per capita of 6.6 percent between 1979 and 2012. At this pace, Chinese real GDP per capita has *doubled* approximately once every 11 years, implying more than three doublings since 1979. Consequently, Chinese real GDP per capita has increased by more than a factor of $2 \times 2 \times 2 = 8$ since 1979! By comparison, it takes about 40 years for U.S. real GDP per capita to double.

China's spectacular growth is largely due to the shift from central planning—in other words, state control of the economy—toward a market economy. Opening to trade in goods and services was just one part of that transition. Farmers and family businesses were allowed to make their own decisions, own private property, and keep the profits from their economic activity. State-owned industries were privatized and China, which previously banned all kinds of foreign capital inflows, became a major destination for foreign investment. Along the way, China improved its technology greatly, enabling its citizens to work in modern factories, which now export to markets around the world.

Foreign direct investment refers to investments by foreign individuals and companies in domestic firms and businesses. To qualify as foreign *direct* investment, this capital flow must generate a large ownership stake in a local firm for the foreign investors. For example, foreign direct investment in China occurs when a foreign company opens a factory in China. It would also count as foreign direct investment if the Chinese factory were jointly owned by the foreign company and some local Chinese investors or a local Chinese company. China receives more foreign direct investment than any other country in the world.

Foreign direct investment refers to investments by foreign individuals and companies in domestic firms and businesses. To qualify as foreign direct investment, these flows need to generate a large foreign ownership stake in the domestic business.

LETTING THE
DATA SPEAK

From IBM to Lenovo

In 1980, almost no families had a computer at home. Personal computers did exist, but they were expensive, hard to use, and were primarily used by technology hobbyists and science geeks. The Internet did not exist. The kind of entertainment one could get from a computer was a game like Pong. Even the game of Tetris wouldn't be invented until 1984.

Between 1980 and 1990, the personal computer reached the mainstream, thanks to gradually improving technology as well as successful marketing. The big bang was the introduc-

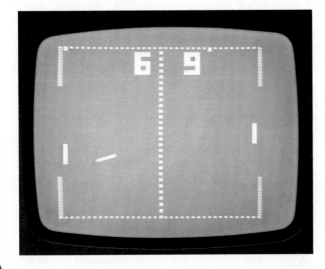

tion of the IBM-PC (model 5150) in 1981. This computer was so successful that it quickly became the industry standard. By the mid-1990s, no self-respecting college student in the developed world still wrote term papers on a typewriter.

The first generation of IBM-PCs was manufactured with mostly U.S. parts and assembled in a U.S. plant. However, even the first IBM-PC had a Japanese monitor. Over time, foreign components came to dominate the business. Mass production of hard disks began in Japan and Korea in the 1980s. Eventually, almost all key components of the personal computer were manufactured outside the United States. Over time, the final assembly also shifted to foreign factories.

Today, IBM is completely out of the business of manufacturing and selling personal computers. The end of IBM's involvement occurred in 2005, when IBM sold its successful laptop business to Lenovo, its Chinese manufacturing partner. So what did IBM do after abandoning its old line of business? IBM did very well by recognizing that its highly skilled U.S. labor force had higher value added—that is, a *comparative advantage*—in providing consulting services rather than in manufacturing machines that low-wage workers could assemble. Today, IBM remains a highly profitable company. Each year it sells approximately $100 billion in consulting and technical services to companies around the world. It has almost 400,000 employees, and the company is worth approximately $200 billion.

> Technology transfer creates one more
> type of cross-country interdependence.

Foreign direct investment is a major conduit for technology transfer, though in most cases this transfer is not the goal of the foreign firm that is making the investment. When a UK company becomes part of a joint venture or opens a factory in China, it brings its know-how and technology to the country. This type of technology transfer enables recipient countries to improve their productivity.

Technology transfer creates one more type of cross-country interdependence. Countries are not only trading goods and services and having their firms and banks borrow from and lend to each other, they are also technologically interlinked. Innovations and technological improvements in one country will ultimately improve productivity in all countries. Moreover, the more interaction there is between these countries—in particular, through foreign direct investment—the faster these improvements will migrate from one to the other. Such transfers are particularly beneficial for countries that start out technologically less advanced, as China did in the late 1970s.

EVIDENCE-BASED ECONOMICS

Q: Are companies like Nike harming workers in Vietnam?

Working on a Vietnamese farm is tough. Wages are very low—approximately $1–$3 per *day* for unskilled labor.[9] And the working conditions on a Vietnamese farm are miserable. The physical labor is grueling, and injuries are common. Benefits like health insurance or pension plans don't exist in the agricultural sector. If you are injured on the job and can't work the next day, you don't get paid. Some children work in the agricultural sector because their families can't afford to send them to school and need the meager income that the children earn.

Unskilled workers in the factories that manufacture Nike products earn little more than the Vietnamese minimum wage, which is $4–$5 per day, depending on the location of the factory.[10] But this is higher than the wage they would earn in the largely unregulated agricultural sector. Some of the factory workers also have free access to rudimentary health clinics. But working conditions are terrible—cramped, noisy, hot rooms, filled with dangerous chemicals and air-borne pollutants. As in the agricultural sector, the factories offer no job security. Sick or injured employees lose their jobs and do not receive unemployment benefits. Working in a factory that makes Nike shoes is a nightmare by the standards of workers in the developed world.

Defenders of globalization emphasize the gains from international trade. At the moment, many Vietnamese workers, with limited human capital and limited access to modern technology, have a comparative advantage in assembly jobs—like work in sneaker and clothing factories. Preventing them from working in these jobs reduces their income. Defenders of free trade point to the agricultural sector and say that Nike is doing

a good thing by giving agricultural workers an alternative job that increases their pay. The factory job provides reliable income and therefore does not depend on the timing of seasonal rains or whether the harvest happens to be good or bad. Famines occur when agricultural production fails, often because of a long stretch of bad weather. Famines generally don't occur in factory towns. Finally, when Nike's subcontractors use foreign direct investment to build new sneaker factories, this facilitates the transfer of new technology to Vietnam.

However, critics of the factory sweatshops in Vietnam point out that these jobs don't even measure up to the jobs that the worst-off workers hold in developed countries. A low-wage worker in the United States earns more than

$50 per day. An unskilled factory worker in Vietnam earns less than a tenth as much. The Vietnam factory wouldn't even come close to passing a U.S. safety inspection. Moreover, many of the factory workers in Vietnam are underage (like the workers in the agricultural sector).

Almost everyone agrees with these facts. But there is a great deal of disagreement about what should be done. Is it possible for Nike to continue to buy shoes from suppliers in Vietnam but require those suppliers to pay higher wages? Suppose that U.S. consumers boycotted Nike's products because of the work arrangements at the factories that supply Nike with sneakers. The U.S. consumers would like Nike's subcontractors to pay the factory workers more and to improve working conditions in those factories. In principle, such improvements could be implemented without necessitating a very large increase in Nike's sneaker prices.

Would the improved working conditions at Nike's subcontractors and higher wages for their workers create unintended negative consequences? One possibility is that because labor costs in Vietnam and other low-wage countries are so low and Nike's profits are so high, these changes would increase wages at the expense of Nike's profits, without much else changing. But most likely, Nike would also lose business because of the need to (modestly) raise its sneaker prices. If Nike does lose some customers, it might end up reducing its sneaker purchases from the Vietnamese subcontractors, leading some of its suppliers to shut down. In this case, Vietnamese workers might actually be hurt. Perhaps Nike would improve conditions at the existing factories in Vietnam, but the subcontractors might stop building new factories in Vietnam, thereby preventing other agricultural workers from transitioning to the relatively well-paid manufacturing sector. Consumers in the United States would like to see the lives of Vietnamese families improve, but in the end, we do not know enough to be able to forecast with accuracy what would happen if Nike and its subcontractors were pressured to raise the wages of workers in Vietnamese sneaker factories. In the most likely scenario, some of these high wages might come out of Nike's profits, but this would be accompanied by a major reduction in demand for Vietnamese labor, thereby increasing, rather than reducing, poverty in the country.

Though it is not clear what would happen if Nike were forced to pay its Vietnamese workers more, it is clear that globalization in general has been an enormous force for good in Vietnam. Like Deng Xiaoping, who initiated market and trade reforms in China after decades of strict central planning, Nguyen Van Linh pursued a similar policy in Vietnam starting in 1988 (2 years after he came to power). As a result of these Vietnamese reforms, trade rapidly expanded, with exports rising from 10 percent of GDP in 1988 to 75 percent of GDP today. Since the reforms were passed, real GDP per capita has grown by about 5.5 percent per year (1988–2013), more than double the pre-reform growth rate.[11] In addition, poverty has fallen precipitously. In 1993, nearly 60 percent of the Vietnamese population lived on less than a (U.S.) dollar a day, compared to only 16 percent of the population in 2006.[12]

Economists believe that sustained growth is one of the key factors that reduces child labor. Exhibit 14.11 shows a strong negative correlation between child labor and GDP per capita: fewer children are forced to, or choose to, work in countries with higher GDP per capita. Consistent with Exhibit 14.11, rising levels of income in Vietnam have coincided with a sharp fall in child labor, and much of the decline in child labor is credited to Vietnam's opening to trade.[13]

Exhibit 14.11 The Relationship Between GDP per Capita and Child Labor (Fraction of children ages 7–14 who are working)

There is a strong negative relationship between GDP per capita and child labor, which is measured as the percentage of children between the ages of 7 and 14 who are working. The red dots represent countries that are identified by name in the exhibit.

Source: Based on Jean Fares and Dhushyanth Raju (2007). "Child Labor Across the Developing World: Patterns and Correlations," World Development Report, World Bank.

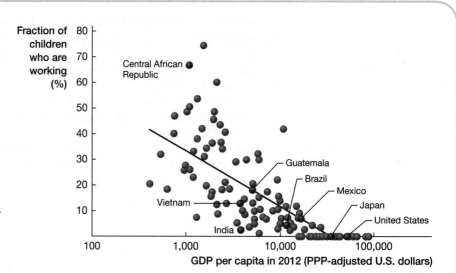

Question	**Answer**	**Data**	**Caveat**
Are companies like Nike harming workers in Vietnam?	The Vietnamese workers that make Nike's sneakers are paid extremely low wages and work in conditions that are unsafe by the standards of developed countries. However, the next-best alternative for many of the workers that produce Nike's sneakers, which is work in the agricultural sector, appears to be even worse.	Agricultural and factory wages in Vietnam, as well as data on trade, growth, poverty, and child labor-force participation.	Nike could improve the quality of life of the workers who manufacture its products if it forced its subcontractors to raise the workers' wages.

Summary

- The process of globalization has produced a highly interconnected world.

- International trade enables us to exploit specialization and comparative advantage. Comparative advantage arises when a person or country has a lower opportunity cost of production than another person or country.

- Globalization and international trade improve the well-being of most people, but many other people are made worse off, especially low-skilled workers in developed countries who lose their jobs to foreign producers.

- A country runs a current account deficit when it has a negative sum of net exports, net payments from abroad for factor payments, and net transfers from abroad. When this happens, the country must have a financial account surplus, as there needs to be a corresponding flow of funds that pays for the current account deficit. This implies a net increase in domestic assets held by foreigners and/or a net decrease in foreign assets held by domestic residents.

- A rapid process of globalization has been under way for several decades, increasing the total volume of international trade. Consequently, consumers and workers around the world can now take better advantage of the gains from international trade. Nevertheless, continued progress in globalization is not guaranteed. In fact, an anti-globalization backlash is now occurring, and some trade agreements are currently being abandoned or re-negotiated.

- Globalization also makes the enormous inequities across nations more visible. We purchase goods and services produced and assembled by workers, sometimes even children, earning a small fraction of the wages of workers in developed economies. The working conditions in factories in the developing world are far worse than those in developed countries. Nevertheless, globalization usually improves the well-being of most low-paid factory workers in foreign countries. Their alternative opportunities for employment are usually worse than these factory jobs in the traded goods sector.

Key Terms

gains from specialization *p. 337*
absolute advantage *p. 338*
comparative advantage *p. 338*
closed economy *p. 343*

open economy *p. 343*
net exports or the trade balance *p. 347*
trade surplus *p. 347*
trade deficit *p. 347*

current account *p. 348*
financial account *p. 350*
net capital outflows *p. 351*
foreign direct investment *p. 353*

Questions

All questions are available in MyEconLab *for practice and instructor assignment.*

1. How does comparative advantage differ from absolute advantage?

2. How does trade allow buyers and sellers to exploit gains from specialization?

3. Engaging in trade increases overall economic efficiency. Does this also imply that everyone in an economy gains from trade equally?

4. Explain the following terms:
   a. Open economy
   b. Closed economy
   c. Imports
   d. Exports
   e. Tariffs

5. Has trade been increasing or decreasing over the past few decades? What could explain why the ratio of imports to GDP in the United States fell sharply after 1929 before rebounding shortly thereafter?

6. How is the trade balance defined? When is a country said to be running a trade deficit or a trade surplus?

7. The international accounting system maintains a clear distinction between residency and citizenship.
   a. Who would be considered a domestic resident of the United States, according to the international accounting system?
   b. Suppose a U.S. citizen lives and works in Nigeria. Would he be considered a "foreigner" or a domestic resident in the U.S. international transactions accounts?

8. List the sources of income-based payments that domestic residents make to foreigners and the ways that domestic residents can receive income-based payments from foreigners.

9. What does the current account include? Describe each of its components. Are all of these components included in GDP? Explain.

10. What is included in a country's financial account? How is the financial account related to the current account?

11. What are net capital outflows? Use an example to explain how they are related to net exports.

12. What is foreign direct investment? Explain with an example. How does foreign direct investment benefit the recipient country?

13. Are multinational companies harming factory workers in the developing world by hiring them at low wages?

Problems

All problems are available in MyEconLab for practice and instructor assignment.

1. The economist Alan Blinder said that any economist who mows his own lawn probably has not understood the concept of comparative advantage. Would you agree with Professor Blinder?

2. You and your roommate are enrolled in the same course: Postmodern Deconstruction of Postmodern Deconstructionism. The course requires a term paper. Since the professor encourages collaboration on the paper, you decide to work on it together, "trading" tasks. In 8 hours, you can type eighteen pages, whereas your roommate can type only ten. If you do outlining instead of typing, in the same 8 hours you can produce six summary outlines of the course readings, while your roommate can produce only two.

   a. Who has the absolute advantage in typing? In outlining? Explain your answers.

   b. Who should do the typing, and who should do the outlining? Explain.

3. Suppose that United States and India are the only two countries in the world. Suppose also that in India, an acre of land can produce 40 tons of sugarcane or 65 bushels of corn per season, while in the United States, an acre of land can produce 20 tons of sugarcane or 150 bushels of corn per season.

   a. Which country has the absolute advantage in the production of sugarcane? Of corn? Explain.

   b. Explain the concept of comparative advantage. What is India's comparative advantage in this case? What about the United States?

   c. Suppose U.S. scientists have developed a groundbreaking new technology that increases the productivity of sugarcane in the United States to 75 tons of sugarcane per acre (and has no effect on U.S. corn productivity or Indian productivity in sugarcane or corn). How does this change India's comparative advantage?

4. Assume that an American worker can produce 5 cars per year or 10 tons of grain per year, whereas a Japanese worker can produce 15 cars per year or 5 tons of grain per year. Assume that labor is the only input used in car and grain production.

   a. Which country has the absolute advantage in producing cars? In producing grain?

   b. For the United States, what is the opportunity cost of producing a car? What is the opportunity cost of producing a ton of grain? Show how you arrived at your numbers.

   c. For Japan, what is the opportunity cost of producing a car? What is the opportunity cost of producing a ton of grain? Show how you arrived at your numbers.

   d. If free trade is allowed, which country will import cars? Which country will import grain? Explain.

5. David Ricardo, the British political economist, used the example of two commodities—wine and cloth—produced by England and Portugal to explain trade. The following table shows the number of labor hours it would take England and Portugal to produce one unit each of wine and cloth:

	Portugal	England
Wine	80	120
Cloth	90	100

   Portugal can produce both wine and cloth using fewer labor hours than England uses. A group of mercantilists (who believe that nations build their wealth by exporting more than they import) suggest that Portugal has nothing to gain from trading with England. Would you agree? Explain your answer.

6. Tire production in the United States has been on the decline, in both absolute and relative terms. Imported tires are replacing most domestically manufactured tires in the market. Trade unions in the United States have claimed that over 7,000 jobs have been lost due to Chinese tire imports. You read a blog post that uses this example to say that this is exactly why countries should not engage in free trade; cheaper imports will flood the domestic market and unemployment in the country will increase. Do you think the blogger's conclusions are entirely correct? Explain.

7. During the 2016 election, Donald Trump argued that China was exploiting the United States. In particular, he decried the large trade deficit with China—in debates, he liked to say that China was "killing" the United States on trade. Is having a trade deficit with another country inherently bad? Explain why a trade deficit may not be a bad thing for the United States. What are the scenarios under which a trade deficit may be a problem?

8. Suppose the following table shows data on transactions between the United States and the rest of the world for

the month of May 2013. Assuming the list is exhaustive, use the information given to fill in the table showing the current and financial accounts for May 2013.

Transaction	Amount
U.S. aid to earthquake-hit Haiti	$8,000,000
Payments made to Indian software companies for services rendered by workers in India to U.S. customers	$850,000
Payments made to U.S. producers for ethanol exports	$3,000,000
Dividend payment from Walmart in China to a U.S. resident	$10,500
Salary earned by a team of IT consultants from the United Kingdom who were working in the United States for a few days	$120,000
Sale of U.S. Treasury bonds from the U.S. Treasury to foreign governments	$15,000,000
Remittances from U.S. residents to other family members in Mexico	$30,000
Payments made to Chinese producers for steel imports	$8,000,000
Purchases of foreign assets by the U.S. government	$1,040,500
A U.S. citizen, who is a resident of Dubai, sends money to a charity in the United States	$30,000

Current and Financial Account for May 2013

	Payments from Foreigners	Payments to Foreigners	Net Payments
Trade in goods and services			
Factor payments			
Net transfer payments			
Current account			
	Increase in domestic assets held by foreigners	Increase in foreign assets held domestically	
Net sales to foreigners			
Financial account			

9. In the fourth quarter of 2016, the U.S. current account deficit was $112.4 billion, while the trade deficit was $132.3 billion.

   a. Why are the trade deficit and the current account deficit different?

   b. Based on the information in this problem, what were U.S. net capital outflows in 2016? Carefully show how you got your answer and explain, in words, the concept of net capital outflows.

   c. Suppose Apple (based in the United States) sold an additional $0.5 billion in iPhones to retailers in Spain. How would this transaction affect the trade deficit? What about net capital outflows? Explain.

   d. How would an increase in the U.S. real interest rate affect the trade deficit? Net capital outflows? Explain.

10. Throughout the 1950s and 1960s, many poor countries pursued a policy called "import-substituting industrialization," or ISI for short. India, and many nations in Africa and Latin America, closed themselves off to trade in order to promote the development of domestic industries. As noted in the *Economist* article "Grinding the Poor" (September 27, 2001), "[o]n the whole, ISI failed; almost everywhere, trade has been good for growth." The article discusses how growth was disappointing in countries that pursued ISI. Nations that were open to trade—primarily in Asia—grew much more rapidly. Based on the discussion in the chapter, speculate on why ISI was ultimately a failure and why integration with the global economy promotes economic growth and development.

11. Foreign direct investment in several sectors in India is still heavily regulated. After much debate, the government of India recently relaxed restrictions on foreign direct investment in the retail sector. Purportedly for reasons like national security and possible job losses, many sectors of the economy (such as defense, nuclear power, and oil refining) are not fully open to foreign direct investment. Suppose you are hired to serve on the government's Working Group on Foreign Direct Investment. What would you suggest to the government? Defend your position.

12. The coffee market is one of the most globalized and volatile commodity markets in existence. In terms of the value of trade, it is second only to oil. Coffee is produced in over seventy countries, primarily lower-income nations in Latin America, Africa, and Asia. In recent years, a movement has developed supporting "fair trade coffee," which seeks to better the conditions and increase the incomes of coffee producers in poor countries.

   Read the following online sources and list the main arguments for and against the fair trade coffee movement, as delineated in the articles. Comment on any similarities you see between fair trade coffee policy and the case of Nike in Vietnam (as discussed in the chapter's Evidence-Based Economics feature).

   "The Fair Trade Debate" in Wikipedia: http://en.wikipedia.org/wiki/Fair_trade_debate

   "Coffee" from Fair Trade International: http://www.fairtrade.net/coffee.html

   "Fair Trade Coffee Enthusiasts Should Confront Reality" from the Cato Institute: http://object.cato.org/sites/cato.org/files/serials/files/cato-journal/2007/1/cj27n1-9.pdf

   "The Pros and Cons of Fair Trade Coffee" from the Organic Consumers Association: http://www.organicconsumers.org/articles/article_4738.cfm

Open Economy Macroeconomics

How did George Soros make $1 billion?

George Soros, one of the world's most renowned investors, challenged the central bank of England in the summer of 1992. In essence, he bet everything he had that the British currency, the pound, would lose value relative to other currencies. Starting in September, the pound plummeted in value. Soros made approximately $1 billion in profits for himself and his investors. How did Soros know that the pound was about to collapse?

CHAPTER OUTLINE

15.1 Exchange Rates

In the previous chapter, we saw that economies around the world are linked through trade and investment. For example, the United States imported about $483 billion of goods and services from China in 2015. But *how* does this trade take place? After all, almost all transactions in the United States are in U.S. dollars, while most transactions in China are in the Chinese currency, the *yuan*, also called the *renminbi*.

Many countries have their own currencies for use in economic transactions: the United Kingdom has the pound, Japan the yen, Mexico the peso, and India the rupee, among others. An exception to the use of a national currency is the euro, a currency used by nineteen European countries (as of 2017). The euro, first introduced in 1999, is the second-most-traded currency after the U.S. dollar.

Nominal Exchange Rates

Walmart sells toys imported from China. How does Walmart decide whether to purchase the toys from China rather than purchasing similar toys from some U.S. toy manufacturer?

To answer this question, we need to understand the concept of the *nominal exchange rate*. The **nominal exchange rate** is the price of one country's currency in units of another country's currency. Specifically, the nominal exchange rate is the number of units of foreign currency that can be purchased with one unit of domestic currency. Sometimes you'll see the nominal exchange rate referred to as simply the "exchange rate" (which is what we did in Chapter 6). In the current chapter, we often use the full name, *nominal* exchange rate, to distinguish the nominal exchange rate from another type of exchange rate that we discuss later in the chapter.

> The **nominal exchange rate** is the price of one country's currency in units of another country's currency.

In the following equation, the nominal exchange rate is represented by the symbol e:

$$e = \frac{\text{Units of foreign currency}}{1 \text{ Unit of domestic currency}}.$$

For instance, if the yuan-per-dollar exchange rate is 6.88 yuan per dollar, then a person holding 1 dollar can exchange the dollar for 6.88 yuan.

$$e = 6.88 \text{ Yuan per dollar} = \frac{6.88 \text{ Yuan}}{1 \text{ Dollar}}.$$

Exhibit 15.1 The Nominal Exchange Rates e and 1/e

The nominal exchange rates e and 1/e for several major currencies on January 27, 2017.

Source: Federal Reserve Board of Governors.

	British Pound per Dollar	Euro per Dollar	Mexican New Peso per Dollar	Swiss Franc per Dollar	Yuan per Dollar
e	0.8	0.93	21.02	0.999	6.88

	Dollar per British Pound	Dollar per Euro	Dollar per Mexican New Peso	Dollar per Swiss Franc	Dollar per Yuan
1/e	1.25	1.07	0.05	1.001	0.15

All Chinese currency features a portrait of Mao Zedong, the first leader of modern China.

The higher the value of e, the more units of foreign currency a dollar buys. When a nominal exchange rate goes up, we say that the domestic currency is *appreciating* against the foreign currency. When a nominal exchange rate goes down, we say that the domestic currency is *depreciating* against the foreign currency.

We can also use the yuan-per-dollar exchange rate to calculate the value of 1 yuan in terms of dollars. When the yuan-per-dollar exchange rate is e, the number of units of dollars that can be purchased with 1 yuan is $1/e$. Put differently, 1 yuan is worth $1/e = 1/6.88 = 0.15$ dollars.

Notice that the appreciation of a currency—a rise in e—always has a flip side. When the dollar appreciates against the yuan, implying that e is rising, the yuan is depreciating against the dollar, implying that $1/e$ is falling.

Exhibit 15.1 shows e and $1/e$ for some key currencies on January 27, 2017. The above discussion and Exhibit 15.1 clarify that both e (yuan per dollar) and $1/e$ (dollar per yuan) convey the same information. In newspapers, you will see exchange rates sometimes expressed as yuan per dollar or euro per dollar and at other times as dollar per yuan or dollar per euro. In this chapter, to avoid confusion, we will stick to the definition above of the exchange rate, e, expressing it as the number of units of foreign currency that can be purchased with one unit of domestic currency, such as yuan per dollar or euro per dollar.

Now let's return to Walmart's *sourcing* decision—should Walmart purchase toys from a Chinese or a U.S. manufacturer? Walmart needs to decide whether a toy sold by a Chinese manufacturer at a unit price of 20 yuan is less expensive than an identical toy sold by a competing U.S. manufacturer at a unit price of $5 (we are ignoring transportation costs for simplicity). To implement this comparison, Walmart makes the yuan and dollar prices comparable by using the nominal exchange rate. For example, on January 27, 2017, the yuan-per-dollar exchange rate was 6.88, so the dollar price of the Chinese-manufactured toy was

$$\text{Dollar cost} = \text{Yuan cost} \times \frac{\text{Dollars}}{\text{Yuan}}$$

$$= \text{Yuan cost} \times \frac{1}{e}$$

$$= 20 \times \frac{1}{6.88}$$

$$= \$2.91.$$

As you can see, the dollar price of the Chinese-manufactured toy is just under $3, which is less than the $5 price of the U.S.-manufactured toy, so it is less expensive to purchase the toy from the Chinese manufacturer.

Flexible, Managed, and Fixed Exchange Rates

Exhibit 15.2 shows historical movements in two nominal exchange rates: yuan-per-dollar and euro-per-dollar. Both nominal exchange rates vary over time.

However, the yuan-per-dollar exchange rate has had long periods in which it hasn't moved at all. For example, the yuan-per-dollar exchange rate was constant—8.28 yuan per dollar—from late 1998 to 2005. Likewise, the yuan-per-dollar exchange rate was nearly constant at 6.82 yuan per dollar between mid-2008 and mid-2010. There have also been some periods when the yuan-per-dollar exchange rate has suddenly jumped in value and other periods when it has been allowed to slowly drift in one direction. For example, from 2005 to mid-2008, the dollar slowly and persistently depreciated against the yuan (so that the yuan-per-dollar exchange rate fell). In contrast, from 2014 to the present, the dollar tended to appreciate against the yuan (so that the yuan-per-dollar exchange rate rose).

The movements in the euro-per-dollar exchange rate don't have the same properties as those in the yuan-per-dollar exchange rate. Most importantly, the euro-per-dollar exchange rate is never completely flat. In addition, the euro-per-dollar exchange rate neither jumps the way the yuan-per-dollar exchange rate did in 2005 nor drifts smoothly in the same direction for years at a time, as the yuan-per-dollar exchange rate did from 2005 to 2008.

These differences arise because the euro-per-dollar exchange rate is determined with little or no government intervention. Each day the euro-per-dollar exchange rate moves up and down as market forces change. This is referred to as a **flexible exchange rate**, or a **floating exchange rate**.

> If the government does not intervene in the foreign exchange market, then the country has a **flexible exchange rate,** which is also referred to as a **floating exchange rate.**

Exhibit 15.2 Yuan-per-Dollar and Euro-per-Dollar Exchange Rates (1999–January 2017)

The yuan-per-dollar exchange rate is managed by the Chinese government, so it is either held fixed or allowed to change in a controlled manner. In contrast, the euro-per-dollar exchange rate floats freely, so its path is set by market forces that fluctuate from day to day.

Source: Federal Reserve Bank of St. Louis.

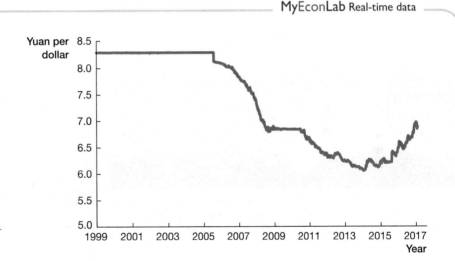

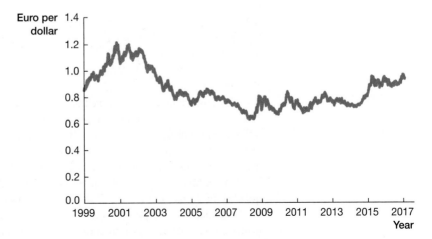

If the government fixes a value for the exchange rate and intervenes to maintain that value, then the country has a **fixed exchange rate**.

If the government intervenes actively to influence the exchange rate, then the country has a **managed exchange rate**.

At the other extreme, a government could fix a value for the exchange rate and intervene to permanently maintain that value. In this case, the country has a **fixed exchange rate**.

There is also a middle case. The yuan-per-dollar exchange rate is not flexible or (permanently) fixed but is instead a **managed exchange rate**: the Chinese government influences its movement. Managed exchange rates can be flat for long periods, but they aren't flat forever. When they do change, those movements tend to be either gentle slow drifts in one direction, or sometimes sharp jumps. For example, the Chinese government allowed the dollar to jump down in value during the summer of 2005 and then slowly depreciate against the yuan from 2005 to 2008. In contrast, since 2014, the Chinese government has allowed the dollar to appreciate against the yuan.

We explain why a country might adopt a managed or a fixed exchange rate later in the chapter. For now, we note only that there are many reasons, among them the belief that managed or fixed exchange rates provide more economic stability domestically and might facilitate international trade.

15.2 The Foreign Exchange Market

The **foreign exchange market** is the global financial market in which currencies are traded and nominal exchange rates are determined.

The **foreign exchange market** is the global financial market in which currencies are traded and nominal exchange rates are determined. To illustrate the role of this market, suppose Air China would like to add five Boeing Dreamliners, each costing $200 million, to its aircraft fleet. To do this, it needs to pay the Boeing Company in dollars. So Air China will go to the foreign exchange market to buy (demand) a total of $1 billion (= 5 × $200 million), offering yuan in return. Because the yuan-per-dollar exchange rate is $e = 6.88$, this means Air China will be paying 6.88 billion yuan in exchange for 1 billion dollars.

As with other markets, the supply and demand curves determine the equilibrium price, which is the equilibrium exchange rate in the foreign exchange market. Exhibit 15.3 illustrates the supply and demand curves in the foreign exchange market. The x-axis represents the quantity of dollars available for transactions in the foreign exchange market. We use the yuan-per-dollar exchange rate on the y-axis to represent the value or "price" of a dollar: how many yuan a dollar will buy. Recall that we are expressing the nominal exchange rate as units of foreign currency per U.S. dollar.

Boeing's Dreamliner costs $200 million per plane. If a Chinese airline tries to buy one, it will need to exchange (e × $200 million) on the foreign exchange market to obtain $200 million. At an exchange rate of $e = 6.88$ yuan per dollar, that amounts to 1.38 billion yuan.

In panel (a) of Exhibit 15.3, the dollar demand curve represents the relationship between the quantity of dollars demanded and the exchange rate. The demand curve represents traders who are trying to buy dollars in the foreign exchange market with yuan. So, Air China's demand for dollars is reflected in this demand curve. Of course, millions of other economic agents will also be trying to obtain dollars by selling yuan. The actions of all these agents make up the dollar demand curve.

To understand why the demand curve for dollars in exchange for yuan is downward-sloping, consider an *appreciation* of the dollar—in other words, a *depreciation* of the yuan. A dollar appreciation would move the exchange rate from *A* to *B* in panel (a) of Exhibit 15.3. The dollar appreciation implies that each dollar buys more yuan, that each yuan buys fewer dollars, and that the price of each Boeing aircraft is now greater in yuan. The Chinese airline's revenues are paid (largely) in yuan, so the relevant price for Air China is the price of the Boeing Dreamliner in yuan. The higher yuan-denominated price for the Dreamliner leads Air China to reduce the quantity of Dreamliners demanded. This implies that the quantity of dollars demanded will fall—with fewer aircraft demanded, fewer dollars will be demanded. We've just shown how an appreciation of the dollar leads to a reduction in the quantity of dollars demanded. Examples like this imply that the demand curve is downward-sloping, as shown in the exhibit.

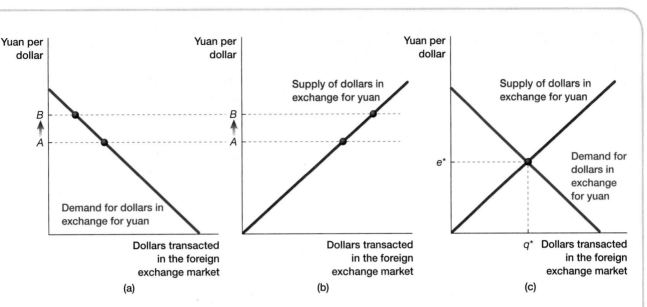

Exhibit 15.3 The Foreign Exchange Market under a Flexible Exchange Rate Regime

The demand for dollars in exchange for yuan in panel (a) is downward-sloping, because a dollar appreciation (a movement from A to B) increases the price of U.S. goods faced by Chinese firms and consumers, reducing the quantity of goods they demand and thereby reducing the quantity of dollars they demand. The supply of dollars in exchange for yuan in panel (b) is upward-sloping, because a dollar appreciation (a movement from A to B) increases the quantity of goods purchased by U.S. buyers from Chinese producers, thus raising the dollar earnings of Chinese producers and the quantity of dollars that they supply to the foreign exchange market. The intersection of the demand and supply curves in panel (c) gives the equilibrium exchange rate, e^*, in a flexible exchange rate regime.

The dollar supply curve, shown in panel (b) of Exhibit 15.3, represents the relationship between the quantity of dollars supplied and the exchange rate. The transactions of traders who are trying to obtain yuan by selling dollars are represented by this dollar supply curve. For example, Chinese manufacturers that export their products are often paid in dollars, and they need to exchange these dollars into yuan so they can pay their workers and suppliers. The transactions of the millions of households and firms supplying dollars in exchange for yuan make up the dollar supply curve.

The reason that the supply curve (for dollars in exchange for yuan) slopes up is related to the reason that the demand curve (for dollars in exchange for yuan) slopes down. When the dollar appreciates (yuan depreciates) and we move from exchange rate A to exchange rate B, each dollar buys more yuan. This implies that the prices of all Chinese products, such as the toys produced by Chinese manufacturers, become less expensive in U.S. dollars—recall that when we draw supply (or demand) curves, we are holding constant all other prices, such as the yuan-denominated price of toys manufactured in China. Because an appreciation of the dollar enables U.S. consumers to pay fewer dollars for each good they import from China, U.S. consumers and companies increase their purchases of Chinese goods. This implies greater dollar revenues for Chinese firms, and thus a greater quantity of dollars supplied by them to the foreign exchange market. To sum up, a rising yuan-per-dollar exchange rate leads to a greater quantity of dollars supplied, so the supply curve is upward-sloping.

The equilibrium exchange rate under a flexible exchange rate regime is given by the foreign exchange equilibrium, which corresponds to the exchange rate that equates the quantity supplied and the quantity demanded. This intersection of the supply and demand curves is shown in panel (c) of Exhibit 15.3 at quantity q^* and price (yuan per dollar) e^*. As already noted, the yuan-per-dollar exchange rate is not flexible but managed, so panel (c) shows

Exhibit 15.4 The Foreign Exchange Market After a Rightward Shift in the Dollar Demand Curve

Increased demand for Boeing aircraft from Air China causes a rightward shift of the demand for dollars in exchange for yuan. This raises the equilibrium nominal exchange rate from e^* to e^{**}.

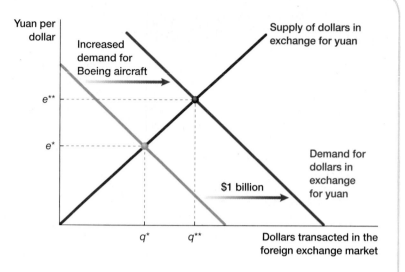

what the yuan-per-dollar exchange rate would be if there were no Chinese government intervention. In fact, the Chinese government has been slowly reducing the scope of its foreign exchange market interventions, leading the yuan-per-dollar market to move closer to the situation that would arise under a flexible exchange rate regime like that shown in panel (c).

What would happen to the equilibrium exchange rate if Air China unexpectedly faced a higher demand for air travel in China? Air China would need more aircraft. For example, its demand curve for aircraft would shift so that, at unchanged prices, it would now demand ten Dreamliners instead of five. In this case, again keeping prices including the exchange rate fixed, Air China's demand for dollars would increase by $5 \times \$200$ million $= \$1$ billion. In terms of Exhibit 15.3, this corresponds to a $1 billion rightward shift of the dollar demand curve, as illustrated in Exhibit 15.4.

Under a flexible exchange rate, the rightward shift in the dollar demand curve causes the equilibrium yuan-per-dollar exchange rate to increase, implying that a dollar will now buy more yuan. Using the terminology introduced earlier, we can see that, with flexible exchange rates, in response to the increased demand for Boeing aircraft, the dollar would appreciate against the yuan (or equivalently, the yuan would depreciate against the dollar).

How Do Governments Intervene in the Foreign Exchange Market?

How does equilibrium work when an exchange rate is not flexible? If a government attempts to control the value of its exchange rate through a managed or fixed exchange rate system, we say that the exchange rate is being "pegged" by the government.

Though this may no longer be the case, Chinese authorities have historically chosen an exchange rate that makes the yuan substantially *undervalued* relative to the dollar. By implication, the dollar is then somewhat *overvalued* relative to the yuan. Exhibit 15.5 illustrates the yuan-per-dollar foreign exchange market and reveals what it means for the yuan to be undervalued and the dollar to be overvalued. The exchange rate is pegged at the level shown by the solid purple line. The dollar is overvalued because the dollar is worth more yuan than it would have been under a flexible exchange rate regime. The flexible equilibrium is still represented by e^*. The pegged exchange rate is above the market-clearing price at the intersection of the supply and demand curves.

At the exchange rate corresponding to the peg, the quantity supplied exceeds the quantity demanded. If the Chinese authorities simply announce the peg and do nothing else, the forces of supply and demand will lower the yuan-per-dollar exchange rate below the peg. Recall that the supply curve represents the quantity of dollars supplied to the yuan-per-dollar foreign exchange market at a particular yuan-per-dollar exchange rate. If that quantity supplied exceeds the quantity demanded at a particular yuan-per-dollar exchange rate, there will be an excess supply of dollars, which will drive down the price of dollars. In

Exhibit 15.5 The Foreign Exchange Market under a Pegged Exchange Rate That Overvalues the Dollar Relative to the Yuan

To support an overvalued dollar (or equivalently an undervalued yuan), the Chinese government would need to soak up the excess supply of dollars by buying dollars in exchange for yuan. The quantity of dollars that must be purchased is given by the difference between the quantity of dollars supplied and the quantity of dollars demanded at the pegged exchange rate.

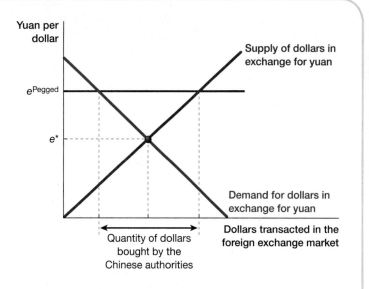

other words, the price of dollars—the exchange rate—will fall, so the dollar will depreciate against the yuan. This process will lower the yuan-per-dollar exchange rate from the peg toward the market-clearing price at the intersection of the supply and demand curves.

This analysis shows that simply announcing a target exchange rate will have little or no effect on the exchange rate that will prevail in the foreign exchange market. Because the quantity of dollars supplied exceeds the quantity of dollars demanded at the pegged yuan-per-dollar exchange rate, Chinese authorities would need to soak up this excess supply by buying dollars and selling yuan. Exhibit 15.5 shows that to maintain the peg above the market-clearing exchange rate—in other words, to keep the dollar overvalued—Chinese authorities would have to continuously purchase dollars and sell yuan.

> Simply announcing a target exchange rate will have little or no effect on the exchange rate that will prevail in the foreign exchange market.

In fact, this is exactly what they did. Between 1990 and 2014, the Chinese central bank increased its holdings of foreign reserves from about $30 billion to $4 trillion. Most of these reserves are in dollars, but the Chinese central bank has bought other currencies as well. The analysis in Exhibit 15.5 shows why dollar purchases were necessary, given the fact that the yuan has been pegged to the dollar at exchange rates that overvalued the dollar and therefore undervalued the yuan.

In the Letting the Data Speak feature on the Chinese exchange rate policy on page 375 we explain in detail why the Chinese government went to all this trouble: an overvalued dollar (undervalued yuan) increases the net exports of China. We also discuss there what happened after 2014, when the Chinese government ended this policy and allowed the yuan-per-dollar exchange rate to move closer to the market-clearing value of e^*.

Defending an Overvalued Exchange Rate

Exhibit 15.5 makes it look easy to defend a fixed exchange rate. The Chinese authorities bought dollars, building up their dollar reserves. In exchange, the Chinese authorities supplied yuan. This was simple to achieve because a country with a national currency, like the Chinese yuan, has the right to print or electronically create as many units of that currency as it wants. So, at least in the short run, defending an undervalued yuan appears feasible. However, it is not as easy to defend an exchange rate when your currency is overvalued.

In many cases, countries try to peg their exchange rate at a level that overvalues their own currency. To see why a country might do so, let's consider the example of Mexico and analyze the peso-dollar exchange rate, with the convention that the exchange rate is measured in pesos per dollar. Why would the Mexican government want the peso to be overvalued and the dollar to be undervalued?

Most countries regularly borrow from foreign lenders. In developing countries like Mexico, these loans are typically denominated in dollars. So the Mexican borrowers receive dollars when they take out their loans and pay back dollars, not pesos, at the end of the loan period. To work through a numerical example, imagine that Mexican borrowers, including the Mexican government and Mexican companies, owe $1 billion to U.S. banks. If the peso-per-dollar exchange rate is 20, meaning that 20 pesos purchase 1 dollar, then Mexican borrowers need 20 billion pesos to pay back their dollar-denominated debts.

Now suppose that at the exchange rate of 20 pesos per dollar, the dollar is undervalued and that its market-clearing price under a flexible exchange rate regime would be 30 pesos per dollar instead. What would happen if the Mexican government allowed the undervalued dollar to appreciate (which is equivalent to allowing the overvalued peso to depreciate)? This situation would have several implications, one of which is that Mexican borrowers would now need to give up 30 billion pesos instead of just 20 billion pesos to pay back their debts of $1 billion. Allowing the dollar to appreciate, and hence the peso to depreciate, has suddenly increased the number of pesos that are needed to pay back the dollar-denominated debts of Mexican borrowers.

Having an overvalued peso also has other benefits for Mexico. An undervalued dollar—hence, an overvalued peso—lowers the cost that Mexican consumers pay in pesos to import goods from the United States. Consequently, the Mexican government can keep prices and inflation low by keeping the dollar undervalued and the peso overvalued. For example, suppose that an iPhone costs $400 to import into Mexico. If the Mexican exchange rate is 10 pesos per dollar, then the local cost will be 4,000 pesos. This is a lower iPhone price (in pesos) than if the peso-dollar exchange rate rises to 20 pesos per dollar. In that case, the local cost of the iPhone doubles to 8,000 pesos. Price increases like this raise the overall inflation rate in Mexico.

Another reason that countries maintain an overvalued exchange rate is because a fall in the value of a currency is often perceived as a failure of government policies. A currency that is depreciating (sometimes confusingly called a "weak currency") is at times perceived to be a sign of a weak government or a weak country. This perception can be a problem for incumbent politicians in democratic countries. For this reason, officials at the U.S. Treasury Department have historically repeated the mantra that they support a "strong dollar policy." The American public doesn't like to hear politicians associate anything "weak" with the United States, including its currency. However, as we have learned, a "weak" currency is exactly what the non-democratic Chinese government pursued until recently.

Whatever their motivations, many governments have intervened in the foreign exchange market to maintain an overvalued national currency. But overvaluation is also costly, as discussed below. In addition, overvalued currencies are much harder to defend than undervalued ones. Exhibit 15.6 plots the situation for an overvalued peso, which implies an undervalued dollar. Exhibit 15.6 is very similar to Exhibit 15.5, except that the solid purple line corresponding to the peg value is now *below* the market-clearing price, e^*, at the intersection of

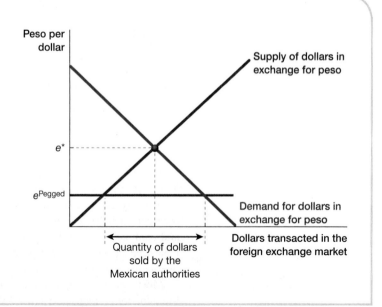

Exhibit 15.6 The Foreign Exchange Market under a Pegged Exchange Rate That Undervalues the Dollar Relative to the Peso

To maintain an undervalued dollar, which is the same thing as an overvalued peso, the Mexican government needs to supply dollars to purchase pesos. The quantity of dollars that must be supplied is given by the difference between the quantity of dollars demanded and the quantity of dollars supplied at the pegged exchange rate.

the supply and demand curves (again marked with the dotted line in the exhibit). Thus the peso-per-dollar exchange rate is below what it would have been under a flexible exchange rate regime, and in particular, the dollar is worth fewer pesos than it would be at the market-clearing price. Hence, the dollar is undervalued and the peso is overvalued.

Exhibit 15.6 illustrates how the Mexican authorities would in principle defend an overvalued peso (and thus keep the dollar undervalued). This exhibit differs from Exhibit 15.5, where the quantity of dollars supplied exceeded the quantity of dollars demanded. In Exhibit 15.6, the quantity of dollars supplied falls short of the quantity of dollars demanded. To maintain the peso-per-dollar exchange rate at the value corresponding to the peg, the Mexican authorities have to sell dollars and purchase pesos. The Mexican authorities can certainly do this if they have substantial dollar reserves. But how long can they keep up this policy?

In the situation depicted in Exhibit 15.5, the Chinese authorities can print or electronically create as many yuan as they want, so they could perpetually supply yuan to buy dollars if they wished. Likewise, Mexican authorities can create as many *pesos* as they want, but sustaining an *overvalued* peso relative to the dollar does not rely on the creation of more pesos. Instead, the Mexican authorities would need to keep selling dollars to sustain an overvalued peso. Because they can't create new dollars, the Mexican authorities have to use their pre-existing dollar reserves, which are limited. If the quantity of dollars they need to supply exceeds their reserves, they won't be able to sustain an overvalued peso. At the moment it becomes clear that their dollar reserves are going to run out, defending the overvalued peso becomes impossible. Whatever their public announcements, the Mexican authorities will then have to give up the peg and allow the peso to depreciate and the dollar to appreciate, which implies that the number of pesos per dollar will rise.

This discussion highlights the observation that overvalued exchange rates can be defended for a while—as long as the dollar reserves of the country defending the exchange

---

CHOICE — & CONSEQUENCE

Fixed Exchange Rates and Corruption

Some developing countries with fixed exchange rates announce an official exchange rate that overvalues their local currency and then ration who gets the privilege of exchanging the local currency for dollars at the overvalued exchange rate. In particular, the situation has some similarities to Exhibit 15.6, which depicts an undervalued dollar and, by implication, an overvalued foreign currency. As in Exhibit 15.6, at the official pegged exchange rate, the supply of dollars falls short of the demand for dollars, but, with rationing, some of the demand for dollars will not be met by the government. The government will pick and choose who gets to sell the local currency at the price that undervalues dollars and overvalues the local currency. In cases like this, a *black market*—the name for the underground market, in this case for dollars—comes into existence. A black market is part of the broader underground economy, which includes all transactions that are hidden from the government. The exchange rate on the black market, which is determined by supply and demand, will be less favorable to sellers of local currency than the official pegged exchange rate.

For instance, in Venezuela in November 2016, the official "Dipro" exchange rate was 10 bolivares per dollar, but the black market exchange rate was more than 1,500 bolivares to the dollar.[1] Hence, a Venezuelan who wanted to sell 1,000 bolivares in exchange for dollars

would get 1,000/10 = $100 at the official exchange rate, but only 1,000/1,500 = $0.67 at the black market exchange rate. As you can see, in this case everybody with bolivares would have liked to purchase dollars at the more advantageous official rate. But the Venezuelan government did not allow this and simply refused to sell dollars at the official exchange rate to all Venezuelans who asked to buy dollars with bolivares. Those who were denied dollars had to either make do without the dollars or pay the much higher price for dollars on the black market—in this case the black market rate was more than 150 times as high.

To further complicate matters, some people who receive dollars at the official exchange rate are likely to turn around and sell them at the much higher black market rate. Such black market sales are illegal, but in most cases the black market transactions are prosecuted only if they are conducted by political enemies of the government. Can you see who benefits from the system?

Not surprisingly, many governments maintain overvalued exchange rates as a way of rewarding friends, cronies, and themselves. They can benefit directly from having access to the official and artificially cheap dollars. The system ultimately collapses, however, because it is inefficient. But while it lasts, politicians and their buddies make billions in profits.

> Market pressure often pushes prices in financial markets, including exchange rates, back to their market-clearing levels, no matter what governments try to do.

rate last. But this scenario cannot continue indefinitely. If the peso-per-dollar exchange rate is too low relative to what supply and demand dictate—meaning that the dollar is undervalued and the peso is overvalued—there will continue to be an excess demand for dollars, and this excess demand will keep draining the dollar reserves of the Mexican authorities who are trying to defend the overvalued peso.

Market pressure often pushes prices in financial markets, including exchange rates, back to their market-clearing levels, no matter what governments try to do. In some cases, this pressure works gradually. In other cases, like the example discussed in our Evidence-Based Economics feature, the pressure ends up generating explosive fallout.

EVIDENCE-BASED ECONOMICS

Q: How did George Soros make $1 billion?

From 1990 to 1992, the British pound had an exchange rate that was pegged against the German mark, the currency that Germany used before its present currency, the euro. The mark-pound exchange rate was initially pegged at a value that required little government intervention. However, in 1992, changing market forces put pressure on the British pound to depreciate. During the summer of 1992, the British authorities spent about $24 billion of foreign currency reserves to defend the pegged value of the pound. The British authorities were running low on foreign currency reserves when a new wave of pound sales hit the market on September 16, 1992. At the end of that day, the British authorities gave up trying to prop up the currency and accepted a sharp depreciation, as shown in Exhibit 15.7. This day came to be known as Black Wednesday.

Exhibit 15.7 The Mark-per-Pound Exchange Rate (January 1991–December 1992)

Changes in economic conditions during 1992 implied that the British pound had become overvalued. British authorities spent their foreign currency reserves trying to defend their overvalued currency, leading to a sharp decline in their reserves in August and especially in early September 1992. On September 16, they gave up on their attempts to prop up the British pound, allowing a sharp depreciation.

Source: Federal Reserve Board of Governors.

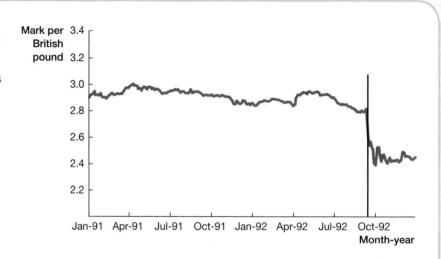

Journalists referred to George Soros as "the man who broke the Bank of England." He had bet against the pound earlier in 1992 and made $1 billion when the pound subsequently fell in value.

The events leading up to Black Wednesday yielded winners and losers. The winners were the currency traders, especially George Soros. He had bet against the pound by borrowing about $10 billion worth of pounds and then using those pounds to purchase German marks. Following Black Wednesday, the German mark became more valuable relative to the pound and, consequently, the $10 billion of pound-denominated debts that Soros owed were cheaper to pay off with appreciated marks. Soros is believed to have made more than $1 billion in profits on these transactions. These trading profits benefited Soros and the investors in his hedge fund.

In making these investments, Soros was employing basic economic reasoning. He understood that the British government was running out of foreign currency reserves, like German marks, in the summer of 1992. Soros was able to generate billions of dollars of additional sales of the British government's foreign currency reserves—Soros used pounds to buy $10 billion worth of marks on the foreign exchange market—which helped force the British authorities' hand. Soros's pound sales and mark purchases accelerated the pace of the British government's reserve losses, convincing the government that it couldn't resist the tide of pound selling.

The losers from Black Wednesday included the British government, which suffered enormous losses because it spent billions of dollars of foreign currency reserves to prop up the pound. By selling foreign currency reserves that would subsequently appreciate against the pound, the British government ended up with trading losses of approximately $6 billion worth of pounds.

Question	**Answer**	**Data**	**Caveat**
How did George Soros make $1 billion?	George Soros bet against an overvalued British pound just before the pound depreciated. Soros borrowed pounds and then used those pounds to buy German marks. On September 16, 1992, a day that came to be known as Black Wednesday, the British authorities succumbed to market pressure and devalued the pound. At that moment, Soros's investments in German marks became more valuable than his pound-denominated debts. Soros was able to forecast the pound's depreciation because British foreign currency reserves were rapidly running down during the summer of 1992.	Exchange rate and reserves data.	George Soros and other speculators have made many bets against currencies they thought were overvalued, but these bets have not all been profitable, because authorities can sometimes successfully defend overvalued exchange rates.

15.3 The Real Exchange Rate and Exports

So far we've focused on the nominal exchange rate. That's the exchange rate that you read about in the newspaper each day and is also the exchange rate that equates quantity supplied and quantity demanded in the foreign exchange market. However, it is a different exchange rate—the so-called *real* exchange rate—that is actually crucial for the macroeconomy and for trade. We now define the concept of the real exchange rate and explain why it plays such an important role in influencing trade flows.

From the Nominal to the Real Exchange Rate

As we have seen, for its sourcing decisions, Walmart compares the costs of domestic manufacturers and foreign manufacturers, adjusting for the exchange rate. For example, holding quality fixed, Walmart compares the implied dollar price of the toy manufactured in China to the dollar price of a similar toy manufactured in the United States. In essence, Walmart is interested in the following ratio:

$$\frac{\text{Dollar price of U.S. toy}}{\text{Dollar price of Chinese toy}}.$$

If this ratio is greater than 1, U.S. toys are more expensive than Chinese toys and Walmart buys from the Chinese supplier. However, if this ratio is less than 1, a U.S. toy is less expensive than a Chinese toy and Walmart buys from the U.S. supplier.

This ratio incorporates two different kinds of information: the prices of the toys in their respective domestic currencies and the yuan-per-dollar exchange rate that enables Walmart to convert yuan prices to dollar prices. The numerator is the price that U.S. suppliers quote Walmart. If the U.S. manufacturer will supply toys to Walmart at $5 per toy, then $5 is the numerator.

To calculate the dollar price of the Chinese toy, we need to take the Chinese price (in yuan) and multiply it by the number of dollars per yuan. Recall that e is the yuan-per-dollar nominal exchange rate. The number of dollars per yuan is given by $1/e$. Thus the dollar price of Chinese toys can be calculated as

$$\text{Dollar price of Chinese toy} = (\text{Yuan price of Chinese toy}) \times \frac{\text{Dollars}}{\text{Yuan}}$$

$$= (\text{Yuan price of Chinese toy}) \times \frac{1}{e}.$$

For example, if a Chinese toy has a price of 20 yuan and the nominal exchange rate is 6.88 yuan per dollar, then the dollar price of the Chinese toy is

$$20 \times \frac{1}{6.88} = \frac{20}{6.88} = \$2.91.$$

Let's put these pieces together. We can now rewrite our initial ratio this way:

$$\frac{\text{Dollar price of U.S. toy}}{\text{Dollar price of Chinese toy}} = \frac{\text{Dollar price of U.S.toy}}{(\text{Yuan price of Chinese toy}) \times \frac{1}{e}}$$

$$= \frac{(\text{Dollar price of U.S. toy}) \times e}{\text{Yuan price of Chinese toy}}.$$

The **real exchange rate** is defined as the ratio of the dollar price of a basket of goods and services in the United States, divided by the dollar price of the same basket of goods and services in a foreign country.

This ratio represents the relative price, adjusted for the exchange rate, of U.S. and Chinese toys. All companies make these calculations when sourcing their products.

Because this ratio is at the heart of every firm's sourcing decisions, economists have developed a special name for it. We define this ratio for a general basket of goods and services and refer to it as the *real exchange rate*. The **real exchange rate** for the United States is defined as the ratio of the dollar price of a basket of goods and services in the United States divided by the *dollar* price of the *same* basket of goods and services in a foreign country, for instance, China. Echoing the previous derivation for the toy example, the overall real exchange rate for the United States and China is written as

$$\frac{\text{Dollar price of U.S. basket}}{\text{Dollar price of Chinese basket}} = \frac{(\text{Dollar price of U.S. basket}) \times e}{\text{Yuan price of Chinese basket}}.$$

The term "Dollar price of a U.S. basket" refers to the price of a basket of goods and services in the United States. The "Yuan price of a Chinese basket" is the price of the *same* basket in China. By using the nominal exchange rate, we make the U.S. basket (priced in dollars) and the Chinese basket (priced in yuan) comparable.

Co-Movement Between the Nominal and the Real Exchange Rates

The preceding equation makes it clear that the real exchange rate depends partially on the nominal exchange rate and partially on the ratio of U.S. prices and Chinese prices. If U.S. and Chinese prices don't respond to a change in the nominal exchange rate, then the real exchange rate should move proportionally with the nominal exchange rate. This is indeed the case in the short run but not necessarily in the long run.

Let's first consider the short-run consequences of a change in the nominal exchange rate. Exhibit 15.8 plots both the nominal exchange rate between British pounds and U.S. dollars (pounds per dollar, normalized to 100 in 1950, in blue) and the real exchange rate between the two currencies (dollar prices in the United States divided by dollar prices in the United Kingdom,

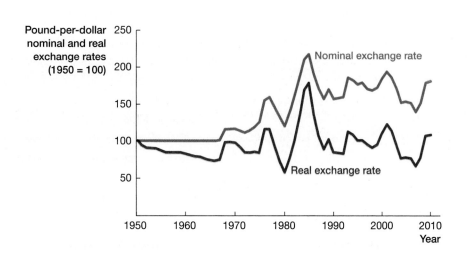

Exhibit 15.8 The Nominal and the Real Pound-per-Dollar Exchange Rates (1950–2010)

Shown are the nominal exchange rate between British pounds and U.S. dollars (pounds per dollar, in blue) and the real exchange rate between the two currencies (dollar prices in the United States divided by *dollar* prices in the United Kingdom, in red). The pound and the dollar were pegged until 1966, so the nominal exchange rate was constant from 1950 to 1966. However, the real exchange rate fell from 1950 to 1966, because prices were rising more slowly in the United States than they were in the United Kingdom. After 1967, the nominal and the real exchange rates seem to move up and down together: when the nominal pound-per-dollar exchange rate rises so that the dollar appreciates, so does the real pound-per-dollar exchange rate. Over the entire period, the real exchange rate keeps falling further behind the nominal exchange rate, because the UK inflation rate has been slightly greater on average than the U.S. inflation rate. Note that both exchange rates are normalized to equal 100 in 1950 (every observation is divided by the value of the same series in 1950 and the result is multiplied by 100).

Source: Alan Heston, Robert Summers, and Bettina Aten, Penn World Table Version 7.1, Center for International Comparisons of Production, Income and Prices at the University of Pennsylvania, July 2012.

> In most circumstances the nominal and real exchange rates appreciate and depreciate together.

also normalized to 100 in 1950, in red). The exhibit reveals that, in the short run, the nominal pound-per-dollar exchange rate moves almost in lock-step with the real exchange rate. In other words, in most circumstances the nominal and real exchange rates appreciate and depreciate together.

However, the exhibit also shows that some movements in the real exchange rate are not associated with changes in the nominal exchange rate. This is easiest to see from 1950 to 1966, when the nominal exchange rate was pegged between the two countries. With the nominal exchange rate temporarily *fixed*, movements in the real exchange rate derive solely from different amounts of inflation in the United States and the United Kingdom. Note that the real exchange rate is the U.S. price index multiplied by the pound-per-dollar nominal exchange rate, all divided by the UK price index. From 1950 to 1966, U.S. inflation was lower than UK inflation, causing the ratio of U.S. prices to UK prices to fall. With a fixed nominal exchange rate, a lower inflation rate in the United States relative to the United Kingdom implies that the real exchange rate fell from 1950 to 1966.

Movements in the real exchange rate arising from differences in the U.S. and UK infla-tion rates have also occurred after 1966 (when the two currencies started floating against each other), but these inflation effects are easy to miss when you look at the exhibit. For floating currencies with modest levels of inflation, most of the year-to-year movement in the real exchange rate derives from movement in the nominal exchange rate and not from cross-country differences in the rate of inflation.

The Real Exchange Rate and Net Exports

The real exchange rate is the key determinant of whether Walmart is stocking its U.S. store shelves with U.S. or Chinese products and whether Shanghai Bailian—a Chinese big-box retailer like Walmart—is stocking its shelves (in China) with U.S. or Chinese products. When the yuan-per-dollar real exchange rate appreciates, U.S. goods become more expen-sive relative to Chinese goods, so more stores in the United States prefer to import from China and more stores in China, like Shanghai Bailian, prefer to buy local products rather than to import from the United States. Exhibit 15.9 summarizes these optimizing decisions.

Exhibit 15.9 The Relationship Between the Real Exchange Rate and Trade Flows

Yuan-per-Dollar Real Exchange Rate	China	United States
Goes up (dollar appreciates and the yuan depreciates)	Import less from United States	Export less to China
	Export more to United States	Import more from China
Goes down (dollar depreciates and the yuan appreciates)	Import more from United States	Export more to China
	Export less to United States	Import less from China

Exhibit 15.10 The Real Exchange Rate (E) and Net Exports

When its real exchange rate appreciates, a country imports more from other countries and exports less to other countries, reducing its net exports. This relationship is shown by the downward-sloping net exports curve, denoted by $NX(E)$. For instance, when the real exchange rate rises from E^* to E_1, net exports fall from 0 to $NX_1 < 0$. Conversely, when the real exchange rate falls from E^* to E_2, net exports rise from 0 to $NX_2 > 0$.

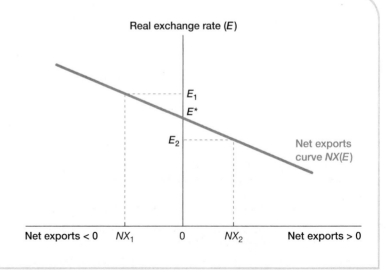

Now recall that net exports are defined as exports minus imports:

$$\text{Net exports} = \text{Exports} - \text{Imports}.$$

Exhibit 15.10 plots the *net exports curve*, denoted by $NX(E)$, which shows the relationship between net exports and the real exchange rate, denoted as E. This relationship is downward-sloping, because when the yuan-per-dollar real exchange rate appreciates (implying a higher value of E), U.S. exports to China tend to fall and U.S. imports from China tend to increase.

LETTING THE
DATA SPEAK

Why Did the Chinese Authorities Keep the Yuan Undervalued?

Our discussion of the yuan-per-dollar nominal exchange rate, which is illustrated in Exhibit 15.5, implies that the yuan was historically undervalued (and the dollar was accordingly historically overvalued). To hold down the value of the yuan (and thereby prop up the value of the dollar), the Chinese authorities sold yuan and purchased dollars (about $4 trillion).

Why would the Chinese authorities try to keep the dollar overvalued? Exhibit 15.10 provides the answer: an overvalued real dollar exchange rate implies greater net exports from China to the United States. Chinese authorities supported an overvalued dollar to boost Chinese exports. A consequence of the overvalued yuan-per-dollar real exchange rate—an exchange rate above the equivalent of E^* in Exhibit 15.10—is the large trade deficit that the United States runs with China. Exhibit 15.11 shows that this trade deficit has exceeded $300 billion. Export growth has been a key pillar of China's growth strategy since the 1980s.

This strategy might boost the rate of Chinese growth, but it does come with costs to China, not to mention the rest of the world. An undervalued Chinese yuan hurts Chinese workers by lowering their buying power because it makes their imports from the rest of the world more expensive. In addition, an undervalued Chinese yuan creates diplomatic problems with China's trading partners. Higher Chinese exports to the United States distort economic activity in the United States by crowding out industries that compete with Chinese manufacturers. This situation creates considerable friction between the United States and China.

These considerations have led the Chinese authorities to abandon their weak yuan policy. In recent years, most analysts, including the International Monetary Fund, have concluded that China is no longer undervaluing its currency by selling yuan and buying dollars. Indeed, we can see this by looking at China's foreign exchange reserves. These reserves peaked in 2014 at almost $4 trillion. If China had kept forcing down the value of the yuan, these foreign exchange reserves would have kept growing. Instead they have fallen from $4 trillion to $3 trillion as of early 2017.

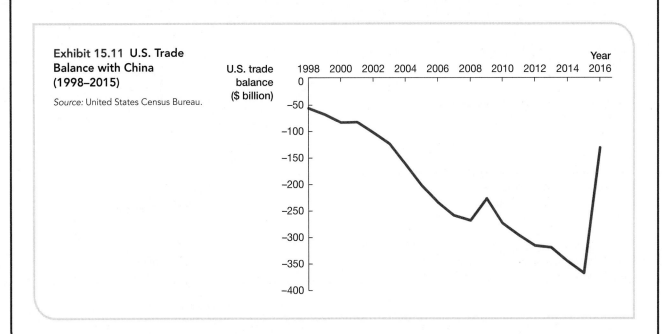

Exhibit 15.11 U.S. Trade Balance with China (1998–2015)

Source: United States Census Bureau.

Notice also that there is a particular value of the real exchange rate, marked as E^* in Exhibit 15.10, at which net exports are equal to zero. When the real exchange rate is above E^*, net exports are negative (a trade deficit), and when the real exchange rate is below E^*, net exports are positive (a trade surplus). The real exchange rate usually can't stay very far above E^*, because large permanent trade deficits tend to be unsustainable. A large permanent trade deficit leads to an ever-rising debt to foreign countries. At some point, foreign countries will get nervous that this debt won't be repaid. When that happens, they will start selling their U.S. assets, driving down the nominal dollar exchange rate, which causes E to fall toward E^*.

15.4 GDP in the Open Economy

We now analyze the macroeconomic implications of changes in the real exchange rate. Let's focus on an appreciation of the real exchange rate. To understand the consequences of this change, let's return to the national income accounting identity, which was introduced in Chapter 5:

$$Y = C + I + G + X - M.$$

Here Y represents GDP, C represents consumption, I represents investment (in plants, equipment, and residential construction), G represents government expenditure, and $X - M$ represents net exports (all for the U.S. economy).

The appreciation of the real exchange rate reduces net exports and causes a decline in GDP—holding all else equal, a decline in $X - M$ on the right-hand side of the national income accounting identity reduces Y or GDP. We can trace out these macroeconomic implications using the labor supply and labor demand diagram introduced in Chapter 9 and used for the analysis of macroeconomic fluctuations in Chapters 12 and 13. Exhibit 15.12 presents the model with downward wage rigidity.

To illustrate how GDP responds to the changes in net exports, suppose that the dollar appreciates and net exports decline. In particular, suppose the foreign demand for certain U.S. products—let's say machine tools—declines because the appreciation of the dollar has made these goods more expensive for foreigners. This decline in demand for machine tools implies that machine-tool producers will shift their labor demand to the left.

Exhibit 15.12 Employment Falls When the Real Exchange Rate Appreciates

A rise in the real exchange rate, E, produces a decline in net exports (such as the move from trade balance to NX_1 in Exhibit 15.10), which reduces the demand for the goods and services supplied by certain domestic producers. Together these forces shift labor demand to the left. With downward rigid wages, the lower labor demand translates into unemployment. Employment falls from L to L_1, and all of those job losses translate into unemployed workers.

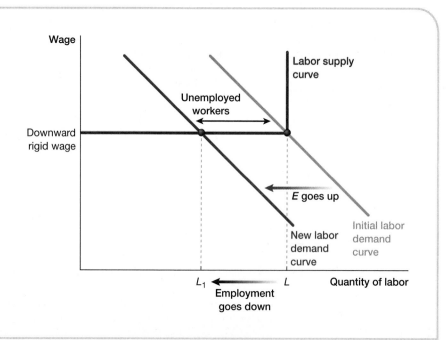

As shown in Exhibit 15.12, the leftward shift of labor demand induced by the appreciation of the dollar will translate into lower employment and a new pool of unemployed workers.

We also need to consider multiplier effects, which were introduced in Chapter 12. For instance, job losses in an export industry will cause unemployment, and the newly unemployed workers will reduce consumption, thereby affecting other industries. In this way, a decline in net exports might have spillover effects, leading to a larger aggregate economic contraction than the direct effect of the reduction in net exports.

Revisiting Black Wednesday

With the help of this discussion, we can revisit the British experience in the early 1990s. As discussed in the Evidence-Based Economics feature, the British pound came to be overvalued relative to the German mark, and this overvaluation eventually led to the sharp depreciation of the pound on Black Wednesday.

The scenario depicted in Exhibits 15.10 and 15.12 reflects the situation of the British economy during 1991 and 1992. The overvalued pound was reducing British GDP. The British economy was effectively at real exchange rate E_1 in Exhibit 15.10 and the corresponding point for employment given by L_1 in Exhibit 15.12.

You might be wondering why the British authorities thought that they could defend the pound despite its overvaluation. They believed that the overvaluation was temporary. The British authorities' optimistic beliefs were not entirely groundless. We have so far explained how a nominal exchange rate depreciation can eliminate overvaluation of a currency. But there is another solution that can occur whether or not a country has a flexible exchange rate. Due to the lower net exports shown in Exhibit 15.10, domestic firms might cut their prices to become more competitive, and this would reduce the ratio of domestic prices to foreign prices. Recall that the real exchange rate is

$$E = \frac{(\text{Domestic prices}) \times e}{\text{Foreign prices}}.$$

A falling ratio of domestic to foreign prices (holding e fixed) would correspond to a falling real exchange rate, boosting net exports, raising labor demand, and increasing GDP.

In 1992, the British authorities anticipated that British prices would fall relative to the prices of their trading partners and that this would eliminate the overvaluation of the pound, because more foreign countries would choose to import goods from the United Kingdom (shifting the demand curve for the pound to the right). However, such domestic price adjustments take a long time to occur, something the British authorities didn't realize at first. By the time they learned this lesson, the overvalued pound had already depressed British net exports and caused a severe recession. As the real exchange rate was showing little sign of improvement and British foreign reserves were running out, the stage was set for Black Wednesday and the sharp depreciation of the pound's nominal exchange rate.

Consistent with the models discussed in this chapter, the depreciation of the pound on Black Wednesday led to a decline in the pound's real exchange rate; an expansion of British net exports and a corresponding increase in the aggregate level of economic activity followed. In fact, the British economy did so well after Black Wednesday, growing on average at 3.6 percent per year during the next 3 years, that some commentators switched to calling the day that Soros broke the pound "White Wednesday." Pegging the pound to the mark had been damaging the UK economy. Letting market forces determine the price of the pound turned out to be the best policy after all.

Interest Rates, Exchange Rates, and Net Exports

We have just discussed how a fall in the United Kingdom's pegged exchange rate (in 1992) stimulated GDP. We now study a situation where the exchange rate is *flexible*, but here, too, the monetary authority can influence the value of the exchange rate and thereby generate a change in GDP. If the monetary authority cuts interest rates, a flexible exchange rate will depreciate, net exports will rise, and GDP will rise too. To understand this process, we combine three concepts: (a) the credit market equilibrium from Chapter 10 (Exhibit 10.5); (b) the determination of net capital outflows and net exports from Chapter 14 (Exhibit 14.9); and (c) the relationship between the real exchange rate and net exports from Exhibit 15.10.

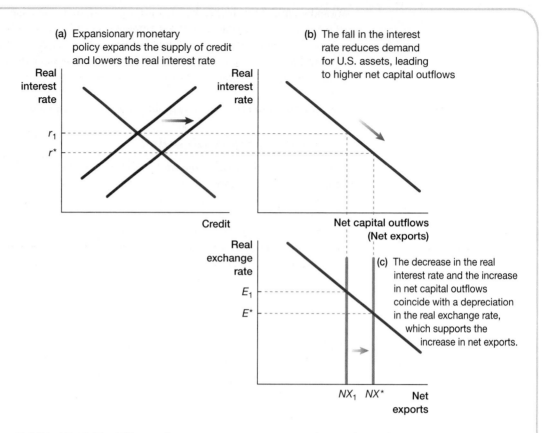

(a) Expansionary monetary policy expands the supply of credit and lowers the real interest rate

(b) The fall in the interest rate reduces demand for U.S. assets, leading to higher net capital outflows

Real interest rate

Real interest rate

r_1

r^*

Credit

Net capital outflows (Net exports)

Real exchange rate

E_1

E^*

(c) The decrease in the real interest rate and the increase in net capital outflows coincide with a depreciation in the real exchange rate, which supports the increase in net exports.

NX_1 NX^* Net exports

Exhibit 15.13 The Effects of Expansionary Monetary Policy under a Flexible Exchange Rate

An expansionary monetary policy increases the supply of credit in panel (a), leading to a lower real interest rate. This causes the economy to move along the downward-sloping line summarizing the relationship between the real interest rate and net capital outflows (net exports) in panel (b). The fall in the real interest rate and the rise in net capital outflows bring about a reduction in the real exchange rate. In equilibrium, net exports rise, as reflected in panels (b) and (c). Net exports rise both because the real exchange rate has fallen and because rising capital outflows must be accompanied by rising net exports.

We combine these three markets in the three panels of Exhibit 15.13. Panel (a) depicts the credit market equilibrium. Before the change in monetary policy, the intersection of the supply of and demand for credit determines the real exchange rate, r_1. Now consider expansionary monetary policy: increasing the supply of credit will lead to a new and lower equilibrium real interest rate, r^*, as shown in this panel. Panel (b) of the exhibit depicts the relationship between the real interest rate and net exports derived in Chapter 14. Recall that a lower real interest rate increases net capital outflows and net exports—these two flows are linked by a national accounting identity, $S - I = NX =$ net capital outflows, as described in Chapter 14.

Panel (b) is lined up with panel (a), so that the real interest rate on the y-axis of panel (a) also gives us the real interest rate that applies in panel (b). Consequently, as the real interest rate falls, we move down along the downward-sloping line in panel (b), generating an increase in net capital outflows and an increase in net exports. This captures the mechanism highlighted in Chapter 14: lower real interest rates lead to more capital outflows as investors seek greater returns abroad, and, because of the national accounting identity, more capital outflow implies greater net exports.

Panel (c) completes the picture by depicting the relationship between the real exchange rate and net exports from Exhibit 15.10. Panel (c) is lined up with panel (b) in such a way that they share the same x-axis, corresponding to net exports. Before the monetary authority reduces interest rates, the real exchange rate is E_1 and net exports are equal to NX_1. As we move along the downward-sloping line in panel (b), we are simultaneously moving along the downward-sloping line in panel (c). The difference is that the y-axis in panel (c) is the real exchange rate, exactly as in Exhibit 15.10. Therefore, the economy is transitioning to a lower real exchange rate, E^*, and also to greater net exports, NX^*.

The movements in panels (b) and (c) are both caused by the decline in real interest rates in panel (a). The fall in interest rates simultaneously causes the real exchange rate to depreciate (panel c), capital outflows to increase (panel b), and net exports to increase (panels b and c). These three panels show how these markets move together in equilibrium. This illustrates how expansionary monetary policy can stimulate GDP by reducing the real interest rate, increasing capital outflows, reducing the real exchange rate, and ultimately increasing net exports.

LETTING THE
DATA SPEAK

The Costs of Fixed Exchange Rates

Both Europe and the United States were plunged into recession during the 2007–2009 financial crisis. The economic contraction and its aftermath have been worse in Europe, as you can see in Exhibit 15.14. In 2015, U.S. real GDP was 9.9 percent *above* its 2007 pre-crisis level. In 2015, eurozone real GDP was just returning to its 2007 pre-crisis level.

Many economists believe that the greater severity and duration of the economic crisis in Europe has in part been due to the inability of European exchange rates to adjust. Since January 1, 1999, major European economies (excluding the United Kingdom) have been part of the eurozone, which means that they use a single currency, the euro. This is referred to as a *currency union*, a form of fixed exchange rate in which, by using the same currency, all of these economies are pegging their exchange rates to one another.

As we have seen, when the exchange rate can change, countries can devalue their currencies and thus increase their net exports, stimulating the economy. This is not possible when a country is a member of a currency union (unless the common currency itself is devalued).

Compounding this problem is the mismatch among the needs of different European economies. Germany has been doing relatively well compared to the rest of Europe. In 2015, German real GDP was 7.1 percent above its 2007 pre-crisis level. Other eurozone economies, such as Greece, Italy, Portugal and Spain, have suffered large declines in GDP. The aggregate real GDP of Greece, Italy, Portugal, and Spain was 8 percent *lower* in 2015 than it was in 2007.

If these economically struggling countries had had independent monetary authorities, they might have adopted highly expansionary monetary policies, stimulating their economies and reducing their real exchange rates. This would have increased their net exports and boosted demand for labor. However, the eurozone currency union has necessitated a one-size-fits-all monetary policy, which has ended up being insufficiently expansionary for Greece, Italy, Portugal, and Spain.

Exhibit 15.14 Real GDP (2007–2015)

This exhibit plots the changes in real GDP for four economic regions: the United States, Germany, the entire eurozone, and a subset of eurozone economies that were particularly hard hit by the financial crisis (Greece, Italy, Portugal, and Spain). All data are normalized to 100 in 2007 to simplify comparisons. This is done by dividing all of the real GDP observations for a country by the value of real GDP for that country in 2007 and then multiplying the result by 100.

Sources: Based on World Bank Databank and International Monetary Fund World Economic Outlook Database.

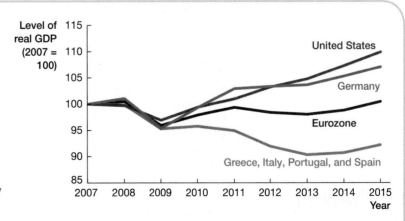

> The Fed can increase net exports by lowering domestic interest rates or can lower net exports by raising domestic interest rates.

In contrast, contractionary monetary policy will have the opposite impact. When the Fed raises the domestic interest rate, capital outflows will decline, the real exchange rate will appreciate, and net exports will decrease.

Thus, depending on its policy needs, the Fed can increase net exports by lowering domestic interest rates or can lower net exports by raising domestic interest rates.

Summary

- The nominal exchange rate is the number of units of foreign currency per unit of domestic currency. The real exchange rate, in contrast, gives the ratio of the dollar price of a basket of goods and services purchased in the United States to the dollar price of the same basket purchased in a foreign country.

- The nominal exchange rate is determined by the supply and demand for a currency in the foreign exchange market. When a Chinese producer sells goods to a U.S. firm and receives dollars, the Chinese firm converts the dollars to the Chinese currency (the yuan) in the foreign exchange market. This is equivalent to demanding yuan and supplying dollars in the foreign exchange market. In contrast, a Chinese firm that imports from the United States would be doing the opposite in the foreign exchange market: supplying yuan and demanding dollars with which it will pay its U.S. trading partners.

- When a country has a flexible exchange rate, changes in the supply and demand for a currency lead to fluctuations in the nominal exchange rate. Many countries, however, manage or fix exchange rates and therefore peg their currencies to another currency, such as the dollar. Under managed or fixed exchange rates, fluctuations in the supply and demand for the currency do not necessarily lead to fluctuations in the exchange rate.

- Though managed or fixed exchange rate systems might appear more stable at first, when the exchange rates they generate are out of line with market forces, these systems can lead to sudden changes in the exchange rate. In the process, they create huge profit opportunities, like the one exploited by the financier George Soros in 1992, when he bet that the British pound would be allowed to depreciate.

- The real exchange rate is a key price for the economy in part because it determines net exports. A real exchange rate greater than 1 implies that U.S. goods and services are more expensive than foreign goods and services. Thus a real exchange rate above 1 discourages exports and encourages imports, reducing net exports.

- A fall in net exports lowers GDP and shifts the labor demand curve to the left.

- Domestic interest rates influence the real exchange rate. A fall in domestic interest rates reduces the appeal of domestic assets to foreign investors, lowering both the nominal and the real exchange rates. The resulting rise in net exports shifts the labor demand curve to the right and increases GDP.

Key Terms

nominal exchange rate *p. 361*

flexible exchange rate, or floating exchange rate *p. 363*

fixed exchange rate *p. 364*

managed exchange rate *p. 364*

foreign exchange market *p. 364*

real exchange rate *p. 372*

Questions

All questions are available in MyEconLab *for practice and instructor assignment.*

1. How is the nominal exchange rate between two currencies defined?

2. When is a currency said to appreciate or depreciate?

3. Distinguish among flexible, fixed, and managed exchange rates.

4. What does the demand curve for dollars show? Why does the demand curve for dollars slope downward?

5. What does the supply curve for dollars show? Why does the supply curve for dollars slope upward?

6. What does it mean to say that, at an exchange rate of $1 = 60 INR, the U.S. dollar is overvalued and the Indian rupee (INR) is undervalued?

7. Why might a country peg its exchange rate at a level that overvalues its own currency?

8. How did George Soros exploit the overvaluation of the British pound?

9. How is the real exchange rate for the United States calculated?

10. How does a change in a country's real exchange rate affect its net exports?

11. All else being equal, explain how an increase in the real interest rate is likely to affect a country's net exports, labor demand, and level of employment.

12. The economy of Freedonia is currently faced with negative net exports and high unemployment. Explain two measures that the Freedonian central bank could take to increase net exports and lower unemployment.

Problems

All problems are available in MyEconLab *for practice and instructor assignment.*

1. Suppose that the country Argonia follows a flexible exchange rate regime. The exchange rate between the Argonian dollar (AGD) and the U.S. dollar (USD) is currently 3 USD = 1 AGD.

   a. Use a graph to show the equilibrium in the foreign exchange market with the U.S.-dollar-per-Argonian-dollar exchange rate on the *y*-axis and the quantity of Argonian dollars on the *x*-axis.

   b. Suppose that the global demand for apricots grown in Argonia increases sharply. Other things being unchanged, how would this affect the value of the Argonian dollar? Use the graph to explain.

2. Recall from Chapter 6 that the Big Mac index is used as a rough measure of purchasing power parity across countries. *The Economist* magazine recently included the Vietnamese dong in its calculation of the Big Mac index. A Big Mac costs $5.06 in the United States but only 60,368 dong or $2.66 in Vietnam (at the current exchange rate). What does this information suggest about the value of the real exchange rate of the U.S. dollar relative to the Vietnamese dong (treating the United States as the domestic economy, so the nominal exchange rate is expressed as dong per dollar)? Is the real exchange rate likely to be greater than or less than 1?

3. In 2011, the government of Argentina developed a new policy (sometimes called the "dollar clamp") to prevent Argentines from exchanging pesos, the local currency, for U.S. dollars. New restrictions hampered currency exchange: for example, buying dollars required advance approval from the national tax authority.

   a. How would you expect these restrictions to affect the foreign exchange market for pesos? Explain using a supply and demand chart, as in Exhibit 15.3, but this time put pesos per dollar on the *y*-axis.

   b. Consider that Argentina has had a tumultuous economic history, with periods of high inflation and economic volatility. In particular, right before the restrictions were put in place, foreign investors (who were holding Argentinian assets) were starting to get skittish. Given this environment, why might the government put these exchange restrictions in place?

   c. Even with the restrictions in place, dollars were still available in the flourishing black market (if you're interested, the twitter feed @dolarblue posts the daily black market exchange rate in Argentina). In these circumstances, would you expect the black market exchange rate (pesos per dollar) to be higher or lower than the official exchange rate? Explain.

   d. At the end of 2015, the new president of Argentina, Mauricio Macri, eliminated the restrictions. Examine a 5-year chart of the pesos-per-dollar exchange rate at: https://www.bloomberg.com/quote/USDARS:CUR. What happened to the official exchange rate when Macri enacted his policy of unrestricted foreign exchange transactions? Explain.

4. The Evidence-Based Economics feature in the chapter discusses how George Soros's hedge fund made money by betting on the devaluation of the British pound. Interestingly, Soros also made money betting against the Thai baht. In 1997, the baht had been continually falling against the U.S. dollar. The Bank of Thailand attempted to defend its overvalued exchange rate by pegging the baht to the U.S. dollar at a rate of 25 bahts per dollar. Explain how each of the following factors made it difficult for the Thai authorities to continue to defend their exchange rate, leading eventually to a sharp devaluation of the baht.

  a. The Thai government's reserves of U.S. dollars fell to a 2-year low in 1997.

  b. A very large quantity of corporate debt in Thailand was denominated in U.S. dollars.

5. Using the net exports curve and the labor demand and labor supply curve, explain how a fall in the real exchange rate can lead to an increase in employment in a country.

6. Econia trades with its neighbors, the countries of Governmentia and Sociologia. In Econia, the currency is called the econ; in Governmentia, the currency is called the gov; and in Sociologia, the currency is the soc. Nominal exchange rates are:

200 econs = 1 gov,
4 socs = 1 gov,
100 econs = 1 soc.

A good that is produced and consumed in all three countries is the Mack Burger. The price of Macks in the three countries is as follows: one Mack costs 2 govs in Governmentia, 16 socs in Sociologia, and 600 econs in Econia.

  a. From the perspective of Governmentia, calculate the real exchange rate in Mack Burgers between Governmentia and Sociologia, using the nominal exchange rate (4 socs per gov) and prices listed above. Explain in words what the number you calculated means.

  b. If these three currencies can be freely traded so that their exchange rates are flexible or floating, can the nominal exchange rates listed above persist over time? Why or why not? [*Hint:* Show that currency traders could make unlimited profits if they could persistently trade at these exchange rates.]

7. *Challenge Problem:* The beautiful, mythical country of Coloradial uses the teo as its currency, and the gritty, post-industrial country of Oheo uses the eren. Exactly 1 year ago, you could get 100 teos in exchange for 5 erens in the foreign exchange market. Since then, though, the real interest rate in Coloradial has increased, while staying constant in Oheo.

  a. All other things being equal, would you expect the eren to have appreciated or depreciated with respect to the teo? In other words, what would you expect to happen to the exchange rate of teo per eren? Explain your reasoning.

  b. Assume that the change in the value of the eren with respect to the teo (appreciation or depreciation, depending on your previous answer) was 50 percent. What is the current nominal exchange rate expressed in teo per eren?

  c. One year ago, you borrowed 100,000 teos from a Coloradial bank at a rate of 3 percent per year. You then traded the 100,000 teos for erens at the nominal exchange rate that prevailed at the time (100 teos = 5 erens), and invested those erens in Oheo at 5 percent interest. After the year was over, your intention was to exchange the erens back for teos, repay the loan to the Coloradial bank, and make a tidy profit. (This strategy is called a "carry trade" and is often popular with foreign exchange traders.)

    i. How much would you have made on this strategy if the interest rates did not change *and* if the exchange rate had not changed from 100 teos = 5 erens?

    ii. What will be your profit (or loss) on the trade given the changes in the exchange rate you found in parts (a) and (b)? (Assume the interest rate you paid to the Coloradial bank was fixed in your loan agreement, and so did not change.)

8. The graph below shows the Japanese-yen-per-U.S.-dollar exchange rate for 2008–2013. The table that follows shows the real interest rates in these two countries during the same period.

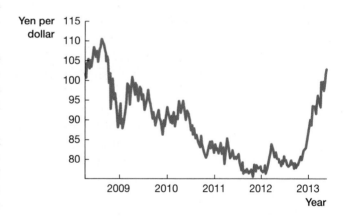

Real Interest Rate in the United States and Japan

Year	2009	2010	2011	2012	2013
United States	2.5	2	1.3	1.5	1.7
Japan	2.2	3.8	3.4	2.3	1.9

What could explain why the U.S. dollar first depreciated and then appreciated with respect to the Japanese yen between 2008 and 2013? Explain your answer with the help of the information given in the table.

9. Since 2008, the dollar has appreciated against the euro.

   a. Suppose that in the short run, the Fed wanted both to weaken the dollar (that is, stop its appreciation and/or cause it to depreciate) and stimulate investment. Based on what you have learned in this chapter and in Chapter 13, discuss whether the Fed can achieve both of these goals simultaneously through monetary policy.

   b. Suppose instead that the European Central Bank conducts contractionary monetary policy. What is the short-run effect, if any, of this policy on the euro-per-dollar nominal exchange rate and on the real exchange rate between the United States and the eurozone? In your answer regarding the real exchange rate, state any assumptions you are making.

10. Thailand and Taiwan are both rapidly growing Asian economies that trade actively with other countries.

    a. Suppose a computer circuit board is the only good produced in Thailand and Taiwan. The circuit board costs 100 baht in Thailand and 200 NT (New Taiwan dollars) in Taiwan. The nominal exchange rate is 2 NT per baht. Calculate the real exchange rate from Thailand's perspective (that is, using Thailand as the domestic economy, so the nominal exchange rate is 2 NT per baht). Show your work. Intuitively, what does this number represent?

    b. The Taiwanese current account with the rest of the world is initially balanced—in other words, it is running neither a deficit nor a surplus. Taiwan alone experiences an economic boom and its real interest rate rises at the same time. Thoroughly explain the mechanisms by which the Taiwanese current account is affected by its boom and the increase in its real interest rate.

    c. Assume that the change in the value of the NT-per-baht exchange rate was 50 percent, which, depending on your answer in part (b), was either appreciation or depreciation. What is the current nominal exchange rate expressed in NT per baht? Show your work.

11. You may have seen the term "capital flight" in news articles about developing countries. Capital flight occurs when foreign investors, often spooked by political instability, lose confidence in a country's assets and decide to sell them. This phenomenon is particularly concerning to the many developing countries that rely on foreign direct investment, which we discussed in Chapter 14.

    a. Using Exhibit 15.13, show how capital flight—a reduction of demand for a country's assets at every interest rate—would affect the real exchange rate. Assume that the domestic credit market (panel (a)) doesn't change, so that the real interest rate is held fixed (for example, the capital flight is caused by political instability). Explain why capital flight is represented by a rightward shift of the curve in panel (b). Then explain how this rightward shift in panel (b) coincides with a movement along the curve in panel (c) and, therefore, a fall in the real exchange rate.

    b. Suppose the local government maintains a fixed exchange rate by changing the domestic interest rate. Faced with capital flight, how would the government need to change the interest rate to maintain its exchange rate? Explain using the charts from part (a) of this problem.

12. Imagine that there are two economies in the world: Bostonia and New Yorkland. Bostonia's currency is the sock and New Yorkland's is the yank. Despite the longstanding rivalry between their citizens, Bostonia and New Yorkland are trading partners.

    a. The Central Bank of New Yorkland decides to conduct contractionary monetary policy. Explain the short-run effect, if any, on the following:

       i. The sock/yank nominal exchange rate

       ii. New Yorkland's net exports

       iii. Bostonia's net exports

    b. GDP in New Yorkland recently plummeted. At first, the citizens in Bostonia cheered, happy to see their rivals taken down a notch. But then an economist (always a killjoy) asserts that the fall in New Yorkland's GDP is likely to hurt Bostonia's GDP in the short run. Could the economist be correct? Why or why not?

13. Sometimes countries abandon their own currency entirely and adopt the currency of another country. For example, Ecuador adopted the U.S. dollar in 2000; El Salvador did the same in 2001. Indeed, because countries often choose the U.S. dollar, this strategy is called "dollarization." Based on the discussion in this chapter and in previous chapters, evaluate "dollarization" as a policy. Why might a government benefit from adopting the U.S. dollar? How might the use of the U.S. dollar limit a country when addressing a domestic economic downturn?

Endnotes

Chapter 1

1. Earnings estimate is from the 2014 census data: http://www.census.gov/content/dam/Census/library/publications/2015/demo/p60-252.pdf.
2. See Facebook's own website: http://newsroom.fb.com/company-info/ and http://www.businessinsider.com/how-much-time-people-spend-on-facebook-per-day-2015-7.
3. Adam Nagourney, "California Imposes First Mandatory Water Restrictions to Deal with Drought," *New York Times,* April 1, 2015, http://www.nytimes.com/2015/04/02/us/california-imposes-first-ever-water-restrictions-to-deal-with-drought.html?_r=0.
4. Ian Lovett, "In California, Stingy Water Users Are Fined, While the Rich Soak," *New York Times*, November 21, 2015, http://www.nytimes.com/2015/11/22/us/stingy-water-users-in-fined-in-drough t-while-the-rich-soak.html.

Chapter 2

1. These data for 2015–2016 are from the College Board: https://trends.collegeboard.org/sites/default/files/2016-trends-college-pricing-web_1.pdf.
2. S. A. Mehr, A. Schachner, R. C. Katz, and E. S. Spelke, "Two Randomized Trials Provide No Consistent Evidence for Nonmusical Cognitive Benefits of Brief Preschool Music Enrichment," *PLoS ONE* 8(12): 2013, e82007. doi:10.1371/journal.pone.0082007.
3. Andrew M. Francis and Hugo M. Mialon, "'A Diamond Is Forever' and Other Fairy Tales: The Relationship Between Wedding Expenses and Marriage Duration," September 15, 2014. Available at the Social Science Research Network: http://ssrn.com/abstract=2501480 or http://dx.doi.org/10.2139/ssrn.2501480.
4. Philip Oreopoulos, "Estimating Average and Local Treatment Effects of Education When Compulsory Schooling Laws Really Matter," *American Economic Review* 96(1): 2006, 152–175.

Chapter 2 Appendix

1. Steven D. Levitt, John A. List, and Sally Sadoff, "The Effect of Performance-Based Incentives on Educational Achievement: Evidence from a Randomized Experiment," NBER Working Paper 22107, Cambridge, MA: National Bureau of Economic Research, 2016.

Chapter 3

1. John Y. Campbell, Tarun Ramadorai, and Benjamin Ranish, "Getting Better or Feeling Better? How Equity Investors Respond to Investment Experience," NBER Working Paper 20000, Cambridge, MA: National Bureau of Economic Research, 2014, http://www.nber.org/papers/w20000.
2. James Frew and Beth Wilson, "Apartment Rents and Locations in Portland, Oregon: 1992–2002," *Journal of Real Estate Research* 29(2): 2007, 201–217.

Chapter 4

1. Chico Harlan, "The Hummer Is Back. Thank Falling Oil Prices," *Washington Post*, November 10, 2014. https://www.washingtonpost.com/news/wonk/wp/2014/11/10/the-hummer-is-back-thank-falling-oil-prices/.
2. Source: International Energy Agency.
3. Source: International Energy Agency.
4. Fred Ferretti, "The Way We Were: A Look Back at the Late Great Gas Shortage," *New York Times,* April 15, 1974, p. 386. Subsequent quotes are from the same article.
5. Stephanie McCrummen and Aymar Jean, "17 Hurt as Computer Sale Turns into Stampede," *Washington Post*, August 17, 2005. http://www.washingtonpost.com/wp-dyn/content/article/2005/08/16/AR2005081600738.htm.

Chapter 5

1. This is based on a population of 321.8 million in 2015 as reported by the U.S. Census Bureau: http://www.census.gov/population/international/data/countryrank/rank.php.
2. Bureau of Labor Statistics, http://www.bls.gov/news.release/archives/empsit_01082016.pdf.
3. Kenneth Rogoff, *The Curse of Cash*, Princeton, NJ: Princeton University Press, 2016.
4. Bureau of Economics Analysis: https://www.bea.gov/newsreleases/national/gdp/2016/pdf/gdp3q16_adv.pdf (Table 9).
5. David H. Autor, "Skills, Education, and the Rise of Earnings Inequality Among the 'Other 99 Percent,'" *Science* 344: 2014, 843–851.
6. Edison Research for the National Election Pool, a consortium of ABC News, The Associated Press, CBS News, CNN, Fox News, and NBC News. The voter survey is based on questionnaires completed by 24,537 voters leaving 350 voting places throughout the United States on Election Day, including 4,398 telephone interviews with early and absentee voters.
7. Daniel Kahneman and Alan B. Krueger, "Developments in the Measurement of Subjective Well-Being," *Journal of Economic Perspectives* 20(1): 2006, 3–24.
8. Betsey Stevenson and Justin Wolfers, "Economic Growth and Subjective Well-Being: Reassessing the Easterlin Paradox," *Brookings Papers on Economic Activity* 1: 2008.

Chapter 6

1. Charles H. Feinstein, *An Economic History of South Africa: Conquest, Discrimination, and Development*, London: Cambridge University Press, 2005.
2. Gordon Moore, "Cramming More Components onto Integrated Circuits," *Electronics Magazine* 38(8): 1965.
3. Fabian Waldinger, "Quality Matters: The Expulsion of Professors and the Consequences for PhD Student Outcomes in Nazi Germany," *Journal of Political Economy* 118(4): 2010, 787–831.

4. James A. Schmitz, "What Determines Productivity? Lessons from the Dramatic Recovery of the U.S. and Canadian Iron Ore Industries Following Their Early 1980s Crisis," *Journal of Political Economy* 113(3): 2005, 582–625.

5. Dambisa Moyo, *Dead Aid,* New York City: Farrar, Straus, and Giroux, 2009.

Chapter 7

1. James Roy Newman, *The World of Mathematics*, vol. 3, North Chelmsford, MA: Courier Corporation, 2000.

2. William D. Nordhaus, "Do Real-Output and Real-Wage Measures Capture Reality? The History of Light Suggests Not," Cowles Foundation Discussion Paper 1078, New Haven, CT: Cowles Foundation for Research in Economics, 1994.

3. Daron Acemoglu and Simon Johnson, "Disease and Development: The Effect of Life Expectancy on Economic Growth," *Journal of Political Economy* 115(6): 2007, 925–985.

4. David E. Bloom and Jeffrey D. Sachs. "Geography, Demography and Economic Growth in Africa," *Brookings Papers on Economic Activity* 2:1998, 207–295.

5. Daron Acemoglu and Simon Johnson. "Disease and Development: The Effect of Life Expectancy on Economic Growth," *Journal of Political Economy* 115(6): 2007, 925–985.

6. Robert Gordon, *The Rise and Fall of American Growth: The U.S. Standard of Living Since the Civil War,* Princeton, NJ: Princeton University Press, 2016.

7. Organisation for Economic Co-operation and Development, "OECD Compendium of Productivity Indicators 2016," Paris: OECD Publishing, 2006, http://dx.doi.org/10.1787/pdtvy-2016-en.

8. Ryan Decker, John Haltiwanger, Ron Jarmin, and Javier Miranda, "The Role of Entrepreneurship in U.S. Job Creation and Economic Dynamism," *Journal of Economic Perspectives* 28(3): 2014, 3–24.

9. For example, Martin Baily, James Manyika, and Shalabh Gupta, "U.S. Productivity Growth: An Optimistic Perspective," *International Productivity Monitor* 25: 2013, 3–12.

10. Anonymous [Thomas R. Malthus], *An Essay on the Principle of Population*, London: J. Johnson, 1798.

11. Emmanuel Saez and Thomas Piketty, "Income Inequality in the United States, 1913–1998," *Quarterly Journal of Economics* 118(1): 2003, 1–39.

12. Claire Pénicaud, "State of the Industry: Results from the 2012 Global Mobile Money Adoption Survey," GSM Association, 2012.

13. Robert Jensen, "The Digital Provide: Information (Technology), Market Performance, and Welfare in the South Indian Fisheries Sector," *Quarterly Journal of Economics* 122(3): 2007, 879–924.

14. Robert M. Solow, "A Contribution to the Theory of Economic Growth," *Quarterly Journal of Economics* 70(1): 1956, 65–94; Trevor W. Swan, "Economic Growth and Capital Accumulation," *Economic Record* 32(2): 1956, 334–361.

Chapter 8

1. Charles-Louis de Secondat Montesquieu, *The Spirit of the Laws, Book XIV*, Chapter 2, 230–235, [1748] 1989.

2. Alfred Marshall, *Principles of Economics, Book IV: The Agents of Production*, Chapter 5, London: Macmillan, 1890.

3. Jeffrey Sachs, "Tropical Underdevelopment," *NBER Working Paper* 8119, Cambridge, MA: National Bureau of Economic Research, 2001.

4. Max Weber, *The Protestant Ethic and the Spirit of Capitalism*, New York: Routledge, [1905] 2001.

5. Samuel P. Huntington, "The Clash of Civilizations?" *Foreign Affairs* 72: 1993, 22–49.

6. Lawrence E. Harrison and Samuel P. Huntington, *Culture Matters: How Values Shape Human Progress*, New York: Basic Books, 2000.

7. Douglass North, *Institutions, Institutional Change and Economic Performance*, Cambridge: Cambridge University Press, 1990.

8. Tim Culpan, "Taiwan's iPads Are Free. The Cases Cost $1,000," *Bloomberg Businessweek*, October 7, 2010.

9. Adam Smith, *An Inquiry into the Nature and Causes of the Wealth of Nations*, London: W. Strahan, 1776.

10. Daron Acemoglu, Suresh Naidu, Pascual Restrepo, and James Robinson, "Democracy Does Cause Economic Growth," NBER Working Paper 20004, Cambridge, MA: National Bureau of Economic Research, 2014.

11. Daron Acemoglu and James A. Robinson, *Why Nations Fail: The Origins of Power, Prosperity and Poverty*, New York: Crown Publishers, 2012.

12. Joseph A. Schumpeter, *Capitalism, Socialism, and Democracy*, New York: Harper & Row, 1942.

13. Daron Acemoglu and James A. Robinson, *Why Nations Fail: The Origins of Power, Prosperity and Poverty*, New York: Crown Publishers, 2012, p. 225.

14. Joel Mokyr, *The Enlightened Economy: An Economic History of Britain 1700–1850*, New Haven, CT: Yale University Press, 2010.

15. Ritva Reinikka and Jakob Svensson, "Local Capture: Evidence from a Central Government Transfer Program in Uganda," *Quarterly Journal of Economics* 119(2): 2004, 679–705.

Chapter 9

1. Anna Richey-Allen, "The Pain of Unemployment," *New York Times*, October 31, 2010.

2. Alan Krueger and Andreas Mueller, "Job Search and Job Finding in a Period of Mass Unemployment: Evidence from High-Frequency Longitudinal Data," Industrial Relations Section Working Paper 562, Princeton, NJ: Princeton University, 2011.

3. John Maynard Keynes, "Economic Possibilities for Our Grandchildren," in *Essays in Persuasion.* London: Macmillan, 1931.

4. https://eh.net/encyclopedia/hours-of-work-in-u-s-history/.

5. Daron Acemoglu and Pascual Restrepo, "Robots and Jobs," MIT Working Paper, Cambridge, MA: Massachusetts Institute of Technology, 2016.

6. David E. Card and Alan Krueger, *Myth and Measurement: The New Economics of the Minimum Wage.* Princeton, NJ: Princeton University Press, 1995.

7. David Card and Alan B. Krueger, "Minimum Wages and Employment: A Case Study of the Fast-Food Industry in New Jersey and Pennsylvania," *American Economic Review* 90(5): 2000, 1397–1420.

8. Alan Krueger, "The Minimum Wage: How Much Is Too Much?" *New York Times,* October 9, 2015.

9. Nathan Hipsman, "Downward Nominal Wage Rigidity: A Double-Density Model," Harvard University Working Paper, Cambridge, MA: Harvard University, 2012.

10. David H. Autor, David Dorn, and Gordon H. Hanson, "The China Syndrome: Local Labor Market Effects of Import Competition in the United States," *American Economic Review* 103(6): 2013, 2121–2168.

11. Based on Mark Aguiar, Mark Bils, Kerwin Charles, and Erik Hurst, "Leisure Luxuries and the Labor Supply of Young Men," Working paper, September 15, 2016. http://www.ssc.wisc.edu/~nwilliam/Econ702_files/abch.pdf.

12. Based on Marcus Hagedorn, Fatih Karahan, Iourii Manovskii, and Kurt Mitman, "Unemployment Benefits and Unemployment in the Great Recession: The Role of Macro Effects," NBER Working Paper 19499, Cambridge, MA: National Bureau of Economic Research, 2013.

13. Stefan Kühn, Santo Milasi, Richard Horne, and Sheena Yoon, "World Employment and Social Outlook 2016: Trends for Youth," International Labour Organization report, Geneva, Switzerland, 2016.

Chapter 10

1. Irving Fisher, "Appreciation and Interest: A Study of the Influence of Monetary Appreciation and Depreciation on the Rate of Interest with Applications to the Bimetallic Controversy and the Theory of Interest," *Publications of the American Economic Association* 11(4): 1896, 331–442.

2. Investment Company Institute, https://www.ici.org/pdf/2015_factbook.pdf.

3. Eugene F. Fama, "Efficient Capital Markets: A Review of Theory and Empirical Work," *Journal of Finance* 25(2): 1970, 383–417.

4. Robert J. Shiller, *Irrational Exuberance*, Princeton, N.J.: Princeton University Press, 2005.

Chapter 11

1. Anthony Cuthbertson, "Bitcoin Now Accepted by 100,000 Merchants Worldwide," *International Business Times,* February 4, 2015.

2. Nathaniel Popper, "Bitcoin Price Soars, Fueled by Speculation and Global Currency Turmoil," *New York Times,* January 3, 2017.

3. Board of Governors of the Federal Reserve.

4. Khaleda Rahman, "Empty Shelves Across Venezuela Due to Tumbling Oil Prices Create a New Industry: People Queuing Up for Goods That Have Probably Run Out Earn More Than Professors," *Daily Mail,* January 15, 2015.

Chapter 12

1. U.S. GDP data for the years before 1947 are available only on an annual basis. Because the 1945 recession occurred within a single year, we don't know how much real GDP declined, but we can estimate it using the annual data. From 1944 to 1946, real GDP fell by 12.7 percent.

2. Kathryn M. Dominguez, Ray C. Fair, and Matthew D. Shapiro, "Forecasting the Depression: Harvard Versus Yale," *American Economic Review* 78(4): 1988, 595–612. The Fisher remarks quoted later in the paragraph are from this paper.

3. Dominguez, Fair, and Shapiro, "Forecasting the Depression."

4. Arthur M. Okun, "Potential GNP: Its Measurement and Significance," 1963, reprinted as Cowles Foundation Paper 190, New Haven, CT: Cowles Foundation, 2016.

5. Arthur C. Pigou, *Industrial Fluctuations*, New York: Macmillan, 1929.

6. Finn E. Kydland and Edward C. Prescott, "Time to Build and Aggregate Fluctuations," *Econometrica* 50(6): 1982, 1345–1370.

7. John M. Keynes, *The General Theory of Employment, Interest and Money*, London: Palgrave Macmillan, 1936.

8. Milton Friedman and Anna J. Schwartz, *A Monetary History of the United States, 1867–1960,* Princeton, NJ: Princeton University Press, 1963.

Chapter 13

1. Federal Open Market Committee, December 2012.

2. William L. Silber, *Volcker: The Triumph of Persistence*, New York: Bloomsbury Press, 2012.

3. Bank of England, "Financial Stability Report," June 2014, Issue 35, online at http://www.bankofengland.co.uk/publications/Documents/fsr/2014/fsrfull1406.pdf.

4. John B. Taylor, "Discretion Versus Policy Rules in Practice," *Carnegie-Rochester Conference Series on Public Policy* 39: 1993, 195–214.

5. Christina Romer and Jared Bernstein, "The Job Impact of the American Recovery and Reinvestment Act." January 9, 2009, online at http://otrans.3cdn.net/ee40602f9a7d8172b8_ozm6bt5oi.pdf.

6. Romer and Bernstein, "The Job Impact of the American Recovery and Reinvestment Act."

7. David S. Johnson, Jonathan A. Parker, and Nicholas S. Souleles. "Household Expenditure and the Income Tax Rebates of 2001," *American Economic Review* 96(5): 2006, 1589–1610.

8. Christian Broda and Jonathan A. Parker. "The Economic Stimulus Payments of 2008 and the Aggregate Demand for Consumption," *Journal of Monetary Economics* 68: 2014, S20–S36.

9. Valerie A. Ramey, "Identifying Government Spending Shocks: It's All in the Timing," *Quarterly Journal of Economics* 126(1): 2011, 1–50.

10. Source: Congressional Budget Office forecast on January 2017.

Chapter 14

1. Steven Greenhouse, "Nike Shoe Plant in Vietnam Is Called Unsafe for Workers," *New York Times,* November 8, 1997. See http://www.nytimes.com/1997/11/08/business/nike-shoe-plant-in-vietnam-is-called-unsafe-for-workers.html?pagewanted=all.

2. John Cushman, "Nike Pledges to End Child Labor and Apply U.S. Rules Abroad," *New York Times,* May 13, 1998. See http://www.nytimes.com/1998/05/13/business/international-business-nike-pledges-to-end-child-labor-and-apply-us-rules-abroad.html.

3. Greg Linden, Kenneth Kraemer, and Jason Dedrick, "Who Captures Value in a Global Innovation Network? The Case of Apple's iPod," *Communications of the ACM* 52(3): 2009, 140–144.

4. Linden, Kraemer, and Dedrick, "Who Captures Value?"

5. The video can be viewed on YouTube: https://www.youtube.com/watch?v=Y3ttxGMQOrY.

6. Jack Ewing, "The Disassembly Line," *New York Times*, July 15, 2014, B1.

7. Jennifer L. Rich, "U.S. Admits That Politics Was Behind Steel Tariffs," *New York Times*, March 14, 2002. See http://www.nytimes.com/2002/03/14/business/us-admits-that-politics-was-behind-steel-tariffs.html.

8. Here is a typical stump speech from the campaign, as transcribed by *Time* magazine (June 28, 2016): http://time.com/4386335/donald-trump-trade-speech-transcript/.

9. Dalila Cervantes-Godoy and Joe Dewbre, "Economic Importance of Agriculture for Sustainable Development and Poverty Reduction: The Case Study of Vietnam," OECD Food, Agriculture and Fisheries Working Paper 23, Paris: Organisation for Economic Co-operation and Development, 2010.

10. Ben Bland, "Vietnam's Factories Grapple with Growing Unrest," *Financial Times*, January 19, 2012. For the 2014 minimum wage data, see http://www.amchamvietnam.com/30442612/vietnams-2014-minimum-wage-adjustment-shows-moderation-15-increase-vs-17-5-increase-in-2012/.

11. Penn World Tables. Alan Heston, Robert Summers, and Bettina Aten, Penn World Table Version 7.1, Center for International Comparisons of Production, Income, and Prices at the University of Pennsylvania, November 2012.

12. Cervantes-Godoy and Dewbre, "Economic Importance."

13. Eric V. Edmonds and Nina Pavcnik, "International Trade and Child Labor: Cross-Country Evidence," *Journal of International Economics* 68(1): 2006, 115–140.

Chapter 15

1. "Venezuela's Currency Is Collapsing on the Black Market Again," *Bloomberg News,* November 1, 2016, available at https://www.bloomberg.com/news/articles/2016-11-01/venezuela-s-currency-is-collapsing-on-the-black-market-again.

Glossary

Absolute advantage A producer has an absolute advantage in producing a good or service if the producer can produce more units per hour than other producers can.

Aggregate demand Aggregate demand is the economy's overall demand for the goods and services that firms produce. Aggregate demand drives the hiring decisions of firms and consequently determines the labor demand curve.

Aggregate production function An aggregate production function describes the relationship between the aggregate GDP of a nation and its factors of production.

Aggregation The process of adding up individual behaviors is referred to as aggregation.

Animal spirits Animal spirits are psychological factors that lead to changes in the mood of consumers or businesses, thereby affecting consumption, investment, and GDP.

Automatic stabilizers Automatic stabilizers are components of the government budget that automatically adjust to smooth out economic fluctuations.

Average The mean, or average, is the sum of all the different values divided by the number of values.

Bank reserves Bank reserves consist of vault cash and reserves held at the Federal Reserve Bank.

Bank run A bank run occurs when a bank experiences an extraordinarily large volume of withdrawals driven by a concern that the bank will run out of liquid assets with which to pay withdrawals.

Bar chart A bar chart uses bars of different heights or lengths to indicate the properties of different groups.

Behavioral economics Behavioral economics jointly analyzes the economic and psychological factors that explain human behavior.

Budget constraint A budget constraint shows the bundles of goods or services that a consumer can choose given her limited budget.

Capital income Capital income is any form of payment that derives from owning physical or financial capital.

Catch-up growth Catch-up growth refers to a process whereby relatively poorer nations increase their incomes by taking advantage of knowledge and technologies already invented in other, more technologically advanced countries.

Causation Causation occurs when one thing directly affects another through a cause-and-effect relationship.

Central bank The central bank is the government institution that monitors financial institutions, controls certain key interest rates, and indirectly controls the money supply. These activities constitute monetary policy.

Closed economy A closed economy does not trade with the rest of the world.

Collective bargaining Collective bargaining refers to contract negotiations between firms and labor unions.

Comparative advantage When a producer providing a good (or service) has a lower opportunity cost per unit produced compared to other producers.

Competitive equilibrium The competitive equilibrium is the crossing point of the supply curve and the demand curve.

Competitive equilibrium price The competitive equilibrium price equates quantity supplied and quantity demanded.

Competitive equilibrium quantity The competitive equilibrium quantity is the quantity that corresponds to the competitive equilibrium price.

Complements Two goods are complements when a fall in the price of one leads to a right shift in the demand curve for the other.

Consumer Price Index (CPI) The Consumer Price Index (CPI) is 100 times the ratio of the cost of buying a basket of consumer goods using target year prices divided by the cost of buying the same basket of consumer goods using base-year prices.

Consumption Consumption is the market value of consumption goods and consumption services that are bought by domestic households.

Contractionary fiscal policy Contractionary fiscal policy uses lower government expenditure and higher taxes to reduce the growth rate of real GDP.

Contractionary monetary policy Contractionary monetary policy slows down growth in bank reserves, raises interest rates, reduces borrowing, slows down growth in the money supply, and reduces the rate of inflation.

Correlation A correlation means that two variables tend to change at the same time.

Cost-benefit analysis Cost-benefit analysis is a calculation that adds up costs and benefits using a common unit of measurement, like dollars.

Countercyclical fiscal policy Countercyclical fiscal policy, which is passed by the legislative branch and signed into law by the executive branch, aims to reduce economic fluctuations by manipulating government expenditures and taxes.

Countercyclical monetary policy Countercyclical monetary policy, which is conducted by the central bank (in the United States, the Fed), attempts to reduce economic fluctuations by manipulating bank reserves and interest rates.

Countercyclical policies Countercyclical policies attempt to reduce the intensity of economic fluctuations and smooth the growth rates of employment, GDP, and prices.

Creative destruction Creative destruction refers to the process by which new technologies replace old ones, new businesses replace established companies, and new skills make old ones redundant.

Credit Credit refers to the loans that the debtor receives.

Credit demand curve The credit demand curve is the schedule that reports the relationship between the quantity of credit demanded and the real interest rate.

Credit market The credit market is where borrowers obtain funds from savers.

Credit supply curve The credit supply curve is the schedule that reports the relationship between the quantity of credit supplied and the real interest rate.

Crowding out Crowding out occurs when rising government expenditure partially or even fully displaces expenditures by households and firms.

Culture hypothesis The culture hypothesis claims that different values and cultural beliefs fundamentally cause the differences in prosperity around the world.

Current account The current account is the sum of net exports, net factor payments from abroad, and net transfers from abroad.

Cyclical unemployment Cyclical unemployment is the deviation of the actual unemployment rate from the natural rate of unemployment.

Data Data are facts, measurements, or statistics that describe the world.

Debtors Debtors, or borrowers, are economic agents who borrow funds.

Deflation The deflation rate is the rate of decrease of a price index.

Demand curve The demand curve plots the quantity demanded at different prices. A demand curve plots the demand schedule.

Demand curve shifts The demand curve shifts when the quantity demanded changes at a given price.

Demand deposits Demand deposits are funds that depositors can access on demand by withdrawing money from the bank, writing checks, or using their debit cards.

Demand schedule A demand schedule is a table that reports the quantity demanded at different prices, holding all else equal.

Demographic transition The demographic transition refers to the decline in fertility and number of children per family that many societies undergo as they transition from agriculture to industry.

Dependent variable A dependent variable is a variable whose value depends on another variable.

Depression Although there is no consensus on the definition, the term depression is typically used to describe a prolonged recession with an unemployment rate of 20% or more.

Diminishing marginal benefit As you consume more of a good, your willingness to pay for an additional unit declines.

Downward wage rigidity Downward wage rigidity arises when workers resist a cut in their wage.

Dynamic equilibrium A dynamic equilibrium traces out the behavior of the economy over time.

Economic agent An economic agent is an individual or a group that makes choices.

Economic expansions Economic expansions are the periods between recessions. Accordingly, an economic expansion begins at the end of one recession and continues until the start of the next recession.

Economic fluctuations or business cycles Short-run changes in the growth of GDP are referred to as economic fluctuations or business cycles.

Economic growth Economic growth, or growth, is the increase in GDP per capita of an economy.

Economic institutions Economic institutions are those aspects of the society's rules that concern economic transactions.

Economics Economics is the study of how agents choose to allocate scarce resources and how those choices affect society.

Efficiency of production Efficiency of production refers to the ability of an economy to produce the maximal amount of output from a given amount of factors of production and knowledge.

Efficiency wages Wages above the lowest pay that workers would accept; employers use them to increase motivation and productivity.

Empirical evidence Empirical evidence consists of facts that are obtained through observation and measurement. Empirical evidence is also called data.

Empiricism Empiricism is analysis that uses data–evidence-based analysis. Economists use data to develop theories, to test theories, to evaluate the success of different government policies, and to determine what is causing things to happen in the world.

Employed A person holding a full-time or part-time paid job is employed.

Equilibrium Equilibrium is the special situation in which everyone is simultaneously optimizing, so nobody would benefit personally by changing his or her own behavior, given the choices of others.

Excess demand When the market price is below the competitive equilibrium price, quantity demanded exceeds quantity supplied, creating excess demand.

Excess supply When the market price is above the competitive equilibrium price, quantity supplied exceeds quantity demanded, creating excess supply.

Expansionary fiscal policy Expansionary fiscal policy uses higher government expenditure and lower taxes to increase the growth rate of real GDP.

Expansionary monetary policy Expansionary monetary policy increases the quantity of bank reserves and lowers interest rates.

Expected real interest rate The expected real interest rate is the nominal interest rate minus the expected rate of inflation.

Experiment An experiment is a controlled method of investigating causal relationships among variables.

Exponential growth Exponential growth refers to a situation in which the growth process can be described by an approximately constant growth rate of a variable such as GDP or GDP per capita.

Exports Exports are the market value of all domestically produced goods and services that are purchased by households, firms, and governments in foreign countries.

Extractive economic institutions Extractive economic institutions do not protect private property rights, do not uphold contracts, and interfere with the workings of markets. They also erect significant entry barriers into businesses and occupations.

Factors of production Factors of production are the inputs to the production process.

Federal funds market The federal funds market refers to the market where banks obtain overnight loans of reserves from one another.

Federal funds market equilibrium The point where the supply and demand curves cross in the federal funds market is the federal funds market equilibrium.

Federal funds rate The federal funds rate is the interest rate that banks charge each other for overnight loans in the federal funds market. The funds being lent are reserves at the Federal Reserve Bank.

Federal Reserve Bank The Federal Reserve Bank, or the Fed, is the name of the central bank in the United States.

Fertility Fertility refers to the number of children per adult or per woman of childbearing age.

Fiat money Fiat money refers to something that is used as legal tender by government decree and is not backed by a physical commodity, like gold or silver.

Financial account The financial account is the increase in domestic assets held by foreigners minus the increase in foreign assets held domestically.

Financial intermediaries Financial intermediaries channel funds from suppliers of financial capital to users of financial capital.

Fixed exchange rate If the government fixes a value for the exchange rate and intervenes to maintain that value, then the country has a fixed exchange rate.

Flexible exchange rate If the government does not intervene in the foreign exchange market, then the country has a flexible exchange rate, which is also referred to as a floating exchange rate.

Foreign direct investment Foreign direct investment refers to investments by foreign individuals and companies in domestic firms and businesses. To qualify as foreign direct investment, these flows need to generate a large foreign ownership stake in the domestic business.

Foreign exchange market The foreign exchange market is the global financial market in which currencies are traded and nominal exchange rates are determined.

Frictional unemployment Frictional unemployment refers to unemployment that arises because workers have imperfect information about available jobs and need to engage in a time-consuming process of job search.

Fundamental causes of prosperity Fundamental causes of prosperity are factors that are at the root of the differences in the proximate causes of prosperity.

Gains from specialization Gains from specialization are the economic gains that society can obtain by having some individuals, regions, or countries specialize in the production of certain goods and services.

GDP deflator The GDP deflator is 100 times the ratio of nominal GDP to real GDP in the same year. It is a measure of how prices of goods and services produced in a country have risen since the base year.

GDP per capita The GDP divided by the total population.

GDP per worker The GDP divided by the number of people in employment.

Geography hypothesis The geography hypothesis claims that differences in geography, climate, and ecology are ultimately responsible for the major differences in prosperity observed across the world.

Government expenditure Government expenditure is the market value of government purchases of goods and services.

Government expenditure multiplier If a \$1 change in government expenditure causes an \$m change in GDP, then the government expenditure multiplier is m.

Government taxation multiplier If a \$1 reduction in taxation causes an \$m increase in GDP, then the government taxation multiplier is m.

Great Depression The Great Depression refers to the severe contraction that started in 1929, reaching a low point for real GDP in 1933. The period of below-trend real GDP did not end until the buildup to World War II in the late 1930s.

Gross domestic product (GDP) The market value of the final goods and services produced in a country during a given period of time.

Gross national product (GNP) Gross national product (GNP) is the market value of production generated by the factors of production—both capital and labor—possessed or owned by the residents of a particular nation.

Growth rate The growth rate is the change in a quantity, for example, GDP per capita, between two dates, relative to the baseline (beginning of period) quantity.

Holding all else equal "Holding all else equal" implies that everything else in the economy is held constant. The Latin phrase *ceteris paribus* means "with other things the same" and is sometimes used in economic writing to mean the same thing as "holding all else equal."

Human capital Each person's stock of skills to produce output of economic value.

Hypotheses Hypotheses are predictions (typically generated by a model) that can be tested with data.

Identity Two variables are related by an identity when the two variables are defined in a way that makes them mathematically identical.

Imports Imports are the market value of all foreign-produced goods and services that are sold to domestic households, domestic firms, and the domestic government.

Inclusive economic institutions Inclusive economic institutions protect private property, uphold law and order, allow and enforce private contracts, and allow free entry into new lines of business and occupations.

Income (or GDP) per worker Income (or GDP) per worker is defined as GDP divided by the number of people in employment.

Income per capita Income per capita is income per person. It is calculated by dividing a nation's aggregate income by the number of people in the country. Income per capita is often referred to as GDP per capita.

Independent variable An independent variable is a variable whose value does not depend on that of another variable; in an experiment it is manipulated by the experimenter.

Industrial Revolution The Industrial Revolution denotes the series of innovations and their implementation in the production process that began at the end of the eighteenth century in Britain.

Inferior good For an inferior good, an increase in income causes the demand curve to shift to the left (holding the good's price fixed), or in other words, causes buyers to buy less of the good.

Inflation expectations Economic agents' inflation expectations are their beliefs about future inflation rates.

Inflation rate The rate of increase in prices is the inflation rate. It is calculated as the year-over-year percentage increase in a price index.

Input An input is a good or service used to produce another good or service.

Insolvent A bank becomes insolvent when the value of the bank's assets is less than the value of its liabilities.

Institutions Institutions are the formal and informal rules governing the organization of a society, including its laws and regulations.

Institutions hypothesis The institutions hypothesis claims that differences in institutions—that is, in the way societies have organized themselves and shaped the incentives of individuals and businesses—are at the root of the differences in prosperity across the world.

Interest rate The interest rate (also referred to as the nominal interest rate), i, is the annual cost of a $1 loan, so $i \times L$ is the annual cost of an $L loan.

Investment Investment is the market value of new physical capital that is bought by domestic households and domestic firms.

Job search Job search refers to the activities that workers undertake to find appropriate jobs.

Labor demand curve The labor demand curve depicts the relationship between the quantity of labor demanded and the wage. The value of the marginal product of labor is also the labor demand curve, because they both show how the quantity of labor demanded varies with the wage.

Labor force The labor force is the sum of all employed and unemployed workers.

Labor force participation rate The labor force participation rate is the percentage of potential workers who are in the labor force.

Labor income Labor income is any form of payment that compensates people for their work.

Labor supply curve The labor supply curve represents the relationship between the quantity of labor supplied and the wage.

Law of Demand In almost all cases, the quantity demanded rises when the price falls (holding all else equal).

Law of Diminishing Marginal Product The Law of Diminishing Marginal Product states that the marginal contribution of a factor of production to GDP diminishes when we increase the quantity used of that factor of production (holding all other factors constant).

Law of Supply In almost all cases, the quantity supplied rises when the price rises (holding all else equal).

Liquidity Liquidity refers to funds available for immediate payment. To express the same concept in a slightly different way, funds are liquid if they are immediately available for payment.

Long-term real interest rate The long-term real interest rate is the long-term nominal interest rate minus the long-term inflation rate.

Macroeconomics Macroeconomics is the study of the economy as a whole. Macroeconomists study economy-wide phenomena, like the growth rate of a country's total economic output, the inflation rate, or the unemployment rate.

Malthusian cycle The Malthusian cycle refers to the pre-industrial pattern in which increases in aggregate income lead to an expanding population, which in turn reduces income per capita and ultimately puts downward pressure on population.

Managed exchange rate If the government intervenes actively to influence the exchange rate, then the country has a managed exchange rate.

Marginal analysis Marginal analysis is a cost-benefit calculation that studies the difference between a feasible alternative and the next feasible alternative.

Marginal cost The extra cost generated by moving from one feasible alternative to the next feasible alternative.

Marginal tax rate The marginal tax rate refers to how much of the last dollar earned is paid out in tax.

Market A market is a group of economic agents who are trading a good or service plus the rules and arrangements for trading.

Market demand curve The market demand curve is the sum of the individual demand curves of all the potential buyers. It plots the relationship between the total quantity demanded and the market price, holding all else equal.

Market price If all sellers and all buyers face the same price, it is referred to as the market price.

Market supply curve The market supply curve is the sum of the individual supply curves of all the potential sellers. It plots the relationship between the total quantity supplied and the market price, holding all else equal.

Market-clearing wage The competitive equilibrium wage is the market-clearing wage. At this wage, every worker who wants a job can find one: the quantity of labor demanded matches the quantity of labor supplied.

Maturity Maturity refers to the time until debt must be repaid.

Maturity transformation Maturity transformation is the process by which banks take short-maturity liabilities and invest in long-maturity assets (long-term investments).

Mean The mean, or average, is the sum of all of the different values divided by the number of values.

Median The median value is calculated by ordering the numbers from least to greatest and then finding the value halfway through the list.

Medium of exchange A medium of exchange is an asset that can be traded for goods and services.

Microeconomics Microeconomics is the study of how individuals, households, firms, and governments make choices, and how those choices affect prices, the allocation of resources, and the well-being of other agents.

Model A model is a simplified description, or representation, of the world. Sometimes, economists will refer to a model as a *theory*. These terms are often used interchangeably.

Money Money is the asset that people use to make and receive payments when buying and selling goods and services.

Money supply The money supply adds together currency in circulation, checking accounts, savings accounts, travelers' checks, and money market accounts. It is sometimes referred to as M2.

Movement along the demand curve If a good's own price changes and its demand curve hasn't shifted, the own price change produces a movement along the demand curve.

Movement along the supply curve If a good's own price changes and its supply curve hasn't shifted, the own price change produces a movement along the supply curve.

Multipliers Multipliers are economic mechanisms that amplify the initial impact of a shock.

National income accounting identity The national income accounting identity, $Y = C + I + G + X - M$, decomposes GDP into consumption + investment + government expenditure + exports − imports.

National income accounts National income accounts measure the level of aggregate economic activity in a country.

National income and product accounts The national income and product accounts is the system of national income accounts that is used by the U.S. government.

Natural experiment A natural experiment is an empirical study in which some process—out of the control of the experimenter—has assigned subjects to control and treatment groups in a random or nearly random way.

Natural rate of unemployment The natural rate of unemployment is the rate around which the actual rate of unemployment fluctuates.

Negative correlation Negative correlation implies that two variables tend to move in opposite directions.

Negatively related Two variables are negatively related if the variables move in opposite directions.

Net benefit The net benefit is the sum of the benefits of choosing an alternative minus the sum of the costs of choosing that alternative.

Net capital outflows Net capital outflows are the difference between investment by the home country in foreign countries and foreign investment in the home country.

Net exports Net exports are the value of a country's exports minus the value of its imports. Net exports are also known as the trade balance.

Nominal exchange rate The nominal exchange rate is the rate at which one currency can be traded for another.

Nominal GDP Nominal GDP is the total value of production (final goods and services), using current market prices to determine the value of each unit that is produced.

Nominal interest rate The interest rate i, is the annual cost of a \$1 loan, so $i \times L$ is the annual cost of an \$$L$ loan.

Nominal wages Actual wages are also called nominal wages, which distinguishes them from wages adjusted for inflation, or **real wages**. To calculate real wages, economists divide nominal wages by a measure of overall prices, for example the Consumer Price Index (CPI).

Normal good For a normal good, an increase in income causes the demand curve to shift to the right (holding the good's price fixed), or in other words, causes consumers to buy more of the good.

Normative economics Normative economics is an analysis that recommends what an individual or society ought to do.

Okun's Law Okun's Law states that the year-to-year change in the rate of unemployment is equal to $-\frac{1}{2} \times (g - 2\%)$, where g represents the annual growth rate of real GDP in percentage points.

Omitted variable An omitted variable is something that has been left out of a study that, if included, would explain why two variables that are in the study are correlated.

One dollar a day per person poverty line The one dollar a day per person poverty line is a measure of absolute poverty used by economists and other social scientists to compare the extent of poverty across countries.

Open economy An open economy trades freely with the rest of the world.

Open market operations If the Fed wishes to increase the level of reserves that private banks hold, it offers to buy government bonds from the private banks, and in return it gives the private banks more electronic reserves. If the Fed wishes to decrease the level of reserves, it offers to sell government bonds to the private banks and in return the private banks give back some of their reserves. By buying or selling government bonds, the Fed shifts the vertical supply curve in the federal funds market and thereby controls the level of reserves. These transactions are referred to as open market operations.

Opportunity cost Opportunity cost is the best alternative use of a resource.

Optimization Optimization means picking the best feasible option, given whatever (limited) information, knowledge, experience, and training the economic agent has. Economists believe that economic agents try to optimize but sometimes make mistakes.

Optimum The optimum is the best feasible choice. In other words, the optimum is the optimal choice.

Perfect price discrimination Perfect price discrimination, also known as first-degree price discrimination, occurs when a firm charges each buyer exactly his or her willingness to pay.

Perfectly competitive market In a perfectly competitive market, (1) sellers all sell an identical good or service, and (2) any individual buyer or any individual seller isn't powerful enough on his or her own to affect the market price of that good or service.

Phillips curve The Phillips curve describes the empirical relationship between employment growth and inflation, showing that employment growth tends to produce more inflation, especially when an economy is near full employment.

Physical capital Any good, including machines and buildings, used for production.

Physical capital stock The physical capital stock of an economy is the value of equipment, structures and other non-labor inputs used in production.

Pie chart A pie chart is a circle split into (non-overlapping) slices. The area of each slice represents the percentage importance of that part of the whole.

Pigouvian subsidies Corrective subsidies, or Pigouvian subsidies, are designed to induce agents who produce positive externalities to increase quantity toward the socially optimal level.

Political creative destruction Political creative destruction refers to the process by which economic growth destabilizes existing regimes and reduces the political power of rulers.

Political institutions Political institutions are the aspects of the society's rules that concern the allocation of political power and the constraints on the exercise of political power.

Positive correlation A positive correlation implies that two variables tend to move in the same direction.

Positive economics Positive economics is analysis that generates objective descriptions or predictions, which can be verified with data.

Positively related Two variables are positively related if the variables move in the same direction.

Potential workers Potential workers include everyone in the general population with three exceptions: children under 16 years of age, people on active duty in the military, and people who are living in institutions where the residents have restricted personal mobility, like long-term medical care facilities or prisons.

Price-taker A price-taker is a buyer or seller who accepts the market price—buyers can't bargain for a lower price and sellers can't bargain for a higher price.

Principle of optimization at the margin The principle of optimization at the margin states that an optimal feasible alternative has the property that moving to it makes you better off and moving away from it makes you worse off.

Private property rights Private property rights mean that individuals can own businesses and assets and their ownership is secure.

Productivity Productivity refers to the value of goods and services that a worker generates for each hour of work.

Proximate causes of prosperity Proximate causes of prosperity are high levels of factors such as human capital, physical capital, and technology that result in a high level of GDP per capita.

Purchasing power parity (PPP) The purchasing power parity (PPP) constructs the cost of a representative basket of commodities in each country and uses these relative costs for comparing income across countries.

Quantity demanded Quantity demanded is the amount of a good that buyers are willing to purchase at a given price.

Quantity supplied Quantity supplied is the amount of a good or service that sellers are willing to sell at a given price.

Quantity theory of money The quantity theory of money assumes that the growth rate of the money supply and the growth rate of nominal GDP are the same over the long run.

Randomization Randomization is the assignment of subjects by chance, rather than by choice, to a treatment group or control group.

Real business cycle theory Real business cycle theory is the school of thought that emphasizes the role of changes in technology in causing economic fluctuations.

Real exchange rate The real exchange rate is defined as the ratio of the dollar price of a basket of goods and services in the United States, divided by the dollar price of the same basket of goods and services in a foreign country.

Real GDP Real GDP is the total value of production (final goods and services), using market prices from a specific base year to determine the value of each unit that is produced.

Real GDP growth Real GDP growth is the growth rate of real GDP.

Real interest rate The real interest rate is the nominal interest rate minus the inflation rate.

Real wage The real wage is the nominal wage divided by a price index, like the consumer price index (CPI).

Realized real interest rate The realized real interest rate is the nominal interest rate minus the realized rate of inflation.

Research and development (R & D) The activities directed at improving scientific knowledge, generating new innovations, or implementing existing knowledge in production to improve the technology of a firm or an economy.

Recession A recession is a period (lasting at least two quarters) in which aggregate economic output falls.

Reverse causality Reverse causality occurs when we mix up the direction of cause and effect.

Saving rate The saving rate designates the fraction of income that is saved.

Scarce resources Scarce resources are things that people want, where the quantity that people want exceeds the quantity that is available.

Scarcity Scarcity is the situation of having unlimited wants in a world of limited resources.

Scientific method The scientific method is the name for the ongoing process that economists and other scientists use to (1) develop models of the world and (2) test those models with data.

Securities Securities are financial contracts. For example, securities may allocate ownership rights of a company (stocks), or promise payments to lenders (bonds).

Seigniorage Government revenue obtained from printing currency is called seigniorage.

Self-fulfilling prophecy A self-fulfilling prophecy is a situation in which the expectations of an event (such as a left shift in labor demand in the future) induce actions that lead to that event.

Sentiments Sentiments include changes in expectations about future economic activity, changes in uncertainty facing firms and households, and fluctuations in animal spirits. Changes in sentiments lead to changes in household consumption and firm investment.

Slope The slope is the change in the value of the variable plotted on the vertical axis divided by the change in the value of the variable plotted on the horizontal axis.

Solvent A bank is solvent when the value of the bank's assets is greater than the value of its liabilities.

Steady-state equilibrium A steady-state equilibrium is an economic equilibrium in which the physical capital stock remains constant over time.

Stockholders' equity Stockholders' equity is the difference between a bank's total assets and its total liabilities.

Store of value A store of value is an asset that enables people to transfer purchasing power into the future.

Structural unemployment Structural unemployment arises when the quantity of labor supplied persistently exceeds the quantity of labor demanded.

Subsistence level The subsistence level is the minimum level of income per person that is generally necessary for the individual to obtain enough calories, shelter, and clothing to survive.

Substitutes Two goods are substitutes when a fall in the price of one leads to a left shift in the demand curve for the other.

Supply curve The supply curve plots the quantity supplied at different prices. A supply curve plots the supply schedule.

Supply curve shifts The supply curve shifts when the quantity supplied changes at a given price.

Supply schedule A supply schedule is a table that reports the quantity supplied at different prices, holding all else equal.

Sustained growth Sustained growth refers to a process whereby GDP per capita grows at a positive and relatively steady rate for long periods of time.

Technological change Technological change is the process of new technologies and new goods and services being invented, introduced, and used in the economy, enabling the economy to achieve a higher level of GDP for given levels of physical capital stock and total efficiency units of labor.

Technology Technology refers to a set of devices and practices that determine how efficiently an economy uses its labor and capital.

Time series graph A time series graph displays data at different points in time.

Total efficiency units of labor Total efficiency units of labor is the product of the total number of workers in the economy and the average human capital of workers.

Trade deficit A trade deficit is an excess of imports over exports and is thus the name given to the trade balance when it is negative.

Trade surplus A trade surplus is an excess of exports over imports and is thus the name given to the trade balance when it is positive.

Trade-off An economic agent faces a trade-off when the agent needs to give up one thing to get something else.

Unemployed A worker is officially unemployed if he or she does not have a job, has actively looked for work in the prior 4 weeks, and is currently available for work.

Unemployment rate The unemployment rate is the percentage of the labor force that is unemployed.

Unit of account A unit of account is a universal yardstick that is used for expressing the worth (price) of different goods and services.

Value added Each firm's value added is the firm's sales revenue minus its purchases of intermediate products from other firms.

Value of marginal product of labor The value of marginal product of labor is the contribution of an additional worker to a firm's revenues.

Variable A variable is a factor that is likely to change or vary.

Wage rigidity Wage rigidity refers to the condition in which the market wage is held above the competitive equilibrium level that would clear the labor market.

Willingness to accept Willingness to accept is the lowest price that a seller is willing to get paid to sell an extra unit of a good. Willingness to accept is the same as the marginal cost of production.

Willingness to pay Willingness to pay is the highest price that a buyer is willing to pay for an extra unit of a good.

Zero correlation Zero correlation implies that two variables have movements that are not related.

Credits

Chapter 1: p. 2: blue Porsche, F1online digitale Bildagentur GmbH/Alamy Stock Photo; p. 5: roller skater, Chase Jarvis/Getty Images; p. 6: whooping crane, Critterbiz/Shutterstock; p. 12 top: cappuccino, By-studio/Fotolia; p. 12 middle left: iPhone, D. Hurst/Alamy Stock Photo; p. 12 middle right: Eiffel Tower, Samott/Fotolia; p. 12 bottom: beach, Wirepec/Fotolia; p. 15: man jumping turnstile, Mauro Speziale/Getty Images.

Chapter 2: p. 20: graduation cap and money, Zimmytws/Shutterstock; p. 22: New York subway map, Martin Shields/Alamy Stock Photo; p. 27: runners, Photos by Sharon/Alamy Stock Photo; p. 28: Christmas package, DK Images/Alamy Stock Photo; p. 28: Macy's ad, Amy Sinns/Alamy Stock Photo; p. 28: red bar chart, Robert Kneschke/Shutterstock; p. 29: bride and groom, nataliakabliuk/Fotolia.

Chapter 3: p. 42: globe concept for commute, Pablo Scapinachis/Shutterstock; p. 45: park bench, Vladimirs Koskins/Shutterstock; p. 53: map of Portland, Oregon, Pearson Education; p. 54: Mount Hood, Portland, Oregon, Vincentlouis/Fotolia; p. 55: Boston-area subway map, based on Ryan Nickum, Estately, Inc.

Chapter 4: p. 58: gas price sign, Eric Glenn/Alamy Stock Photo; p. 60: flowers, DutchScenery/Fotolia; p. 60: two gas signs, Lynne Sladky/AP Images; p. 62: Hummer and smart car, Gudellaphoto/Fotolia; p. 63: stadium crowd, Monjiro/Fotolia; p. 66: Spam, Helen Sessions/Alamy Stock Photo; p. 69: oil rig, Paul Andrew Lawrence/Alamy Stock Photo; p. 73: oil refinery burning, John Moore/Getty Images; p. 79: Hess gas station, ClassicStock/Alamy Stock Photo; p. 79: sorry no gas sign, Everett Collection/Newsco.

Chapter 5: p. 88: Victoria Falls, TanArt/Shutterstock; p. 88: jobless men, Franklin D. Roosevelt Presidential Library and Museum; p. 89: Ford Focus, Mark Scheuern/Alamy Stock Photo; p. 92 (left): Ford Mustang, Mark Scheuern/Alamy Stock Photo; p. 92 (right): Ford Mustang, Bill Pugliano/Getty Images; p. 92 (bottom): We Can Do It!, US National Archives/Alamy Stock Photo; p. 93: Dell logo, PSL Images/Alamy Stock Photo; p. 93: Best Buy logo, PSL Images/Alamy Stock Photo; p. 99: money house, OlegDoroshin/Shutterstock; p. 99: weather icon, Pk74/Fotolia; p. 100: Costa Concordia, Reuters/Alamy Stock Photo; p. 101: mother/child, WavebreakMediaMicro/Fotolia; p. 102: power plant, Doin Oakenhelm/Fotolia.

Chapter 6: p. 116 (left): teacher/class, Sergio Azenha/Alamy Stock Photo; p. 116 (right): class in India, Sergio Azenha/Alamy Stock Photo; p. 122: mother bathing child, Jake Lyell/Alamy Stock Photo; p. 129: interactive glasses, Naeblys/Shutterstock.

Chapter 7: p. 140: arrow over dollar signs, Mathagraphics/Shutterstock; p. 144: balls of money, PM Images/Getty Images; p. 147 (top): Singapore skyline, ESB Professional/Shutterstock; p. 147 (bottom): Nairobi slum, John Warburton-Lee Photography/Alamy Stock Photo; p. 152: saving rate, Donskarpo/Shutterstock; p. 153: table in hands, Violetkaipa/Shutterstock; p. 154: syringe/hands, Alexander Raths/Shutterstock; p. 156: arrow over dollar signs (re-use), Mathagraphics/Shutterstock.

Chapter 8: p. 176: glass globe, FikMik/Shutterstock; p. 182: satellite image of North and South Korea, Universal Images Group North America LLC/Alamy Stock Photo; p. 183: cartoon of general, Pearson Education, Inc.; p. 190: access is denied/computer, Worker/Shutterstock; p. 192: house in floating village, Tommy Trenchard/Alamy Stock Photo; p. 197: Angelina Jolie, REUTERS/Boris Heger/UNHCR/Handout; p. 197: cartoon of general, Pearson Education, Inc.; p. 200: map of Nogales border between Arizona and Mexico, Pearson Education, Inc.

Chapter 9: p. 202: Sears Store Closing Sale, Kristoffer Tripplaar/Alamy Stock Photo; p. 207: three barbers, Luis Artus/Getty Images; p. 209 (top): permanent waving, Topical Press Agency/Getty Images; p. 209 (bottom); dark-haired woman, SvetlanaFedoseyeva/Shutterstock; p. 215: workers smashing, Mary Evans Picture Library/Alamy Stock Photo; p. 217: striking teachers, AP Photo/Thibault Camus.

Chapter 10: p. 228: bank, Pete Spiro/Shutterstock; p. 234: pirates, ClassicStock/Alamy Stock Photo; p. 243: FDIC seal, MCT/Newscom; p. 244: Northern Rock, John Giles/AP Images.

Chapter 11: p. 252: money kite, Keystone/Getty Images; p. 254: $100 bill, Vladimir Voronin/Fotolia; p. 254: gold coins, Fullempty/Fotolia; p. 254: stack of paper money, Ekostsov/Fotolia; p. 255: demand note (left, top), HA.com; p. 255 (left, bottom): US Department of the Treasury; p. 255: bitcoin, Julia Tsokur/Shutterstock; p. 256: Yap stone money, dbimages/Alamy Stock Photo; p. 260: shortage of goods, Anadolu Agency/Getty images; p. 261: Zimbabwe 100 billion dollar bill, Katherine Welles/Shutterstock; p. 262 (bottom): German inflation currency, Pearson Education, Inc.; p. 264: Janet Yellen, dpa picture alliance/Alamy Stock Photo; p. 269: Federal Reserve headquarters, Adamparent/Fotolia; p. 269: Bank of America sign, Jon Hicks/Corbis Documentary/Getty images; p. 273: Airbus A380, Goncalo Diniz/Alamy Stock Photo; p. 276: Federal Reserve headquarters, Adamparent/Fotolia.

Chapter 12: p. 280: foreclosed home, rSnapshotPhotos/Shutterstock; p. 285: woman with children, Farm Security Administration/Office of War Information Photograph Collection, Library of Congress Prints and Photographs; p. 289: forklift, Alexey Fursov/Shutterstock.

Chapter 13: p. 308: American Recovery and Reinvestment Act, Norma Jean Gargasz/Alamy Stock Photo; p. 308: William McChesney Martin Jr., Dennis Brack/Newscom; p. 318: Paul Volcker, AP Photo/Chick Harrity; p. 319: housing bubbles, Gino Santa Maria/Shutterstock; p. 329: Bridge to Nowhere, Ron Niebrugge/Alamy Stock Photo; p. 330 (left): Pearl Habor, Library of Congress Prints and Photographs; p. 330 (right): Sputnik, NASA.

Chapter 14: p. 336: black Nike running shoes, Sergio Azenha/Alamy Stock Photo; p. 337: Tom Hanks/Castaway, Moviestore collection Ltd./Alamy Stock Photo; p. 340: Steve Jobs, Paul Sakuma/AP Photo; p. 341: women working an assembly line, AP Photo; p. 344: clothing label, JohnKwan/Shutterstock; p. 701: laptop, Georgejmclittle/Fotolia; p. 349: treasury bond, HA.com; p. 353: pong screenshot, INTERFOTO/Alamy Stock Photo; p. 354 (bottom): workers sewing jeans, SCPhotos/Alamy Stock Photo.

Chapter 15: p. 360: UK sterling money notes, Marcus/Fotolia; p. 361: Yuan, Chinese currency, Dave Newman/Shutterstock; p. 364: Boeing 787 Dreamliner, Peter Carey/Alamy Stock Photo; p. 371: George Soros, Europa Newswire/Alamy Stock Photo.

Index

Note: Key terms and the page number on which they are defined appear in **boldface.**